An Introduction to

LANGUAGE

Fifth Edition

To Disa, Emily, and Zachary

An Introduction to

LANGUAGE

Fifth Edition

Victoria Fromkin

University of California, Los Angeles

Robert Rodman

North Carolina State University, Raleigh

Harcourt Brace College Publishers

Fort Worth   Philadelphia   San Diego   New York   Orlando   Austin   San Antonio
Toronto   Montreal   London   Sydney   Tokyo

Editor in Chief	*Ted Buchholz*
Acquisitions Editor	*Michael Rosenberg*
Developmental Editor	*Christine Caperton*
Project Editor	*Angela Williams*
Production Manager	*Cynthia Young*
Book Designer	*Brian Salisbury*
Photo/Permissions Editor	*Shirley Webster*

Cover photo: Picasso. Harlequin. 1915, New York, MOMA. Giraudon/Art Resource, N.Y. ©1993 ARS, N.Y./SPADEM

Address for Editorial Correspondence
Harcourt Brace College Publishers, 301 Commerce Street, Suite 3700, Fort Worth, TX 76102

Address for Orders
Harcourt Brace & Company, 6277 Sea Harbor Drive, Orlando, FL 32887
1-800-782-4479, or 1-800-433-0001 (in Florida)

ISBN: 0–03–054983–3
Library of Congress Catalogue Number: 92–70637

Printed in the United States of America

5 6 7 8 9 0 1 2 016 9 8 7 6 5 4

Preface

Interest in linguistics—the study of human language—has existed throughout history. Many of the questions discussed in this book have been asked for thousands of years. What is language? What do you know when you know a language? What is the origin of language? Is language unique to the human species? Why are there many languages? Where do they come from? How are they related? How do children learn language? Are some languages (or dialects) superior to others? Are some languages simpler than others? What do all languages have in common? What is the neurological basis of human language? What parts of the brain are concerned with language? Can computers be taught to speak and understand human language? These are only a few of the questions that have piqued human curiosity about language.

In addition to a philosophical interest in such questions, there are many other reasons why linguists, psychologists, philosophers, educators, sociologists, legal experts, neurologists, communication engineers, and computer scientists need to understand the nature of human language. Linguistics provides a theoretical basis for practical applications that includes the diagnosis and treatment of language disorders such as aphasia and dyslexia, the planning of "language arts" curricula in schools, the fight against illiteracy, the learning of foreign languages, the simplification of legal language, and the development of computerized speech products.

For these reasons the first four editions of this textbook were directed toward students of many disciplines. The book has been used in both linguistic and nonlinguistic courses, at all levels from freshman through graduate courses, for majors in fields as diverse as computer science, English, foreign languages, speech pathology, anthropology, communications, and philosophy. The fifth edition continues this approach and adds material to make it suitable for an even wider audience. It also reflects new developments in linguistics and related fields since the fourth edition.

Unlike the fourth edition, the book is divided into five parts: The Nature of Human Language, Grammatical Aspects of Language, Social Aspects of Language, Biological Aspects of Language, and Language in the Computer Age.

Part One, the opening chapter, establishes the framework for what follows by discussing linguistic knowledge, grammars, linguistic creativity, language universals, nonhuman communication, and the origin of language.

Part Two, Chapters 2 through 6, examines the kinds of linguistic knowledge that all speakers, from Arabic to Zulu, possess. There are chapters on words and word formation (morphology), sentence structure (syntax), meaning (semantics), and the sound patterns of language (phonetics and phonology). These chapters have been substantially revised since the fourth edition to take into account recent changes in linguistic theory. In addition, there is greater emphasis on linguistic data and less on the formalisms used in different theories since these are usually covered in more advanced courses.

In Part Three, Chapter 7, we consider language variation and the study of ethnic minority and social dialects. Attitudes toward language and how it reflects the views and mores of society are included in an expanded section of this chapter. Another section on Language and Sexism reflects a growing concern with this topic. Chapters 8 and 9 discuss language change or historical linguistics and the nature and development of writing.

Part Four has also been expanded and updated to reflect the rapid changes occurring in our understanding of the biological basis of language. Chapter 10 covers language acquisition of spoken and sign languages by hearing and deaf infants, respectively. The section on attempts to teach language to chimpanzees (and one gorilla) traces the entire fifty-year history of this endeavor, from outset to the present. Chapter 11, on Brain, Mind and Language, and Chapter 12, on Computer Processing of Human Language, in Part Five, have also been extensively revised in keeping with the exciting new discoveries in these research areas.

As in previous editions, the primary concern has been with basic ideas rather than detailed expositions. The textbook assumes no previous knowledge on the part of the reader. A list of references at the end of each chapter is included to accommodate any reader who wishes to pursue the subject in more depth. Each chapter concludes with a summary and exercises to enhance the student's interest in and comprehension of the textual material. A glossary of technical terms introduced in the book is found in the appendix.

We are deeply grateful to the individuals too numerous to mention who have sent us suggestions, corrections, criticisms, cartoons, language data, and exercises, all of which we have tried to incorporate in this new edition. We owe special thanks to Sean Boisen, Joseph Bogen, John Bremer, Aaron Broadwell, Carole Chaski, Abby Cohn, Thomas Cornell, A. R. Damasio, Hanna Damasio, William Edmondson, Sheila Embleton, Barbara A. Fennell, Lila Gleitman, Shelly Harrison, Bruce Hayes, John Holm, Nina Hyams, Patricia Keating, S. Martin Keleti, John E. Koontz, Jouko Lindstedt, Walter E. Meyers, Pamela Munro, Natalie Maynor (and her students), Laura Petitto, John Phillips, Alexis Manaster-Ramer, John A. Rea, Eric Schiller, Russ Schuh, Thomas F. Shannon, Emily Sityar, Edward Stabler, David Stampe, Donca Steriade, Timothy Stowell, Anna Szabolcsi, Allen C. Wechsler, and Guido Vanden Wyngaerd. Many of these individuals responded to specific queries sent by electronic mail over the Linguistic Network, and we thank Network editors Anthony Aristar and Helen Dry.

The responsibility for errors in fact or judgment is, of course, ours alone. We continue to be indebted to the instructors who have used the earlier editions and to their students, without whom there would be no fifth edition.

V.F.
R.R.

Contents

CHAPTER 3   **Syntax: The Sentence Patterns of Language**

CHAPTER 4   Semantics: The Meanings of Language

CHAPTER 5   **Phonetics: The Sounds of Language**

CHAPTER 6 **Phonology: The Sound Patterns of Language**

PART 3
Social Aspects of Language

CHAPTER 7   Language in Society

CHAPTER 8 **Language Change: The Syllables of Time**

CHAPTER 11 Human Processing: Brain, Mind, and Language

PART 5

Language in the Computer Age

CHAPTER 12   **Computer Processing of Human Language**

APPENDIX   **Glossary**

PART 1
The Nature of Human Language

Reflecting on . . . Noam Chomsky's ideas on the innateness of the fundamentals of grammar in the human mind, I saw that any innate features of the language capacity must be a set of biological structures, selected in the course of the evolution of the human brain . . .

S. E. Luria, *A Slot Machine, A Broken Test Tube, An Autobiography.*

Language is not an abstract construction of the learned, or of dictionary-makers, but is something arising out of the work, needs, ties, joys, affections, tastes, of long generations of humanity, and has its bases broad and low, close to the ground.

Walt Whitman

CHAPTER 1
What Is Language?

When we study human language, we are approaching what some might call the "human essence," the distinctive qualities of mind that are, so far as we know, unique to man.

Noam Chomsky, *Language and Mind*

By permission of Johnny Hart and Creators Syndicate, Inc.

Whatever else people do when they come together—whether they play, fight, make love, or make automobiles—they talk. We live in a world of language. We talk to our friends, our associates, our wives and husbands, our lovers, our teachers, our parents and in-laws. We talk to bus drivers and total strangers. We talk face to face and over the telephone, and everyone responds with more talk. Television and radio further swell this torrent of words. Hardly a moment of our waking lives is free from words, and even in our dreams we talk and are talked to. We also talk when there is no one to answer. Some of us talk aloud in our sleep. We talk to our pets and sometimes to ourselves.

The possession of language, perhaps more than any other attribute, distinguishes humans from other animals. To understand our humanity one must understand the nature of language that makes us human. According to the philosophy expressed in the myths and religions of many peoples, it is language that is the source of human life and power. To some people of Africa, a newborn child is a kuntu, a "thing," not yet a muntu, a "person." Only by the act of learning does the child become a human being. Thus, according to this tradition, we all become "human" because we all know at least one language. But what does it mean to "know" a language?

Linguistic Knowledge

When you know a language, you can speak and be understood by others who know that language. This means you have the capacity to produce sounds that signify certain meanings and to understand or interpret the sounds produced by others. We are referring to normal-hearing individuals. Deaf persons produce and understand sign languages just as hearing persons produce and understand spoken languages.

Everyone knows a language. Five-year-old children are almost as proficient at speaking and understanding as are their parents. Yet the ability to carry out the simplest conversation requires profound knowledge that most speakers are unaware of. This is as true of speakers of Japanese as of English, of Armenian as of Navajo. A speaker of English can produce a sentence having two relative clauses without knowing what a relative clause is, like

> My goddaughter who was born in Sweden and who now lives in Vermont is named Disa, after a Viking queen.

In a parallel fashion, a child can walk without understanding or being able to explain the principles of balance and support, or the neurophysiological control mechanisms that permit one to do so. The fact that we may know something unconsciously is not unique to language.

What, then, do speakers of English or Quechua or French or Mohawk or Arabic know?

Knowledge of the Sound System

B.C. By Johnny Hart

By permission of Johnny Hart and Creators Syndicate, Inc.

Knowing a language means knowing what sounds are in that language and what sounds are not. This unconscious knowledge is revealed by the way speakers of one language pronounce words from another language. If you speak only English, for example, you may substitute an English sound for a non-English sound when pronouncing "foreign" words. Most English speakers pronounce the name *Bach* with a final *k* sound because the sound represented by the letters *ch* in German is not an English sound. If you pronounce it as the Germans do, you are using a sound outside the English sound system. French people speaking English often pronounce words like *this* and *that* as if they were spelled *zis* and *zat*. The English sound represented by the initial letters *th* is not part of the French sound system, and the French mispronunciation reveals the speakers' unconscious knowledge of this fact.

Knowing the sound system of a language includes more than knowing the **inventory** of sounds: it includes knowing which sounds may start a word, end a word, and follow each other. The name of a former president of Ghana was *Nkrumah*, pronounced with an initial sound identical to the sound ending the English word *sing* (for most Americans). Most speakers of English mispronounce it (by Ghanaian standards) by inserting a short vowel before or after the *n* sound. Similarly, the first name of the New Zealand mystery writer Ngaio Marsh is usually mispronounced in this way. The reason for these "errors" is that no word in English begins with the *ng* sound. Children who learn English discover this fact about our language, just as Ghanaian and Australian children learn that words in their language may begin with the *ng* sound.

We will learn more about sound systems in Chapters 5 and 6.

Knowledge of the Meaning of Words

> The minute I set eyes on an animal I know what it is. I don't have to reflect a moment; the right name comes out instantly . . . I seem to know just by the shape of the creature and the way it acts what animal it is. When the dodo came along he [Adam] thought it was a wildcat . . . But I saved him . . . I just spoke up in a quite natural way . . . and said "Well, I do declare if there isn't the dodo!"
>
> Mark Twain, *Eve's Diary*

Knowing the sounds and sound patterns in our language constitutes only one part of our linguistic knowledge. In addition, knowing a language is knowing that certain sound sequences **signify** certain concepts or **meanings.** Speakers of English know what *boy* means and that it means something different from *toy* or *girl* or *pterodactyl*. Knowing a language is therefore knowing how to relate sounds and meanings.

If you do not know a language, the sounds spoken to you will be mainly incomprehensible, because the relationship between speech sounds and the meanings they represent is, for the most part, an **arbitrary** one. You have to learn (when you are acquiring the language) that the sounds represented by the letters *house* (in

the written form of the language) signify the concept ; if you know French,

this same meaning is represented by *maison;* if you know Twi, it is represented by ɔdaŋ; if you know Russian, by *dom;* if you know Spanish, by *casa.* Similarly, the

concept ⟨hand drawing⟩ is represented by *hand* in English, *main* in French, *nsa* is Twi, and

ruka in Russian.

The following are words in some different languages. How many of them can you understand?

a. kyinii
b. doakam
c. odun
d. asa
e. toowq
f. bolna
g. wartawan
h. inaminatu
i. yawwa

Speakers of the languages from which these words are taken know that they have the following meanings:

a. a large parasol (in a Ghanaian language, Twi)
b. living creature (in the native American language, Papago)
c. wood (in Turkish)
d. morning (in Japanese)
e. is seeing (in a California Indian language, Luiseño)
f. to speak (in a Pakistani language, Urdu); to ache (in Russian)
g. reporter (in Indonesian)
h. teacher (in a Venezuelan Indian language, Warao)
i. right on! (in a Nigerian language, Hausa)

These examples show that the sounds of words are only given meaning by the language in which they occur. Mark Twain satirizes the idea that something is called X because it looks like X or called Y because it sounds like Y in the quotation at the beginning of this section. Neither the shape nor the other physical attributes of objects determine their pronunciation in any language. As the cartoon on page 7 illustrates, a pterodactyl could have been called a ron.

This arbitrary relationship between the **form** (sounds) and **meaning** (concept) of a word in spoken language is also true of the sign languages used by the deaf. If you see someone using a sign language you do not know, it is doubtful that you will understand the message from the signs alone. A person who knows Chinese Sign Language would find it difficult to understand American Sign Language. Signs that may have originally been **mimetic** (similar to miming) or **iconic** (with a nonarbitrary relationship between form and meaning) change historically as do words, and the iconicity is lost. These signs become **conventional,** so knowing the shape or movement of the hands does not reveal the meaning of the gestures in sign languages.

HERMAN Copyright 1991 Jim Unger. Reprinted with permission of Universal Press Syndicate. All rights reserved.

There is, however, some **"sound symbolism"** in language—that is, words whose pronunciation suggests the meaning. A few words in most languages are **onomatopoeic**—the sounds of the words supposedly imitate the sounds of nature. Even here, the sounds differ from one language to another, reflecting the particular sound system of the language. In English we say *cockadoodledoo* to represent the rooster's crow, but in Russian they say *kukuriku*.

Sometimes particular sound sequences seem to relate to a particular concept. In English many words beginning with *gl* relate to sight, such as *glare, glint, gleam, glitter, glossy, glaze, glance, glimmer, glimpse,* and *glisten*. However, such words are a very small part of any language, and *gl* may have nothing to do with "sight" in another language, or even in other words in English, such as *gladiator, glucose, glory, glycerine, globe,* and so on.

English speakers know the *gl* words that relate to sight and those that do not; they know the onomatopoeic words, and all the words in the basic vocabulary of the language. There are no speakers of English who know all 450,000 words listed in *Webster's Third New International Dictionary;* but even if there were and that were all they knew, they would not know English. Imagine trying to learn a foreign language by buying a dictionary and memorizing words. No matter how many words you learned, you would not be able to form the simplest phrases or sentences in the language or understand a native speaker. No one speaks in isolated words. (Of course, you could search in your traveler's dictionary for individual words to find out how to say something like "car—gas—where?" After many tries, a native might understand this question and then point in the direction of a gas station. If you were answered with a sentence, however, you probably would not understand what was said or be able to look it up, because you would not know where one word ended and another began.) Chapter 4 will further explore word meanings.

The Creativity of Linguistic Knowledge

By permission of Johnny Hart and Creators Syndicate, Inc.

Knowledge of a language enables you to combine words to form phrases, and phrases to form sentences. You cannot buy a dictionary of any language with all its sentences, because no dictionary can list all the possible sentences. Knowing a language means being able to produce new sentences never spoken before and to understand sentences never heard before. The linguist Noam Chomsky refers to this ability as part of the "creative aspect" of language use. Not every speaker of a language can create great literature, but you, and all persons who know a language, can and do "create" new sentences when you speak and understand new sentences "created" by others.

This 'creative ability' is due to the fact that language use is not limited to stimulus-response behavior. It's true that if someone steps on our toes we will "automatically" respond with a scream or gasp or grunt, but these sounds are really not part of language; they are involuntary reactions to stimuli. After we automatically cry out, we can say "That was some clumsy act, you big oaf" or "Thank you very much for stepping on my toe because I was afraid I had elephantiasis and now that I can feel it hurt I know it isn't so," or any one of an infinite number of sentences, because the particular sentence we produce is not controlled by any stimulus.

Even some involuntary cries like *ouch* are constrained by our own language system, as are the filled pauses that are sprinkled through conversational speech—*er* or *uh* or *you know* in English. They contain only the sounds found in the language. French speakers, for example, often fill their pauses with the vowel sound that starts with their word for egg—*oeuf*—a sound that does not occur in English.

Knowing a language includes knowing what sentences are appropriate in various situations. Saying "Hamburger costs $2.00 a pound" after someone has just stepped on your toe would hardly be an appropriate response, although it would be possible.

Consider the following sentence:

> Daniel Boone decided to become a pioneer because he dreamed of pigeon-toed giraffes and cross-eyed elephants dancing in pink skirts and green berets on the wind-swept plains of the Midwest.

You may not believe the sentence; you may question its logic; but you can understand it, although you probably never heard or read it before now.

Knowledge of a language, then, makes it possible to understand and produce new sentences. If you counted the number of sentences in this book that you have seen or heard before, the number would be small. Next time you write an essay or a letter, see how many of your sentences are new. Few sentences are stored in your brain, to be "pulled out" to fit some situation or matched with some sentence that you hear. Novel sentences never spoken or heard before cannot be in your memory.

Simple memorization of all the possible sentences in a language is impossible in principle. If for every sentence in the language a longer sentence can be formed, then there is no limit to the length of any sentence and therefore no limit to the number of sentences. In English you can say:

> This is the house.

or

> This is the house that Jack built.

or

> This is the malt that lay in the house that Jack built.

or

> This is the dog that chased the cat that killed the rat that ate the malt that lay in the house that Jack built.

and you need not stop there. How long, then, is the longest sentence? A speaker of English can say:

> The old man came.

or

> The old, old, old, old, old man came.

How many "olds" are too many? Seven? Twenty-three?

It is true that the longer these sentences become, the less likely we would be to hear or to say them. A sentence with 276 occurrences of "old" would be highly unlikely in either speech or writing, even to describe Methuselah; but such a sentence is theoretically possible. That is, if you know English, you have the knowledge to add any number of adjectives as modifiers to a noun.

All human languages permit their speakers to form indefinitely long sentences; "creativity" is a universal property of human language.

To memorize and store an infinite set of sentences would require an infinite storage capacity. However, the brain is finite, and even if it were not, we could not store novel sentences.

Knowledge of Sentences and Nonsentences

When you learn a language you must learn something finite—your vocabulary is finite (however large it may be)—and that can be stored. If sentences in a language were formed by putting one word after another in any order, then language could simply be a set of words. You can see that words are not enough by examining the following strings of words:

(1)   a. John kissed the little old lady who owned the shaggy dog.
b. Who owned the shaggy dog John kissed the little old lady.
c. John is difficult to love.
d. It is difficult to love John.
e. John is anxious to go.
f. It is anxious to go John.
g. John, who was a student, flunked his exams.
h. Exams his flunked student a was who John.

If you were asked to put a star or asterisk before the examples that seemed "funny" or "no good" to you, which ones would you star?[1] Our "intuitive" knowledge about what is or is not an allowable sentence in English convinces us to star b, f, and h. Which ones did you star?

Would you agree with the following judgments?

(2)   a. What he did was climb a tree.
b. *What he thought was want a sports car.
c. Drink your beer and go home!

---

[1]The asterisk is used before examples that speakers reject for any reason. This notation will be used throughout the book.

d. *What are drinking and go home?
e. I expect them to arrive a week from next Thursday.
f. *I expect a week from next Thursday to arrive them.
g. Linus lost his security blanket.
h. *Lost Linus security blanket his.

If you starred the same ones we did, then you agree that not all strings of words constitute sentences in a language, and knowledge of a language determines which are and which are not. Therefore, in addition to knowing the words of the language, linguistic knowledge must include "rules" for forming sentences and making judgments like those you made about the examples in (1) and (2). These rules must be finite in length and finite in number so that they can be stored in our finite brains; yet they must permit us to form and understand an infinite set of new sentences, as we discussed earlier. The nature of these rules will be discussed in Chapter 3.

A language, then, consists of all the sounds, words, and possible sentences. When you know a language, you know the sounds, the words, and the rules for their combination.

Linguistic Knowledge and Performance

"What's one and one and one and one and one and one and one and one and one and one?"
"I don't know," said Alice. "I lost count."
"She can't do Addition," the Red Queen interrupted.

Lewis Carroll, *Through the Looking-Glass*

PEANUTS reprinted by permission of UFS, Inc.

Speakers' linguistic knowledge permits them to form longer and longer sentences by joining sentences and phrases together or adding modifiers to a noun. Whether you stop at three, five, or eighteen adjectives, it is impossible to limit the number you could add if desired. Very long sentences are theoretically possible, but they are highly improbable. Evidently there is a difference between having the knowledge necessary to produce sentences of a language and applying this knowledge. It is a difference between what you *know,* which is your linguistic **competence,** and how you *use* this knowledge in actual speech production and comprehension, which is your linguistic **performance.**

Speakers of all languages have the knowledge to understand or produce sentences of any length. When they attempt to use that knowledge, though—when they perform linguistically—there are physiological and psychological reasons that limit the number of adjectives, adverbs, clauses, and so on. They may run out of breath, their audience may leave, they may lose track of what they have said, and of course, no one lives forever.

When we speak we usually have a certain message to convey. At some stage in the act of producing speech we must organize our thoughts into strings of words. But sometimes the message gets garbled. We may stammer, or pause, or produce "slips of the tongue." We may even sound like Tarzan in the cartoon by Gary Larson, who illustrates the difference between linguistic knowledge and the way we use that knowledge in performance.

THE FAR SIDE copyright 1991, 1987, and 1986 Universal Press Syndicate. Reprinted with permission. All rights reserved.

Linguistic knowledge is, for the most part, *not* conscious knowledge. The linguistic system—the sounds, structures, meanings, words, and rules for putting them all together—is learned subconsciously with no awareness that rules are being learned. Just as we may be unconscious of the rules that allow us to stand or walk, to crawl on all fours if we choose, to jump or catch a baseball, or to ride a bicycle, our unconscious ability to speak and understand and to make judgments about sentences reveals our knowledge of the rules of our language. This knowledge represents a complex cognitive system. The nature of this system is what this book is all about.

What Is Grammar?

> We use the term "grammar" with a systematic ambiguity. On the one hand, the term refers to the explicit theory constructed by the linguist and proposed as a description of the speaker's competence. On the other hand, [it refers] to this competence itself.
>
> N. Chomsky and M. Halle, *The Sound Pattern of English*

Descriptive Grammars

The sounds and sound patterns, the basic units of meaning, such as words, and the rules to combine them to form new sentences constitute the **grammar** of a language. The grammar, then, is what we know; it represents our linguistic competence. To understand the nature of language we must understand the nature of this internalized, unconscious set of rules, which is part of every grammar of every language.

Every human being who speaks a language knows its grammar. When linguists wish to describe a language, they attempt to describe the grammar of the language that exists in the minds of its speakers. There may be some differences among speakers' knowledge, but there must be shared knowledge, because it is this grammar that makes it possible to communicate through language. To the extent that the linguist's description is a true model of the speakers' linguistic capacity, it will be a successful description of the grammar and of the language itself. Such a model is called a **descriptive grammar.** It does not tell you how you *should* speak; it describes your basic linguistic knowledge. It explains how it is possible for you to speak and understand, and it tells what you know about the sounds, words, phrases, and sentences of your language.

We have used the word *grammar* in two ways: the first in reference to the grammar speakers have in their brains; the second as the model or description of this internalized grammar. Almost 2000 years ago the Greek grammarian Dionysius Thrax defined grammar as that which permits us either to speak a language or to speak about a language. From now on we will not differentiate these two meanings, because the linguist's descriptive grammar is an attempt at a formal statement (or theory) of the speakers' grammar.

When we say in later chapters that there is a rule in the grammar—such as "Every sentence has a noun phrase subject and a verb phrase predicate"—we posit the rule in both the "mental" grammar and the model of it, the linguist's grammar.

When we say that a sentence is **grammatical,** we mean that it conforms to the rules of both grammars; conversely, an **ungrammatical** (starred) sentence deviates in some way from these rules. If, however, we posit a rule for English that does not agree with your intuitions as a speaker, then the grammar we are describing is in some way different from the grammar that represents your linguistic competence; that is, your language is not the one we are describing. No language or variety of a language (called a dialect) is superior to any other in a linguistic sense. Every grammar is equally complex and logical and capable of producing an infinite set of sentences to express any thought. If something can be expressed in one language or one dialect, it can be expressed in any other language or dialect. It might involve different means and different words, but it can be expressed.

No grammar, therefore no language, is either superior or inferior to any other. Languages of technologically undeveloped cultures are not primitive or ill-formed in any way.

Prescriptive Grammars

I don't want to talk grammar. I want to talk like a lady.

G. B. Shaw, *Pygmalion*

Reprinted with special permission of North America Syndicate.

The views expressed in the section above are not those of all grammarians now or in the past. From ancient times until the present, "purists" have believed that language change is corruption and that there are certain "correct" forms that all educated people should use in speaking and writing. The Greek Alexandrians in the first century, the Arabic scholars at Basra in the eighth century, and numerous English grammarians of the eighteenth and nineteenth centuries held this view. They wished to *prescribe* rather than describe the rules of grammar, which gave rise to the writing of **prescriptive grammars.**

With the rise of capitalism, a new middle class emerged who wanted their children to speak the dialect of the "upper" classes. This desire led to the publication of many prescriptive grammars. In 1762 an influential grammar, *A Short Introduction to English Grammar with Critical Notes,* was written by Bishop Robert Lowth.

Lowth, influenced by Latin grammar and by personal preference, prescribed a number of new rules for English. Before the publication of his grammar, practically everyone—upper-class, middle-class, and lower-class speakers of English—said *I don't have none, You was wrong about that,* and *Mathilda is fatter than me.* Lowth, however, decided that "two negatives make a positive" and therefore one should say *I don't have any;* that even when *you* is singular it should be followed by the plural *were;* and that *I* not *me, he* not *him, they* not *them,* and so forth should follow *than* in comparative constructions. Many of these "rules" were based on Latin grammar, which had already given way to different rules in the languages that developed from Latin. Because Lowth was influential and because the rising new class wanted to speak "properly," many of these new rules were legislated into English grammar, at least for the "prestige" dialect. Grammars such as Lowth wrote are quite different from the descriptive grammars we have been discussing. Their goal is not to describe the rules people know, but to tell them what rules they should know.

In 1908, a grammarian, Thomas R. Lounsbury, wrote: "There seems to have been in every period in the past, as there is now, a distinct apprehension in the minds of very many worthy persons that the English tongue is always in the condition approaching collapse and that arduous efforts must be put forth persistently to save it from destruction."

Today our bookstores are filled with books by language "purists" attempting to do just that. Edwin Newman, for example, in his books *Strictly Speaking,* and *A Civil Tongue* rails against those who use the word *hopefully* to mean "I hope," as in "Hopefully, it will not rain tomorrow," instead of using it "properly" to mean "with hope." What Newman fails to recognize is that language changes in the course of time and words change meaning, and the meaning of *hopefully* has been broadened for most English speakers to include both usages. Other "saviors" of the English language blame television, the schools, and even the National Council of Teachers of English for failing to preserve the standard language, and they mount attacks against those college and university professors who suggest that Black English and other dialects are viable, living, complete languages. Although not mentioned by name, the authors of this textbook would clearly be among those who would be criticized by these new prescriptivists.

There is even a literary organization dedicated to the proper use of the English language, called the Unicorn Society of Lake Superior State College, which issues an annual "dishonor list" of words and phrases of which they do not approve, including the word "medication," which they say "We can no longer afford. It's too expensive. We've got to get back to the cheaper 'medicine.'"[2] At least these guardians of the English language have a sense of humor; but they as well as the other prescriptivists are bound to fail. Language is vigorous and dynamic and constantly changing. All languages and dialects are expressive, complete, and logical, as much so as they were 200 or 2000 years ago. If sentences are muddled, it is not because of the language but because of the speakers. Prescriptivists should be more

[2]Los Angeles *Times,* Jan. 2, 1978, Part 1, p. 21.

concerned about the thinking of the speakers than about the language they use. "Hopefully" this book will convince you of this idea.

Linguists object to prescriptivism for a number of reasons. The views are elitist, in that they assume that the linguistic grammars and usages of a particular group in society (usually the more affluent and those with political power) are the only correct ones. Prescriptivists, for the most part, seem to have little knowledge of the history of the language and less about the nature of language, the fact that all dialects are rule governed and that what is grammatical in one language may be ungrammatical in another (equally prestigious) language.

Teaching Grammars

By permission of Johnny Hart and Creators Syndicate, Inc.

The grammar of a language is different from a **teaching grammar,** which is used to learn another language or dialect. In countries where it is advantageous to speak a "prestige" dialect, people who do not speak it natively may wish to learn it. Teaching grammars state explicitly the rules of the language, list the words and their pronunciations, and aid in learning a new language or dialect. As an adult, it is difficult to learn a second language without being instructed. Teaching grammars assume that the student already knows one language and compares the grammar of the target language with the grammar of the native language. The meaning of a word is given by providing a **gloss**—the parallel word in the student's native language, such as *maison,* "house" in French. It is assumed that the student knows the meaning of the gloss "house," and so the meaning of the word *maison.*

Sounds of the target language that do not occur in the native language are often described by reference to known sounds. Thus the student might be aided in producing the French sound *u* in the word *tu* by instructions such as "Round your lips while producing the vowel sound in *tea.*"

The rules on how to put words together to form the grammatical sentences also refer to the learners' knowledge of their native language. Thus the teaching grammar *Learn Zulu* by Sibusiso Nyembezi states that "The difference between singular and plural is not at the end of the word but at the beginning of it," and warns that

"Zulu does not have the indefinite and definite articles 'a' and 'the.'" Such statements assume students know the rules of their own grammar. Although they might be prescriptive in the sense that they attempt to teach the student what is or is not a grammatical construction in the new language, their aim is different from grammars that attempt to change the rules or usage of a language already learned.

This book is not primarily concerned with either prescriptive or teaching grammars. The matter, however, is considered in Chapter 7 in the discussion of standard and nonstandard dialects.

Language Universals

> In a grammar there are parts which pertain to all languages; these components form what is called the general grammar. In addition to these general (universal) parts, there are those which belong only to one particular language; and these constitute the particular grammars of each language.
>
> Du Marsais, c. 1750

The way we are using the word *grammar* differs in another way from its most common meaning. In our sense, the grammar includes everything speakers know about their language—the sound system, called **phonology;** the system of meanings, called **semantics;** the rules of word formation, called **morphology;** and the rules of sentence formation, called **syntax.** It also, of course, includes the vocabulary of words—the dictionary or **lexicon.** Many people think of the grammar of a language as referring solely to the syntactic rules. This latter sense is what students usually mean when they talk about their class in "English grammar."

Our aim is more in keeping with that stated in 1784 by the grammarian John Fell in "Essay Towards an English Grammar": "It is certainly the business of a grammarian to find out, and not to make, the laws of a language." This business is just what the linguist attempts—to find out the laws of a language, and the laws that pertain to all languages. Those laws that pertain to all human languages, representing the universal properties of language, constitute a **universal grammar.**

Throughout the ages, philosophers and linguists have been divided on the question of whether there are universal properties that hold for all human languages and are unique to them. Most modern linguists are on the side of the "universalists," finding common, universal properties in the grammars of all languages. Such properties may be said to constitute a "universal" grammar of human language.

About 1630, the German philosopher Alsted first used the term *general grammar* as distinct from special grammar. He believed that the function of a general grammar was to reveal those features "which relate to the method and etiology of grammatical concepts. They are common to all languages." Pointing out that "general grammar is the pattern 'norma' of every particular grammar whatsoever," he implored "eminent linguists to employ their insight in this matter."[3]

[3]V. Salmon, "Review of *Cartesian Linguistics* by N. Chomsky." *Journal of Linguistics* 5 (1969): 165–187.

Three and a half centuries before Alsted, the scholar Robert Kilwardby held that linguists should be concerned with discovering the nature of language in general. So concerned was Kilwardby with universal grammar that he excluded considerations of the characteristics of particular languages, which he believed to be as "irrelevant to a science of grammar as the material of the measuring rod or the physical characteristics of objects were to geometry."[4] Kilwardby was perhaps too much of a universalist; the particular properties of individual languages are relevant to the discovery of language universals, and they are of interest for their own sake.

Someone attempting to study Latin, Greek, French, or Swahili as a second language may assert, in frustration, that those ancient scholars were so hidden in their ivory towers that they confused reality with idle speculation; yet the more we investigate this question, the more evidence accumulates to support Chomsky's view that there is a universal grammar, which is part of the human biologically endowed language faculty. It may be thought of "as a system of principles which characterizes the class of possible grammars by specifying how particular grammars are organized (what are the components and their relations), how the different rules of these components are constructed, how they interact, and so on."[5]

To discover the nature of this Universal Grammar whose principles characterize all human languages is the major aim of **linguistic theory.** The linguist's goal is to discover the "laws of human language" as the physicist's goal is to discover the "laws of the physical universe." The complexity of language, a product of the human brain, undoubtedly means this goal will never be fully achieved. Just as Newtonian physics was enlarged by Einsteinian physics, so the linguistic theory of Universal Grammar develops, and new discoveries, some of which are discussed in this book, shed new light on what human language is.

Animal "Languages"

No matter how eloquently a dog may bark, he cannot tell you that his parents were poor but honest.

Bertrand Russell

Whether language is the exclusive property of the human species is an interesting question. The idea of talking animals probably is as old and as widespread among human societies as language is itself. No culture lacks a legend in which some animal plays a speaking role. All over West Africa, children listen to folk tales in which a "spider-man" is the hero. "Coyote" is a favorite figure in many Native American tales, and there is hardly an animal who does not figure in Aesop's famous fables. Hugh Lofting's fictional Doctor Doolittle's major accomplishment was his ability to communicate with animals.

[4]Ibid.
[5]Noam Chomsky, *Language and Responsibility* (based on conversations with Misou Ronat), New York: Pantheon, 1979, p. 180.

If language is viewed only as a system of communication, then many species communicate. Humans also use systems other than their language to relate to each other and to send "messages." The question is whether the kinds of grammars which represent linguistic knowledge acquired by children with no external instruction, and which are used creatively rather than as responses to internal or external stimuli, are unique to the human animal.

"Talking" Parrots

Copyright © 1991 by Chronicle Features.

Most humans who acquire language utilize speech sounds to express meanings, but such sounds are not a necessary aspect of language, as evidenced by the sign languages of the deaf. The use of speech sounds is therefore not a basic part of what we have been calling language. The chirping of birds, the squeaking of dolphins, and the dancing of bees may potentially represent systems similar to human languages. If animal communication systems are not like human language, it will not be due to a lack of speech.

Conversely, when animals vocally imitate human utterances, it does not mean they possess language. Language is a system that relates sounds (or gestures) to meanings. "Talking" birds such as parrots and mynah birds are capable of faithfully reproducing words and phrases of human language that they have heard; but when a parrot says "Polly wants a cracker," she may really want a ham sandwich or a drink of water or nothing at all. A bird that has learned to say "hello" or "goodbye" is as likely to use one as the other, regardless of whether people are arriving or departing. The bird's utterances carry no meaning. They are speaking neither English nor their own language when they sound like us.

Talking birds do not dissect the sounds of their imitations into discrete units. *Polly* and *Molly* do not rhyme for a parrot. They are as different as *hello* and *goodbye* (or as similar). One property of all human languages (which will be discussed further in Chapter 5) is the "discreteness" of the speech or gestural units, which are ordered and reordered, combined and split apart. A parrot says what it is taught, or what it hears, and no more. If Polly learns "Polly wants a cracker" and "Polly wants a doughnut" and also learns to imitate the single words *whiskey* and *bagel,* she will not spontaneously produce, as children do, "Polly wants whiskey" or "Polly wants a bagel" or "Polly wants whiskey and a bagel." If she learns *cat* and *cats* and *dog* and *dogs* and then learns the word *parrot,* she will be unable to form the plural *parrots;* nor can a parrot form an unlimited set of utterances from a finite set of units. Therefore, the ability to produce sounds similar to those used in human language cannot be equated with the ability to learn a human language.

The Birds and the Bees

> The birds and animals are all friendly to each other, and there are no disputes about anything. They all talk, and they all talk to me, but it must be a foreign language for I cannot make out a word they say.
>
> Mark Twain, *Eve's Diary*

Most animals possess some kind of "signaling" communication system. Among the spiders there is a complex system for courtship. The male spider, before he approaches his lady love, goes through an elaborate series of gestures to inform her that he is indeed a spider and not a crumb or a fly to be eaten. These gestures are invariant. One never finds a "creative" spider changing or adding to the particular courtship ritual of his species.

A similar kind of "gesture" language is found among the fiddler crabs. There are forty different varieties, and each variety uses its own particular claw-waving movement to signal to another member of its "clan." The timing, movement, and posture of the body never change from one time to another or from one crab to another within the particular variety. Whatever the signal means, it is fixed. Only one meaning can be conveyed. There is not an infinite set of fiddler crab "sentences."

The imitative sounds of talking birds have little in common with human language, but the calls and songs of many species of birds do have a communicative function, and they resemble human languages in that there may be "dialects" within the same species. Bird **calls** (consisting of one or more short notes) convey messages associated with the immediate environment, such as danger, feeding, nesting, flocking, and so on. Bird **songs** (more complex patterns of notes) are used to "stake out" territory and to attract mates. There is no evidence of any internal structure to these songs, nor can they be segmented into independently meaningful parts as words of human language can be. In a study of the territorial song of the European robin,[6] it was discovered that the rival robins paid attention only to the alternation between high-pitched and low-pitched notes, and which came first did not matter. The message varies only to the extent of how strongly the robin feels about his possession and to what extent he is prepared to defend it and start a family in that territory. The different alternations therefore express "intensity" and nothing more. The robin is creative in his ability to sing the same thing in many different ways, but not creative in his ability to use the same "units" of the system to express many different messages with different meanings.

To what degree human language is biologically conditioned (or **innate**) and to what degree it is learned is one of the fundamental questions of linguistics. The songs of some species of birds appear to be innate. This question will be discussed in Chapter 11, which deals with language and the brain.

Despite certain superficial similarities to human language, bird calls and songs are fundamentally different kinds of communicative systems. The number of messages that can be conveyed is finite, and messages are stimulus controlled.

This distinction is also true of the system of communication used by honeybees. A forager bee is able to return to the hive and tell other bees where a source of food is located. It does so by forming a dance on a wall of the hive that reveals the location and quality of the food source. For one species of Italian honeybee, the dancing behavior may assume one of three possible patterns: *round* (which indicates locations near the hive, within twenty feet or so), *sickle* (which indicates locations at twenty- to sixty-feet distance from the hive), and *tail-wagging* (for distances that exceed sixty feet). The number of repetitions per minute of the basic pattern in the tail-wagging dance indicates the precise distance; the slower the repetition rate, the longer the distance.

The bees' dance is an effective system of communication for bees. It is capable, in principle, of infinitely many different messages, like human language; but unlike human language, the system is confined to a single subject—distance from the hive. The inflexibility was shown by an experimenter who forced a bee to walk to the food source. When the bee returned to the hive, it indicated a distance twenty-five times farther away than the food source actually was. The bee had no way of communicating the special circumstances in its message. This absence of creativity makes the bees' dance qualitatively different from human language.

In the seventeenth century, the philosopher and mathematician René Descartes pointed out that the communication systems of animals are qualitatively different from the language used by humans:

[6]R. G. Busnel and J. Bremond, "Recherche du Support de l'Information dans le Signal Acoustique de Défense Territoriale du Rougegorge," *C. R. Acad. Sci. Paris* 254 (1962): 2236–2238.

> It is a very remarkable fact that there are none so depraved and stupid, without even excepting idiots, that they cannot arrange different words together, forming of them a statement by which they make known their thoughts; while, on the other hand, there is no other animal, however perfect and fortunately circumstanced it may be, which can do the same.[7]

Descartes goes on to state that one of the major differences between humans and animals is that human use of language is not just a response to external, or even internal, emotional stimuli, as are the sounds and gestures of animals. He warns against confusing human use of language with "natural movements which betray passions and may be . . . manifested by animals."

To hold that animals communicate by systems qualitatively different from human language systems is not to claim human superiority. Humans are not inferior to the one-celled amoeba because they cannot reproduce by splitting in two; they are just different sexually. All the studies of animal communication systems, including those of chimpanzees (discussed in Chapter 10), provide evidence for Descartes' distinction between other animal communication systems and the linguistic creative ability possessed by the human animal.

In the Beginning: The Origin of Language

> Nothing, no doubt, would be more interesting than to know from historical documents the exact process by which the first man began to lisp his first words, and thus to be rid for ever of all the theories on the origin of speech.
>
> M. Muller, *1871*

If language is unique to our species, a natural question is how it arose. All religions and mythologies contain stories of language origin. Philosophers through the ages have argued the question. Scholarly works have been written on the subject. Prizes have been awarded for the "best answer" to this eternally perplexing problem. Theories of divine origin, evolutionary development, and language as a human invention have all been suggested.

The difficulties inherent in answering this question are immense. Anthropologists think that the species has existed for at least one million years, and perhaps for as long as five or six million years. But the earliest deciphered written records are barely six thousand years old, dating from the writings of the Sumerians of 4000 B.C.E. These records appear so late in the history of the development of language that they provide no clue to its origin.

For these reasons, scholars in the latter part of the nineteenth century, who were only interested in "hard science," ridiculed, ignored, and even banned discussions of language origin. In 1886, the Linguistic Society of Paris passed a resolution "outlawing" any papers concerned with this subject.

---

[7]René Descartes, "Discourse on Method," V. In *The Philosophical Works of Descartes,* Vol. I, trans. by E. S. Haldane and G. R. Ross. Cambridge, England: Cambridge University Press, 1967, p. 116.

Despite the difficulty of finding scientific evidence, speculations on language origin have provided valuable insights into the nature and development of language, which prompted the learned scholar Otto Jespersen to state that "linguistic science cannot refrain forever from asking about the whence (and about the whither) of linguistic evolution." A brief look at some of these speculative notions will reveal this.

God's Gift to Mankind?

> And out of the ground the Lord God formed every beast of the field, and every fowl of the air, and brought them unto Adam to see what he would call them; and whatsoever Adam called every living creature, that was the name thereof.
>
> *Genesis 2:19*

According to Judeo-Christian beliefs, God gave Adam the power to name all things. Similar beliefs are found throughout the world. According to the Egyptians, the creator of speech was the god Thoth. Babylonians believed the language giver was the god Nabu, and the Hindus attributed our unique language ability to a female god; Brahma was the creator of the universe, but language was given to us by his wife, Sarasvati.

Belief in the divine origin of language is closely intertwined with the magical properties that have been associated with language and the spoken word. Children in all cultures utter "magic" words like *abracadabra* to ward off evil or bring good luck. Despite the childish jingle "Sticks and stones may break my bones, but names will never hurt me," name-calling is insulting, cause for legal punishment, and feared. In some cultures, when certain words are used, one is required to counter them by "knocking on wood."

In many religions only special languages may be used in prayers and rituals. The Hindu priests of the fifth century B.C.E. believed that the original pronunciations of Vedic Sanskrit had to be used. This led to important linguistic study, since their language had already changed greatly since the hymns of the Vedas had been written. The first linguist known to us is Panini, who, in the fourth century B.C.E. wrote a detailed grammar of Sanskrit in which the phonological rules revealed the earlier pronunciation for use in religious worship.

While myths and customs and superstitions do not tell us very much about language origin, they do tell us about the importance ascribed to language.

There is no way to "prove" or "disprove" the divine origin of language, just as one cannot argue scientifically for or against the existence of God.

The First Language

> Imagine the Lord talking French! Aside from a few odd words in Hebrew, I took it completely for granted that God had never spoken anything but the most dignified English.
>
> Clarence Day, *Life with Father*

Among the proponents of the divine origin theory a great interest arose in the language used by God, Adam, and Eve. For millennia, "scientific" experiments have reportedly been devised to verify particular theories of the first language. In the fifth century B.C.E. the Greek historian Herodotus reported that the Egyptian Pharaoh Psammetichus (664–610 B.C.E.) sought to determine the most primitive "natural" language by experimental methods. The monarch was said to have placed two infants in an isolated mountain hut, to be cared for by a mute servant. The Pharaoh believed that without any linguistic input the children would develop their own language and would thus reveal the original tongue of man. Patiently the Egyptian waited for the children to become old enough to talk. According to the story, the first word uttered was *bekos,* the word for "bread" in Phrygian, the language spoken in a province of Phrygia in the northwest corner of what is now modern Turkey. This ancient language, which has long since died out, was thought, on the basis of this "experiment," to be the original language.

History is replete with other proposals. In the thirteenth century, the Holy Roman Emperor Frederick II of Hohenstaufen was said to have carried out a similar test, but the children died before they uttered a single word. James IV of Scotland (1473–1513), however, supposedly succeeded in replicating the experiment with the surprising results, according to legend, that the Scottish children "spak very guid Ebrew," providing "scientific evidence" that Hebrew was the language used in the Garden of Eden.

But J.G. Becanus in the sixteenth century argued that German must have been the primeval language, since God would have used the most perfect language. In 1830 the lexicographer Noah Webster asserted that the "proto-language" must have been Chaldee (Aramaic), the language spoken in Jerusalem during the time of Jesus. In 1887, Joseph Elkins maintained that "there is no other language which can be more reasonably assumed to be the speech first used in the world's gray morning than can Chinese."

The belief that all languages originated from a single source—the **monogenetic** theory of language origin—is not only found in the Tower of Babel story in Genesis, but also in a similar legend of the Toltecs, early inhabitants of Mexico, and in the myths of other peoples as well.

We are no further along today in discovering the original language (or languages) than was Psammetichus, given the obscurities of prehistory.

Human Invention or the Cries of Nature?

> Language was born in the courting days of mankind; the first utterances of speech I fancy to myself like something between the nightly love lyrics of puss upon the tiles and the melodious love songs of the nightingale.

Otto Jespersen, *Language, Its Nature, Development and Origin*

The Greeks speculated about everything in the universe, including language. The earliest surviving linguistic treatise which deals with the origin and nature of language is Plato's *Cratylus*. A commonly held view among the classical Greeks, expressed by Socrates in this dialogue, was that at some ancient time there was a "legislator" who gave the correct, natural name to everything, and that words "echoed" the essence of their meanings.

Despite all the contrary evidence, the idea that the earliest form of language was imitative, or "echoic," was proposed up to the twentieth century. Called the *bow-wow* theory, it claimed that a dog would be designated by the word *bow-wow* because of the sounds of his bark.

A parallel view states that language at first consisted of emotional ejaculations of pain, fear, surprise, pleasure, anger, and so on. This proposal that the earliest manifestations of language were "cries of nature" was proposed by Jean Jacques Rousseau in the middle of the eighteenth century.

Another hypothesis suggests that language arose out of the rhythmical grunts of men working together. A more charming view was suggested by Jespersen who proposed that language derived from song as an expressive rather than a communicative need, with love being the greatest stimulus for language development.

Just as with the beliefs in a divine origin of language, these proposals are untestable. Other approaches to the evolution of language as part of the science of biology are discussed in Chapter 11. The debate is unsettled and it continues.

What We Know About Language

There are many things we do not yet know about the nature and origin of language. The science of linguistics is concerned with these questions. The investigations of linguists throughout history and the analysis of spoken languages date back at least to 1600 B.C. in Mesopotamia. We have learned a great deal since that time. A number of facts pertaining to all languages can now be stated.

1. Wherever humans exist, language exists.
2. There are no "primitive" languages—all languages are equally complex and equally capable of expressing any idea in the universe. The vocabulary of any language can be expanded to include new words for new concepts.
3. All languages change through time.
4. The relationships between the sounds and meanings of spoken languages and between the gestures (signs) and meanings of sign languages are for the most part arbitrary.
5. All human languages utilize a finite set of discrete sounds (or gestures) that are combined to form meaningful elements or words, which themselves form an infinite set of possible sentences.
6. All grammars contain rules for the formation of words and sentences of a similar kind.

7. Every spoken language includes discrete sound segments like *p, n,* or *a,* which can all be defined by a finite set of sound properties or features. Every spoken language has a class of vowels and a class of consonants.

8. Similar grammatical categories (for example, noun, verb) are found in all languages.

9. There are semantic universals, such as "male" or "female," "animate" or "human," found in every language in the world.

10. Every language has a way of referring to past time, negating, forming questions, issuing commands, and so on.

11. Speakers of all languages are capable of producing and comprehending an infinite set of sentences. Syntactic universals reveal that every language has a way of forming sentences such as:

    Linguistics is an interesting subject.
    I know that linguistics is an interesting subject.
    You know that I know that linguistics is an interesting subject.
    Cecilia knows that you know that I know that linguistics is an interesting subject.
    Is it a fact that Cecilia knows that you know that I know that linguistics is an interesting subject?

12. Any normal child, born anywhere in the world, of any racial, geographical, social, or economic heritage, is capable of learning any language to which he or she is exposed. The differences we find among languages cannot be due to biological reasons.

It seems that Alsted and Du Marsais (and we could add many other "universalists" from all ages) were not spinning idle thoughts. We all speak "human language."

Summary

We are all intimately familiar with at least one language, our own. Yet few of us ever stop to consider what we know when we know a language. There is no book that contains the English or Russian or Zulu language. The words of a language can be listed in a dictionary, but not all the sentences, and a language consists of these sentences as well as words. Speakers use a finite set of rules to produce and understand an infinite set of "possible" sentences.

These rules comprise the **grammar** of a language, which is learned when you "acquire" the language and includes the sound system (the **phonology**), and *morphology* how words may be combined into phrases and sentences (the **syntax**), the ways in which sounds and meanings are related (the **semantics**), and the words or **lexicon.** The sounds and meanings of these words are related in an **arbitrary** fashion. If you had never heard the word *syntax* you would not, by its sounds, know what it meant. Language, then, is a system that relates sounds with meanings, and when you know a language you know this system.

This knowledge (linguistic **competence**) is different from behavior (linguistic **performance**). If you woke up one morning and decided to stop talking (as the Trappist monks did after they took a "vow of silence"), you would still have knowledge of your language. This ability or competence underlies linguistic behavior. If you do not know the language, you cannot speak it; but if you know the language, you may choose not to speak.

Grammars are of three kinds. The **descriptive grammar** of a language represents the unconscious linguistic knowledge or capacity of its speakers. Such a grammar is a model of the "mental grammar" every speaker of the language knows. It does not teach the rules of the language; it describes the rules that are already known. A grammar that attempts to legislate what your grammar should be is called a **prescriptive grammar.** It prescribes; it does not describe, except incidentally. **Teaching grammars** are written to help people learn a foreign language or a dialect of their own language.

The more linguists investigate the thousands of languages of the world and describe the ways in which they differ from each other, the more they discover that these differences are limited. There are linguistic universals that pertain to all parts of grammars, the ways in which these parts are related, and the forms of rules. These principles comprise **universal grammar,** which forms the basis of the specific grammars of all possible human languages.

If language is defined merely as a system of communication, then language is not unique to humans. There are, however, certain characteristics of human language not found in the communication systems of any other species. A basic property of human language is its **creative aspect**—a speaker's ability to combine the basic linguistic units to form an *infinite* set of "well-formed" grammatical sentences, most of which are novel, never before produced or heard.

The fact that deaf children learn language shows that the ability to hear or produce sounds is not a necessary prerequisite for language learning. Further, the ability to imitate the sounds of human language is not a sufficient basis for learning language; "talking" birds imitate sounds but can neither segment these sounds into smaller units, nor understand what they are imitating, nor produce new utterances to convey their thoughts.

Birds, bees, crabs, spiders, and most other creatures communicate in some way, but the information imparted is severely limited and stimulus-bound, confined to a small set of messages. The system of language represented by intricate mental grammars, which are not stimulus-bound and which generate infinite messages, is unique to the human species.

The idea that language was God's gift to humanity is found in religions throughout the world. The continuing belief in the miraculous powers of language is tied to this notion. The assumption of the divine origin of language stimulated interest in discovering the first primeval language. There are legendary "experiments" in which children were isolated in the belief that their first words would reveal the original language.

Opposing views suggest that language is a human invention. The Greeks believed that an ancient "legislator" gave the true names to all things. Others have suggested that language developed from "cries of nature," or "early gestures," or onomatopoeic words, or even from songs to express love.

All of these proposals are untestable. The cooperative efforts of linguists and evolutionary biologists and neurologists may in time provide some answers to this intriguing question. Because of linguistic research throughout history, we do know a great deal about the nature of language and its use.

References For Further Reading

Bolinger, Dwight. 1980. *Language—The Loaded Weapon: The Use and Abuse of Language Today.* London: Longman.

Chomsky, Noam. 1986. *Knowledge of Language: Its Nature, Origin, and Use.* New York and London: Praeger.

Chomsky, Noam. 1975. *Reflections on Language.* New York: Pantheon Books.

Chomsky, Noam. 1972. *Language and Mind.* Enlarged ed. New York: Harcourt Brace Jovanovich.

Crystal, David. 1984. *Who Cares About Usage?* New York: Penguin.

Hall, Robert A. 1950. *Leave Your Language Alone.* Ithaca, N.Y.: Linguistica.

Gould, J.L. and C.G. Gould. 1983. "Can a Bee Behave Intelligently?" *New Scientist* 98: 84–87.

Milroy, James, and Lesley Milroy. 1985. *Authority in Language: Investigating Language Prescription and Standardisation.* London: Routledge & Kegan Paul.

Newmeyer, Frederick J. 1983. *Grammatical Theory: Its Limits and Possibilities.* Chicago, Ill.: University of Chicago Press.

Nunberg, Geoffrey. 1983. "The decline of grammar." *Atlantic Monthly,* December.

Safire, William. 1980. *On age.* New York: Avon Books.

Sebeok, T.A., ed. 1977. *How Animals Communicate.* Bloomington, Ind.: Indiana University Press.

Shopen, Timothy and Joseph M. Williams, eds. 1980. *Standards and Dialects in English.* Rowley, Mass: Newbury House.

Stam, J. 1976. *Inquiries into the Origin of Language: The Fate of a Question.* New York: Harper & Row.

Von Frisch, K. 1967. *The Dance Language and Orientation of Bees,* trans. by L.E. Chadwick. Cambridge, Mass: Belknap Press of Harvard University Press.

Exercises

---

1. An English speaker's knowledge includes the sound sequences of the language. When new products are put on the market, the manufacturers have to think up new names for them that conform to the allowable sound patterns. Suppose you were hired by a manufacturer of soap products to name five new products. What names might you come up with? List them.

We are interested not in the spelling of the words but in how they are pronounced. Therefore, describe in any way you can how the words you list should be pronounced. Suppose, for example, you named one soap powder *Blick*. You could describe the sounds in any of the following ways:

> *bl* as in *blood, i* as in *pit, ck* as in *stick*
> *bli* as in *bliss, ck* as in *tick*
> *b* as in *boy, lick* as in *lick*

2. Consider the following sentences. Put a star (∗) after those that do not seem to conform to the rules of your grammar, that are ungrammatical for you. State, if you can, why you think the sentence is ungrammatical.

a. Robin forced the sheriff go.
b. Napoleon forced Josephine to go.
c. The Devil made Faust go.
d. He passed by a large sum of money.
e. He came by a large sum of money.
f. He came a large sum of money by.
g. Did in a corner little Jack Horner sit?
h. Elizabeth is resembled by Charles.
i. Nancy is eager to please.
j. It is easy to frighten Emily.
k. It is eager to love a kitten.
l. That birds can fly amazes.
m. The fact that you are late to class is surprising.
n. Has the nurse slept the baby yet?
o. I was surprised for you to get married.
p. I wonder who and Mary went swimming.
q. Myself bit John.

3. It was pointed out in this chapter that a small set of words in languages may be onomatopoeic; that is, their sounds "imitate" what they refer to. *Ding-dong, tick-tock, bang, zing, swish,* and *plop* are such words in English. Construct a list of ten new words. Test them on at least five friends to see if they are truly "nonarbitrary" as to sound and meaning.

(1)	(6)
(2)	(7)
(3)	(8)
(4)	(9)
(5)	(10)

4. Although sounds and meanings of most words in all languages are arbitrarily related, there are some communication systems in which the "signs" unambiguously reveal their "meaning."

    a. Describe (or draw) five different signs that directly show what they mean. Example: a road sign indicating an S curve.

    b. Describe any other communication system that, like language, consists of arbitrary symbols. Example: traffic signals, where red means stop and green means go.

5. Consider these two statements:

> I learned a new word today.
> I learned a new sentence today.

Do you think the two statements are equally probable, and if not, why not?

6. What do the barking of dogs, the meowing of cats, and the singing of birds have in common with human language? What are some of the basic differences?

7. A wolf is able to express subtle gradations of emotion by different positions of the ears, the lips, and the tail. There are eleven postures of the tail that express such emotions as self-confidence, confident threat, lack of tension, uncertain threat, depression, defensiveness, active submission, and complete submission. This system seems to be complex. Suppose there were a thousand different emotions that the wolf could express in this way. Would you then say a wolf had a language similar to a human's? If not, why not?

8. Suppose you taught a dog to *heel, sit up, beg, roll over, play dead, stay, jump,* and *bark* on command, using the italicized words as cues. Would you be teaching it language? Why or why not?

9. State some "rule of grammar" that you have learned is the "correct" way to say something, but that you do not generally use in speaking. For example, you may have heard that *It's me* is incorrect and that the correct form is *It's I*. Nevertheless you always use *me* in such sentences, your friends do also, and in fact, *It's I* sounds odd to you.

Write a short essay presenting arguments against someone who tells you that you are wrong. Discuss how this disagreement demonstrates the difference between descriptive and prescriptive grammars.

PART 2
Grammatical Aspects of Language

We may think of a grammar, represented somehow in the mind, as a system that specifies the phonetic, syntactic, and semantic properties of an infinite class of potential sentences. The child knows the language so determined by the grammar that [has been] acquired. This grammar is a representation of . . . "intrinsic competence."

N. Chomsky, *"On Cognitive Structures and Their Development: A Reply to Piaget"*

CHAPTER 2
Morphology: The Words of Language

A word is dead
When it is said,
Some say.
I say it just
Begins to live
That day.

    Emily Dickinson, *"A Word"*

Every speaker of every language knows thousands, even tens of thousands of words. The words we know are part of our linguistic knowledge, a component of our mental grammars.

When you know a word you know both its pronunciation and its meaning. If you hear someone utter the sounds represented by the string of letters *morpheme* and don't know that it means "smallest unit of linguistic meaning," you don't know that word. Once you learn that this particular sound sequence has such a meaning, if you store that knowledge in your mental **lexicon** (the Greek word for *dictionary*), you now know the word *morpheme*.

Just as a particular string of sounds must be united with a meaning in order for it to be a word, so a concept or meaning must be united with specific sounds. Knowing a word means knowing both how to pronounce it and its meaning. Someone who doesn't know English would not know where one word begins or ends in hearing an utterance like *Thecatsatonthemat*. Without knowledge of the language, it isn't even possible to tell how many words have been said. A speaker of English, however, has no difficulty in segmenting the sounds into the individual words: *the, cat, sat, on, the,* and *mat.* Similarly, someone who doesn't know the American Indian language, Potawatomi, would not know whether *kwapmuknanuk* (which means "They see us") was one, two, or more words. It is, in fact, only one word.

The form (sounds or pronunciation) and the meaning of a word are inseparable; they are like two sides of a coin. Thus, synonyms like *couch* and *sofa* are two words because their identical meanings are represented by two different strings of sounds; homonyms like *crab* the crustacean, and *crab* the verb meaning "to complain," with identical pronunciations but with different meanings, are two words. This was pointed out by the nineteenth century Swiss linguist Ferdinand de Saussure, who discussed the **arbitrary** union between the sounds (form) and meaning (concept) of the **linguistic sign,** or word.

Before 1955, *googol* did not exist as an English word. Now, at least among mathematicians and scientists, it is a word. The word was "coined" by the nine-year-old nephew of Dr. Edward Kasner, an American mathematician, to mean "the number 1 followed by 100 zeros," a number equal to 10^{100}. The number existed before the word was invented, but no single word represented this particular numerical concept. When the concept and sounds of "googol" were united, a word was born. From this word another word, *googolplex,* was formed to mean "1 followed by a googol of zeros."

Of course, not all speakers of English know this word, but since some speakers know its form (pronunciation) and its meaning, it can be referred to as an English word.

Sometimes we think we know a word even though we don't know what it means. It is hard to find an English speaker who hasn't heard the word *antidisestablishmentarianism;* and most will tell you that it is the longest word in the English language. Yet, many of these same persons are unsure as to its meaning. According to the way we have defined what it means to "know a word"—pairing a string of sounds with a particular meaning—such individuals do not really know this word.

Note that information about the longest or shortest word in the language is not part of linguistic knowledge of a language, but general conceptual knowledge *about* a language. Children do not learn such facts the way they learn the sound/meaning correspondences of the words *of* their language. Both children and adults have to be told that *antidisestablishmentarianism* is the longest word in English or discover it through an analysis of a dictionary. As we shall see in Chapter 10, children learn words like *elephant, disappear, mother,* and all the other words they know without being taught them explicitly.

Since each word is a sound-meaning unit, each word stored in our mental dictionaries must be listed with its unique phonological representation, which determines its pronunciation, and with its meaning. For literate speakers, the spelling or **orthography** of most of the words we know is also in our lexicons.

Each word listed in your mental dictionary must include other information as well, such as whether it is a noun, a pronoun, a verb, an adjective, an adverb, a preposition, a conjunction. That is, it must specify its **grammatical category,** or **syntactic class.** You may not consciously know that a form like *love* is listed as both a verb and a noun, but a speaker has such knowledge, as shown by the phrases *I love you* and *You are the love of my life.* If such information is not in the mental dictionary, we would not know how to form grammatical sentences, nor be able to distinguish grammatical from ungrammatical sentences. The classes of words, the syntactic categories—such as nouns, verbs, adjectives, and so on—will be discussed in more detail in Chapter 3. The semantic properties of words, which represent their meanings, will be discussed in Chapter 4.

Dictionaries

Dictionary, n. A malevolent literary device for cramping the growth of a language and making it hard and inelastic.

Ambrose Bierce, *The Devil's Dictionary*

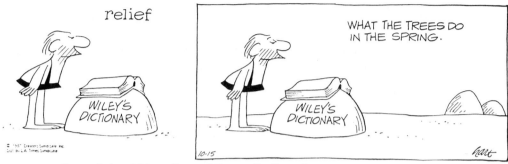

By permission of Johnny Hart and Creators Syndicate, Inc.

The dictionaries that one buys in a bookstore contain some of the information found in our mental dictionaries. The first dictionary to be printed in England was the Latin-English *Promptuorium parvulorum* in 1499; another Latin-English dictionary by Sir Thomas Elyot was published in 1538. Noah Webster, who lived from 1758 until 1843, published *An American Dictionary of the English Language* in two volumes in 1828. It included 70,000 entries.

One of the best efforts at lexicography (defined as "the editing or making of a dictionary" in *Webster's Third New Dictionary of the English Language: Unabridged*) was the *Dictionary of the English Language* by Dr. Samuel Johnson, published in 1755 in two volumes.

The aim of most early lexicographers, whom Dr. Johnson called "harmless drudges," was to "prescribe" rather than "describe" the words of a language, to be, as in the stated aim of one Webster's dictionary, the "supreme authority" of the 'correct' pronunciation and meaning of a word. It is to Johnson's credit that in his Preface he stated he could not construct the language but could only "register the language."

Although probably no speaker of English knows all the 450,000 words listed in *Webster's Third,* all speakers know more about the words in their mental dictionaries than can be found in any published dictionary. Chapter 3 will discuss some of the syntactic information that must be part of a speaker's lexical knowledge but which is not found in even the *Oxford English Dictionary* (often referred to as the *OED*), called the greatest lexicographic work ever produced.[1]

All dictionaries, from the *OED* to the more commonly used 'collegiate dictionaries,' provide the following information about each word: (1) spelling, (2) the 'standard' pronunciation, (3) definitions to represent the word's one or more meanings, and (4) parts of speech, e.g., noun, verb, preposition. Other information may be

---

[1]The title page of the *OED* states: *The Oxford English Dictionary: A New English Dictionary on historical principles; founded mainly on the materials collected by the Philological Society. Edited by James A. H. Marry with the assistance of many scholars and men (sic) of science. 1888–1933.* A new edition of the *OED* was published in 1989 and a computerized edition of the 1933 volumes is now available.

included such as the etymology or history of the word, whether the word is non-standard (such as *ain't*) or slang, vulgar, or obsolete. Many dictionaries provide quotations from published literature to illustrate the given definitions, as was first done by Johnson.

It is interesting to think that scholarly lexicographers spend years writing dictionaries that include information that young children store in their mental dictionaries with great ease.

Classes of Words

THE FAMILY CIRCUS®   **By Bil Keane**

"Adverbs are used to mortify adjectives."

Reprinted with special permission of King Features Syndicate.

Lexical Content Words

In English, nouns, verbs, adjectives, and adverbs make up the largest part of the vocabulary. They are the **content** words of a language, which are sometimes called the **open class** words because we can and regularly do add new words to these classes. *Googol,* for example, was added to the class of nouns. A new verb, *download,* which means to transfer information from a large computer to a smaller computer, entered English with the computer revolution. New adverbs like *weather-*

wise and *saleswise* have been added in recent years, as well as adjectives like *biodegradable*.

Function Words

Other syntactic categories include 'grammatical' or 'function' words. Conjunctions, like *and* and *or,* prepositions, like *in* or *of,* the articles *the* and *a/an,* and pronouns have been referred to as being **closed class** words. It is not easy to think of new conjunctions or prepositions or pronouns that have recently entered the language. The small set of personal pronouns such as *I, me, mine, he, she,* and so on, are part of this class. With the growth of the feminist movement, some proposals have been made for adding a new neutral singular pronoun, which would be neither masculine nor feminine, and which could be used as the general, or **generic,** form. If such a pronoun existed it might have prevented the department chairperson in a large university from making the incongruous statement: "We will hire the best person for the job regardless of his sex." The UCLA psychologist Donald MacKay has suggested that we use "e," pronounced like the letter name, for this pronoun with various alternative forms; others point out that *they* and *their* are already being used as neutral third person singular forms, as in "Anyone can do it if they try hard enough" or "Everyone can do their best." The use of the various forms of *they* is reported to be Standard British English used on the BBC (British Broadcasting System) with *anyone* and *everyone* now considered either singular or plural, similar to such words as *committee* or *government.*

These classes of content and function words appear to have psychological and neurological validity. Some brain-damaged patients have greater difficulty in using or understanding or reading function words than content words. Some interpret a word like *in* to mean *inn,* or *which* to mean *witch,* when asked to read and use such words in sentences. Other patients do just the opposite. Such effects of brain damage on language will be discussed further in Chapter 11. We mention this here merely to show that linguistic analysis of words is attested to by researchers in other areas of science. Note that the important feature of these two classes is their function rather than their degree of "openness." What is an 'open class' in one language may be 'closed' in another. In Akan, the major language spoken in Ghana, for example, there are only a handful of 'adjectives'; most English adjectives are in the verb class in Akan. Instead of saying "The sun is bright today," an Akan speaker will say "The sun brightens today."

Word Sets

Most wonderful of all are words, and how they make friends one with another

O. Henry

Words may be related to each other in a special way. Consider the words below, which are all related in both sound and meaning. You may not know the meaning of some of them but you will when you read Chapters 5 and 6.

phone	phonologist	allophone
phonetic	phonological	telephone
phonetician	phonic	telephonic
phonetics	phoneme	euphonious
phonology	phonemic	

Phon is a minimal form in that it can't be divided into more elemental structures. *Ph* doesn't mean anything, and *pho,* though it may be pronounced like *foe,* has no relation in meaning to it, and *on* is not the preposition spelled *o n*. But all the words on the list contain *phon* as part of their structure. Even if that part of the word is pronounced differently in the words above, the same element, *phon,* is present, with its identical meaning, "pertaining to sound," in all these words.

Notice further that in the following pairs of words the meanings of all the words in column B consist of the meanings of the words in column A plus the meaning "not":

A	**B**
desirable	undesirable
likely	unlikely
inspired	uninspired
happy	unhappy
developed	undeveloped
sophisticated	unsophisticated

Webster's Third New International Dictionary lists about 2700 adjectives beginning with *un.*

The *Luann* cartoon shown below reflects the knowledge that speakers have about the meaning of *un.*

Reprinted with special permission of North America Syndicate.

If the most elemental units of meaning, the basic linguistic signs, are assumed to be the words of a language, it would be a coincidence that *un* has the same meaning in all the column B words, or that *phon* has the same meaning in all the words in the preceding list. But this is no coincidence. The words *undesirable, unlikely, uninspired, unhappy,* and the others in column B consist of at least two meaningful units: *un + desirable, un + likely,* and so on.

It is also a fact about words that their internal structure is subject to rules. Thus *uneaten, unadmired,* and *ungrammatical* are words in English, but **eatenun, *admiredun,* and **grammaticalun* (to mean "not eaten," "not admired," "not grammatical") are not, because we do not form a negative meaning of a word by **suffixing** *un* (that is, by adding it to the end of the word), but by **prefixing** it (that is, by adding it to the beginning).

The study of the internal structure of words, and of the rules by which words are formed, is called **morphology.** Knowledge of a language implies knowledge of its morphology.

Morphemes: The Minimal Units of Meaning

"They gave it me," Humpty Dumpty continued, "for an un-birthday present."
"I beg your pardon?" Alice said with a puzzled air.
"I'm not offended," said Humpty Dumpty.
"I mean, what is an un-birthday present?"
"A present given when it isn't your birthday, of course."

Lewis Carroll, *Through the Looking-Glass*

When Samuel Goldwyn, the pioneer moviemaker, announced: "In two words: im-possible" he was reflecting the common view that words are the basic meaningful elements in a language. We have already seen that this cannot be so, since some words are formed by combining a number of distinct units of meaning. The traditional term for the most elemental unit of grammatical form is **morpheme.** The word is derived from the Greek word, *morphe,* meaning "form." Linguistically speaking, then, Goldwyn should have said: "In two morphemes: im-possible."

A single word may be composed of one or more morphemes:

one morpheme	boy
	desire
two morphemes	boy + ish
	desire + able
three morphemes	boy + ish + ness
	desire + able + ity
four morphemes	gentle + man + li + ness
	un + desire + able + ity

more than four   un + gentle + man + li + ness
anti + dis + establish + ment + ari + an + ism[2]

A morpheme may be represented by a single sound, such as the morpheme *a* meaning "without" as in *amoral* or *asexual* or by a single syllable, such as *child* and *ish* in *child + ish*. A morpheme, however, may be represented by more than one syllable: by two syllables, as in *aardvark, lady, water;* or by three syllables, as in *Hackensack* or *crocodile;* or by four or more syllables, as in *salamander*. Although we haven't yet given a definition for the term *syllable,* most speakers of English know intuitively how many syllables there are in a morpheme or a word.

A morpheme may be defined as the minimal linguistic sign, a grammatical unit in which there is an arbitrary union of a sound and a meaning that cannot be further analyzed. As we shall see, this may be too simple a definition, but it will serve our purposes for now. Every word in every language is composed of one or more morphemes.

Bound and Free Morphemes

THE FAMILY CIRCUS®   By Bil Keane

"Mommy said to behave, so I'm bein' as hayve as I can."

Reprinted with special permission of King Features Syndicate.

[2]Some speakers have even more morphemes for this word than are shown here.

Prefixes and Suffixes

The examples given above show that some morphemes like *boy, desire, gentle,* and *man* can constitute words by themselves. Other morphemes like *-ish, -able, -ness, -ly, dis-, trans-,* and *un-* are never words but always parts of words. Thus, *un-* is like *pre-* (*prefix, predetermine, prejudge, prearrange*), and *dis-* (*disallow, disobey, disapprove, dislike*), and *bi-* (*bipolar, bisexual, bivalved*); it occurs only before other morphemes. Such morphemes are called **prefixes.**

Prefixing is very widespread in the languages of the world. In Isthmus Zapotec, for example, the plural morpheme *ka-* is a prefix:

zigi	"chin"	kazigi	"chins"
zike	"shoulder"	kazike	"shoulders"
diaga	"ear"	kadiaga	"ears"

Other morphemes occur only as **suffixes,** after other morphemes. English examples of such morphemes are *-er* (as in *singer, performer, reader,* and *beautifier*), *-ist* (in *typist, copyist, pianist, novelist, collaborationist,* and *linguist*) and *-ly* (as in *manly, bastardly, sickly, spectacularly,* and *friendly*), to mention only a few.

These prefix and suffix morphemes have traditionally been called **bound** morphemes, because they cannot occur "unattached," as distinct from **free** morphemes like *man, bastard, sick, prove, allow,* and so on. Of course in speaking we seldom use even free morphemes alone. We combine all morphemes into larger units—phrases and sentences.

In all languages morphemes are the minimal linguistic signs. In Turkish, if you add *-ak* to a verb, you derive a noun, as in:

dur	"to stop"	dur + ak	"stopping place"
bat	"to sink"	bat + ak	"sinking place" or "marsh/swamp"

In English, in order to express reciprocal action we use the phrase *each other,* as in *understand each other, love each other.* In Turkish, one simply adds a morpheme to the verb:

anla	"understand"	anla + s	"understand each other"
sev	"love"	sev + is	"love each other"

The "reciprocal" suffix in these examples is pronounced as *s* after a vowel and as *is* after a consonant. This is similar to the process in English in which we use *a* as the indefinite article morpheme before a noun beginning with a consonant, as in *a dog,* and *an* before a noun beginning with a vowel, as in *an apple.* We will discuss the various pronunciations of morphemes in Chapter 6.

In Piro, an Arawakan language spoken in Peru, a single morpheme, *kaka,* can be added to a verb to express the meaning "cause to":

cokoruha	"to harpoon"	cokoruha + kaka	"cause to harpoon"
salwa	"to visit"	salwa + kaka	"cause to visit"

In Karok, a Native American language spoken in the Pacific Northwest, one forms a locative adverbial meaning "in, on" or "at" by adding -*ak* to a noun:

ikrivaam	"house"	ikrivaamak	"in a house"

Note that it is accidental that both Turkish and Karok have a suffix -*ak*. Despite the similarity in form, the two meanings are different. Similarly, the reciprocal suffix -*s* in Turkish is similar in form to the English plural -*s*. Also in Karok, the suffix -*ara* has the same meaning as the English -*y,* that is, "characterized by":

aptiik	"branch"	aptikara	"branchy"

These examples exemplify the arbitrary nature of the linguistic sign.

In Russian the suffix -*shchik* (pronounced like the beginning of the word *she* followed by *chick*) added to a noun is similar in meaning to the English suffix -*er* in words like *reader, teacher,* or *rider,* which when added to a verb means "one who—". The Russian suffix, however, is added to nouns, not verbs, as shown in the following examples.

Russian		**Russian**	
atom	"atom"	atomshchik	"atom-warmonger"
baraban	"drum"	barabanshchik	"drummer"
kalambur	"pun"	kalamburshchik	"punner"
beton	"concrete"	betonshchik	"concrete worker"
lom	"scrap"	lomshchik	"salvage collector"

The examples given above from different languages also illustrate "free" morphemes like *boy* in English: *dur* in Turkish, *salwa* in Piro, and *lom* in Russian.

Infixes

Some languages also have **infixes,** morphemes that are inserted into other morphemes. Bontoc, a language spoken in the Philippines, is such a language, as is illustrated by the following:

Nouns/Adjectives		**Verbs**	
fikas	"strong"	fumikas	"to be strong"
kilad	"red"	kumilad	"to be red"
fusul	"enemy"	fumusul	"to be an enemy"

In this language the infix -*um*- is inserted after the first consonant of the noun or adjective. Thus, a speaker of Bontoc who learns that *pusi* means "poor," would understand the meaning of *pumusi*, "to be poor," on hearing the word for the first time. Just as an English speaker who learns the verb *sneet* would know that *sneeter* is one who sneets, a Bontoc speaker who knows that *ngumitad* means "to be dark" would know that the adjective "dark" must be *ngitad*.

Circumfixes

There are also languages which have **circumfixes,** morphemes which are attached to a root or stem morpheme both initially and finally. These are sometimes called **discontinuous morphemes.** In Chickasaw, a Muskogean language spoken in Oklahoma, the negative is formed by using both a prefix *ik-* and the suffix *-o.* Note that the final vowel of the declarative is deleted before the negative suffix is added. Examples of this circumfixing are:

Declarative		**Negative**	
chokm + a	"he is good"	ik + chokm + o	"he isn't good"
lakn + a	"it is yellow"	ik + lakn + o	"it isn't yellow"
pall + i	"it is hot"	ik + pall + o	"it isn't hot"
tiww + i	"he opens (it)"	ik + tiww + o	"he doesn't open (it)"

An example of a more familiar 'circumfixing' language is German. The past participle of regular verbs is formed by adding the prefix *ge-* and the suffix *-t* to the verb root. Thus, this circumfix added to the verb root *lieb* "love" produces *geliebt,* "loved" (or "beloved," when used as an adjective).

Huckles and Ceives

We have defined a morpheme as the basic element of meaning, a phonological form that is arbitrarily united with a particular meaning and that cannot be analyzed into simpler elements. This definition has presented problems for linguistic analysis for many years, although it holds for most of the morphemes in a language. Consider words like *cranberry, huckleberry,* and *boysenberry.* The *berry* part is no problem, but *huckle* and *boysen* occur only with *berry,* as did *cran* until the drink *Cranapple* juice came on the market, and other morphologically complex words using *cran-* followed. *Lukewarm* is another word with two stem morphemes, with *luke* occurring only in this word, because it is not the same morpheme as the name *Luke.*

To account for bound forms like *huckle-, boysen-,* and *luke-*, we have to redefine the notion "morpheme." Some morphemes are not meaningful in isolation but acquire meaning only in combination with other specific morphemes. Thus the morpheme *huckle,* when joined with *berry,* has the meaning of a special kind of berry which is small, round, and purplish-blue; *luke* when combined with *warm* has the meaning "sort of" or "somewhat," and so on.

Just as there are some morphemes which occur only in a single word (that is, combined with another morpheme), there are other morphemes which occur in many words, combining with different morphemes, but for which it is very difficult

THE FAMILY CIRCUS®   By Bil Keane

3-12

Copyright 1988
Cowles Syndicate, Inc.

"We're on the outskirts of the city now."
"When will we be on the inskirts?"

Reprinted with special permission of King Features Syndicate.

to find a constant meaning. How would you define the *-ceive* in *receive, perceive, conceive,* and *deceive,* or the *-mit* in *remit, permit, commit, submit, transmit,* and *admit?*

There are other words that seem to be composed of prefix + stem morphemes in which the stems like the *cran-* or *-ceive* never occur alone, but always with a regular prefix. Thus we find *inept,* but no **ept, inane,* but no **ane, incest,* but no **cest, inert* but no **ert, disgusted,* but no **gusted.*

Similarly, the stems of *upholster, downhearted,* and *outlandish* do not occur by themselves: *holster and *hearted (with these meanings), and *landish* (except as the maiden name of V. A. Fromkin) are not free morphemes. In addition, *downholster, uphearted,* and *inlandish,* their 'opposites,' are not found in any English lexicon.

To complicate things a little further, there are words like *strawberry* in which the *straw* has no relationship to any other kind of *straw, gooseberry,* which is unrelated to *goose,* and *blackberry,* which may be blue or red. While some of these words may have historical origins, there is no present meaningful connection. The *Oxford English Dictionary* entry for the word *strawberry* states that "The reason for the name has been variously conjectured. One explanation refers the first element to Straw . . . a particle of straw or chaff, a mote describing the appearance of the achenes scattered over the surface of the strawberry." That may be true of the word's origin, but today, the *straw-* in *strawberry* is not the same morpheme as that found in *strawlike* or *straw-colored.*

A morpheme, like a word, is a linguistic sign—its meaning must be constant. The morpheme *-er* means "one who does" in words like *singer, painter, lover,* and *worker,* but the same sounds represent the "comparative" morpheme, meaning "more," in *nicer, prettier,* and *taller.* Thus, two different morphemes may have the same form, that is, may be pronounced identically but be two morphemes because they have different meanings. The same sounds may occur in another word and not represent any separate morpheme as is shown by the final syllable in *butcher; er* does not represent any morpheme, since a butcher is not one who butches. (In an earlier form of English the word *butcher* was *bucker,* "one who dresses bucks." The *-er* in this word was then a separate morpheme.) Similarly, in *water* the *-er* is not a distinct morpheme ending; *butcher* and *water* are single morphemes, or **mono-morphemic** words. This follows from the concept of the morpheme as a sound-meaning unit.

All morphemes, then, are bound or free. Affixes (prefixes, suffixes, and infixes) are bound morphemes. Non-affix lexical content morphemes, called **root** morphemes, such as *boy* or *cran,* can be bound or free. We can illustrate these facts as follows:

	Free	**Bound**
Root	dog, cat, aardvark, corduroy, run, bottle, hot, separate, phone, museum, school . . . (and 1000s more)	huckle(berry), (dis)gruntle, (un)couth, (non)chalance, (per)ceive, (in)ept, (re)mit, (in)cest, (homo)geneous . . . (and a few more)
Affix		(friend)ship, (lead)ership, re(do), homo(geneous), hetero(geneous), trans-(sex)-ual, (sad)ly, (tall)-ish, (a)moral (and many others)

(Note that there are some morpheme types not listed in this chart, such as the *-ing* in *going* or *the* or *and.*)

Rules of Word Formation

"I never heard of 'Uglification,'" Alice ventured to say. "What is it?"

The Gryphon lifted up both its paws in surprise. "Never heard of uglifying!" it exclaimed. "You know what to beautify is, I suppose?"

"Yes," said Alice doubtfully: "it means—to make—anything—prettier."

"Well, then," the Gryphon went on, "if you don't know what to uglify is, you are a simpleton."

Lewis Carroll, *Alice in Wonderland*

When the Mock Turtle listed the different branches of Arithmetic for Alice as "Ambition, Distraction, Uglification, and Derision," Alice was very confused. She wasn't really a simpleton, since *uglification* was not a common word in English until Lewis Carroll used it. There are many ways in which words enter a language. Some of these are discussed in Chapter 8 on language change.

Lexical Gaps

We have already noted that there are gaps in the lexicon such as *googol,* 'words' which are not in the dictionary but which can be added. Some of the gaps are due to the fact that a permissible sound sequence has no meaning attached to it (like *blick,* or *slarm,* or *krobe*). Note that the sequence of sounds must be in keeping with the constraints of the language. **bnick* is not a 'gap' because no word in English can begin with a *bn.* We will discuss such constraints in Chapter 6.

Other gaps are due to the fact that possible combinations of morphemes have not been made (like *ugly + ify* or *linguistic + ism*). Morphemes can be combined in this way because there are **morphological rules** in every language that determine how morphemes combine to form new words.

The Mock Turtle added *-ify* to the adjective *ugly* and formed a verb. Many verbs in English have been formed in this way: *purify, amplify, simplify, falsify.* The suffix *-ify* conjoined with nouns also forms verbs: *objectify, glorify, personify.* Notice that the Mock Turtle went even further; he added the suffix *-cation* to *uglify* and formed a noun, *uglification,* as in *glorification, simplification, falsification,* and *purification.*

Derivational Morphology

There are morphemes in English that are called **derivational morphemes** because when they are conjoined to other morphemes (or words) a new word is derived, or formed. The derived word may have a different meaning than the original word and may even be in a different grammatical class than the underived word. Thus, when a verb is suffixed with *-able,* the result is an adjective, as in *desire* + *able* or *adore* + *able*. Or, when the suffix *-en* is added to an adjective, a verb may be derived, as in *dark* + *en*. One may form a noun from an adjective, as in *sweet* + *ie*. A few other examples are:

Noun To Adjective	Verb To Noun	Adjective To Adverb	Noun To Verb
boy + ish	acquitt + al	exact + ly	moral + ize
virtu + ous	clear + ance	quiet + ly	vaccin + ate
Elizabeth + an	accus + ation		brand + ish
pictur + esque	confer + ence		haste + n
affection + ate	sing + er		
health + ful	conform + ist		
alcohol + ic	predict + ion		
life + like	free + dom		

Not all derivational morphemes cause a change in grammatical class. Many prefixes fall into this category:

a + moral	mono + theism
auto + biography	re + print
ex + wife	semi + annual
super + human	sub + minimal

There are also suffixes of this type:

vicar + age	New Jersey + ite
long + er	fadd + ist
short + est	music + ian
Americ + an	pun + ster

New words may enter the dictionary in this fashion, created by the application of morphological rules. It is often the case that when such a word as, for example, *Commun* + *ist* enters the language, other possible complex forms will not, such as *Commun* + *ite* (as in *Trotsky* + *ite*) or *Commun* + *ian* (as in *grammar* + *ian*). There may however exist alternative forms: for example, *Chomskyan* and *Chomsky-ist* and perhaps even *Chomskyite* (all meaning "follower of Chomsky's views of linguistics"). *Linguist* and *linguistician* are both used, but note that the possible word *linguite* is not. The redundancy of such alternative forms, all of which conform to the regular rules of word formation, may explain some of the accidental gaps in the lexicon. This further shows that the actual words in the language constitute only a subset of the possible words.

There are many other derivational morphemes in English and other languages, such as the suffixes meaning "diminutive," as in the words *pig* + *let* and *sap* + *ling*.

Some of the morphological rules are **productive,** meaning that they can be used freely to form new words from the list of free and bound morphemes. The suffix *-able* appears to be a morpheme that can be conjoined with any verb to derive an adjective with the meaning of the verb and the meaning of *-able*, which is something like "able to be" as in *accept + able, blam(e) + able, pass + able, change + able, breath + able, adapt + able,* and so on. The meaning of *-able* has also been given as "fit for doing" or "fit for being done."

Such a rule might be stated as:

(1) VERB + able = "able to be VERB-ed"
e.g. accept + able = "able to be accepted"

The productivity of this rule is illustrated by the fact that we find *-able* in such morphologically complex words as *un + speakabl(e) + y* and *un + come + at + able*.

We have already noted that there is a morpheme in English meaning "not" which has the form *un-* and which, when combined with adjectives like *afraid, fit, free, smooth, American,* and *British,* forms the **antonyms,** or negatives, of these adjectives; for example, *unafraid, unfit, un-American,* and so on.

We can also add the prefix *un-* to derived words that have been formed by morphological rules:

un + believe + able
un + accept + able
un + talk + about + able
un + keep + off + able
un + speak + able

The rule that forms these words may be stated as:

(2) un + ADJECTIVE = "not-ADJECTIVE"

This seems to account for all the examples cited. Yet we find *happy* and *unhappy, cowardly* and *uncowardly,* but not *sad* and **unsad* or *brave* and **unbrave.* The starred forms that follow may be merely **accidental gaps** in the lexicon. If someone refers to a person as being **unsad* we would know that the person referred to was "not sad," and an **unbrave* person would not be brave. But, as the linguist Sandra Thompson points out, it may be the case that the "un-Rule" is not as productive for adjectives composed of just one morpheme as for adjectives that are themselves derived from verbs.[3]

The rule seems to be freely applicable to an adjectival form derived from a verb, as in *unenlightened, unsimplified, uncharacterized, unauthorized, undistinguished,* and so on.

It is true, however, that one cannot always know the meaning of the words derived from free and derivational morphemes from the morphemes themselves.

[3]S.A. Thompson, "On the Issue of Productivity in the Lexikon," *Kritikon Litterarum* 4 (1975): 332–349.

Thompson has also pointed out that the *un-* forms of the following have unpredictable meanings:

unloosen	"loosen, let loose"
unrip	"rip, undo by ripping"
undo	"reverse doing"
untread	"go back through in the same steps"
unearth	"dig up"
unfrock	"deprive (a cleric) of ecclesiastic rank"
unnerve	"fluster"

Therefore, although the words in a language are not the most elemental sound-meaning units, they (plus the morphemes) must be listed in our dictionaries. The morphological rules also are in the grammar, revealing the relation between words and providing the means for forming new words.

Morphological rules may be more or less productive. The rule that adds an *-er* to verbs in English to produce a noun meaning "one who performs an action (once or habitually)" appears to be a very productive morphological rule; most English verbs accept this suffix: *lover, hunter, predictor* (notice that *-or* and *-er* have the same pronunciation), *examiner, exam-taker, analyzer,* and so forth.

Now consider the following:

sincerity	from	*sincere*
warmth	from	*warm*
moisten	from	*moist*

The suffix *-ity* is found in many other words in English, like *chastity, scarcity,* and *curiosity;* and *-th* occurs in *health, wealth, depth, width,* and *growth.* We find *-en* in *sadden, ripen, redden, weaken, deepen.* Still, the phrase **The fiercity of the lion* sounds somewhat strange, as does the sentence **I'm going to thinnen the sauce.* Someone may use the word *coolth,* but, as Thompson points out, when such words as *fiercity, thinnen, fullen,* or *coolth* are used, usually it is either an error or an attempt at humor.

It is possible that in such cases a morphological rule that was once productive (as shown by the existence of related pairs like *scarce/scarcity*) is no longer so. Our knowledge of the related pairs, however, may permit us to use these examples in forming new words, by analogy with the existing lexical items.

"Pullet Surprises"

That speakers of a language know the morphemes of that language and the rules for word formation is shown as much by the "errors" made as by the nondeviant forms produced. Morphemes combine to form words. These words form our internal

DRABBLE reprinted by permission of UFS, Inc.

dictionaries. No speaker of a language knows all the words. Given our knowledge of the morphemes of the language and the morphological rules, we can often guess the meaning of a word we do not know. Sometimes we guess wrong.

Amsel Greene collected errors made by her students in vocabulary-building classes and published them in a book called *Pullet Surprises*.[4] The title is taken from a sentence written by one of her high-school students: "In 1957 Eugene O'Neill won a Pullet Surprise." What is most interesting about these errors is how much they reveal about the students' knowledge of English morphology. Consider the creativity of these students in the following examples:

Word	**Student's Definition**
deciduous	"able to make up one's mind"
longevity	"being very tall"
fortuitous	"well protected"
gubernatorial	"to do with peanuts"
bibliography	"holy geography"
adamant	"pertaining to original sin"
diatribe	"food for the whole clan"
polyglot	"more than one glot"
gullible	"to do with sea birds"
homogeneous	"devoted to home life"

The student who used the word *indefatigable* in the sentence

She tried many reducing diets, but remained indefatigable.

clearly shows morphological knowledge: *in,* meaning "not" as in *ineffective; de* meaning "off" as in *decapitate; fat,* as in "fat"; *able,* as in *able;* and combined meaning, "not able to take the fat off."

[4]Amsel Greene, *Pullet Surprises,* Glenview, Ill.: Scott, Foresman & Co., 1969.

Word Coinage

As we have seen, new words may be added to the vocabulary or lexicon of a language by derivational processes. New words may also enter a language in a variety of other ways. Some are created outright to fit some purpose. Madison Avenue has added many new words to English, such as *Kodak, nylon, Orlon,* and *Dacron.* Specific brand names such as *Xerox, Kleenex, Jell-O, Frigidaire, Brillo* and *Vaseline* are now sometimes used as the generic name for different brands of these types of products. Notice that some of these words were created from existing words: *Kleenex* from the word *clean* and *Jell-O* from *gel,* for example.

Compounds

... the Houynhnms have no Word in their Language to express any thing that is evil, except what they borrow from the Deformities or ill Qualities of the Yahoos. Thus they denote the Folly of a Servant, an Omission of a Child, a Stone that cuts their feet, a Continuance of foul or unseasonable Weather, and the like, by adding to each the Epithet of Yahoo. For instance, Hnhm Yahoo, Whnaholm Yahoo, Ynlhmnawihlma Yahoo, and an ill contrived House, Ynholmhnmrohlnw Yahoo.

Jonathan Swift, *Gulliver's Travels*

PEANUTS reprinted by permission of UFS, Inc.

New words may be formed by stringing together other words to create **compound** words. There is almost no limit on the kinds of combinations that occur in English, as the following list of compounds shows:

	-Adjective	-Noun	-Verb
Adjective-	bittersweet	poorhouse	highborn
Noun-	headstrong	rainbow	spoonfeed
Verb-	carryall	pickpocket	sleepwalk

Frigidaire is a compound formed by combining the adjective *frigid* with the noun *air.*

When the two words are in the same grammatical category, the compound will be in this category: noun + noun—*girlfriend, fighter-bomber, paper clip, elevator-operator, landlord, mailman;* adjective + adjective—*icy-cold, red-hot,* and *worldly-wise.* In many cases, when the two words fall into different categories, the class of the second or final word will be the grammatical category of the compound: noun + adjective—*headstrong, watertight, lifelong;* verb + noun—*pickpocket, pinchpenny, daredevil, sawbones.* On the other hand, compounds formed with a preposition are in the category of the nonprepositional part of the compound: *over-take, hanger-on, undertake, sundown, afterbirth, downfall, uplift.*

Though two-word compounds are the most common in English, it would be difficult to state an upper limit: Consider *three-time loser, four-dimensional space-time, sergeant-at-arms, mother-of-pearl, man about town, master of ceremonies,* and *daughter-in-law.*

Spelling does not tell us what sequence of words constitutes a compound; whether a compound is spelled with a space between the two words, with a hyphen, or with no separation at all is idiosyncratic, as shown, for example, in *blackbird, gold-tail,* and *smoke screen.*

Meaning of Compounds

One of the interesting things about a compound is that you cannot always tell by the words it contains what the compound means. The meaning of a compound is not always the sum of the meanings of its parts; a *blackboard* may be green or white.

By permission of Johnny Hart and Creators Syndicate, Inc.

Everyone who wears a red coat is not a *Redcoat,* either. The difference between the sentences *She has a red coat in her closet* and *She has a Redcoat in her closet* could be highly significant under certain circumstances.

Other similarly constructed compounds show that, underlying the juxtaposition of words, different grammatical relations are expressed. A *boathouse* is a house for boats, but a *cathouse* is not a house for cats. A *jumping bean* is a bean that jumps, a *falling star* is a "star" that falls, and a *magnifying glass* is a glass that magnifies; but a *looking glass* is not a glass that looks, nor is an *eating apple* an apple that eats, and *laughing gas* does not laugh.

In all these examples, the meaning of each compound includes at least to some extent the meanings of the individual parts. However, there are other compounds that do not seem to relate to the meanings of the individual parts at all. A *jack-in-a-box* is a tropical tree, and a *turncoat* is a traitor. A *highbrow* does not necessarily have a high brow, nor does a *bigwig* have a big wig, nor does an *egghead* have an egg-shaped head.

As we pointed out earlier in the discussion of the prefix *un-,* the meaning of many compounds must be learned as if they were individual simple words. Some of the meanings may be figured out, but not all. If you had never heard the word *hunchback,* it might be possible to infer the meaning; but if you had never heard the word *flatfoot,* it is doubtful you would know it means "detective" or "policeman," even though the origin of the word, once you know the meaning, can be figured out.

Therefore, the words as well as the morphemes must be listed in our dictionaries. The morphological rules also are in the grammar, revealing the relations between words and providing the means for forming new words. Dr. Seuss uses the rules of compounding when he explains that "when tweetle beetles battle with paddles in a puddle, they call it a *tweetle beetle puddle paddle battle* ."[5]

Universality of Compounding

Other languages have rules for conjoining words to form compounds, as seen by French *cure-dent,* "toothpick"; German *Panzerkraftwagen,* "armored car"; Russian *cetyrexetaznyi,* "four-storied"; Spanish *tocadiscos,* "record player." In the Native American language Papago the word meaning "thing" is *haʔichu,* and it combines with *doakam,* "living creatures," to form the compound *haʔichu doakam,* "animal life."

In Twi, by combining the word meaning "son" or "child," *ɔba,* with the word meaning "chief," *ɔhene,* one derives the compound *ɔheneba,* meaning "prince." By adding the word "house," *ofi,* to *ɔhene,* the word meaning "palace," *ahemfi* is derived. The other changes that occur in the Twi compounds are due to phonological and morphological rules in the language.

In Thai, the word "cat" is *mɛɛw,* the word for "watch" (in the sense of "to watch over") is *fâw,* and the word for "house" is *bâan.* The word for "watch cat" (like a watchdog) is the compound *mɛɛwfâwbâan*—literally, "catwatchhouse."

Compounding is therefore a common and frequent process for enlarging the vocabulary of all languages.

[5]Dr. Seuss, *Fox in Sox,* New York: Random House, 1965, p. 51.

Acronyms

Acronyms are words derived from the initials of several words. Such words are pronounced as the spelling indicates: NASA from *N*ational *A*eronautics and *S*pace *A*gency, UNESCO from *U*nited *N*ational *E*ducational, *S*cientific, and *C*ultural *O*rganization, and UNICEF from *U*nited *N*ations *I*nternational *C*hildren's *E*mergency *F*und. *Radar* from "*r*adio *d*etecting *a*nd *r*anging," *laser* from "*l*ight *a*mplification by *s*timulated *e*mission of *r*adiation," and *scuba* from "*s*elf-*c*ontained *u*nderwater *b*reathing *a*pparatus," show the creative efforts of word coiners, as does *snafu,* which was coined by soldiers in World War II and is rendered in polite circles as "situation normal, all fouled up." A new acronym which has recently been added to the English language and which is sadly used very frequently these days is AIDS from the initials of *A*cquired *I*mmune *D*eficiency *S*yndrome. When the string of letters is not easily pronounced as a word, the acronym is produced by sounding out each letter, as in NFL for *N*ational *F*ootball *L*eague or UCLA (*U*niversity of *C*alifornia, *L*os *A*ngeles), which may also be pronounced as if it were spelled *youcla.*

Blends

Blends are compounds that are "less than" compounds. *Smog,* from *smoke + fog; motel,* from *motor + hotel;* and *urinalysis,* from *urine + analysis* are examples of blends that have attained full lexical status in English. The word *Cranapple* may be a blend of *cranberry + apple. Broasted,* from *broiled + roasted,* is a blend that has limited acceptance in the language, as does Lewis Carroll's *chortle,* from *chuckle + snort.* Carroll is famous for both the coining and the blending of words. In *Through the Looking-Glass* he describes the "meanings" of the made-up words in "Jabberwocky" as follows:

> . . . "Brillig" means four o'clock in the afternoon—the time when you begin broiling things for dinner. . . . "Slithy" means "lithe and slimy." . . . You see it's like a portmanteau—there are two meanings packed up into one word. . . ."Toves" are something like badgers—they're something like lizards—and they're something like corkscrews . . . also they make their nests under sun-dials—also they live on cheese. . . . To "gyre" is to go round and round like a gyroscope. To "gimble" is to make holes like a gimlet. And "the wabe" is the grass-plot round a sun-dial. . . . It's called "wabe" . . . because it goes a long way before it and a long way behind it. . . . "Mimsy" is "flimsy and miserable" (there's another pormanteau . . . for you).

Carroll's "portmanteaus" are what we have called blends, and such words can become part of the regular lexicon.

Back-Formations

Copyright © by Mell Lazarus.

New words may be formed from existing words by "subtracting" an affix thought to be part of the old word; that is, ignorance sometimes can be creative. Thus, *peddle* was derived from *peddler* on the mistaken assumption that the *er* was the "agentive" suffix. Such words are called **back-formations.** The verbs *hawk, stoke, swindle,* and *edit* all came into the language as back-formations—of *hawker, stoker, swindler,* and *editor. Pea* was derived from a singular word, *pease,* by speakers who thought *pease* was a plural. Language purists sometimes rail against back-formations and cite *enthuse* (from *enthusiasm*) and *ept* (from *inept*) as examples of language corruption; but language cannot be corrupt (although the speakers who use it may be), and many words have entered the language this way.

Some word coinage, similar to the kind of wrong morphemic analysis that produces back-formations, is deliberate. The word *bikini* is from the Bikini atoll of the Marshall Islands. Because the first syllable *bi-* in other words, like *bipolar*, means "two," some clever person called a topless bathing suit a *monokini*. Historically, a number of new words have entered the English lexicon in this way. Based on analogy with such pairs as *act/action, exempt/exemption, revise/revision*, new words *resurrect, preempt*, and *televise* were formed from the existing words *resurrection, preemption*, and *television*.

Abbreviations

Abbreviations of longer words or phrases also may become "lexicalized"; *nark* for *narcotics agent, tec* (or *dick*) for *detective; telly*, the British word for *television, prof* for *professor, piano* for *pianoforte*, and *gym* for *gymnasium* are only a few examples of such "short forms" that are now used as whole words. Other examples are *ad, bike, math, gas, phone, bus*, and *van*. This process is sometimes called **clipping.**

Words from Names

The creativity of word coinage (or vocabulary addition) is also revealed by the number of words in the English vocabulary that derive from proper names of individuals or places.

Willard R. Espy[6] has compiled a book of 1500 such words. They include some old favorites:

sandwich	Named for the fourth Earl of Sandwich, who put his food between two slices of bread so that he could eat while he gambled.
robot	After the mechanical creatures in the Czech writer Karel Capek's play *R.U.R.*, the initials standing for "Rossum's Universal Robots."
gargantuan	Named for Gargantua, the creature with a huge appetite created by Rabelais.
jumbo	After an elephant brought to the United States by P. T. Barnum. ("Jumbo olives" need not be as big as an elephant, however.)

Espy admits to ignorance of the Susan, an unknown servant, from whom we derived the compound *lazy susan*, or the Betty or Charlotte or Chuck from whom we got *brown betty, charlotte russe*, or *chuck wagon*. He does point out that *denim* was named for the material used for overalls and carpeting, which originally was imported "de Nîmes" ("from Nimes") in France, and *argyle* from the kind of socks worn by the chiefs of Argyll of the Campbell clan in Scotland.

---

[6]W. R. Espy, *O Thou Improper, Thou Uncommon Noun: An Etymology of Words That Once Were Names,* New York: Clarkson N. Potter, 1978.

Grammatical Morphemes

"... and even ... the patriotic archbishop of Canterbury found it advisable—"
"Found what?" said the Duck
"Found it," the Mouse replied rather crossly; "of course you know what 'it' means."
"I know what 'it' means well enough, when I find a thing," said the Duck; "it's generally a frog or a worm. The question is, what did the archbishop find?"

Lewis Carroll, *Alice's Adventures in Wonderland*

"My boy, Grand-père is not the one to ask about such things. I have lived eighty-seven peaceful and happy years in Montoire-sur-le-Loir without the past anterior verb form."
Drawing by Everett Opie; ©1973 The New Yorker Magazine, Inc.

Morphological rules for combining morphemes into words differ from the syntactic rules of a language which determine how words are combined to form sentences to be discussed in Chapter 3. There is, however, an interesting relationship between morphology and syntax. In the discussion of derivational morphology, we saw that certain aspects of morphology have syntactic implications in that nouns can be derived from verbs, verbs from adjectives, adjectives from nouns, and so on. There are other ways in which morphology is dependent on syntax.

When we combine words to form sentences, these sentences are combinations of morphemes, but some of these morphemes, similar to *-ceive* or *-mit,* which were shown to derive a meaning only when combined with other morphemes in a word, derive a meaning only when combined with other morphemes in a sentence. For example, what is the meaning of *it* in the sentence *It's hot in July,* or in *The Archbishop found it advisable?* What is the meaning of *to* in *He wanted her to go? To* has a **grammatical** "meaning" as an infinitive marker, and it is also a morpheme required by the syntactic, sentence-formation rules of the language. Similarly for *have* in *Cows **have** walked here,* which is a grammatical marker for the "present perfect"; and for the different forms of *be* in both *The baby **is** crying* and *The baby's diaper **was** changed,* which function, respectively, as a "progressive" marker and a "passive voice" marker.

Inflectional Morphemes

"LOOKS LIKE WE SPEND MOST OF OUR TIME INGING...
YOU KNOW, LIKE SLEEPING, EATING, RUNNING, CLIMBING..."

DENNIS THE MENACE® used by permission of Hank Ketcham and ©by North America Syndicate.

Many languages, including English to some extent, contain "bound" morphemes that, like *to,* are for the most part purely grammatical markers, representing such concepts as "tense," "number," "gender," "case," and so forth.

Such "bound" grammatical morphemes are called **inflectional morphemes:** they never change the syntactic category of the words or morphemes to which they are attached. They are always attached to complete words. Consider the forms of the verb in the following sentences:

(a) I sail the ocean blue.
(b) He sails the ocean blue.
(c) John sailed the ocean blue.
(d) John has sailed the ocean blue.
(e) John is sailing the ocean blue.

In sentence (b) the *s* at the end of the verb is an "agreement" marker; it signifies that the subject of the verb is "third person," is "singular," and that the verb is in the "present tense." It doesn't add any "lexical meaning." The *-ed* and *-ing* endings are morphemes required by the syntactic rules of the language to signal "tense" or "aspect."

English is no longer a highly inflected language. But we do have other inflectional endings. The plurality of many count nouns, for example, is usually marked by a plural suffix attached to the singular noun, as in *boy/boys* and *cat/cats.* At the present stage of English history, there are a total of eight bound inflectional affixes:

English Inflectional Morphemes		**Examples**
-s	third person singular present	She wait-s at home.
-ed	past tense	She wait-ed at home.
-ing	progressive	She is eat-ing the donut.
-en	past participle	Mary has eat-en the donuts.
-s	plural	She ate the donut-s.
-'s	possessive	Disa's hair is short.
-er	comparative	Disa has short-er hair than Karin.
-est	superlative	Disa has the short-est hair.

Inflectional morphemes in English typically follow derivational morphemes. Thus, to the derivationally complex word *un + like + ly + hood* one can add a plural ending to form *un + like + ly + hood + s* but not **unlikeslyhood.* However, with 'compounds' such as those previously discussed, the situation is complicated. Thus, for many speakers, the plural of *mother-in-law* is *mothers-in-law* whereas the possessive form is *mother-in-law's.*

Some languages are highly inflective. Finnish nouns, for example, have many different inflectional endings, as shown in the following example (don't be concerned if you don't know what all the specific case endings mean):[7]

[7]Examples are from L. Campbell, "Generative Phonology vs. Finnish Phonology: Retrospect and prospect," *Texas Linguistic Forum* 5 (1977): 21–58.

mantere	nominative singular (sg.)
mantereen	genitive (possessive) sg.
manteretta	partitive sg.
mantereena	essive sg.
mantereeseen	illative sg.
mantereita	partitive plural (pl.)
mantereisiin	illative pl.
mantereiden	genitive pl.

Exceptions and Suppletions

PEANUTS reprinted by permission of UFS, Inc.

There are no regular rules to determine the plural forms of exceptional nouns like *child/children, man/men, sheep/sheep, criterion/criteria,* so also there are no regular rules to specify the past tense of verbs like *sing/sang* or *bring/brought.*

When, as children, we are acquiring (or constructing) the grammar, we have to learn specifically that the plural of *man* is *men* and that the past of *go* is *went.* For this reason we often hear children say *mans* and *goed;* they first learn the regular rules, and until they learn the exceptions to these rules, they apply them generally to all the nouns and verbs. These children's errors, in fact, support our position that the regular rules exist.

The irregular forms, then, must be listed separately in our mental dictionaries, as **suppletive forms.** When a new word enters the language it is the regular inflectional rules that apply. The plural of *Bic* is *Bics,* not **Bicken.*

The past tense of the verb *hit,* as in the sentence *Yesterday John hit the roof,* and the plural of the noun *sheep,* as in *The sheep are in the meadow,* show that some morphemes seem to have no phonological shape at all. We know that *hit* in the above sentence is *hit + past* because of the time adverb *yesterday,* and we know that *sheep* is the phonetic form of *sheep + plural* because of the plural verb form *are.* Thousands of years ago the Hindu grammarians suggested that some morphemes have a **zero-form;** that is, they have no phonological representation. In our view, however, because we would like to hold to the definition of a morpheme as a constant sound-meaning form, we will suggest that the morpheme *hit* is marked as both present and past in the dictionary, and the morpheme *sheep* is marked as both singular and plural.

Morphology and Syntax

Some grammatical relations can be expressed either inflectionally (morphologically) or syntactically (as part of the sentence structure, which will be further discussed in Chapter 3). We can see this in the following sentences:

England's queen is Elizabeth II.   The Queen of England is Elizabeth II.
He loves books.   He is a lover of books.
The planes which fly are red.   The flying planes are red.
He is hungrier than she.   He is more hungry than she.

Perhaps some of you form the comparative of *beastly* only by adding *-er. Beastlier* is often used interchangeably with *more beastly*. There are speakers who say either. We know the rule that determines when either form of the comparative can be used or when just one can be used, as pointed out by Lewis Carroll:

> "'Curiouser and curiouser!' cried Alice (she was so much surprised, that for the moment she quite forgot how to speak good English)."

It is interesting to note that what one language signals with inflectional affixes, another does with word order and another with "function words." For example, in English, the sentence *Maxim defends Victor* means something different from *Victor defends Maxim*. The word order is very important. In Russian, all the following sentences mean "Maxim defends Victor":

Maksim zasčisčajet Viktora.
Maksim Viktora zasčisčajet.
Viktora Maksim zasčisčajet.
Viktora zasčisčajet Maksim.
Zasčisčajet Maksim Viktora.
Zasčisčajet Viktora Maksim.

The inflectional suffix *-a* added to the name *Viktor* to derive *Viktora* shows that Victor, not Maxim, is defended.

In English, to convey the future meaning of a verb we must use a function word *will*, as in *John will come Monday*. In French, the verb is inflected for future tense. Notice the difference between "John is coming Monday," *Jean* **vient** *lundi* and "John will come Monday," *Jean* **viendra** *lundi*. Similarly, where English uses the grammatical markers *have* and *be*, mentioned above, other languages use affixing to achieve the same meaning, as illustrated with Indonesian:

dokter mem + *eriksa saja*   "The doctor examines me."
saja dip + *eriksa oleh dokter*   "I was examined by the doctor."

In discussing derivational and compounding morphology, we noted that knowing the meaning of the distinct morphemes may not always reveal the meaning of the morphologically complex word. This problem is not true of inflectional morphology. If we know the meaning of the word *linguist,* we also know the meaning of the plural form *linguists;* if we know the meaning of the verb *analyze,* we know the meaning of *analyzed* and *analyzes* and *analyzing.* This fact is another difference between derivational and inflectional morphology.

The grammar of the language that is internalized by the language learner includes the morphemes and the derived words of the language. The morphological rules of the grammar permit you to use and understand the morphemes and words in forming and understanding sentences, and in forming and understanding new words.

Summary

Knowing a language means knowing the words of that language. When you know a word you know both its **form** (sound) and its **meaning;** these are inseparable parts of the **linguistic sign.** Each word is stored in our mental dictionaries with information on its pronunciation (phonological representation), its meaning (semantic properties), and its syntactic class or category specification.

Words are not the most elemental sound-meaning units; some words are structurally complex. The most elemental grammatical units in a language are *morphemes.* Thus, *moralizers* is an English word composed of four morphemes: *moral + ize + er + s.*

The study of word formation and the internal structure of words is called **morphology.** Part of one's linguistic competence includes knowledge of the language's morphology—the morphemes, words, their pronunciation, their meanings, and how they are combined. Morphemes combine according to the morphological rules of the language.

Some morphemes are *bound* in that they must be joined to other morphemes, are always parts of words and never words by themselves. Other morphemes are *free* in that they need not be attached to other morphemes. *Free, king, serf,* and *bore* are free morphemes; *-dom,* as in *freedom, kingdom, serfdom,* and *boredom* is a bound morpheme. **Affixes,** that is **prefixes, suffixes, infixes,** and **circumfixes,** are bound morphemes.

Some morphemes, like *huckle* in *huckleberry* and *-ceive* in *perceive* or *receive,* have constant phonological form but meanings determined only by the words in which they occur. They are thus also bound morphemes.

Lexical content or **root** morphemes constitute the major word classes—nouns, verbs, adjectives, adverbs. These are **open class** items because their classes are easily added to.

Morphemes may also be classified as **derivational** or **inflectional. Derivational morphological rules** are lexical rules of word formation. **Inflectional morphemes** are determined by the rules of syntax. They are added to complete words, simple **monomorphemic** words or complex **polymorphemic** words (i.e., words with more than one morpheme). Derivational morphemes can change the syntactic category of the word with which they combine; adding *-ish* to the noun *boy* derives an adjective, for example. Inflectional morphemes never change the syntactic category of the word.

Some grammatical morphemes or "function words," together with the bound inflectional morphemes constitute a **closed class;** they are inserted into sentences according to the syntactic structure. The past tense morpheme, often written as *d,* is added as a suffix to a verb, and the future tense morpheme, *will,* is inserted in a sentence according to the syntactic rules of the English.

Grammars also include ways of increasing the vocabulary, of adding new words and morphemes to the lexicon. Words can be coined outright so that former nonsense words or possible but nonoccurring words can become words. Morphological **compounding** rules combine two or more morphemes or words to form complex compounds, like *lamb chop, deep-sea diver,* and *ne'er-do-well.* Frequently the meaning of compounds cannot be predicted from the meanings of their individual morphemes.

Acronyms are words derived from the initials of several words—like AWOL, which came into the language as the initials for "*a*way *witho*ut *l*eave." **Blends** are similar to compounds but usually combine shortened forms of two or more morphemes or words. *Carpeteria* is a store selling carpets and the name derives from *carpet* plus the end of *cafeteria.* **Back-formations, abbreviations** and words formed from proper nouns also add to our given stock of words.

While the particular morphemes and the particular morphological rules are language-dependent, the same general processes occur in all languages.

References for Further Reading

Aronoff, Mark. 1976. *Word Formation in Generative Grammar.* Cambridge, Mass: MIT Press.

Bauer, Laurie. 1983. *English Word-formation.* Cambridge, England: Cambridge University Press.

Jensen, John T. 1990. *Morphology: Word Structure in Generative Grammar.* Amsterdam/Philadelphia: John Benjamins Publishing.

Marchand, Hans. 1969. *The Categories and Types of Present-Day English Word-Formation,* 2nd ed. Munich: C.H. Beck'sche Verlagsbuchhandlung.

Matthews, P.H. 1976. *Morphology: An Introduction to the Theory of Word Structure.* Cambridge, England: Cambridge University Press.

Spencer, Andrew. 1991. *Morphological Theory: An Introduction to Word Structure in Generative Grammar.* London: Basil Blackwell.

Exercises

1. Divide these words by placing a + between their separate morphemes. (Some of the words may be *monomorphemic* and therefore indivisible.)

    Example: replaces re + place + s

    a. retroactive _____

    b. befriended _____

    c. televise _____

    d. margin _____

    e. endearment _____

    f. psychology _____

    g. unpalatable _____

    h. holiday _____

    i. grandmother _____

    j. morphemic _____

2. A. Consider the following nouns in Zulu:

umfazi	"married woman"	abafazi	"married women"
umfani	"boy"	abafani	"boys"
umzali	"parent"	abazali	"parents"
umfundisi	"teacher"	abafundisi	"teachers"
umbazi	"carver"	ababazi	"carvers"
umlimi	"farmer"	abalimi	"farmers"
umdlali	"player"	abadlali	"players"
umfundi	"reader"	abafundi	"readers"

    a. What is the morpheme meaning "singular" in Zulu? _____

    b. What is the morpheme meaning "plural" in Zulu? _____

    c. List all the Zulu morphemes which occur in the words above:

    Zulu   meaning

B. In Zulu, some nouns are derived from verbs. Consider the following verbs which are composed of a stem + a verbal suffix.

fundisa	"to teach"	funda	"to read"
lima	"to cultivate"	baza	"to carve"

d. What is the derivational suffix morpheme which specifies the category verb? _____

e. What is the nominal suffix morpheme?_____

f. State the morphological "noun formation rule" in Zulu.

_____

_____

g. What is the stem morpheme meaning "read"? _____

h. What is the stem morpheme meaning "carve"? _____

3. Match each expression under A with the one statement under B that characterizes it.

A
a. noisy crow
b. eat crow
c. scarecrow
d. the crow
e. crowlike
f. crows

B
1. compound noun
2. root morpheme plus derivational prefix
3. phrase consisting of adjective plus noun
4. root morpheme plus inflectional affix
5. root morpheme plus derivational suffix
6. grammatical morpheme followed by lexical morpheme
7. idiom

4. Write the one proper description from the list under B for the italicized part of each word in A.

A
a. terror*ized*   _____
b. un*civil*ized   _____
c. terror*ize*   _____
d. *luke*warm   _____

B
(1) free root
(2) bound root
(3) inflectional suffix
(4) derivational suffix
(5) inflectional prefix
(6) derivational prefix
(7) inflectional infix
(8) derivational infix

5. The following infinitive and past participle verb forms are found in Dutch.

Root	Infinitive	Past Participle	
wandel	wandelen	gewandeld	"walk"
duw	duwen	geduwd	"push"
zag	zagen	gezagd	"saw"
stofzuig	stofzuigen	gestofzuigd	"vacuum-clean"

With reference to the morphological processes of prefixing, suffixing, infixing, and circumfixing discussed in this chapter and the specific morphemes involved:

a. State the morphological rule for forming an infinitive in Dutch.
b. State the morphological rule for forming the Dutch past participle form.

6. Here are some Japanese verb forms given in Roman alphabet forms rather than in the Japanese orthography. They represent two different styles (informal and formal) of present tense verbs.

	Informal	Formal	Basic Verb Stem
"call"	yobu	yobimasu	_____
"write"	kaku	kakimasu	_____
"eat"	taberu	tabemasu	_____
"see"	miru	mimasu	_____
"lend"	kasu	kashimasu	_____
"wait"	matsu	machimasu	_____
"leave"	deru	demasu	_____
"go out"	dekakeru	dekakemasu	_____
"read"	yomu	yomimasu	_____
"die"	shinu	shinimasu	_____
"close"	shimeru	shimemasu	_____
"wear"	kiru	kimasu	_____

a. List the underlying or basic verb stems for each of these Japanese verbs.
b. State the rule for deriving the present tense informal verb forms from the underlying verb stems.
c. State the rule for deriving the present tense formal verb forms from the underlying verb stems.
d. State a rule that will derive the formal forms from the informal forms.

7. Below are some sentences in Swahili:

mtoto	amefika	"The child has arrived."
mtoto	anafika	"The child is arriving."
mtoto	atafika	"The child will arrive."
watoto	wamefika	"The children have arrived."
watoto	wanafika	"The children are arriving."
watoto	watafika	"The children will arrive."
mtu	amelala	"The man has slept."
mtu	analala	"The man is sleeping."
mtu	atalala	"The man will sleep."
watu	wamelala	"The men have slept."
watu	wanalala	"The men are sleeping."
watu	watalala	"The men will sleep."
kisu	kimeanguka	"The knife has fallen."
kisu	kinaanguka	"The knife is falling."
kisu	kitaanguka	"The knife will fall."
visu	vimeanguka	"The knives have fallen."
visu	vinaanguka	"The knives are falling."
visu	vitaanguka	"The knives will fall."
kikapu	kimeanguka	"The basket has fallen."
kikapu	kinaanguka	"The basket is falling."
kikapu	kitaanguka	"The basket will fall."
vikapu	vimeanguka	"The baskets have fallen."
vikapu	vinaanguka	"The baskets are falling."
vikapu	vitaanguka	"The baskets will fall."

One of the characteristic features of Swahili (and Bantu languages in general) is the existence of noun classes. There are specific singular and plural prefixes that occur with the nouns in each class. These prefixes are also used for purposes of agreement between the subject-noun and the verb. In the sentences given, two of these classes are included (there are many more in the language).

a. Identify all the morphemes you can detect, and give their meanings.

> Example: -toto "child"
> > m- noun prefix attached to singular nouns of Class I
> > a-prefix attached to verbs when the subject is a singular noun of Class I

Be sure to look for the other noun and verb markers, including tense markers.

b. How is the "verb" constructed? That is, what kinds of morphemes are strung together and in what order?

c. How would you say in Swahili:

(1) The child is falling. ——————————————————

(2) The baskets have arrived. _____

(3) The man will fall. _____

8. One morphological process not discussed in this chapter is called **reduplication,** which occurs in a number of languages. The following examples from Samoan exemplify this kind of morphological rule.

manao	"he wishes"	mananao	"they wish"
matua	"he is old"	matutua	"they are old"
malosi	"he is strong"	malolosi	"they are strong"
punou	"he bends"	punonou	"they bend"
atamaki	"he is wise"	atamamaki	"they are wise"
savali	"he travels"	pepese	"they sing"
laga	"he weaves"		

a. What is the Samoan for:

   (1) they weave _____

   (2) they travel _____

   (3) he sings _____

b. Formulate a general statement (a morphological rule) that states how to form the plural verb form from the singular verb form.

9. Below are listed some words followed by incorrect definitions. (All these errors are taken from Amsel Greene's *Pullet Surprises.*)

Word	Student Definition
stalemate	"husband or wife no longer interested"
effusive	"able to be merged"
tenet	"a group of ten singers"
dermatology	"a study of derms"
ingenious	"not very smart"
finesse	"a female fish"

For each of these incorrect definitions, give some possible reasons why the students made the guesses they did. Where you can exemplify by reference to other words or morphemes, giving their meanings, do so.

10. Dal Yoo[8] expresses the belief that abbreviations and acronyms occur in the United States more than in any other country. He refers, for example, to the

---

[8]Dal Yoo, "The World of Abbreviations and Acronyms," *Verbatim: The Language Quarterly* (Summer 1991):4–5.

acronyms generated in the 1991 Gulf war, by both pro- and antiwar demonstrations such as SMASH "*S*tudents *M*obilized *A*gainst *S*addam *H*ussein" and SCUD "*S*adly *C*onfused *U*npatriotic *D*emonstrators." He also refers to a neon sign on a downtown high-rise building in Philadelphia reading PSFS for "*P*hiladelphia *S*avings *F*und *S*ociety" which was referred to by a local tour guide as meaning, instead, "*P*hiladelphia *S*mells *F*unny *S*ometimes." Dr. Yoo is a medical doctor who writes: "When I have no idea what the patient has, I apply my favorite of all the abbreviations, GOK syndrome '*G*od *O*nly *K*nows'." Such acronyms show how innovative our linguistic ability is.

a. List ten acronyms currently in use in English. Do not use the ones given in the text.
b. Invent ten new acronyms (listing the words as well as the initials).

CHAPTER 3
Syntax: The Sentence Patterns of Language

The grammar of the language determines the properties of each of the sentences of the language . . . The language is the set of sentences that are described by the grammar . . . the grammar "generates" the sentences it describes and their structural descriptions . . . When we speak of the linguist's grammar as a "generative grammar," we mean only that it is sufficiently explicit to determine how sentences of the language are in fact characterized by the grammar.

Noam Chomsky, *Rules and Representations*

"We get a lot of foreign visitors."

HERMAN copyright 1991 Jim Unger. Reprinted with permission of Universal Press Syndicate. All rights reserved.

Knowing a language includes the ability to put words together to form phrases and sentences that express our thoughts. That part of the grammar that represents a speaker's knowledge of the structure of phrases and sentences is called **syntax.** The aim of this chapter is to present some of the syntactic phenomena that are found in all human languages. Most of the examples and the specific structures will be from the syntax of English but the principles which account for these kinds of structures are universal.

The meaning of a sentence depends to a great extent on the meaning of the words of which it is composed. But the structure of the sentence also contributes to its meaning. Word order, for example, can change the meaning. The sentence

> Salome danced for Herod.

does not have the same meaning as

> Herod danced for Salome.

Sometimes, however, a change of word order has no effect on meaning.

> Jack Horner stuck in his thumb.
> Jack Horner stuck his thumb in.

The grammars of all languages include **rules of syntax** which reflect speakers' knowledge of these facts.

Grammatical or Ungrammatical?

The syntactic rules of a grammar also account for the fact that even though the following sequence is made up of meaningful words, it has no meaning.

> for danced Herod Salome

In English and in every language, every sentence is a sequence of words, but not every sequence of words is a sentence. Sequences of words that conform to the rules of syntax are said to be **well formed** or **grammatical** and those which violate the syntactic rules are therefore **ill formed** and **ungrammatical.**

What Grammaticality Is Based On

You do not have to be a linguist to know that

> The boy kissed the girl.

is a "good" sentence, but that something is wrong with

> *Girl the boy the kissed.

Reprinted with special permission of King Features Syndicate.

In Chapter 1 you were asked to indicate strings of words as grammatical or ungrammatical according to your linguistic intuitions. Here is another list of word sequences. Disregarding the sentence meanings, use *your* knowledge of English and place an asterisk in front of the ones that strike you as peculiar or funny in some way.

(1)   (a) The boy found the ball
(b) The boy found quickly
(c) The boy found in the house
(d) The boy found the ball in the house
(e) Disa slept the baby
(f) Disa slept soundly
(g) Zack believes Robert to be a gentleman
(h) Zack believes to be a gentleman
(i) Zack tries Robert to be a gentleman
(j) Zack tries to be a gentleman
(k) Zack wants to be a gentleman
(l) Zack wants Robert to be a gentleman
(m) Jack and Jill ran up the hill
(n) Jack and Jill ran up the bill
(o) Jack and Jill ran the hill up
(p) Jack and Jill ran the bill up
(q) Up the hill ran Jack and Jill
(r) Up the bill ran Jack and Jill

We predict that speakers of English will "star" **b, c, e, h, i, o, r.** If we are right, this shows that grammaticality judgments are not idiosyncratic or capricious but are determined by rules that are shared by the speakers of a language.

The syntactic rules that account for the ability to make these judgments include, in addition to rules of word order, other constraints. For example, the rules specify that *found* must be followed directly by an expression like *the ball* but not by *quickly* or *in the house* as illustrated in **a–d.** The verb *sleep* patterns differently than *find* in that it may be followed solely by a word like *soundly* but not by other kinds of phrases such as *the baby* as shown in **e** and **f.** Examples **g–l** show that *believe* and *try* function in opposite fashion while *want* exhibits yet a third pattern. Finally, the word order rules that constrain phrases such as *run up the hill* differ from those concerning *run up the bill* as seen in **m–r.**

Sentences are not simply random strings of words; they conform to specific patterns determined by the syntactic rules of the language. This is true of all human languages, as shown by the fact that speakers can distinguish grammatical from ungrammatical combinations of words in their language, and can often "fix up" ungrammatical strings of words to make them grammatical.

What Grammaticality Is Not Based On

> . . . The fundamental aim in the linguistic analysis of a language L is to separate the grammatical sequences which are sentences of L from the ungrammatical sequences which are not sentences of L and to study the structure of the grammatical sequences.
>
> Noam Chomsky, *Syntactic Structures*

Grammaticality is *not* based on what is taught in school but on the rules acquired or constructed unconsciously as children. Much grammatical knowledge is "in place" before we learn to read.

The ability to make grammaticality judgments does not depend on having heard the sentence before. You may never have heard or read the sentence

Enormous crickets in pink socks danced at the prom.

but your syntactic knowledge will tell you that it is grammatical.

Grammaticality judgments do not depend on whether the sentence is meaningful or not, as shown by the following sentences:

Colorless green ideas sleep furiously.
A verb crumpled the milk.

Although these sentences do not make much sense, they are syntactically well formed. They sound "funny," but they differ in their "funniness" from the following strings of words:

*Furiously sleep ideas green colorless.
*Milk the crumpled verb a.

You may understand ungrammatical sequences even though you know they are not well formed. To most English speakers

*The boy quickly in the house the ball found

is interpretable although these same speakers recognize that the word order is irregular. On the other hand, grammatical sentences may be uninterpretable if they include nonsense strings, that is, words with no agreed-on meaning, as shown by the first two lines of "Jabberwocky" by Lewis Carroll:

> *'Twas brillig, and the slithy toves*
> *Did gyre and gimble in the wabe;*

Such nonsense poetry is amusing because the sentences "obey" syntactic rules and sound like good English. Ungrammatical strings of nonsense words are not entertaining:

> **Toves slithy the and brillig 'twas*
> *wabe the in gimble and gyre did . . .*

Grammaticality does not depend on the truth of sentences either—if it did, lying would be impossible—nor on whether real objects are being discussed, nor on whether something is possible or not. Untrue sentences can be grammatical, sentences discussing unicorns can be grammatical, and sentences referring to pregnant fathers can be grammatical.

Unconscious knowledge of the syntactic rules of grammars permits speakers to make grammaticality judgments.

What Else Do You Know About Syntax?

Reprinted with special permission of North America Syndicate.

Syntactic knowledge goes beyond being able to decide which strings are grammatical and which are not. It accounts for the double meaning, or *ambiguity,* of expressions like the one illustrated in the cartoon above. The humor of the cartoon depends on the ambiguity of the phrase *synthetic buffalo hides,* which can mean buffalo hides that are synthetic, or hides of synthetic buffalo. This is an example of **structural ambiguity** which is revealed in the following two diagrams of these phrases.

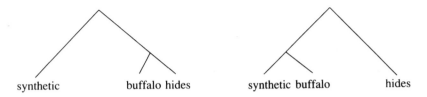

synthetic   buffalo hides   synthetic buffalo   hides

The difference in meaning is due to the different structures which are permitted by the rules of syntax, rather than to any ambiguous word. The following sentences also have more than one meaning due to structural ambiguity:

> The children drew five squares and triangles.
> Visiting professors can be interesting.
> The boy saw the man with the telescope.

The first sentence may be understood as referring to five squares and five triangles or five squares and any number of triangles. You should have no difficulty providing the different meanings for the other two sentences.

Contrast these sentences with

> This will make you smart.

The two interpretations of this sentence are due to the two meanings of *smart*— "clever" or "burning sensation." Such *lexical* or word-based ambiguities, as opposed to *structural* ambiguities will be discussed further in Chapter 4.

Syntactic knowledge also enables us to determine how different parts of a sentence are related. Consider the following sentences:

> Mary hired Bill.
> Bill was hired by Mary.
> Bill hired Mary.

Mary is understood to be the employer and *Bill* the employee in the first two sentences, but the opposite holds true in the third sentence. Syntactic rules reveal the relations between the words of a sentence, and tell us when structural differences result in meaning differences and when they do not.

There are other kinds of sentences with structures differing from each other in which the meaning remains constant as in the following:

> It is fun for Vicki to please Disa.
> Pleasing Disa is fun for Vicki.
> Disa is fun for Vicki to please.

The syntac c rules of English determine when changes in structure retain or change the meaning of sentences.

It is also the syntactic rules which permit speakers to produce and understand an unlimited number of sentences never produced or heard before, what was referred to in Chapter 1 as the creative aspect of language use.

Thus, the syntactic rules in a grammar must at least account for:

1. the grammaticality of sentences
2. word order
3. structural ambiguity
4. the meaning relations between words in a sentence
5. the similarity of meaning of sentences with different structures
6. speakers' creative ability to produce and understand any of an infinite set of possible sentences.

A major goal of linguistics is to show clearly and explicitly how syntactic rules account for this knowledge. A theory of grammar must provide a complete characterization of what speakers implicitly know about their language.

Sentence Structure

Syntactic rules determine the order of words in a sentence. In English an article like *the* or *an* precedes a noun like *animal,* but sentences are more than words placed one after another like beads on a string. As *synthetic buffalo hides* showed, the words of a sentence can be divided into two or more groups, and within each group the words can be divided into subgroups, and so on, until only single words remain. For example, the sentence

The child found the puppy.

may be subdivided into *the child* and *found the puppy,* corresponding to the "subject" and "predicate" of the sentence. Further subdivisions may occur until only the individual words of the sentence remain, as shown in the following "tree" diagram:

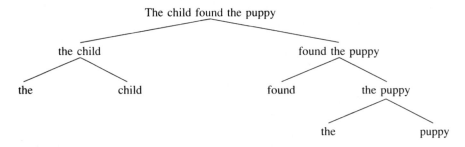

The "tree" is upside down with its "root" being the entire sentence, *The child found the puppy,* and its "leaves" being the individual words, *the, child, found, the,*

puppy. In addition to the linear order of words in a sentence, a tree diagram also exhibits the subgroupings and sub-subgroupings of the words in the sentence, the **hierarchical structure.**

The tree diagram shows among other things that the phrase *found the puppy* is naturally divided into the two groups, *found* and *the puppy.* A different division, say *found the* and *puppy,* is unnatural in the sense that speakers of English would not use *found the* by itself or as an answer to the question "What did you find?" An answer might be "the puppy" but not *found the.* Notice that one can also move *the puppy* and say *The puppy was found by the child,* but there is no way to change the original sentence by moving *found the* as a single structure. Such "tests" show that *the puppy* is a natural subgrouping of words whereas *found the* is not.

Only one tree representation can be drawn for the sentence, *The child found the puppy.* But the phrase, *synthetic buffalo hides,* has two possible trees:

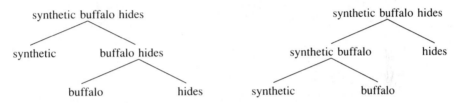

Each tree corresponds to one of the possible meanings. Thus, structural ambiguity can be explicity accounted for by multiple tree structures.

Syntactic Categories

Each of the natural groupings in the diagram on page 78 is a member of a large family of similar expressions. For example, *the child* belongs to a family that includes *the police officer, your neighbor, this yellow cat, he,* and countless others. Each member of this family can be substituted for *the child* without affecting the grammaticality of the sentence, although the meanings of course would change.

> A police officer found the puppy.
> Your neighbor found the puppy.
> This yellow cat found the puppy.
> He found the puppy.

A family of expressions that can substitute for one another without loss of grammaticality is called a **syntactic category.**

The child, a police officer, and so on belong to the syntactic category **Noun Phrase (NP),** one of several syntactic categories in English and every other language in the world. Noun Phrases may function as "subject" or "object" in a sentence and only Noun Phrases may do so. NPs always contain some form of a noun (common noun like *boy,* proper noun like *John,* or pronoun like *he*). Since *he* is a

" I MISS THE GOOD OLD DAYS WHEN ALL WE HAD TO WORRY ABOUT WAS NOUNS AND VERBS."

single word, you may question our calling it a *phrase,* but technically a syntactic phrase can consist of one or more words.

Part of the syntactic component of a grammar is the specification of the syntactic categories in the language since this constitutes part of speakers' knowledge. That is, speakers of English know that items **a, b, e, f,** and **g** in (**2**) are Noun Phrases even if they have never heard the term before.

(**2**) (a) a bird
(b) the red banjo
(c) have a nice day

(d) with a balloon

(e) the woman who was laughing

(f) it

(g) John

(h) run

You can test this claim by inserting each expression into the context "Who found _____ ?" and " _____ was lost." The ones that are grammatical contain the NPs, because only NPs can function as subject and direct object.

There are other syntactic categories. The expression *found the puppy* is a **Verb Phrase (VP).** Verb Phrases always contain a Verb, which may be followed by other categories, such as Noun Phrases. This shows that one syntactic category may contain other syntactic categories. In (3), the Verb Phrases are those which can complete the sentence, "The child _____ ."

(3)   (a) saw a clown

(b) a bird

(c) slept

(d) smart

(e) is smart

(f) found the cake

(g) found the cake in the cupboard

Inserting **a, c, e, f,** and **g** will produce grammatical sentences whereas the insertion of **b** or **d** would result in an ungrammatical string. Thus, **a, c, e, f,** and **g** are Verb Phrases.

Other syntactic categories we will encounter in this section are **Sentence (S), Article (Art), Noun (N),** and **Verb (V).** Some of these syntactic categories should be familiar; they have traditionally been called "parts of speech." All languages have such syntactic categories; in fact, categories such as Noun, Verb, and Noun Phrase are universally found in the grammars of all human languages. Speakers know the syntactic categories of their language, even if they do not know the technical terms.

Phrase Structure Trees

> Who climbs the Grammar-Tree distinctly knows
> Where Noun and Verb and Participle grows.
>
> John Dryden, *"The Sixth Satyr of Juvenal"*

The fact that *The child found the puppy* belongs to the syntactic category of Sentence, that *the child* and *the puppy* are Noun Phrases, that *found the puppy* is a Verb Phrase, and so on, can be illustrated in a tree diagram by specifying the syntactic category label of each word grouping.

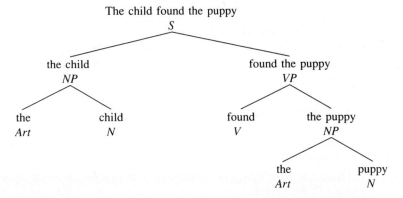

A diagram with syntactic category information provided is called a **Phrase Structure Tree.** This tree shows that a sentence is both a linear string of words and a hierarchical structure with phrases nested in phrases.

Three aspects of speakers' syntactic knowledge of sentence structure are disclosed in phrase structure trees:

1. the linear order of the words in the sentence
2. the groupings of words into syntactic categories
3. the hierarchical structure of the syntactic categories (e.g. a Sentence is made up of a Noun Phrase followed by a Verb Phrase, a Verb Phrase may be composed of a Verb followed by a Noun Phrase and so on)

Every sentence of English and of every human language can be represented by a phrase structure tree that explicitly reveals these properties. Phrase structure representation is not some arbitrary way of "diagramming" sentences invented by English teachers to torment students. These trees represent in precise notational form the linguistic properties that are part of speakers' mental grammars.

The phrase structure tree above is correct, but it is redundant. The word *child* is repeated three times in the tree, *puppy* is repeated four times, and so on. We can streamline the tree by writing the words only once at the bottom of the diagram. Only the syntactic categories to which the words belong need to remain at the higher levels.

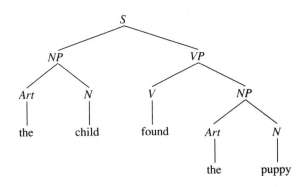

No information is lost in this simplified version. The syntactic category of each individual word appears immediately above that word. In this way *the* is shown to be an Article, *child* a Noun, and so on. The lowest categories in the tree, those immediately above the words, are called **lexical categories.** In Chapter 2 we discussed the fact that the syntactic category of each word is listed in our mental dictionaries. We now see how this information functions in the syntax of the language. We have not given a definition of these categories. All traditional definitions fail. In the sentence, *Seeing is believing, seeing* and *believing* are nouns but are neither "persons, places, nor things." The grammar of the language and the syntactic rules define these categories.

The larger syntactic categories such as Verb Phrase (VP) are identified as consisting of all the words below that point or **node** in the tree. The VP in the above phrase structure tree consists of *found* together with *the* and *puppy,* which is consistent with our observation that *found the puppy* is a VP.

The phrase structure tree also states implicitly what combinations of words are not syntactic categories. For example, since there is no point or node above the words *found* and *the* which connects them, the two words do not constitute a syntactic category, which is in keeping with the intuitions of speakers of English which we discussed earlier.

The phrase structure tree also makes clear that some syntactic categories are composed of combinations of other syntactic categories. The Sentence, *The child found the puppy,* consists of a Noun Phrase, *the child,* and a Verb Phrase, *found the puppy.* The Verb Phrase, *found the puppy,* consists of the Verb *found* and the Noun Phrase *the puppy.* Although the Article *the* and the Noun *puppy* together constitute a Noun Phrase, individually neither is an NP.

A syntactic category includes **all** the smaller categories beneath it in the tree. For example, an S is composed of an NP followed by a VP. An S is also an Art followed by an N followed by a V followed by an Art followed by an N. The "all" is important; an S is **not** simply Art N V Art as that would omit the final N which is a part of the S (that is, *the boy found the* is not a Sentence).

More Phrase Structure Trees

> The structure of every sentence is a lesson in logic.
>
> John Stuart Mill, *Inaugural address at St. Andres.*

Every language contains sentences of varying phrase structure. The phrase structure tree on the following page differs from the previous tree not only in the words which terminate it but also in its syntactic categories and structure.

This tree shows that a Verb Phrase may also consist of a Verb followed by a Noun Phrase followed by a **Prepositional Phrase (PP).** A Prepositional Phrase is shown to consist of a **Preposition (P)** followed by a Noun Phrase. This tree also illustrates that Noun Phrases may occur in three different structural positions: immediately below the S, below the VP, and below the PP.

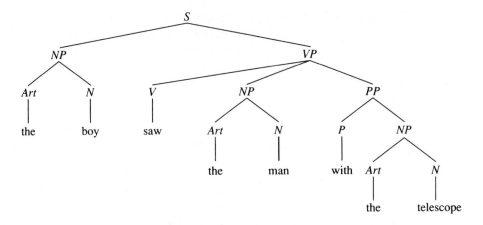

Just as tree structures reveal ambiguities as shown above by such phrases as *synthetic buffalo hides*, they also account for other ambiguities as in sentences like *The boy saw the man with the telescope.* One meaning of this sentence—"the boy used a telescope to see the man"—is shown in the phrase structure tree above by the attachment of the PP directly under the VP. This shows that the PP modifies the Verb *saw.*

In its other meaning, "the boy saw a man who had a telescope in his possession," the PP *with the telescope* modifies the Noun *man.* This is made explicit in the following phrase structure tree, where the PP is part of the NP that includes *the man.*

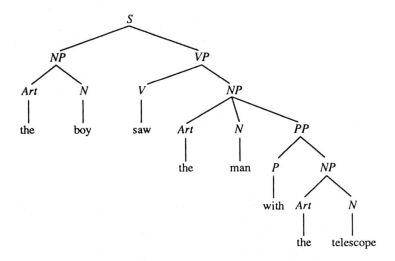

The capacity of phrase structure trees to reveal such ambiguities is further evidence that these structures reflect linguistic knowledge.

The Infinitude of Language

> So, naturalists observe, a flea
> Hath smaller fleas that on him prey;
> And these have smaller fleas still to bite 'em,
> And so proceed ad infinitum.
>
> Jonathan Swift, *"On Poetry. A Rhapsody"*

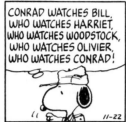

PEANUTS reprinted by permission of UFS, Inc.

There is no longest sentence in any language, because speakers can lengthen any sentence by various means, such as adding an adjective or, as in Snoopy's sentence, adding clauses. Even children know how to produce and understand very long sentences, and know how to make them even longer, as illustrated by the children's rhyme about the house that Jack built.

> *This is the farmer sowing the corn,*
> *that kept the cock that crowed in the morn,*
> *that waked the priest all shaven and shorn,*
> *that married the man all tattered and torn,*
> *that kissed the maiden all forlorn,*
> *that milked the cow with the crumpled horn,*
> *that tossed the dog,*
> *that worried the cat,*
> *that killed the rat,*
> *that ate the malt,*
> *that lay in the house that Jack built.*

This rhyme begins with the line *This is the house that Jack built,* continues by lengthening it to *This is the malt that lay in the house that Jack built,* and so on.

You can add any of the following phrases to the beginning of the rhyme and still have a grammatical, even longer, sentence:

> I think that . . .
> What is the name of the unicorn that noticed that . . .
> Ask someone if . . .
> Do you know whether . . .

This limitless aspect of language is also reflected in phrase structure trees. We have already seen that an NP may appear in several different positions in a tree; it may be immediately under a PP, which PP may occur immediately under a higher NP, as in *the man with the telescope.* The sentence, *The girl with the feather on the ribbon on the brim,* as shown in the phrase structure tree below illustrates that one can repeat the number of NPs under PPs under NPs without a limit. This property of all human languages is called **recursion.**

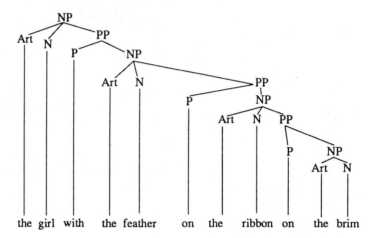

This phrase structure tree for the Noun Phrase illustrates that any syntactic category may be represented by a phrase structure tree, that is, be the topmost node. It also illustrates the recursion of the NP within PP within NP and so on. (The reason this property is called a recursive property is because a syntactic category may **recur** over and over in a sentence.)

The NP diagrammed above, though cumbersome, violates no rules of syntax and is a grammatical Noun Phrase. Moreover, it can be made even longer by expanding the final NP—*the brim*—by adding another PP—*of her hat*—to derive the longer phrase—*the girl with the feather on the ribbon on the brim of her hat.*

Recursion is common in all languages. It allows speakers to "recycle" syntactic categories in the same sentence. With a small number of categories, an infinite set of sentences can be represented.

This linguistic property also illustrates the difference between competence and performance discussed in Chapter 1. All speakers of English have as part of their linguistic competence—their mental grammars—the ability to put NPs in PPs in NPs ad infinitum. But as the structures grow longer and longer they become increasingly difficult to produce and understand. This could be due to short-term memory limitations, muscular fatigue, breathlessness, or any number of performance factors.

Thus while recursive rules give a speaker access to infinitely many sentences, no speaker utters or hears an infinite number in a lifetime; nor is any sentence of infinite length although there is no upper limit in principle on sentence length. It is this recursive property of grammars which accounts for the creative aspect of language use, since it permits speakers to produce and understand sentences never spoken before. Since such sentences cannot be stored in our minds, they must be produced by a finite set of rules which can be stored.

Phrase Structure Rules

Everyone who is master of the language he speaks . . . may form new . . .
phrases, provided they coincide with the genius of the language.

Michaelis, *Dissertation* (1769)

When we look at other phrase structure trees of English, we see certain patterns emerging. In ordinary sentences, the S is always subdivided into NP VP. NPs always contain Nouns, VPs always contain Verbs, PPs consist of a Preposition followed by a Noun Phrase.

Of all logically possible tree structures, few actually occur, just as all word combinations do not constitute sentences in a language or even grammatical phrases. For example, a nonoccurring tree structure in English is:

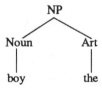

Since this is known to be ungrammatical by all speakers of the language, the grammar, if it is adequately to account for a speaker's competence, must make such facts explicit. To do this, grammars include **Phrase Structure Rules** which specify the constituency of syntactic categories in the language.

For example, in English a Noun Phrase (NP) can be an Article (Art) followed by a Noun (N). Thus a "piece" of a tree, called a *subtree,* may look like this:

NP
Art   N
the   bus

The Phrase Structure Rule which makes this explicit can be stated as:

NP→ Art N

This rule conveys two facts:

(a) A Noun Phrase can be an Article followed by a Noun.
(b) An Article followed by a Noun is a Noun Phrase.

The left side of the arrow is the category whose components are defined on the right side. The right side of the arrow also shows the linear order of these components. Phrase Structure Rules make explicit speakers' knowledge of the order of words and the grouping of words into syntactic categories.

    The phrase structure trees of the previous section show that the following Phrase Structure Rules are part of the grammar of English.

(a) VP→V NP
(b) VP→V NP PP

Rule **a** states that a Verb Phrase can be a Verb followed by a Noun Phrase. Rule **b** states that a Verb Phrase can also be a Verb followed by a Noun Phrase followed by a Prepositional Phrase. These rules are *general* statements, which do not refer to any specific Verb Phrase, Verb, Noun Phrase, or Prepositional Phrase.

    Rules **a** and **b** can be summed up in one statement: A Verb Phrase may be a Verb followed by a Noun Phrase, which may be followed by a Prepositional Phrase. The Prepositional Phrase may or may not be there. By putting parentheses around the optional element, we can abbreviate rules **a** and **b** with a single rule:

    VP→V NP (PP)

In fact the NP is also optional, as shown in the following trees:

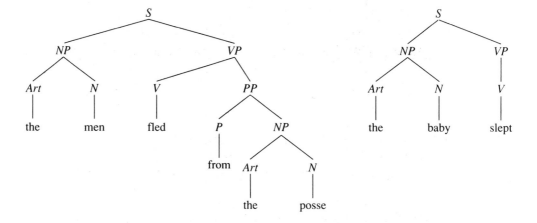

In the first case we have a Verb Phrase consisting of a Verb plus a Prepositional Phrase, corresponding to the rule VP→V PP. In the second case, the Verb Phrase consists of a Verb alone, corresponding to the rule VP→V. All the facts about the Verb Phrase we have seen so far are revealed in the single rule:

VP→V (NP) (PP)

This rule states that a Verb Phrase may consist of a Verb followed optionally by a Noun Phrase and/or a Prepositional Phrase.

Other rules of English that are evident are:

S→NP VP
PP→P NP

Growing Trees: The Relationship Between Phrase Structure Rules and Phrase Structure Trees

I think that I shall never see
A poem lovely as a tree

Joyce Kilmer, *"Trees"*

Phrase Structure Trees may not be as lovely to look at as the trees Kilmer was thinking of, but if a poem is written in grammatical English, its phrases and sentences can be represented by trees and those trees can be specified by Phrase Structure Rules.

The rules that we have discussed, repeated here, define some of the phrase structure trees of English.

S→NP VP
NP→Art N
VP→V (NP) (PP)
PP→P NP

The rules may also be viewed as a way to construct Phrase Structure Trees which characterize the syntactic structure of sentences. Certain conventions as to how to do this have been developed. One convention is that the tree starts with the category S at the top or "root." Another convention specifies how the rules are to be applied: Find a rule with an S on the left side of the arrow, and "apply" it by putting the categories that are on the right side of the arrow in that rule directly below the S, as shown here:

Convention also dictates that to construct a grammatical sentence we continue to apply any rule that can apply until we are left only with categories that never appear on the left-hand side of any rule, like Art, N, and so on. Thus we can start applying the NP rule to produce:

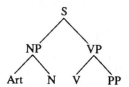

The categories at the bottom are Art, N and VP, but only VP occurs to the left of an arrow in the set of rules. The VP rule is actually four rules abbreviated by parentheses. They are:

VP→V
VP→V NP
VP→V PP
VP→V NP PP

Any one of them may be chosen to apply next; the order in which the rules appear in the grammar is irrelevant. Suppose VP→V PP is chosen to apply. Then the tree has grown to look like this:

As stated above, convention dictates that we continue in this way until none of the categories at the bottom of the tree appear on the left-hand side of any rule. Thus the PP must be expanded into a P and an NP, and that NP expanded into an Art and an N. We can use a rule as many times as it can apply. In this tree, the NP rule was used twice. After we have applied all the rules which can apply, the tree looks like this:

The categories that occur to the left of the arrow in a phrase structure rule are called **phrasal categories;** categories that *never* occur on the left side of any rule are **lexical categories.** Phrase Structure Trees always have lexical categories at the bottom since the rules must apply until no phrasal categories remain unexpanded. The lexical categories are traditionally called "the parts of speech," and include Articles, Nouns, Verbs, Prepositions and so on.

The previous tree structure corresponds to a very large number of sentences because each lexical category may contain many words. This is particularly true of the major "open class" categories discussed in Chapter 2, such as Noun or Verb. This tree structure underlies the following sentences and millions more.

> The boat sailed up the river.
> A girl laughed at the monkey.
> The sheepdog rolled in the mud.
> The lions roared in the jungle.

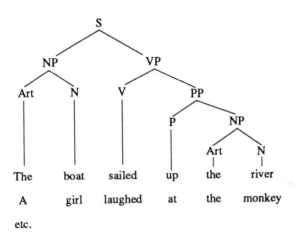

At any point during the growth of a tree, any rule may be used providing its left side category occurs somewhere at the bottom of the tree. At the point where we chose the rule VP→ V PP, we could equally well have chosen VP→ V or VP→ V NP PP. This would have resulted in a different tree which, when the lexical categories were filled, would have been the structure for such sentences as:

> The boys left (VP→ V)
> The wind swept the kite into the sky. (VP→ V NP PP)

Since there are an infinite number of possible sentences in every language, there are limitless numbers of trees, but only a finite set of Phrase Structure Rules which specify the trees allowed by the grammar of the language.

These rules and the way we have suggested they can be applied to specify trees are part of one's linguistic competence. It is not suggested that as we use our knowledge we apply the rules of our mental grammar in this way; the production of utterances is part of performance. We are attempting to characterize the kinds of syntactic phenomena and the hierarchical structure of sentences found in human language.

Trees That Won't Grow

THE FAR SIDE copyright 1991, 1987 & 1986 UNIVERSAL PRESS SYNDICATE. Reprinted with permission. All rights reserved.

Just as speakers know which structures and strings of words are permitted by the syntax of their language, they know which are not. Such knowledge is specified implicitly by the Phrase Structure Rules.

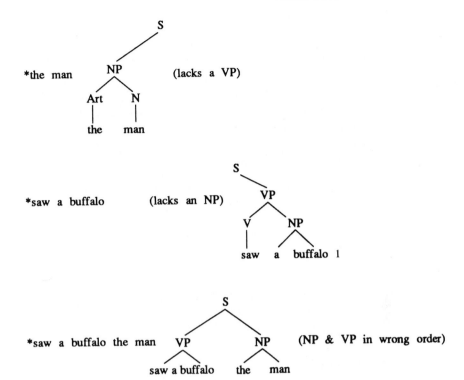

If the Rule S→NP VP were the only S rule in the grammar of English, the word sequences above and their corresponding structures would not constitute English sentences.

Similarly, *boy the*

cannot be an NP in English because no NP rule of English syntax specifies that an article can follow a noun.

Other languages have different Phrase Structure Rules, hence different tree structures. In Swedish the article may follow the Noun in some NPs, for example, in *mannen* "the man" (*mann* "man" + *en* "the"). The ungrammatical tree of English is found to be a grammatical tree structure in Swedish:

¹Nonpertinent parts of the tree are sometimes omitted, in this case the Art and N of the NP, *a buffalo*.

There are languages that have "post-positions" which function like prepositions of English but come after the Noun Phrase instead of preceding it. In Japanese *Tokyo kara* means "from Tokyo." The following tree, which does not occur in English, is found in Japanese:

The grammar of Japanese contains the Phrase Structure Rule

PP→NP P

but not the rule

PP→P NP

Such differences between these languages and English are reflected in the Phrase Structure Rules of the respective grammars.

In English the Verb is always the first member of the Verb Phrase, as can be seen from the VP rule. In German, however, the Verb may occur in the final position of the Verb Phrase in some circumstances. German contains sentences such as

Ich glaube dass Tristan Isolde liebt

which, if translated word for word, would be "I believe that Tristan Isolde loves," meaning "I believe that Tristan loves Isolde." This particular characteristic of German inspired Mark Twain to write:

Whenever the literary German dives into a sentence, that is the last you are going to see of him till he emerges on the other side of the Atlantic with his Verb in his mouth.[2]

Despite these differences in detail, all grammars of all languages have the *type* of rule we are calling Phrase Structure Rules that determine the structure of phrases and sentences of the language and its syntactic categories.

[2]Mark Twain, *A Connecticut Yankee in King Arthur's Court,* New York: Harper's, 1889.

More Phrase Structure Rules

Reprinted with special permission of North America Syndicate.

There are many sentences of English whose structure is not accounted for by the Phrase Structure Rules given so far, including:

(a) The man with the hat smiled.
(b) A large fierce black dog looked out the window.

In (a), the Noun Phrase is more than just an article followed by a noun; the NP rule stated earlier can not account for (a) since the Noun is modified by the Prepositional Phrase *with the hat.* In (b) the Noun *dog* is preceded by adjectives which the NP rule doesn't mention.

The NP in sentence (a), *the man with the hat,* is similar to *the man with the telescope* (see page 84), and has the following structure:

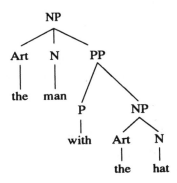

Each NP in the example *the girl with the feather on the ribbon on the brim of her hat* on page 86 also has this structure, as do many other NPs.

The NP rule can be modified to include the option of a Prepositional Phrase:

    NP→Art N (PP)

Since NPs may contain one or more adjectives, English includes the lexical category **Adjective (Adj),** corresponding to words like *large* and *black*. With the addition of this category we can now give a Phrase Structure Tree for (b):

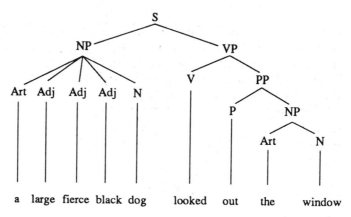

This tree indicates the need to change the NP rule once again, this time to contain optional Adjectives:

    NP→Art (Adj)* N (PP)

The asterisk on (Adj) means "zero, one or more." It is different than the asterisk used to indicate ungrammaticality.

This complex rule actually abbreviates an infinite number of NP rules, including the following:

NP→Art N	The dog
NP→Art Adj N	The big dog
NP→Art Adj Adj N	The big black dog
NP→Art Adj Adj Adj N	The big black shaggy dog

The rule accounts for the fact, discussed in Chapter 1, that there is no limit in principle to the number of adjectives that may precede a noun in English. All languages have rules that use this asterisk.

Heads of Phrases

We can now summarize all the Phrase Structure Rules for the grammar of English presented so far:

$$S \rightarrow NP\ VP$$
$$NP \rightarrow Art\ (Adj)^*\ N\ (PP)$$
$$VP \rightarrow V\ (NP)\ (PP)$$
$$PP \rightarrow P\ NP$$

With these rules we can characterize infinitely many sentence structures of English. Phrase structure rules with recursive properties such as the NP and PP rule explain how language is "creative," and how speakers with "finite" minds have the ability to produce and understand an infinite set of sentences. The rules presented here are only a fraction of the rules needed for a complete description of the language.

Many generalizations about English are contained in these rules. For example, Noun Phrases always contain a Noun, Prepositional Phrases a Preposition, and Verb Phrases a Verb. Put more succinctly, X phrases always contain an X, where X stands for Noun, Preposition or Verb. The X of an X phrase is called the **head** of that phrase. Thus the head of a Noun Phrase is a Noun, of a Prepositional Phrase a Preposition, and so on, which is not surprising. Every phrasal category must contain at a minimum its lexical category head. It may, of course, contain other elements. A VP may or may not include an NP or a PP but it must always contain a Verb.

A theory of Phrase Structure called **X-bar theory** has been developed to capture the "head-centered" characteristics of phrase structure rules. The references at the end of the chapter include sources for further pursuit of this subject.

The Lexicon

We next went to the School of Languages, where three Professors sat in Consultation upon improving that of their own Country.

The first Project was to shorten Discourse by cutting Polysyllables into one, and leaving out Verbs and Participles; because in Reality all things imaginable are but Nouns.

The other was a Scheme for entirely abolishing all Words whatsoever; and this was urged as a great Advantage in Point of Health as well as Brevity. For it is plain, that every Word we speak is in some degree a Diminution of our Lungs by Corrosion.

Jonathan Swift, *Gulliver's Travels*

The learned professors of languages in Laputa proposed a scheme for abolishing all words, thinking it would be more convenient if "Men [were] to carry about them such Things as were necessary to express the particular Business they are to discourse on." We doubt that this scheme could ever come to fruition, even in Laputa, not only because it would be difficult to carry around an unobservable *atom* or an abstract *loyalty,* but because our thoughts are expressed by sentences that have structure and cannot be represented by things pulled from a sack.

Speakers of any language know thousands of words. They know how to pronounce them in all contexts, they know their meaning (see Chapter 4), and they know how to combine them in Phrases or Sentences, which means that they know their *syntactic category* (or *word class,* or "part of speech"). All of this knowledge is contained in the component of the grammar called the **Lexicon,** discussed in Chapter 2.

As stated there, the Lexicon contains all the words and morphemes in our vocabulary and can be thought of as our "mental dictionary." Together with the Phrase Structure Rules, the Lexicon provides the information needed for complete, well formed Phrase Structure Trees. The Phrase Structure Rules account for the entire tree except for the words at the bottom. The words in the tree belong to the same syntactic categories that appear immediately above them. Through *lexical insertion,* words of the specified category are chosen from the Lexicon and put into the tree. Only words that are specified as verbs in the Lexicon are inserted under a node labeled *verb,* and so on. Words such as *fish,* which belong to two or more categories, have separate entries in the Lexicon.

Subcategorization

The Lexicon contains more syntactic information than merely the lexical category of each word. If it did not, speakers of English would be unable to make the following grammaticality distinctions.

> The boy found the ball
> *The boy found quickly
> *The boy found in the house
> The boy found the ball in the house

The verb *find* is a **transitive** verb. A transitive verb must be followed by a Noun Phrase, its "direct object." This additional specification is called **subcategorization** and is also included in the lexical entry of each word.

Most words in the Lexicon are subcategorized for certain contexts. Subcategorization accounts for the ungrammaticality of:

> *John put the milk
> *Disa slept the baby

The Verb *put* occurs with *both* a Noun Phrase and a Prepositional Phrase, as in *John put the milk* **in the refrigerator.** *Sleep* is an **intransitive verb,** so it cannot be followed by an NP. This information is included as the subcategorization of each word.

Other categories besides verbs are subcategorized. For example, within the NP, the Noun *belief* is subcategorized for both a PP or an S, as shown by the following two examples:

> the belief in freedom of speech
> the belief that freedom of speech is a basic right

The Noun *sympathy,* however, is subcategorized for a PP, but not an S:

> their sympathy for the victims
> *their sympathy that the victims are so poor

Knowledge about subcategorization may be accounted for in the Lexicon as follows:

A Fragment of the Lexicon	**Comments**
put, V, _____ NP PP	*put* is a Verb and must be followed by both an NP and a PP within the Verb Phrase
find, V, _____ NP	*find* is a Verb and must be followed by an NP within the Verb Phrase
sleep, V, _____	*sleep* is a Verb and must not be followed by any category within the Verb Phrase
belief, N, _____ (PP), _____ (S)	*belief* is a Noun and may be followed by either a PP or an S within the Noun Phrase
sympathy, N, _____ (PP)	*sympathy* is a Noun and may be followed by a PP within the Noun Phrase

Just as lexical insertion ensures that Verbs are inserted under a V node in a tree, Nouns under an N node, and so on, it also ensures that, for example, intransitive verbs such as *sleep* can only appear in trees in which the VP has no direct object. Similarly, *put* could only occur in trees where it would be followed by an NP and a PP within the Verb Phrase, and so on.

More Lexical Differences

As we have seen, different words engender different syntactic behavior, and this aspect of speaker knowledge is represented in the Lexicon. The verbs of English occur in a wide variety of syntactic patterns. For example, the verbs *want* and *force* appear to be similar when we consider such sentences as

> The conductor wanted the passengers to leave.
> The conductor forced the passengers to leave.

but they differ in another syntactic context:

> The conductor wanted to leave.
> *The conductor forced to leave

Try exhibits a third pattern differing from both *want* and *force* in that it is never followed directly by an NP:

> *The conductor tried the passengers to leave

Try is, however, similar to *want,* but not *force,* in that it can be directly followed by an infinitive (i.e., the "to" form of the verb):

> The conductor tried to leave.

These different syntactic patterns of the verbs must also be specified in the Lexicon.

The examples given show only a single verb for each pattern, but each verb cited is representative of a class of verbs. For example, *expect, need,* and *wish* pattern like *want; allow, order, persuade* pattern like *force;* and *condescend, decide,* and *manage* pattern like *try.*

Another instance of syntactically based lexical difference is found in the patterns in which *believe* and *say* appear, which, incidentally, are quite different than those of *want-, force-* and *try-*class verbs:

> The teachers believe Susan is outstanding.
> The teachers say Susan is outstanding.
>
> The teachers believe Susan to be outstanding.
> *The teachers say Susan to be outstanding.

Both *believe* and *say* may be followed by a complete sentence. However, only *believe* can be followed by a "sentence" in which the verb occurs as an infinitive. As in the previous case, these patterns are representative of classes of verbs: *suppose* and *think* are like *believe; forget* and *insist* are like *say.*

A generalization emerges when the following examples are considered:

> The teachers believe themselves to be outstanding.
> *The teachers say themselves to be outstanding.

*Believe-*class verbs, but not *say-*class verbs can be followed by a **reflexive pronoun,** a pronoun ending with *-self.* The differences in syntactic patterns are part of the lexical representation of these verbs.

The Lexicon is a key component in the grammar, containing vast amounts of information on individual words.

Transformational Rules

> Method consists entirely in properly ordering and arranging the things to which we should pay attention.
>
> René Descartes, *Oeuvres,* Vol. X

The Phrase Structure Rules presented so far characterize an infinite number of different kinds of sentences; yet there remain many types of common sentences not accounted for. Consider sentences like the following:

By permission of Johnny Hart and Creators Syndicate, Inc.

The boy is sleeping.
The boy can sleep.
The boy will sleep.

Words like *is, can,* and *will* are in a class of **Auxiliary Verbs** or **Auxiliary (Aux)**, which includes *be* and *have* as well as *may, might, would, could* and several others. In English classes, they may be called "helping verbs" or "modals." They occur in such structures as this one:

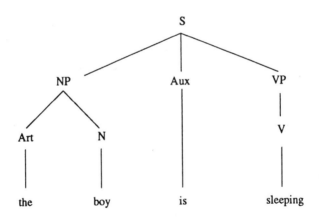

Another S rule can account for such sentences.

S→NP Aux VP

Now consider some other sentences which include Auxiliaries:

Is the boy sleeping?   (Cf. The boy is sleeping)
Can the boy sleep?   (Cf. The boy can sleep)
Will the boy sleep?   (Cf. The boy will sleep)

The "interrogative" or question sentences are related to their "declarative" counterparts in a simple way. In the questions the Aux occurs at the beginning of the sentence rather than after the subject NP. The two sentences may be said to be

transformationally related or related by an operation called a **Transformation** or a **Transformational Rule.**

The following declarative/interrogative sets of sentences show an interesting fact about languages.

> The boy who is sleeping was dreaming.
> Was the boy who is sleeping dreaming?
> *Is the boy who sleeping was dreaming?

> The boy who can sleep will dream.
> Will the boy who can sleep dream?
> *Can the boy who sleep will dream?

The ungrammatical sentences show that in forming questions it is the Auxiliary of the topmost S, that is, the Aux following the entire first NP that appears at the front of the sentence, not simply the first Auxiliary in the sentence. This is illustrated in the following simplified Phrase Structure Trees.

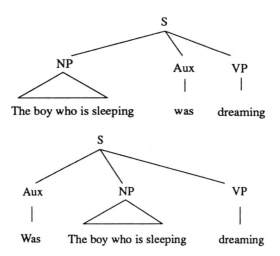

This is further evidence that syntactic categories like Noun Phrase are basic structures in language. Rules refer to such structures because rules, such as the one for forming questions, are **structure dependent.** This is not only true in English. Similar constraints and similar rules occur in other languages, as shown by the following sentences in Spanish.[3]

> El hombre está en la casa.
> The man is in the house.

[3]Examples from Chomsky's *Language and Problems of Knowledge: The Managua Lectures,* Cambridge, Mass.: MIT Press, 1988.

Está el hombre en la casa?
Is the man in the house?

El hombre está contento.
The man is happy.

Está el hombre contento?
Is the man happy?

El hombre, que está contento, está en la casa.
The man, who is happy, is in the house.

Está el hombre, que está contento, en la casa?
Is the man, who is happy, in the house?

*Está el hombre, que contento, está en la casa?
Is the man, who happy, is in the house?

As we shall see in Chapter 10, children have knowledge of structures and structure dependencies from a very early age without anyone teaching them these facts about the syntax of their language.

Long-Distance Relationships

Anyone who has had a girl- or boyfriend or a spouse living in another city probably cringes at the idea of long-distance relationships. But they are indispensable to the grammar of English.

Consider first the following sentences:

The guy seems kind of cute.
The guys seem kind of cute.

The verb has an "s" added whenever the subject is third person singular. Such a relationship is called **agreement** or **subject-verb agreement.**

Now consider these sentences:

The guy we met at the party next door *seems* kind of cute.
The guys we met at the party next door *seem* kind of cute.

The verb *seem* must agree with the subject, *guy* or *guys,* and that agreement takes place over a long distance. In the examples above, the "distance" encompassed *we met at the party next door,* but there is no limit to how many words may intervene, as the following sentence illustrates:

The guys (guy) we met at the party next door that lasted until three A.M. and was finally broken up by the cops who were called by the neighbors seem (seems) kind of cute.

This aspect of linguistic competence is explained by the phrase structure tree of such a sentence, which is shown below omitting much detail:

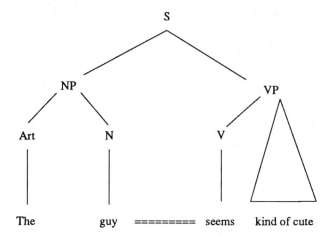

In the tree, "= = = = = = = =" represents the intervening structure which may, in principle, be indefinitely long and complex. But speakers of English know that agreement depends on sentence structure, not the linear order of words. Agreement is between the noun head of the NP immediately below the S and the verb head of the VP immediately below the S. Other material can be ignored as far as the rule of agreement is concerned, although in actual performance, if the distance is too great, the speaker may forget what the head noun was.

The NP immediately below an S in a phrase structure tree is the **subject** of that Sentence. In the tree above, *The guy* = = = = = = = = is the subject. This definition generally corresponds to the notion "subject" as commonly understood but note that here it is given an explicit definition in terms of the structure of the Phrase Structure Tree. The Verb immediately below the VP, which is immediately below the S, is the **main verb** of the S. In the tree above, the Main Verb is *seems*. Agreement is thus a relationship between the head of the Subject NP and the Main Verb of the S.

"Wh–" Sentences

Who's on first?
That's right!

Bud Abbott and Lou Costello

A different long-distance relationship is illustrated by the following sentences:

Helen said the senator wanted to hire her aide.
Helen said the senator wanted to hire who?
Who did Helen say the senator wanted to hire?

Either of the last two sentences might be spoken by someone who didn't hear all of the first sentence. Note, however, that the *who* which replaced *her aide* in the second sentence appears at the front of the third sentence. One way suggested by some linguists to account for this fact is a transformation that moves the wh- word to the front of the sentence, the same transformation that moves Aux to the front in other types of questions.

In both the second and third sentences, the *who* functions as the NP object of *hire* even though in the third sentence there is a long distance between *who* and the verb it originally followed. As in the case of agreement, the distance can be indefinitely long:

> Who did Helen say the senator wanted the congressman to try to convince the Speaker of the House to get the Vice President to hire?

Unlike the agreement rule, the nature of the intervening structure makes a difference in sentences with *wh-* words like *who, when, what,* and *which,* as shown in the following:

> Emily paid a visit to the senator that wants to hire who?
> *Who did Emily pay a visit to the senator that wants to hire?
> Miss Marple asked Sherlock whether Poirot had solved the crime.
> Who did Miss Marple ask whether Poirot had solved the crime?
> *Who did Miss Marple ask Sherlock whether had solved the crime?
> *What did Miss Marple ask Sherlock whether Poirot had solved?

> Sam Spade insulted the fat man's henchman.
> Who did Sam Spade insult?
> Whose henchman did Sam Spade insult?
> *Whose did Sam Spade insult henchman?

> Alice talked to the white rabbit in the afternoon.
> Who talked to the white rabbit in the afternoon?
> Who did Alice talk to when?
> When did Alice talk to whom?
> *Who when did Alice talk to?
> *When to whom did Alice talk?

The constraints on the formation of Wh- questions are rather complicated. If this were a book on English syntax, the rules would have to be made explicit. The examples above are presented here simply to give some idea of the complexity of syntactic knowledge that speakers of a language possess.

Recursion Revisited

Earlier we observed that recursion gives language its infinite aspect and accounts for much linguistic creativity. The following cartoon illustrates yet another type of

By permission of Johnny Hart and Creators Syndicate, Inc.

recursion in which the syntactic category Sentence is the recurring element. That is, we find sentences occurring within sentences occurring within sentences. The sentence in the final box of the cartoon consists of five sentences combined together as shown:

You mean you didn't know (that) I knew she didn't know you knew that?

To see what the phrase structure of the "B.C." cartoon sentence is, let us first examine a similar but simpler case. Consider *You mean that you knew that I knew.*

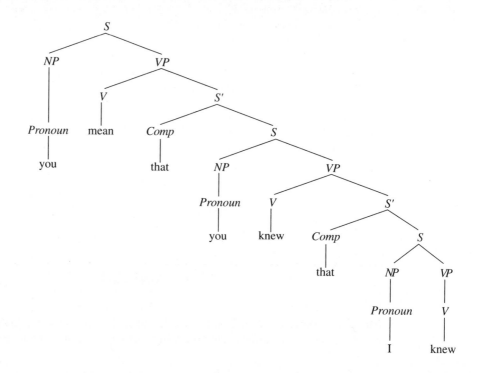

In this tree the final sentence, *I knew,* is in the higher sentence, *you knew. . . ,* which itself is in the highest sentence, *You mean. . . .* The lower sentences are **embedded** in the higher ones.

Three more phrase structure rules and two additional syntactic categories— **S'** (pronounced "S-bar") and **Complementizer (Comp)** can account for this structure.

NP → Pronoun
VP → V S'
S' → (Comp) S

The first rule states that Noun Phrases may be Pronouns. The second states that a Verb Phrase may be a Verb followed by S' and the third that an S' may be a Complementizer followed by a Sentence. The following sentence and its Phrase Structure Tree illustrate these rules:

He believes that she loves the cat.

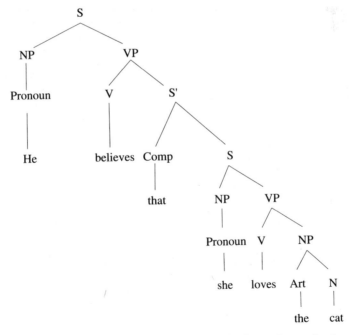

Comp is optional in the S' rule since *He believes she loves the cat* is also grammatical.

Up to this point the syntactic categories we have seen correspond, to a greater or lesser degree, to familiar concepts from traditional "grammar." For example, NPs are traditionally called "subjects" or "objects"; VPs are often called "predicates." However, the category S' illustrates the abstract nature of syntax required to account for speakers' linguistic knowledge.

The recursion on S happens because S occurs on both the left side of phrase structure rules, in S→NP VP, as well as the right side, in S'→(Comp) S.

A summary of all the phrase structure rules presented in this chapter is given below.

```
S   → NP (Aux) VP
S'  → (Comp) S
NP → Art (Adj)*N (PP)
NP → Pronoun
VP → V (NP) (PP)
VP → V S'
PP → P NP
```

These rules do not constitute all the rules that speakers of English know. Speakers of English know many other rules of this kind, and produce many sentences and phrase structures using rules other than these.

More About Sentence Structure

> Normal human minds are such that . . . without the help of anybody, they will produce 1000 (sentences) they never heard spoke of . . . inventing and saying such things as they never heard from their masters, nor any mouth.
> Huarte De San Juan, c. 1530–1592

There are many more structure-dependent relationships in language than can be discussed in an introductory text. In this section we will examine another of these. Consider the following pairs of sentences:

The boy kissed the girl. / The girl was kissed by the boy.
The child saw the puppy. / The puppy was seen by the child.

The first of each pair is an **active** sentence; the second is **passive.** There is a systematic relationship between the structure of an active/passive pair:

(1) The subject of the passive sentence corresponds to the direct object of the active sentence.

(2) In the passive sentence a form of the verb *to be* appears in front of the main verb which occurs in its "participle" form (the form that occurs after the auxiliary verb *have* as in *Politicians have kissed many babies*).

(3) The subject of the active sentence appears in the passive sentence in a prepositional phrase headed by the preposition *by.*

We have already defined "subject" as the NP immediately below S. The **direct object** of a sentence is the NP immediately below the VP immediately below the S, as illustrated below:

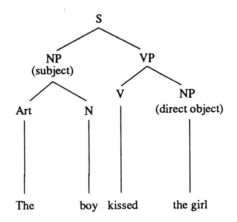

Active sentences of the form

> Subject V Direct Object

have passive counterparts

> Direct Object *be* V-participle *by* Subject

where the *be* agrees with the Direct Object, which functions as the Subject of the passive sentence. The following abbreviated trees illustrate the active/passive relationship:

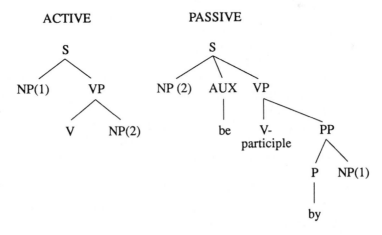

That this is a structure-dependent relationship may be seen by making up a nonsense sentence such as

> The jabberwocky snicker-snacked the wabe.

and observing that the passive is

> The wabe was snicker-snacked by the jabberwocky.

The form of *to be* that occurs in passive sentences is an Auxiliary as shown by forming questions from passive sentences, and observing that the same pattern is followed with *be* as Aux (cf. page 101). Thus the corresponding question of

> The wabe was snicker-snacked by the jabberwocky.

is

> Was the wabe snicker-snacked by the jabberwocky?

The syntax of all human languages is complex. It is not the aim of an introductory text to present the specific details of these complexities or even the arguments in support of some of the concepts we have presented in this chapter. Our aim is rather to expose the syntactic complexities of English or any language, and point out that children learn the syntax of their language at a very early age and mature speakers exhibit full knowledge of their grammar without being aware of their linguistic competence.

Types of Languages

> All the Oriental nations jam tongue and words together in the throat, like the Hebrews and Syrians. All the Mediterranean peoples push their enunciation forward to the palate, like the Greeks and the Asians. All the Occidentals break their words on the teeth, like the Italians and Spaniards. . . .
>
> Isadore of Seville, 7th century C.E.

There are many ways to classify languages. One way, to be discussed in Chapter 8, is according to the language "family." This method would be like classifying people according to whether they were Smiths, Johnsons, Fromkins, or Rodmans. Another way of classifying languages is by certain linguistic traits, regardless of family. With people, this method would be like classifying them according to height and weight, or hair and eye color.

Every language has sentences that include a Subject (S),[4] an Object (O), and a Verb (V), although some sentences do not have all three elements. Languages have been classified according to the "basic" or most common order in which these occur in the language.

There are six possible orders—SOV (Subject, Object, Verb), SVO, VSO, VOS, OVS, OSV—permitting six possible language types. Here are examples of some of the languages in these classes.[5]

---

[4]In this section *only,* S will abbreviate Subject rather than Sentence.
[5]The examples of VOS, OVS, and OSV languages are from G. K. Pullum, "Languages with Object Before Subject: A Comment and a Catalogue," *Linguistics* 19 (1981): 147–155.

SVO: English, French, Swahili, Hausa, Thai
VSO: Tagalog, Irish, (Classical) Arabic, (Biblical) Hebrew
SOV: Turkish, Japanese, Persian, Georgian, Eskimo
OVS: Apalai (Brazil), Barasano (Colombia), Panare (Venezuela)
OSV: Apurina and Xavante (Brazil)
VOS: Cakchiquel (Guatemala), Huave (Mexico), Coeur d'Alene (Idaho)

The most frequent word orders found in languages of the world are SVO, VSO, and SOV. The "basic" VSO and SOV sentences may be illustrated as follows:

VSO Tagalog: Sumagot siya sa propesor
answered he   the professor
"He answered the professor."
SOV Turkish: Romalilar barbarlari yendiler
Romans   barbarians defeated
"The Romans defeated the Barbarians."

Languages with OVS, OSV and VOS basic word order are much rarer.

The order of other sentence components in a language is most frequently correlated with the language type. If a language is of a type in which the Verb precedes the Object—a "VO" language, which includes SVO, VSO, or VOS—then the Auxiliary Verb tends to precede the Verb, Adverbs tend to follow the Verb, and Prepositions tend to precede the Noun, among other such ordering relationships. English exhibits all these tendencies.

In "OV" languages, most of which are SOV, the opposite tendency occurs: Auxiliary Verbs tend to follow the Verb, Adverbs tend to precede the Verb, and there are "Postpositions," which are "Prepositions" that follow the noun. Japanese, an SOV language, has Postpositions, as we saw in a previous section. Also, in Japanese, the Auxiliary Verb follows the Verb, as illustrated by the following sentence:

Akiko wa   sakana   o   tabete   iru
Akiko *topic*   fish   *object*   eating   is
       marker   *marker*
"Akiko is eating fish."

It must be emphasized that the correlations between language type and the word order of syntactic categories in sentences are "tendencies," not inviolable rules, and different languages follow them to a greater or lesser degree.

The knowledge that speakers of the various languages have about word order is revealed in the particular Phrase Structure Rules of the language. In English, an SVO language, the V precedes its NP Object: VP→V NP. In Turkish or Japanese, SOV languages, the NP Object precedes the Verb in the corresponding Phrase Structure Rule of that language. Similarly, the rule PP→P NP occurs in SVO languages, whereas the rule PP→NP P is the correlate occurring in SOV languages.

If a language is, say, SVO, this does not mean that SVO is the only possible word order. Yoda, the Jedi Master from the motion picture *Return of the Jedi,* speaks a strange but perfectly understandable style of English that achieves its eccentricity by being OSV. Some of Yoda's utterances are:

> Sick I've become.
> Strong with the Force you are.
> Your father he is.
> When nine hundred years you reach, look as good you will not.

Despite the differences, languages share many commonalities, referred to as "Language Universals" in Chapter 1. All languages have Verbs; all languages have NPs that may function as Subjects and Objects; all languages have Phrase Structure Rules that show word order and the constituency of syntactic categories; all languages have structure-dependent relationships. We will suggest in later chapters that such linguistic universals are biologically based and help account for how children manage to learn grammars at an early age.

Summary

Speakers of a language recognize the grammatical sentences of their language and know how the words in a grammatical sentence must be arranged. All speakers are capable of producing and understanding an unlimited number of new sentences never before spoken or heard. They also recognize ambiguities, know when different sentences mean the same thing, and correctly perceive the meaning relations in a sentence. This kind of knowledge is accounted for in the grammar by the **rules of syntax.**

Sentences have structure that can be represented by **Phrase Structure Trees** containing **Syntactic Categories.** Such a representation reveals the linear order of words, and the constituency of each syntactic category. Syntactic categories are either **Phrasal Categories,** such as NP and VP, which can be decomposed into other syntactic categories, or **Lexical Categories,** such as Noun and Verb, which correspond to the words of the language.

A linguistic grammar is a formally stated, explicit description of the mental grammar or speaker's linguistic competence. **Phrase Structure Rules** characterize the basic phrase structure trees of the language, including such facts as that a Noun Phrase may be an Article followed by a Noun, but never (in English) a Noun followed by an Article. Phrase structure rules reveal that every phrasal category contains, at a minimum, its lexical category head, and may contain other elements. Thus, Noun Phrases must contain Nouns, and so on.

Phrase Structure Rules may be **recursive.** A recursive rule or set of rules repeats on the right side of the arrow a category that appears on the left side. Recursive rules allow the same syntactic category to appear repeatedly in a phrase structure tree, which reflects a speaker's ability to produce sentences without length limitations.

The **Lexicon** represents the knowledge speakers have about the vocabulary of their language, including the syntactic category of words, what elements may co-occur together—expressed as **subcategorization** restrictions—and whether certain syntactic rules apply or not.

The grammar includes rules that reveal structural patterning, such as the relationship between a declarative and its corresponding interrogative sentence. Certain patterns occur over unbounded distances within a sentence, such as subject-verb agreement and **wh-** question formation. Some linguists use **transformational rules** to account for the movement of Aux or *wh- words* to the beginning of interrogative sentences.

Languages of the world may be classified according to the order in which the Subject, Object, and Verb commonly occur in a sentence. English, for example, is SVO or Subject-Verb-Object. Whatever basic word order a language has is reflected in the particular set of Phrase Structure Rules for that language.

To capture the knowledge speakers have about the syntax of their language, the grammar requires, at a minimum, Phrase Structure Rules, a Lexicon richly endowed with pertinent facts about individual words, and a set of rules describing the structure-dependent patterning that occurs throughout the language.

References for Further Reading

Akmajian, A., R. A. Demers, and R. M. Harnish. 1979. *Linguistics: An Introduction to Language and Communication,* 2d ed. Cambridge, Mass: M.I.T. Press.

Chomsky, Noam. 1957. *Syntactic Structures.* The Hague: Mouton.

Chomsky, Noam. 1965. *Aspects of the Theory of Syntax.* Cambridge, Mass: M.I.T. Press.

Chomsky, Noam. 1972. *Language and Mind,* rev. ed. New York: Harcourt Brace Jovanovich.

Chomsky, Noam. 1982. *Some Concepts and Consequences of the Theory of Government and Binding.* Cambridge, Mass: M.I.T. Press.

Gazdar, Gerald, E. Klein, G. Pullum, and I. Sag. 1985. *Generalized Phrase Structure Grammar.* Cambridge, Mass: Harvard University Press.

Haegeman, Liliane. 1991. *Introduction to Government and Binding Theory.* Oxford, England: Basil Blackwell.

Horrocks, Geoffrey. 1987. *Generative Grammar.* New York: Longman Inc.

Jackendoff, R. S. 1977. *X-bar Syntax: A Study of Phrase Structure.* Cambridge, Mass: M.I.T. Press.

McCawley, James D. 1988. *The Syntactic Phenomena of English,* Vols. I, II. Chicago: University of Chicago Press.

Newmeyer, Frederick J. 1981. *Linguistic Theory in America: The First Quarter Century of Transformational-Generative Grammar.* New York: Academic Press.

Radford, Andrew. 1988. *Transformational Grammar.* New York: Cambridge University Press.

Sells, Peter. 1985. *Lectures on Contemporary Syntactic Theories: An Introduction to Government-Binding Theory, Generalized Phrase Structure Grammar, and Lexical-Functional Grammar.* Stanford, Calif: Center for the Study of Language and Information. Ventura Hall. Stanford University.

Stockwell, R. P. 1977. *Foundations of Syntactic Theory.* Englewood Cliffs, N.J.: Prentice-Hall.

Stockwell, R. P., M. Bean, and D. Elliot. 1977. *Workbook for Foundations of Syntactic Theory*. Englewood Cliffs, N.J.: Prentice-Hall.

Van Riemsdijk, Henk, and E. Williams. 1986. *Introduction to the Theory of Grammar*. Cambridge, Mass.: M.I.T. Press.

Exercises

1. Besides distinguishing grammatical from ungrammatical strings, the rules of syntax account for other kinds of linguistic knowledge, such as

   a. when a sentence is structurally ambiguous.
   b. when two sentences of different structure mean the same thing.
   c. what the meaning relations are in sentences.

   In each case a–c, draw on your own linguistic knowledge of English to provide an example different than the ones in the chapter, and explain why your example illustrates the point. If you know a language other than English, provide examples in that language, if possible.

   a. Structural ambiguity:
   b. Paraphrases:
   c. Meaning relations:

2. Consider the following sentences:

   a. I hate war.
   b. You know that I hate war.
   c. He knows that you know that I hate war.

      A. Write another sentence that includes sentence *c.*
      B. What does this set of sentences reveal about the nature of language?
      C. How is this characteristic of human language related to the difference between linguistic competence and performance? (Hint: Review these concepts in Chapter 1.)

3. Paraphrase each of the following sentences in two different ways to show that you understand the ambiguity involved:

      Example: Smoking grass can be nauseating.
        i. Putting grass in a pipe and smoking it can make you sick.
       ii. Fumes from smoldering grass can make you sick.

   a. Dick finally decided on the boat.
        i.
       ii.
   b. The professor's appointment was shocking.
        i.
       ii.

    c. The design has big squares and circles.
       i.
      ii.
    d. That sheepdog is too hairy to eat.
       i.
      ii.
    e. Could this be the invisible man's hair tonic?
       i.
      ii.
    f. The governor is a dirty street fighter.
       i.
      ii.
    g. I cannot recommend him too highly.
       i.
      ii.
    h. Terry loves his wife and so do I.
       i.
      ii.
    i. They said she would go yesterday.
       i.
      ii.

4. Using the example *The boy saw the man with the telescope* as a model, draw two Phrase Structure Trees representing the two meanings of the sentence:

    The magician touched the child with the wand.

Meaning 1:

Tree 1:

Meaning 2:

Tree 2:

5. In the spaces provided write out the phrase structure rules that the following seven rules abbreviate, expanding the NP rule with Adj for zero, one, and two Adjectives.

S' → (Comp) S	VP → V (NP) (PP)
S → NP (Aux) VP	VP → V S'
NP→ Art (Adj)* N (PP)	PP → P NP
NP→ Pronoun	

a.   b.
c.   d.
e.   f.
g.   h.
i.   j.
k.   l.
m.   n.
o.   p.
q.

6. In all languages, sentences can occur within sentences. For example, in exercise 2; sentence *b* contains sentence *a,* and sentence *c* contains sentence *b*. Put another way, sentence *a* is *embedded* in sentence *b,* and sentence *b* is embedded in sentence *c*. Sometimes embedded sentences appear slightly changed from their "normal" form, but you should be able to recognize and underline the embedded sentences in the examples below. Underline in the non-English sentences, when given, not in the translations. (The first one is done as an example):

a. Yesterday I noticed <u>my accountant repairing the toilet</u>.
b. Becky said that Jake would play the piano.
c. I deplore the fact that bats have wings.
d. That Guinevere loves Lorian is known to all my friends.
e. Who promised the teacher that Maxine wouldn't be absent?
f. It's ridiculous that he washes his own Rolls-Royce.
g. The woman asked for the waiter to bring a glass of ice water.
h. The person who answers this question will win $100.
i. The idea of Romeo marrying a 13 year old is upsetting.
j. I gave my hat to the nurse who helped me cut my hair.
k. For your children to spend all your royalty payments on recreational drugs is a shame.
l. Give this fork to the person I'm getting the pie for.
m. khăw chyâ   waă   khruu maa. (Thai)
   He   believe *complementizer* teacher come
   He believes the teacher is coming.
n. Je me demande quand il partira. (French)
   I me ask   when he will leave
   I wonder when he'll leave.
o. Jan zei dat Piet dit boek niet heeft gelezen. (Dutch)
   Jan said that Piet this book not has   read
   Jan said that Piet has not read this book.

7. Following the patterns of the various tree examples in the text, especially in the two sections on Phrase Structure Rules, draw Phrase Structure Trees for the following sentences:

   a. The puppy found the child.
   b. A very frightened passenger landed the crippled airplane.
   c. The house on the hill collapsed in the wind.
   d. The ice melted.
   e. The hot sun melted the ice.
   f. A quaint old ivy-covered house appeared.
   g. The old tree swayed in the wind.
   h. The children put the toy in the box.
   i. The reporter realized that the senator lied.

8. Use the rules on page 108 to create five phrase structure trees of sentences of 6, 7, 8, 9, and 10 words in length not given in the chapter. Use your own "mental lexicon" to fill in the bottom of the tree.

9. We stated that the rules of syntax specify all and only the grammatical sentences of the language. Why is it important to say "only"? What would be wrong with a grammar that specified as grammatical sentences all of the truly grammatical ones plus a few that were not grammatical?

10. Here is a set of made-up Phrase Structure Rules. The "initial" symbol is still S, and the "terminal symbols" (the ones that do not appear to the left of an arrow) are actual words:

    (i) S→A B C
    (ii) A→*the*
    (iii) B→*children*
    (iv) C→*ran*
    (v) C→C *and* D
    (vi) D→*ran and* D
    (vii) D→*ran*

    a. Give three Phrase Structure Trees that these rules characterize.
    b. How many phrase structure trees could these rules characterize? (*Hint:* Look for recursive rules.)

11. Because languages have recursive properties, there is no limit to the potential length of sentences, and the set of sentences of any language is infinite. Give two examples (different from the ones in the text) of:

a. Noun Phrase recursion
b. Verb Phrase recursion
c. Sentence recursion

In one example the relevant category should appear twice, and in the other example at least three times. Draw one of the Phrase Structure Trees in each case, being careful to illustrate the recursion.

12. Referring to exercise 7(a)–7(i), write down the head of each NP and VP. For example, in 7(a), the NP, *the puppy,* has the head *puppy;* the VP, *found the puppy,* has the head *found;* and the NP, *the child,* has the head *child.*

   b.
   c.
   d.
   e.
   f.
   g.
   h.
   i.

13. In terms of subcategorization, explain why the following are ungrammatical.

   a. *The man located
   b. *Jesus wept the apostles
   c. *Robert is hopeful of his children
   d. *Robert is fond that his children love animals
   e. *The children laughed the man

14. We only considered transitive verbs in the chapter, ones subcategorized in the Lexicon like *find:*

   find, V, _____ NP

   There are also *ditransitive* verbs in English, ones that may be followed by two NPs, such as *give:*

   The emperor gave the vassal a castle.

   Think of three other ditransitive verbs in English.

   i.
   ii.
   iii.

(continued on following page)

In the space provided below, write the lexical entry for one of these verbs, following the pattern of *find* above:

15. In addition to the examples given in the chapter, write down one additional verb in each of the following verb classes:

    a. *want* class:
    b. *force* class:
    c. *try* class:
    d. *believe* class:
    e. *say* class:

16. All of the *Wh-* words exhibit the "long-distance" behavior illustrated with *who* in the chapter. Invent three sentences beginning with *what, which,* and *where,* in which the wh- word is not in its "logical" position within the sentence. Give both versions of your sentence. Here is an example with the wh- word *when: When could Marcy catch a flight out of here?* from *Marcy could catch a flight out of here when?*

    a.
    b.
    c.

17. There are many systematic, structure-dependent relationships among sentences, such as the one discussed in the chapter between actives and passive sentences. Here is another example, based on the ditransitive verbs mentioned in Exercise 14:

    The boy *wrote* the senator a letter.
    The boy *wrote* a letter to the senator.

    A philanthropist *gave* the Animal Rights movement $1,000,000.
    A philanthropist *gave* $1,000,000 to the Animal Rights movement.

Describe the relationship between the first and second members of the pairs of sentences in a way similar to the way the active/passive relationship is described on page 108.

18. State at least three differences between English and the following languages, using just the sentence(s) given. Ignore lexical differences—that is, the different vocabulary. Then give the language *type:* SVO, SOV, and so on. Here is an example:

Thai: dèg   khon   níi   kamlang   kin.
       boy *classifier* this   *progressive* eat
"This boy is eating."

      mǎa   tua   nán   kin   khâaw.
      dog *classifier* that   eat   rice
"That dog ate rice."

Three differences are: (1) Thai has "classifiers." They have no English equivalent. (2) The demonstratives "this" and "that" follow the noun in Thai, but precede the noun in English. (3) The "progressive" is expressed by a separate word in Thai. The verb does not change form. In English, the progressive is indicated by the presence of the verb *to be* and the adding of *-ing* to the verb. Thai is an SVO language.

a. French:

    cet   homme   intelligent   comprendra   la question.
    this   man   intelligent   will understand the question
"This intelligent man will understand the question."

    ces   hommes   intelligents   comprendront   les questions
    these   men   intelligent   will understand the questions.
"These intelligent men will understand the questions."

b. Japanese:

    watashi ga   sakana   o   tabete   iru
    I   *subject* fish   *object* eat (*ing*) am
             marker   *marker*
"I am eating fish."

c. Swahili:

    mtoto   alivunja kikombe
    m-   toto   a-   li-   vunja   ki-   kombe
    class child   he   *past*   break   *class*   cup
    marker   *marker*
"The child broke the cup."

    watoto   wanavunja   vikombe
    wa-   toto   wa- na-   vunja   vi-   kombe
    class   child   they *present* break   *class* cup
    marker   *marker*
"The children break the cups."

d. Korean:

    kɨ   sonyɔ-nɨn wɨyu-lɨl   masi-ass-ta
    kɨ   sonyɔn- nɨn wɨyu- lɨl   masi- ass-   ta
    the boy   *subject* milk *object* drink *past* *assertion*
                 marker   *marker*
"The boy drank milk."

kɨ-nɨn	muɔs-lɨl	mɔk-ass-nya			
kɨ	nɨn	muɔs-	lɨl	mɔk-	ass-	nya
he	*subject marker*	what	*object marker*	eat	*past*	*question*

"What did he eat?"

e. Tagalog:

nakita	ni	Pedro	-ng		puno	na	ang	bus
saw	*article*	Pedro	*complementizer*		full	already	*topic marker*	bus

"Pedro saw the bus was already full."

CHAPTER 4
Semantics: The Meanings of Language

Language without meaning is meaningless.

Roman Jakobson

By permission of Johnny Hart and Creators Syndicate, Inc.

For thousands of years philosophers have been pondering the meaning of "meaning"; yet speakers of a language can understand what is said to them and can produce strings of words that convey meaning.

Learning a language includes learning the "agreed-upon" meanings of certain strings of sounds and learning how to combine these meaningful units into larger units that also convey meaning. We are not free to change the meanings of these words at will, for if we did we would be unable to communicate with anyone.

Humpty Dumpty, however, was unwilling to accept this fact when he said:

"There's glory for you!"

"I don't know what you mean by 'glory,'" Alice said.

Humpty Dumpty smiled contemptuously. "Of course you don't—till I tell you. I meant 'there's a nice knock-down argument for you!'"

"But 'glory' doesn't mean 'a nice knock-down argument,'" Alice objected.

"When *I* use a word," Humpty Dumpty said, in rather a scornful tone, "it means just what I choose it to mean—neither more nor less."

> "The question is," said Alice, "whether you *can* make words mean so many different things."

Alice is quite right. You cannot make words mean what they do not mean. Of course, if you wish to redefine the meaning of each word as you use it, you are free to do so, but you would be making an artificial, clumsy use of language, and most people would not wait around long to talk to you.

Fortunately there are few Humpty Dumptys; all the speakers of a language share the basic vocabulary—the sounds and meanings of words. All speakers know how to combine words to produce phrase and sentence meaning. The study of the linguistic meaning of words, phrases, and sentences is called **semantics.**

Word Meaning

> "My name is Alice . . . "
> "It's a stupid name enough!" Humpty Dumpty interrupted impatiently. "What does it mean?"
> "Must a name mean something?" Alice asked doubtfully.
> "Of course it must," Humpty Dumpty said with a short laugh. "My name means the shape I am—and a good handsome shape it is, too. With a name like yours, you might be any shape, almost."
>
> Lewis Carroll, *Through the Looking-Glass*

Dictionaries are filled with words and their meanings. So is the head of every human being who speaks a language. You are a walking dictionary. You know the meaning of thousands of words. Your knowledge of their meanings permits you to use them to express your thoughts and to understand them when heard, even though you probably seldom stop and ask yourself: "What does *boy* mean?" or "What does *walk* mean?" The meaning of words is part of linguistic knowledge and is therefore a part of the grammar. Your mental storehouse of information about words and morphemes is what we have been calling the **Lexicon.**

Semantic Properties

Words and morphemes have meanings. We shall talk about the meaning of words, even though words may be composed of several morphemes, as noted in Chapter 2.
Suppose someone said:

The assassin was stopped before he got to Mr. Thwacklehurst.

If the word *assassin* is in your mental dictionary, you know that it was some *person* who was prevented from *murdering* some *prominent person* named Thwacklehurst. Your knowledge of the meaning of *assassin* tells you that it was not an animal that tried to kill the man and that Thwacklehurst was not likely to be a little old man who owned a tobacco shop. In other words, your knowledge of the meaning of *assassin*

By permission of Johnny Hart and Creators Syndicate, Inc.

includes knowing that the individual to whom that word refers is *human,* is a *murderer,* and is a killer of *prominent people.* These pieces of information, then, are some of the **semantic properties** of the word upon which speakers of the language agree. The meaning of all nouns, verbs, adjectives, and adverbs—the "content words"—and even some of the "function words" such as *with* or *over* can at least partially be specified by such properties.

The same semantic property may be part of the meaning of many different words. "Female" is a semantic property that helps to define

tigress	hen	actress	maiden
doe	mare	debutante	widow
ewe	vixen	girl	woman

The words in the last two columns are also distinguished by the semantic property "human," which is also found in

| doctor | dean | professor | bachelor | parent | baby | child |

The meanings of the last two of these words are also specified as "young." That is, part of the meaning of the words *baby* and *child* is that they are "human" and "young." (We will continue to indicate words by using *italics* and semantic "properties" by using double quotation marks.)

The meanings of words have other properties. The word *father* has the properties "male" and "adult," as do *uncle* and *bachelor;* but *father* also has the property "parent," which distinguishes it from the other two words.

Mare, in addition to "female" and "animal," must also denote a property of "horseness." Words have general semantic properties such as "human" or "parent," as well as more specific properties that give the word its particular meaning.

The same semantic property may occur in words of different categories. "Female" is part of the meaning of the noun *mother,* of the verb *breast-feed,* and of the adjective *pregnant.* "Cause" is a verbal property of *darken, kill, uglify,* and so on.

darken	cause to become dark
kill	cause to die
uglify	cause to become ugly

Other semantic properties of verbs are shown in the following table:

Semantic Property	Verbs Having It
motion	bring, fall, plod, walk, run . . .
contact	hit, kiss, touch . . .
creation	build, imagine, make . . .
sense	see, hear, feel . . .

For the most part no two words have exactly the same meaning (but see the discussion of synonyms below). Additional semantic properties make for finer and finer distinctions in meaning. *Plod* is distinguished from *walk* by the property "slow," and *stalk* from *plod* by a property such as "purposeful."

The humor of the cartoon at the head of this section is that the verb "roll over" has a specific semantic property, something like "activity about the longest axis." The snake's attempt to roll about its shortest axis indicates trouble with semantic *properties*.

Evidence for Semantic Properties

Semantic properties are not directly observable. Their existence must be inferred from linguistic evidence. One source of such evidence is found in the speech errors, or "slips of the tongue," that we all produce. Consider the following unintentional word substitutions that some speakers have actually spoken.

Intended Utterance	Actual Utterance (Error)
bridge of the nose	bridge of the neck
when my gums bled	when my tongues bled
he came too late	he came too early
Mary was young	Mary was early
the lady with the dachshund	the lady with the Volkswagen
that's a horse of another color	that's a horse of another race
he has to pay her alimony	he has to pay her rent

These errors and thousands we and others have collected reveal that the incorrectly substituted words are not random substitutions but share some semantic property with the intended words. *Nose* and *neck, gums* and *tongues* are all "body parts" or "parts of the head." *Young, early,* and *late* are related to "time." *Dachshund* and *Volkswagen* are both "German" and "small." The semantic relationships between *color* and *race* and even between *alimony* and *rent* are rather obvious.

The semantic properties that describe the linguistic meaning of a word should not be confused with other non-linguistic properties, such as physical properties. Scientists know that water is composed of hydrogen and oxygen but such knowledge is not part of a word's meaning. We know that water is an essential ingredient of lemonade or a bath. We need not know any of these things, though, to know what the word *water* means, and to be able to use and understand this word in a sentence.

Semantic Properties and the Lexicon

As discussed in Chapter 2, the Lexicon is the part of the grammar that contains the knowledge speakers have about individual words and morphemes, including semantic properties. Words that share a semantic property are said to be in a semantic class, for example, the semantic class of "female" words. Semantic classes may "intersect," such as the class of words with the properties "female" and "young," which class is an intersection of the female class with the young class. The words *girl* or *filly* would be members of this class. In some cases, the presence of one semantic property can be inferred from the presence or absence of another. For example, words with the property "human" also have the property "animate".

One way of expressing these facts about semantic properties is through the use of **semantic features.** Semantic features are a formal or notational device for expressing the presence or absence of semantic properties by pluses and minuses. For example, the lexical entries for words such as *father, girl* and *mare* would appear as follows (with other information omitted):

woman	**father**	**girl**	**mare**	**stalk**
+ female	+ male	+ female	+ female	+ motion
+ human	+ human	+ human	− human	+ slow
− young	+ parent	+ young	− young	+ purposeful
. . .	. . .	. . .	+ horseness	. . .
			. . .	

Intersecting classes share the same features; members of the class of words referring to human females are marked "plus" for the features *human* and *female.* Some features need not be specifically mentioned. For example if a word is [+ human] it is "automatically" [+ animate]. This generalization can be expressed as a **redundancy rule,** which is part of the Lexicon:

A word that is [+ human] is [+ animate]

This rule specifies that [+ animate] need not be specified in the lexical entry for *father, girl, professor,* etc. since it can be inferred from the feature [+ human].

Some semantic redundancy rules infer "negative" properties. For example, if something is "human" it is not "abstract"; an activity that is "slow" is not "fast." Thus we can state the following two redundancy rules:

A word that is [+ human] is [− abstract]
A word that is [+ slow] is [− fast]

Thus without further specification in the lexicon, *woman* is [− abstract], and the verb *crawl,* which is [+ slow], is also [− fast] by the second redundancy rule.

More Semantic Relationships

GARFIELD® reprinted by permission of UFS, Inc.

Our linguistic knowledge about words, their semantic properties, and the relationships among them are illustrated by the Garfield cartoon, which shows that "small" is a semantic property of *morsel,* but not of *glob.*

Consider the following knowledge about words that speakers of English have:

> If something *swims,* it is in a liquid.
> If something is *splashed,* it is a liquid.

If you say you saw a bug swimming in a container of "goop," anyone who understands English would agree that *goop* is surely a liquid, that is, has the semantic feature [+liquid]. Even without knowing what goop refers to, you know you can talk about pouring goop, drinking goop, or plugging a hole where goop is leaking out and forming droplets. The words *pour, drink, leak,* and *droplet* are all used with items relating to the property "liquid."

Similarly, we would know that "sawing goop in half," "melting goop," or "bending goop" are semantically ill-formed expressions because none of these activities apply sensibly to objects that are [+liquid].

In some languages, the fact that certain verbs can occur appropriately with certain nouns is reflected in the verb morphology. For example in the Native American language Navajo, there are different verb forms for objects with different semantic properties. The verbal form *šánléh* is used with words with semantic features [+long], [+flexible], such as *rope;* whereas the verb form *šántúh* is used for words like *spear,* which is [+long], [−flexible].

Homonyms and Ambiguity

> "Mine is a long and sad tale!" said the Mouse, turning to Alice and sighing.
> "It is a long tail, certainly," said Alice, looking with wonder at the Mouse's tail, "but why do you call it sad?"
>
> **Lewis Carroll,** *Alice's Adventures in Wonderland*

©1983 Newspaper Enterprise Association, Inc.

We observed in Chapter 2 that knowing a word means knowing both its sounds (pronunciation or "form") and its meaning. Both are crucial in determining whether two "words" are the same or different. If two "words" differ in pronunciation but have the same meaning, such as *sofa* and *couch,* they are different words. Likewise, two "words" with identical pronunciation but significantly different meanings, such as *tale* and *tail,* are also considered different words. Spelling is not relevant, only pronunciation. Thus, *bat* the animal and *bat* for hitting baseballs are also different words.

Words like the two *bat*s are called **homonyms.** Homonyms are different words that are pronounced the same, but may or may not be spelled the same. *To, too,* and *two* are homonyms because they are pronounced the same, despite their spelling differences.

Homonyms can create ambiguity. A word or a sentence is **ambiguous** if it can be understood or interpreted in more than one way. The sentence

> She cannot bear children.

may mean "She is unable to give birth to children" or "She cannot tolerate children." The ambiguity is due to the two words *bear* with two different meanings. Sometimes additional context can help to disambiguate the sentence:

> She cannot bear children if they are noisy.
> She cannot bear children because she is sterile.

Both words *bear* in the above sentences are verbs. There is another homonym *bear,* the animal, which is a noun with different semantic properties. The adjective *bare,* despite its different spelling, is a homonym of these words because it too has a different meaning. *Bare,* as a verb, is yet another homonym.

Homonyms are good candidates for humor as well as for confusion.

> "How is bread made?"
> "I know *that*!" Alice cried eagerly.
> "You take some flour—"
> "Where do you pick the flower?" the White Queen asked. "In a garden, or in the hedges?"
> "Well, it isn't *picked* at all," Alice explained; "it's *ground*—"
> "How many acres of ground?" said the White Queen.

The humor of this passage is due to the two sets of homonyms: *flower* and *flour* and the two meanings of *ground*. Alice means *ground* as the past tense of *grind*, whereas the White Queen is interpreting *ground* to mean "earth."

Thus, sentences may be ambiguous because they contain one or more ambiguous words. This is called **lexical ambiguity.** Other examples of such lexically ambiguous sentences are:

(a) The Rabbi married my sister.
(b) Do you smoke after sex?
(c) It takes two mice to screw in a light bulb.

Item c is also an example of **structural ambiguity,** which was examined in Chapter 3 on syntax, in which the two or more meanings are not the result of lexical ambiguity but of two or more *structures* underlying the same string of words. The word *screw* has two meanings, and the sentences have two structures:

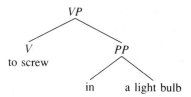

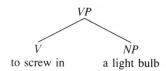

Another somewhat different instance of homonyms occurs with *have* and *be*. In the following sentences both are verbs:

(a) Robert *has* a dog named Cecelia.
(b) Dogs *are* intelligent animals.

Both also occur as auxiliaries. In addition, the auxiliary *be* has two homonyms, one that occurs with "-ing" forms and one that indicates the passive voice:

(c) Cecelia *has* seen ten squirrels today.
(d) They *are* running fast.
(e) The women *were* given gifts by Senator Snort.

Ambiguity may also result from the use of these homonyms, as illustrated in the sentence

(f) They are moving sidewalks.

When *are* is understood as a verb (called a **copula** when used in this way), *moving* is an adjective modifying *sidewalks.* The overall meaning is something like "those things are sidewalks that move." If *are* is an auxiliary, then the meaning is "those workers are relocating the sidewalks."

Synonyms and Paraphrases

> Does he wear a turban, a fez or a hat?
> Does he sleep on a mattress, a bed or a mat, or a Cot,
> The Akond of Swat?
> Can he write a letter concisely clear,
> Without a speck or a smudge or smear or Blot,
> The Akond of Swat?
>
> Edward Lear, *"The Akond of Swat"*

There are not only words that sound the same but have different meanings; there are also words that sound different but have the same or nearly the same meaning. Such words are called **synonyms.** There are dictionaries of synonyms that contain many hundreds of entries, such as:

> apathetic/phlegmatic/passive/sluggish/indifferent
> pedigree/ancestry/genealogy/descent/lineage

It has been said that there are no perfect synonyms—that is, no two words ever have *exactly* the same meaning. Still, the following pairs of sentences have very similar meanings.

(a) He's sitting on the sofa. / He's sitting on the couch.
(b) I'll be happy to come. / I'll be glad to come.
(c) *Tale* and *tail* are homonyms. / *Tale* and *tail* are homophones.

Some individuals may always use *sofa* instead of *couch,* but if they know the two words, they will understand both sentences and interpret them to mean the same thing. The degree of semantic similarity between words depends to a great extent on the number of semantic properties they share. *Sofa* and *couch* refer to the same type of object and share most, if not all, of their semantic properties.

The word *homophone* is a synonym for the word *homonym,* and in writing the previous section of this book, we chose more or less arbitrarily which term to use, and then used it consistently. We could easily have used *homophone* for the same concept.

There are words with many semantic properties in common which are neither synonyms nor near synonyms. *Man* and *boy* both refer to male humans; the meaning of *boy* includes the additional semantic property of "youth," whereby it differs from the meaning of *man.* Thus the semantic system of English permits you to say *A sofa is a couch* or *A couch is a sofa* but not *A man is a boy* or *A boy is a man,* except when you wish to describe "boylike" qualities of the man or "manlike" qualities of the boy.

A word may have several closely related but slightly different meanings. Such a word is said to be **polysemous.** It is not unusual for a polysemous word to share one of its meanings with another word, a kind of partial synonymy. For example *mature* and *ripe* are polysemous words which are synonyms when applied to fruit, but not when applied to animals. *Deep* and *profound* are another such pair. Both may apply to thought, but only *deep* applies to water.

Sometimes words that are ordinarily opposites can mean the same thing in certain contexts; thus a *good* scare is the same as a *bad* scare. Similarly, a word with a positive meaning in one form, such as the adjective *perfect,* when used adverbially, undergoes a "weakening" effect, so that a "perfectly good bicycle" is neither perfect nor always good. "Perfectly good" means something more like "adequate."

When synonyms occur in otherwise identical sentences, the sentences will be paraphrases. Sentences are **paraphrases** if they have the same meaning (except possibly for minor differences in emphasis). Thus the use of synonyms may create **lexical paraphrase,** just as the use of homonyms may create lexical ambiguity.

Sentences may also be paraphrases because of *structural differences* that are not essential to their meaning. Several examples were cited in the syntax chapter, such as:

> The girl kissed the boy. / The boy was kissed by the girl.

Although there may be a difference in the emphasis in these two sentences—in the second the emphasis is on what happened to the boy, whereas in the first the emphasis is on what the girl did—the meaning relations between the verb *kiss* and the two noun phrases are the same in both cases, and on this basis the two sentences are paraphrases of each other.

Antonyms

> As a rule, man is a fool;
> When it's hot, he wants it cool;
> When it's cool, he wants it hot;
> Always wanting what is not.
>
> Anonymous

The meaning of a word may be partially defined by saying what it is *not. Male* means *not female. Dead* means *not alive.* Words that are opposite in meaning are often called **antonyms.** Ironically, the basic property of two words that are antonyms is that they share all but one semantic property. *Beautiful* and *tall* are not antonyms; *beautiful* and *ugly,* or *tall* and *short,* are. The property they do not share is present in one and absent in the other.

There are several kinds of antonymy. There are **complementary pairs:**

alive/dead   present/absent   awake/asleep

They are complementary in that *not alive = dead* and *not dead = alive,* and so on.
There are **gradable** pairs of antonyms:

big/small   hot/cold   fast/slow   happy/sad

With gradable pairs the negative of one word is not synonymous with the other. For
example, someone who is *not happy* is not necessarily *sad.* It is also true of gradable antonyms that more of one is less of another. More bigness is less smallness;
wider is less narrow, and taller is less short. Another characteristic of many pairs of
gradable antonyms is that one is **marked** and the other **unmarked.** The unmarked
member is the one used in questions of degree. We ask, "How *high* is it?" (not "How
low is it?") or "How *tall* is she?" We answer "One thousand feet high" or "Five feet
tall" but never "Five feet short," except humorously. *High* and *tall* are the unmarked
members of *high/low* and *tall/short.* Notice that the meaning of these adjectives and
other similar ones is relative. The words themselves provide no information about
absolute size. Because of our knowledge of the language, and of things in the world,
this relativity normally causes no confusion. Thus we know that "a small elephant"
is much bigger than "a large mouse."
    Another kind of "opposite" involves pairs like

give/receive   buy/sell   teacher/pupil

They are called **relational opposites,** and they display symmetry in their meaning.
If X *gives* Y to Z, then Z *receives* Y from X. If X is Y's *teacher,* then Y is X's *pupil.*
Pairs of words ending in *-er* and *-ee* are usually relational opposites. If Mary is
Bill's employ*er,* then Bill is Mary's employ*ee.*
    Comparative forms of gradable pairs of adjectives often form relational pairs.
Thus, if Sally is *taller* than Alfred, then Alfred is *shorter* than Sally. If a Cadillac is
more expensive than a Ford, then a Ford is *cheaper* than a Cadillac.
    If meanings of words were indissoluble wholes, there would be no way to make
the interpretations that we do. We know that *big* and *red* are not opposites because
they have too few semantic properties in common. They are both adjectives, but *big*
is the semantic class involving size, whereas *red* is a color. On the other hand, *buy/
sell* are relational opposites because both contain the semantic property "transfer of
goods or services," and they differ only in one property, "direction of transfer."
    Semantic redundancy rules such as those discussed above can reveal knowledge
about antonyms. Consider:

    A word that is [+ married] is [− single]
    A word that is [+ single] is [− married]

These rules show that any word that bears the semantic property "married," such as *wife*, is understood to lack the semantic property "single"; and conversely, any word that bears the semantic property "single," such as *bachelor*, will not have the property "married."

Formation of Antonyms

Reprinted by permission: Tribune Media Services.

In English there are a number of ways to form antonyms. You can add the prefix *un:*

> likely/unlikely   able/unable   fortunate/unfortunate

or you can add *non:*

> entity/nonentity   conformist/nonconformist

or you can add *in:*

> tolerant/intolerant   discreet/indiscreet   decent/indecent

Other prefixes may also be used to form negative words morphologically: *il-*, as in *illegal, mis-,* as in *misbehave, dis-,* as in *displease.* The suffix *-less,* as in *toothless,* also negates the meaning of a stem morpheme.

Because we know the semantic properties of words, we know when two words are antonyms, synonyms, or homonyms, or are unrelated in meaning.

Names

> Her name was McGill and she called herself Lil
> But everyone knew her as Nancy.
>
> John Lennon and Paul McCartney, *"Rocky Raccoon"* [1]

[1] © 1969 by Northern Songs Ltd. All rights for the U.S.A., Mexico, and the Philippines controlled by Maclen Music, Inc., c/o ATV Music Corp. Used by permission; all rights reserved.

Reprinted with special permission of North America Syndicate.

"What's in a name?" is a question that has occupied philosophers of language for centuries. Plato was concerned with whether names were "natural," though the question did not bother Adam when he named the animals; Humpty Dumpty thought his name meant his shape, and in part it does.

Usually when we think of names we think of names of people or places, which are **proper names.** We do not think of *Canis familiaris* as being named "dog." Still, the old view persists that all words name some object, though that object may be abstract. This view presents difficulties. We are unable to identify the objects named by *sincerity* or *forgetfulness,* not to mention *into, brave,* and *think.*

Proper names can refer to objects. The objects may be extant, such as those designated by

> Disa Karin Viktoria Lubker
> Lake Michigan
> The Empire State Building

or extinct, such as

> Socrates
> Troy

or even fictional

> Sherlock Holmes
> Dr. John H. Watson
> Oz

Proper names are **definite,** which means they refer to a unique object insofar as the speaker and listener are concerned. If I say

> Mary Smith is coming to dinner.

my spouse understands Mary Smith to refer to our friend Mary Smith, and not to one of the dozens of Mary Smiths in the phone book.

Because they are inherently definite, proper names in English are not in general preceded by *the:*

> *the John Smith
> *the California

There are some exceptions, such as the names of rivers, ships, and erected structures:

> the Mississippi
> the *Queen Mary*
> the Empire State Building
> the Eiffel Tower
> the Golden Gate Bridge

and there are special cases such as *the John Smiths* to refer to the family of John Smith. Also, for the sake of clarity or literary effect, it is possible to precede a proper name by an article if the resulting noun phrase is followed by a modifying expression such as a prepositional phrase or a sentence:

> The Paris of the 1920s . . .
> The New York that everyone knows and loves . . .

In some languages, such as Greek and Hungarian, articles normally occur before proper names. Thus we find in Greek:

> O Spiros agapai tin Sophia

which is literally "The Spiro loves the Sophie," where *O* is the masculine nominative form of the definite article and *tin* the feminine accusative form. This indicates that some of the restrictions we observed are particular to English, and may be due to syntactic rather than semantic rules of language.

Proper names cannot usually be pluralized, though they can be plural, like *the Great Lakes* or *the Pleiades*. There are exceptions, such as *the John Smiths* already mentioned or expressions like *the Linguistics Department has three Bobs,* meaning three people named Bob, but they are special locutions used in particular circumstances. Because proper names generally refer to unique objects, it is not surprising that they occur mainly in the singular.

For the same reason, proper names cannot in general be preceded by adjectives. Many adjectives have the semantic effect of narrowing down the field of reference, so that the noun phrase *a red house* is a more specific description than simply *a house;* but what proper names refer to is already completely narrowed down, so modification by adjectives seems peculiar. Again, as in all these cases, extenuating circumstances give rise to exceptions. Language is nothing if not flexible, and we find expressions such as *young John* used to discriminate between two people named John. We also find adjectives applied to emphasize some quality of the object referred to, such as *the wicked Borgias* or *the brilliant Professor Einstein.*

Names may be coined or drawn from the stock of names that the language provides; but once a proper name is coined, it cannot be pluralized or preceded by *the* or any adjective (except for cases like those cited above), and it will be used to refer uniquely, for these rules are among the many rules already in the grammar, and speakers know they apply to all proper names, even new ones.

Phrase and Sentence Meaning

"Then you should say what you mean," the March Hare went on.

"I do," Alice hastily replied, "at least—I mean what I say—that's the same thing, you know."

"Not the same thing a bit!" said the Hatter. "You might just as well say that 'I see what I eat' is the same thing as 'I eat what I see'!"

"You might just as well say," added the March Hare, "that 'I like what I get' is the same thing as 'I get what I like'!"

"You might just as well say," added the Dormouse . . . "that 'I breathe when I sleep' is the same thing as 'I sleep when I breathe'!"

"It *is* the same thing with you," said the Hatter.

Lewis Carroll, *Alice's Adventures in Wonderland*

Words and morphemes are the smallest meaningful units in language. For the most part, however, we communicate in phrases and sentences, which also have meaning. The meaning of a phrase or sentence depends on both the meaning of its words and how these words are structurally combined. (Idioms are exceptional and will be discussed later.) Some of the semantic knowledge we have about words can be applied to sentences. Words are synonyms; sentences are paraphrases. Words may be homonyms; sentences may be ambiguous. Words have opposites; sentences can be negated. Words are used for naming purposes; sentences can be used that way too. Both words and sentences can be used to refer to, or point out, objects; and both may have some further meaning beyond this referring capability, as we shall see in a later section.

Combining Words into Sentences

. . . I placed all my words with their interpretations in alphabetical order. And thus in a few days, by the help of a very faithful memory, I got some insight into their language.

Jonathan Swift, *Gulliver's Travels*

Although it is widely believed that learning a language is merely learning the words of that language and what they mean—a myth apparently accepted by Gulliver—there is more to it than that, as you know if you have ever tried to learn a foreign language. We comprehend sentences because we know the meaning of individual words, *and we know rules for combining their meanings.*

We know the meanings of *red* and *balloon*. The semantic rule to interpret the combination *red balloon* adds the property "redness" to the properties of *balloon*. The phrase *the red balloon,* because of the presence of the definite article *the,* means "a particular instance of redness and balloonness." A semantic rule for the interpretation of *the* accounts for this.

The phrase *large balloon* would be interpreted by a different semantic rule, because part of the meaning of *large* is that it is a relative concept. *Large balloon* means *"large for a balloon."* What is large for a balloon may be small for a house and gargantuan for a cockroach; yet we correctly comprehend the meanings of *large balloon, large house,* and *large cockroach.*

There are many more rules involved in the semantics of noun phrases. Because noun phrases may contain prepositional phrases, semantic rules are needed for such expressions as *The house with the white picket fence.* We have seen how the rules account for *the house,* and *the white picket fence.* The semantic rule for prepositions indicates that two objects stand in a relationship determined by the meaning of the particular preposition. For *with,* that relationship is "accompanies" or "is part of." A preposition like *on* means a certain spatial relationship, and so on for other prepositions.

The syntactic structure of a phrase is important to its meaning. *The dog on the bed* has a different meaning than *the bed on the dog* ; *red brick* is different than *brick red.*

The last example shows that the syntactic notion *head,* examined in the previous chapter, plays a significant role in semantic rules. Since *brick* is the head of the noun phrase *the red brick,* the meaning of *a red brick* is a certain kind of brick. On the other hand, *red* is the head of the expression *brick red,* and the meaning of *brick red* is a certain kind of red.

The semantic rules for adjectives are complex. A *good friend* is a kind of friend, just as a *red brick* is a kind of a brick. But a *false friend* is not any kind of a friend at all. The semantic rules for *good* and *false* are quite different when these words modify *friend.* A third kind of rule governs adjectives like *alleged;* the meaning of *alleged murderer* is someone accused of murder, but the semantic rules in this case do not tell us whether an alleged murderer is or is not a murderer.

Meanings build on meanings. Noun phrases are combinations of meanings of nouns, adjectives, articles, and even sentences. (The Noun Phrase *the fact he knew too much* is a combination of *the, fact,* and the sentence *he knew too much.*) In turn, sentences are combinations of Noun Phrases, Verb Phrases, and so on. All these combinations make sense because the semantic rules of grammar combine the meanings of the parts to give the meaning of the whole. (In some cases, such as in idioms, the whole is not the sum of its parts as will be shown later.)

Thematic Roles

By permission of Johnny Hart and Creators Syndicate, Inc.

In Chapter 3 we observed that verbs are subcategorized for zero, one, or two Noun Phrase "objects," which stand in a certain meaning relation to the verb. *Sleep* was an example of a zero object or intransitive verb; *find* was subcategorized for one object, and *put* for two.

A verb is related in various ways to the constituents in a sentence. The relations depend on the meaning of the particular verb. For example the NP *the boy* in *the boy found a red brick* is called the **agent** or "doer" of the action of finding. The NP *a red brick* is the **theme** (sometimes called **patient**) or "recipient" of the action. (The boldfaced words are technical terms of semantic theory.) Part of the meaning of *find* is that its subject is an agent and its direct object is a theme. That fact is reflected in the entry for *find* in the lexicon.

The noun phrases within a verb phrase whose head is *put* have the relation of theme and **location.** In the verb phrase *put the red brick on the wall, the red brick* is the theme and *on the wall* is the location. The entire verb phrase is interpreted to mean that the theme of *put* changes its position to the location. The location, itself a prepositional phrase, will have its own meaning, which is combined with the meaning of *put* and the meaning of *the red brick. Put*'s subject is also an agent, so that in *The boy put the red brick on the wall,* "the boy" performs the action. Semantic rules do all this work, revealing speaker knowledge about the meaning of such sentences.

The semantic relationships that we have called *theme, agent,* and *location* are among the **thematic roles** of the verb. Other thematic roles are **goal,** where the action is directed, **source,** where the action originated, and **instrument,** an object used to accomplish the action. Consider the following example:

The boy carried the red brick from the wall to the wagon.

The boy is the agent; *the red brick* is the theme; *the wall* is the source; *the wagon* is the goal. In

The boy broke a window with the red brick.

The boy is again the agent, *a window* is the theme, and *the red brick* is the instrument. These examples show that the same noun phrase (*the red brick*) can function as a different thematic role depending on the sentence.

The lexical entries for *find* and *put* would now look something like this:

> find, V, _____ NP, (Agent, Theme)
> put, V, _____ NP PP, (Agent, Theme, Location)

The thematic roles are contained in parentheses. The first one states that the subject is an agent. The remaining thematic roles belong to the categories for which the verb is subcategorized. The direct object of both *find* and *put* will be a theme. The Prepositional Phrase for which *put* subcategorizes will be a location.

Our knowledge of verbs includes their syntactic category, how they are subcategorized, and the thematic roles that their NP subject and object(s) have, and this knowledge is explicitly represented in the lexicon.

Thematic roles are the same in sentences that are paraphrases. In both these sentences

> The dog bit the man.
> The man was bitten by the dog.

the dog is the agent and *the man* is the theme.

Thematic roles may remain the same in sentences that are *not* paraphrases, as in the following instances:

> The boy opened the door with the key.
> The key opened the door.
> The door opened.

In all three of these sentences, *the door* is the theme, the thing that gets opened. In the first two sentences, *the key,* despite its different structural positions, retains the thematic role of instrument.

The three examples illustrate the fact that English allows many different thematic roles to be the subject of the sentence (that is, the first NP under the S). These sentences had as subjects an agent (*the boy*), an instrument (*the key*), and a theme (*the door*). The sentences below illustrate other kinds of subjects.

> This hotel forbids dogs.
> It seems that Samson has lost his strength.

In the first example, *this hotel* has the thematic role of location. In the second, the subject *it* is "semantically empty," and lacks a thematic role entirely.

Contrast English with German. German is much "stingier" about which thematic roles can be subjects. For example, in order to express the idea "this hotel forbids dogs," a German speaker would have to say:

In diesem Hotel sind Hunde verboten.

literally, "in this hotel are dogs forbidden." German does not permit the thematic role of location to occur as a subject; it must be expressed as a prepositional phrase. If we translated the English sentence word for word into German, the results would be ungrammatical in German:

*Dieses Hotel verbietet Hunde

Differences such as these between English and German show that learning a foreign language is not a matter of simple word-for-word translation. You must learn the grammar, and that includes learning the syntax and semantics and how the two interact.

In many languages thematic roles are reflected in the **case** assumed by the noun. The *case,* or *grammatical case,* of a noun is the particular morphological shape that it takes. English does not have an extensive case system, but the possessive form of a noun, as in *the boy's red brick,* is called the genitive or possessive case.

In languages such as Finnish, the noun assumes a morphological shape according to its thematic role in the sentence. For example, in Finnish, *koulu-* is the root meaning "school," and *-sta* is a case ending that means "directional source." Thus *koulusta* means "from the school." Similarly, *kouluun (koulu + un)* means "to the school."

Some of the information carried by grammatical case in languages like Finnish is borne by prepositions in English. Thus *from* and *to* often indicate the thematic roles of source and goal. Instrument is marked by *with,* location by prepositions such as *on* and *in,* and agent by *by* in passive sentences. The role of theme is generally unaccompanied by a preposition, as is agent when it is the structural subject of the sentence. What we are calling thematic roles in this section has sometimes been studied as *case theory.*

In German, case distinctions appear on articles, as well as on nouns and adjectives. Thus in

Sie liebt den Mann.

"She loves the man," the article *den* is in the accusative case. In the nominative case it would be *der.* Languages with a rich system of case are often more constraining as to which thematic roles can occur in subject position. German, as we saw above, is one such language.

A universal principle has been proposed called the **theta-criterion,** which states in part that a particular thematic role may occur only once in a sentence. Thus sentences like

*The boy opened the door with the key with a lock-pick

are semantically anomalous because two noun phrases bear the thematic role of instrument.

In English the thematic role of possessive is indicated two ways syntactically: either as *the boy's red hat* or as *the red hat of the boy*. However, **the boy's red hat of Bill* is semantically anomalous according to the theta-criterion because both *the boy* and *Bill* have the thematic role of possessor.

Irrespective of how we label the semantic relations that exist between verbs and noun phrases, they are part of every speaker's linguistic competence and account for much of the meaning in language.

Semantics and Syntax

"HE CAN SMELL BETTER THAN WE CAN, BUT HE USUALLY SMELLS WORSE."

DENNIS THE MENACE® used by permission of Hank Ketcham and © by North America Syndicate.

Syntax is concerned with how words are combined to form phrases and sentences; semantics is concerned with what these combinations mean. The theta-criterion, discussed in the previous section, is an instance in which semantics and syntax interact: the semantic constraint that no thematic role may occur more than once has the effect of restricting the NPs and PPs that may follow the verb in a Verb Phrase.

We saw in the previous section that the same meaning may be expressed syntactically in more than one way; the semantic property of possession may be expressed by the genitive case such as *England's king,* or by an "of" construct such as *the king of England.* Paraphrases result when the same meaning is expressed by different syntactic structures.

A similar situation arises with certain semantic concepts such as "ability," "permission," or "obligation." These may be expressed syntactically by means of "auxiliary" or "helping" verbs.

> He can go.
> He may go.
> He must go.

They may also be expressed without the auxiliaries:

> He is able to go. / He has the ability to go.
> He is permitted to go. / He has permission to go.
> He is obliged to go. / He has an obligation to go.

Active-passive pairs constitute another common type of paraphrase:

> The child found the puppy.
> The puppy was found by the child.

This relationship between actives and passives is based on syntactic structure as discussed in Chapter 3. However some active sentences do not have a well-formed passive counterpart. For example:

> John resembles Bill.
> The book cost ten dollars.

cannot be "passivized" to give

> *Bill was resembled by John
> *Ten dollars was cost by the book

Semantically, when the subject of an active sentence is in a state described by the verb and direct object, there is no passive paraphrase. Since *John* is in a state of resembling Bill—John doesn't do anything—the sentence fails to passivize. This shows how the semantics of verbal relationships may affect syntactic relationships.

Note that the following two sentences have different meanings:

> The Greeks who were philosophers liked to talk.
> The Greeks, who were philosophers, liked to talk.

The first means that among the Greeks, the ones who were philosophers liked to talk. The second means that all Greeks were philosophers and liked to talk. Both sentences contain the "relative clause," *who were philosophers,* but in different syntactic structures. The difference in syntax makes the difference in meaning, though both sentences contain the same words in the same sequence. The following two trees provides one way of demonstrating the syntactic difference.

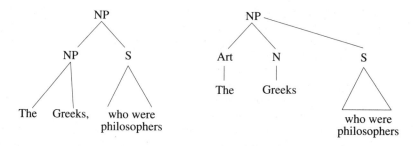

Another example of how syntax and semantics interact has to do with **reflexive** pronouns, such as *herself* or *themselves.* The meaning of a reflexive pronoun always refers back to some "antecedent." In *Jane bit herself, herself* refers to Jane. Syntactically, reflexive pronouns and their antecedents must occur under the same S in the Phrase Structure Tree. Compare the Phrase Structure Tree of *Jane bit herself* with the Phrase Structure Tree of **Jane said that herself slept:*

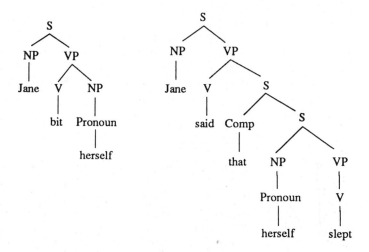

In the second tree, *Jane* is in the topmost S, but *herself* is in a different, embedded S. Syntactic and semantic rules do not allow the pronoun to be reflexive. The interaction between the rules tells us that in *Jane bit her,* the pronoun *her* cannot refer to Jane; it must refer to some other person.

Sentence structure also plays a role in determining when a pronoun and a noun phrase in different clauses can be **coreferential,** that is, refer to the same object. For example in

> John believes that he is a genius.

the pronoun *he* can be interpreted as John or as some person other than John. However in

> He believes that John is a genius.

the coreferential interpretation is impossible. *John* and *he* cannot refer to the same person. A pronoun cannot occur to the left of the noun phrase if the two refer to the same person. However, the rule is not that simple. In the sentence

> The fact that he is considered a genius bothers John.

he and *John* can be interpreted as coreferential. A somewhat complicated semantic rule that refers to sentence structure is at work here. A precise statement of this rule goes beyond the scope of this introductory text. The point is that syntax and semantics interrelate in complex ways.

We have knowledge of syntactic rules, semantic rules, and of how these rules interact. The fact that we have this knowledge is demonstrated by our ability to make judgments of grammaticality, recognize ambiguities and paraphrases, and know what the antecedents of pronouns are.

The "Truth" of Sentences

> . . . Having Occasion to talk of Lying and false Representation, it was with much Difficulty that he comprehended what I meant . . . For he argued thus: That the Use of Speech was to make us understand one another and to receive Information of Facts; now if any one said the Thing which was not, these Ends were defeated; because I cannot properly be said to understand him . . . And these were all the Notions he had concerning that Faculty of Lying, so perfectly well understood, and so universally practiced among human Creatures.
>
> Jonathan Swift, *Gulliver's Travels*

We have seen how sentence meaning is partially based on the meanings of its words and phrases. Knowing the meaning of a declarative sentence means knowing under what circumstances that sentence would be true. Those "circumstances" are called the **truth conditions** of the sentence.

In the world as we know it, the sentence

> The Declaration of Independence was signed in 1776.

is true, and the sentence

The Declaration of Independence was signed in 1976.

is false. We know the meaning of both sentences equally well, and knowing their meaning means knowing their truth conditions. We compare their truth conditions with "the real world" or historical fact, and can thus say which one is true and which one false.

You can, however, understand well-formed sentences of your language without knowing their truth value. Knowing the truth conditions is not the same as knowing the actual facts. Rather, the truth conditions, the meaning, permit you to examine the world and learn the actual facts. If you did not know the linguistic meaning—if the sentence were in an unknown language—you could never determine its truth, even if you had memorized an encyclopedia. You may not know the truth of

The Mecklenburg Charter was signed in 1770.

but if you know its meaning you know *in principle* how to discover its truth, even if you do not have the means to actually do so. For example, consider the sentence

The moon is made of green cheese.

We knew before space travel that going to the moon would test the truth of the sentence.

Now consider this sentence:

Rufus believes that the Declaration of Independence was signed in 1976.

This sentence is true if some individual named Rufus does indeed believe the statement, and it is false if he does not. Those are its truth conditions.

It does not matter that a subpart of the sentence is false. An entire sentence may be true even if one or more of its parts are false, and vice versa. Truth is determined by the semantic rules which permit you to combine the subparts of a sentence and still know under what conditions the sentence is true or false.

Knowing a language includes knowing the semantic rules for combining meanings and the conditions under which sentences are true or false.

Sometimes knowing the truth of one sentence **entails** the truth of another sentence. For example if you know it is true that

Corday assassinated Marat.

then you know that it is true that

Marat is dead.

The sentence *The brick is red* entails *The brick is not white; Mortimer is a bachelor* entails *Mortimer is male,* and so on. These entailments are part of the semantic rules we have been discussing. Much of what we know about the world comes about from knowing the entailments of true sentences.

Sense and Reference

> It is natural . . . to think of there being connected with a sign . . . besides . . .
> the reference of the sign, also what I should like to call the sense of the sign . . .
>
> **Gottlob Frege,** *On Sense and Reference*

Just as knowing the meaning of a declarative sentence means knowing how to determine its truth value, knowing the meaning of certain noun phrases means knowing how to discover what objects the noun phrases refer to. For example in the sentence

The boy put the red brick on the wall.

knowing the meaning of *the red brick* enables us to identify the object being referred to and see if it is really a brick that is red. As with the truth of sentences, we need only know, *in principle,* how to identify the object; a blindfolded person would comprehend the meaning of the phrase as well as someone who was actually looking at the boy putting the red brick on the wall, if they both knew English.

The object "pointed to" in such a Noun Phrase is called its **referent,** and the Noun Phrase is said to have **reference.**

For many Noun Phrases there is more to meaning than just reference. For example, *the red brick* and *the first brick from the right* may refer to the same object, that is, may be **coreferential.** Nevertheless we would be reluctant to say that the two expressions have the same meaning because they have the same reference. There is some additional meaning to these expressions, which is often termed **sense.** Thus Noun Phrases may have *sense* and *reference,* which together comprise the meaning of the Noun Phrase. Knowing the sense of a Noun Phrase allows you to identify its referent. Sometimes the term **extension** is used for *reference,* and **intension** for *sense.*

It has been argued that the meaning of certain proper names is equivalent to reference alone. Thus a name like Kelly Jones points out a certain person, its referent, but seems to have little meaning beyond that. Nonetheless some proper names do seem to have meaning over and above their ability to refer. Humpty Dumpty suggested that his name means "a good round shape." Certainly, the name *Sue* has the semantic property "female" as evinced by the humor in "A Boy Named Sue," a song sung by Johnny Cash. *The Pacific Ocean* has the semantic properties of *ocean,* and even such names as *Fido* and *Bossie* are associated with dogs and cows, respectively.

While some proper nouns appear to have reference but no sense, other noun phrases have sense, but no reference. If not, we would be unable to understand sentences like these:

The present king of France is bald.
By the year 3000, our descendants will have left Earth.

Speakers of English can understand these sentences, even though France now has no king, and our descendants of a millennium from now do not exist.

When Rules Are Broken

For all a rhetorician's rules
Teach nothing but to name his tools.

Samuel Butler, *Hudibras*

The rules of language are not laws of nature. Only by a "miracle" can the laws of nature be broken, but the rules of language are broken every day by everybody. This lawlessness is not human perversity, but rather another way in which language is put to use.

There are three kinds of rule violation that we will discuss: **anomaly,** a violation of semantic rules to create "nonsense"; **metaphor,** or nonliteral meaning; and **idioms,** in which the meaning of an expression may be unrelated to the meaning of its parts.

Anomaly: No Sense and Nonsense

Don't tell me of a man's being able to talk sense; everyone can talk sense. Can he talk nonsense?

William Pitt

If in a conversation someone said to you

My brother is an only child.

you might think that he was making a joke or that he did not know the meaning of the words he was using. You would know that the sentence was strange, or **anomalous;** yet it is certainly an English sentence. It conforms to all the grammatical rules of the language. It is strange because it represents a contradiction; the meaning of *brother* includes the fact that the individual referred to is a male human who has at least one sibling.

The sentence

That bachelor is pregnant.

is anomalous for similar reasons; the word *bachelor* contains the semantic property "male," whereas the word "pregnant" has the semantic property "female." Through a semantic redundancy rule, *pregnant* will also be marked [−male]. The anomaly arises from trying to equate something that is [+male] with something that is [−male].

The semantic properties of words determine what other words they can be combined with. One sentence that is used by linguists to illustrate this fact is

> Colorless green ideas sleep furiously.[2]

The sentence seems to obey all the syntactic rules of English. The subject is *color-less green ideas* and the predicate is *sleep furiously*. It has the same syntactic structure as the sentence

> Dark green leaves rustle furiously.

but there is obviously something wrong *semantically* with the sentence. The meaning of *colorless* includes the semantic property "without color," but it is combined with the adjective *green,* which has the property "green in color." How can something be both "without color" and "green in color" simultaneously? Other such semantic violations also occur in the sentence.

There are other sentences that sound like English sentences but make no sense at all because they include words that have no meaning; they are **uninterpretable.** One can only interpret them if one dreams up some meaning for each "no-sense" word. Lewis Carroll's "Jabberwocky" is probably the most famous poem in which most of the content words have no meaning—they do not exist in the Lexicon of the grammar. Still, all the sentences "sound" as if they should be or could be English sentences:

> *'Twas brillig, and the slithy toves*
>   *Did gyre and gimble in the wabe;*
> *All mimsy were the borogoves,*
>   *And the mome raths outgrabe.*
>
>   . . .
>
> *He took his vorpal sword in hand:*
>   *Long time the manxome foe he sought—*
> *So rested he by the Tumtum tree,*
>   *And stood awhile in thought.*

Without knowing what *vorpal* means, you nevertheless know that

> He took his vorpal sword in hand.

means the same thing as

> He took his sword, which was vorpal, in hand.
> It was in his hand that he took his vorpal sword.

Knowing the language, and assuming that *vorpal* means the same thing in the three sentences (because the same sounds are used), you can decide that the "truth values" of the three sentences are identical. In other words, you are able to decide that two things mean the same thing even though you do not know what either one means. You decide by assuming that the semantic properties of *vorpal* are the same whenever it is used.

[2]Noam Chomsky, *Syntactic Structures,* The Hague: Mouton, 1957.

We now see why Alice commented, when she had read "Jabberwocky":

> "It seems very pretty, but it's *rather* hard to understand!" (You see she didn't like to confess, even to herself, that she couldn't make it out at all.) "Somehow it seems to fill my head with ideas—only I don't exactly know what they are! However, *somebody* killed *something:* that's clear, at any rate—"

The semantic properties of words show up in other ways in sentence construction. For example, if the meaning of a word includes the semantic property "human" in English, we can replace it by one sort of pronoun but not another. This semantic feature determines that we call a boy *he* and a table *it,* and not vice versa.

According to Mark Twain, Eve had such knowledge in her grammar, for she writes in her diary:

> If this reptile is a man, it ain't an *it,* is it? That wouldn't be grammatical, would it? I think it would be *he.* In that case one would parse it thus: nominative *he;* dative, *him;* possessive, *his'n.*

The linguist Samuel Levin has shown that in poetry semantic violations may form strange but interesting aesthetic images. He cites Dylan Thomas's phrase *a grief ago* as an example. *Ago* is ordinarily used with words specified by some temporal semantic feature:

a week ago		*a table ago
an hour ago	but not	*a dream ago
a month ago		*a mother ago
a century ago		

When Thomas used the word *grief* with *ago* he was adding a durational feature to *grief* for poetic effect.

In the poetry of e. e. cummings there are phrases like

> the six subjunctive crumbs twitch
> a man . . . wearing a round jeer for a hat
> children building this rainman out of snow.

Though all of these phrases violate some semantic rules, we can understand them; it is the breaking of the rules that creates the imagery desired. The ability to understand these phrases and at the same time recognize their anomalous or deviant nature shows knowledge of the semantic system and semantic properties of the language.

Metaphor

> Our doubts are traitors.
>
> Shakespeare

Walls have ears.

Cervantes

The night has a thousand eyes
and the day but one.

Frances William Bourdillon

Sometimes the breaking of semantic rules can be used to convey a particular idea. *Walls have ears* is certainly anomalous, but it can be interpreted as meaning "you can be overheard even when you think nobody is listening." In some sense the sentence is ambiguous, but the literal meaning is so unlikely that listeners stretch their imagination for another interpretation. That "stretching" is based on semantic properties that are inferred or that provide some kind of resemblance. Such nonliteral interpretations of sentences are called **metaphor.**

The literal meaning of a sentence such as

My new car is a lemon.

is anomalous. You could, if driven to the wall (another metaphor), provide some literal interpretation that is plausible if given sufficient context. For example, the *new car* may be a miniature toy carved out of a piece of citrus fruit. The more common meaning, however, would be metaphorical and interpreted as referring to a newly purchased automobile that breaks down and requires constant repairs. The imagination stretching in this case may relate to the semantic property "tastes sour" that *lemon* possesses.

Metaphors are not necessarily anomalous when taken literally. The literal meaning of the sentence

Dr. Jekyll is a butcher.

is that a physician named Jekyll also works as a retailer of meats or a slaughterer of animals used for food. The metaphorical meaning is that the doctor named Jekyll is harmful, possibly murderous, and apt to operate unnecessarily.

Similarly, the sentence

John is a snake in the grass.

can be interpreted literally to refer to a pet snake on the lawn named John. Metaphorically the sentence has nothing to do with a scaly, limbless reptile.

To interpret metaphors we need to understand both the literal meaning and facts about the world. To understand the metaphor

Time is money.

it is necessary to know that in our society we are often paid according to the number of hours or days worked. To recognize that the sentence

> Jack is a pussycat.

has a different meaning than

> Jack is a tiger.

requires knowledge that the metaphorical meaning of each sentence does *not* depend on the semantic property "feline." Rather, other semantic properties of these two words are referred to.

Metaphorical use of language is language creativity at its highest. Nevertheless, the basis of metaphorical use is the ordinary linguistic knowledge about words, their semantic properties, and their combining powers that all speakers possess.

Idioms

PEANUTS reprinted by permission of UFS, Inc.

Knowing a language includes knowing the morphemes, simple words, compound words, and their meanings. In addition it means knowing fixed phrases, consisting of more than one word, with meanings that cannot be inferred from the meanings of the individual words. The usual semantic rules for combining meanings do not apply. Such expressions are called **idioms.** All languages contain many idiomatic phrases, as in these English examples:

> sell down the river
> haul over the coals
> eat my hat
> let their hair down
> put his foot in his mouth
> throw her weight around
> snap out of it
> cut it out
> hit it off
> get it off
> bite your tongue
> give a piece of your mind

Idioms are similar in structure to ordinary phrases except that they tend to be frozen in form and do not readily enter into other combinations or allow the word order to change. Thus,

> (a) She put her foot in her mouth.

has the same structure as

> (b) She put her bracelet in her drawer.

but whereas

> The drawer in which she put her bracelet was hers.
> Her bracelet was put in her drawer.

are sentences related to sentence (b)

> The mouth in which she put her foot was hers.
> Her foot was put in her mouth.

do not have the idiomatic sense of sentence (a).

On the other hand, the words of some idioms can be moved without affecting the idiomatic sense:

> The FBI kept tabs on radicals.
> Tabs were kept on radicals by the FBI.
> Radicals were kept tabs on by the FBI.

Idioms can break the rules on combining semantic properties. The object of *eat* must usually be something with the semantic property "edible," but in

he ate his hat
eat your heart out

this restriction is violated.

Idioms, grammatically as well as semantically, have special characteristics. They must be entered into the Lexicon or mental dictionary as single "items," with their meanings specified, and speakers must learn the special restrictions on their use in sentences.

Many idioms may have originated as metaphorical expressions that "took hold" in the language and became frozen in their form and meaning.

Discourse Meaning

Put your discourse into some frame, and start not so wildly from my affair.

William Shakespeare, *Hamlet*

Linguistic knowledge accounts for speakers' ability to combine phonemes into morphemes, morphemes into words, and words into sentences. Knowing a language also permits combining sentences together to express complex thoughts and ideas. This linguistic ability makes language an excellent medium for communication. These larger linguistic units are called **discourse.**

The study of discourse, or **discourse analysis,** involves many aspects of *linguistic performance* and of "sociolinguistics" (taken up in chapter 7), as well as linguistic competence. Discourse analysis involves questions of style, appropriateness, cohesiveness, rhetorical force, topic/subtopic structure, differences between written and spoken discourse, and so on.

Pronouns

The 911 operator, trying to get a description of the gunman, asked, "What kind of clothes does he have on?"

Mr. Morawski, thinking the question pertained to Mr. McClure, [the victim, who lay dying of a gunshot wound], answered, "He has a bloody shirt with blue jeans, purple striped shirt."

The 911 operator then gave police that description [the victim's] of a gunman.

The News and Observer, Raleigh, North Carolina, 1/21/89

Pronouns may be used in place of *Noun Phrases* or may be used to refer to an entity presumably known to the discourse participants. When that presumption fails, miscommunication such as the one at the head of this section may result.

Consider the following "mini-discourse":

> It seems that the man loves the woman.
> Many people think he loves her.

In the most "natural" interpretation, *he* refers to *the man,* its **antecedent,** with which it is *coreferential.* Similarly, *her* refers to *the woman.*

Pronominalization occurs both in sentences and across the sentences of a discourse. Within a sentence, the sentence structure limits the choice of pronoun. We saw previously that a reflexive pronoun must be used if both it and its antecedent are in the same S in the Phrase Structure Tree. Likewise we saw that sentence structure also dictates whether a pronoun and Noun Phrase can be interpreted as coreferential.

In a discourse, context plays a primary role in pronoun interpretation. In the mini-discourse example, *her* could conceivably refer to a person other than "the woman," a person identified contextually, say with a gesture. In such a case *her* would be spoken with added emphasis:

> Many people think he loves HER!

As far as syntactic rules are concerned, pronouns are Noun Phrases, and may occur anywhere that a Noun Phrase may occur. Semantic rules of varying complexity establish whether a pronoun and some other Noun Phrase in the discourse can be interpreted as coreferential. A minimum condition of coreferentiality is that the pronoun and its antecedent have the same semantic feature values for the semantic properties of number and gender.

When semantic rules and contextual interpretation determine that a pronoun is coreferential with a Noun Phrase, we say that the pronoun is **bound** to that Noun Phrase antecedent. When a pronoun refers to some object not explicitly mentioned in the discourse, it is said to be **free** or **unbound.** The reference of a free pronoun may be determined by context. First and second person nonreflexive pronouns are always free. Reflexive pronouns, sometimes called **anaphors,** are always bound. They require an antecedent in the sentence.

In the preceding example, semantic rules permit *her* to be bound either to *the woman,* or to be a free pronoun, referring to some person not explicitly mentioned. The ultimate interpretation is context-dependent. On the other hand, if the second sentence were

> Everyone thinks that he loves him.

the pronoun *him* could only be interpreted as free, since there is no antecedent that has the semantic properties of *him.*

It would not be "ungrammatical" if the discourse went this way:

> It seems that the man loves the woman.
> Everyone thinks that the man loves the woman.

However most people would think that such a discourse sounds "stilted." Often in discourse the use of pronouns is a stylistic decision, that is, governed by usage rules of performance.

Missing Parts

Reprinted with special permission of North America Syndicate.

Performance discourse conventions permit us to "violate" in regular ways many of the rules of grammar. For example, the rules of syntax would not generate as a well-formed sentence *My uncle has, too,* but in the following discourse it is perfectly acceptable:

> First speaker: My aunt has been dieting strenuously.
> Second speaker: My uncle has, too.

The second speaker is understood to mean "My uncle has been dieting strenuously." The missing part of the verb phrase is understood from previous discourse.
Entire sentences may be "filled in" this way:

> First speaker: My aunt has been dieting strenuously, and she has lost a good deal
>   of weight.
> Second speaker: My mother has, too.

The second speaker can be understood to have meant "My mother has been dieting strenuously, and she has lost a good deal of weight." Rules of discourse not only provide the missing parts of the verb phrase, but provide the entire second sentence meaning.

Much discourse is "telegraphic" in nature. Verb phrases are not specifically mentioned, entire clauses are left out, pronouns abound, "you know" is everywhere. People still understand people, and part of the reason is that rules of grammar and rules of discourse combine with contextual knowledge to fill in missing gaps and make the discourse cohere.

The Articles *the* and *a*

There are discourse rules that apply regularly, such as those that determine the occurrence of the articles *the* and *a*. The article *the* is used to indicate that the referent of a noun phrase is agreed upon by speaker and listener. If someone says

> I saw the boy.

PEANUTS reprinted by permission of UFS, Inc.

it is assumed that a certain boy is being discussed. No such assumption accompanies

> I saw a boy.

which is more of a description of what was seen than a reference to a particular individual.

Often a discourse will begin with the use of indefinite articles, and once everyone agrees on the referents, definite articles start to appear. A short example illustrates this transition:

> I saw *a* boy and *a* girl holding hands and kissing.
> Oh, it sounds lovely.
> Yes, *the* boy was quite tall and handsome, and he seemed to like *the* girl a lot.

These examples show that some rules of discourse are similar to grammatical rules in that a violation produces unacceptable results. If the final sentence of this discourse were

> Yes, a boy was quite tall and handsome, and he seemed to like a girl a lot.

most speakers would find it unacceptable.

Maxims of Conversation

> Though this be madness, yet there is method in't.
> William Shakespeare, *Hamlet*

Speakers recognize when a series of sentences "hangs together" or when it is "disjointed." The discourse below, which gave rise to Polonius' remark quoted at the head of this section, does not seem quite right—it is not **coherent.**

> POLONIUS: What do you read, my lord?
> HAMLET: Words, words, words.
> POLONIUS: What is the matter, my lord?
> HAMLET: Between who?

POLONIUS: I mean, the matter that you read, my lord.

HAMLET: Slanders, sir: for the satirical rogue says here that old men have grey beards, that their faces are wrinkled, their eyes purging thick amber and plum-tree gum, and that they have a plentiful lack of wit, together with most weak hams: all which, sir, though I most powerfully and potently believe, yet I hold it not honesty to have it thus set down; for yourself, sir, should grow old as I am, if like a crab you could go backward.[3]

Hamlet, who is feigning insanity, refuses to answer Polonius' questions "in good faith." He has violated certain conversational conventions or **maxims of conversation.**[4] One such maxim, the **cooperative principle,** states that a speaker's contribution to the discourse should be as informative as is required—neither more nor less. Hamlet has violated this maxim in both ways. In answering "Words, words, words" to the question of what is being read, he is providing too little information. His final remark goes to the other extreme in providing more information than required.

He also violates the **maxim of relevance,** when he "misinterprets" the question about the reading matter as a matter between two individuals.

The "run on" nature of Hamlet's final remark is another source of incoherence. This effect is increased in the final sentence by the somewhat bizarre choice of phrasing to compare growing younger with walking backward.

Conversational conventions such as the requirement to "be relevant" allow the various sentence meanings to be sensibly connected into discourse meaning, much as rules of sentence grammar allow word meanings to be sensibly (and grammatically) connected into sentence meaning.

Most of the rules of grammar we have studied are for phrases and sentences. Such rules interact heavily with nonlinguistic knowledge in discourse.

Pragmatics

[3]*Hamlet,* Act II, Scene ii.

[4]These maxims were first discussed by H. Paul Grice in the William James Lectures delivered at Harvard University in 1967.

The "context" of an utterance is often necessary in order to understand it. We saw this in the discussion of ambiguous sentences and discourse. For example consider a sign that states:

> Best place to take a leak.

In the context of a radiator repair garage, only one meaning is reasonable. Posted near toilet facilities at a campsite, the other meaning is most likely.

Even innocent-seeming sentences such as

> John believes he is a genius.

are ambiguous, as it is unclear in the absence of context whether *he* is a bound pronoun coreferential with John, or a free pronoun that refers to some other person.

Context includes the speaker, hearer, and any third parties present, along with their beliefs, and their beliefs about what the others believe. It includes what has been previously uttered, the physical environment, the "topic" of conversation, the time of day, and so on, ad infinitum. Almost any imaginable extralinguistic factor may, under appropriate circumstances, influence the way language is interpreted.

The general study of how context influences the interpretation of meaning is called **pragmatics.** Pragmatics has to do with people's *use* of language in contexts. It may thus be considered to be a part of what we have been calling *linguistic performance.*

Speech Acts

PEANUTS reprinted by permission of UFS, Inc.

You can do things with speech. You can make promises, lay bets, issue warnings, christen boats, place names in nomination, offer congratulations, or swear testimony. By saying *I warn you that there is a sheepdog in the closet,* you not only say something, you *warn* someone. Verbs like *bet, promise, warn,* and so on are **performative verbs.** Using them in a sentence does something extra over and above the statement.

There are hundreds of performative verbs in every language. The following sentences illustrate their usage:

> I *bet* you five dollars the Yankees win.
> I *challenge* you to a match.

I *dare* you to step over this line.
I *fine* you $100 for possession of oregano.
I *move* that we adjourn.
I *nominate* Batman for mayor of Gotham City.
I *promise* to improve.
I *resign!*

In all these sentences the speaker is the subject (that is, they are in "first person") who by uttering the sentence is accomplishing some additional action, such as daring, nominating, or resigning. Also, all these sentences are affirmative, declarative, and in the present tense. They are typical **performative sentences.**

An informal test to see whether a sentence contains a performative verb is to begin it with the words *I hereby.* . . . Only performative sentences sound right when begun this way. Compare *I hereby apologize to you* with the somewhat strange *I hereby know you.* The first is generally taken as an act of apologizing. In all the examples given, insertion of *hereby* would be acceptable. As the cartoon at the beginning of this section shows, Snoopy is aware that using *hereby* will ensure that his statement is taken as an act of despising.

Actually, every utterance is some kind of speech act. Even when there is no explicit performative verb, as in *It is raining,* we recognize an implicit performance of *stating.* On the other hand, *Is it raining?* is a performance of *questioning,* just as *Leave!* is a performance of *ordering.* In all these instances we could use, if we chose, an actual performative verb: *I state that it is raining; I ask if it is raining; I order you to leave.*

The study of how we do things with sentences is the study of **speech acts.** In studying speech acts, we are acutely aware of the importance of the *context of the utterance.* In some circumstances *There is a sheepdog in the closet* is a warning, but the same sentence may be a promise or even a mere statement of fact, depending on circumstances. We call this purpose—a warning, a promise, a threat, or whatever—the **illocutionary force** of a speech act.

Speech act theory aims to tell us when we appear to ask questions but are really giving orders, or when we say one thing with special (sarcastic) intonation and mean the opposite. Thus, at a dinner table, the question *Can you pass the salt?* means the order *Pass the salt!* It is not a request for information, and *yes* is an inappropriate response.

Because the illocutionary force of a speech act depends on the context of the utterance, speech act theory is a part of pragmatics.

Presuppositions

You mentioned your name as if I should recognize it, but beyond the obvious facts that you are a bachelor, a solicitor, a Freemason, and an asthmatic, I know nothing whatever about you.

Sir Arthur Conan Doyle, *"The Norwood Builder," The Memoirs of Sherlock Holmes*

Speakers often make implicit assumptions about the real world, and the sense of an utterance may depend on those assumptions, which some linguists term **presuppositions.** Consider the following sentences:

(a) Have you stopped hugging your sheepdog?
(b) Who bought the badminton set?
(c) John doesn't write poems anymore.
(d) The present King of France is bald.
(e) Would you like another beer?

In sentence (a) the speaker has *presupposed* that the listener has at some past time hugged his sheepdog. In (b) there is the presupposition that someone has already bought a badminton set, and in (c) it is assumed that John once wrote poetry.

We have already run across the somewhat odd (d), which we decided we could understand even though France does not currently have a king. The use of the definite article *the* usually presupposes an existing referent. When presuppositions are inconsistent with the actual state of the world, the utterance is felt to be strange, unless a fictional setting is agreed upon by the conversants, as in a play, for example.

Sentence (e) presupposes or implies that you have already had at least one beer. Part of the meaning of the word *another* includes this presupposition. The Hatter in *Alice's Adventures in Wonderland* appears not to understand presuppositions.

> "Take some more tea," the March Hare said to Alice, very earnestly.
> "I've had nothing yet," Alice replied in an offended tone, "so I can't take more."
> "You mean you can't take *less*," said the Hatter: "It's very easy to take *more* than nothing."

The humor in this passage comes from the fact that knowing English includes knowing the meaning of the word *more*, which in this usage presupposes some earlier amount.

These phenomena may also be described as **implication** or **entailment.** Part of the meaning of *more* implies or entails that there has already been something. The definite article *the*, in these terms, entails or implies the existence of the referent within the current context.

Presuppositions can be used to communicate information indirectly. If someone says *My brother is rich*, we assume that person has a brother, even though that fact is not explicitly stated. Much of the information that is exchanged in a conversation or discourse is of this kind. Often, after a conversation has ended, we will realize that some fact was imparted to us that was not specifically mentioned. That fact is often a presupposition.

The use of language in a courtroom is restricted so that presuppositions cannot influence the court or jury. The famous type of question, *Have you stopped beating your wife?* is disallowed in court, because accepting the validity of the question means accepting its presuppositions; the question imparts "information" in a way that is difficult to cross-examine and even difficult to detect. Presuppositions are so much a part of natural discourse that they become second nature and we do not think of them, any more than we are directly aware of the many other rules and maxims that govern language and its use in context.

Deixis

DENNIS THE MENACE® used by permission of Hank Ketcham and © by North America Syndicate.

In all languages there are many words and expressions whose reference relies entirely on the circumstances of the utterance and can only be understood in light of these circumstances. This aspect of pragmatics is called **deixis** (pronounced "dike-sis"). First and second person pronouns such as

my   mine   you   your   yours   we   ours   us

are always deictic because they are free pronouns and their reference is entirely dependent on context. You must know who the speaker and listener are in order to interpret them.

Third person pronouns are deictic if they are *free*. If they are *bound,* their reference is known from preceding dialogue. One peculiar exception is the "pronoun" *it* when used in sentences such as

It appears as though sheepdogs are the missing link.
The patriotic archbishop of Canterbury found it advisable . . .

In these cases the *it* does not function as a true pronoun by referring to some entity. Rather, as discussed in Chapter 2 in the section on Inflectional Morphemes, the *it* is a grammatical morpheme, a place-holder as it were, required to satisfy the English rules of syntax.

Expressions such as

> this person
> that man
> these women
> those children

are deictic, for they require pragmatic information in order for the listener to make a "referential connection" and understand what is meant. The above examples illustrate **person deixis.** They also show that the use of **demonstrative articles** like *this* and *that* is deictic.

There is also **time deixis** and **place deixis.** The following examples are all deictic expressions of time:

now	then	tomorrow
this time	that time	seven days ago
two weeks from now	last week	next April

In order to understand what specific times such expressions refer to, we need to know when the utterance was said. Clearly, *next week* has a different reference when uttered today than a month from today. If you found an advertising leaflet on the street that said "BIG SALE NEXT WEEK" with no date given, you would not know whether the sale had already taken place.

Expressions of place deixis require contextual information about the place of the utterance, as shown by the following examples:

here	there	this place
that place	this ranch	those towers over there
this city	these parks	yonder mountains

The "Dennis the Menace" cartoon at the beginning of this section indicates what can happen if deictic expressions are misinterpreted.

Directional terms such as

> before/behind   left/right   front/back

are deictic insofar as you need to know which way the speaker is facing. In Japanese the verb *kuru* "come" can only be used for motion toward the place of utterance. A Japanese speaker cannot call up a friend and ask

> May I *kuru* to your house?

as you might, in English, ask "May I come to your house?" The correct verb is *iku,* "go," which indicates motion away from the place of utterance. These verbs thus have a deictic aspect to their meaning.

Deixis abounds in language use and marks one of the boundaries of semantics and pragmatics. The pronoun *I* certainly has a meaning independent of context—its semantic meaning, which is "the speaker"; but context is necessary to know who the speaker is, hence what "I" refers to.

Summary

Knowing a language is knowing how to produce and understand sentences with particular meanings. The study of linguistic meaning, called **semantics,** is concerned with the meaning of morphemes, words, phrases, sentences and discourses.

The meanings of morphemes and words are defined in part by their **semantic properties,** whose presence or absence is indicated by use of **semantic features.** Relationships between semantic properties, such as that "human" implies "animate," can be expressed through **redundancy rules.**

When two words have the same sounds but different meanings, they are **homonyms** (for example *bear* and *bare*). The use of homonyms may result in **ambiguity,** which occurs when an utterance has more than one meaning. Ambiguity may also arise due to sentence structure, as in *synthetic buffalo hides.*

When two words have the same meaning but different sounds, they are **synonyms** (for example *sofa* and *couch*). The use of synonyms may result in **paraphrase,** which occurs when two different utterances have the same meaning. Paraphrase may also arise when sentences differ structurally in ways that do not affect meaning, as in *Hail, Richard, England's king/Hail, Richard, king of England.*

A word that has several meanings is **polysemous.** For example *good* means "well behaved" in *good child,* and "sound" in *good investment.* Words may be partially synonymous in that they share one or more of their meanings with other words.

Two words that are "opposite" in meaning are **antonyms.** Antonyms have the same semantic properties except for the one that accounts for their oppositeness. There are antonymous pairs that are **complementary** (*alive/dead*), **gradable** (*hot/cold*), and **relational opposites** (*buy/sell, employer/employee*).

Proper names are special morphemes used to designate particular objects uniquely; that is, they are **definite.** Proper names cannot ordinarily be preceded by an article or an adjective, or be pluralized, in English.

Languages have rules for combining the meanings of parts into the meaning of the whole. For example, *red balloon* has the semantic properties of *balloon* combined with the semantic property of *red* in an "additive" manner. Such combinations are not always additive. The phrase *counterfeit dollar* does not simply have the semantic properties of *dollar* plus something else.

Sentence meaning is determined in part by the **thematic roles** of the noun phrases to the verb. These semantic relationships indicate who, to whom, toward what, from which, with what, and so on, to make up sentence meaning.

In building larger meanings from smaller meanings, the semantic rules interact with the syntactic rules of the language. For example, if a Noun Phrase and a nonreflexive pronoun occur within the same S, semantic rules cannot interpret them to be **coreferential,** that is, having the same referent. Thus in *Mary bit her,* the *her* refers to someone other than Mary.

The meaning of a sentence determines under what conditions the sentence is true or false. You can understand a sentence without knowing its "truth value," but you cannot determine the truth value without knowing the meaning. Often, the truth of one sentence **entails** the truth of another. If the sentence *I managed to kiss my sheepdog* is true, then the sentence *I kissed my sheepdog* is also true by the semantic rules for entailment.

Words, phrases, and sentences have **sense** and can be used to **refer.** Frege showed that meaning is more than reference alone. Some meaningful expressions (for example, *the present King of France*) have sense but no reference.

Sentences are **anomalous** when they deviate from certain semantic rules. *The six subjunctive crumbs twitched* and *The stone ran* are anomalous. Other sentences are **uninterpretable** because they contain "words" without meaning, such as *An orkish sluck blecked nokishly.*

Many sentences have both a literal and nonliteral or **metaphorical** interpretation. *He's out in left field* may be a literal description of a baseball player or a metaphorical description of someone mentally deranged.

Idioms are phrases whose meaning is *not* the combination of the meanings of the individual words (for example, *put her foot in her mouth*). Idioms often violate co-occurrence restrictions of semantic properties.

Discourse consists of several sentences, and discourse semantics is concerned with the meaning relations among them, for example, when a pronoun in one sentence has the same referent as a fully expressed Noun Phrase in another sentence, or when a "missing part" can be understood from something previously said.

Well structured discourse follows certain rules and **maxims,** such as "be relevant," that make the discourse **coherent.** There are also grammatical rules that affect discourse, such as those which determine when to use the definite article *the*.

The general study of how context affects linguistic interpretation is **pragmatics.** Pragmatics includes **speech acts, presuppositions,** and **deixis.** Speech act theory is the study of what an utterance does beyond just saying something. The effect of what is done is called the **illocutionary force** of the utterance. For example, use of a **performative verb** like *bequeath* may be an act of bequeathing, which may even have legal status.

Presuppositions are implicit assumptions that accompany certain utterances. *Have you stopped hugging Sue?* carries with it the presupposition that at one time you hugged Sue.

Deictic terms such as *you, there, now* require knowledge of the circumstances (the person, place, or time) of the utterance to be interpreted referentially.

Everything you know about linguistic meaning is included in the semantic system of your grammar.

References for Further Reading

Austin, J. L. 1962. *How to Do Things with Words.* Cambridge, Mass.: Harvard University Press.

Brown, G., and G. Yule. 1983. *Discourse analysis.* Cambridge, England: Cambridge University Press.

Chierchia, Gennaro, and Sally McConnell-Ginet. 1990. *Meaning and Grammar: An Introduction to Syntax.* Cambridge, Mass.: MIT Press.

Davidson, D., and G. Harman, eds. 1972. *Semantics of Natural Languages.* Dordrecht, The Netherlands: Reidel.

Green, Georgia M. 1989. *Pragmatics and Natural Language Understanding.* Hillsdale, N.J.: Lawrence Erlbaum Associates.

Hawkins, John A. 1985. *A Comparative Typology of English and German.* Austin: University of Texas Press.

Hurford, J. R., and B. Heasley. 1983. *Semantics: A Coursebook.* Cambridge, England: Cambridge University Press.

Jackendoff, Ray. 1983. *Semantics and Cognition.* Cambridge, Mass.: MIT Press.

Katz, J. 1972. *Semantic Theory.* New York: Harper & Row.

Levinson, S. C. 1983. *Pragmatics.* Cambridge, England: Cambridge University Press.

Lyons, J. 1977. *Semantics.* Cambridge, England: Cambridge University Press.

Searle, John R. 1969. *Speech Acts: An Essay in the Philosophy of Language.* Cambridge, England: Cambridge University Press.

Sperber, D., and D. Wilson. 1986. *Relevance: Communication and Cognition.* Oxford, England: Basil Blackwell.

Exercises

---

1. For each group of words given below, state what semantic property or properties are shared by the (a) words and the (b) words, and what semantic property or properties distinguish between the classes of (a) words and (b) words.

> Example: a. widow, mother, sister, aunt, seamstress
> b. widower, father, brother, uncle, tailor
> The (a) and (b) words are "human."
> The (a) words are "female" and the (b) words are "male."

A. a. bachelor, man, son, paperboy, pope, chief
    b. bull, rooster, drake, ram

    The (a) and (b) words are _____.

    The (a) words are _____.

    The (b) words are _____.

B. a. table, stone, pencil, cup, house, ship, car
    b. milk, alcohol, rice, soup, mud

    The (a) and (b) words are _____.

    The (a) words are _____.

    The (b) words are _____.

C. a. book, temple, mountain, road, tractor
    b. idea, love, charity, sincerity, bravery, fear

    The (a) and (b) words are _____.

    The (a) words are _____.

    The (b) words are _____.

D. a. pine, elm, ash, weeping willow, sycamore
    b. rose, dandelion, aster, tulip, daisy

    The (a) and (b) words are _____.

    The (a) words are _____.

    The (b) words are _____.

E. a. book, letter, encyclopedia, novel, notebook, dictionary
    b. typewriter, pencil, ballpoint, crayon, quill, charcoal, chalk

    The (a) and (b) words are _____.

    The (a) words are _____.

    The (b) words are _____.

F. a. walk, run, skip, jump, hop, swim
    b. fly, skate, ski, ride, cycle, canoe, hang-glide

The (a) and (b) words are _____.

The (a) words are _____.

The (b) words are _____.

G. a. ask, tell, say, talk, converse
    b. shout, whisper, mutter, drawl, holler

The (a) and (b) words are _____.

The (a) words are _____.

The (b) words are _____.

H. a. alive, asleep, dead, married, pregnant
    b. tall, smart, interesting, bad, tired

The (a) and (b) words are _____.

The (a) words are _____.

The (b) words are _____.

I. a. alleged, counterfeit, false, putative, accused
    b. red, large, cheerful, pretty, stupid
       (*Hint:* Is an alleged murderer always a murderer?)

The (a) and (b) words are _____.

The (a) words are _____.

The (b) words are _____.

2. Explain the semantic ambiguity of the following sentences by providing two sentences that paraphrase the two meanings. Example: *She can't bear children* can mean either *She can't give birth to children* or *She can't tolerate children.*

a. He waited by the bank.

Meaning one: _____.

Meaning two: _____.

b. Is he really that kind?

Meaning one: _____.

Meaning two: _____.

c. The proprietor of the fish store was the sole owner.

Meaning one: _____.

Meaning two: _____.

d. The long drill was boring.

Meaning one: _____.

Meaning two: _____.

e. When he got the clear title to the land, it was a good deed.

Meaning one: _____.

Meaning two: _____.

f. It takes a good ruler to make a straight line.

Meaning one: _____.

Meaning two: _____.

g. He saw that gasoline can explode.

Meaning one: _____.

Meaning two: _____.

3. The following sentences are ambiguous when written. After figuring out the ambiguity, circle the letter of the ones that can be disambiguated in speech by special intonation or pauses.

a. The lamb is too hot to eat.
b. Old men and women will be served first.
c. Kissing girls is what Stephen likes best.
d. They are moving sidewalks.
e. Becky left directions for Jack to follow.
f. John loves Richard more than Martha.

4. There are several kinds of antonymy. By writing a *c, g,* or *r* in column *C,* indicate whether the pairs in columns *A* and *B* are complementary, gradable, or relational opposites:

A	**B**	**C**
good	bad	
expensive	cheap	
parent	offspring	
beautiful	ugly	
false	true	
lessor	lessee	
pass	fail	
hot	cold	

(continued on following page)

A	B	C
legal	illegal	
larger	smaller	
poor	rich	
fast	slow	
asleep	awake	
husband	wife	
rude	polite	

5. The following sentences consist of a verb, its noun phrase subject, and various objects. Identify the thematic relation of each noun phrase by writing the letter *a, t, l, i, s,* or *g* above the noun, standing for *agent, theme, location, instrument, source,* or *goal.*

> $\qquad\qquad\quad$ *a* $\qquad\quad$ *t* $\qquad\qquad$ *s*
> Example: *The boy took the books from the cupboard with a*
> $\qquad\qquad\qquad\qquad$ *i*
> *handcart.*

a. Mary found a ball in the house.

b. The children ran from the playground to the wading pool.

c. One of the men unlocked all the doors with a paper clip.

d. John melted the ice with a blowtorch.

e. The sun melted the ice.

f. The ice melted.

g. Broken ice still melts in the sun.

h. The farmer's daughter loaded hay onto the truck.

i. The farmer's daughter loaded the hay with a pitchfork.

j. The hay was loaded on the truck by the farmer.

6. It is often the case that the subject of the sentence has the thematic role of agent, as can be seen in the previous exercise. With verbs like *receive,* however, the subject is not the agent. Think of five other verbs in which the subject is clearly not the agent. Can you identify the actual thematic role of the subject in your examples? For instance, we would surmise that the subject of *receive* has the thematic role of goal.

i. _____ ii. _____ iii. _____

iv. _____ v. _____

7. Some linguists and philosophers distinguish between two kinds of truthful statements: one follows from the definition or meaning of a word; the other simply happens to be true in the world as we know it. Thus, *kings are monarchs* is true because the word *king* has the semantic property "monarch" as part of its meaning; but *kings are rich* is circumstantially true. We can imagine a poor king, but a king who is not a monarch is not truly a king. Sentences like *kings are monarchs* are said to be **analytic,** true by virtue of meaning alone. Write *A* by any of the following sentences that are analytic, and *T* by the ones that are not analytic.

a. Queens are monarchs.   _____

b. Queens are female.   _____

c. Queens are mothers.   _____

d. Dogs are four-legged.   _____

e. Dogs are animals.   _____

f. Cats are felines.   _____

g. Cats are stupid.   _____

h. George Washington is George Washington.   _____

i. George Washington was the first president.   _____

j. Uncles are male.   _____

8. The opposite of *analytic* (see previous exercise) is **contradictory.** A sentence that is false due to the meaning of its words alone is contradictory. *Kings are female* is an example. Write a *C* by the contradictory sentences and *F* by sentences that are not contradictory.

a. My aunt is a man.   _____

b. Witches are wicked.   _____

c. My brother is an only child.   _____

d. The evening star isn't the morning star.   _____

e. The evening star isn't the evening star.   _____

f. Babies are adults.   _____

g. Babies can lift one ton.   _____

h. Puppies are human.   _____

i. My bachelor friends are all married.   _____

j. My bachelor friends are all lonely.   _____

9. In sports and games many expressions are "performative." By shouting *you're out,* the first base umpire performs an act. Think up a half-dozen or so similar examples and explicate their use.

10. A criterion of a "performance sentence" is whether you can begin it with *I hereby.* Notice that if you say sentence *a* aloud it sounds like a genuine apology, but to say sentence *b* aloud sounds funny because you cannot perform an act of knowing:

a. I hereby apologize to you.

b. I hereby know you.

Test whether the following sentences are performance sentences by inserting *hereby* and seeing whether they sound "right." Circle the letter of any that are performance sentences.

c. I testify that she met the agent.

d. I know that she met the agent.

e. I suppose the Yankees will win.

f. He bet her $2500 that Reagan would win.

g. I dismiss the class.

h. I teach the class.

i. We promise to leave early.

j. I owe the I.R.S. $1,000,000.

k. I bequeath $1,000,000 to the I.R.S.

l. I swore I didn't do it.

m. I swear I didn't do it.

11. The following sentences make certain presuppositions. What are they? (The first one has been done for you.)

a. The police ordered the minors to stop drinking.

Presupposition: <u>The minors were drinking.</u>

b. Please take me out to the ball game again.

Presupposition: _____

c. Valerie regretted not receiving a new T-bird for Labor Day.

Presupposition: _____

d. That her pet turtle ran away made Emily very sad.

Presupposition: _____

e. The administration forgot that the professors support the students. (Compare *The administration believes that the professors support the students,* in which there is no such presupposition.)

Presupposition: _____

f. It is strange that the United States invaded Cambodia in 1970.

Presupposition: _____

g. Isn't it strange that the United States invaded Cambodia in 1970?

Presupposition: _____

h. Disa wants more popcorn.

Presupposition: _____

i. Why don't pigs have wings?

Presupposition: _____

j. Who discovered America in 1492?

Presupposition: _____

12. A. Consider the following "facts" and then answer the questions:

Roses are red and bralkions are too.
Booth shot Lincoln and Czolgosz, McKinley.
Casca stabbed Caesar and so did Cinna.
Frodo was exhausted as was Sam.

(1) What color are bralkions?   _____

(2) What did Czolgosz do to McKinley? _____

(3) What did Cinna do to Caesar?   _____

(4) What state was Sam in?   _____

B. Now consider these facts and answer the questions:

Black Beauty was a stallion.
Mary is a widow.
John remembered to send Mary a birthday card.
John didn't remember to send Jane a birthday card.
Flipper is walking.
(T = true; F = false)

(5) Black Beauty was male?   T____   F____

(6) Mary was never married?   T____   F____

(7) John sent Mary a card?   T____   F____

(8) John sent Jane a card?   T____   F____

(9) Flipper has legs?   T____   F____

Part A illustrates your ability to interpret meanings when syntactic rules have deleted parts of the sentence; Part B illustrates your knowledge of semantic features and presupposition.

13. Circle any deictic expression in the following sentences. (All sentences do not include such expressions)

   a. I saw her standing there.
   b. Dogs are animals.
   c. Yesterday, all my troubles seemed so far away.
   d. The name of this rock band is "The Beatles."
   e. The Declaration of Independence was signed in 1776.
   f. The Declaration of Independence was signed last year.
   g. Copper conducts electricity.
   h. The treasure chest is on the right.
   i. These are the times that try men's souls.
   j. There is a tide in the affairs of men which taken at the flood leads on to fortune.

14. State for each pronoun in the following sentences whether it is free, bound, or either bound or free. Consider each sentence independently.

   Example: John finds himself in love with her.
          himself—bound; her—free
   Example: John said that he loved her.
          he—bound or free; her—free

   a. Louise said to herself in the mirror: "I'm so ugly."
   b. The fact that he considers her pretty pleases Maria.
   c. Whenever I see you, I think of her.
   d. John discovered that a picture of himself was hanging in the Post Office, and that fact bugged him, but it pleased her.
   e. It seems that she and he will never stop arguing with them.
   f. Persons are prohibited from picking flowers from any but their own graves. (On a sign in a cemetery)

15. We passed lightly over the distinction between homonymy (different words with the same pronunciation) and polysemy (one word with more than one meaning). In practice, it is not always easy to make this distinction. For instance, are the two meanings of *fathom,* as illustrated in the cartoon below, an example of homonymy or polysemy?

   Dictionary writers must make thousands of decisions of this kind. In a dictionary, homophonous words have separate entries, whereas the various

By permission of Johnny Hart and Creators Syndicate, Inc.

meanings of a polysemous word occur within the same entry.[5] Using any up-to-date dictionary, look up ten sets of homophones (some homophones have four or five entries; for example, *peak*). Then look up ten polysemous words with five or more given meanings (for example, *gauge*). List both sets with their meanings.

16. The following sentences may be either lexically or structurally ambiguous, or both. Provide paraphrases showing you comprehend all the meanings.

> Example: I saw him walking by the bank.
> Meaning one: I saw him and he was walking by the river bank.
> Meaning two: I saw him and he was walking by the financial institution.
> Meaning three: I was walking by the river bank when I saw him.
> Meaning four: I was walking by the financial institution when I saw him.

  a. We laughed at the colorful ball.
  b. He was knocked over by the punch.
  c. The police were urged to stop drinking by the fifth.
  d. I said I would file it on Thursday.
  e. I cannot recommend visiting professors too highly.
  f. The license fee for pets owned by senior citizens who have not been altered is $1.50. (Actual notice)
  g. What looks better on a handsome man than a Tux? Nothing! (Attributed to Mae West)

[5]Often, word etymologies are used as the basis for decision. If two different meanings of a form come from historically different sources, the forms are considered to be homophones and receive separate entries.

CHAPTER 5
Phonetics: The Sounds of Language

Phonetics is concerned with describing the speech sounds that occur in the languages of the world. We want to know what these sounds are, how they fall into patterns, and how they change in different circumstances . . . The first job of a phonetician is . . . to try to find out what people are doing when they are talking and when they are listening to speech.

Peter Ladefoged, *A Course in Phonetics* 1982, 2d Edition

When we speak or understand someone speaking a language we know, the sounds produced or heard are related to specific meanings by the language system. When we hear a language we do not know, it sounds like gibberish. As mentioned in Chapter 2, we don't know where one word ends and another begins.

In the earlier chapters we discussed the fact that knowing a language means knowing the meaning of the sounds which represent morphemes, words, phrases, and sentences. Knowing a language also includes knowing what sounds are in the language and how they may be "strung" together to form these meaningful units. Although the sounds of French or Xhosa or Quechua are uninterpretable to someone who does not speak those languages, and although there may be some sounds in one language that are not in another, the sounds of all the languages of the world together constitute a limited set. This chapter will discuss these speech sounds, how they are produced, and how they may be characterized.

Sound Segments

The study of the speech sounds that occur in all human languages to represent meanings is called **phonetics.** To describe these sounds it is necessary to decide what an "individual sound" is and how each sound differs from all others.

This is not as easy as it may seem. A speaker of English "knows" that there are three sounds in the word *cat,* the initial sound represented by the letter *c,* the second by *a,* and the final sound by *t.* Yet, physically the word is just one continuous sound. You can **segment** the one sound into parts because you know English. The ability to analyze a word into its individual sound segments does not depend on knowledge of how the word is spelled. Both *not* and *knot* have three sounds even

"Keep out! Keep out! K-E-E-P O-U-T."

HERMAN copyright 1991 Jim Unger. Reprinted with permission of Universal Press Syndicate. All rights reserved.

though the first sound in *knot* is represented by the two letters, *kn*. Similarly, the printed word *psycho* has six letters which represent only four sounds—*ps, y, ch, o.*

If you heard someone clearing their[1] throat you would be unable to segment the sound into a sequence of discrete units because the sounds produced are not sounds in the language. This is not because it is a single continuous sound; you do not produce one sound, then another, then another when you say the word *cat.* You move your organs of speech continuously and produce a continuous signal.

Although the sounds we produce and hear and comprehend during speech are continuous, everyone throughout history who has attempted to analyze language has recognized that speech utterances can be segmented into individual units. According to an ancient Hindu myth, the god Indra, in response to an appeal made by the other gods, attempted for the first time to segment speech into its separate elements. After he accomplished this feat, according to the myth, the sounds could be regarded as language. Indra thus may be the first phonetician.

Speakers of English can, despite the Herman cartoon, separate *keep out* into two words because they know the language. We do not, however, pause between words

---

[1]We will use the pronouns *they, their,* and *them* as the singular or plural form when referring generally to either male or female. This use was mentioned in Chapter 2 and will be discussed further in Chapter 7.

even though we sometimes have that illusion. Children learning a language reveal this problem. The two-year-old child of one of the authors of this book when told by his mother to *Hold on* when he was going down a flight of stairs replied, *I'm holding don,* not knowing where the word "break" was. In the course of history, the errors in deciding where a boundary falls between two words can change the form of words. At an earlier stage of English, the word *apron* was *napron;* it was misperceived in the phrase, *a napron,* as *an apron* by so many speakers, it lost its initial *n.*

The lack of actual breaks between words and individual sounds often makes us think that speakers of foreign languages "run their words together" not realizing that we do also. X-ray motion pictures of someone speaking make this lack of breaks in the "speech chain" very clear. One can see the tongue, jaw and lips in continuous motion while the "individual sounds" are being produced.

Yet, if you know a language you have no difficulty segmenting the continuous sounds. In this way, speech is similar to music. A person who has not studied music cannot write the sequence of individual notes combined by a violinist into one changing continuous sound. A trained musician, however, finds it a simple task. Every human speaker, without special training, can segment a speech signal. Just as one cannot analyze a musical passage without musical knowledge, so also linguistic knowledge is required to segment speech into pieces.

Identity of Speech Sounds

"Boy, he must think we're pretty
stupid to fall for that again."

RUBES by Leigh Rubin. By permission of Leigh Rubin and Creators Syndicate.

The task is even more complicated because no two speakers ever say the "same thing" identically. The speech signal produced when one speaker says *cat* will not be exactly the same as the signal produced by another speaker's *cat* or even the repetition of the word by the same speaker. Yet, speakers understand each other because they know the same language.

Our knowledge of a language determines when we judge physically different sounds to be the same; we know which aspects or properties of the signal are linguistically important and which are not. For example, if someone coughs in the middle of saying "How (cough) are you"? a listener will interpret this simply as "How are you?" If you look at a picture of the physical signal produced, called a **sound spectrogram,** you will notice that the two utterances are very different. Despite acoustic differences, the phonetic properties that distinguish one sound, such as *b* from *d* in English remain fairly constant across all English speakers and times.

In Chapter One, language and speech were distinguished. Our linguistic knowledge, our mental grammar, makes it possible to ignore nonlinguistic differences in speech. Furthermore we are capable of making many sounds that we know intuitively are not speech sounds in our language. Many English speakers can make a clicking sound which writers sometimes represent as *tsk tsk tsk*. But these sounds are not part of the English sound system. They never occur as part of the words of the sentences we produce. It is, in fact, difficult for many English speakers to combine this clicking sound with other sounds. Yet clicks are speech sounds in Xhosa, Zulu, Sotho, and Khoikhoi—languages spoken in southern Africa—just like the *k* or *t* in English. Speakers of those languages have no difficulty producing them as parts of words. *Xhosa,* the name of a language spoken in South Africa, begins with one of these clicks. Thus, *tsk* is a speech sound in Xhosa but not in English. The sound represented by the letters *th* in the word *think* is a speech sound in English but not in French. The sound produced with a closed mouth when we are trying to clear a tickle in our throats is not a speech sound in any language, nor is the sound produced when we sneeze.

The science of phonetics attempts to describe all the sounds used in human language—sounds that constitute a subset of the totality of sounds that humans are capable of producing.

The process by which we use our linguistic knowledge to produce a meaningful utterance is a very complicated one. It can be viewed as a chain of events starting with an idea or message in the brain or mind of the speaker and ending with a similar message in the brain of the hearer. The message is put into a form that is dictated by the language we are speaking. It must then be transmitted by nerve signals to the organs of speech articulation, which produce the different physical sounds.

Speech sounds can be described at any stage in this chain of events. The study of the physical properties of the sounds themselves is called **acoustic phonetics** and the study of the way listeners perceive these sounds is called **auditory phonetics,** both of which will be discussed in later chapters. **Articulatory phonetics** is the study of how the vocal tract produces the sounds of language, which will be the primary concern in this chapter.

Spelling and Speech

The one-l lama,
He's a priest.
The two-l llama,
He's a beast.

And I will bet
A silk pajama
There isn't any
Three-l lllama.

Ogden Nash[2]

Drawing by Leo Cullum © 1988 The New Yorker Magazine, Inc.

[2]"The Lama" from *Verses from 1929 On* by Ogden Nash. Reprinted by permission of Curtis Brown Ltd., London, on behalf of the Estate of Ogden Nash.

Beware of heard, a dreadful word
That looks like beard and sounds like bird.
And dead: it's said like bed, not bead;
For goodness' sake, don't call it deed!
Watchout for meat and great and threat.
(They rhyme with suite and straight and debt.)
A moth is not a moth in mother,
Nor both in bother, broth in brother.

                                        Anonymous

Alphabetic spelling represents the pronunciations of words. But it is often the case that the sounds of the words in a language are rather unsystematically represented by **orthography**—that is, by spelling. In this chapter, in discussing the way different sounds are produced, it may therefore be confusing and rather difficult to refer to the sounds as spelled in English words. This difficulty is apparent when we look at the orthographic representation of English words.

Suppose all Earthlings were destroyed by some horrible catastrophe, and years later Martian astronauts exploring Earth discovered some fragments of English writing that included the following sentence:

Did he believe that Caesar could see the people seize the seas?

How would a Martian linguist decide that **e, ie, ae, ee, eo, ei,** and **ea** all represented the same sound? To add to the confusion, later this sentence might crop up:

The silly amoeba stole the key to the machine.

English speakers learn how to pronounce these words when learning to read and write and know that *y, oe, ey,* and *i* also represent the same sound as the boldface letters in the first sentence.

The Phonetic Alphabet

The English have no respect for their language, and will not teach their children to speak it. They cannot spell it because they have nothing to spell it with but an old foreign alphabet of which only the consonants—and not all of them—have any agreed speech value.

                          G.B. Shaw, *Preface to Pygmalion*

The discrepancy between spelling and sounds gave rise to a movement of "spelling reformers" called orthoepists. They wanted to revise the alphabet so that one letter would correspond to one sound and one sound to one letter, thus simplifying spelling. This is a **phonetic alphabet.**

By permission of Johnny Hart and Creators Syndicate, Inc.

George Bernard Shaw followed in the footsteps of three centuries of spelling reformers in England. In typical Shavian manner he pointed out that we could use the English spelling system to spell *fish* as *ghoti* —the *gh* like the sound in *enough,* the *o* like the sound in *women,* and the *ti* like the sound in *nation.* Shaw was so concerned about English spelling that he included a provision in his will for a new "Proposed English Alphabet" to be administered by a "Public Trustee" who would have the duty of seeking and publishing a more efficient alphabet. This alphabet was to have at least forty letters to enable "the said language to be written without indicating single sounds by groups of letters or by diacritical marks." After Shaw's death in 1950, 450 designs for such an alphabet were submitted from all parts of the globe. Four alphabets were judged to be equally good, and the £500 sterling prize was divided among their designers. An "expert" collaborated with these four to produce the alphabet designated in Shaw's will. Shaw also stipulated in his will that his play *Androcles and the Lion* be published in the new alphabet, with "the original Doctor Johnson's lettering opposite the transliteration page by page and a glossary of the two alphabets." This version of the play was published in 1962.

If we look at English spelling, it is easy to understand why there is a need for a phonetic alphabet. Different letters may represent a single sound, as shown in the following instances:

t*o*   **t***oo*   **tw***o*   thr***ough*   thr***e**w   cl***ue*   sh***oe*

A single letter may represent different sounds:

d***a***me   d***a***d   f***a***ther   c***a***ll   vill***a***ge   m***a***ny

A combination of letters may represent a single sound:

*sh*oot	*ch*aracter	***Th***omas	*ph*ysics
ei*th*er	d*ea*l	rou*gh*	na*ti*on
c*oa*t	gla*ci*al	***th***eater	pl*ai*n

Some letters have no sound at all in certain words:

*m*nemonic	*w*hole	resi*g*n	*gh*ost
*p*terodactyl	*w*rite	hol*e*	corp*s*
*p*sychology	s*w*ord	de*b*t	*g*naw
bou*gh*	lam*b*	is*l*and	*k*not

Some sounds are not represented in the spelling. In many words the letter *u* represents a *y* sound followed by a *u* sound:

c*u*te   (compare: c*oo*t)
f*u*tile   (compare: r*u*le)
*u*tility   (compare: *U*zbek)

One letter may represent two sounds; the final *x* in *Xerox* represents a *k* followed by an *s*.

Whether we support or oppose spelling reform in English, it is clear that to describe the sounds of English, or any other language, we cannot depend on the spelling of words. The alphabets designed to fulfill Shaw's will were not the first phonetic alphabets. One of the earliest was produced by Robert Robinson in 1617. In Shaw's lifetime, the phonetician Henry Sweet, the prototype for Shaw's own Henry Higgins in the play *Pygmalion,* which many people know from the musical play or movie *My Fair Lady,* produced a phonetic alphabet.

In 1888 the interest in the scientific description of speech sounds led the **International Phonetics Association (IPA)** to develop a phonetic alphabet that could be used to symbolize the sounds found in all languages. Since many languages use a Roman alphabet like that used in the English writing system, the IPA phonetic symbols were based on the Roman letters. These phonetic symbols have a consistent value unlike ordinary letters which may or may not represent the same sounds in the same or different languages.

The original IPA phonetic alphabet was the primary one used all over the world by phoneticians, language teachers, speech pathologists, linguists, and anyone wishing to symbolize the "spoken word" until 1989 when, from August eighteenth to the twenty-first, approximately 120 members of the Association met in Kiel, West Germany, to work on revisions. The symbols which will be used in this text are those from the revised IPA alphabet unless otherwise noted.

It is of course impossible to construct any set of symbols that will specify all the minute differences between sounds. Even Shaw recognized this when in his will he directed his Trustee

> to bear in mind that the proposed British Alphabet does not pretend to be exhaustive as it contains only sixteen vowels whereas by infinitesimal movements of the tongue countless different vowels can be produced all of them in use among speakers of English who utter the same vowels no oftener than they make the same fingerprints.

Even if we could specify all the details of different pronunciations, we would not want to. As mentioned above, a basic fact about speech is that no two utterances are ever physically the same. If a speaker says "Good morning" on Monday and again on Tuesday there will be some slight differences in the sounds he produces on the two days. In fact, if he says "Good morning" twice in succession on the same day, the two utterances will not be physically identical. If another speaker says "Good morning" the physical sounds (that is, the acoustic signal) produced will also differ from that produced by the first speaker. Yet all the "Good mornings" are considered by speakers of English to be repetitions of the same utterance.

This is an interesting fact about language. Some differences in the sounds of an utterance are important when one is trying to comprehend what is being said, and other differences can be ignored. Even though we never produce or hear exactly the same utterance twice, speakers know when two utterances are *linguistically* the same or different. Some properties of the sounds are therefore more important linguistically than others.

A phonetic alphabet should include enough symbols to represent the "crucial" linguistic differences. At the same time it should not, and cannot, include noncrucial differences, since such differences are infinitely varied.

TABLE 5.1

A Phonetic Alphabet for English Pronunciation

Consonants								Vowels			
p	pill	t	till	k	kill			i	beet	ɪ	bit
b	bill	d	dill	g	gill			e	bait	ɛ	bet
m	mill	n	nil	ŋ	ring			u	boot	ʊ	foot
f	feel	s	seal	h	heal			o	boat	ɔ	bore
v	veal	z	zeal	l	leaf			æ	bat		
θ	thigh	č	chill	r	reef			ʌ	but	a	pot/bar
ð	thy	ǰ	Jill	j	you			aj	bite	ə	sofa
š	shill	ʍ	which	w	witch			ɔj	boy	aw/æw	bout
ž	azure										

A list of phonetic symbols which can be used to represent speech sounds of English is given in Table 5.1. The symbols omit many details about the sounds and how they are produced in different words, and in different places in words. These symbols are meant to be used by persons knowing English. These are not all the phonetic symbols needed for English sounds; when we discuss the sounds in more detail later in the chapter we will add appropriate symbols. At the end of the chapter we list all the symbols needed for English pronunciation with examples of the words in which these sounds occur.

The symbol [ə] is called a **schwa.** It will be used in this book only to represent unstressed vowels, as illustrated in Table 5.1. (Note that there is great variation in the way speakers of English produce this vowel, but it is phonetically similar to the wedge symbol [ʌ], which will be used only in stressed syllables.)

Speakers of different English dialects pronounce some words differently. For example, some of you may pronounce the words *which* and *witch* identically. If you do, the initial sound of both words is symbolized by *w* in the chart. Some speakers of English pronounce *bought* and *pot* with the same vowel; others pronounce them with the vowel sounds in *bore* and *bar,* respectively. We have thus listed both words in the chart of symbols. English dialect differences will be discussed more fully in Chapter 7.

Some of the symbols in Table 5.1 are those traditionally used by linguists in the United States in place of IPA symbols:

U.S.		IPA
š	=	ʃ
ž	=	ʒ
č	=	tʃ
ǰ	=	dʒ
ʊ	=	ʋ

Using these symbols, we can now unambiguously represent the pronunciation of words. For example, words spelled with *ou* may have different pronunciations. To distinguish between the symbols representing sounds and the alphabet letters, we put the phonetic symbols between brackets:

Spelling	Pronunciation
though	[ðo]
thought	[θɔt]
rough	[rʌf]
bough	[baw]
through	[θru]
would	[wʊd]

Notice that only in *rough* do the letters *gh* represent any sound; that is, the sound [f]. Notice also that *ou* represents six different sounds, and *th* two different sounds. The *l* in *would*, like the *gh* in all but one of the words above, is not pronounced at all.

We will continue to use square brackets around the phonetic **transcription** to distinguish it from ordinary spelling.

Articulatory Phonetics

The principles of pronunciation are those general laws of articulation which determine the character, and fix the boundaries of every language; as in every system of speaking, however irregular, the organs must necessarily fall into some common mode of enunciation or the purpose of Providence in the gift of speech would be absolutely defeated. These laws, like every other object of philosophical inquiry, are only to be traced by an attentive observation and enumeration of particulars . . .

John Walker (1823)[3]

All the sounds symbolized in Table 5.1 and all speech sounds in the languages of the world are produced by the upper respiratory tract. To understand the nature of language it is necessary to understand the nature of these sounds and how they are produced. Articulatory phonetics attempts to provide a framework to do so.

Airstream Mechanisms

The production of any speech sound (or any sound at all) involves the movement of an airstream. Most speech sounds are produced by pushing lung air out of the body

---

[3]John Walker, *A Critical Pronouncing Dictionary and Expositor of the English Language,* London: A. Wilson, 1823. The 26th edition, from which this quote is taken, was published posthumously. Walker died in 1807.

through the mouth and sometimes also through the nose. Since lung air is used, these sounds are called **pulmonic** sounds; since the air is pushed **out,** they are called **egressive.** The majority of sounds used in languages of the world are thus produced by a **pulmonic egressive** airstream mechanism. All the sounds in English are produced in this manner.

Other airstream mechanisms are used in other languages to produce sounds called **ejectives, implosives,** and **clicks.** Instead of lung air, the body of air in the mouth may be moved. When this air is sucked in instead of flowing out, **ingressive** sounds, like implosives and clicks, are produced. When the air in the mouth is pushed out, ejectives are produced; they are therefore also **egressive** sounds. Implosives and ejectives are produced by a **glottalic airstream mechanism,** while clicks are produced by a **velaric airstream mechanism.** Ejectives are found in many American Indian languages as well as African and Caucasian languages. Implosives also occur in the languages of the American Indians and throughout Africa, India, and Pakistan. Clicks occur in the Southern Bantu languages such as Xhosa and Zulu, and in the languages spoken by the Bushmen and Khoikhoi. A detailed description of these different airstream mechanisms goes beyond the requirements of an introductory text. They are mentioned to show that sounds can be classified according to the airstream mechanism used to produce them. In the rest of this chapter we will be discussing only sounds produced by a pulmonic egressive airstream mechanism.

Voiced and Voiceless Sounds

The airstream from the lungs moves up through the trachea, or windpipe, and through the opening between the vocal cords, which is called the **glottis.** (See Figure 5–1)

If the vocal cords are apart, the airstream is not obstructed at the glottis and it passes freely into the **supraglottal** cavities (the parts of the vocal tract above the glottis). The sounds produced in this way are **voiceless** sounds. The sounds represented by **[p], [t], [k],** and **[s]** in the English words *seep* [sip], *seat* [sit], and *seek* [sik] are voiceless sounds.

If the vocal cords are together, the airstream forces its way through and causes them to **vibrate.** Such sounds are called **voiced** sounds and are illustrated by the sounds **[b], [d], [g],** and **[z]** in the words *cob* [kab], *cod* [kad], *cog* [kag], and *daze* [dez]. If you put a finger in each ear and say "z-z-z-z-z" you can feel the vibrations of the vocal cords. If you now say "s-s-s-s-s" you will not feel these vibrations (although you might hear a hissing sound in your mouth). When you whisper, you are making all the speech sounds voiceless. The voiced/voiceless distinction is a very important one in English. It is this phonetic feature or property that distinguishes between word pairs like the following:

rope/robe	*fate/fade*	*rack/rag*	*wreath/wreathe*
[rop]/[rob]	[fet]/[fed]	[ræk]/[ræg]	[riθ]/[rið]

The first word of each pair ends with a voiceless sound and the second word with a voiced sound. All other aspects of the sounds of these words are identical; the position of the lips and tongue is the same in each of the paired words.

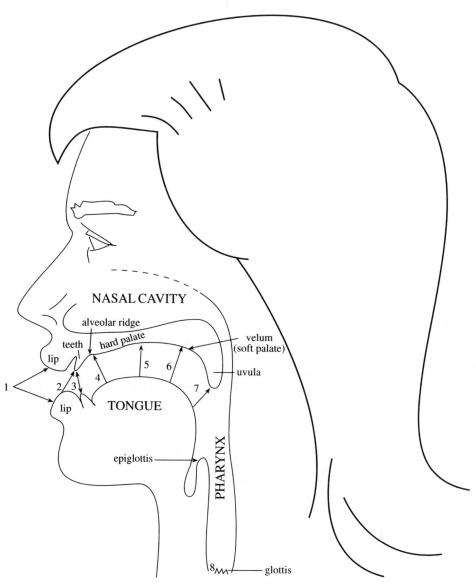

Figure 5–1.
The vocal tract; places of articulation are marked.
1. bilabial;   2. labiodental;   3. interdental;   4. alveolar;   5. (alveo) palatal;   6. velar;
7. uvular;   8. glottal.

The voiced/voiceless distinction is also shown in the following pairs; the first word begins with a voiceless sound and the second with a voiced sound:

fine/vine *seal/zeal* *choke/joke*
[fajn]/[vajn] [sil/zil] [čok]/[ǰok]

The initial sounds of the first words of the following pairs are also voiceless, and for many speakers of English, the second words begin with voiced sounds. (We will discuss other differences between the initial [p] and [b] sounds below; the phonetic transcriptions of many of these words have been simplified to help the reader grasp basic concepts and may include other details in later sections of this chapter and Chapter 6.)

peat/beat *tune/dune* *cane/gain*
[pit]/[bit] [tun]/[dun] [ken]/[gen]

The state of the vocal cords during speech thus permits us to classify speech sounds into two large classes—**voiced** and **voiceless.**

Sounds must differ from each other in ways other than voicing, because although [p], [t], [k] are all voiceless, and [b], [d], [g] are all voiced, each sound is distinct from all the others.

Nasal and Oral Sounds

If you say *rip* [rɪp] *rib* [rɪb], and *rim* [rɪm], you will notice that the final sounds [p], [b], and [m] are all produced by closing the lips. [p] differs from [b] because in producing the voiceless [p] the vocal cords are apart; the glottis is open. [b] is voiced because the vocal cords are together and vibrating. If you put your hands over your ears and keep your lips together prolonging the pronunciation of the [b] in *rib* you will feel the hum of the vibrations while your lips are closed. You will not feel such vibrations if you keep your lips together before releasing them in producing the [p] of *rip* because [p] is voiceless. If you do the same in producing a prolonged "m-m-m-m" in *rim* you will see that [m] is also a voiced sound. What, then, distinguishes the *m* from the *b?*

[m] is a **nasal** sound. When you produce [m], air escapes not only through the mouth (when you open your lips) but also through the nose.

In Figure 5–1 notice that the roof of the mouth is divided into the **hard palate** and the **soft palate** or **velum.** The hard palate is the bony structure at the front of the mouth. You can feel this hard palate with your finger. As you move your finger back you can feel the section of the palate where the flesh becomes soft and is movable. This soft, movable part is called the **velum.** Hanging down from the end of the soft palate, or velum, is the **uvula,** which you can see in a mirror if you open your mouth wide and say "aaah". When the velum is raised all the way to touch the back of the throat, the passage through the nose is cut off. When the nasal passage is blocked in this way, the air can escape only through the mouth. Sounds produced this way are called **oral** sounds. **[p]** and **[b]** are oral sounds. When the velum is lowered, air escapes through the nose as well as the mouth; sounds produced this way are called **nasal** sounds. **[m]**, **[n]**, and **[ŋ]** are the nasal consonants of English. The diagrams in Figure 5–2 show the position of the lips and the velum when [m], [b] and [p] are articulated.

THE FAR SIDE By GARY LARSON

Final page of the Medical Boards

The same nasal/oral difference occurs in *beet* [bit] and *meat* [mit], *dear* [dir] and *near* [nir]; in [b] and [d] the velum is raised preventing the air from flowing through the nose whereas in [m] and [n] the velum is down, letting the air go through both the nose and the mouth when the closure is released. [m], [n] and [ŋ] are therefore **nasal** sounds and [b], [d], and [g] are **oral** sounds.

The **phonetic features** or properties permit the classification of all speech sounds into four classes: voiced, voiceless, nasal, oral. One sound may belong to more than one class, as shown in Table 5.2.

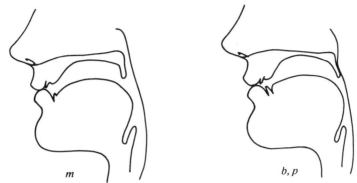

Figure 5–2
Position of lips and velum for *m* (lips together, velum down) and *b* or *p* (lips together, velum up).

TABLE 5.2
Classes of Speech Sounds

	Oral	Nasal
Voiced	b d g	m n ŋ
Voiceless	p t k	*

*Nasal consonants in English are usually voiced. Both voiced and voiceless nasal sounds occur in other languages, as will be discussed below.

Places of Articulation

[b], [d], [g] are all voiced nonnasal (oral) sounds, [p], [t] and [k] are all voiceless oral sounds, and [m], [n] and [ŋ] are voiced nasals. We know they are distinct because we recognize *brew* [bru], *drew* [dru], and *grew* [gru], and *robe* [rob], *road* [rod], and *rogue* [rog] as different words with different meanings. This is also true of *pole* [pol], *toll* [tol] and *coal* [kol], and *Kim* [kɪm], *kin* [kɪn] and *king* [kɪŋ]. What is it that distinguishes one from the other? Different sounds result when we change the shape of the oral cavity by moving the lips and tongue, the **articulators** changing the **place of articulation** in the oral cavity. The major **place** features are given below.

Labials

When we produce a [p], [b], or [m] we **articulate** by bringing both lips together. These sounds are therefore called **bilabials.**

We also use our lips to form [f] and [v] as in *fine* [fajn] and *vine* [vajn]. To produce these sounds we articulate by touching the bottom lip to the upper teeth, which is why these sounds are called **labiodental, labio-** referring to lips and **dental** to teeth.

The class of **labial** consonants in English consists of the three bilabials **[b]**, **[p]**, and **[m]** and the two labiodentals **[f]** and **[v]**.

Interdentals

To produce the voiceless [θ] and the voiced [ð], both of which sounds are represented orthographically by the *th* in the words *thin* [θɪn], *ether* [iθər], *then* [ðɛn] and *either* [iðər], the tip of the tongue is inserted between the upper and lower teeth. These are **interdental** ("between the teeth") sounds.

Alveolars

To articulate a **[d], [n], [t], [s],** or **[z]**, the tongue is raised to the bony tooth ridge, called the **alveolar ridge** (see Figure 5–1). Sounds produced by raising the front part of the tongue to the alveolar ridge are thus called **alveolar** sounds. If you say *do* [du], *new* [nu], *two* [tu], *Sue* [su], *zoo* [zu], you will notice that the first sounds in all these words are alveolar sounds. The [t] and [s] are voiceless alveolar sounds, and the [d], [z], and [n] are voiced. Only [n] is nasal.

Velars

Another class of sounds is produced by raising the back of the tongue to the soft palate or velum. The initial and final sounds of the words *kick* [kɪk], *gig* [gɪg], and the final sounds of the words *back* [bæk], *bag* [bæg], and *bang* [bæŋ] are produced in this way and are called **velar** sounds. The [k] is a voiceless, oral velar; the [g] is a voiced oral velar, and the [ŋ] (which never occurs at the beginning of words in English) is a voiced nasal velar.

Palatals

To produce the sounds in the middle of the words *mesher* [mɛšər] and *measure* [mɛžər], the front part of the tongue is raised to a point on the hard palate just behind the alveolar ridge. [š], the voiceless sound in *mesher* (spelled *sh*) and [ž], the voiced sound in *measure* (spelled *s*) are **palatal** sounds. In English the voiced palatal never begins words (except in words borrowed from the French like *genre* or *gendarme* which some English speakers produce with a French pronunciation). The voiceless palatal sound begins the words *shoe* [šu] and *sure* [šur] and ends the words *rush* [rʌš] and *push* [pʊš]. (These palatal sounds are also referred to as **alveopalatals.**)

Coronals

Just as bilabial and labiodental sounds can be classified together as labial sounds, the alveolar and palatal sounds may also be grouped together as **coronal,** sharing the common property of being articulated by raising the tongue blade toward the hard palate.

Manners of Articulation

We have described a number of phonetic properties that divide speech sounds into several overlapping classes. Yet we are still unable to distinguish [t] from [s] since both are voiceless oral alveolar sounds.

The voiced/voiceless and oral/nasal features do not refer to the movement or position of the tongue, teeth, or lips. Rather they reflect the way the airstream is affected as it travels from the lungs up and out of the mouth and nose. Such features or phonetic properties have traditionally been referred to as **manners of articulation** or simply **manner** features.

Other manner features distinguish sounds like [t] and [s] which are both voiceless alveolar sounds; the meanings of *tale* [tel] and *sale* [sel] differ solely because of the manner in which they are produced. Other classes of sounds are also distinguished by such phonetic properties.

Stops and Continuants

Once the airstream enters the oral cavity, it may be stopped, it may be partially obstructed, or it may flow freely out of the mouth. Sounds that are *stopped completely* in the oral cavity for a brief period are, not surprisingly, called **stops.** These can be distinguished from all other speech sounds which are called **continuants** because the stream of air continues without complete interruption through the mouth opening.

[p], [b], [m], [t], [d], [n], [k], [g], and [ŋ] in the words *top* [tap], *bomb* [bam], *dune* [dun], *keg* [kɛg], and *king* [kɪŋ] are stops that occur in English.

In the production of the nasal stops **[n], [m], [ŋ]**, the airflow is blocked completely in the mouth but continues to 'escape' through the nose. The phonetic feature, continuant, refers to the air flow through the oral cavity; therefore, nasal consonants are stops because the passage of air **through the mouth** is stopped completely.

The nonnasal or oral stops are also called **plosives** because the air that is blocked in the mouth "explodes" when the closure is released. This explosion does not occur during the production of the nasal stops because the air has an "escape route" through the nose.

[p], [b], and **[m]** are bilabial stops, with the airstream stopped at the mouth by the complete closure of the lips.

[t], [d], and **[n]** are alveolar stops; the airstream is stopped by the tongue making a complete closure at the alveolar ridge.

[k], [g], and **[ŋ]** are velar stops with the complete closure at the velum.

In Quechua, a major language spoken in Bolivia and Peru, one also finds **uvular** stops which are produced when the back of the tongue is raised and moved backward to form a complete closure with the uvula. The letter **q** in words in this language, as in the language name, usually represents a uvular stop, which may occur voiced or voiceless.

All speech sounds are either in the class of continuants or stops (noncontinuants), which of course intersect with other classes. Table 5.3 shows the classification of some of the sounds in English according to the Place of Articulation features and the Manner features discussed so far.

TABLE 5.3
Place and Manner Feature Classes
(The voiceless sound is on the left, the voiced on the right)

	LABIALS			**CORONALS**		
	Bilabial	**Labiodental**	**Interdental**	**Alveolar**	**Palatal**	**Velar**
Stop						
Oral	p b			t d		k g
Nasal	m			n		ŋ
Continuants		f v	θ ð	s z	š ž	

Aspirated and Unaspirated Sounds

In the discussion of the phonetic properties or features that are used to distinguish and define speech sounds, we were faced with certain problems. We used one symbol [p] to represent the voiceless bilabial stop, one symbol [t] to represent the voiceless alveolar stop, and the symbol [k] to represent the voiceless velar stop. We did not distinguish, for example, the initial sound in the word *pit* from the second sound in the word *spit*. There is, however, a difference in these two stops.

During the production of voiceless sounds the glottis is open and the air passes freely through the opening between the vocal cords. When a voiceless sound is followed by a voiced sound such as a vowel, the vocal cords must close in order to permit them to vibrate.

Voiceless sounds fall into two classes depending on the "timing" of the vocal cord closure. In English when we pronounce the word *pit,* there is a brief period of voicelessness immediately after the *p* sound is released. That is, after the lips come apart the vocal cords remain open for a very short time. Such sounds are called **aspirated** because an extra puff of air is produced.

When we pronounce the *p* in *spit,* however, the vocal cords start vibrating as soon as the lips are opened. Such sounds are called **unaspirated.** The **t** in *tick* and the **k** in *kin* are also aspirated voiceless stops, while the **t** in *stick* and the **k** in *skin* are unaspirated. If you hold a strip of paper in front of your lips and say *pit*, a puff of air (the aspiration) will push the paper. The paper will not move when you say *spit.*

When a fully voiced [b] is produced, the vocal cords vibrate throughout the articulation.

Figure 5–3 shows in diagrammatic form the timing of the articulators (in this case the lips) in relation to the state of the vocal cords. Notice that in the production of the voiced **b,** the vocal cords are vibrating throughout the closure of the lips and continue to vibrate for the vowel production after the lips are opened. Most English speakers do not voice initial [b] to the full extent. Because we heavily aspirate an initial [p], there is no difficulty in distinguishing these two sounds. In the aspirated or unaspirated **p** in *spin*, the vocal cords are open during the lip closure and come together and start vibrating as soon as the lips open. In the production of the aspirated **p** in *pin* the vocal cords remain apart for a brief period after the lip closure is released.

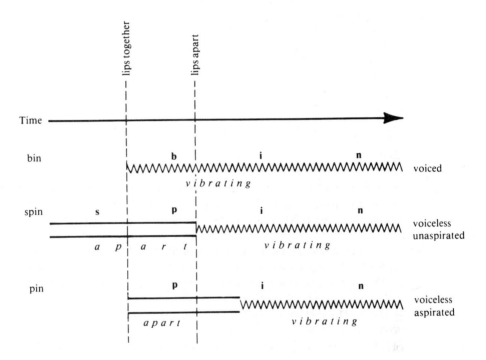

Figure 5–3
Timing of articulators and vocal cord vibration for voiced, voiceless unaspirated, and voiceless aspirated stops.

Aspirated sounds are indicated by following the phonetic symbol with a raised [h] as in the following examples:

pate	[pʰet]	*spate*	[spet]
tale	[tʰel]	*stale*	[stel]
kale	[kʰel]	*scale*	[skel]

Fricatives

In the production of some sounds, the airstream is not completely stopped but is obstructed from flowing freely. If you put your hand in front of your mouth and produce an [s], [z], [f], [v], [θ], [ð], [š], or [ž] sound, you will feel the air coming out of your mouth. The passage in the mouth through which the air must pass, however, is very narrow, causing **friction** or turbulence. Such sounds are called **fricatives.** (They are also sometimes referred to as **spirants,** from the Latin word *spirare,* "to blow".)

In the production of the labiodental fricatives [f] and [v], the friction is created at the lips, where a narrow passage permits the air to escape.

[s] and [z] are alveolar fricatives with the friction created at the alveolar ridge.

The palatal or alveopalatal fricatives, [š] and [ž], such as those in *mesher* [mɛšər] and *measure* [mɛžər], are produced with friction created as the air passes through the narrow opening behind the alveolar ridge.

In the production of the interdental fricatives [θ] and [ð], represented by *th* in *thin* and *then,* the friction occurs at the opening between the tongue and teeth.

Most dialects of modern English do not include velar fricatives, although they occurred in an earlier stage of English in such words as *right, knight, enough,* and *through,* where the *gh* occurs in the spelling. If you raise the back of the tongue as if you were about to produce a [g] or [k], but stop just short of touching the velum, you will produce a velar fricative. The *ch* ending in the German pronunciation of the composer's name, *Bach,* is a velar fricative. Some speakers of modern English substitute a voiceless velar fricative in words like *bucket* and a voiced velar fricative in such words as *wagon* for the velar stops that occur for other speakers in those words. [x] is the IPA symbol for the voiceless velar fricative and [ɣ] for the voiced velar fricative.

In some languages of the world, such as French, *uvular fricatives* occur as the sound represented by *r* in French words such as *rouge* "red" or *rose* "pink". In Arabic *pharyngeal fricatives* are produced by pulling the tongue root towards the back wall of the pharynx. It is difficult to pull the tongue far enough to make a complete pharyngeal stop closure, but both voiced and voiceless pharyngeal fricatives can be produced and can be distinguished from velar fricatives.

All fricatives are continuants; although the airstream is obstructed as it passes through the oral cavity, it is not completely stopped.

Affricates

Some sounds are produced by a stop closure followed immediately by a slow release of the closure characteristic of a fricative. These sounds are called **affricates.** The sounds that begin and end the words *church* and *judge* are voiceless and voiced affricates, respectively. Phonetically, an affricate is a sequence of a stop plus a fricative. Thus, the *ch* in *church* is the same as the sound combination [t] + [š] as shown by observing that in fast speech *white shoes* and *why choose* may be pronounced identically. The voiceless and voiced affricates may be symbolized as [tš] (IPA [tʃ]) and [dž] (IPA [dʒ]), respectively. In the American tradition, [č], [ǰ] are the more commonly used symbols for these sounds, and the ones used in this book.

Because the air is stopped completely during the initial articulation of an affricate, these sounds are noncontinuant and classified as stops.

Liquids

In the production of the sounds [l] and [r], there is some obstruction of the airstream in the mouth, but not enough to cause any real constriction or friction. These sounds are called **liquids.**

[l] is a **lateral** liquid, the tongue is raised to the alveolar ridge, but the sides of the tongue are down permitting the air to escape laterally over the sides of the tongue.

The sound [r] is produced in a variety of ways. Many English speakers produce **r** by curling the tip of the tongue back behind the alveolar ridge. Such sounds are called **retroflex** sounds.

In some languages, the *r* may be **trill,** which is produced by the tip of the tongue vibrating against the roof of the mouth. A trilled [r] occurs in many languages, such as Spanish. In addition to the alveolar trill, uvular trills occur, produced by vibrating the uvula. Some French speakers use uvular trills instead of uvular fricatives.

In other languages the **r** is produced by a single **tap** or a **flap** of the tongue against the alveolar ridge. In Spanish both the trilled and tapped **r** occur. Some speakers of British English pronounce the *r* in the word *very* with a flap. It sounds like a "very fast" *d.* Most American speakers produce a flap instead of a [t] or [d] in words like *writer* or *rider,* or *latter* or *ladder.* The IPA symbol for the alveolar tap or flap is [ɾ].

In English, [l] and [r] are regularly voiced. When they follow voiceless sounds, as in *please* and *price,* they may be automatically "devoiced." Many languages of the world have a voiceless **l.** Welsh is such language; the name *Lloyd* in Welsh starts with the voiceless **l.**

Some languages may lack liquids entirely, or have only a single one. The Cantonese dialect of Chinese has the single liquid [l]. Some English words are difficult for Cantonese speakers to pronounce, and they may substitute an [l] for an [r] when speaking English.

The reason why speakers in languages with only one liquid tend to use that sound as a substitute for the sound that does not occur in their language is because of the acoustic similarity of these sounds. This likeness is why they are grouped together in one class and why they function as a single class of sounds in certain circumstances. For example, in English, the only two consonants that occur after an initial [k], [g], [p], or [b] are the liquids [l] and [r]. Thus we have *crate* [kret], *clock* [klak], *plate* [plet], *prate* [pret], *bleak* [blik], *break* [brek], but no word starting with [ps], [bt], [pk], and so on. (Notice that in words like *psychology* or *pterodactyl* the "p" is not pronounced. Similarly in *knight* or *knot* the "k" is not pronounced, although at an earlier stage of English, it was.)

Glides

The sounds [j] and [w], the initial sounds of *you* and *woo* [wu] are produced with little or no obstruction of the airstream in the mouth. When occurring in a word, they must always be either preceded or followed directly by a vowel. In articulating [j] or [w], the tongue moves rapidly in gliding fashion either toward or away from a neighboring vowel, hence the term **glide.** Glides are transition sounds that are sometimes called **semivowels.** They are **sonorants** because like the other sounds in this class the air is essentially unobstructed as it moves through the oral cavity. They differ from vowels which are also sonorant in that they do not form the peak of a syllable. We shall discuss this further below.

[j] is a **palatal glide;** the blade of the tongue is raised toward the hard palate in a position almost identical to that in producing the vowel sound [i] in the word *beat* [bit]. In pronouncing *you* [ju], the tongue moves rapidly from the **[j]** to the **[u]** vowel.

The glide **[w]** is produced by both raising the back of the tongue toward the velum and simultaneously rounding the lips. It is thus a **labio–velar** glide, or a rounded velar glide. In the dialect of English where speakers have different pronunciations for the words *which* and *witch,* the velar glide in the first word is voiceless [ʍ] (an "upside down" *w*), and in the second word it is voiced **[w].** The position of the tongue and the lips for **[w]** is similar to that for producing the vowel sound in *lute* [lut], but the **[w]** is a glide because the tongue moves quickly to the vowel that follows.

The **[h]** sound that starts words such as *house* [haws], *who* [hu] and *hair* [her] is also a glide. The glottis is open as in the production of voiceless sounds. No other modification of the airstream mechanisms occurs in the mouth. In fact, the tongue and lips are usually in the position for the production of the following vowel as the airstream passes through the open glottis. The air or noise produced at the glottis is heard as **h** and, for this reason, is sometimes classified as a **voiceless glottal fricative.** However, the **[h]** differs from "true" consonants in that there is no obstruction in the oral cavity. It also differs from vowels which are articulated by moving the tongue. When it is both preceded and followed by a vowel in English it is often voiced, as in *ahead* and *cohabit.*

If the air is stopped completely at the glottis by tightly closed vocal cords, the sound produced is a **glottal stop.** This is the sound sometimes used instead of **[t]** in *button* and *Latin.* It also may occur in colloquial speech at the end of words like *don't, won't* or *can't.* In one American dialect it regularly replaces the "tt" sound in words like *bottle* or *glottal.* If you say "ah-ah-ah-ah-" with one "ah" right after another but do not sustain the vowel sound, you will be producing glottal stops between the vowels. The IPA symbol for a glottal stop looks something like a question mark without the dot on the bottom [ʔ]. Like the **[h],** it differs from both consonants and vowels and therefore may be classified as a glide. Because the air is completely blocked at the glottis, some linguists classify it as a stop.

Syllabic Sounds

Every language of the world contains the two basic classes of speech sounds often referred to by the cover terms **consonants** (C) and **vowels** (V). In the production of consonants the flow of air is obstructed as it travels through the mouth. Vowels are produced with no oral obstruction whatsoever. Oral and nasal stops, fricatives, affricates, liquids, and glides all have some degree of obstruction and are therefore consonants.

As mentioned above, vowels and glides are similar in their phonetic properties. Vowels, however, as distinct from glides, usually constitute the "main core" or the **nucleus** of syllables. Because they constitute syllable peaks, vowels are in a class of syllabic speech sounds, whereas glides are nonsyllabic.

Liquids and nasals can be syllabic—that is, they may constitute separate syllables, as in the words *medal, feather, mutton,* or *rhythm;* or they may be nonsyllabic, as in the words *lead, read, deal, dear, name,* or *mean.*

Vowels

HIGGINS: Tired of listening to sounds?
PICKERING: Yes. It's a fearful strain. I rather fancied myself because I can pronounce twenty-four distinct vowel sounds, but your hundred and thirty beat me. I can't hear a bit of difference between most of them.
HIGGINS: Oh, that comes with practice. You hear no difference at first, but you keep on listening and presently you find they're all as different as A from B.

G. B. Shaw, *Pygmalion*

© 1980 Newspaper Enterprise Association, Inc.

The quality of vowels is determined by the particular configuration of the vocal tract. Different parts of the tongue may be raised or lowered. The lips may be spread or pursed. The passage through which the air travels, however, is never so narrow as to obstruct the free flow of the airstream.

Vowel sounds carry pitch and loudness; you can sing vowels. They may be long or short. Vowels can "stand alone"—they can be produced without any consonants before or after them. You can say the vowels of *beat,* [bit], *bit* [bɪt], or *boot* [but] for example, without the initial [b] or the final [t].

There have been many different schemes for describing vowel sounds. They may be described by articulatory features, as in classifying consonants. Many beginning students of phonetics find this method more difficult to apply to vowel articulations than to consonant articulations. In producing a [t] you can feel your tongue touch the alveolar ridge. When you make a [p] you can feel your two lips come together, or you can watch the lips move in a mirror. Because vowels are produced without any articulators touching or even coming close together it is often difficult to figure out just what is happening. One of the authors of this book, at the beginning of her graduate work, almost gave up the idea of becoming a linguist because she could not understand what was meant by "front," "back," "high," and "low" vowels.

These terms do have meaning, though. If you watch an X-ray movie of someone talking, you can see why vowels have traditionally been classified according to three questions:

1. How high is the tongue?
2. What part of the tongue is involved; that is, what part is raised or lowered?
3. What is the position of the lips?

There are other distinguishing features, such as length and nasalization, which we will discuss below.

Tongue Position

The three diagrams in Figure 5–4 show that the tongue in the production of the vowels in the words *he* [hi] and *who* [hu] is very high in the mouth; in [hi] it is the front part of the tongue that is raised, and in [hu] it is the back part of the tongue. (Prolong the vowels of these words and try to feel your tongue rise.)

To produce the vowel sound of *hah* [ha], the back of the tongue is lowered. (The reason a doctor examining your throat may ask you to say "ah" is that the tongue is low and easy to see over.) This vowel is therefore a low, back vowel.

The vowels [ɪ] and [ʊ] in the words *hit* [hɪt] and *put* [pʊt] are similar to those in *he* [hi] and *who* [hu] with slightly lowered tongue positions.

The vowel [æ] in *hat* [hæt] is produced with the front part of the tongue lowered, similar to the low vowel like [a], but with the front rather than the back part of the tongue lowered.

The vowels [e] and [o] in *bait* [bet] and *boat* [bot] are **mid vowels,** produced by raising the tongue to a position midway between the high and low vowels discussed above. [ɛ] and [ɔ] in the words *bet* [bɛt] and *bore* [bɔr] are also mid vowels, produced with a slightly lower tongue position than [e] and [o].

To produce the vowel [ʌ] in the word *butt* [bʌt] or the **schwa** vowel [ə] which occurs in the second syllable of the words *sofa* [sofə] or *Rosa* [rozə], the tongue is neither high nor low, front nor back. These are mid, central vowels as shown in Figure 5–5.

Lip Rounding

Vowels also differ as to whether the lips are rounded. The vowels [u], [ʊ], [o], [ɔ], in *boot, put, boat,* and *bore* are produced with the back of the tongue at decreasing heights. These back vowels are all pronounced with the lips pursed or **rounded.** The low vowel [a] in the words *bar, bah, aha* is the only English back vowel that occurs without lip rounding. All non-back vowels in English are also unrounded.

Figure 5–5 places these vowels on a **vowel chart** specifying the part of the tongue from front to back on the horizontal axis, and the height of the tongue on the vertical axis.

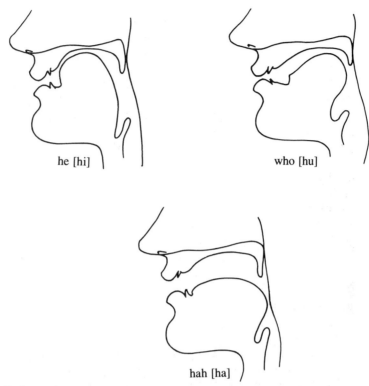

he [hi]   who [hu]

hah [ha]

Figure 5–4
Position of the tongue in producing the vowels in *he, who,* and *hah.*

As shown, there are no front-rounded vowels in English. This is not true of all languages. French and Swedish, for example, have both front- and back-rounded vowels. In English a high back unrounded vowel does not occur, but in Mandarin Chinese, in Japanese, in the Cameroonian language FeʔFeʔ, and in many other languages, this vowel is part of the phonetic inventory of sounds. There is a Chinese word meaning "four" with an initial [s] followed by a vowel similar to the one in *boot* but with nonrounded spread lips. This Chinese word is distinguished from the word meaning "speed" pronounced like the English word *sue* with a high back-rounded vowel.

As already mentioned, but perhaps worth repeating, because of the many dialects of English, the Vowels in Figure 5–5 do not represent all the vowels of all dialects. British RP (a particular dialect spoken in England) has a low-rounded back vowel in the word *hot,* which is symbolized as [ɒ] and contrasts with the unrounded low back vowel [a] in *bah.* The long, tense vowels in British RP are all diphthongs. Thus the vowel in *bay* is [eʲ] and the vowel in *bow* is [oʷ], as is true for some dialects of American English. These are just a few examples of dialect differences which occur primarily in the pronunciation of vowels.

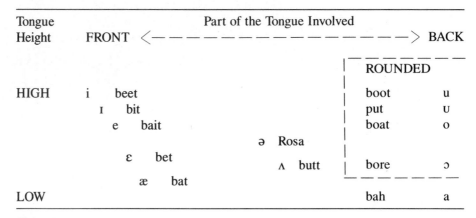

Figure 5–5
Classification of American English vowels.

Diphthongs

Many languages, including English, have vowels called **diphthongs** which can also be described as a sequence of two sounds, vowel + glide. The vowels we have studied so far are all simple vowels called **monophthongs.** The vowel sounds in the words *bite* [bajt] and *rye* [raj] are produced with the **[a]** vowel sound of *father* followed by the **[j]** glide. The vowels in *bout* [bawt], *brow* [braw], and *hour* [awr] are produced by some speakers of English with a similar **[a]** sound followed by the glide **[w].** Some speakers of English produce this diphthong as [æw], with the front low unrounded vowel instead of the back vowel. The third diphthong that occurs in English is the vowel sound in *boy* [bɔj] and *soil* [sɔjl] which is the vowel that occurs in *bore* (without the [r]) followed by the palatal glide **[j]**, [ɔj].

Nasalization of Vowels

Vowels, like consonants, can be produced with a raised velum that prevents the air from escaping through the nose, or with a lowered velum that permits air to pass through the nasal passage. When the nasal passage is blocked, **oral** vowels are produced; when the nasal passage is open, **nasal** or **nasalized** vowels are produced. In English, nasal vowels occur before nasal consonants, and oral vowels occur before oral consonants.[4]

The words, *bean, bin, bane, Ben, ban, boon, bun, bone, beam, bam, boom, bing, bang,* and *bong* are examples of words that contain nasalized vowels. To show the nasalization of a vowel in a phonetic transcription a **diacritic** mark [˜] is placed over the vowel, as in *bean* [bĩn] and *bone* [bõn].

---

[4]In fast colloquial speech some speakers drop the nasal consonant when it occurs before voiceless stops such as in *hint* or *camp,* leaving just the nasal vowel, but the words originate with nasal consonants.

In languages like French, Polish, and Portuguese, nasalized vowels may occur when no nasal consonant is adjacent. In French for example, the word meaning "year" is *an* [ā] and the word for "sound" is *son* [sō]. The *n* in the spelling is not pronounced but indicates in these words that the vowels are nasalized.

Prosodic Suprasegmental Features

Speech sounds which are identical as to their place or manner features may differ in duration (length), pitch, or loudness. A vowel can be lengthened by prolonging it. A consonant is made long by maintaining the closure or obstruction for a longer period of time.

When we speak we also change the **pitch** of our voice. The pitch produced depends upon how fast the vocal cords vibrate; the faster they vibrate, the higher the pitch. In physical or acoustic terms, pitch is referred to as the **fundamental frequency** of the sound signal.

We are also able to change the loudness of the sounds and sound sequences. In many languages, some syllables or vowels are produced more loudly with a simultaneous change in pitch (usually higher) and longer duration than other vowels in the word or sentence. They are referred to as **stressed** or **accented** vowels or syllables. For example, the first syllable of *digest,* the noun meaning "summation of articles" or a "journal" is stressed, while in *digest,* the verb meaning "to absorb food," the second syllable is stressed. Stress can be marked in a number of ways, for example, by putting an "accent" mark over the stressed vowel.

In Chapter 6, we will further discuss features like **length, pitch,** and the complex feature **stress** and how they are used in various languages to distinguish the meaning of words and sentences. Such features are often referred to as **prosodic** or **suprasegmental** features. In this chapter we will illustrate the use of such prosodic features by a discussion of vowel length as it pertains to the phonetic distinction of the vowels of English and the use of pitch as a **tone** feature in other languages.

Long and Short (Tense and Lax Vowels)

Figure 5–5 shows that the vowel [i] is produced with a slightly higher tongue position than [ɪ]. This is also true for [e] and [ɛ], [u] and [ʊ], and [o] and [ɔ]. These pairs of vowels are also distinguished by length with the vowel in the first word of the following pairs longer in duration than the vowel in the second word. **Long** vowels in English are also produced with greater tension of the tongue muscles than their **short** counterparts and are therefore also referred to as **tense** vowels. We will use the long/short distinction when referring to them in this book.

Long (Tense)		**Short (Lax)**	
i	beat	ɪ	bit
e	bait	ɛ	bet
u	boot	ʊ	put
o	boat	ɔ	bore

Long tense vowels are sometimes also slightly diphthongized for some speakers of English whose tense front vowels are followed by a short **[j]** glide [iʲ], [eʲ], and whose tense back vowels by a short **[w]** glide [uʷ] and [oʷ].

In some languages there are vowels and/or consonants that differ phonetically from each other only by duration. That is, neither height of the tongue nor tenseness distinguishes the vowel from its counterpart in pairs of words which contrast in meaning. It is customary to transcribe this difference either by doubling the symbol or by the use of a diacritic "colon" after the segment, as for example [aa] or [a:], [bb] or [b:].[5] Since English long vowels differ qualitatively from their paired short vowels, we are using different symbols to distinguish them.

Tone and Intonation

Speakers of all languages vary the pitch of their voices when they talk; the pitch produced depends upon how fast the vocal cords vibrate; the faster they vibrate, the higher the pitch.

The way pitch is used linguistically differs from language to language. In English, it doesn't much matter whether you say *cat* with a high pitch or a low pitch. It will still mean "cat." But if you say [ba] with a high pitch in Nupe (a language spoken in Nigeria), it will mean "to be sour," whereas if you say [ba] with a low pitch, it will mean "to count." Languages that use the pitch of individual vowels or syllables to contrast meanings of words are called **tone** languages.

The majority of the languages in the world are tone languages. There are more than 1000 tone languages in Africa alone; many languages of Asia, such as Chinese, Thai, and Burmese, are tone languages, as are many Native American languages.

Thai is a language that has contrasting pitches or tones. The same string of "segmental" sounds represented by [naa] will mean different things if one says the sounds with a low pitch, a mid pitch, a high pitch, a falling pitch from high to low, or a rising pitch from low to high. Thai therefore has five linguistic tones.

[naa]	[—]	low tone	"a nickname"
[naa]	[—]	mid tone	"rice paddy"
[naa]	[—]	high tone	"young maternal uncle or aunt"
[naa]	[⌐]	falling tone	"face"
[naa]	[◡]	rising tone	"thick"

Diacritics are used to represent distinctive tones in the phonetic transcriptions.

[ˋ]	L	low tone	
[ˉ]	M	mid tone	
[ˊ]	H	high tone	
[ˆ]	HL	falling tone	(High to Low)
[ˇ]	LH	rising tone	(Low to High)

[5]Long or doubled segments may be referred to as **geminate.**

We can use these diacritics placed above the vowels to represent the tonal contrasts in any language where the pitch of the vowel is important in conveying meaning as illustrated by the three contrastive tones in Nupe:

[bá]   "be sour"   [bā]   "cut"   [bà]   "count"
H   M   L

Akan, sometimes called Twi, the major language of Ghana, has two tones which are shown in the contrasting two syllables words.

dù à   [_]   "tail"   dù á   [¯]   "tree"
| | | |
L L   L H
kɔ̀ tɔ́   [¯]   "go buy"   kɔ́ tɔ̀   [¯]   "crab"
| | | |
L H   H L

In some tone languages the pitch of each tone is "level"; in others, the direction of the pitch (whether it glides from high to low, or from low to high) is important. Tones that "glide" are called **contour tones;** tones that do not are called **level** or **register tones.** The contour tones of Thai are represented by using for a falling tone a high tone followed by a low tone, and a rising tone is a low followed by a high.

In a tone language it is not the absolute pitch of the syllables that is important but the relations among the pitches of different syllables. After all, some individual speakers have high-pitched voices, others low-pitched, and others medium-pitched. In many tone languages we find a falling-off of the pitch, or a "downdrifting."

In the following sentence in Twi, the **relative pitch** rather than the absolute pitch is important.

"Kofi searches for a little food for his friend's child."

Kòfí   hwèhwɛ́   áduàŋ   kàkrá mà   ǹ' ádàmfò   bá.
| | | | | | | | | | | | | |
LH   L   H   H L   L H   L   L H L L   H

The actual pitches of these syllables would be rather different from each other, as shown on the next page (the higher the number, the higher the pitch):

7		fí						
6				hwέ	á			
5	Kò					krá		
4			hwὲ				á	
3				duàŋ	kà			bá
2						mà ǹ'		
1							dàmfò	

The lowering of the pitch is called **downdrift.** In languages with downdrift—and many tone languages in Africa are downdrift languages—a high tone that occurs after a low tone, or a low tone after a high tone, is lower in pitch than the preceding similarly marked tone. Notice that the first high tone in the sentence is given the pitch value 7. The next high tone (which occurs after an intervening low tone) is 6; that is, it is lower in pitch than the first high tone.

This example shows that in analyzing tones, just as in analyzing segments, all the physical properties need not be considered; only essential features are important in language—in this case, whether the tone is "high" or "low" in relation to the other pitches, but not the specific pitch of that tone.

Languages that are not tone languages, such as English, are called **intonation** languages. The pitch contour of the utterance varies, but in an intonation language as opposed to a tone language pitch is not used to distinguish words from each other. Chapter 6 will discuss **intonation** in greater detail.

Diacritics

In the sections on vowel nasalization, prosodic features, and tone we presented a number of **diacritic** marks which can be used to modify the basic phonetic symbols. A [˜] over the vowel was used to mark vowel nasalization, the doubling of a symbol or a [:] after the symbol to show length, an acute accent to show stress and various accent marks to show tones.

Other diacritics provide additional ways of showing phonetic differences between speech sounds.

To differentiate a voiceless lateral liquid like the sound written *ll* in *Lloyd* as spoken in Welsh, the symbol [̥] is placed under the segmental symbol. Thus in Welsh the name is pronounced [l̥ɔjd] and in English it is pronounced [lɔjd].

Cover symbols are used when a class of sounds are referred to. A capital C is often used to represent the class of consonants, V for the class of vowels, G for glides, and L for liquids. A syllabic consonant may also be specified as C. And a rounded consonant which often occurs before a rounded vowel by a superscript small [ʷ].

We can summarize these diacritics and additional symbols as follows:

C = Consonant   C: = long C   Cʷ = rounded C
V = Vowel   V: = long V   V̂   = nasalized
L = Liquid   L̥   = voiceless   L̩   = syllabic
G = Glide   V́   = stressed V

Tones:

V́ = High   V̀ = Low   V̄ = Mid
V̌ = Rising   V̂ = Falling

Phonetic Symbols for American English Consonants

Table 5.4 classifies the phonetic symbols for American English Consonants according to place and manner of articulation features.

Table 5.5 shows the sound/spelling correspondences for American English consonants and vowels. (Note that all possible spellings are not given; these, however should provide enough examples to help students pair sounds and English orthography.)

Some of these pronunciations may differ from yours, making some of the examples confusing. For example, as mentioned above, some speakers of American English pronounce the words *cot* and *caught* identically. In the dialect described here, *cot* and *caught* are pronounced differently, so *cot* is given as an example for the symbol [a]. Many speakers who pronounce *cot* and *caught* identically pronounce

TABLE 5.4
Classification of Phonetic Symbols for American English Nonvowel Sounds

	Bilabial	Labiodental	Interdental	Alveolar	Palatal	Velar	Glottal
Stop (oral)							
voiceless unaspirated	p			t		k	
voiceless aspirated	pʰ			tʰ		kʰ	
voiced	b			d		g	
Nasal (stop)	m			n		ŋ	
Fricative							
voiceless		f	θ	s	š		
voiced		v	ð	z	ž		
Affricate							
voiceless					č		
voiced					ǰ		
Glide							
voiceless						ʍ	h
voiced					j	w	
Liquid				l r			

TABLE 5.5
Phonetic Symbol/English Spelling Correspondences

Consonants

Symbol	Examples
p	s*p*it ti*p* a*pp*le am*p*le
pʰ	*p*it *p*rick *p*laque ap*p*ear
b	*b*it ta*b* *b*rat *b*u*bb*le
m	*m*itt ta*m* s*m*ack E*mm*y ca*m*p co*mb*
t	s*t*ick pi*t* kiss*ed* wri*t*e
tʰ	*t*ick in*t*end p*t*erodactyl a*tt*ack
d	*D*ick ca*d* *d*rip love*d* ri*d*e
n	*n*ick ki*n* s*n*ow *mn*emo*n*ic *gn*ostic *pn*eumatic *kn*ow
k	s*k*in sti*ck* s*c*at criti*que* e*x*ceed
kʰ	*c*url *k*in *ch*arisma *c*ritic me*ch*anic *c*lose
g	*g*irl bur*g* lon*g*er Pittsbur*gh*
ŋ	si*ng* thi*n*k fi*n*ger
f	*f*at *ph*iloso*ph*y *f*lat *ph*logiston co*ff*ee ree*f* cou*gh*
v	*v*at do*v*e gra*v*el
s	*s*ip *s*kip *p*sychology pas*s* pat*s* democra*cy* *sc*issors fa*s*ten de*c*eive de*s*cent
z	*z*ip ja*zz* ra*z*or pad*s* kis*s*es *X*erox de*s*ign la*z*y sci*ss*ors mai*ze*
θ	*th*igh *th*rough wra*th* e*th*er Ma*tth*ew
ð	*th*y *th*eir wea*th*er la*the* ei*th*er
š	*sh*oe mu*sh* mi*ss*ion na*t*ion fi*sh* gla*ci*al *s*ure
ž	mea*s*ure vi*s*ion a*z*ure ca*s*ual deci*s*ion rou*ge* (for those who do not pronounce this word with the final sound of *judge*)
č	*ch*oke ma*tch* fea*t*ure ri*ch* righ*t*eous
ǰ	*j*udge mi*dg*et *G*eorge ma*g*istrate resi*d*ual
l	*l*eaf fee*l* ca*ll* sing*le*
r	*r*eef fea*r* Pa*r*is singe*r*
j	*y*ou *y*es f*eu*d *u*se
w	*w*itch s*w*im q*u*een
ʍ	*wh*ich *wh*ere *wh*ale (for speakers who pronounce *which* differently than *witch*)
h	*h*at *wh*o *wh*ole re*h*ash
	bo*tt*le bu*tt*on glo*tt*al (for some speakers)

Vowels

i	b*ee*t b*ea*t b*e* rec*ei*ve k*ey* bel*ie*ve am*oe*ba p*eo*ple C*ae*sar Vasel*i*ne ser*e*ne
ɪ	b*i*t cons*i*st *i*njury b*i*n
e	b*a*te b*ai*t r*ay* gr*ea*t *ei*ght g*au*ge r*ei*gn th*ey*
ɛ	b*e*t ser*e*nity s*ay*s g*ue*st d*ea*d s*ai*d
æ	p*a*n *a*ct l*au*gh comr*a*de
u	b*oo*t l*u*te wh*o* s*ew*er thr*ough* t*o* t*oo* tw*o* m*o*ve L*ou*
ʊ	p*u*t f*oo*t b*u*tcher c*oul*d
ʌ	c*u*t t*ou*gh am*o*ng *o*ven d*oe*s c*o*ver fl*oo*d
o	c*oa*t g*o* b*eau* gr*ow* th*ough* t*oe* *ow*n *o*ver
ɔ	c*augh*t st*a*lk c*o*re s*aw* b*a*ll *awe*
a	c*o*t f*a*ther p*a*lm serg*ea*nt h*o*nor h*o*spital mel*o*dic
ə	sof*a* *a*lone symph*o*ny s*u*ppose mel*o*dy tedi*ou*s th*e* Americ*a*
aj	b*i*te s*igh*t b*y* d*ie* d*ye* St*ei*n *ai*sle ch*oi*r l*i*ar *is*land h*ei*ght s*ig*n
aw, æw	ab*ou*t br*ow*n d*ou*bt c*ow*ard
ɔj	b*oy* d*oi*ly

car and *core* with different vowels. If you use the vowel of *car* to say *cot* and the vowel of *core* to say *caught* you will be approximating the dialect that distinguishes the two words. There are also a number of English dialects in which an *r* sound is not pronounced unless it occurs before a vowel. Speakers of this dialect would pronounce the word *car* without the [r]. The selection of the dialect used in this book is rather arbitrary; it is in fact a mixture of a number of dialects in an attempt to provide at least the major symbols that can be used to describe dialects of American English. We are aware that this may present problems for speakers of different dialects and we apologize for this but we have not figured out a way to solve this problem satisfactorily.

The symbols given in the list are not sufficient to represent the pronunciation of words in all languages. The symbol [x], for example, is needed for the voiceless velar fricative in the German word *Bach,* and [ʁ] for the French uvular fricative. English does not have rounded front vowels, but languages such as French and Swedish do. French front rounded vowels can be symbolized as follows:

[y] as in *tu* [ty] "you" (singular)	The tongue position as for [i] but the lips are rounded
[ø] as in *bleu* [blø] "blue"	The tongue position as for [e] but the lips are rounded
[œ] as in *heure* "hour"	The tongue position as in [ɛ] but the lips are rounded

The phonetic properties and features we have discussed are broad terms covering many even finer distinctions. In this chapter we are merely attempting to present a general view as to how such phonetic properties differentiate the sounds found in human languages, and how they are produced.

Summary

The science of speech sounds is called **phonetics**. It aims to provide the set of features or properties that can be used to describe and distinguish all the sounds used in human language.

When we speak, the physical sounds we produce are continuous stretches of sound, which are the physical representations of strings of **discrete linguistic segments.**

The discrepancy between spelling and sounds in English and other languages motivated the development of **phonetic alphabets** in which one letter corresponds to one sound. The major phonetic alphabet in use is that of the **International Phonetic Association (IPA)** which includes modified Roman letters and diacritics by means of which the sounds of all human languages can be represented.

All human speech sounds fall into classes according to their phonetic properties or features; that is, according to how they are produced. During the production of **voiced** sounds the vocal cords are together and vibrating whereas in **voiceless** sounds the vocal cords or glottis is open and non-vibrating. Voiceless sounds may also be **aspirated** or **unaspirated**. Classes of sounds which differ according to their **manner of articulation** also include **oral** and **nasal** sounds, **continuants** or **stops. Non-sonorant continuants** are **fricatives;** the class of **sonorant** continuants include, **vowels, glides,** and **liquids.**

Speech sounds also are distinguished according to **place of articulation** including **labial, alveolar, palatal** (or **palatoalveolar**), **velar, uvular,** and **glottal** sounds.

Vowels form the nucleus of syllables and are therefore **syllabic.** They differ according to the position of the tongue and lips: **high, mid,** or **low** tongue; **front** or **back** of the tongue; **rounded** or **unrounded** lips.

Length, pitch and **loudness** are **prosodic** or **suprasegmental** features which also differentiate sounds. The vowels in English may be **long** or **short, stressed** (longer, higher in pitch and louder) or **unstressed.** In many languages the pitch of the vowel or syllable is linguistically significant in distinguishing the meaning of words. Such languages are called **tone** languages as opposed to **intonation** languages in which pitch is never used to contrast words.

Diacritics to specify such properties as **nasalization, length, voicelessness, syllabicity, stress, tone,** or **rounding** may be combined with the phonetic symbols for more detailed phonetic transcriptions.

By means of these phonetic features one can describe all speech sounds. There are general and regular processes (rules) in languages of the world that utilize the classes of sounds distinguished by these phonetic properties.

References For Further Reading

Abercrombie, David. 1967. *Elements of General Phonetics*. Chicago: Aldine.

Catford, J.C. 1977. *Fundamental Problems in Phonetics*. Bloomington, Indiana: Indiana University Press.

Clark, John, and Colin Yallop. 1990. *An Introduction to Phonetics and Phonology*. Oxford: Blackwell.

Crystal, David. 1985. *A Dictionary of Linguistics and Phonetics*. Oxford: Blackwell.

International Phonetic Association. 1989. *Principles of the International Phonetics Association,* rev. ed. London: IPA.

Ladefoged, Peter. 1993. *A Course in Phonetics,* 3rd ed. Fort Worth: Harcourt Brace Jovanovich.

MacKay, Ian R.A. 1987. *Phonetics: The Science of Speech Production,* 2nd ed. Boston: Little Brown.

Pullum, Geoffrey K. and William A. Ladusaw. 1986. *Phonetic Symbol Guide*. Chicago: University of Chicago Press.

Exercises

1. Write the phonetic symbol for the first sound in each of the following words, according to the way you pronounce it.

Examples: ooze [u]   psycho   [s]

a. judge	[ ]	f. thought	[ ]
b. Thomas	[ ]	g. contact	[ ]
c. though	[ ]	h. phone	[ ]
d. easy	[ ]	i. civic	[ ]
e. pneumonia	[ ]	j. usury	[ ]

2. Write the phonetic symbol for the *last* sound in each of the following words:

a. fleece	[ ]	f. cow	[ ]
b. neigh	[ ]	g. rough	[ ]
c. long	[ ]	h. cheese	[ ]
d. health	[ ]	i. bleached	[ ]
e. watch	[ ]	j. rags	[ ]

3. Write the following words in phonetic transcription, according to your pronunciation.

Example: gnome [nõm]

a. physics	f. marry
b. merry	g. tease
c. weather	h. heath
d. coat	i. Mary
e. yellow	j. "your name"

4. Below is a phonetic transcription of one of the verses in the poem "The Walrus and the Carpenter" by Lewis Carroll. The speaker who transcribed it may not have exactly the same pronunciation as you; there are many alternate correct versions. However, there is *one* major error in each line that is an impossible pronunciation for any American English speaker. The error may consist of an extra symbol, a missing symbol, or a wrong symbol in the word.

Write the word in which the error occurs in the *correct* phonetic transcription.

Corrected Word

a. ðə tʰãjm hæz cʌm   [kʰʌm   ]

b. ðə wɔlrəs sed

  c. tʰu tʰɔlk əv mɛ̃ni θĩŋz
  d. əv šuz ãnd šɪps
  e. æ̃nd silĩŋ wæx
  f. əv kʰæbəgəz æ̃nd kʰĩnz
  g. æ̃nd waj ðə si ɪs bɔjlĩŋ hat
  h. æ̃nd wɛθər pʰɪgz hæv wĩŋz

5. Write the symbol that corresponds to each of the following phonetic descriptions; then give an English word that contains this sound.

>   Example: voiced alveolar stop   [d]   *dog*

  a. voiceless bilabial unaspirated stop
  b. low front vowel
  c. lateral liquid
  d. velar nasal
  e. voiced interdental fricative
  f. voiceless affricate
  g. palatal glide
  h. mid lax front vowel
  i. high back tense vowel

6. In each of the following pairs of words, the bold italicized sounds differ by one or more phonetic properties (features). State the differences and, in addition, state what properties they have in common.

>   Example: phone–phonic   The *o* in *phone* is mid, tense, round.
>   The *o* in *phonic* is low, unround.
>   Both are back vowels.

  a. ba*th*–ba*th*e
  b. redu*c*e–redu*c*tion
  c. c*oo*l–c*o*ld
  d. wi*f*e–wi*v*es
  e. cat*s*–dog*s*
  f. i*m*polite–i*n*decent

7. Write a phonetic transcription of the italized words in the following stanzas from a poem by Richard Krogh.

I take it you already ***know***
Of ***tough*** and ***bough*** and ***cough*** and ***dough?***
Some may stumble, but not ***you,***
On ***hiccough, thorough, slough*** and ***through?***
So now you are ready, perhaps,

To learn of less familiar traps?
Beware of *heard,* a dreadful *word*
That looks like *beard* and sounds like *bird.*
And *dead;* it's *said* like *bed,* not *bead;*
For goodness' sake, don't call it *deed!*
Watch out for *meat* and *great* and *threat.*
(They rhyme with *suite* and *straight* and *debt.*)
A *moth* is not a moth in *mother,*
Nor *both* in *bother, broth* in *brother.*

8. For each group of sounds listed below, state the phonetic feature or features which they all share.

       Example: [p] [b] [m]   Feature: labial, stop, consonant

  a. [g] [p] [t] [d] [k] [b]
  b. [u] [ʊ] [o] [ɔ]
  c. [i] [ɪ] [e] [ɛ] [æ]
  d. [t] [s] [š] [p] [k] [č] [f] [h]
  e. [v] [z] [ž] [j] [ŋ] [g] [d] [b] [l] [r] [w] [ǰ]
  f. [t] [d] [s] [š] [n] [č] [ǰ]

9. Match the sounds under column A with one or more phonetic properties from column B as illustrated in the first one.

A	B
[u] 5, 8	1. velar
[θ]	2. nasal
[s]	3. coronal
[b]	4. stop
[l]	5. rounded
[t]	6. voiceless
[a]	7. back
[m]	8. liquid
	9. labial

10. Write the following sentences in regular English spelling.

  a. nõm čãmski ɪz ə līŋgwɪst hu tʰičəz æt ɛ̃m aj tʰi
  b. fõnɛtɪks ɪz ðə stʌdi ʌv spič sãw̃ndz
  c. ɔl lǽŋgwɪǰəz juz sãw̃ndz pʰrodust baj ðə ʌpər rɛspərətɔri sɪstə̃m

d. ɪn wʌn dajəlɛkt ʌv ɪ̃ŋglɪš kʰat ðə nãw̃n ænd kʰɔt ðə vʌrb ar pʰronãw̃nst ðə sẽm

e. sʌm pʰipəl θɪ̃ŋk fõnɛtɪks ɪz vɛri ɪ̃ntərɛstɪ̃ŋ

f. vɪktɔrijə frãmkɪn ænd rabərt radmə̃n ar ðə ɔθərz ʌv ðɪs tɛksbʊk

11. What phonetic property or feature distinguish the sets of sounds in column A from those in Column B.

A	B	
[i] [ɪ]	[u] [ʊ]	_____
[p] [t] [k] [s] [f]	[b] [d] [g] [z] [v]	_____
[p] [b] [m]	[t] [d] [n] [k] [g] [ŋ]	_____
[i] [ɪ] [u] [ʊ]	[e] [ɛ] [o] [ɔ] [æ] [a]	_____
[f] [v] [s] [z] [š] [ž]	[č] [ǰ]	_____
[b] [d] [g] [z] [ǰ]	[l] [r] [m] [n] [ŋ]	_____
[i] [ɪ] [e] [ɛ] [æ]	[u] [ʊ] [o] [ɔ] [a]	_____

CHAPTER 6
Phonology: The Sound Patterns of Language

Speech is human, silence is divine, yet also brutish and dead; therefore we must learn both arts.

Thomas Carlyle (1795–1881)

Phonology is the study of telephone etiquette.

A high school student[1]

Linguists are interested in how sound systems may vary, and in the ways they are similar, in the phonetic and phonological universals found in all languages. The same relatively small set of phonetic properties or features characterizes all human speech sounds; the same classes of these sounds are utilized in languages spoken from the Arctic Circle to the Cape of Good Hope, and the same kinds of regular patterns of speech sounds occur all over the world. When you learn a language, you learn which speech sounds occur in your language and how they pattern according to regular rules.

Phonology is concerned with this kind of linguistic knowledge. Phonetics is a part of phonology, and, as discussed in the previous chapter, provides the means for describing speech sounds; phonologists study the ways in which these speech sounds form systems and patterns in human language. The phonology of a language is then the system and pattern of the speech sounds. We see that the word *phonology* is used in two ways, either as the *study* of sound patterns in language or as *the sound patterns* themselves.

Phonological knowledge permits a speaker to produce sounds which form meaningful utterances, to recognize a foreign "accent," to make up new words, to add the appropriate phonetic segments to form plurals and past tenses, to produce "aspirated" and "unaspirated" voiceless stops in the appropriate context, to know what is or is not a sound in one's language, and to know that different phonetic strings may represent the same "meaningful unit." Since the grammar of the language represents the totality of one's linguistic knowledge, knowledge of the sound patterns—the phonological component—must be part of this grammar. In this chapter we shall discuss the kinds of things that speakers know about the sound system of their language—their phonological knowledge.

[1]As reported in Amsel Greene, *Pullet Surprises,* Glenview, Ill.: Scott, Foresman & Co., 1969.

216

Phonemes: The Phonological Units of Language

> In the physical world the naive speaker and hearer actualize and are sensitive to sounds, but what they feel themselves to be pronouncing and hearing are "phonemes."
>
> Edward Sapir, 1933

Phonological knowledge goes beyond the ability to produce all the phonetically different sounds of a language. It includes this ability, of course. A speaker of English can produce the sound [θ] and knows that this sound occurs in English, in words like *thin* [θĭn], *ether* [iθər], or *bath* [bæθ]. English speakers may or may not be able to produce a "click" or a velar fricative, but even if they can, they know that such sounds are not part of the phonetic inventory of English. Many speakers are unable to produce such "foreign" sounds. French speakers similarly know that [θ] is not part of the phonetic inventory of French and often find it difficult to pronounce a word like *thin* [θĭn], pronouncing it [sĭn].

An English speaker also knows that [ð], the voiced counterpart of [θ], is a sound of English, occurring in words like *either* [iðər], *then* [ðɛ̆n], and *bathe* [beð].

Knowing the sounds (the phonetic units) of a language is only a small part of phonological knowledge.

In Chapters 1 and 2 we discussed the fact that knowing a language implies knowing the set of words that comprise the vocabulary, or lexicon, of that language. You might know fewer or more words than your next-door neighbor, but each word you have learned is stored in your memory as part of the grammar of the language. When you know a word, you know both its **form** (the sounds that represent it) and its **meaning.** We have already seen that the relationship between the form and the meaning of a word is arbitrary. You must learn both: knowing the meaning does not tell you its pronunciation, and knowing how to say it does not tell you what it means (if you did not know already).

Consider the forms and meanings of the following English words:

sip	fine	chunk
zip	vine	junk

Each word differs from the other words in both form and meaning. The difference between *sip* and *zip* is "signaled" by the fact that the initial sound of the first word is *s* [s] and the initial sound of the second word is *z* [z]. The forms of the two words—that is, their sounds—are identical except for the initial consonants. [s] and [z] can therefore distinguish or contrast words. They are distinctive sounds in English. Such distinctive sounds are called **phonemes.**

We see from the contrast between *fine* and *vine* and between *chunk* and *junk* that [f], [v], [č], and [ǰ] must also be phonemes in English for the same reason—because substituting a [v] for [f] or a [č] for [ǰ] produces a different word.

Minimal Pairs

A first rule of thumb to determine the phonemes of any language is to see whether substituting one sound for another results in a different word. If it does, the two sounds represent different phonemes. When two different forms are identical in every way except for one sound segment that occurs in the same place in the string, the two words are called a **minimal pair.** *Sink* and *zink* are a minimal pair, as are *fine* and *vine,* and *chunk* and *junk.* Note that *seed* [sid] and *soup* [sup] are not a minimal pair because they differ in two sounds, the vowels and the final consonants. Nor are *bar* [bar] and *rod* [rad] a minimal pair because although only one sound differs in the two words, the [b] occurs initially and the [d] occurs finally. Of course we can find many minimal pairs which show that [b] and [d] are phonemes in English:

beed	[bid]	*deed*	[did]
bowl	[bol]	*dole*	[dol]
rube	[rub]	*rude*	[rud]
lobe	[lob]	*load*	[lod]

Substituting a [d] for a [b] changes both the phonetic form and its meaning. [b] and [d] also contrast with [g] as is shown by the following:

bill/dill/gill   rib/rid/rig

Therefore [b], [d], and [g] are all phonemes in English and *bill, dill,* and *gill* constitute a **minimal set.** We have many minimal sets in English, which makes it relatively "easy" to determine what the English phonemes are. All the following words are identical except for the vowels; therefore each vowel represents a phoneme.

beat	[bit]	[i]	boot	[but]	[u]
bit	[bɪt]	[ɪ]	but	[bʌt]	[ʌ]
bait	[bet]	[e]	boat	[bot]	[o]
bet	[bɛt]	[ɛ]	bought	[bɔt]	[ɔ]
bat	[bæt]	[æ]	bout	[bawt]	[aw]
bite	[bajt]	[aj]	bot[2]	[bat]	[a]

It can also be demonstrated that [ʊ] and [ɔj], which are not part of the minimal set listed above, are phonemes of English by other minimal pairs in which these vowels contrast meanings, such as *book* [bʊk] and *beak* [bik], *look* [lʊk] and *leak* [lik], *boy* [bɔj] and *buy* [baj], or *soil* [sɔjl] and *sail* [sel]. Note that in Chapter 5, the diphthong

---

[2]A *bot* is the larva of a botfly.

[ɔj], and also the diphthongs [aj] and [aw] were considered to be single vowel sounds although each includes an off-glide. This is why they are included as single phonemes in the minimal sets above. A further illustration of how they contrast is shown in the set:

bile   bowel   boil
[bajl]   [bawl]   [bɔjl]

As the B.C. cartoon shows, the contrasts among

crick   [ɪ]   *creek*   [i]   *crook*   [ʊ]   *croak*   [o]

illustrate that there are other minimal sets in English. *Crack* [æ], *crock* [a], and *crake* [e] (a short-billed bird) are also members of this contrasting set.

By permission of Johnny Hart and Creators Syndicate, Inc.

For some speakers, *crick* and *creek* are pronounced identically, another example of regional dialect differences; but most speakers of this dialect still contrast the vowels in *beat* and *bit,* so these high front vowels are phonemes in their dialect. Although [bat], for some speakers, and [bʊt] are not actual words in English, they are sequences or strings of sounds, all of which represent phonemes, and the sequences of these phonemes are permissible in English. (We will discuss permissible sequences below.) We might then say that they are **nonsense words** (permissible forms with no meanings) or **possible words.** Similarly, *creck* [krɛk], *cruke* [kruk], *cruk* [krʌk], and *crike* [krajk] are nonexistent but possible words in English.

Madison Avenue advertisers constantly take advantage of the fact that they can use possible but nonoccurring words for the names of new products. We would hardly expect a new product to come on the market with the name [xik], because [x] (the voiceless velar fricative) is not a phoneme in English. Nor would a new soap be called *Zhleet* [žlit], because in English, the voiced palatal fricative [ž] can not occur initially before a liquid. Possible but nonoccurring words such as *Bic* [bɪk], before it was coined as a brand name, are **accidental gaps** in the vocabulary. An accidental gap is a form that "obeys" all the phonological rules of the language—it includes native phonemes in a permitted order—but has no meaning. An actual, occurring word is a combination of both a permitted form and a meaning.

Further examples of minimal pairs in English provide evidence for other phonemes. Change in the phonetic form produces a different word. When such a change is the result of the substitution of just one sound segment, the two different segments must represent different phonemes. There is no other way to account for these particular meaning contrasts.

In trying to determine the set of contrastive phonemes in a language it is not always possible to find minimal pairs, because there may be accidental gaps. For example, in English, there are very few minimal pairs in which the phonemes [θ] and [ð] contrast; they occur medially in *ether* and *either* and finally in *teeth* and *teethe* and in a few more pairs. (See if you can think of them.) But even if these pairs did not occur, we find that [θ] and [ð] each contrasts with other sounds in the language, for example *thick* [θɪk] / *sick* [sɪk] and *though* [ðo] / *dough* [do], we can conclude that these two sounds are contrastive in English and are therefore phonemes. Note also that one cannot substitute the voiced and voiceless interdental fricatives in the words in which they do occur without producing nonsense forms; for example, if we substitute the voiced [ð] for the voiceless [θ] in *thick,* we get [ðɪk] which has no meaning.

Free Variation

In Chapter 5 we noted that some speakers of English substitute a glottal stop for the [t] at the end of words such as *don't* or *can't* or in the middle of words like *bottle* or *button*. The substitution of the glottal stop does not change the meanings; [dõnt] and [dõnʔ] do not **contrast** in meaning, nor do [batəl] or [baʔəl]. A glottal stop is therefore not a phoneme in English since it is not a distinctive sound. These sounds [t] and [ʔ] are in **free variation** in these words.

Similarly, at the end of a word, a stop consonant may be released or unreleased. That is, it will not change the meaning of the word *rope* if in pronouncing it, you keep your lips together or open them. An unreleased stop is transcribed phonetically with the diacritic [˺] after it, as [rop˺]. Thus in English unreleased stops do not contrast with released stops. Released and unreleased stops occur in **free variation.** You may freely use one or the other. Released stops are not distinct phonemes in English.

There is another way in which two sounds may be in free variation. In English a substitution of [i] for [ɛ] in *economics* does not change the meaning of the word. Some speakers pronounce the word with an initial [i] and others with an initial [ɛ]. However, [i] and [ɛ] are not in free variation in other words, since we can not substitute [i] and [ɛ] for each other in other words, such as *beat* [bit] and *bet* [bɛt]. *Did you beat the drum?* does not mean the same thing as *Did you bet the drum?* An old song of the 1930s was based on the notion of free variation:

> You say either [iðər] and I say [ajðər],
> You say [niðər] and I say [najðər],
> [iðər] [ajðər] [niðər] [najðər],
> let's call the whole thing off.

Distinctive Features

Even if we do not consciously know which phonetic properties or features distinguish the contrasting sounds, we know which sound segments represent phonemes in the phonological system of our language. Phonetics provides the means to describe these sounds, showing how they differ; phonology tells us which sounds function as phonemes to contrast the meanings of words.

In order for two phonetic forms to differ and to contrast meanings, there must be some phonetic difference between the substituted sounds. The minimal pairs *seal* [sil] and *zeal* [zil] show that [s] and [z] represent two contrasting phonemes in English. From the discussion of phonetics in Chapter 5, we know that the only difference between [s] and [z] is a voicing difference; [s] is voiceless and [z] is voiced. It is this phonetic feature that distinguishes the two words. Voicing thus plays a special role in English (and in many other languages). It also distinguishes *feel* and *veal* [f]/[v] and *cap* and *cab* [p]/[b]. When a feature distinguishes one phoneme from another it is a **distinctive feature** (or a phonemic feature). When two words are exactly alike phonetically except for one feature, the phonetic difference is **distinctive,** since this difference alone accounts for the contrast or difference in meaning.

Binary Valued Features

Note that one can think of voicing or voicelessness as the presence or absence of a **single feature,** voicing. A feature can be thought of as having two values, + which signifies its presence and − which signifies its absence. [b] is therefore [+voiced] and [p] is [−voiced]. Similarly, the presence or absence of nasality can be designated as [+nasal] or [−nasal] (oral), with [m] being [+nasal] and [b] or [p] being [−nasal]. All the phonetic features can be specified in this manner.

The phonetic symbols we have been using are therefore **cover symbols** for a set or bundle of distinctive features, a shorthand method of specifying the phonetic properties of the segment. A more explicit description of [p][b][m] may thus be given as:

	p	b	m
Stop	+	+	+
Labial	+	+	+
Voiced	−	+	+
Nasal	−	−	+

A phonetic feature is distinctive when the + value of that feature found in certain words contrasts with the − value of that feature in other words.

The minimal pairs given below illustrate some of the distinctive features in the phonological system of English.

bat	[bæt]	mat	[mæt]	The difference between *bat* and *mat* is due only to the difference in nasality between [b] and [m]. [b] and [m] are identical in all features except for the fact that [b] is oral or [−nasal] and [m] is nasal or [+ nasal]. Therefore nasality or [±nasal] is a distinctive feature of English consonants.
rack	[ræk]	rock	[rak]	The two words are distinguished only because [æ] is a front vowel and [a] is a back vowel. They are both low, unrounded vowels. [±back] is therefore a distinctive feature of English vowels.
see	[si]	zee	[zi]	The difference is due to the voicelessness of the [s] in contrast to the voicing of the [z]. Therefore voicing ([± voiced]) is a distinctive feature of English consonants.

Sounds That Are Not Phonemes

In Chapter 5 it was shown that *phonetically* both oral and nasalized vowels occur in English. The following examples show this.

bean	[bĩn]	bead	[bid]
roam	[rõm]	robe	[rob]

Nasalized vowels occur in English syllables only before nasal consonants. If one substituted an oral vowel for the nasal vowels in *bean* and *roam* the meanings of the two words would not be changed. Try to say these words keeping your velum up until your tongue makes the stop closure of the [n] or your lips come together for the [m]. It will not be easy because in English we automatically lower the velum when producing vowels before nasals in the same syllable.

There is a general principle or **rule** in the phonology of English that tells us when nasalized vowels occur—always before [+nasal] consonants, never before [−nasal] oral consonants. This shows that the oral vowels in English differ phonemically from each other whereas the differences between the oral vowels and their nasal counterparts do not. This is because there is no principle or rule to predict when for example [i] occurs instead of [e] or [u] or [a] or any of the other vowel phonemes. We must learn that [i] occurs in *beat* and [e] in *bait*. We do not have to learn that the nasalized version of [i] occurs in *beam, bean, bing* ([bĩm] [bĩn] [bĩŋ]) or that the nasalized [u] occurs in *boom* [bũm] or *boon* [bũn]. Rather, we generalize from the occurrences of oral and nasal vowels in English that [i] and [u] are nasalized before nasal consonants, as are all the other vowels.

The rule, or general principle, that predicts when a vowel phoneme will be realized as an oral vowel phone and when the same vowel phoneme will be a nasalized phone is exemplified in the following sets of words and nonwords:

Words					**Nonwords**		
bee	[bi]	bead	[bid]	bean	[bĩn]	*[bĩ]	*[bĩd]	*[bin]
lay	[le]	lace	[les]	lame	[lẽm]	*[lẽ]	*[lẽs]	*[lem]
baa	[bæ]	bad	[bæd]	bang	[bǽŋ]	*[bǽ]	*[bǽd]	*[bæŋ]

As these words illustrate, in English, oral vowels occur in final position and before nonnasal consonants; nasalized vowels occur only before nasal consonants. The "nonwords" show us that nasalized vowels do not occur finally or before nonnasal consonants. Therefore oral vowels and their nasalized counterparts never contrast. Nasalization of vowels in English is predictable by a rule, which can be stated as:

> **Vowel Nasalization Rule: Nasalize a vowel or diphthong (vowel + glide) when it occurs before a nasal consonant.**

The value (+ or −) of the feature [± nasal] is predictable for the class of vowel segments in English. When a feature value is predictable by a general principle or rule, it is not a distinctive or phonemic feature for that class of segments. Therefore, the feature [± nasal] is not a distinctive feature for English vowels, although it is distinctive for English consonants.

We have seen that nasalized vowels do occur phonetically. We can conclude, then, that there is no one-to-one correspondence between phonetic segments and phonemes in a language. From the examples given above we see that one phoneme may be realized phonetically (that is, pronounced) as more than one phonetic segment. Each vowel phoneme in English is realized as either an oral vowel or a nasal vowel, depending on its context.

Phonemes, Phones, and Allophones

Some new terminology may help to clarify things. A phonetic unit or segment is called a **phone.** A **phoneme** is a more abstract unit. One must know the phonological rules of the language to know how to pronounce a phoneme, since in one context it may be realized as one phone (for example, [i]) and in another context as a different phone (for example, [ĩ]). To distinguish between phonemes and phones we will use slashes / / to enclose phonemic segments or phonemic transcriptions of words and will continue to use the square brackets [ ] for phonetic segments or phonetic transcriptions. Thus, we will represent the vowel phoneme in *bead* and *bean* as /i/ in both words /bid/ and /bin/, respectively. This phoneme is pronounced (or realized) as [i] in *bead* [bid] and [ĩ] in *bean* [bĩn].

Phonemes are the **underlying** mental representations of the phonological units of a language, the units used to represent the forms of words in our mental lexicons. These phonemic **underlying** representations of words, together with the phonological rules of the language, determine their pronunciation.

We have seen that a single phoneme may be phonetically realized or pronounced as two or more phones. The different phones that "represent" or are **derived** from one phoneme are called the **allophones** of that phoneme. An **allophone** is therefore a **predictable phonetic variant** of a phoneme. In English, each vowel phoneme has both an oral and a nasalized allophone. The choice of the allophone is not random or haphazard; it is **rule-governed,** as illustrated by the general principle determining the occurrence of oral and nasalized vowels in English. No one is explicitly taught these rules. They are "constructed" by the learner; language acquisition, to a certain extent, is rule construction. Speakers probably do not know that they know these rules; yet they produce the nasalized allophones of the vowel phonemes automatically whenever they occur before nasal consonants. Much knowledge is unconscious knowledge and requires scientific investigation to understand it.

Complementary Distribution

When two or more sounds never occur in the same phonemic context or environment they are said to be in **complementary distribution.** The examples of the words and nonwords given on page 223 illustrate the complementary distribution of the oral and nasalized allophones of English phonemes. This is further shown in Table 6.1.

When oral vowels occur, nasal vowels do not occur, and vice versa. It is in this sense that the phones are said to complement each other or to be in complementary distribution.

The concept of complementary distribution is illustrated by Clark Kent and Superman, who represent in different form only one person. When Clark Kent is present, Superman is not; when Superman is present, Clark Kent is not. Clark Kent and Superman are therefore in complementary distribution, just as [i] and [ĩ] are in complementary distribution. Of course there is a difference between their "distribution" and the two allophones of the phoneme /i/ since Kent and Superman can occur in the same environment (for example, talking to Lois Lane) whereas [i] and [ĩ] never occur in the same environment or under the same conditions.

One may then define a phoneme as a set of phonetically similar sounds which are in complementary distribution with each other. Note that the phones must be phonetically similar, that is, share most of the same feature values. In English, the velar nasal [ŋ] and the glottal glide [h] are in complementary distribution; [ŋ] is not found word initially and [h] does not occur word finally. But they share very few

TABLE 6.1

Distribution of Oral and Nasal Vowels in English Syllables

	In Final Position	Before Nasal Consonants	Before Oral Consonants
Oral vowels	Yes	No	Yes
Nasal vowels	No	Yes	No

feature values; [ŋ] is a velar nasal voiced stop; [h] is a glottal voiceless glide. Therefore, they are not allophones of the same phoneme; /ŋ/ and /h/ are different phonemes.

Predictability of Redundant Features

When a feature is predictable by rule, it is a **redundant** feature. Nasality is a redundant feature in English vowels, but is a nonredundant (distinctive or phonemic) feature for English consonants. We have to learn that the word meaning "mean" begins with a nasal bilabial stop [m] and that the word meaning "bean" begins with an oral bilabial stop [b]. But we do not have to learn that the vowels in *bean* and *mean* and *comb* and *sing* and so on are nasalized since they occur before nasal consonants and are thus redundantly, predictably nasal.

This is not the case in all languages. In French, nasality is a distinctive feature for both vowels and consonants: *gars* pronounced [ga] "lad" contrasts with *gant* [gã] which means "glove", and *bal* [bal] "dance" contrasts with *mal* [mal] "evil/pain". In Chapter 5, other examples of French nasalized vowels are presented. Thus, French has both oral and nasal consonant phonemes and vowel phonemes; English has oral and nasal consonant phonemes, but only oral vowel phonemes. Both languages, however, have oral and nasal consonant and vowel phones.

In the Ghanaian language Akan (or Twi), nasalized and oral vowels occur both phonetically and phonemically; nasalization is a distinctive feature for vowels in Akan, as the following examples illustrate:

[ka]	"bite"	[kã]	"speak"
[fi]	"come from"	[fĩ]	"dirty"
[tu]	"pull"	[tũ]	"hole/den"
[nsa]	"hand"	[nsã]	"liquor"
[či]	"hate"	[čĩ]	"squeeze"
[pam]	"sew"	[pãm]	"confederate"

These examples show that vowel nasalization is not predictable in Akan. As shown by the last minimal pair—[pam] / [pãm]—there is no rule that nasalizes vowels before nasal consonants. We also find word-final oral vowels contrasting with word-final nasalized vowels (after identical initial consonants). The change of form—the substitution of nasalized for oral vowels, or vice versa—does change the meaning. Both oral and nasal vowel phonemes must therefore exist in Akan.

Notice that two languages may have the same phonetic segments (phones) but have two different phonemic systems. Both oral and nasalized vowels exist in English and Akan phonetically; English has no nasalized vowel phonemes, but Akan does. The same phonetic segments function differently in the two languages. Nasalization of vowels in English is *redundant and nondistinctive;* nasalization of vowels in Akan is *nonredundant and distinctive.*

We can further illustrate the fact that two languages can have the same set of phonetic segments with different phonemic systems by examining the voiceless stops. In the previous chapter we pointed out that in English both aspirated and unaspirated voiceless stops occur. The voiceless aspirated stops [pʰ] [tʰ] [kʰ] and the voiceless unaspirated stops [p] [t] [k] are in complementary distribution in English. Aspiration is a redundant, nondistinctive feature in English; aspiration is predictable as is shown by the environments or contexts in which they occur:

Word (or Syllable) Initially Before a Stressed Vowel			**After a Word (or Syllable) Initial /S/**		
[pʰ]	**[tʰ]**	**[kʰ]**	**[p]**	**[t]**	**[k]**
pill	till	kill	spill	still	skill
[pʰɪl]	[tʰɪl]	[kʰɪl]	[spɪl]	[stɪl]	[skɪl]
par	tar	car	spar	star	scar
[pʰar]	[tʰar]	[kʰar]	[spar]	[star]	[skar]

Despite the phonetic difference between the unaspirated and aspirated phones, speakers of English (if they are not analyzing the sounds as linguists or phoneticians) usually consider the [pʰ] in *pill* and the [p] in *spill* to be the "same" sound, just as they consider the [i] and [ī] that represent the phoneme /i/ in *bead* and *bean* to be the "same." They do so because the difference between them, in this case the feature *aspiration,* is **predictable, redundant, nondistinctive,** and **nonphonemic** (all equivalent terms). The aspirated and the nonaspirated phones are in complementary distribution. Voiceless stops are always aspirated when they occur at the beginning of a syllable before stressed vowels, and they are always unaspirated after an initial /s/. This distribution is a fact about English phonology. There are two *p* sounds (or phones) in English, but only one *p* phoneme. (This arrangement is also true of *t* and *k*.) A phoneme is an **abstract unit.** We do not utter phonemes; we produce phones. /p/ is a phoneme in English that is realized phonetically (pronounced) as either [p] or [pʰ]. [p] and [pʰ] are allophones of the phoneme /p/. Another way of stating this fact is to say that the [p] and [pʰ] are **derived** from /p/ by a rule:

> **Aspiration Rule: Aspirate a voiceless stop—/p/, /t/, or /k/—when it occurs syllable initially before a stressed vowel.**

The discussion on oral and nasalized vowels pointed out that the same phones (phonetic segments) can occur in two languages but pattern differently because the phonemic system is different. Aspiration of voiceless stops further illustrates this fact. Both aspirated and unaspirated voiceless stops occur in English and Thai (the major language spoken in Thailand), but they function differently in the two languages. Aspiration in English is not a phonemic or distinctive feature, because its presence or absence is predictable. In Thai, however, it is not predictable, as the following examples show:

Voiceless		**Voiceless**	
Unaspirated		**Aspirated**	
[paa]	*forest*	[pʰaa]	*to split*
[tam]	*to pound*	[tʰam]	*to do*
[kat]	*to bite*	[kʰat]	*to interrupt*

The voiceless unaspirated and the voiceless aspirated stops in Thai are not in complementary distribution. They occur in the same positions in the minimal pairs above; they contrast and are therefore phonemes in Thai. In both English and Thai the phones [p][t][k][pʰ][tʰ] [kʰ] occur. In English they represent the phonemes /p/ /t/ and /k/; in Thai they represent the phonemes /p/ /t/ /k/ /pʰ/ /tʰ/ /kʰ/. [±aspiration] is a distinctive feature in Thai; it is a nondistinctive redundant feature in English.

The phonetic facts alone do not reveal what is distinctive or phonemic. **The phonetic representation of utterances shows what speakers know about the pronunciation of utterances; the phonemic representation of utterances shows what the speakers know about the abstract underlying phonology.** That *pot*/ *pat* and *spot*/*spat* are transcribed with an identical /p/ reveals the fact that English speakers consider the [pʰ] in *pot* [pʰat] and the [p] in *spot* [spat] to be phonetic manifestations of the same phoneme /p/.

In learning a language a child learns which features are distinctive in that language and which are not. One phonetic feature may be distinctive for one class of sounds but predictable or nondistinctive for another class of sounds, as, for example, the feature nasality in English. [+nasal] is a distinctive feature for English consonants but a nondistinctive, predictable phonetic feature for English vowels. In French, it is distinctive for both consonants and vowels. Aspiration in English is predictable, nondistinctive for any class of sounds.

Unpredictability of Phonemic Features

In Chapter 5, we mentioned in the discussion on prosodic features that the length of a segment (whether a consonant or vowel is long or short) may be linguistically important. We also pointed out that in English, the long vowels /i/ /e/ /u/ /o/ are also higher and tenser than their short vowel counterparts /ɪ/ /ɛ/ /ʊ/ /ɔ/. Since the phonemic long vowels also differ as to the height of the tongue and tenseness, they are qualitatively as well as quantitatively distinct from the short vowels, which is why we use different phonetic symbols to represent them.

In other languages, long and short vowels occur which are identical except for length. Thus, length can be a nonpredictable distinctive feature which must be specified in the underlying phonemic representations of words in which they occur contrastively.

Vowel length is phonemic in Danish, Finnish, Arabic, and Korean. Consider the following "minimal pairs" in Korean:

il	"day"	i:l	"word"
seda	"to count"	se:da	"strong"
kul	"oyster"	ku:l	"tunnel"

Vowel length is also phonemic in Japanese as shown by the following:

| biru | "building" | tsuji | "a proper name" |
| bi:ru | "beer" | tsu:ji | "moving one's bowels" |

When teaching at a university in Japan, one of the authors of this book inadvertantly pronounced Ms. Tsuji's name as Tsu:ji-san. (The -*san* is a suffix used to show respect). The effect of this error quickly taught him to understand the phonemic nature of vowel length in Japanese.

Consonant length also is contrastive in Japanese. A consonant may be lengthened by prolonging the closure: a long *t* [t:] or [tt] can be produced by holding the tongue against the alveolar ridge twice as long as for a short *t* [t]. The following minimal pairs illustrate that length is a phonemic feature for Japanese consonants:

| šite | "doing" | šitte | "knowing" |
| saki | "ahead" | sakki | "before" |

Luganda, an African language, also contrasts long and short consonants; /kkula/ means "treasure" and /kula/ means "grow up". (In both these words the first vowel is produced with a high pitch and the second with a low pitch.)

The Italian word for "grandfather" is *nonno* /nonno/ contrasting with the word for "ninth" which is *nono* /nono/.

In English, consonants may be pronounced long if they occur across word boundaries. Many English speakers will produce a longer closure of the /t/ in *white tie* than in *why tie?* In such cases the [t:] is in free variation with a short [t]. Length is not a distinctive feature for English consonants.

The longer duration of two identical consonants or vowels can be symbolized by the colon, e.g. /t:/ or /a:/ or by doubling the segment, i.e. /tt/ or /aa/. Such long segments are sometimes referred to as **geminates.**

The grammar of a language includes the kind of information we have been discussing: what the distinctive phonemic units of the language are, which phonetic features are phonemic or distinctive, and which are nonphonemic or predictable. These phonological facts are represented by the underlying phonemic representations and the phonological rules specifying the occurrence of nondistinctive phonetic features, that is, the allophones of the underlying phonemes. Thus, a grammar of French would not include a /θ/ as part of the phonemic representation of any word, just as a grammar of English would not include an /x/. English would have one voiceless labial stop phoneme, /p/, but Thai would have two, /p/ and /pʰ/. Both would include /b/. These examples show that two languages may have the same phonetic segments but a different set of phonemes. The grammar must account for both the phonemes in the language and the way they are pronounced.

More on Redundancies

The value of some features of a single phoneme is predictable or redundant due to the specification of the other features of that segment. That is, given the presence of certain feature values one can predict the value of other features in that segment.

In English, as pointed out in the preceding chapter, all front vowels are predictably nonround, and the nonlow back vowels are predictably round. Unlike French, there are no rounded front vowels in English. We can thus say that if a vowel in English is specified as [−back] it is also redundantly, predictably [−round]. There is no need to specify the value of redundant features in the phonemic representation of words. In marking the feature values for [−back] vowels in English, one can, then, omit the [−round] marking. A blank would indicate that the value of that feature is predictable by a phonological rule of the language.

Similarly, in English all nasal consonant phonemes are predictably voiced. Thus voicing is nondistinctive for nasal consonants and need not be specified in marking the value of the voicing feature for this set of phonemes. Phonetically in English, the nasal phonemes may be devoiced when they occur after a syllable initial /s/ as in *snoop,* which phonemically is /snup/ and phonetically may be [snup]. The devoicing is, however, predictable from the context.

This can be accounted for by the following:

Redundancy Rule: If a phoneme is [+nasal] it is also [+voiced].

In Burmese, however we find the following minimal pairs:

| /ma/ | [ma] | "health" | /m̥a/ | [m̥a] | "order" |
| /na/ | [na] | "pain" | /n̥a/ | [n̥a] | "nostril" |

The fact that some nasal phonemes are [+voiced] and others [−voiced] must be specified in Burmese; the English redundancy rule does not occur in the grammar of Burmese. We can illustrate this phonological difference between English and Burmese in the following phonemic distinctive feature **matrices:**

	Burmese:	**/m/**	**/m̥/**	**English:**	**/m/**
Nasal		+	+		+
Labial		+	+		+
Voicing		+	−		

Note that the value for the voicing feature is left blank for the English phoneme /m/ since the [+] value for this feature is specified by the redundancy rule given above.

As noted earlier, the value of some features in a segment is predictable because of the segments which precede or follow; the phonological context determines the value of the feature rather than the presence of other feature values in that segment. Aspiration cannot be predicted in isolation but only when a voiceless stop occurs in a word, since the presence or absence of the feature depends on where the voiceless stop occurs and what precedes or follows it. It is determined by its phonemic environment. Similarly, the oral or nasal quality of a vowel depends on its environment. If it is followed by a nasal consonant it is predictably [+nasal].

For certain classes of sounds, the values of some features are **universally** implied for all languages. Thus, all stops—[− continuant] segments—are universally and predictably [− syllabic], regardless of their phonemic context.

Sequential Constraints

Drawing by Jack Ziegler, © 1986 The New Yorker Magazine, Inc.

Suppose you were given four cards, each of which had a different phoneme of English printed on it:

k   b   l   ɪ

If you were asked to arrange these cards to form all the "possible" words that these four phonemes could form, you might order them as follows:

b   l   ɪ   k
k   l   ɪ   b
b   ɪ   l   k
k   ɪ   l   b

These arrangements are the only permissible ones for these phonemes in English. */lbkɪ/, */ɪlbk/, */bkɪl/, and */ɪlkb/ are not possible words in the language. Although /blɪk/ and /klɪb/ are not existing words (you will not find them in a dictionary), if you heard someone say:

"I just bought a beautiful new *blick.*"

you might ask: "What's a 'blick'?" If you heard someone say:

"I just bought a beautiful new *bkli.*"

you would probably reply, "What did you say?"

Your knowledge of English "tells" you that certain strings of phonemes are permissible and others are not. After a consonant like /b/, /g/, /k/, or /p/, another stop consonant is not permitted by the rules of the grammar. If a word begins with an /l/ or an /r/, every speaker "knows" that the next segment must be a vowel. That is why */lbɪk/ does not sound like an English word. It violates the restrictions on the sequencing of phonemes.

Other such constraints exist in English. If the initial sounds of *chill* or *Jill* begin a word, the next sound must be a vowel. /čat/ or /čon/ or /čæk/ are possible words in English, as are /ǰæl/ or /ǰot/ or /ǰalɪk/, but */člit/ and */ǰpurz/ are not. No more than three sequential consonants can occur at the beginning of a word, and these three are restricted to /s/ + /p, t, k/ + /l, r, w, y/. There are even restrictions if this condition is met. For example, /stl/ is not a permitted sequence, so *stlick* is not a possible word in English, but *strick* is.

Other languages have different sequential restrictions. In Polish *zl* is a permissible combination, as in *zloty,* a unit of currency.

Syllable Structure

The constraints on sequences of segments are called **phonotactic** constraints or simply the phonotactics of the language. If we examine the phonotactics of English we find that word phonotactics are in fact based on syllable phonotactics. That is, only the clusters that can begin a syllable can begin a word, and only a cluster that can end a syllable can end a word. Medially in a multisyllabic word, the clusters consist of a syllable final + syllable initial sequences. Words like *instruct*/ɪnstrʌkt/ with the medial cluster /nstr/ or *explicit*/ɛksplɪsɪt/with the medial cluster /kspl/ can be divided into well-formed syllables /ɪn $ strʌkt/ and /ɛk $ splɪs $ ɪt/ (using $ to symbolize a syllable boundary). We, as speakers of English, know that "constluct" is not a possible word because the second syllable starts with a nonpermissible sequence /stl/ or /tl/. Syllables, then, are important phonological units.

All languages have constraints on the permitted sequences of phonemes though different languages have different constraints. Children learn these rules when they learn the language, just as they learn what the phonemes are and how they are related to phonetic segments. In Asante Twi, a word may end only in a vowel or a nasal consonant. /pik/ is not a possible Twi word, because it breaks the sequential rules of the language, and /ŋŋu/ is not a possible word in English for similar reasons, although it is an actual word in Twi.

Speakers of all languages have the same kinds of knowledge. They know what sounds are part of the language, what the phonemes are, and what phonemic and phonetic sequences may occur. The specific sounds and sound sequences may differ, but the phonological systems include similar kinds of rules.

Natural Classes

The rules in English phonology which determine the conditions under which vowels are nasalized or voiceless stops are aspirated are general rules. They apply to classes of sounds. They also apply to all the words in the vocabulary of the language, and they even apply to nonsense words that are not in the language but could enter the language (like *sint, peeg,* or *sparg,* which would be /sɪnt/, /pig/ and /sparg/ phonemically and [sĩnt], [pʰig] and [sparg] phonetically.

There are also less general rules found in all languages and there may also be exceptions to these general rules. But what is of greater interest is that the more we examine the phonologies of the many thousands of languages of the world, the more we find similar phonological rules which apply to the same broad general classes of sounds, like the ones we have mentioned—nasals, voiceless stops, alveolars, labials, and so on.

For example, many languages of the world include the rule that nasalizes vowels before nasal consonants. One need not include a list of the individual sounds to which the rule applies or the sounds which result from its application. We stated the rule above as:

Nasalize a vowel when it occurs before a nasal consonant.

This rule will apply to all vowel phonemes when they occur in a context before any segment marked [+ nasal], and will add the feature [+ nasal] to the feature matrix of the vowels.

Another rule that occurs frequently in the world's languages changes the place of articulation of nasal consonants to the place of articulation of a following consonant. Thus, an /n/ will become an [m] before a /p/ or /b/ and will become a velar [ŋ] before a /k/ or /g/. When two sequential segments agree in their place of articulation they are called **homorganic consonants.** This **homorganic nasal rule** occurs in Akan as well as English and many other languages. We will see some examples of how it is applied later in the chapter.

Many languages have rules which refer to [+ voiced] and [− voiced] sounds. Note that the aspiration rule in English applies to the class of voiceless stops. As in the vowel nasality rule, we did not list the individual segments in the rule since it applies not to /p/ as opposed to /t/ and /k/ but to all the voiceless stops.

That we find such similar rules which apply to the same classes of sounds across languages is not surprising since such rules often have phonetic explanations and these classes of sounds are defined by phonetic features. For this reason such classes are called **natural classes** of speech sounds.

Children find it easier to learn a rule (or construct it) that applies to a natural class of sounds; they do not have to remember the individual sounds, simply the features that these sounds share.

This fact about phonological rules and natural classes illustrates why individual phonemic segments are better regarded as combinations or complexes of features than as indissoluble whole segments. If such segments are not specified as feature matrices, the similarities among /p/, /t/, and /k/ or /m/, /n/, and /ŋ/ would not be revealed. It would appear that it should be just as easy for a child to learn a rule such as

(a) Nasalize vowels before /p/, /i/, or /z/

as to learn a rule such as

(b) Nasalize vowels before /m/, /n/, or /ŋ/

Rule (a) has no phonetic explanation whereas rule (b) does. It is easier to lower the velum to produce a nasalized vowel in anticipation of a following nasal consonant than to prevent the velum from lowering before the consonant closure.

This does not mean, however, that no language has a rule which applies to a single sound. One finds complex rules in languages including rules that apply to an individual member of a class, but rules pertaining to natural classes occur more frequently and an explanation is provided for this fact by reference to phonetic properties.

Major Class Features

In Chapter 5 we mentioned that the sounds of all the languages of the world fall into two major natural classes—consonants and vowels (often referred to by the cover symbols C and V). Other classes of sounds which contain subclasses were also referred to. The class of labial sounds includes the class of bilabial sounds— /b/ /p/ /m/—as well as the labio-dentals—/f/ and /v/. Coronals include the alveolars—/d/ /t/ /n/ /s/ /z/—the palatals /š/ /ž/—and the affricates—/č/ /ǰ/. Thus, for example, a /b/ is both [+bilabial] and [+labial]. We will see below that these "super" classes are natural classes in that they function in general rules in many of the world's languages.

There are other natural "super" classes of sounds that are referred to in phonological rules which require features not yet referred to in order to specify the members of these classes. Some of these are discussed in the sections that follow.

Obstruents and Sonorants

The nonnasal stops, the fricatives, and the affricates form a major class of sounds. Because the airstream cannot escape through the nose, it is either fully obstructed in its passage through the vocal tract, as in nonnasal stops and affricates, or partially obstructed in the production of fricatives. These sounds are called **obstruents** and are distinguished from the other major class of sounds, which are called **sonorants.**

Nasal stops are sonorant because although the air is blocked in the mouth, it continues to resonate and move through the nose.

The liquids /l/ and /r/, the glides /w/ and /j/ and vowels are sonorants because the air resonates without being stopped.

Fricatives are continuant obstruents because although the air is not completely stopped in its passage through the oral cavity, it is obstructed, causing the friction noted above.

Nonnasal stops and affricates are noncontinuant obstruents; there is complete blockage of the air during the production of these sounds. The closure of a stop is released abruptly, as opposed to the closure of an affricate, which is released gradually, causing friction.

This one **binary** or "two-valued" (+ or −) feature, [±sonorant], provides a way to contrast these two classes in all languages in the world. Obstruents, then, are [−sonorant].

[+consonantal] Sounds Nasals and liquids for the reasons given above are [+sonorant] sounds; yet they resemble the obstruents in that the oral cavity is constricted during their articulation. Obstruents, liquids, and nasals form a natural class of [+consonantal] sounds which differ phonetically from the [−consonantal] class which includes vowels and glides.

[+syllabic] Sounds In Chapter 5, vowels and glides were distinguished by the feature *syllabic*. Vowels are [+syllabic] and glides [j] [w] [h] and [ʔ] are [−syllabic]. We noted, also, that liquids such as /l/ and /r/ and nasals such as /m/ and /n/ can be syllabic as shown by the words *Rachel* [rečl̩], *friar* [frajr̩], *rhythm* [rɪðm̩], and *listen* [lɪsn̩]. Using the features *consonantal* and *sonorant,* we are now able to distinguish the natural intersecting classes of consonants, nasals, liquids, glides, and vowels as shown in Table 6.2.

TABLE 6.2
Feature Specification of Major Natural Classes of Sounds

	Obstruents O	*Nasals* N	*Liquids* L	*Glides* G	*Vowels* V
Features					
Consonantal	+	+	+	−	−
Sonorant	−	+	+	+	+
Syllabic	−	+ / −	+ / −	−	+
Nasal	−	+	−	−	−

Sibilants

Another class of sounds which functions as a natural class in phonological rules is characterized by an acoustic, rather than an articulatory property of its members. The friction created in the production of the fricatives in the words *sit* [sɪt], *zip* [zɪp], *shoe* [šu], *leisure* [ližər], and *measure* [mɛžər] and the affricates in the words *church* [čʌrč] and *judge* [ǰʌǰ] causes a "hissing" sound. These sounds are in a class of **sibilants,** a natural class that we will refer to in the discussion of the English plural rule. We see again that a phonological segment may be a member of a number of classes; for example, /s/ is a member of the class of [+obstruent]s, [+consonantal]s, [+alveolar]s, [+coronal]s, [−stop]s, [+continuant]s, [+sibilants]s, and so on.

Feature Specifications for American English Consonants and Vowels

Using the phonetic properties or features provided in Chapter 5 and the additional features in this chapter, we can provide **feature matrices** for all the phonemes in English using the + or − value for each feature. One then can easily identify the members of each class of phonemes by selecting all the segments marked + or − for a single feature. Thus, the class of stops, /p b m t d n k g n č ǰ/, are those phonemes marked [−continuant] on the Consonant chart; the class of high vowels, / i ɪ u ʊ / are marked [+high] in the vowel feature chart.

TABLE 6.3
Phonemic Features of American
English Stressed Vowels

Features	i	ɪ	e	ɛ	æ	u	ʊ	o	ɔ	a	ʌ
high	+	+	−	−	−	+	+	−	−	−	−
low	−	−	−	−	+	−	−	−	−	+	−
back	−	−	−	−	−	+	+	+	+	+	+
rounded	−	−	−	−	−	+	+	+	+	−	−
tense/long	+	−	+	−	−	+	−	+	−	−	−

TABLE 6.4
Phonemic Features of American English Consonants

Features	p	b	m	t	d	n	k	g	ŋ	f	v	θ	ð	s	z	š	ž	č	ǰ	l	r	j	w	h
Consonantal	+	+	+	+	+	+	+	+	+	+	+	+	+	+	+	+	+	+	+	+	+	−	−	−
Sonorant	−	−	+	−	−	+	−	−	+	−	−	−	−	−	−	−	−	−	−	+	+	+	+	+
Syllabic	−	−	−/+	−	−	−/+	−	−	−/+	−	−	−	−	−	−	−	−	−	−	−/+	−/+	−	−	−
Nasal	−	−	+	−	−	+	−	−	+	−	−	−	−	−	−	−	−	−	−	−	−	−	−	−
Voiced	−	+	+	−	+	+	−	+	+	−	+	−	+	−	+	−	+	−	+	+	+	+	+	−
Continuant	−	−	−	−	−	−	−	−	−	+	+	+	+	+	+	+	+	−	−	+	+	+	+	+
Labial	+	+	+	−	−	−	−	−	−	+	+	−	−	−	−	−	−	−	−	−	−	−	+	−
Alveolar	−	−	−	+	+	+	−	−	−	−	−	−	−	+	+	−	−	−	−	+	+	−	−	−
Palatal	−	−	−	−	−	−	−	−	−	−	−	−	−	−	−	+	+	+	+	−	−	+	−	−
Velar	−	−	−	−	−	−	+	+	+	−	−	−	−	−	−	−	−	−	−	−	−	−	−	−
Coronal	−	−	−	+	+	+	−	−	−	−	−	+	+	+	+	+	+	+	+	+	−	−	−	−
Sibilant	−	−	−	−	−	−	−	−	−	−	−	−	−	+	+	+	+	+	+	−	−	−	−	−

Note: The [+voicing] feature value is redundant for English nasals, liquids, and glides (except for /h/) and could have been left blank for this reason. The feature specifications for [±coronal] and [±sibilant] are also redundant. These redundant predictable feature specifications are provided simply to illustrate the segments in these natural classes. Note that we have not included the allophones [pʰ tʰ kʰ], since the aspiration is predictable at the beginning of syllables and these phones are not distinct phonemes in English.

More on Prosodic Phonology

Intonation

By permission of Johnny Hart and Creators Syndicate, Inc.

In Chapter 5, the use of pitch as a phonetic feature was discussed in reference to tone languages and intonation languages. In this chapter we have discussed the use of phonetic features to distinguish meaning. We can now see that pitch can be a phonemic feature in languages such as Chinese, or Thai, or Akan. Such relative pitches are referred to phonologically as contrasting tones. We also pointed out that there are languages that are not tone languages, such as English. Pitch may still play an important role. It is the **pitch contour** or **intonation** of the phrase or sentence that is important.

In English, syntactic differences may be shown by different intonation contours. We say *John is going* as a statement with a falling pitch, but as a question with the pitch rising at the end of the sentence.

A sentence which is ambiguous when it is written may be unambiguous when spoken. For example:

(a) Tristram left directions for Isolde to follow.

If Tristram wanted Isolde to follow him, the sentence would be pronounced with the rise in pitch on the first syllable of *follow,* followed by a fall in pitch, as in (b).

(b) Tristram left directions for Isolde to follow.

The sentence can also mean that Tristram left a set of directions he wanted Isolde to use. If this is the intention, the highest pitch comes on the second syllable of directions, as in c:

(c) Tristram left directions for Isolde to follow.

The way we have indicated pitch is of course highly oversimplified. Before the big rise in pitch the voice does not remain on the same monotone low pitch. These pitch diagrams indicate merely when there is a special change in pitch.

Thus pitch plays an important role in both tone languages and intonation languages, but in different ways.

Word Stress

By permission of Johnny Hart and Creators Syndicate, Inc.

In English and many other languages, one or more of the syllables in each content word (words other than the "little words" like *to, the, a, of,* and so on) are stressed. The stressed syllable is marked by ´ in the following examples:

pérvert	(noun)	as in	"My neighbor is a pervert."
pervért	(verb)	as in	"Don't pervert the idea."
súbject	(noun)	as in	"Let's change the subject."
subjéct	(verb)	as in	"He'll subject us to criticism."[3]

In some words, more than one vowel is stressed, but if so, one of these stressed vowels receives greater stress than the others. We have indicated the most highly stressed vowel by an acute accent over the vowel (we say this vowel receives the **accent,** or **primary stress,** or **main stress**); the other stressed vowels are indicated by marking a grave accent ` over the vowels (these vowels receive **secondary stress**).

rèsignátion	lìnguístics	sỳstemátic
fùndaméntal	ìntrodúctory	rèvolútion

Generally, speakers of a language know which syllable receives primary stress or accent, which receives secondary stress, and which are not stressed at all; it is part of their knowledge of the language.

The stress pattern of a word may differ from dialect to dialect. For example, in most varieties of American English the word *láboratòry* has two stressed syllables; in one dialect of British English it receives only one stress [ləbórətri]. Because the

---

[3]These minimal pairs show that stress is contrastive in English; it distinguishes between nouns and verbs.

vowel qualities in English are closely related to whether they are stressed or not, the British vowels differ from the American vowels in this word; in fact, in the British version one vowel "drops out" completely because it is not stressed.

Just as stressed syllables in poetry reveal the **metrical structure** of the verse, phonological stress patterns relate to the metrical structure of a language.

There are a number of ways used to represent stress. Above we used grave and acute accent marks. We can also specify which syllable in the word is stressed by marking the syllable **s** if strongly stressed, **w** if weakly stressed and unmarked if unstressed.

s   w   w   s
resignation   systematic

Stress is also sometimes shown by placing a "1" over the primary stressed syllable, a "2" over the syllable with secondary stress, with unstressed vowels unmarked.

2   1   2   1   1   2
fundamental   introductory   secondary

Stress is a property of a syllable rather than a segment, so it is a prosodic or suprasegmental feature.

To produce a stressed a syllable, one may change the pitch (usually by raising it), make the syllable louder, or make it longer. We often use all three of these phonetic features to stress a syllable.

Sentence and Phrase Stress

© Howie Schneider.

When words are combined into phrases and sentences, one of the syllables receives greater stress than all others. That is, just as there is only one primary stress in a word spoken in isolation (for example, in a list), only one of the vowels in a phrase (or sentence) receives primary stress or accent; all the other stressed vowels are "reduced" to secondary stress. A syllable that receives the main stress when the word is not in a phrase may have only secondary stress in a phrase, as is illustrated by these examples:

1	1	1	2

tight + rope→tightrope ("a rope for acrobatics")

1	1	2	1

tight + rope→tight rope ("a rope drawn taut")

1	1	1 2

hot + dog→hotdog ("frankfurter")

1	1	2 1

hot + dog→hot dog ("an overheated dog")

1	1	1 2

red + coat→Redcoat ("a British soldier")

1	1	2 1

red + coat→red coat ("a coat that is red")

1	1	1	2

white + house→White House ("the President's house")

1	1	2	1

white + house→white house ("a house painted white")

In English we place primary stress on an adjective followed by a noun when the two words are combined in a compound noun (usually, but not always, written as one word), but we place the stress on the noun when the words are not joined in this way. The differences between the pairs above are therefore predictable:

Compound Noun	Adjective + Noun
tightrope	tight rope
Redcoat	red coat
hotdog	hot dog
White House	white house

These minimal pairs show that stress may be predictable if phonological rules include nonphonological information; that is, the phonology is not independent of the rest of the grammar. The stress differences between the noun and verb pairs (*subject* as noun and verb) discussed in the previous section are also predictable from the word category.

In the English sentences we used to illustrate intonation contours, we may also describe the differences by referring to the word on which the main stress is placed, as in the following examples:

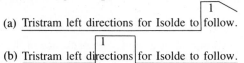

(a) Tristram left directions for Isolde to follow.

(b) Tristram left directions for Isolde to follow.

In sentence (a) the primary stress is on the word *follow,* and in (b) the primary stress is on *directions*.

The Rules of Phonology

> No rule is so general which admits not some exception.
> Robert Burton, *The Anatomy of Melancholy*

> But that to come
> Shall all be done by the rule.
> Shakespeare, *Antony and Cleopatra*

All who know a language know its basic vocabulary, the phonemic representations of words, their phonetic pronunciations, and what these forms mean. This knowledge is "stored" in mental dictionaries.

If you want to refer to the concept "pot," you say [pʰat] not [tʰat]. You know what sounds represent the meaning you wish to express. You must know that the word meaning "pot" starts with a /p/ rather than a /t/ or a /k/, or you would not be understood. You also know that the initial /p/ is pronounced as a [pʰ], because part of your phonological knowledge is the fact that all syllable-initial voiceless stops before stressed vowels are aspirated. It is not necessary to specify the /p/ as an aspirated [pʰ] in your mental dictionary; there is a general rule that will add this feature. The inclusion of the feature [+ aspiration] in the description of the initial segment of this word would be redundant. The fact that the initial voiceless stop is aspirated is not a fact about the word *pot* but about all words that begin with voiceless stops.

The relationship between the phonemic representations that are stored and the phonetic representations that reflect the pronunciation of these words is "rule-governed." These **phonological rules** relate the **minimally specified** phonemic representation to the phonetic representation and are part of a speaker's knowledge of the language. The phonemic representations of words in the mental grammar are minimally specified because the predictable features or feature values are not included. This reveals the redundancy of such features, a fact about the knowledge speakers have of the phonology.

The phonemic representation need only include the nonpredictable distinctive features of the string of phonemes that represent the words. The phonetic representation **derived** by applying these rules includes all the linguistically relevant phonetic aspects of the sounds. It does not include all the physical properties of the sounds of an utterance, because the physical signal may vary in many ways that have little to do with the phonological system. The absolute pitch of the sounds, the rate of speech, or its loudness is not linguistically significant. The phonetic transcription is therefore also an abstraction from the physical signal; it includes the nonvariant phonetic aspects of the utterances, those features that remain relatively the same from speaker to speaker and from one time to another.

The Formalization of Phonological Rules

> Form follows function.
> Slogan of the Bauhaus school of architecture

The nasalization rule and the aspiration rule, presented earlier in this chapter, make certain predictions about English pronunciation. We repeat them with some slight changes, for easy reference.

(1) Nasalize vowels and diphthongs before nasals.
(2) Aspirate voiceless stops before stressed vowels at the beginning of a word or syllable.

Both rules specify the **class of sounds** affected by the rules:

in (1) vowels and diphthongs
in (2) voiceless stops

Both rules state what **phonetic changes** are to occur:

in (1) nasalize (change from [− nasal] to [+ nasal])
in (2) aspirate (change from a blank to [+ aspirated])

Both rules specify the **context** or **phonemic environment** of the relevant sounds:

in (1) before nasals
in (2) before stressed vowels at the beginning of a word or syllable

All three kinds of information—segments affected, phonemic environment, phonetic change—must be included in the statement of a phonological rule, or it would not explicitly state the regularities that constitute speakers' phonological knowledge. The rules of grammar written by linguists or posited as being in the grammar should explicitly characterize the actual rules known unconsciously by speakers of the language.

How can we state these rules in the most explicit and simple way? With the development of linguistic theory, **technical notations** began to be used as in other sciences, both to simplify the theoretical statements and to reveal the "laws" of language. Every physicist knows that $E = mc^2$ means "Energy equals mass times the square of the velocity of light."

The phonological rules we have considered so far have been stated in words like the sentence used to "translate" the formula in physics. We have used a few special symbols or "formal devices" or "formal notations" in specifying the + or − values of features and in applying the **cover symbols** like C, V, L, and G to the classes of consonants, vowels, liquids, and glides. The phonetic symbols themselves are technical terms; /e/ represents a "front, mid, tense, unrounded vowel" in the same sense as "*E*" in physics represents "energy" and "*m*" represents "mass." Slashes—/ /—show that the symbols represent phonemes; brackets—[ ]—enclose phonetic segments or phones.

Other such notations can be used to **formalize** phonological rules. These special symbols are part of the theory of phonology. They do more than merely save paper or abbreviate long statements. They provide a way to express the generalizations of the language that may be obscured otherwise.

Similar to the way we use " = " instead of "equals" in mathematical equations and formulas, we will use an arrow "→" to represent the change that the rule specifies. The segment on the left of the arrow "becomes" or "is" or "is changed to" whatever is on the right of the arrow in the specified environment. The vowel nasalization rule can then be written as:

V→[+ nasal] before a [+ nasal]

What occurs on the left side of the arrow fulfills the first requirement for a rule: it specifies the class of sounds affected by the rule. What occurs on the right side of the arrow specifies the change that occurs, thus fulfilling the second requirement of a phonological rule.

To fulfill the third requirement of a rule—the phonological environment or context where the rule will apply—we can formalize the notions of "environment" or "in the environment" and the notions of "before" and "after" since it is also important to specify whether the vowels to be nasalized occur before or after a nasal. In some languages, nasalization occurs after rather than before nasal segments. We will use the following notations:

/ **to mean "in the environment of"**

____ **placed before or after the relevant segment(s) that determine the change**

Using these notations we can write the above rule:

V→ [+nasal]/____ [+nasal]

This rule reads in words:

"A vowel becomes or is nasalized in the environment (/) before (____) a nasal segment."

The Aspiration Rule states that the environment in which a voiceless stop is to become aspirated is at the beginning of a syllable. We can use the symbol $ to represent a syllable **boundary.** Generally aspiration occurs only if the following vowel is **stressed.** The /p/ in *pit* and *repeat* is aspirated but the /p/ in *in $ spect* or *com $ pass* is usually unaspirated (although if aspirated it will not change meaning since aspiration is nonphonemic). Using the feature [+ stress] to indicate a stressed syllable and the feature complex [− consonantal, + syllabic, + stress] we can formalize this rule as:

$$\begin{bmatrix} - \text{continuant} \\ - \text{voiced} \end{bmatrix} \rightarrow [+ \text{aspirated}] / \$ \_\_\_\_ \begin{bmatrix} - \text{consonantal} \\ + \text{stress} \end{bmatrix}$$

We can also symbolize a stressed vowel as V́, as stated above in the section on diacritics.

This rule is somewhat oversimplified since a syllable initial voiceless stop before a liquid—/l/ or /r/—followed by a stressed vowel is also aspirated. We can use the parentheses notation used in the syntax chapter to specify that a liquid may or may not follow the stop. The rewritten rule looks like this:

$$\begin{bmatrix} -\text{continuant} \\ -\text{voiced} \end{bmatrix} \rightarrow [+\text{aspirated}] \; / \; \$ \; \underline{\hspace{1cm}} \; (L) \; \acute{V}$$

Because every word-initial segment is also syllable initial, the rule applies to word-initial voiceless stops. Note that we do not have to write two rules, one for word-initial voiceless stops and one for syllable-initial voiceless stops before stressed vowels. Where one rule will suffice, to state the process in two rules would obscure the generalization we wish to capture.

In the sections below on the kinds of phonological rules which occur in the world's languages, the formalization of rules will be illustrated further.

Assimilation Rules

The vowel nasalization rule is an **assimilation** rule; it *assimilates* one segment to another by "copying" or "spreading" a feature of a sequential phoneme on to its neighboring segment, thus making the two phones more similar. Assimilation rules are, for the most part, caused by articulatory or physiological processes. There is a tendency when we speak to increase the **ease of articulation,** that is, to make it easier to move the articulators. We noted above that it is "easier" to lower the velum while a vowel is being pronounced before a nasal stop closure than to wait for the articulators to come together. The vowel nasalization rule is thus an assimilation rule.

Assimilation rules in languages reflect what phoneticians often call **coarticulation**—the spreading of phonetic features either in anticipation of sounds or the perseveration of articulatory processes. This "sloppiness" tendency may become regularized as rules of the language.

The following example illustrates how the English vowel nasalization rule applies to the phonemic representation of words and shows the assimilatory nature of the rule; that is, the [−nasal] feature value of the vowel in the phonemic representation changes to a [+nasal] in the phonetic representation:

	"Bob"			**"bomb"**		
Phonemic representation	/b	a	b/	/b	a	m/
Nasality: phonemic feature value	−	−	−	−	−	+
Apply nasal rule	NA*				↓	
Nasality: phonetic feature value	−	−	−	−	+	+
Phonetic representation	[b	a	b]	[b	ã	m]

*NA = "not applicable."

The nasalization rule applies wherever it is applicable.

There are many other examples of assimilation rules in English and other languages. There is an **optional** ("free variation") rule in English that, particularly in fast speech, devoices the nasals and liquids in words like *snow* /sno/ [sn̥o], *slow* /slo/ [sl̥o], *smart* /smart/ [sm̥art], *probe* /prob/ [pʰr̥ob], and so on. The feature [− voiced] of the /s/ or /p/ carries over onto the following segment. Because voiceless nasals and liquids do not occur phonemically—do not contrast with voiced sonorants—the vocal cords can "afford" to be "sluggish." The devoicing will not change the meaning of the words; [slat] and [sl̥at] both mean "slot."

Vowels may also become devoiced or voiceless in a voiceless environment. In Japanese, high vowels are devoiced when preceded and followed by voiceless obstruents; in words like *sukiyaki* the /u/ becomes [u̥]. This assimilation rule can be stated as follows:

$$
\begin{bmatrix} - \text{ consonantal} \\ + \text{ syllabic} \end{bmatrix} \rightarrow [- \text{ voiced}] \ / \begin{bmatrix} - \text{ sonorant} \\ - \text{ voiced} \end{bmatrix} - \begin{bmatrix} - \text{ sonorant} \\ - \text{ voiced} \end{bmatrix}
$$

This rule states that any Japanese vowel (segment that is nonconsonantal and syllabic) becomes devoiced ([− voiced]) in the environment of, or when it occurs (/) between, voiceless obstruents.[4] Notice that the dash does not occur immediately after the slash or at the end of the rule, but between the segment matrices represented as [− sonorant, − voiced].

This rule includes the three kinds of information required:

a . the class of sounds affected: vowels ($\begin{bmatrix} - \text{ consonantal} \\ + \text{ syllabic} \end{bmatrix}$)

b . the phonemic environment: between two obstruents

c . the phonetic change: devoicing $\begin{bmatrix} - \text{ consonantal} \\ + \text{ syllabic} \\ + \text{ voiced} \end{bmatrix}$ becomes $\begin{bmatrix} - \text{ consonantal} \\ + \text{ syllabic} \\ - \text{ voiced} \end{bmatrix}$

The rule does not specify the class of segments to the left of the arrow as [+ voiced] because phonemically all vowels in Japanese are voiced. It therefore simply has to include the change on the right side of the arrow.

We can illustrate the application of this rule in Japanese as we did the vowel nasalization rule in English:

	"sukiyaki"
Phonemic Representation	/s u k i j a k i/
Voicing: phonemic feature value	− + − + + + − +
Apply Devoicing rule	↓
Voicing: phonetic feature value	− − − + + + − +
Phonetic Representation	[s u̥ k i j a k i]

[4]The rule applies most often to high vowels but may apply to other vowels as well.

The English vowel nasalization and devoicing rules and the Japanese devoicing rule change feature specifications. That is, in English the [− nasal] value of phonemic vowels is changed to [+ nasal] phonetically when they occur before nasals through a spreading process. Vowels in Japanese are phonemically voiced, and the rule changes vowels that occur in the specified environment into phonetically voiceless segments.

The rules we have discussed are phonetically plausible, as are other assimilation rules, and can be explained by natural phonetic processes. This fact does not mean that all these rules have to occur in all languages. In fact, if they always occurred they would not have to be learned at all; they would apply automatically and universally, and therefore would not have to be included in the grammar of any particular language. They are not, however, universal.

There is a nasal assimilation rule in Akan that nasalizes voiced stops when they follow nasal consonants, as shown in the following example:

/ɔ́ bá/   [ɔ̀bá]   "he comes"   /ɔ̀ m̀ bá/   [ɔ̀mmá]   "he doesn't come"
he come   *he not come*

The /b/ of the verb "come" becomes an [m] when it follows the negative /m/.

This assimilation rule also has a phonetic explanation; the velum is lowered to produce the nasal consonant and remains down during the following stop. Although it is a phonetically "natural" assimilation rule, it does not occur in the grammar of English; the word *amber,* for example, shows an [m] followed by a [b]. A child learning Akan must learn this rule, just as a child learning English learns to nasalize all vowels before nasal consonants, a rule that does not occur in the grammar of Akan.

Assimilation rules such as the ones we have discussed in English, Japanese, and Akan often have the function of changing the value of phonemic features. They are feature-changing or feature-spreading rules. Although nasality is nondistinctive for vowels in English, it is a distinctive feature for consonants, and the nasalization rule therefore changes a feature value.

The Akan rule is a feature-changing rule that states that [m] is an allophone of /b/ as well as an allophone of /m/. Thus, there is no one-to-one relationship between phonemes and their allophones. This fact can be illustrated in another way:

We will provide more examples of this one-to-many or many-to-one mapping between phonemes and allophones below.

Dissimilation Rules

It is understandable why assimilation rules are found in so many languages. As pointed out above, they permit greater ease of articulation. It might seem strange then to learn that one also finds **dissimilation** rules in languages, rules in which a segment becomes **less** similar to another segment rather than more similar. But such rules do exist. They also have a "natural" explanation, often from the point of view of the **hearer** rather than the speaker. That is, in listening to speech, if sounds are too similar, we may miss the contrast.

A 'classic' example of dissimilation occurred in Latin and the results of this process show up in modern day English. There was a derivational suffix *-alis* in Latin that was added to nouns to form adjectives. When the suffix was added to a noun which contained the liquid /l/ the suffix was changed to *-aris,* that is, the liquid /l/ was changed to the liquid /r/. These words came into English as adjectives ending in *-al* or in its dissimilated form *-ar* as shown in the following examples:

-al	**-ar**
anecdot-al	angul-ar
annu-al	annul-ar
ment-al	column-ar
pen-al	perpendicul-ar
spiritu-al	simil-ar
ven-al	vel-ar

As *columnar* illustrates, the /l/ need not be the consonant directly preceding the dissimilated segment.

Dissimilation rules are quite rare but they do occur, as shown by the examples above. The African language Kikuyu also has a dissimilation rule in which a prefix added to a verb begins with a velar fricative if the verb begins with stop but with a velar stop if the verb begins with a continuant.

Feature Addition Rules

Some phonological rules are neither assimilation nor dissimilation rules. The aspiration rule in English, shown on page 244, which aspirates voiceless stops in certain contexts, simply adds a nondistinctive feature. Aspiration is neither present nor absent in any phonemic feature matrices in English. This fact was pointed out above when we discussed why /p/ and /b/ were distinguished by the feature [± voiced] rather than by the feature [± aspirated]. The assimilation rules do not add new features but change phonemic feature values, whereas the aspiration rule adds a new feature not present in phonemic matrices.

/p/ and /b/ (and all such symbols) are simply cover symbols that do not reveal the phonemic distinctions. In the phonemic and phonetic feature matrices, these differences are made explicit, as shown in the following phonemic matrices:

	/p/	**/b/**	
Consonantal	+	+	
Continuant	−	−	
Labial	+	+	
Voiced	−	+	← distinctive difference

The nondistinctive feature "aspiration" is not included in these phonemic representations because aspiration is predictable.

In the phonemic representations of all three words there is no feature value specified for the nondistinctive feature [± aspirated]. Phonemically, /p/ and /b/ are neither "aspirated" nor "unaspirated." The specification of this feature depends on the context of the /p/—where it occurs in a word. The aspiration rule can apply only to the voiceless stops /p/, /t/, /k/, because the specification of the class of sounds on the left of the arrow is unique to this class, but only when one of these segments occurs in the environment specified after the slash, at the beginning of a syllable (/$—) before a stressed vowel. The rule thus adds the [+ aspirated] designation to the voiceless stops in words like *pin, tin, kin, peal, teal, keel, repeal, intend,* and *rekindle* but does nothing to *spin, steal, skin, penumbra, terrific, collect,* and so on, or to any of the voiced stops.

Segment Deletion and Addition Rules

In addition to assimilation and dissimilation (feature-changing) and feature-addition rules, phonological rules can delete or add entire phonemic segments. In French, for example, as demonstrated by Sanford Schane,[5] word-final consonants are deleted when the following word begins with a consonant (oral or nasal) or a liquid, but are retained when the following word begins with a vowel or a glide, as illustrated in Table 6.5:

TABLE 6.5
Distribution of Word Final Consonants in French

Before a consonant:	/pətit tablo/ /noz tablo/	[peti tablo] [no tablo]	"small picture" "our pictures"
Before a liquid:	/pətit livr/ /noz livr/	[pəti livr] [no livr]	"small book" "our books"
Before a nasal:	/pətit navet/ /noz navets/	[pəti navɛ] [no navɛ]	"small turnip" "our turnips"
Before a vowel:	/pətit ami/ /noz amis/	[pətit ami] [noz ami]	"small friend" "our friends"
Before a glide:	/pətit wazo/ /noz wazo/	[pətit wazo] [noz wazo]	"small bird" "our birds"

Table 6.5 represents a general rule in French applying to all word-final consonants. We distinguished these five classes of sounds by the features *consonantal, sonorant, syllabic* and *nasal.* We noted that oral and nasal consonants and liquids

[5]Sanford Schane, *French Phonology and Morphology,* Cambridge, Mass: M.I.T. Press, 1968.

were specified as [+ consonantal] and vowels and glides as [− consonantal]. We can now see why such "super classes" or "cover features" are important. Using the symbol ∅ to represent the "null" unit (or zero) and # as "word boundary," we can state the French rule simply as:

[+consonantal]→∅/ _____ ## [+consonantal]

This rule can be "translated" into words as:

> **A consonantal segment (obstruent, liquid or nasal) is deleted or becomes null (→∅) in the environment (/) at the end of a word (___ #) which is followed by a word beginning with an obstruent or liquid or nasal (# [+ consonantal]).**

or simply as "Delete a consonant before a word beginning with a consonant."

In Schane's complete analysis, many words that are pronounced with a final consonant actually have a vowel as their word-final segment in phonemic representation. The vowel prevents the rule of word-final consonant deletion from applying. The vowel itself is deleted by another, later rule. Given this rule in the grammar of French, *petit* would be phonemically /pətit/. It need not be additionally represented as /pəti/, because the rule determines the phonetic shape of the word.

"Deletion rules" also show up as **optional rules** in fast speech or casual speech in English. They result, for example, in the common contractions changing *he is* [hi ɪz] to *he's* [hiz] or *I will* [aj wɪl] to *I'll* [ajl]. In ordinary everyday speech most of us also "delete" the unstressed vowels that are shown in bold type in words like the following:

    mys**te**ry   general   mem**o**ry   funeral   vig**o**rous   Barb**a**ra

These words in casual speech sound as if they were written:

    mystry   genral   memry   funral   vigrous   Barbra

Phonological rules therefore can be either optional or obligatory.

Phonological rules may also add whole segments. In Spanish, a rule inserts an [e] at the beginning of a word that otherwise would begin with an [s] followed by another consonant. For example, the word meaning "to transcribe" in Spanish is *transcribir,* and the word meaning "to endorse" is *subscribir.* Both of these words consist of a prefix followed by *scribir,* which means "to write." Without a prefix, however, "to write" is not **scribir* but *escribir;* the segment [e] has been added to the word-initial /skr/ cluster. You will not find a word in Spanish beginning with [sp] or [st] or [sk]; the [e] insertion rule produces the phonetic forms of *escuela* "school," *estampa* "stamp," *España* "Spain," and *espina* "spine," from the phonemic representations that begin with /sk/, /st/, and /sp/.

Movement (Metathesis) Rules

Phonological rules may also move phonemes from one place in the string to another. Such rules are called **metathesis rules.** They are less common, but they do exist.

In some dialects of English, for example, the word *ask* is pronounced [æks], but the word *asking* is pronounced [æskiŋ]. In these dialects a metathesis rule "switches" the /s/ and /k/ in certain contexts. It is interesting that in Old English the verb was *aksian,* with the /k/ preceding the /s/. An historical metathesis rule switched these two consonants, producing *ask* in most dialects of English. Children's speech shows many cases of metathesis (which are later corrected as the child approaches the adult grammar): *aminal* [æmənəl] for *animal* and *pusketti* [pʰəskɛti] for *spaghetti* are common children's pronunciations.

In Hebrew there is a metathesis rule that reverses a pronoun-final consonant with the first consonant of the following verb if the verb starts with a sibilant. These reversals are in "reflexive" verb forms, as shown in the following examples:

Nonsibilant— **Initial Verbs**		**Sibilant—** **Initial Verbs**	
kabel	"to accept"	*tsadek*	"to justify"
lehit-kabel	"to be accepted"	*lehits-tadek*	"to apologize"
		(not **lehit-tsadek*)	
pater	"to fire"	*šameš*	"to use for"
lehit-pater	"to resign"	*lehiš-tameš*	"to use"
		(not **lehit-šameš*)	
bayeš	"to shame"	*sader*	"to arrange"
lehit-bayeš	"to be ashamed"	*lehis-tader*	"to arrange
		(not **lehit-sader*)	oneself"

We see, then, that phonological rules may produce the following alterations:

1. **Change feature values** (vowel nasalization rule in English).
2. **Add new features** (aspiration in English).
3. **Delete segments** (final consonant deletion in French).
4. **Add segments** (vowel insertion in Spanish).
5. **Reorder segments** (metathesis rule in Hebrew).

These rules, when applied to the phonemic representations of words and phrases, result in phonetic forms that may differ substantially from the phonemic forms. If such differences were unpredictable, we would find it difficult to explain how we can understand what we hear or how we produce utterances that represent the meanings we wish to convey. The more we look at languages, however, the more we see that many aspects of the phonetic forms of utterances which appear at first to be irregular and unpredictable are actually rule-governed. We learn, or construct, these rules when we are learning the language as children. The rules represent "patterns," or general principles.

From One to Many and from Many to One

The discussion on how phonemic representations of utterances are realized phonetically included an example from the African Ghanaian language Akan, to show that the relationship between a phoneme and its allophonic realization may be complex. The same phone may be an allophone of two or more phonemes, as [m] was shown to be an allophone of both /b/ and /m/ in Akan.

We can also illustrate this complex mapping relationship in English. Consider the vowels in the following pairs of words:

	A		**B**	
/i/	comp**e**te	[i]	comp**e**tition	[ə]
/ɪ/	med**i**cinal	[ɪ]	med**i**cine	[ə]
/e/	main**tai**n	[e]	main**te**nance	[ə]
/ɛ/	tel**e**graph	[ɛ]	tel**e**graphy	[ə]
/æ/	an**a**lysis	[æ]	an**a**lytic	[ə]
/a/	s**o**lid	[a]	s**o**lidity	[ə]
/o/	ph**o**ne	[o]	ph**o**netic	[ə]
/u/	Talm**u**dic	[u]	Talm**u**d	[ə]

In column A all the bold-faced vowels are stressed vowels with a variety of different vowel phones; in column B all the bold-faced unstressed vowels are pronounced [ə]; yet the "reduced" vowels of column B must be derived from different underlying phonemes, because when they are stressed they show up as different vowels in column A. If the vowel of *compete* were not phonemically /i/, there would be no way to account for the particular quality of the stressed vowel. We might say that [ə] is an allophone of all English vowel phonemes. The rule to derive the schwa can be stated simply as:

Change a vowel to a [ə] when it is unstressed.

This rule is oversimplified, because when an unstressed vowel occurs as the final segment of some words it retains its full vowel quality, as shown in words like *confetti, motto,* or *democracy.* In some dialects, all unstressed vowels are reduced.

The rule that "reduces" unstressed vowels to schwas is another example of a rule that changes feature values.

In a phonological description of a language that we do not know, it is not always possible to determine from the phonetic transcription what the phonemic representation is. However, given the phonemic representation and the phonological rules, we can always derive the correct phonetic transcription. Of course, in our internal, mental grammars this derivation is no problem, because the words are listed phonemically and we know the rules of the language.

Another example will illustrate this aspect of phonology. In English, /t/ and /d/ are both phonemes, as is illustrated by the minimal pairs *tie/die* and *bat/bad.* When /t/ or /d/ occurs between a stressed and an unstressed vowel they both become a flap [D].[6] For many speakers of English, *writer* and *rider* are pronounced identically as [rajDər]; yet these speakers know that *writer* has a phonemic /t/ because of *write* /rajt/, whereas *rider* has a phonemic /d/ because of *ride* /rajd/. The "flap rule" may be stated informally.

---

[6]The IPA symbol for the flap is [ɾ].

An alveolar stop becomes a voiced flap when preceded by a stressed vowel and followed by an unstressed vowel.

The application of this rule is illustrated as follows:

Phonemic Representation	write /rajt/	writer /rajt + ər/ ↓	ride /rajd/	rider /rajd + ər/ ↓
Apply Rule	NA	D	NA	D
Phonetic Representation	[rajt]	[rajDər]	[rajd]	[rajDər]

    We are omitting other phonetic details that are also determined by phonological rules, such as the fact that in *ride* the vowel is slightly longer than in *write* because it is followed by a voiced [d], which is a phonetic rule in many languages. We are using the example only to illustrate the fact that two distinct phonemes may be realized phonetically as the same sound.

    Such cases show that we cannot arrive at a phonological analysis by simply inspecting the phonetic representation of utterances. If we just looked for minimal pairs as the only evidence for phonology, we would have to conclude that [D] is a phoneme in English because it contrasts phonetically with other phonetic units: *riper* [rajpər], *rhymer* [rājmər], *riser* [rajzər], and so forth. Grammars are much more complex than this pairing shows. The fact that *write* and *ride* change their phonetic forms when suffixes are added shows that there is an intricate mapping between phonemic representations of words and phonetic pronunciations.

    Notice that in the case of the "schwa rule" and the "flap rule" the allophones derived from the different phonemes by rule are different in features from all other phonemes in the language. That is, there is no [D] phoneme, but there is a [D] phone.

    The English "flap rule" also illustrates an important phonological process called **neutralization;** the voicing contrast between /t/ and /d/ is *neutralized* in the specified environment. That is, /t/ never contrasts with /d/ in the environment between a stressed and an unstressed vowel.

    Similar rules showing there is no one-to-one relation between phonemes and phones are found in other languages. In both Russian and German, when voiced obstruents occur at the end of a word or syllable, they become voiceless. Both voiced and voiceless obstruents do occur in German as phonemes, as is shown by the following minimal pair:

Tier   [ti:r]   "animal"   *dir*   [di:r]   "to you"

At the end of a word, however, only [t] occurs; the words meaning "bundle" *Bund*[7] /bʊnd/ and "colorful" *bunt* /bʊnt/ are phonetically identical and pronounced [būnt].

The German devoicing rule, like the vowel reduction rule in English and the homorganic nasal rule, changes the specifications of features. In German, the phonemic representation of the final stop in *Bund* is /d/, specified as [+ voiced]; it is changed by rule to [− voiced] to derive the phonetic [t] in word-final position.

This rule in German further illustrates that we cannot decide what the phonemic representation of a word is, given only the phonetic form; [būnt] can be derived from either /bʊnd/ or /bʊnt/. However, given the phonemic representations and the rules of the language, the phonetic forms are automatically derived.

The Function of Phonological Rules

The function of the phonological rules in a grammar is to provide the phonetic information necessary for the pronunciation of utterances. We may illustrate this point in the following way:

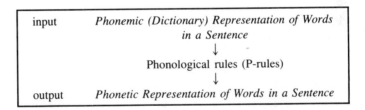

That is, the input to the P-rules is the phonemic representation; the P-rules apply to or operate on the phonemic strings and produce as output the phonetic representation.

The application of rules in this way is called a **derivation.** We have given a number of examples of derivations, which show how phonemically oral vowels become nasalized, how phonemically unaspirated voiceless stops become aspirated, how constrastive voiced and voiceless alveolar stops in English merge to become flaps, and how German voiced obstruents are devoiced. A derivation is thus an explicit way of showing both the effects of a phonological rule and the function of phonological rules (which we can abbreviate as P-rules) in a grammar.

All the examples of derivations we have so far considered show the applications of just one phonological rule. It must be the case, however, that more than one rule may apply to a word. For example, the word *tempest* is phonemically /tɛmpəst/ but phonetically [tʰɛ̃mpəst]. Three rules apply to it: the aspiration rule, the vowel nasalization rule, and the schwa rule. We can derive the phonetic form from the phonemic representation as follows:

---

[7]In German, nouns are capitalized in written form.

Underlying Phonemic Representation	/ t	ε	m	p	ε	s	t /
Aspiration Rule	tʰ						
Nasalization Rule		ɛ̃					
Schwa Rule					ə		
Surface Phonetic Representation	[tʰ	ɛ̃	m	p	ə	s	t]

We are using phonetic symbols instead of matrices in which the feature values are changed. These derivatives are equivalent, however, as long as we understand that a phonetic symbol is a *cover term* representing a matrix with all distinctive features marked either + or − (unless, of course, the feature is nondistinctive, such as the nasality value for phonemic vowels in English).

Slips of the Tongue: Evidence for Phonological Rules

By permission of Johnny Hart and Creators Syndicate, Inc.

"Slips of the tongue" or "speech errors" in which we deviate in some way from the intended utterance show phonological rules in action. Some of these tongue slips are called **spoonerisms,** after William Archibald Spooner, a distinguished head of an Oxford College in the early 1900s who is reported to have said to a class of students, "You have hissed my mystery lecture" instead of the intended "You have missed my history lecture," "You have tasted the whole worm" instead of "You have wasted the whole term," and other such errors. We all make speech errors, however, and they tell us interesting things about language and its use. Consider the following speech errors:

Intended Utterance	**Actual Utterance**
(1) gone to seed	god to seen
[gɔ̃n tə sid]	[gɔd tə sĩn]
(2) stick in the mud	smuck in the tid
[stɪk ĩn ðə mʌd]	[smʌk ĩn ðə tʰɪd]
(3) speech production	preach seduction
[spič pʰrədʌkšə̃n]	[pʰrič sədʌkšə̃n]

In the first example, the final consonants of the first and third words were reversed. Notice that the reversal of the consonants also changed the nasality of the vowels. The first vowel /ɔ/ was a nasalized [ɔ̃] in the intended utterance; in the actual utterance the nasalization was "lost," because it no longer occurred before a nasal consonant. The vowel in the third word, which was the nonnasal [i] in the intended utterance, became [ĩ] in the error, because it was followed by /n/. The nasalization rule applied.

In the other two errors, we see the application of the aspiration rule. In the intended *stick,* the /t/ would have been realized as unaspirated because it is not syllable-initial; when it was switched with the /m/ in *mud,* it was pronounced as the aspirated [tʰ], because it occurred initially. The third example also illustrates the application of the aspiration rule in performance.

The Pronunciation of Morphemes

We noted that a single morpheme may have different pronunciations, that is, different phonetic forms, in different contexts. Thus *write* /rajt/ is pronounced [rajt] but is pronounced [rajDɹ̩] when the suffix -*er* is added.

We also saw that in French a morpheme such as /noz/ meaning "our" is pronounced [no] before words beginning with [+ consonantal] sounds and as [noz] before word initial [− consonantal] sounds.

We also saw that in English, **underlying** phonemic vowels "reduce" to schwa [ə] when they are unstressed. The particular phonetic forms of some morphemes are determined by regular phonological rules that refer only to the phonemic context as is true of the alternate vowel forms of the following sets:

m[ɛ]l[ə]dy   h[a]rm[ə]ny   s[ɪ]mph[ə]ny
m[ə]l[o]dious   h[a]rm[o]nious   s[ɪ]mph[o]nious
m[ə]l[a]dic   h[a]rm[a]nic   s[ɪ]mph[a]nic

The vowel rules that determine these pronunciations are rather complicated and beyond the scope of this text. The examples are presented simply to show that the morphemes in "melody," "harmony," and "symphony" vary phonetically in these words.

Another example of a morpheme in English with different phonetic forms is the plural morpheme. In the following examples, all the nouns in column **A** end in voiced nonsibilant sounds, and to form their plurals you add the voiced [z]. All the words in column **B** end in voiceless nonsibilant sounds, and you add a voiceless [s]. The words in **C** end in both voiced and voiceless sibilants, which form their plurals with the insertion of a schwa followed by [z].

A	B	C	D
cab	cap	bus	child
cad	cat	bush	ox
bag	back	buzz	mouse
love	cuff	garage	sheep
lathe	faith	match	criterion
cam		badge	
can			
bang			
call			
bar			
spa			
boy			

Children do not have to learn the plural rule by memorizing the individual sounds that require the [z] or [s] or [əz] plural ending, because these sounds form natural classes. A grammar that included lists of these sounds would not reveal the regularities in the language or what a speaker knows about the regular plural formation rule.

The regular plural rule does not work for a word like *child,* which in the plural is *children,* or for *ox,* which becomes *oxen,* or for *sheep,* which is unchanged phonologically in the plural. *Child, ox,* and *sheep* are exceptions to the regular rule. We learn these exceptional plurals when learning the language.

If the grammar represented each unexceptional or regular word in both its singular and plural forms—for example, *cat* /kæt/, *cats* /kæts/; *cap* /kæp/, *caps* /kæps/; and so on—it would imply that the plurals of *cat* and *cap* were as irregular as the plurals of *child* and *ox.* Of course, they are not. If a new toy appeared on the market called a *glick* /glɪk/, a young child who wanted two of them would ask for two *glicks* /glɪks/ and not two *glicken,* even if the child had never heard the word *glicks.* The child knows the regular rule to form plurals. An experiment conducted by the linguist Jean Berko Gleason showed that very young children can apply this rule to words they never have heard previously. This fact is further discussed in Chapter 10. A grammar that describes such knowledge (the internalized mental grammar) must then include the general rule.

This rule, which determines the phonetic representation or pronunciation of the plural morpheme, is somewhat different from some of the other phonological rules we have discussed. The "aspiration rule" in English applies to a word whenever the phonological description is met; it is not the case, for example, that a /t/ is aspirated only if it is part of a particular morpheme. The "flap rule," which changes the phonetic forms of the morphemes *write* and *ride* when a suffix is added, is also completely automatic, depending solely on the phonological environment. The plural rule, however, applies only to the inflectional plural morpheme. To see that it is not "purely" phonological in nature, consider the following words:

race	[res]	ray	[re]	ray + pl.	[rez]	*[res]
sauce	[sɔs]	saw	[sɔ]	saw + pl.	[sɔz]	*[sɔs]
rice	[rajs]	rye	[raj]	rye + pl.	[rajz]	*[rajs]

The examples show that the [z] in the plural is not determined by the phonological context, because in an identical context an [s] occurs.

Morphophonemics

© 1981 Newspaper Enterprise Association, Inc.

The rule that determines the phonetic form of the plural morpheme has traditionally been called a **morphophonemic rule,** because its application is determined by both the morphology and the phonology. When a morpheme has alternate phonetic forms, these forms are called **allomorphs** by some linguists. [z], [s], and [əz] would be allomorphs of the regular plural morpheme, and determined by rule.

To show how such a rule may be applied, assume that the regular, productive, plural morpheme has the phonological form /z/, with the meaning "plural." The regular "plural rule" can be stated in a simple way:

(a) Insert a [ə] before the plural ending when a regular noun ends in a sibilant— /s/, /z/, /š/, /ž/, /č/, or /ǰ/.

(b) Change the voiced /z/ to voiceless [s] when it is preceded by a voiceless sound.

If neither (a) nor (b) applies, then /z/ will be realized as [z]; no segments will be added and no features will be changed.

	bus + pl.	*butt* + pl.	*bug* + pl.
Phonemic *Representation*	/bʌs + z/	/bʌt + z/	/bʌg + z/
	↓		
apply rule (a)	ə	NA*	NA
apply rule (b)	NA	s	NA
Phonetic *Representation*	[bʌsəz]	[bʌts]	[bʌgz]

*NA means "not applicable."

The plural formation rule will derive the phonetic forms of plurals for all regular nouns (remember, this plural is /z/).

As we have formulated these rules, (a) must be applied before (b). If we applied the two parts of the rule in reverse order, we would derive incorrect phonetic forms:

Phonemic Representation	/bʌs + z/
	↓
apply rule (b)	s
apply rule (a)	ə
Phonetic Representation	*[bʌsəs]

The plural formation rule illustrates once again that phonological rules can insert entire segments into the phonemic string: a [ə] is added by the first rule. It also illustrates the importance of *ordered rules* in phonology.

An examination of the rule for the formation of the past tense of verbs in English shows some interesting parallels with the plural formation of nouns.

A	**B**	**C**	**D**
grab	reap	state	is
hug	peak	raid	run
seethe	unearth		sing
love	huff		have
buzz	kiss		go
rouge	wish		hit
judge	pitch		
fan			
ram			
long			
kill			
care			
tie			
bow			
hoe			

The productive regular past tense morpheme in English is /d/, *phonemically,* but [d] (column **A**), [t] (column **B**), or [əd] (column **C**) *phonetically,* again depending on the final phoneme of the verb to which it is attached. **D** column verbs are exceptions.

The past tense rule in English, like the plural formation rule, must include morphological information. Notice that after a vowel or diphthong the form of the past tense is always [d], even though no phonological rule would be violated if a [t] were added, as shown by the words *tight, bout, rote.* When the word is a verb, and when the final alveolar represents the past tense morpheme, however, it must be a voiced [d] and not a voiceless [t].

There is a plausible explanation for why a [ə] is inserted in the past tense of regular verbs ending with alveolar stops (and in nouns ending with sibilants).

Because in English we do not contrast long and short consonants, it is difficult for English speakers to perceive a difference in consonantal length. If we added a [z] to *squeeze* we would get [skwizz], which would be hard for English speakers to distinguish from [skwiz]; similarly, if we added [d] to *load,* it would be [lodd] phonetically in the past and [lod] in the present, which would also be difficult to perceive.

More Sequential Constraints

Some of the sequential constraints on phonemes that were discussed previously may show up as morphophonemic rules. The English homorganic nasal constraint applies between some morphemes as well as within a morpheme. The negative prefix *in-,* which, like *un-,* means "not," has three allomorphs:

[ɪn] before vowels:	inexcusable, inattentive, inorganic
and alveolars:	intolerable, indefinable, insurmountable
[ɪm] before labials:	impossible, imbalance
[ɪŋ] before velars:	incomplete, inglorious

The pronunciation of this morpheme is often revealed by the spelling as *im-* when it is prefixed to morphemes beginning with /p/ or /b/. Because we have no letter "ŋ" in our alphabet (although it exists in alphabets used in other languages), the velar [ŋ] is written as *n* in words like *incomplete.* You may not realize that you pronounce the *n* in *inconceivable, inglorious, incongruous,* and other such words as [ŋ] because your homorganic nasal rule is as unconscious as other rules in your grammar. It is the job of linguists and phoneticians to bring such rules to consciousness or to reveal them as part of the grammar. If you say these words in normal tempo without pausing after the *in-,* you should feel the back of your tongue rise to touch the velum.

In Akan the negative morpheme also has three nasal allomorphs: [m] before /p/, [n] before /t/, and [ŋ] before /k/, as is shown in the following cases:

mɪ pɛ	"I like"	mɪ mpɛ	"I don't like"
mɪ tɪ	"I speak"	mɪ ntɪ	"I don't speak"
mɪ kɔ	"I go"	mɪ ŋkɔ	"I don't go"

We see, then, that one morpheme may have different phonetic forms or allomorphs. We have also seen that more than one morpheme may occur in the language with the same meaning but different forms—like *in-, un-,* and *not* (all meaning "not"). It is not possible to predict which of these forms will occur, so they are separate synonymous morphemes. It is only when the phonetic form is predictable by general rule that we find different phonetic forms of a single morpheme.

The plural and past tense formation rules both change feature values of segments (for example, the voiced /z/ and /d/ to voiceless [s] and [t] after voiceless sounds) and also insert a [ə] in given environments. The nasal homorganic rule is also a feature-changing rule. Because the allomorph [ɪn] occurs before vowels, where there is no consonant following by which we can determine the place of articulation features, the phonemic representation of this morpheme is /ɪn/ and the rule will assimilate the /n/ to a following consonant by changing feature values of the /n/.

In some cases different phonetic forms of the same morpheme may be derived by segment deletion rules, as in the following examples:

	A		**B**
sign	[sajn]	signature	[sɪgnəčər]
design	[dəzajn]	designation	[dɛzɪgnešən]
paradigm	[pʰærədajm]	paradigmatic	[pʰærədɪgmæDək]

In none of the words in column **A** is there a phonetic [g], but in each corresponding word in column **B** a [g] occurs. Our knowledge of English phonology accounts for these phonetic differences. The "[g]–no [g]" alternation is regular, and we apply it to words that we never have heard before. Suppose someone says:

"He was a salignant [səlɪgnənt] man."

Even if you do not know what the word means, you might ask (perhaps to hide your ignorance):

"Why, did he salign [səlajn] somebody?"

It is highly doubtful that a speaker of English would pronounce the verb form with the -*ant* dropped as [səlɪgn], because the phonological rules of English would "delete" the /g/ when it occurred in this context. This rule might be stated as:

Delete a /g/ when it occurs before a final nasal consonant.[8]

Given this rule, the phonemic representation of the stems in *sign/signature, design/ designation, resign/resignation, repugn/repugnant, phlegm/phlegmatic, paradigm/ paradigmatic,* and *diaphragm/diaphragmatic* will include a phonemic /g/ that will be deleted by the regular rule if a suffix is not added. By stating the class of sounds that follow the /g/ (nasal consonants) rather than any specific nasal consonant, the rule deletes the /g/ before both /m/ and /n/.

The phonological rules that delete whole segments, add segments and features, and change features also account for the various phonetic forms of some morphemes. This point can be further illustrated by the following words:

	A			**B**	
bomb	/bamb/	[bãm]	bombardier	/bambədir/	[bãmbədir]
iamb	/ajæmb/	[ajæ̃m]	iambic	/ajæmbɪk/	[ajæmbək]
crumb	/krʌmb/	[kʰrʌ̃m]	crumble	/krʌmbl/	[kʰrʌ̃mbəl]

---

[8]The /g/ may be deleted under other circumstances as well, as indicated by its absence in *signing* and *signer.*

A speaker of English knows when to pronounce a /b/ and when not to. The relationship between the pronunciation of the **A** words and their **B** counterparts is regular and can be accounted for by the following rule:

> Delete a word-final /b/ when it occurs after an /m/.

Notice that the underlying phonemic representation of the **A** and **B** stems is the same.

Phonemic Representation	/bamb/	/bamb + adir/	/bʌlb/
apply /b/ deletion rule	ø	NA	NA
unstressed vowel rule	NA	ə	NA
nasalization rule	ã	ã	NA
Phonetic Representation	[bãm]	[bãmbədir]	[bʌlb]

The rules that delete the segments are general phonological rules, but their application to phonemic representations results in deriving different phonetic forms of the same morpheme.

Summary

Part of one's knowledge of a language is knowledge of the **phonology** or sound system of that language—the inventory of **phones,** the phonetic segments that occur in the language, and the ways in which they pattern. It is this patterning that determines the inventory of **phonemes**—the segments that differentiate words.

Phonetic segments are enclosed in square brackets, [ ], and phonemes between slashes, / /. When phones occur in **complementary distribution,** they are **allophones**—predictable phonetic variants—of phonemes. For example, in English, aspirated voiceless stops such as the initial sounds in the words *pill, till,* and *kill* are in complementary distribution (never occur in the same phonological environment) as the unaspirated voiceless stops following the 's' /s/ in *spill, still,* and *skill;* thus the aspirated 'p,' 't,' and 'k' ([pʰ], [tʰ], [kʰ]) and the unaspirated [p], [t], and [k] are allophones of the phonemes /p/, /t/, and /k/, respectively. On the other hand, phones which occur in the same environment and which differentiate words, like the [b] and [m] in *beat* [bit] and *meat* [mit] represent two distinct phonemes, /b/ and /m/.

Phonological segments—phonemes and phones—are composed of phonetic features or properties, such as the presence or absence of *voicing, nasality, labiality,* and *continuance,* which distinguish one segment from another. When this phonetic difference contrasts words, such as the nasality of /m/ versus the oral (non-nasality) of /b/, it is a **distinctive feature.** Thus, in English, the **binary valued** feature [± nasal] [± voicing] are distinctive features, whereas aspiration is not.

A tool that a linguist (or a student of linguistics) can use to discover the phonemes in a language is to look for **minimal pairs,** words which are distinguished by a single phone occurring in the same position. Some pairs, such as *beat* and *meat,* contrast by means of a single distinctive feature, in this case, [± nasal], where /b/ is [− nasal] and /m/ is [+ nasal]. Other minimal pairs may show sounds contrasting in more than one feature, for example, *rip* versus *rim,* where /p/ is [− voiced, − nasal] and /m/ is [+ voiced, + nasal]. The /b/–/m/ contrast shows [± nasal] is a distinctive feature in English. Some sounds differ phonetically but are nonphonemic because they are in **free variation,** which means that either sound may occur in the identical environment without changing the meaning of the word. The glottal stop [ʔ] in English is in free variation with the [t] in words like *don't* or *bottle* and is therefore not a phoneme in English.

Phonetic features which are **predictable** are nondistinctive and **redundant.** The nasality of vowels in English is a redundant feature since all vowels are nasalized before nasal consonants. One can thus predict the + or − value of this feature in vowels.

Phonetic features which are **nondistinctive** in one language may be distinctive in another. Aspiration is distinctive in Thai and nondistinctive in English; both aspirated voiceless stops and unaspirated voiceless stops are phonemes in Thai.

The phonology of a language also includes constraints on the **sequences** of phonemes in the language, as exemplified by the fact that in English two stop consonants may not occur together at the beginning of a word; similarly, the final sound of the word *sing,* the velar nasal, never occurs word initially. These sequential constraints determine what are *possible* but nonoccurring words in a language, and what phonetic strings are "impossible" or "illegal." For example, *blick* [blɪk] is not now an English word but it could become one, whereas *kbli* [kbli] or *ngos* [ŋos] could not. These possible but nonoccurring words constitute **accidental gaps.**

Words in some languages may also be phonemically distinguished by **prosodic** or **suprasegmental** features, such as **pitch, stress,** and segment **duration** or **length.** Languages in which syllables or words are contrasted by pitch are called **tone** languages. **Intonation** languages may use pitch variations to distinguish meanings of phrases and sentences.

In English, words and phrases may be differentiated by **stress,** as in the contrast between the noun *pérvert* in which the first syllable is stressed, and the verb *pervért* in which the final syllable is stressed. In the compound noun *hótdog* versus the adjective + noun phrase *hot dóg,* the former is stressed on *hot,* the latter on *dog.*

Vowel length and **consonant length** may be phonemic features. Both are contrastive in Japanese, Finnish, Italian, and many other languages.

The relationship between the **phonemic representation** of words and sentences and the **phonetic representation** (the pronunciation of these words and sentences) is determined by general **phonological rules.**

Phonological rules in a grammar apply to phonemic strings and alter them in various ways to **derive** their phonetic pronunciation:

1. They may be **assimilation rules** that change feature values of segments, thus spreading phonetic properties. The rule that nasalizes vowels in English before nasal consonants is such a rule.

2. They may be **dissimilation** rules that change feature values to make two phonemes in a string more dissimilar like the Latin liquid rule.
3. They may add nondistinctive features that are predictable from the context. The rule that aspirates voiceless stops at the beginning of words and syllables in English is such a rule, since aspiration is a nonphonemic, nondistinctive, and predictable **redundant** feature.
4. They may **insert** segments that are not present in the phonemic string. The rule in Spanish that inserts an [e] before word initial /s/ consonant clusters is an example of an addition or insertion rule.
5. They may **delete** phonemic segments in certain contexts. Contraction rules in English are deletion rules.
6. They may transpose or move segments in a string. These **metathesis** rules occur in many languages like Hebrew. The rule in certain American dialects that changes an /sk/ to [ks] in final position is also a metathesis rule.

Phonological rules often refer to entire classes of sounds rather than to individual sounds. These are **natural classes,** characterized by the phonetic properties or features that pertain to all the members of each class, such as voiceless sounds, voiced sounds, stops, fricatives, consonants, vowels, or, using + 's and − 's, the class specified as [− voiced] or [+ consonantal] or [− continuant] or [+ nasal].

In the writing of rules, linguists use **formal notations** and **devices** that reveal linguistic generalizations of phonological processes. Features are used rather than whole segments, and other devices such as **arrows** and **parentheses.**

A morpheme may have different phonetic representations; these are determined by the **morphophonemic** and phonological rules of the language. Thus the regular plural morpheme is phonetically [z] or [s] or [əz], depending on the final phoneme of the noun to which it is attached.

The phonological and morphophonemic rules in a language show that the phonemic shape of words or phrases is not identical with their phonetic form. The phonemes are not the actual phonetic sounds, but are abstract mental constructs that are realized as sounds by the operation of rules such as those described above. No one teaches us these rules. And yet all speakers of a language know the phonology of their language better than any linguist who tries to describe it. The linguist's job is to make explicit what we know unconsciously about the sound pattern of our language.

References For Further Reading

Anderson, Stephen R. 1974. *The Organization of Phonology*. New York: Academic Press.

Anderson, S.R. 1985. *Phonology in the Twentieth Century: Theories of Rules and Theories of Representations*. Chicago: University of Chicago Press.

Chomsky, N., and M. Halle. 1968. *The Sound Pattern of English*. New York: Harper & Row.

Clark, John, and Colin Yallop. 1990. *An Introduction to Phonetics and Phonology*. Oxford, England: Basil Blackwell.

Clements, George N., and Samuel Jay Keyser, 1983. *CV Phonology: A Generative Theory of the Syllable*. Cambridge, Mass: MIT Press.

Dell, François. 1980. *Generative Phonology*. London, England: Cambridge University Press.

Goldsmith, John A. 1989. *Autosegmental and metrical phonology: A new synthesis*. Oxford, England: Basil Blackwell.

Hogg, Richard, and C.B. McCully. 1987. *Metrical Phonology: A Coursebook*. Cambridge, England: Cambridge University Press.

Hyman, Larry M. 1975. *Phonology: Theory and Analysis*. New York: Holt, Rinehart & Winston.

Kenstowicz, Michael, and Charles Kisseberth, 1979. *Generative Phonology: Description and Theory*. New York: Academic Press.

van der Hulst, Harry, and Norval Smith (Eds.) 1982. *The structure of phonological representations: Part 1*. Dordrecht, Netherlands: Foris Publications.

Exercises

1. Consider the distribution of [r] and [l] in Korean in the following words:

rupi	"ruby"	mul	"water"
kiri	"road"	pal	"big"
saram	"person"	səul	"Seoul"
irɯmi*	"name"	ilkop	"seven"
ratio	"radio"	ipalsa	"barber"

   *[ɯ] is a high back unrounded vowel. It does not affect
   your analysis in this problem.

   Are [r] and [l] allophones of one or two phonemes? State your reasons, and give the rule to derive the surface phones if you conclude that they are allophonic.

2. In Southern Kongo, a Bantu language spoken in Angola, the nonpalatal segments [t, s, z] are in complementary distribution with their palatal counterparts [č, š, ž], as shown in the following words:

[tobola]	"to bore a hole"	[čina]	"to cut"
[tanu]	"five"	[čiba]	"banana"
[kesoka]	"to be cut"	[nkoši]	"lion"
[kasu]	"emaciation"	[nselele]	"termite"
[kunezulu]	"heaven"	[ažimola]	"alms"
[nzwetu]	"our"	[lolonži]	"to wash house"
[zevo]	"then"	[zenga]	"to cut"
[žima]	"to stretch"		

   a. State the distribution of each pair of segments given below. (Assume that the nonoccurrence of [t] before [e] is an *accidental gap*.)

      Example: [t]—[č]: [t] occurs before the back vowels [o, a, u]; [č] occurs before [i].

      [s]—[š]
      [z]—[ž]

   b. When two allophones can be derived from one phoneme, one selects as the underlying segment the allophone that makes the rules and the phonemic feature complexes as simple as possible. For example, deriving the unaspirated and aspirated voiceless stops in English from an underlying /p/ makes aspiration redundant and unnecessary as a phonemic feature value. If /pʰ/ were the phoneme, the phonemic features would be more complex. Using such considerations, state which phones should be used as the basic phoneme for each pair of nonpalatal and palatal segments in Southern Kongo.

c. State the *one* phonological rule that will derive all the phonetic segments from the phonemes. Do not state a separate rule for each phoneme, but a general rule for all three phonemes you listed in b.

3. In some dialects of English the following words have different vowels, as is shown by the phonetic transcriptions.

A		**B**		**C**	
bite	[bʌjt]	bide	[bajd]	die	[daj]
rice	[rʌjs]	rise	[rajz]	by	[baj]
ripe	[rʌjp]	bribe	[brajb]	sigh	[saj]
wife	[wʌjf]	wives	[wajvz]	rye	[raj]
dike	[dʌjk]	dime	[dajm]	guy	[gaj]
		nine	[najn]		
		rile	[rajl]		
		dire	[dajr]		
		writhe	[rajð]		

a. How may the classes of sounds that end the words in columns **A** and **B** be characterized? That is, what feature specifies all the final segments in **A** and all the final segments in **B**?

b. How do the words in column **C** differ from those in columns **A** and **B**?

c. Are [ʌj] and [aj] in complementary distribution? Give your reasons.

d. If [ʌj] and [aj] are allophones of one phoneme, should they be derived from /ʌj/ or /aj/? Why?

e. Give the phonetic representations of the following:

life _____ lives _____ lie _____

file _____ bike _____ lice _____

f. State the rule that will relate the phonemic representations to the phonetic representations of the words given above.

4. Pairs like *top* and *chop, dunk* and *junk, so* and *show* reveal that /t/ and /č/, /d/ and /ǰ/, and /s/ and /š/ are distinct phonemes in English. Although it is difficult to find a minimal pair to distinguish /z/ and /ž/, they occur in similar if not identical environments, such as *razor* and *azure*. Consider these same pairs of nonpalatalized and palatalized consonants in the following data. (The palatal forms are optional forms that often occur in casual speech.)

Nonpalatalized		**Palatalized**	
[hɪt mi]	"hit me"	[hɪč ju]	"hit you"
[lid hĩm]	"lead him"	[liǰ ju]	"lead you"
[pʰæs ʌs]	"pass us"	[pʰæš ju]	"pass you"
[luz ðɛ̃m]	"lose them"	[luž ju]	"lose you"

State the rule that specifies when /t/, /d/, /s/, and /z/ become palatalized as [č], [ǰ], [š], and [ž]. Use feature notations to reveal generalizations.

5. The following sets of minimal pairs show that English /p/ and /b/ contrast in initial, medial, and final positions.

Initial	*Medial*	*Final*
pit/bit	rapid/rabid	cap/cab

Find similar sets of minimal pairs for each pair of consonants given:

a. /k/–/g/
b. /m/–/n/
c. /l/–/r/
d. /b/–/v/
e. /b/–/m/
f. /p/–/f/
g. /s/–/š/
h. /č/–/ǰ/
i. /s/–/z/

6. Here are some words in Japanese. [č] is the voiceless palatal affricate that occurs in the English word *church* and [ts] is an alveolar affricate which does not occur in English as a single sound but is similar to the sequence of the word final [t] followed by the word initial [s] in the phrase *hot summer* [hatsʌ̃mər].

tatami	'mat'	tomodači	'friend'	uči	'house'
tegami	'letter'	totemo	'very'	otoko	'male'
čiči	'father'	tsukue	'desk'	tetsudau	'help'
šita	'under'	ato	'later'	matsu	'wait'
natsu	'summer'	tsutsumu	'wrap'	čizu	'map'
kata	'person'	tatemono	'building'	te	'hand'

In addition, Japanese words (except for certain loan words) never contain the phonetic sequences *[ti] or *[tu]. Consider [č] and [ts] to be single phones.

a. Based on these data, are [t], [č], and [ts] in complementary distribution?
b. State the distribution, first in words, then using features, of these phones.

c. Give a phonemic analysis of these data insofar as [t], [č], and [ts] are concerned. That is, identify the phonemes, and the allophones.

d. Give the phonemic representation of the Japanese words given below.

tatami	tsukue	tsutsumu
tomodači	tetsudau	čizu
uči	šita	kata
tegami	ato	koto
totemo	matsu	tatemono
otoko	deguši	te
hiči	natsu	tsuri

7. Consider the following English verbs. Those in column **A** have stress on the next-to-last syllable (called the *penultimate*), whereas the verbs in column **B** have their last syllable stressed.

A	**B**	**C**
astonish	collapse	explain
exit	exist	erase
imagine	torment	surprise
cancel	revolt	combine
elicit	adopt	careen
practice	insist	atone
solicit	contort	equate

a. Transcribe the words under **A, B,** and **C** phonemically.

b. State a rule that predicts where stress occurs in these verbs.

c. In the verbs in column **C,** stress also occurs on the final syllable. What must you add to the rule to account for this fact? (*Hint:* For the forms in columns **A** and **B,** the final consonants had to be considered; for the forms in column **C,** consider the vowels.)

8. Below are listed ten "words." Some are English words, some are not words now but could be (they are "possible words"), and others are definitely "foreign" (they violate English sequential constraints).

Write the English words in regular spelling. Mark the other words "foreign" or "possible." For each word you mark as "foreign," state your reason.

	Word	**Possible**	**"Foreign"**	**Reason**
Example:				
[θrot]	throat			
[slig]		X		
[lsig]			X	No English word can begin with a liquid followed by an obstruent.

Word	Possible	"Foreign"	Reason

a. [pʰril]
b. [skrič]
c. [know]
d. [may]
e. [gnostɪk]
f. [jūnəkɔrn]
g. [fruit]
h. [blaft]
i. [ŋar]
j. [æpəpʰlɛksi]

9. Consider the following data from Finnish:

a.	[ku:zi]	'six'		g.	[li:sa]	'Lisa'	
b.	[kudot]	'failures'		h.	[madon]	'of a worm'	
c.	[kate]	'cover'		i.	[maton]	'of a rug'	
d.	[katot]	'roofs'		j.	[ratas]	'wheel'	
e.	[kade]	'envious'		k.	[li:za]	'Lisa'	
f.	[ku:si]	'six'		l.	[radan]	'of a track'	

(1) Do [s] and [z] represent different phonemes?
(2) Do [d] and [t]?
(3) Are the sounds in each pair in complementary distribution?
(4) Are they in free variation?
(5) State the distribution of each phone.

10. Examine the following sounds in the Greek words listed below.

[x] voiceless velar fricative
[k] voiceless velar stop
[c] voiceless palatal stop
[ç] voiceless palatal fricative

Which of these sounds are contrastive and which are in complementary distribution? State the phonetic environments in which each of the sounds occur.

a.	[kano]	'do'		j.	[kori]	'daughter'
b.	[xano]	'lose'		k.	[xori]	'dances'
c.	[çino]	'pour'		l.	[xrima]	'money'
d.	[cino]	'move'		m.	[krima]	'shame'
e.	[kali]	'charms'		n.	[xufta]	'handful'
f.	[xali]	'plaight'		o.	[kufeta]	'bonbons'
g.	[çeli]	'eel'		p.	[oçi]	'no'
h.	[ceri]	'candle'				
i.	[çeri]	'hand'				

11. The following words are found in Paku, a language spoken by the Pakuni in the NBC television series "Land of the Lost'. (The language was created by V. Fromkin.) v́ = [+ stress]

a.	ótu	'evil' (N)	h.	mpósa	'hairless'
b.	túsa	'evil' (Adj)	i.	ámpo	'hairless one'
c.	etógo	'cactus' (sg)	j.	ãmpóni	'hairless ones'
d.	etogóni	'cactus' (pl)	k.	ámi	'mother'
e.	Páku	'Paku' (sg)	l.	ãmíni	'mothers'
f.	Pakúni	'Paku' (pl)	m.	áda	'father'
g.	épo	'hair'	n.	adáni	'fathers'

(1) Is stress predictable? If so, what is the rule?
(2) Is nasalization a distinctive feature for vowels? Give the reasons for your answer.

12. Consider these phonetic forms of Hebrew words:

[v]–[b]		[f]–[p]	
bika	"lamented"	litef	"stroked"
mugbal	"limited"	sefer	"book"
šavar	"broke" (masc.)	sataf	"washed"
šavra	"broke" (fem.)	para	"cow"
ʔikev	"delayed"	mitpaxat	"handkerchief"
bara	"created"	haʔalpim	"the Alps"

Assume that these words and their phonetic sequences are representative of what may occur in Hebrew. In your answers below, consider classes of sounds rather than individual sounds.

a. Are [b] and [v] allophones of one phoneme? (*Hint:* Are they in complementary distribution?)
b. Does the same rule, or lack of a rule, that describes the distribution of [b] and [v] apply to [p] and [f]? If not, why not?
c. Here is a word with one phone missing. A blank appears in place of the missing sound: hid____ik.

Check the one correct statement.

(1) [b] but not [v] could occur in the empty slot.	( )
(2) [v] but not [b] could occur in the empty slot.	( )
(3) Either [b] or [v] could occur in the empty slot.	( )
(4) Neither [b] nor [v] could occur in the empty slot.	( )

d. Which one of the following statements is correct about the incomplete word ____ana?

  (1) [f] but not [p] could occur in the empty slot.   (   )
  (2) [p] but not [f] could occur in the empty slot.   (   )
  (3) Either [p] or [f] could fill the blank.   (   )
  (4) Neither [p] nor [f] could fill the blank.   (   )

  e. Now consider the following possible words (in phonetic transcription):

      laval   surva   labal   palar   falu   razif

      If these words actually occurred in Hebrew, would they:

      (1) Force you to revise the conclusions about the distribution of labial stops and fricatives you reached on the basis of the first group of words given above?   (   )
      (2) Support your original conclusions?   (   )
      (3) Neither support nor disprove your original conclusions?   (   )

13. In the African language Maninka, the suffix *-li* has more than one pronunciation (like the *-ed* past tense ending on English verbs, as in *reaped* [t], *robbed* [d], and *raided* [əd]). This suffix is similar to the derivational suffix *-ing,* which, when added to the verb *cook,* makes it a noun as in "Her cooking was great," or the suffix *-ion,* which also derives a verb from a noun as in *create + ion,* permitting "the creation of the word."

    Consider these data from Maninka:

bugo	"hit"	bugoli	"hitting"
dila	"repair"	dilali	"repairing"
don	"come in"	donni	"coming in"
dumu	"eat"	dumuni	"eating"
gwen	"chase"	gwenni	"chasing"

  a. What are the two forms of the morpheme meaning "the _____ing"?

    (1) _____   (2) _____

  b. Can you predict which phonetic form will occur? If so, state the rule.
  c. What are the "-ing" forms for the following verbs?

      da   "lie down"_____   famu   "understand"_____

      men   "hear"   _____   sunogo "sleep"_____

14. Consider the following phonetic data from the Bantu language Luganda. (The data have been somewhat altered to make the problem easier.) In each line, the same root or stem morpheme occurs in both columns **A** and **B,** but it has one prefix in column **A,** meaning "a" or "an," and another prefix in column **B,** meaning "little."

A		B	
[ēnato]	"a canoe"	[akaato]	"little canoe"
[ēnapo]	"a house"	[akaapo]	"little house"
[ēnobi]	"an animal"	[akaoobi]	"little animal"
[ēmpipi]	"a kidney"	[akapipi]	"little kidney"
[ēŋkoosa]	"a feather"	[akakoosa]	"little feather"
[ēmmāāmmo]	"a peg"	[akabāāmmo]	"little peg"
[ēŋŋōōmme]	"a horn"	[akagōōmme]	"little horn"
[ēnnīmiro]	"a garden"	[akadīmiro]	"little garden"
[ēnugēni]	"a stranger"	[akatabi]	"little branch"

In answering the following questions, base your answers on only these forms. Assume that all the words in the language follow the regularities shown here.

You may need to use scratch paper to work out your analysis before writing your answers in the space provided. (*Hint:* The phonemic representation of the morpheme meaning "little" is /aka/.)

a. Are nasal vowels in Luganda phonemic? _____

Are they predictable? _____

b. Is the phonemic representation of the morpheme meaning "garden" /dimiro/?

c. What is the phonemic representation of the morpheme meaning

"canoe"? _____

d. Are [p] and [b] allophones of one phoneme?

e. If /am/ represents a bound prefix morpheme in Luganda, can you conclude that [amdano] is a possible phonetic form for a word in this language starting with this prefix?

f. Is there a phonological homorganic nasal rule in Luganda?

g. If the phonetic representation of the word meaning "little boy" is [akapoobe], give the phonemic and phonetic representations for "a boy."

Phonemic _____   Phonetic _____

h. Which of the following forms is the *phonemic* representation for the prefix meaning "a" or "an"?

(1) /en/   (2) /ēn/   (3) /ēm/   (4) /em/   (5) /eŋ/

i. What is the *phonetic* representation of the word meaning "a branch"?

_____

j. What is the *phonemic* representation of the word meaning "little stranger"?

_____

k. State in general terms any phonological rules revealed by the Luganda data.

PART 3
Social Aspects of Language

Speech is civilization itself. The word, even the most contradictious word, preserves contact—it is silence which isolates.

Thomas Mann, *The Magic Mountain*

Children raised in isolation do not use language; it is used by human beings in a social context, communicating their needs, ideas, and emotions to one another. . . .

William Labov, *Sociolinguistic Patterns*

CHAPTER 7
Language in Society

Language is a city to the building of which every human being brought a stone.

Ralph Waldo Emerson, *Letters and Social Aims*

Dialects

Within any recognizable speech community, variations are normally found on all levels of linguistic structure—phonological, grammatical, and lexical. Some of the variations are correlated with geographical location...some...may... depend on the identity of the person spoken to or spoken about...Other variations are correlated with the identity of the speaker. These include cases of difference between men's and women's speech...linguistic variation may also be correlated with the social status of the speakers [or] with other facts in the social and cultural context.

William Bright[1]

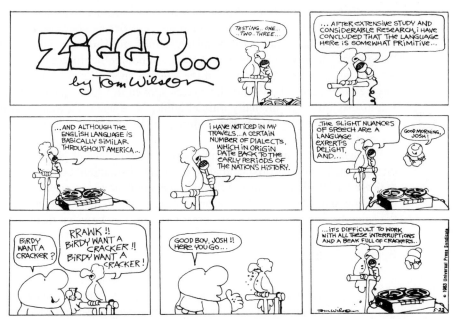

ZIGGY copyright 1983 ZIGGY & FRIENDS, INC. Distributed by Universal Press Syndicate. Reprinted with permission. All rights reserved.

[1]W. Bright, *Variation & Change in Language: Essays by William Bright*, A.S. Dil, ed. Stanford, Calif.: Stanford University Press, 1976, p. 32.

All speakers of English can talk to each other and pretty much understand each other; yet no two speak exactly alike. Some differences are due to age, sex, state of health, size, personality, emotional state, and personal idiosyncrasies. That each person speaks somewhat differently from all others is shown by our ability to recognize acquaintances by hearing them talk. The unique characteristics of the language of an individual speaker are referred to as the speaker's **idiolect.** English may then be said to consist of 400,000,000 idiolects, or the number equal to the number of speakers of English.

Beyond these individual differences, the language of a group of people may show regular variations from that used by other groups of speakers of that language. When the English of speakers in different geographical regions and from different social groups shows *systematic* differences, the groups are said to speak different **dialects** of the same language. The dialects of a single language may thus be defined as **mutually intelligible** forms of a language that differ in **systematic** ways from each other.

It is not always easy to decide whether the systematic differences between two speech communities reflect two dialects or two different languages. A rule-of-thumb definition can be used: "When dialects become mutually unintelligible—when the speakers of one dialect group can no longer understand the speakers of another dialect group—these 'dialects' become different languages." However, to define "mutually intelligible" is itself a difficult task. Danes speaking Danish and Norwegians speaking Norwegian and Swedes speaking Swedish can converse with each other; yet Danish and Norwegian and Swedish are considered separate languages because they are spoken in separate countries and because there are regular differences in their grammars. Similarly, Hindi and Urdu are mutually intelligible "languages" spoken in Pakistan and India, although the differences between them are not much greater than between the English spoken in America and Australia. On the other hand, the various languages spoken in China, such as Mandarin and Cantonese, although mutually unintelligible, have been referred to as dialects of Chinese because they are spoken within a single country and have a common writing system.

Because neither mutual intelligibility nor the existence of political boundaries is decisive, it is not surprising that a clear-cut distinction between language and dialects has evaded linguistic scholars. We shall, however, use the rule-of-thumb definition and refer to dialects of one language as mutually intelligible versions of the same basic grammar, with systematic differences between them.

Regional Dialects

Phonetics . . . the science of speech. That's my profession. . . . (I) can spot an Irishman or a Yorkshireman by his brogue. I can place any man within six miles. I can place him within two miles in London. Sometimes within two streets.

George Bernard Shaw, *Pygmalion*

Dialectal diversity develops when people are separated from each other geographically and socially. The changes that occur in the language spoken in one area or group do not necessarily spread to another. Within a single group of speakers who are in regular contact with one another, the changes are spread among the group and "relearned" by their children. When some communication barrier separates groups of speakers—be it a physical barrier such as an ocean or a mountain range, or social barriers of a political, racial, class, or religious kind—linguistic changes are not easily spread and dialectal differences are reinforced.

Dialect differences tend to increase proportionately to the degree of **communicative isolation** between the groups. Communicative isolation refers to a situation such as existed among America, Australia, and England in the eighteenth century. There was some contact through commerce and emigration, but an Australian was less likely to talk to an Englishman than to another Australian. Today the isolation is less pronounced because of the mass media and travel by jet, but even within one country, regionalisms persist. In fact, there is no evidence to show that any **dialect leveling** occurs due to the mass media, and recent studies even suggest that dialect variation is increasing, particularly in urban areas.

Changes in the grammar do not take place all at once within the speech community. They take place gradually, often originating in one region and slowly spreading to others, and often taking place throughout the lives of several generations of speakers.

A change that occurs in one region and fails to spread to other regions of the language community gives rise to dialect differences. When enough such differences give the language spoken in a particular region (for example, the city of Boston or the southern area of the United States) its own "flavor," that version of the language is referred to as a regional dialect.

Accents

Regional phonological or phonetic distinctions are often referred to as different **accents.** A person is said to have a Boston accent, a Southern accent, a Brooklyn accent, a Midwestern drawl, and so on. Thus, *accent* refers to the characteristics of speech that convey information about the speaker's dialect, which may reveal in what country or what part of the country the speaker grew up or to which sociolinguistic group the speaker belongs. People in the United States often refer to someone as having a British accent or an Australian accent; in Britain they refer to an American accent.

The term *accent* is also used to refer to the speech of someone who speaks a language nonnatively; for example, a French person speaking English is described as having a French accent. In this sense, accent refers to phonological differences or "interference" from a different language spoken elsewhere. Unlike the regional dialectal accents, such "foreign" accents do not reflect differences in the language of the community where the language was acquired.

Dialects of English

The educated Southerner has no use for an r except at the beginning of a word.

Mark Twain, *Life on the Mississippi*

Regional dialects tell us a great deal about how languages change, which will be discussed at greater length in the next chapter. The origins of many regional dialects of American English can be traced to the people who first settled North America in the seventeenth and eighteenth centuries. The early settlers came from different parts of England, speaking different dialects. Therefore regional dialect differences existed in the first colonies.

By the time of the American Revolution, there were three major dialect areas in the British colonies: the Northern dialect spoken in New England and around the Hudson River; the Midland dialect spoken in Pennsylvania; and the Southern dialect. These dialects differed from each other, and from the English spoken in England, in systematic ways. Some of the changes that occurred in British English spread to the colonies; others did not.

How regional dialects developed may be illustrated by changes in the pronunciation of words with an *r*. The British in southern England were already dropping their *r*'s before consonants and at the ends of words as early as the eighteenth century. Words such as *farm, farther,* and *father* were pronounced as [fa:m], [fa:ðə], and [fa:ðə], respectively. By the end of the eighteenth century, this practice was a general rule among the early settlers in New England and the southern Atlantic seaboard. Close commercial ties were maintained between the New England colonies and London, and Southerners sent their children to England to be educated, which reinforced the "*r*-dropping" rule. The "*r*-less" dialect still spoken today in Boston, New York, and Savannah maintained this characteristic. Later settlers, however, came from northern England, where the *r* had been retained; as the frontier moved westward so did the *r*.

Pioneers from all three dialect areas spread westward. The intermingling of their dialects "leveled" or "submerged" many of their dialectal differences, which is why the English used in large sections of the Midwest and the West is similar.

In addition to the English settlers, other waves of immigration brought speakers of other dialects and other languages to different regions. Each group left its imprint on the language of the communities in which they settled—the Germans who in the last half of the eighteenth century settled the southeastern section of Pennsylvania, the Welsh west of Philadelphia, the Germans and Scotch-Irish in the section of the state called the Midlands area.

The last half of the twentieth century has brought hundreds of thousands of Spanish-speaking immigrants from Cuba, Puerto Rico, Central America, and Mexico to both east and west coasts of the United States. It is estimated that a majority of Southern Californians will be native Spanish speakers by the year 2000. In addition, English is being enriched by the languages spoken by the large numbers of new residents coming from the Pacific Rim countries of Japan, China, Korea, Samoa, Malaysia, Viet Nam, Thailand, the Philippines, and Indonesia. Large new groups of Russian and Armenian speakers also contribute to the richness of the vocabulary and culture of American cities. Students in one high school in Los Angeles come from homes in which sixty-seven different languages are spoken.

The language of the regions where the new immigrants settle may thus be differentially affected by the native languages of the settlers further adding to the varieties of American English.

English is the most widely spoken language in the world if one counts all those who use it as a native language or as a second or third language. It is the national language of a number of countries, such as the United States, large parts of Canada, the British Isles, Australia, New Zealand. For many years it was the official language in countries which were once colonies of Britain, including India, Nigeria, Ghana, Kenya and the other "anglophone" countries of Africa. Different dialects of English are spoken in these countries for the reasons discussed above.

Phonological Differences

> I have noticed in traveling about the country a good many differences in the pronunciation of common words. . . . Now what I want to know is whether there is any right or wrong about this matter. . . . If one way is right, why don't we all pronounce that way and compel the other fellow to do the same? If there isn't any right or wrong, why do some persons make so much fuss about it?
>
> Letter quoted in "The Standard American," *in J. V. Williamson and V. M. Burke, eds.,*
> *A Various Language*

A comparison between the "*r*-less" dialect and other dialects illustrates phonological differences between dialects. There are many such differences in the United States, which created difficulties for the authors of this book in writing Chapter 5, where we had to illustrate the different sounds of English by reference to words in which the sounds occur. As mentioned earlier, some students pronounce *caught* as /kɔt/ with the vowel /ɔ/ and *cot* as /kat/ with /a/, whereas other students will pronounce them identically. Some readers pronounce *Mary, marry,* and *merry* identically; others pronounce all three words differently as /meri/, /mæri/, and /mɛri/; and still others pronounce two of them the same. In the southern area of the country, *creek* is pronounced with a tense /i/ as /krik/, and in the north Midlands, it is pronounced with a lax /ɪ/ as /krɪk/. Many speakers of American English pronounce *pin* and *pen* identically, whereas others pronounce the first as /pɪn/ and the second as /pɛn/. If variety is indeed the spice of life, then American English dialects add zest to our existence.

As mentioned in Chapter 5, the pronunciation of British English differs in systematic ways from that spoken in Standard American English. Britain, however, has many regional dialects. The British vowels described in the phonetics chapter on p. 201 are the ones used by speakers of the most prestigious British dialect.[2] In this dialect, /h/ is pronounced at the beginning of both *head* and *herb,* whereas in American English dialects it is not pronounced in the second word. In some English dialects, the /h/ is regularly dropped from most words in which it is pronounced in American, such as *house,* pronounced /aws/, and *hero,* pronounced /iro/.

There are many other phonological differences found in the many dialects of English used around the world.

Lexical Differences

Regional dialects may differ in the words people use for the same object, as well as in phonology. Hans Kurath,[3] an eminent dialectologist, in his paper "What Do You Call It?" asked:

> Do you call it a *pail* or a *bucket?* Do you draw water from a *faucet* or from a *spigot?* Do you pull down the *blinds,* the *shades,* or the *curtains* when it gets dark? Do you *wheel* the baby, or do you *ride* it or *roll* it? In a *baby carriage,* a *buggy,* a *coach,* or a *cab?*

People take a *lift* to the *first floor* (our *second floor*) in England, but an *elevator* in the United States; they get five gallons of *petrol* (not *gas*) in London; in Britain a *public school* is "private" (you have to pay), and if a student showed up there wearing *pants* ("underpants") instead of *trousers* ("pants"), he would be sent home to get dressed. If you ask for a *tonic* in Boston, you will get a drink called *soda* or *soda-pop* in Los Angeles; and a *freeway* in Los Angeles is a *thruway* in New York, a *parkway* in New Jersey, a *motorway* in England, and an *expressway* or *turnpike* in other dialect areas.

Dialect Atlases

Kurath produced **dialect maps** and **dialect atlases** of a region (an example of which may be seen in Figure 7.1), on which dialect differences are geographically plotted. For instance, black dots may mark every village whose speakers retain the voiceless /ʍ/ pronunciation of *wheelbarrow,* and white dots where voiced /w/ is pronounced. The black dots often fall together, as do the white dots. These concentrations define **dialect areas.** A line drawn on the map separating the areas is called

[2]This dialect is often referred to as RP, standing for "received pronunciation" because it was once considered to be the dialect used in court and "received by" the British king and queen.
[3]Hans Kurath, *"What Do You Call It?"* In Juanita V. Williamson and Virginia M. Burke, eds., *A Various Language: Perspective on American Dialects,* New York: Holt, Rinehart and Winston, 1971.

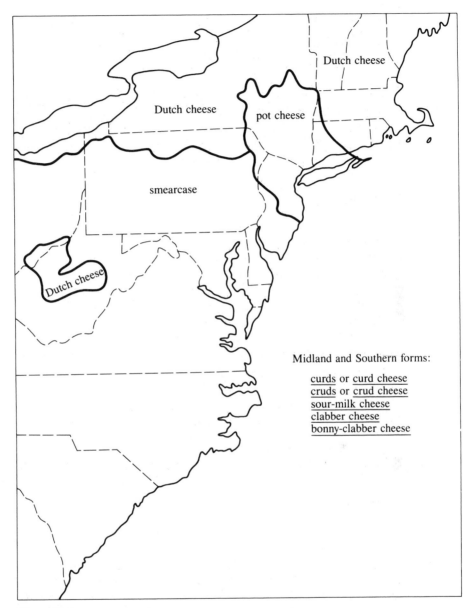

Figure 7–1

A dialect map from Hans Kurath's *A Word Geography of the Eastern United States,* showing the isoglosses separating the use of different words which refer to the same cheese.

an **isogloss.** When you "cross" an isogloss, you are passing from one dialect area to another. Sometimes several isoglosses will coincide, often at a political boundary or at a natural boundary such as a river or mountain range. Linguists call these groupings a **bundle of isoglosses.** Such a bundle will define a particular regional dialect.

The first volume of a long-awaited *Dictionary of Regional English* by Frederick G. Cassidy was published in 1985. This work represents years of research and scholarship by Cassidy and other American dialectologists and promises to be a major resource for those interested in American English dialectal differences.

Syntactic Differences

Systematic syntactic differences also distinguish dialects. In most American dialects sentences may be conjoined as follows:

John will eat and Mary will eat → John and Mary will eat.

In the Ozark dialect the following conjunction is also possible:

John will eat and Mary will eat → John will eat and Mary.

Speakers of some American dialects say *Have them come early!* where others would say *Have them to come early!* Some American speakers use *gotten* in a sentence such as *He should have gotten to school on time;* in British English, only the form *got* occurs. In a number of American English dialects the pronoun *I* occurs when *me* would be used in other dialects. This difference is a syntactically conditioned morphological difference.

Dialect 1	**Dialect 2**
between you and I	between you and me
Won't he let you and I swim?	Won't he let you and me swim?

In British English the pronoun *it* in the sentence *I could have done it* can be deleted to form *I could have done,* which is not permitted in the American English grammar.

With all such differences we are still able to understand speakers of another dialect. Even though regional dialects differ as to pronunciation, vocabulary, and syntactic rules, they are minor differences when compared with the totality of the grammar. The largest part of the vocabulary, the sound–meaning relations of words and the syntactic rules, are shared, which is why dialects of one language are mutually intelligible.

The "Standard"

> We don't talk fancy grammar and eat anchovy toast. But to live under the kitchen doesn't say we aren't educated.
>
> Mary Norton, *The Borrowers*

> Standard English is the customary use of a community when it is recognized and accepted as the customary use of the community. Beyond this is the larger field of good English, any English that justifies itself by accomplishing its end, by hitting the mark.
>
> George Philip Krapp, *Modern English: Its Growth and Present Use*

Even though every language is a composite of dialects, many people talk and think about a language as if it were a "well-defined" fixed system with various dialects diverging from this norm. Such was the view of Mario Pei,[4] the author of a number of books on language that were quite popular at one time. He accused the editors of *Webster's Third New International Dictionary,* published in 1961, of confusing "to the point of obliteration the older distinction between standard, substandard, colloquial, vulgar, and slang," attributing to them the view that "Good and bad, right and wrong, correct and incorrect no longer exist" (p. 82).

Language Purists

> A woman who utters such depressing and disgusting sounds has no right to be anywhere—no right to live. Remember that you are a human being with a soul and the divine gift of articulate speech: that your native language is the language of Shakespeare and Milton and The Bible; and don't sit there crooning like a bilious pigeon.
>
> George Bernard Shaw, *Pygmalion*

Prescriptive grammarians, or language "purists," usually consider the dialect used by political leaders and the upper socioeconomic classes, the dialect used for literature or printed documents, the dialect taught in the schools, as the correct form of the language.

Otto Jespersen, the great Danish linguist, ridiculed the view that a particular dialect is better than any other when he wrote: "We set up as the best language that which is bound in the best writers, and count as the best writers those that best write the language. We are therefore no further advanced than before."[5]

The dominant or prestige dialect is often called the standard dialect. **Standard American English (SAE)** is a dialect of English that many Americans *almost*

---

[4]M. Pei, "A Loss for Words," *Saturday Review.* Nov. 14 (1964): 82–84.
[5]O. Jesperson, *Mankind, Nation, and Individual,* Bloomington, Indiana: Indiana University Press, 1925 (reprinted 1964).

speak; divergences from this "norm" are labeled "Philadelphia dialect," "Chicago dialect," "Black English," and so on.

SAE is an idealization. Nobody speaks this dialect; and if somebody did, we would not know it, because SAE is not defined precisely. Several years ago there was an entire conference devoted to one subject: a precise definition of SAE. This meeting did not succeed in satisfying everyone as to what SAE should be. It used to be the case that the language used by national newsbroadcasters represented SAE, but today many of these people speak a regional dialect, or themselves "violate" the English preferred by the purists.

Deviations from this "standard" that no one can define, let alone use, are seen by many as reflecting a "language crisis." Edwin Newman, in his best seller *Strictly Speaking,* asks "Will Americans be the death of English?" and answers "My mature, considered opinion is that it will." All this fuss is reminiscent of Mark Twain's cable to the Associated Press, after reading his obituary: "The reports of my death are greatly exaggerated."

The idea that language change equals corruption goes back at least as far as the Greek grammarians at Alexandria, of around 100–200 B.C.E. They were concerned that the Greek spoken in their time was different from the Greek of Homer, and they believed that the earlier forms were purer. They also tried to "correct" the imperfections but failed as miserably as do any modern counterparts. Similarly, the Moslem Arabic grammarians working at Basra in the eighth and ninth centuries C.E. attempted to purify Arabic to restore it to the perfection of Arabic in the Koran.

For many years after the American Revolution, British writers and journalists railed against American English. Thomas Jefferson was an early target in a commentary on his *Notes on the State of Virginia,* which appeared in the *London Review:*

> For shame, Mr. Jefferson! Why, after trampling upon the honour of our country, and representing it as little better than a land of barbarism—why, we say, perpetually trample also upon the very grammar of our language. . . . Freely, good sir, we will forgive all your attacks, impotent as they are illiberal, upon our *national character;* but for the future spare—O spare, we beseech you, our mother-tongue!

The fears of the British journalists in 1787 proved unfounded, and so will the fears of Edwin Newman. One dialect is neither better nor worse than another, nor purer nor more corrupt; it is simply different.

Banned Languages

Language purists wish to stem change in language or dialect differentiation because of their false belief that some languages are better than others or that change leads to corruption. Languages and dialects have also been banned as a means of political control. Russian was the only legal language permitted by the Russian tsars who banned the use of Ukrainian, Lithuanian, Georgian, Armenian, Azerbaijan, and all the other languages spoken by national groups under the rule of Russia.

Cajun English was banned in southern Louisiana by practice if not by law until about twenty years ago. Individuals over the age of fifty years report that they were often punished in school if they spoke in French even though many of them had never heard English before attending school.

For many years, American Indian languages were banned in Federal and state schools on Native Indian reservations. Japanese movies and songs were once banned in Korea, and Faroese in the Faroe Islands. In a recent discussion among linguists via a computer network called Linguist Net, various degrees of the banning of languages and dialects were reported to exist or to have existed in many countries throughout history.

In France, a notion of the "standard" as the only correct form of the language is propagated by an official academy of "scholars" who determine what usages constitute the "official French language." A number of years ago, this Academy enacted a law forbidding the use of "Franglais" words in advertising (words of English origin like *le parking, le weekend, le hotdog*) but the French continue to use them. Many of the hundreds of local village dialects (called *patois* [patwa] by the Academy) are actually separate languages, derived from Latin (as are French, Spanish, and Italian). There were political as well as misguided linguistic motivations behind the efforts to maintain only one official language.

In the past (and to some extent in the present) a Frenchman or Frenchwoman from the provinces who wished to succeed in French society nearly always had to learn Parisian French and be bidialectal. In recent years in France the regional "nationalist" movements made a major demand for the right to use their own languages in their schools and for official business. In the section of France known as l'Occitanie, the popular singers sing in the regional language, Languedoc, both as a protest against the official "standard language" policy and as part of the cultural revival movement. Here is the final chorus of a popular song sung in Languedoc (shown below with its French and English translations):

Languedoc	French	English
Mas perqué, perqué	Mais pourquoi, pourquoi	But why, why
M'an pas dit à	Ne m'a-t-on pas dit à	Did they not speak to
l'escóla	l'école	me at school
La lega de mon pais?	La langue de mon pays?	The language of my country?

In the province of Brittany in France there has also been a strong movement for the use of Breton in the schools, as opposed to the "standard" French. Breton is not even in the same language family as French, which is a Romance language; Breton is a Celtic language in the same family as Irish, Gaelic, and Welsh. (We will discuss such family groupings in Chapter 8.) It is not, however, the structure of the language or the genetic family grouping that has led to the Breton movement. It is rather the pride of a people who speak a language or a dialect not considered as good as the "standard," and their efforts to change this political view of language use.

These efforts have proved successful. In 1982, the newly elected French government decreed that the languages and cultures of Brittany (Breton), the southern Languedoc region, and other areas would be promoted through schooling, exhibitions, and festivals. No longer would school children who spoke Breton be punished by having to wear a wooden shoe tied around their necks, as had been the custom.

There is no reference to a national language in the Constitution of the United States. John Adams proposed that a national academy be established, similar to the French Academy, to standardize American English, but this view was roundly rejected as not in keeping with the goals of "liberty and justice for all."

In recent years in the United States a movement has arisen in the attempt to establish English as an official language by amending the Constitution. An "Official English" initiative was passed by the electorate in California in 1986, in Colorado, Florida, and Arizona in 1988, and in Alabama in 1990. Such measures have also been adopted by seventeen state legislatures. This kind of linguistic "chauvinism" is opposed by civil rights minority group advocates who point out that such measures prevent large numbers of non-English speakers from participating in the electoral process if ballots and other educational material are printed only in English. Leading educators also oppose such moves since they could halt programs in bilingual education which are proving to be effective as means both to educate nonnative speakers and to aid their acquisition of English.

The attempts to ban certain languages and dialects should not be equated with the efforts on the part of certain peoples to preserve their own languages and cultures. This attempt to slow down or reverse the dying out of a language is illustrated by the French in Quebec. But such "anti-linguicide" moves should not include the banning of any use of a language.

A dramatic example of the efforts to revive not only a dying but a dead language occurred in Israel. An Academy of the Hebrew Language in Israel was established to accomplish this task never before done in the history of humanity—to revive an ancient written language to serve the daily colloquial needs of the people. Twenty-three lexicologists work with the Bible and the Talmud in order to add new words to the language. While there is some attempt to keep the language "pure," the academy has given way to popular pressure. Thus, a bank check is called a *check* /čɛk/ in the singular and pluralized by adding the Hebrew suffix to form *check-im*, although the Hebrew word *hamcha* was proposed. Similarly, *lipstick* has triumphed over *faton* and *pajama* over *chalifatsheina*.

No academy and no guardians of language purity can stem language change, nor should anyone attempt to do so, since such change does not mean corruption. The fact that for the great majority of American English speakers *criteria* and *data* are now mass nouns like *information* is no cause for concern. Information can include one fact or many facts, but one would still say "The information is" For some speakers it is equally correct to say "The criteria is" or "The criteria are." Those who say "The data are" would or could say "The datum (singular) is."

A standard dialect (or prestige dialect) of a particular language may have social functions—to bind people together or to provide a common written form for multi-dialectal speakers. It is, however, neither more expressive, more logical, more complex, nor more regular than any other dialect or language. Any judgments, therefore, as to the superiority or inferiority of a particular dialect or language are social judgments, not linguistic or scientific ones.

Black English

> For some blacks and some whites (notice the infamous all has been omitted) it is not a matter of you say e-ther and we say i-ther, but rather: . . . You kiss your children, and we give 'em some sugar . . . You cook a pan of spinach, and we burn a mess of greens. You wear clothes, and we wear threads . . . You call the police, and we drop a dime. You say wow! We say ain't that a blip. You care, love and hurt, and we care, love and hurt.
>
> Sandra Haggerty, *Los Angeles Times,* April 2, 1973.

KUDZU by Doug Marlette. By permission of Doug Marlette and Creators Syndicate.

Whereas the majority of United States dialects are, to a great extent, free from stigma, especially the many regional dialects, one dialect of North American English has been a victim of prejudicial ignorance. This dialect (actually a group of closely related dialects) is spoken by a large section of non-middle-class African Americans; it is usually referred to as Black English (BE) or Negro English or Non-standard Negro English. The distinguishing features of this English dialect persist for social, educational, and economic reasons. The historical discrimination against black Americans[6] has created ghetto living and segregated schools. Where social isolation exists, dialect differences are intensified. In addition, particularly in recent years, many blacks no longer consider their dialect to be inferior, and it has become a means of positive black identification.

Since the onset of the civil-rights movement in the 1960s, Black English has been the focus of national attention. There are critics who attempt to equate the use of Black English with inferior "genetic" intelligence and "cultural deprivation,"

---

[6]As used here, "American" refers to the United States.

justifying these incorrect notions by stating that BE is a "deficient, illogical, and incomplete" language. Such epithets cannot be applied to any language, and they are as unscientific in reference to BE as to Russian, Chinese, or Standard American English. The cultural-deprivation myth is as false as the idea that some dialects or languages are inferior. A person may be "deprived" of one cultural background but rich in another.

Some people, white and black, think they can identify someone's race by hearing an unseen person talk, believing that different races inherently speak differently. This assumption is equally false; a black child raised in an upper-class British household will speak that dialect of English. A white child raised in an environment where Black English is spoken will speak Black English. Children construct grammars based on the language they hear.

There are, however, systematic differences between BE and SAE, just as there are systematic differences between Australian and American English.

Phonology of Black English

Some of the differences between BE and SAE phonology are as follows:

1. Like a number of dialects of both British and American English, BE includes a rule which **deletes /r/** except before a vowel. Pairs of words like *guard* and *god, nor* and *gnaw, sore* and *saw, poor* and *pa, fort* and *fought,* and *court* and *caught* are pronounced identically in BE because of the presence of this phonological rule in the grammar.
2. There is also an **l-deletion Rule** for some speakers of BE creating homophones like *toll* and *toe, all* and *awe, help* and *hep.*
3. A regular **Consonant Cluster Simplification** rule in BE simplifies consonant clusters, particularly at the ends of words and when one of the two consonants is an alveolar (/t/, /d/, /s/, /z/). The application of this rule may delete the past tense morpheme so that *meant* and *mend* are both pronounced as *men* and *past* and *passed (pass + ed)* may both be pronounced like *pass.* When speakers of this dialect say *I pass the test yesterday,* they are not showing an ignorance of past and present, but are pronouncing the past tense according to this rule in their grammar.

   The deletion rule is optional; it does not always apply, and studies have shown that it is more likely to apply when the final [t] or [d] does not represent the past tense morpheme, as in nouns like *paste* [pes] as opposed to verbs like *chased* [cest] where the final past tense [t] will not always be deleted. This has also been found true with final [s] or [z], which will be retained more often by speakers of BE in words like *seats* /sit + s/ where the /s/ represents "plural" than in words like *Keats* /kit/ where it is more likely to be deleted.
4. BE shares with many regional dialects the lack of any distinction between /ɪ/ and /ɛ/ before nasal consonants, producing identical pronunciations of *pin* and

pen, bin and *Ben, tin* and *ten,* and so on. The vowel used in these words is roughly between the [ɪ] of *pit* and the [ɛ] of *pet.*

5. In BE the phonemic distinction between /aj/ and /aw/ has been lost, both having become /a/. Thus *why* and *wow* are pronounced [wa].

6. Another change has reduced the /oy/ (particularly before /l/) to the simple vowel [o] without the glide, so that *boil* and *boy* are pronounced [bo].

7. A regular feature is the change of a /θ/ to /f/ and /ð/ to /v/ so that *Ruth* is pronounced [ruf] and *brother* is pronounced [brʌvər]. This [θ]–[f] correspondence also is true of some dialects of British English, where /θ/ is not even a phoneme in the language. *Think* is regularly [fiŋk] in Cockney English.

All these differences are systematic and "rule governed" and similar to sound changes that have taken place in languages all over the world, including Standard English.

Syntactic Differences between BE and SAE

Syntactic differences, as noted above, also exist between dialects. It is the syntactic differences that have often been used to illustrate the "illogic" of BE, and yet it is just such differences that point up the fact that BE is as syntactically complex and as "logical" as SAE.

Double Negatives

Following the lead of early "prescriptive" grammarians, some "scholars" and teachers conclude that it is illogical to say *he don't know nothing* because two negatives make a positive.

Since such negative constructions occur in BE, it has been concluded by some "educators" that speakers of BE are deficient because they use language "illogically." These so-called educators fail to point out that 'double negatives' are part of many current white dialects in the English-speaking world, and were the standard in an earlier stage of English. Furthermore, multiple negation is the regular rule in many other languages of the world.

Deletion of the Verb "Be"

In most cases, if, in Standard English the verb can be contracted, in Black English sentences it is deleted, as shown in the following sentences:

SAE	BE
He is nice/He's nice.	He nice.
They are mine/They're mine.	They mine.
I am going to do it/I'm gonna do it.	I gonna do it.[7]

---

[7]Sentences taken from W. Labov, *The Logic of Nonstandard English,* Georgetown University, 20th Annual Round Table, No. 22, 1969.

Habitual "Be"

In Black English, an uninflected form of *be* is required if the speaker is referring to **habitual** action. In SAE, the sentence *John is happy* can be interpreted to mean John is happy at the moment and may be generally happy. To make the distinction clear in SAE, one would have to say *John is generally happy*. In BE, this distinction is made syntactically, as follows:

John be happy.	"John is always happy."
John happy.	"John is happy now."
He be late.	"He is habitually late"
He late.	"He is late this time."
Do you be tired?	"Are you generally tired?"
You tired?	"Are you tired now?"

This syntactic distinction between habitual aspect and nonhabitual occurs in languages other than BE, but not in SAE. It has been suggested that the uninflected *be* is the result of a convergence of similar rules in African, Creole, and Irish English sources.[8]

There are many more differences between the grammars of BE and SAE than those we have discussed. But the ones we have listed are enough to show the "regularity" of BE and to dispel the notion that there is anything "illogical" or "primitive" about this dialect.

The study of Black English is important for nonlinguists, such as teachers, as well as for linguists. There would be less of a communication breakdown between teachers and their students who speak Black English if this dialect were not considered to be an inferior version of the standard. Children who read *your mother* as *you muvver* would be more likely to respond positively to the statement "In the dialect we are using, the 'th' sound is pronounced [ð] not [v] as it is in yours" than they would to a teacher who expressed an attitude of contempt toward their grammar.

Another reason for studying these dialects is that such study shows the extent to which dialects differ and leads to a better knowledge of human language. Furthermore, the history of any dialect reveals important information about language change in general, as will be discussed in the next chapter.

History of Black English

It is simple to date the beginning of Black English—the first blacks arrived in Virginia in 1619. There are, however, different theories as to the factors that led to the systematic differences between Black English and other American English dialects.

One view suggests that Black English originated when the African slaves learned English from their colonial masters as a second language. Although the basic

[8]John Holm, *Pidgins and Creoles,* Vols. 1 & 2, Cambridge, England: Cambridge University Press, 1988, 1989.

grammar was learned, many surface differences persisted, which were reflected in the grammars constructed by the children of the slaves, who heard English primarily from their parents. Had the children been exposed to the English spoken by the whites, their grammars would have been more similar if not identical to the general Southern dialect. The dialect differences persisted and grew because blacks in America were isolated by social and racial barriers. The proponents of this theory point to the fact that the grammars of Black English and Standard American English are basically identical except for a few syntactic and phonological rules, which produce surface differences.

Another view which is receiving increasing support is that many of the unique features of Black English are traceable to influences of the African languages spoken by the slaves. During the seventeenth and eighteenth centuries, Africans who spoke different languages were purposefully grouped together to discourage communication and to prevent slave revolts. In order to communicate, the slaves were forced to use the one common language all had access to, namely, English. They invented a simplified form—called a pidgin (to be discussed below)—which incorporated many features from West African languages. According to this view, the differences between BE and other dialects are due more to basic syntactic differences than to surface distinctions.

It is apparent that Black English is closer to the Southern dialect of English than to other dialects. The theory that suggests that the Negro slaves learned the English of white Southerners as a second language explains these similarities. They might also be explained by the fact that for many decades a large number of Southern white children were raised by black women and played with black children. It is not unlikely that many of the distinguishing features of Southern dialects were acquired from Black English in this way. A publication of the American Dialect Society in 1908–1909 makes this point clearly:

> For my part, after a somewhat careful study of east Alabama dialect, I am convinced that the speech of the white people, the dialect I have spoken all my life and the one I tried to record here, is more largely colored by the language of the negroes [sic] than by any other single influence.[9]

The two-way interchange still goes on. Standard American English is constantly enriched by words, phrases, and usage originating in Black English; and Black English, whatever its origins, is influenced by the changes that go on in the many other dialects of English.

Hispanic English

A major group of American English dialects is spoken by native Spanish speakers or their descendants. The dialects spoken by Puerto Rican and Cuban immigrants

[9]L. W. Payne, "A Word-List from East Alabama," *Dialect Notes* 3(1909): 279–328, 343–391.

or their children are somewhat different from each other and also from those spoken by Mexican Americans in the Southwest and California, called Chicano English (ChE), although they share many features.

These dialects are spoken mainly by bilingual speakers, and the Spanish influence is reinforced by border contact between the United States and Mexico and the social cohesion of a large segment of this population. Like BE, ChE is not simply an incorrect version of SAE; it differs systematically.

In addition to using ChE, many bilingual Hispanics switch from English to Spanish and vice versa, sometimes within a single sentence, a process called **code-switching.**

ChE is, like other dialects, the result of many factors, a major one being the influence of Spanish. Phonological differences between ChE and SAE reveal this influence. Chapters 5 and 6 discussed the fact that English has eleven stressed vowel phonemes (not counting the three diphthongs): /i, ɪ, e, ɛ, æ, u, ʊ, o, ɔ, a, ʌ/. Spanish, however, has only five: /i, e, u, o, a/. Chicano speakers substitute the Spanish vowel system for the English, producing a number of homophones that have distinct pronunciations in SAE. Thus *ship* and *sheep* are both pronounced like *sheep* /šip/, *rid* is pronounced like *read* /rid/, and so on.

Here are other systematic differences:[10]

1. Alternation of *ch* /č/ and *sh* /š/; *show* is pronounced as if spelled with a *ch* /čo/ and *check* as if spelled with an *sh* /šɛk/.
2. Devoicing of some consonants, such as /z/ in *easy* /isi/ and *guys* /gajs/.
3. /t/ for /θ/ and /d/ for /ð/ word initially, as in /tiŋ/ for *thing* and /de/ for *they.*
4. Word-final consonant cluster simplification. *War* and *ward* are both pronounced /war/; *star* and *start* are /star/. This process may also delete past tense suffixes (*poked* becomes /pok/) and third person singular agreement (*He loves her* becomes *he love her*), by a process similar to that in BE.

Prosodic aspects of speech in ChE, that is, the suprasegmentals such as stress and intonation, also differ from SAE. Stress, for example, may occur on a different syllable in ChE than in SAE.

The Spanish sequential constraint, which does not permit a word to begin with an /s/ cluster, is sometimes carried over to ChE. Thus, *scare* may be pronounced *escare* /ɛsker/.

There are also regular syntactic differences between ChE and SAE. In Spanish, a negative sentence includes a negative morpheme before the verb even if another negative appears; thus, in ChE, "double negatives" occur:

SAE	ChE
I don't have any money.	I don have no money.
I don't want anything.	I no want nothin.

[10]Joyce Penfield and Jacob L. Ornstein-Galicia, *Chicano English: An Ethnic Contact,* Philadelphia, Pa.: John Benjamins, 1985.

Another regular difference between ChE and SAE is in the use of the comparative *more* to mean *more often,* as in the following:

SAE	**ChE**
I use English more often.	More I use English.
They use Spanish more often.	They use more Spanish.

Lexical differences also occur, such as the use of *borrow* in ChE for *lend* in SAE (*Borrow me a pencil*) as well as many other substitutions.

Many Chicano speakers (and speakers of Black English) are bidialectal; they can use either ChE (or BE) or SAE, depending on the social situation. The use of these dialects thus is clearly not evidence of language deviance but of language expertise.

Lingua Francas

Language is a steed that carries one into a far country.

Arab proverb

Many areas of the world are populated by people speaking divergent languages. In such areas, where groups desire social or commercial communication, one language is often used by common agreement. Such a language is called a **lingua franca.**

In medieval times, a trade language came into use in the Mediterranean ports, based largely on the medieval languages that became modern Italian and Provencal. This came to be called Lingua Franca, "Frankish language." The term *lingua franca* was generalized to other languages similarly used. Thus, any language can be a lingua franca.

English has been called "the lingua franca of the whole world," French, at one time, was "the lingua franca of diplomacy," and Latin and Greek were the lingua francas of Christianity in the West and East, respectively, for a millennium. Among Jews, Yiddish has long served as a lingua franca.

More frequently, lingua francas serve as "trade languages." East Africa is populated by hundreds of tribes, each speaking its own language, but most Africans of this area learn at least some Swahili as a second language, and this lingua franca is used and understood in nearly every marketplace. A similar situation exists in West Africa, where Hausa is the lingua franca.

Hindi and Urdu are the lingua francas of India and Pakistan, respectively. The linguistic situation of this area of the world is so complex that there are often regional lingua francas—usually the popular dialects near commercial centers. The same situation existed in Imperial China.

In modern China, the Chinese language as a whole is often referred to as *Zhongwen,* which technically refers to the written language, whereas *Zhongguo hua* refers to the spoken language. Ninety-four percent of the people living in the People's

Republic of China are said to speak Han languages, which can be divided into eight major dialects (or language groups) that for the most part are mutually unintelligible. Within each group there are hundreds of dialects. In addition to these Han languages, there are more than fifty "national minority" languages, including the five principal ones: Mongolian, Uighur, Tibetan, Zhuang, and Korean. The situation is clearly complex, and for this reason an extensive language reform policy was inaugurated to spread a standard language, called *Putonghua,* which embodies the pronunciation of the Beijing (Peking) dialect, the grammar of Northern Chinese dialects, and the vocabulary of modern colloquial Chinese. The native languages and dialects are not considered inferior; rather, the approach is to spread the "common speech" (the literal meaning of Putonghua) so that all may communicate with each other in this lingua franca.

Certain lingua francas arise naturally; others are developed by government policy and intervention. In many places of the world, however, people still cannot speak with neighbors only a few miles away.

Pidgins and Creoles

> Padi dɛm; kɔntri; una ɔl we de na Rom.
> Mɛk una ɔl kak una yes. A Kam bɛr siza,
> a nɔ kam prez am.

William Shakespeare, *Julius Caesar III: ii,* translated to Krio by Thomas Decker

Pidgins

A lingua franca is typically a language with a broad base of native speakers, likely to be used and learned by persons whose native language is in the same language family. Often in history, however, traders and missionaries from one part of the world have visited and attempted to communicate with peoples residing in another area. In such cases the contact is too specialized, and the cultures too widely separated for the usual kind of lingua franca to arise. Instead, the two (or possibly more) groups use their native languages as a basis for a rudimentary language of few lexical items and less complex grammatical rules. Such a "marginal language" is called a **pidgin.**

There are a number of such languages in the world, including a large number of English-based pidgins. One such pidgin, called **Tok Pisin,** originally was called Melanesian Pidgin English. It is widely used in Papua New Guinea. Like most pidgins, many of its lexical items and much of its structure are based on only one language of the two or more contact languages, in this case English. The variety of Tok Pisin used as a primary language in urban centers is more highly developed and more complex than the Tok Pisin used as a lingua franca in remote areas. Papers in Tok Pisin have been presented at linguistics conferences in Papua New Guinea and it is commonly used for debates in the parliament of the country.

Further Studies in Pigeon English
Drawing by J.B. Handlesman ©1990 The New Yorker Magazine, Inc.

Although pidgins are in some sense rudimentary, they are not devoid of grammar. The phonological system is rule-governed, as in any human language. The inventory of phonemes is generally small, and each phoneme may have many allophonic pronunciations. In Tok Pisin, for example, [č], [š], and [s] are all possible pronunciations of the phoneme /s/; [masin], [mašin], and [mačin] all mean "machine."

Tok Pisin has its own writing system, its own literature, and its own newspapers and radio programs, and it has even been used to address a United Nations meeting.

With their small vocabularies, however, pidgins are not good at expressing fine distinctions of meaning. Many lexical items bear a heavy semantic burden, with context being relied upon to remove ambiguity. Much circumlocution and metaphorical extension is necessary. All of these factors combine to give pidgins a unique flavor. What could be a friendlier definition of "friend" than the Australian aborigine's *him brother belong me,* or more poetic than this description of the sun: *lamp belong Jesus?* A policeman is *gubmint catchum-fella,* whiskers are *grass belong face,* and when a man is thirsty *him belly allatime burn.*

Pidgin has come to have negative connotations, perhaps because the best-known pidgins are all associated with European colonial empires. The *Encyclopedia Britannica* once described Pidgin English as "an unruly bastard jargon, filled with nursery imbecilities, vulgarisms and corruptions." It no longer uses such a definition. In recent times there is greater recognition of the fact that pidgins reflect human creative linguistic ability, as is beautifully revealed by the Chinese servant asking whether his master's prize sow had given birth to a litter: *Him cow pig have kittens?*

Some people would like to eradicate pidgins. A pidgin spoken on New Zealand by the Maoris was replaced, through massive education, by Standard English, and the use of Chinese Pidgin English was forbidden by the government of China. Its use had died out by the end of the nineteenth century because the Chinese gained access to learning Standard English which proved to be more useful in communicating with non-Chinese speakers.

Pidgins have been unjustly maligned; they may serve a useful function.[11] For example, a New Guinean can learn Tok Pisin well enough in six months to begin many kinds of semiprofessional training. To learn English for the same purpose might require ten times as long. In an area with over 800 mutually unintelligible languages, Tok Pisin plays a vital role in unifying similar cultures.

During the seventeenth, eighteenth, and nineteenth centuries many pidgins sprang up along the coasts of China, Africa, and the New World to accommodate the Europeans. Chinook Jargon is a pidginized American Indian language used by various tribes of the Pacific Northwest to carry on trade. Some linguists have suggested that Proto-Germanic (the earliest form of the Germanic languages) was originally a pidgin, arguing that ordinary linguistic change cannot account for certain striking differences between the Germanic tongues and other Indo-European languages. They theorized that in the first millennium B.C.E. the primitive Germanic tribes that resided along the Baltic Sea traded with the more sophisticated, seagoing cultures. The two people communicated by means of a pidgin, which either grossly affected Proto-Germanic, or actually became Proto-Germanic. If this is true, English, German, Dutch, and Yiddish had humble beginnings as a pidgin.

Case, tense, mood, and voice are generally absent from pidgins. One cannot, however, speak an English pidgin by merely using English without inflecting verbs or declining pronouns. Pidgins are not "baby talk" or Hollywood's version of American Indians talking English. *Me Tarzan, you Jane* may be understood, but it is not pidgin as it is used in West Africa.

Pidgins are simple, but are rule governed. In Tok Pisin, most verbs that take a direct object must have the suffix -m or -im, even if the direct object is absent; here are some examples of the results of the application of this "rule" of the language:

[11]Robert A. Hall, *Hands Off Pidgin English,* New South Wales: Pacific Publications, 1955.

| Tok Pisin: | Mi driman long kilim wanpela snek. |
| English: | I dreamed that I killed a snake. |

| Tok Pisin: | Bandarap em i kukim. |
| English: | Bandarap cooked (it). |

Other rules determine word order, which, as in English, is usually quite strict in pidgins because of the lack of case endings on nouns.

The set of pronouns is often simpler in pidgins. In Cameroonian Pidgin (CP), which is also an English-based pidgin, for example, the pronoun system does not show gender or all the case differences that exist in standard English (SE).[12]

	CP			**SE**	
a	mi	ma	I	me	my
yu	yu	yu	you	you	your
i	i/am	i	he	him	his
i	i/am	i	she	her	her
wi	wi	wi	we	us	our
wuna	wuna	wuna	you	you	your
dɛm	dɛm/am	dɛm	they	them	their

Pidgins also may have fewer prepositions than the languages on which they are based. In CP, for example, *fɔ* means "to," "at," "in," "for," and "from," as shown in the following examples:

Gif di buk fɔ mi.	"Give the book to me."
I dei fɔ fam.	"She is at the farm."
Dɛm dei fɔ chɔs.	"They are in the church."
Du dis wan fɔ mi, a bɛg.	"Do this for me, please."
Di mɔni dei fɔ tebul.	"The money is on the table."
You fit muf tɛn frangk fɔ ma kwa.	"You can take ten francs from my bag."

Characteristics of pidgins differ in detail from one pidgin to another, and often vary depending on the native language of the pidgin speaker. Thus the verb generally comes at the end of a sentence for a Japanese speaker of Hawaiian Pidgin English (as in *The poor people all potato eat*), whereas a Filipino speaker of this pidgin puts it before the subject (*Work hard these people*).

Creoles

One distinguishing characteristic of pidgin languages is that no one learns them as native speakers. When a pidgin comes to be adopted by a community as its native

[12]The data from CP are from Loreto Todd, *Modern Englishes: Pidgins & Creoles,* Oxford, England: Basil Blackwell, 1984.

tongue, and children learn it as a first language, that language is called a **creole;** the pidgin has become **creolized.**

The term *creole* comes originally from the Portuguese meaning "a white man of European descent born and raised in a tropical or semitropical colony . . . The term was . . . subsequently applied to certain languages spoken . . . in and around the Caribbean and in West Africa, and then more generally to other similar languages."[13]

Creoles often arose on slave plantations in certain areas where Africans of many different tribes could communicate only via the plantation pidgin. Haitian Creole, based on French, developed in this way, as did the "English" spoken in parts of Jamaica. Gullah is an English-based creole spoken by the descendants of African slaves on islands off the coast of Georgia and South Carolina. Louisiana Creole, related to Haitian Creole, is spoken by large numbers of blacks and whites in Louisiana. Krio, the language spoken by as many as 200,000 Sierra Leoneans, developed, at least in part, from an English-based pidgin.

Creoles become fully developed languages, having more lexical items and a broader array of grammatical distinctions than pidgins. In time, they become languages as complete in every way as other languages.

The study of pidgins and creoles has contributed a great deal to our understanding of the nature of human language and the genetically determined constraints on grammars.

Styles, Slang, and Jargon

> Slang is language which takes off its coat, spits on its hands—and goes to work.
>
> Carl Sandburg

Styles

Most speakers of a language know many "dialects." They use one "dialect" when out with friends, another when on a job interview or presenting a report in class, and another when talking to their parents. These "situation dialects" are called **styles.**

Nearly everybody has at least an informal and a formal style. In an informal style the rules of contraction are used more often, the syntactic rules of negation and agreement may be altered, and many words are used that do not occur in the formal style. Many speakers have the ability to use a number of different styles, ranging between the two extremes of formal and informal. Speakers of minority dialects sometimes display virtuosic ability to slide back and forth along a continuum of styles that range from the informal patterns learned in a ghetto to "formal standard."

[13]Suzanne Romaine, *Pidgin and Creole Languages,* London and New York: Longman, 1988, p. 38.

When Labov was studying Black English used by Harlem youths, he encountered difficulties because the youths (subconsciously) adopted a different style in the presence of white strangers. It took time and effort to gain their confidence to the point where they would "forget" that their conversations were being recorded and so use their less formal style.

Many cultures have rules of social behavior that strictly govern style. In some Indo-European languages there is the distinction between "you (familiar)" and "you (polite)." German *du* and French *tu* are to be used only with "intimates"; *Sie* and *vous* are more formal and used with nonintimates. French even has a verb *tutoyer*, which means "to use the *tu* form," and German uses the verb *duzen* to express the informal or less honorific style of speaking.

Other languages have a much more elaborate code of style usage. Speakers of Thai use *kin* "eat" to their intimates, informally; but *thaan* "eat" is used informally with strangers, *rabprathaan* "eat" on formal occasions or when conversing with dignitaries or esteemed persons (such as parents), and *chan* "eat" when referring to Buddhist monks. Japanese and Javanese are also languages with elaborate styles that must be adhered to in certain social situations.

Slang

> Police are notorious for creating new words by shortening existing ones, such as *perp* for *perpetrator, ped* for *pedestrian* and *wit* for *witness*. More baffling to court reporters is the gang member who . . . might testify that he was in his *hoopty* around *dimday* when some *mud duck* with a *tray-eight* tried to *take him out of the box*. Translation: The man was in his car about dusk when a woman armed with a .38 caliber gun tried to kill him.
>
> Los Angeles Times, August 11, 1986.

One mark of an informal style is the frequent occurrence of **slang.** Almost everyone uses slang on some occasions, but it is not easy to define the word. Slang has been defined as "one of those things that everybody can recognize and nobody can define."[14] The use of slang, or colloquial language, introduces many new words into the language by recombining old words into new meanings. *Spaced out, right on, hangup,* and *rip-off* have all gained a degree of acceptance. Slang may also introduce an entirely new word, such as *barf, flub,* and *pooped.* Finally, slang often consists of ascribing totally new meanings to old words. *Grass* and *pot* widened their meaning to "marijuana"; *pig* and *fuzz* are derogatory terms for "policeman"; *rap, cool, dig, stoned, bread,* and *split* have all extended their semantic domain.

The words we have cited sound "slangy" because they have not gained total acceptability. Words such as *dwindle, freshman, glib,* and *mob* are former slang words that in time overcame their "unsavory" origin. It is not always easy to know where to draw the line between "slang" words and "regular" words. This confusion seems always to have been around. In 1890, John S. Farmer, coeditor with W. E.

---

[14]Paul Roberts, *Understanding English*, New York: Harper & Row, 1958, p. 342.

Henley of *Slang and Its Analogues,* remarked: "The borderland between slang and the 'Queen's English' is an ill-defined territory, the limits of which have never been clearly mapped out."

One generation's slang is another generation's standard vocabulary. *Fan* (as in "Dodger fan") was once a slang term, short for *fanatic. Phone,* too, was once a slangy, clipped version of *telephone,* as *TV* was of *television.* In Shakespeare's time, *fretful* and *dwindle* were slang, and more recently *blimp* and *hot dog* were both "hard-core" slang.

The use of slang varies from region to region, so slang in New York and slang in Los Angeles differ. The word *slang* itself is slang in British English for "scold."

Slang words and phrases are often "invented" in keeping with new ideas and customs. They may represent "in" attitudes better than the more conservative items of the vocabulary. Their importance is shown by the fact that it was thought necessary to give the returning Viet Nam prisoners of war a glossary of eighty-six new slang words and phrases, from *acid* to *zonked.* The words on this list—prepared by the Air Force—had come into use during only five years. Furthermore, by the time this book is published, many of these terms may have passed out of the language, and many new ones will have been added.

A number of slang words have entered English from the "underworld," such as *crack* for a special form of cocaine, *payola, C-note, G-man, to hang paper* ("to write 'bum' checks"), *sawbuck,* and so forth.

The now ordinary French word meaning "head," *tête,* was once a slang word derived from the Latin *testa,* which meant "earthen pot." Some slang words seem to hang on and on in the language, though, never changing their status from slang to "respectable." Shakespeare used the expression *beat it* to mean "scram" (or more politely, "leave!"), and *beat it* would be considered by most English speakers still to be a slang expression. Similarly, the use of the word *pig* for "policeman" goes back at least as far as 1785, when a writer of the time called a Bow Street police officer a "China Street pig."

Jargon and Argot

> It is common knowledge that students have a language that is quite peculiar to them and that is not understood very well outside student society . . . But if the code of behaviour somewhere is particularly lively, then the language of the students is all the richer for it—and vice versa.
>
> Friedrich Ch. Laukhard (1792)

Practically every conceivable science, profession, trade, and occupation has its own set of words, some of which are considered to be "slang" and others "technical," depending on the status of the people using these "in" words. Such words are sometimes called **jargon** or **argot.** Linguistic jargon, some of which is used in this book, consists of terms such as *phoneme, morpheme, case, lexicon, phrase structure rule,* and so on.

The existence of argots or jargons is illustrated by the story of a seaman witness being cross-examined at a trial, who was asked if he knew the plaintiff. Indicating that he did not know what *plaintiff* meant brought a chide from the attorney: "You mean you came into this court as a witness and don't know what 'plaintiff' means?" Later the sailor was asked where he was standing when the boat lurched. "Abaft the binnacle," was the reply, and to the attorney's questioning stare he responded: "You mean you came into this court and don't know where abaft the binnacle is?"

Because the jargon terms used by different professional groups are so extensive (and so obscure in meaning), court reporters in the Los Angeles Criminal Courts Building have a library that includes books on medical terms, guns, trade names, and computer jargon, as well as street slang.

The computer age not only ushered in a technological revolution; it also introduced a huge jargon of "computerese" used by computer "hackers," including the words *modem* (a blend of *modulator* and *demodulator*), *bit* (a contraction of *binary digit*), *byte* (a collection of some number of bits), *floppy* (a noun or adjective referring to a flexible *disk*), *ROM* (an acronym for *Read Only Memory*), *RAM* (an acronym for *Random Access Memory*), *morf* (an abbreviation for the question *Male or female?*), and *OOPS* (an acronym for *Object Oriented Program Systems.*).

Many jargon terms pass into the standard language. Jargon, like slang, spreads from a narrow group until it is used and understood by a large segment of the population. In fact, it is not always possible to distinguish between what is jargon and what is slang, as illustrated in the book *Slang U: The Official Dictionary of College Slang,*[15] a collection of slang used on the campus of the University of California, Los Angeles, by Professor Munroe and the students in her UCLA Honors Collegium seminar. One can not tell from the hundreds of entries in this collection which of the entries are used solely by UCLA students, which by the definitions above would make it a UCLA student jargon. It is highly probable that the word *fossil,* meaning a "person who has been a college student for more than four years" is used in this way only at UCLA or on college campuses, but certainly the term *prick,* referring to a "mean, offensive, inconsiderate, rude person (usually, a male)" is used as a general slang term on and off university campuses.

Taboo or Not Taboo?

Sex is a four-letter word.
　　Bumper sticker slogan

A recent item in a newspaper included the following paragraph (the names have been deleted to protect the guilty):

"This is not a Sunday school, but it is a school of law," the judge said in warning the defendants he would not tolerate the "use of expletives during jury selec-

---

[15]Pamela Munro (ed.), *Slang U,* New York: Harmony Books, 1990.

tion." "I'm not going to have my fellow citizens and prospective jurors subjected to filthy language," the judge added.

How can language be filthy? In fact, how can it be clean? The filth or beauty of language must be in the ear of the listener, or in the collective ear of society.

There cannot be anything about a particular string of sounds that makes it intrinsically clean or dirty, ugly or beautiful. If you say that you pricked your finger when sewing, no one would raise an eyebrow; but if you refer to your professor as a prick, the judge quoted above would undoubtedly censure this "dirty" word.

Certain words in all societies are considered **taboo**—they are not to be used, or at least, not in "polite company." The word *taboo* was borrowed from Tongan, a Polynesian language, in which it refers to acts that are forbidden or to be avoided. When an act is taboo, reference to this act may also become taboo. That is, first you are forbidden to do something; then you are forbidden to talk about it.

What acts or words are forbidden reflect the particular customs and views of the society. Some words may be used in certain circumstances and not in others; for example, among the Zuni Indians, it is improper to use the word *takka,* meaning "frogs," during a religious ceremony; a complex compound word must be used instead, which literally translated would be "several-are-sitting-in-a-shallow-basin-where-they-are-in-liquid."[16]

In certain societies, words that have religious connotations are considered profane if used outside of formal or religious ceremonies. Christians are forbidden to "take the Lord's name in vain," and this prohibition has been extended to the use of curses, which are believed to have magical powers. Thus *hell* and *damn* are changed to *heck* and *darn,* perhaps with the belief or hope that this change will fool the "powers that be." In England the word *bloody* is a taboo word, perhaps because it originally referred to the blood of Christ. The Oxford English Dictionary states that *bloody* has been in general colloquial use from the Restoration and is "now constantly in the mouths of the lowest classes, but by respectable people considered 'a horrid word' on a par with obscene or profane language, and usually printed in the newspapers 'b _____ y.'" It further states that the origin of the term is not quite certain. This uncertainty itself gives us a clue about "dirty" words: people who use them often do not know why they are taboo, only that they are, and to some extent, this is why they remain in the language, to give vent to strong emotion.

Words relating to sex, sex organs, and natural bodily functions make up a large part of the set of taboo words of many cultures. Some languages have no native words to mean "sexual intercourse" but do borrow such words from neighboring people. Other languages have many words for this common and universal act, most of which are considered taboo.

Two or more words or expressions can have the same linguistic meaning, with one acceptable and the others the cause of embarrassment or horror. In English, words borrowed from Latin sound "scientific" and therefore appear to be technical

---

[16]Peter Farb, *Word Play,* New York: Bantam, 1975, p. 85.

and "clean," whereas native Anglo-Saxon counterparts are taboo. This fact reflects the opinion that the vocabulary used by the upper classes was superior to that used by the lower classes, a distinction going back at least to the Norman Conquest in 1066, when, as Farb puts it, "a duchess perspired and expectorated and menstruated—while a kitchen maid sweated and spat and bled."

There is no linguistic reason why the word *vagina* is "clean" whereas *cunt* is "dirty"; or why *prick* or *cock* is taboo, but *penis* is acknowledged as referring to part of the male anatomy; or why everyone *defecates,* but only vulgar people *shit.* Many people even avoid words like *breast, intercourse,* and *testicles* as much as words like *tits, fuck,* and *balls.* There is no linguistic basis for such views, but pointing this fact out does not imply advocating the use or nonuse of any such words.

Euphemisms

> Banish the use of the four letter words
>   Whose meaning is never obscure.
> The Anglos, the Saxons, those bawdy old birds
>   Were vulgar, obscene, and impure.
> But cherish the use of the weaseling phrase
>   That never quite says what it means;
> You'd better be known for your hypocrite ways
>   Than vulgar, impure, and obscene.
>
>   Ogden Nash, *"Ode to the Four Letter Words"*

The existence of taboo words or taboo ideas stimulates the creation of **euphemisms.** A euphemism is a word or phrase that replaces a taboo word or serves to avoid frightening or unpleasant subjects. In many societies, because death is feared, there are a number of euphemisms related to this subject. People are less apt to *die* and more apt to *pass on* or *pass away.* Those who take care of your *loved ones* who have passed away are more likely to be *funeral directors* than *morticians* or *undertakers.*

Ogden Nash's poem, quoted above, exhorts against such euphemisms, as another verse demonstrates:

> *When in calling, plain speaking is out;*
> *When the ladies (God bless 'em) are milling about,*
> *You may wet, make water, or empty the glass;*
> *You can powder your nose, or the "johnny" will pass.*
> *It's a drain for the lily, or man about dog*
> *When everyone's drunk, it's condensing the fog;*
> *But sure as the devil, that word with a hiss,*
> *It's only in Shakespeare that characters _____.*

There are scholars who are as bemused as Ogden Nash with the attitudes revealed by the use of euphemisms in society. A journal, *Maledicta,* subtitled "The International Journal of Verbal Aggression" and edited by Reinhold Aman, "specializes in uncensored glossaries and studies of all offensive and negatively valued words and expressions, in all languages and from all cultures, past and present." A review of this journal by Bill Katz in the *Library Journal* (November 1977) points out, "The history of the dirty word or phrase is the focus of this substantial . . . journal [whose articles] are written in a scholarly yet entertaining fashion by professors . . . as well as by a few outsiders."

A scholarly study of Australian English euphemisms shows the considerable creativity involved:[17]

urinate: drain the dragon
              syphon the python
              water the horse
              squeeze the lemon
              drain the spuds
              wring the rattlesnake
              shake hands with wife's best friend
              point Percy at the porcelain
              train Terence on the terracotta

have intercourse: shag
              root
              crack a fat
              dip the wick
              play hospital
              hide the ferret
              play cars and garages
              hide the egg roll (sausage, salami)
              boil bangers
              slip a length
              go off like a beltfed motor
              go like a rat up a rhododendron
              go like a rat up a drain pipe
              have a northwest cocktail

These euphemisms, as well as the difference between the accepted Latinate "genteel" terms and the "dirty" Anglo-Saxon terms, show that a word or phrase not only has a linguistic **denotative meaning** but also has a **connotative meaning**, reflecting attitudes, emotions, value judgments, and so on. In learning a language, children learn which words are "taboo," and these taboo words differ from one child to another, depending on the value system accepted in the family or group in which the child grows up.

[17]Jay Powell, Paper delivered at the Western Conference of Linguistics, University of Oregon, 1972.

Racial and National Epithets

The use of epithets for people of different religions, nationalities, or color tell us something about the users of these words. The word *boy* is not a taboo word when used generally, but when a twenty-year-old white man calls a forty-year-old black man "boy," the word takes on an additional meaning; it reflects the racist attitude of the speaker. So also words like *kike, wop, nigger,* and so forth express racist and chauvinist views of society. If racial and national and religious bigotry and oppression did not exist, then in time these words would either die out or lose their racist connotations.

Language And Sexism

doctor, n. . . . a man of great learning.

The American College Dictionary, 1947

A businessman is aggressive; a businesswoman is pushy. A businessman is good on details; she's picky . . . He follows through; she doesn't know when to quit. He stands firm; she's hard . . . His judgments are her prejudices. He is a man of the world; she's been around. He isn't afraid to say what is on his mind; she's mouthy. He exercises authority diligently; she's power mad. He's closemouthed; she's secretive. He climbed the ladder of success; she slept her way to the top.

From "How to Tell A Businessman from a Businesswoman,"
Graduate School of Management, UCLA, The Balloon XXII, (6).

The discussion of obscenities, blasphemies, taboo words, and euphemisms showed that words of a language cannot be intrinsically good or bad but may reflect individual or societal values. In addition, one speaker may use a word with positive connotations while another may select a different word with negative connotations to refer to the same person. For example, the same individual may be referred to as a *terrorist* by one group and as a *freedom fighter* by another. A woman may be called a *castrating female* (or *ballsy women's libber*) or may be referred to as a *courageous feminist advocate*. The words we use to refer to certain individuals or groups reflect our individual nonlinguistic attitudes and may also reflect the culture and views of society.

Language reflects sexism in society. Language itself is not sexist, just as it is not obscene; but it can connote sexist attitudes as well as attitudes about social taboos or racism.

Dictionaries often give clues to social attitudes. In the 1969 edition of the *American Heritage Dictionary,* examples used to illustrate the meaning of words include "manly courage" and "masculine charm." Women do not fare as well, as exemplified by "womanish tears" and "feminine wiles." In *Webster's New World Dictionary of the American Language* (1961), *honorarium* is defined as "a payment to a professional man for services on which no fee is set or legally obtainable."

Sections in history textbooks still in use are headed "Pioneers and Their Wives"; children read that "courageous pioneers crossed the country in covered wagons with their wives, children, and cattle." Presumably women are not considered to be as courageous as their husbands.

As late as the 1965–1968 eleventh edition, Bowker Company (New York) was still publishing *American Men of Science: A Biographical Dictionary,* edited by Jaques Cottell Press. The editors were much in advance of Columbia University. Until 1972, the women's faculty toilet doors were labeled "Women," whereas the men's doors were labeled "Officers of Instruction."

Language also reflects sexism in society by the way we interpret neutral (non-gender-specific) terms. Most people, hearing *My cousin is a professor* (or *a doctor,* or *the Chancellor of the University,* or *a steel worker*), assume the cousin is a man. This assumption has nothing to do with the English language but a great deal to do with the fact that, historically, women have not been prominent in these positions. Similarly, if you heard someone say *My cousin is a nurse* (or *elementary school teacher,* or *clerk-typist,* or *houseworker*), you would probably conclude that the speaker's cousin is a woman. It is less evident why the sentence *My neighbor is a blonde* is understood as referring to a woman; perhaps the physical characteristics of women in our society assume greater importance than those of men because women are constantly exploited as sex objects.

Studies analyzing the language used by men in reference to women, which often has derogatory or sexual connotations, indicate that such terms go far back into history, and sometimes enter the language with no pejorative implications but gradually gain them. Thus, from Old English *huswif* "housewife," the word *hussy* was derived. In their original employment, "a laundress made beds, a needlewoman came to sew, a spinster tended the spinning wheel, and a nurse cared for the sick. But all apparently acquired secondary duties in some households, because all became euphemisms for a mistress or a prostitute at some time during their existence."[18]

Words for women—all with abusive or sexual overtones—abound: *dish, tomato, piece, piece of ass, chick, piece of tail, bunny, pussy, pussycat, bitch, doll, slut, cow,* to name just a few. Far fewer such pejorative terms exist for men.

Marked and Unmarked Forms

Long afterward, Oedipus, old and blinded, walked the roads. He smelled a familiar smell. It was the Sphinx. Oedipus said, "I want to ask one question. Why didn't I recognize my mother?" "You gave the wrong answer," said the Sphinx. "But that was what made everything possible," said Oedipus. "No," she said. "When I asked, 'What walks on four legs in the morning, two at noon, and three in the evening,' you answered, 'Man.' You didn't say anything about woman." "When you say Man," said Oedipus, "you include women too. Everyone knows that." She said, "That's what you think."

Muriel Rukeyser, *Myth*

[18]Muriel R. Schulz, "The Semantic Derogation of Woman." In B. Thorne and N. Henley, eds., *Language and Sex.* Rowley, Mass.: Newbury House Publishers, 1975, pp. 66–67.

PEANUTS reprinted by permission of UFS, Inc.

One striking fact about the asymmetry between male and female terms in many languages is that when there are male/female pairs, the male form for the most part is **unmarked** and the female term is created by adding a bound morpheme or by compounding. We have many such examples in English:

Male	**Female**
prince	princess
author	authoress
count	countess
actor	actress
host	hostess
poet	poetess
heir	heiress
hero	heroine
Paul	Pauline

Given these asymmetries, **folk etymologies** (nonscientific speculations about the origin of words) arise that misinterpret a number of nonsexist words. For example, *female* is not the feminine form of *male,* but came into English from the Latin word *femina,* with the same morpheme *fe* that occurs in the Latin *fecundus* meaning "fertile" (originally derived from an Indo-European word meaning "to give suck to"). It entered English through the Old French word *femme* and its diminutive form *femelle* "little woman."

Other male/female gender pairs have interesting meaning differences. Although a *governor* governs a state, a *governess* takes care of children; a *mistress,* in its most widely used meaning, is not a female master, nor is a *majorette* a woman major. We talk of "unwed mothers" but not "unwed fathers," of "career women" but not "career men," because there has been historically no stigma for a bachelor to father a child, and men are supposed to have careers. It is only recently that the term *househusband* has come into being, again reflecting changes in social customs.

Possibly as a protest against the reference to new and important ideas as being *seminal* (from *semen*), Clare Booth Luce updated Ibsen's drama *A Doll's House* by having Nora tell her husband that she is pregnant "in the way only men are supposed to get pregnant." When he asks "Men pregnant?" she replies, "With ideas. Pregnancies there (she taps her head) are masculine. And a very superior form of labor. Pregnancies here (she taps her stomach) are feminine—a very inferior form of labor."

Neutral nongender words become compounded when the basic form becomes associated with either sex. Thus, people talk of a *male nurse* because it is expected that a nurse will be a female, and for parallel reasons we have the compounds *lady doctor, career woman,* and *woman athlete.*

The Generic "He"

The unmarked, or male, nouns also serve as general terms, as do the male pronouns. The *brotherhood of man* includes women, but *sisterhood* does not include men.

When Thomas Jefferson wrote in the Declaration of Independence that "all *men* are created equal" and "governments are instituted among *men* deriving their just powers from the consent of the governed" he was not using *men* as a general term to include women. His use of the word *men* was precise at the time that women could not vote. In the sixteenth and seventeenth centuries, masculine pronouns were not used as the **generic** terms; the various forms of *he* were used when referring to males, and of *she* when referring to females. The pronoun *they* was used to refer to people of either sex even if the referent was a singular noun, as shown by Lord Chesterfield's statement in 1759: "If a person is born of a gloomy temper . . . they cannot help it."

By the eighteenth century, grammarians (males to be sure) created the rule designating the male pronouns as the general term, and it wasn't until the nineteenth century that the rule was applied widely, after an act of Parliament in Britain in 1850 sanctioned its use. But this generic use of *he* was ignored. In 1879, women doctors were barred from membership in the all-male Massachusetts Medical Society on the basis that the bylaws of the organization referred to members by the pronoun *he*.

Changes in English are taking place which reflect the feminist movement and the growing awareness on the part of both men and women that language may reflect attitudes of society and reinforce stereotypes and bias. More and more the word *people* is replacing *mankind*, *personnel* is used instead of *manpower*, *nurturing* instead of *mothering* and *to operate* instead of *to man*. *Chair* or *moderator* is used instead of *chairman* (particularly by those who do not like the "clumsiness" of *chairperson*) and terms like *postal worker*, *firefighter*, and *public safety officer* are replacing *mailman*, *fireman*, and *policeman*.

More Asymmetries

Other linguistic asymmetries exist, such as the fact that most women continue to adopt their husbands' names in marriage. This name change can be traced back to early (and to a great extent, current) legal practices. Thus we often refer to a woman as Mrs. Jack Fromkin, but seldom refer to a man as Mr. Vicki Fromkin, except in an insulting sense. We talk of Professor and Mrs. John Smith but seldom, if ever, of Mr. and Dr. Mary Jones. At a UCLA alumni association dinner, place cards designated where "Dr. Fromkin" and "Mrs. Fromkin" were to sit, although both individuals have doctoral degrees.

It is insulting to a woman to be called a *spinster* or an *old maid,* but it is not insulting to a man to be called a *bachelor.* There is nothing inherently pejorative about the word *spinster.* The connotations reflect the different views society has about an unmarried woman as opposed to an unmarried man. It is not the language that is sexist; it is society.

Female Language

An increasing number of researchers have been investigating language and sex and language and sexism. One area of research concerns the differences between male and female speech styles. In Japanese, male and female speech comprise two distinct dialects of the language. So different are these two styles that "seeing eye" guide dogs in Japan are trained in English, because the sex of the owner is not known in advance and it is easier and more socially acceptable for a blind person to use English than the "wrong" sex's language style.

In the Muskogean language, Koasati, spoken in Louisiana, words that end in an /s/ when spoken by men, end in /l/ or /n/ when used by women; for example, the word meaning "lift it" is *lakawhol* for women and *lakawhos* for men. Early explorers reported that the men and women of the Carib Indians used different dialects. In Chiquita, a Bolivian language, the grammar of male language includes a noun class gender distinction, with names for males and supernatural beings morphologically marked in one way, and nouns referring to females marked in another.

DENNIS THE MENACE

"WHEN A LADY NEVER MARRIES, "THEN WHEN A MAN NEVER
SHE'S AN *OLD MAID*." MARRIES, IS HE AN OLD BUTLER?"

DENNIS THE MENACE® used by permission of Hank Ketcham and © by North American Syndicate.

There is nothing inherently wrong in the development of different styles, which may include intonation, phonology, syntax, and lexicon. It is wrong, however, to continue stereotypes regarding female speech, which are more myths than truth. For example, a common stereotype is that women talk a lot; yet controlled studies show just the opposite is true when men and women are together. That is, in mixed groups, the women seem to talk less than the men.

One characteristic of female speech is the higher pitch used by women, due, to a great extent, to the shorter vocal tracts of women. But, a study conducted by the phonetician Caroline Henton showed that the difference in pitch between male and female British voices was, on the average, greater than could be accounted for by physiology alone, suggesting that some social factor must be involved during the acquisition period, or perhaps during puberty at the time when male voices "change."

This chapter has stressed the fact that language is neither good nor evil but its use may be one or the other. If one views women or Blacks or Hispanics as inferior, then special speech characteristics will be viewed as inferior. Furthermore, when society itself institutionalizes such attitudes, the language reflects this. When everyone in society is truly equal, and treated as such, there will be little concern for the asymmetries which exist in language.

Summary

Every person has their own individual way of speaking, called an **idiolect.** The language used by a group of speakers may also show systematic differences called a **dialect.** The dialects of a language are the mutually intelligible forms of that language which differ in systematic ways from each other. Dialects develop and are reinforced because languages change, and the changes that occur in one group or area may differ from those that occur in another. **Regional dialects** and **social dialects** develop for this reason. Some of the differences in the regional dialects of America may be traced to the different dialects spoken by the colonial settlers from England; those from southern England who arrived first spoke one dialect and those from the north spoke another. In addition, the colonists who maintained close contact with England reflected the changes occurring in British English while earlier forms were preserved among Americans who spread westward and broke communication contact with England and the Atlantic coast. The study of regional dialects has produced **dialect atlases** with **dialect maps** showing the areas where specific dialectal characteristics occur in the speech of the region. Each area is delineated by a boundary line called an **isogloss.**

Dialect differences include phonological or pronunciation differences (often called **accents**), vocabulary distinctions, and syntactic rule differences. The grammar differences between dialects are not as great as the similarities that are shared, thus permitting speakers of different dialects to communicate with each other.

In many countries, one dialect or dialect group is viewed as the **standard,** such as **Standard American English** (SAE). While this particular dialect is not linguistically superior, it may be considered by some language "purists" to be the only "correct" form of the language. Such a view has led to the idea that some nonstandard dialects are "deficient," as is erroneously suggested regarding **Black English,** a dialect used by a some African Americans. A study of Black English shows it to be as logical, complete, rule-governed, and expressive as any other dialect. This is also true of the dialects spoken by Hispanic Americans, whose native language (or that of their parents) is Spanish. One such dialect spoken in the southwest referred to as **Chicano English** (ChE) shows interesting systematic phonological and syntactic differences from SAE stemming from the influence of Spanish.

Attempts to legislate the use of a particular dialect or language have been made throughout history and exist today even extending to the banning of the use of languages other than the "accepted" one.

In areas where many languages are spoken, one language may become a **lingua franca** to ease communication among the people. In other cases, where traders or missionaries or travelers need to communicate with people who speak a language unknown to them, a **pidgin** may develop, based on one language which is simplified lexically, phonologically, and syntactically. When a pidgin is widely used, and is learned by children as their first language, it is **creolized.** The grammars of **creole** languages are similar to those of other languages, and languages of creole origin now exist in many parts of the world.

Besides regional and social dialects, speakers may use different **styles** of their dialect depending on the particular context. **Slang** is not often used in formal situations or writing, but is widely used in speech; **argot** and **jargon** refer to the unique vocabulary used by professional or trade groups not shared "outside."

In all societies certain acts or behaviors are frowned on, forbidden, or considered taboo. The words or expressions referring to these **taboo** acts are then also avoided, or considered "dirty." Language itself cannot be obscene or clean; the views toward specific words or linguistic expressions reflect the attitudes of a culture or society toward the behaviors and actions of the language users. At times slang words may be taboo whereas scientific or standard terms with the same meaning are acceptable in "polite society." Taboo words and acts give rise to **euphemisms,** which are words or phrases that replace the expressions to be avoided. Thus, *powder room* is a euphemism for *toilet,* which itself started as a euphemism for *lavatory,* which is now more acceptable than its replacement.

Just as the use of some words may reflect society's views toward sex or natural bodily functions, or religious beliefs, so also some words may reflect racist, chauvinist, and sexist attitudes in society. The language itself is not racist or sexist but reflects these views of various sectors of a society. Such terms, however, may perpetuate and reinforce biased views, and be demeaning and insulting to those addressed. Popular movements and changes in the institutions of society may then be reflected in changes in the language.

References for Further Reading

Baugh, John. 1983. *Black Street Speech*. Austin, Tex.: University of Texas.

Bickerton, Derek. 1981. *Roots of Language*. Ann Arbor, Mich.: Karoma.

Cassidy, Frederick G. 1985. *Dictionary of American Regional English*. Cambridge, Mass.: Belknap Press, Harvard University.

Coates, Jennifer. 1986. *Women, Men and Language: A Sociolinguistic Account of Sex Differences in Language*. London and New York: Longman.

Dillard, J.L. 1972. *Black English: Its History and Usage in the United States*. New York: Random House.

Ferguson, Charles, and Shirley Brice Health (Eds.) 1981. *Language in the USA*. Cambridge, England: Cambridge University Press.

Folb, Edith. 1980. *Runnin' Down Some Lines: The Language and Culture of Black Teenagers*. Cambridge, Mass.: Harvard University Press.

Frank, Francine, and Frank Ashen. 1983. *Language and the Sexes*. Albany, New York: State University of New York Press.

Holm, John. 1988–1989. *Pidgins and Creoles*, Vols. 1–2. Cambridge, England: Cambridge University Press.

Labov, William. 1969. *The Logic of Nonstandard English*. Georgetown University 20th Annual Round Table, Monograph Series on Languages and Linguistics, No. 22.

Michaels, Leonard, and Christopher Ricks (Eds.). 1980. *The State of the Language*. Berkeley, Calif.: University of California Press.

Miller, Casey, and Kate Swift. 1980. *The Handbook of Nonsexist Writing*. New York: Barnes & Noble.

Mulhausler, Peter. 1986. *Pidgin and Creole Linguistics*. Oxford, England: Basil Blackwell.

Munro, Pamela. 1990. *Slang U: The Official Dictionary of College Slang*. New York: Harmony Books.

Newmeyer, Frederick J. (Ed.). 1988. *Linguistics: The Cambridge Survey, Vol. IV. Language: The Socio-cultural Context*. Cambridge, England: Cambridge University Press.

Penfield, Joyce, and Jacob L. Ornstein-Galicia. 1985. *Chicano English: An Ethnic Contact Dialect*. Amsterdam/Philadelphia: John Benjamins Publishing Co.

Reed, Carroll E. 1977. *Dialects of American English* (Rev. Ed.). Amherst, Mass.: University of Massachusetts Press.

Romaine, Suzanne. 1988. *Pidgin & Creole Languages*. London and New York: Longman.

Shopen, Timothy, and Joseph M. Williams (Eds.). 1981. *Style and Variables in English*. Cambridge, Mass.: Winthrop Publishers.

Spears, Richard A. 1981. *Slang and Euphemism: A Dictionary of Oaths, Curses, Insults, Sexual Slang and Metaphor, Racial Slurs, Drug Talk, Homosexual Lingo, and Related Matter*. New York: Jonathan David Publishers.

Tannen, Deborah. 1990. *You Just Don't Understand: Women and Men in Conversation*. New York: Ballantine.

Todd, Loreto. 1984. *Modern Englishes: Pidgins & Creoles*. Oxford, England: Basil Blackwell.

Trudgill, Peter. 1977. *Sociolinguistics*. Middlesex, England: Penguin Books.

Williamson, Juanita V., and Virginia M. Burke. 1971. *A Various Language: Perspectives on American Dialects*. New York: Holt, Rinehart and Winston.

Exercises

1. Each pair of words is pronounced as shown phonetically in at least one American English dialect. Write in phonetic transcription your pronunciation of each word that you pronounce differently.

a.	"horse"	[hɔrs]	_____	"hoarse"	[hors]	_____
b.	"morning"	[mɔrnɪŋ]	_____	"mourning"	[mornɪ̃ŋ]	_____
c.	"for"	[fɔr]	_____	"four"	[for]	_____
d.	"ice"	[ʌjs]	_____	"eyes"	[ajz]	_____
e.	"knife"	[nʌjf]	_____	"knives"	[najvz]	_____
f.	"mute"	[mjut]	_____	"nude"	[njud]	_____
g.	"din"	[dɪ̃n]	_____	"den"	[dɛ̃n]	_____
h.	"hog"	[hɔg]	_____	"hot"	[hat]	_____
i.	"marry"	[mæri]	_____	"Mary"	[meri]	_____
j.	"merry"	[mɛri]	_____	"marry"	[mæri]	_____
k.	"rot"	[rat]	_____	"wrought"	[rɔt]	_____
l.	"lease"	[lis]	_____	"grease" (v.)	[griz]	_____
m.	"what"	[ʌat]	_____	"watt"	[wat]	_____
n.	"ant"	[æ̃nt]	_____	"aunt"	[ãnt]	_____
o.	"creek"	[kʰrɪk]	_____	"creak"	[kʰrik]	_____

2. Below is a passage from *The Gospel According to St. Mark* in Cameroon English Pidgin. See how much you are able to understand before consulting the English translation given below. State some of the similarities and differences between CEP and SAE.

   1. Di fos tok fo di gud nuus fo Jesus Christ God yi Pikin.
   2. I bi sem as i di tok fo di buk fo Isaiah, God yi nchinda (Prophet), "Lukam, mi a di sen man nchinda fo bifo yoa fes weh yi go fix yoa rud fan."
   3. Di vos fo som man di krai fo bush: "Fix di ples weh Papa God di go, mek yi rud tret."

   Translation:

   1. The beginning of the gospel of Jesus Christ, the Son of God;
   2. As it is written in the book of Isaiah the prophet, Behold, I send my messenger before thy face, which shall prepare thy way before thee.
   3. The voice of one crying in the wilderness, Prepare ye the way of the Lord, make his paths straight.

3. In the period from 1890 to 1904, *Slang and Its Analogues* by J. S. Farmer and W. E. Henley was published in seven volumes. The following entries are included in this dictionary. For each item (1) state whether the word or phrase

still exists; (2) if not, state what the modern slang term would be; (3) if the word remains but its meaning has changed, provide the modern meaning.

all out: completely, as in "All out the best." (The expression goes back to as early as 1300.)

to have apartments to let: be an idiot; one who is empty-headed.

been there: in "Oh, yes, I've been there." Applied to a man who is shrewd and who has had many experiences.

belly-button: the navel.

berkeleys: a woman's breasts.

bitch: most offensive appellation that can be given to a woman, even more provoking than that of *whore.*

once in a blue moon: extremely seldom.

boss: master; one who directs.

bread: employment (1785—"out of bread" = "out of work.")

claim: to steal.

cut dirt: to escape.

dog cheap: of little worth. (Used in 1616 by Dekker: "Three things there are Dog-cheap, learning, poorman's sweat, and oathes.")

funeral: as in "It's not my funeral." "It's no business of mine."

to get over: to seduce, to fascinate.

groovy: settled in habit; limited in mind.

grub: food.

head: toilet (nautical use only).

hook: to marry.

hump: to spoil.

hush money: money paid for silence; blackmail.

itch: to be sexually excited.

jam: a sweetheart or a mistress.

leg bags: stockings.

to lie low: to keep quiet; to bide one's time.

to lift a leg on: to have sexual intercourse.

looby: a fool.

malady of France: syphilis (used by Shakespeare in 1599).

nix: nothing.

noddle: the head.

old: money. (1900—"Perhaps it's somebody you owe a bit of the old to, Jack.")

to pill: talk platitudes.

pipe layer: a political intriguer; a schemer.

poky: cramped, stuffy, stupid.

pot: a quart; a large sum; a prize; a urinal; to excel.

puny: a freshman.

puss-gentleman: an effeminate.

4. Suppose someone asked you to help compile items for a new dictionary of slang. List ten "slang" words that you know, and provide a short definition for each.

1)
2)
3)
4)
5)
6)
7)
8)
9)
10)

5. Below are given some words used in British English for which different words are usually used in American English. See if you can match the British and American equivalents.

British		**American**	
a. clothes peg	k. biscuits	A. candy	K. baby buggy
b. braces	l. queue	B. truck	L. elevator
c. lift	m. torch	C. line	M. can
d. pram	n. underground	D. main street	N. cop
e. waistcoat	o. high street	E. crackers	O. wake up
f. shop assistant	p. crisps	F. suspenders	P. trunk
g. sweets	q. lorry	G. wrench	Q. vest
h. boot (of car)	r. holiday	H. flashlight	R. subway
i. bobby	s. tin	I. potato chips	S. clothes pin
j. spanner	t. knock up	J. vacation	T. clerk

6. This chapter has discussed various types of dialects that represent mutually intelligible systematic variations of a single language. In addition to such dialects, which arise historically, "secret" languages are invented that "distort" the language, often to prevent understanding by those who have not learned the language "game."

Pig Latin is a common language game of English; but even Pig Latin has dialects, forms of the "language game" with different rules.

A. Consider the following data from three dialects of Pig Latin, each with its own rule applied to words beginning with vowels:

	Dialect 1	**Dialect 2**	**Dialect 3**
"eat"	[itme]	[ithe]	[ite]
"arc"	[arkme]	[arkhe]	[arke]

(1) State the rule that accounts for the Pig Latin forms in each dialect.

Dialect 1:
Dialect 2:
Dialect 3:

(2) How would you say *honest, admire,* and *illegal* in each dialect? Give the phonetic transcription of the Pig Latin forms.

honest   1._____   2._____   3._____

admire   1._____   2._____   3._____

illegal   1._____   2._____   3._____

B. In one dialect of Pig Latin, the word "strike" is pronounced [ajkstre], and in another dialect it is pronounced [trajkse]. In the first dialect "slot" is pronounced [atsle] and in the second dialect, it is pronounced [latse].

(1) State the rules for each of these dialects that account for these different Pig Latin forms of the same words.

Dialect 1:
Dialect 2:

(2) Give the phonetic transcriptions for the following words in both dialects.

	1	2
spot		
crisis		
scratch		

7. Thousands of language games such as Pig Latin exist in the world's languages. In some, a suffix is added to each word; in others a syllable is inserted after each vowel; there are rhyming games and games in which phonemes are reversed. There is a game used by the Walbiri, natives of central Australia, in which the meanings of words are distorted rather than the phonological forms. In this language, all nouns, verbs, pronouns, and adjectives are replaced by their semantic opposites. Thus, the sentence *Those men are small* means *This woman is big.* These language games provide evidence for the phonemes, words, morphemes, semantic features, and so on that are posited by linguists for descriptive grammars.

Below are some sentences representing different English language games. Write each sentence in its undistorted form; state the language-game "rule."

a. /aj-o tʊk-o maj-o dɔg-o awt-o sajd-o/
b. /hirli ɪzli əli mɔrli kamliplɪliketljədli gemli/

   c. Mary-shmary can-shman talk-shmalk in-shmin rhyme-shmyme.

   d. Betpetterper latepate thanpan nevpeverper.

   e. thop-e fop-oot bop-all stop-a dop-i op-um blop-ew dop-own /ðapə fapʊt bapɔl stape dapi apəm blapu dapawn/

   f. /kʌbæn jʌbu spʌbik ðʌbɪs kʌbajnd ʌbəv ʌbɪŋglʌbɪš/ (This sentence is in "Ubby Dubby" from a children's television program popular in the 1970s.)

8. Compile a list of argot (or jargon) terms from some profession or trade (for example, lawyer, musician, doctor, longshoreman, and so forth). Give a definition for each term in "nonjargon" terms.

9. "Translate" the first paragraph of any well-known document or speech—such as the Declaration of Independence, the Gettysburg Address, or the Preamble to the Constitution—into informal, colloquial language.

CHAPTER 8
Language Change: The Syllables of Time

The language of this country being always upon the flux, the Struldbruggs of one age do not understand those of another, neither are they able after two hundred years to hold any conversation (farther than by a few general words) with their neighbors the mortals, and thus they lie under the disadvantage of living like foreigners in their own country.

Jonathan Swift, *Gulliver's Travels*

All living languages change with time. It is fortunate that they do so rather slowly compared to the human life span. It would be inconvenient to have to relearn our native language every twenty years. In the field of astronomy we find a similar situation. Because of the movement of individual stars, the stellar configurations we call constellations are continuously changing their shape. Fifty thousand years from now we would find it difficult to recognize Orion or the Big Dipper; but from year to year the changes are not noticeable. Linguistic change is also slow, in human—if not astronomical—terms. If we were to turn on a radio and miraculously receive a broadcast in our "native language" from the year 3000, we would probably think we had tuned in some foreign language station; yet from year to year we hardly notice any change in our language.

Many of the changes are revealed when languages have written records. We know a great deal of the history of English because it has been written for about 1000 years. Old English, spoken in England around the end of the first millennium, is scarcely recognizable as English. (Of course, our linguistic ancestors did not call their language Old English!) A speaker of Modern English would find the language unintelligible. There are college courses in which Old English is studied as a foreign language.

The following excerpt from Caedmon's "Hymn," composed in the seventh century C.E., shows why Old English is studied as a "foreign" language:

> *Nū sculon herigean heofonrīces Weard,*
> *Now we must praise heaven-kingdom's Guardian,*
>
> *Meotodes meahte ond his mōdgeþanc,*
> *The Creator's might and his mind-plans,*
>
> *weorc Wuldorfæder, swā hē wundra gehwæs,*
> *the work of the glory-father, when he of wonders of every one,*
>
> *ēce Drihten, ōr onstealde.*
> *eternal lord the beginning established.*

A line from *Beowulf* further illustrates why Old English must be translated for us to enjoy (the letter þ, called "thorn," is pronounced like the *th* in *think*):

Wolde guman findan þone þe him on sweofote sare geteode
He wanted to find the man who harmed him while he slept

Approximately 500 years after *Beowulf,* Chaucer wrote *The Canterbury Tales* in what is now called Middle English, spoken from around 1100 to 1500. It is more easily understood by present-day readers, as seen by looking at the opening of the *Tales.*

Whan that Aprille with his shoures soote
The droghte of March hath perced to the roote . . .
When April with its sweet showers
The drought of March has pierced to the root . . .

Two hundred years after Chaucer, in a language that can be considered an earlier form of Modern English, Shakespeare's Hamlet says:

A man may fish with the worm that hath eat of a king, and eat of the fish that hath fed of that worm.

Shakespeare wrote in the sixteenth century. A passage from *Everyman,* written about 1485, illustrates why it is claimed that Modern English was already spoken by 1500:

The Summoning of Everyman called it is,
That of our lives and ending shows
How transitory we be all day.
The matter is wonder precious,
But the intent of it is more gracious
And sweet to bear away.

The division of English into Old English (449–1100 C.E.), Middle English (1100–1500), and Modern English (1500–present) is somewhat arbitrary, being marked by the dates of events in English history, such as the Norman Conquest of 1066, that profoundly influenced the English language. Thus the history of English and the changes that occurred in the language reflect, to some extent, nonlinguistic history.

The changes in the history of the English language are reflected in the following dates:

449–1066 Old English	449	Saxons invade Britain
	658	Caedmon's "Hymn"
	8th C	*Beowulf*
	1066	Norman Conquest
1066–1500 Middle English	1387	*Canterbury Tales*
	1476	Caxton's printing press
	1500	Great vowel shift
1500–Modern English		

Changes in a language are changes in the grammars of the speakers of the language, and are perpetuated when new generations of children learn the language by acquiring the new grammar. An examination of the changes that have occurred in English during the past 1500 years shows changes in the phonology, morphology, syntax, lexicon, and semantic components of the grammar. No part of the grammar remains the same over the course of history. Although most of the examples in this chapter are from English, the histories of all languages show similar changes.

The Regularity of Sound Change

> That's not a regular rule: you invented it just now.
>
> Lewis Carroll, *Alice's Adventures in Wonderland*

The southern United States represents a major dialect area of American English. For example, words pronounced with the diphthong /aj/ in nonsouthern English will usually be pronounced with the monophthong /a/ in the South. Thus, you may be greeted by /ha/ instead of /haj/ "hi" in Atlanta, where many residents will also order apple or pecan /pa/ "pie." This /aj/–/a/ correspondence between these two dialects is an example of a **regular sound correspondence;** when /aj/ occurs in a word in nonsouthern dialects, /a/ occurs in the southern dialect.

The different pronunciations of *I, pie,* and so on did not always exist in English. This chapter will discuss how such dialect differences arose and why the sound differences are usually regular and not confined to just a few words.

In Chaucer's time, over 600 years ago, the small rodent we call a mouse [maws] was called a *mūs* [mu:s], and this mūs may have lived in someone's *hūs* [hu:s], which is the way *house* [haws] was pronounced at that time. In general, where we now pronounce [aw], speakers of Chaucer's time pronounced [u:]. This is a regular correspondence like the one between [aj] and [a:]. Thus *out* [awt] was pronounced *ūt* [u:t], *south* [sawθ] was pronounced [su:θ], and so on. Many such regular correspondences can be found, relating older and newer forms of English. All languages exhibit similar correspondences in their history.

Regular sound correspondences are also found among different languages as well as among dialects of one language. If you have studied a Romance language such as French or Spanish, you may have noticed that where an English word begins with *f,* the corresponding word in a Romance language often has a *p.* Thus *father* is French *père,* Spanish *padre;* and English *fish* is French *poisson,* Spanish *pescado.* This *f–p* correspondence is another example of a regular sound correspondence.[1]

The Native American languages Cree and Ojibwa show a *t–n* correspondence: Cree *atim,* Ojibwa *anim,* "dog"; Cree *nitim,* Ojibwa *ninim,* "my sister-in-law."

---

[1]The individual histories of English and the Romance languages have somewhat obscured the regularity of this correspondence, but even so it is striking.

Languages change in time, and the regular sound correspondences we observe between older and modern forms of a language, or between two dialects or two related languages, are due to changes in the languages' phonological system that affect certain sounds, or classes of sounds, rather than individual words. Centuries ago, as illustrated above, English underwent a sound shift in which [u:] became [aw]. We observe regularity precisely because *sounds* change, not words.

The process of sound shift can also account for dialect differences. At an earlier stage of American English a sound change of [aj] to [a:] took place among certain speakers in the southern region of the country. The change did not spread, perhaps because these speakers were somewhat isolated, or perhaps because the pronunciation of [a:] for [aj] became a "regionalism" that others did not imitate. Whatever the case, many dialect differences in pronunciation result from a sound shift whose spread is limited.

Regional dialect differences in pronunciation arise from the natural linguistic phenomenon of sound change. Many of the world's modern languages were at first regional dialects that became widely spoken and survived as separate languages. The Romance languages were once dialects of Latin spoken in the Roman Empire. As discussed in Chapter 7, there is nothing "degenerate" or "illiterate" about regional pronunciations. They are simply a result of natural sound change that failed to spread.

English and German are languages said to be **genetically related** because they developed from the same "parent" language. All genetically related languages were dialects of the same language at an earlier stage. Regular sound correspondences between languages indicate this fact. Consider the diagram in Figure 8–1 on page 324.

Suppose the phonemic inventory of Language L included the sound A, and the speakers of this language split into two groups with little contact between them. Perhaps half of them migrated to the other side of a mountain or ocean. One group underwent a sound shift A→B: words in L which were pronounced with an A now were pronounced with a B (for example, pronouncing /aw/ in the place of /u:/). The other group underwent a different sound shift of A→C. When the sound shifts are complete, there are two languages (or different dialects) L1 and L2, which exhibit the sound correspondence B↔C. The B↔C correspondence shows that the two languages descended from a common source, the parent language L. (Chance alone cannot explain a regular sound correspondence.)

If records of L were available, it would be possible to observe a regular sound correspondence between L and L1, namely A↔B, and between L and L2, namely A↔C. Such observations would confirm the relatedness of L1 and L2.

Similar circumstances resulted in the *f–p* correspondence between English and the Romance languages. Speakers of Indo-European, the language from which both English and French descended, once divided into smaller groups. One of those groups underwent a sound change of *p→f*. Their descendants eventually spoke "Germanic" languages (for example, English and German). Other Indo-Europeans, whose descendants spoke Romance languages, did not experience the change. This ancient sound change resulted in the *f–p* sound correspondence.

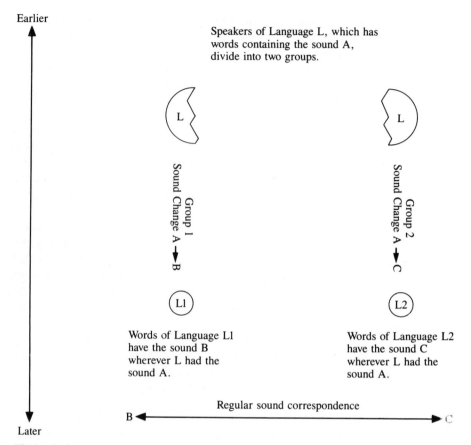

Figure 8–1
How a regular sound correspondence arises.

Phonological Change

> Etymologists . . . for whom vowels did not matter and who cared not a jot for consonants.
>
> Voltaire

Regular sound correspondences illustrate changes in the phonological system. In earlier chapters we discussed speakers' knowledge of their phonological system including knowledge of the phonemes and phonological rules of the language. Any of these aspects of the phonology is subject to change.

Speakers of most Modern English dialects know that /x/, the velar fricative, is not part of their phonemic inventory. In the history of English this sound was lost. *Night* was once pronounced [nɪxt], *drought* was pronounced [druxt], and *saw* was pronounced [saux]. This phonological change—the loss of /x/—took place between the times of Chaucer and Shakespeare. All words once pronounced with an /x/ no longer include this sound. In some cases it disappeared, as in *night* and *light*. In other cases the /x/ became a /k/, as in *elk* (Old English *eolh* [ɛɔlx]). In yet other cases it became a vowel, as in *hollow* (Old English *holh* [hɔlx]) or *sorrow* (Old English *sorh* [sɔrx]). There are dialects of Modern English such as Scottish that have retained the /x/ sound in some words, such as *loch* [lɔx] meaning "lake."

These examples show that the **inventory** of sounds can change by the loss of phonemes. The inventory can also change by the *addition* of new phonemes. Old English did not have the phoneme /ž/ of *leisure* [ližər] or *confusion* [kə̃nfjužə̃n]. Through a process of "palatalization," certain occurrences of /z/ were pronounced as [ž]. Eventually the [ž] sound became a phoneme in its own right, reinforced by the fact that it is a common phoneme in French, which exerted a major influence on English after the Norman Conquest.

A phonetically predictable allophone may become a distinctive phoneme. In Old English the phoneme /f/ was pronounced as [f] in initial and final word position, but as [v] between two vowels. Just as [p] and [pʰ] are allophones of the same /p/ phoneme in modern English, [f] and [v] were variants of the phoneme [f] in Old English. Both [f] and geminate /f:/ occurred between vowels; for example, /ofer/ "over" was pronounced [ɔvɛr] and /of:a/ (a person's name) was pronounced [ɔf:a]. (Geminate /f:/ was not voiced between vowels.) When the geminate [f:] was simplified to [f], a contrast between [f] and [v] was created. In addition, other [f]/[v] contrasts arose, and [v] became a separate phoneme /v/.

This example shows that phonemes may be lost (/x/), or added (/ž/), or result from a change in the status of allophones (the allophones of /f/—[f] and [v]— becoming separate phonemes /f/ and /v/).

Such changes occur in the history of all languages. Neither /č/ nor /š/ were phonemes of Latin, but /č/ is a phoneme of modern Italian and /š/ a phoneme of modern French, both of which evolved from Latin. In an older stage of Russian the phoneme /æ/ occurred, but in modern Russian, [æ] is merely an allophone of /a/. Thus a phoneme was lost due to a change in the allophones.

Phonological Rules

An interaction of phonological rules may result in the addition or loss of phonemes, and in changes in the lexicon. For example, the nouns *house* and *bath* were once differentiated from the verbs *house* and *bathe* by the fact that the verbs ended with a short vowel sound (still reflected in the spelling). Furthermore, a rule in English (alluded to above in relation to [f] and [v]) said: "When a voiceless consonant phoneme occurs between two vowels, voice that consonant." Thus the /s/, which was followed by a vowel in the verb *house,* was pronounced [z], and the /θ/ in the verb *bathe* was pronounced [ð] for the same reason.

Later a rule was added to the grammar of English deleting unstressed short vowels at the end of words. The final vowel was thus deleted from the verbs *house* and *bathe,* which resulted in the present pronunciation with final voiced consonants. The addition of this rule also resulted in the new phonemes /z/ and /ð/. Prior to this change, they were simply the allophones of the phonemes /s/ and /θ/ between vowels.

Eventually, both the unstressed vowel deletion rule and the intervocalic-voicing rule were lost from the grammar of English. Thus the set of phonological rules can change both by addition and loss of rules.

Five hundred years ago, Fante, a language of Ghana, did not have the sounds [ts] or [dz] ([ts] is a *single* sound, a voiceless alveolar affricate; [dz] is a voiced alveolar affricate). The *addition* of a phonological rule to the language "created" these sounds; this rule said "pronounce a /d/ as [dz] and a /t/ as [ts] when these phonemes occur before /i/." The addition of this rule to the grammar of Fante did not create new phonemes; [dz] and [ts] are predictable phonetic realizations of the underlying phonemes /d/ and /t/. That is, they are allophones of /d/ and /t/. The grammar, however, was changed in that a new rule was added.

The addition of phonological rules can result in dialect differences. In Chapter 7 we discussed the addition of an "*r*-dropping" rule in English that did not spread throughout the language (/r/ is not pronounced unless followed by a vowel). Today, we see the effect of that rule in the "*r*-less" pronunciation of British English and of American English dialects spoken in the Boston area and the southern United States.

From the standpoint of the language as a whole, phonological changes occur gradually over the course of many generations of speakers, although a given speaker's grammar may or may not reflect the change. The changes are not "planned" any more than we are presently planning what changes will take place in English by the year 2300. Speakers are aware of the changes only through dialect differences.

The Great Vowel Shift

A major change in the history of English that resulted in new phonemic representations of words and morphemes took place approximately between 1400 and 1600. It is known as the **Great Vowel Shift.** The seven long, or tense, vowels of Middle English underwent the following change:

Shift			**Example**			
Middle English		Modern English	Middle English		Modern English	
[i:]	→	[aj]	[mi:s]	→	[majs]	*mice*
[u:]	→	[aw]	[mu:s]	→	[maws]	*mouse*
[e:]	→	[i:]	[ge:s]	→	[gi:s]	*geese*
[o:]	→	[u:]	[go:s]	→	[gu:s]	*goose*
[ɛ:]	→	[e:]	[brɛ:ken]	→	[bre:k]	*break*
[ɔ:]	→	[o:]	[brɔ:ken]	→	[bro:k]	*broke*
[a:]	→	[e:]	[na:mə]	→	[ne:m]	*name*

By diagramming the Great Vowel Shift on a vowel chart (Figure 8.2), we can see that the highest vowels [i:] and [u:] "fell off" to become the diphthongs [aj] and

[aw], while the long vowels underwent an increase in tongue height, as if to fill in the space left when the highest vowels became diphthongs. In addition, [a] was "fronted."

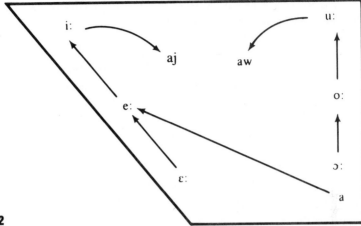

Figure 8–2
The Great Vowel Shift.

These changes are among the most dramatic examples of regular sound shift. The phonemic representation of many thousands of words changed. Today, some reflection of this vowel shift is seen in the alternating forms of morphemes in English: *please, pleasant; serene, serenity; sane, sanity; crime, criminal; sign, signal;* and so on. In each pair of words, the first had a long vowel in Middle English and is therefore pronounced differently today.

The Great Vowel Shift is a primary source of many of the spelling "inconsistencies" of English, because our spelling system still reflects the way words were spelled before the Great Vowel Shift took place.

Morphological Change

Of all the words of witch's doom
There's none so bad as which and whom.
The man who kills both which and whom
Will be enshrined in our Who's Whom.

                              Fletcher Knebel

Like phonological rules, rules of morphology may be lost, added, or changed. We can observe some of these changes by comparing older and newer forms of the language, or by looking at different dialects.

The suffix *-ize*, which changes nouns and adjectives into verbs meaning "to make _____ ," as in *finalize* "to make final," is changing to become "productive" in American English. Speakers are attaching this suffix to more and more words that previously did not take it. Words like *privatize* "to make private" and *rigidize* "to make rigid" are achieving the status of *optimize, stabilize,* and *vitalize.* This change in the morphology of American English is reflected in additions to the lexicon. The change seems to be upsetting the neoprescriptivists. In his book *A Civil Tongue*[2] Edwin Newman devotes an entire chapter, entitled "Ize Front," to lamenting this change in the use of *-ize.*

Extensive changes in rules of morphology have occurred in the history of the Indo-European languages. In Classical Latin there was a complex system of *case endings,* which were added to the noun stem according to its function in the sentence. Latin had seven cases. Below are the different forms (the *declension*) for the noun *lupus* "wolf" for six of the cases (the "locative" case is not shown because its use was restricted to place names):

Case	Noun Stem	Case Ending			
nominative	lup	+	us	lupus	The *wolf* runs.
genitive	lup	+	i	lupi	A sheep in *wolf's* clothing.
dative	lup	+	ō	lupō	Give food *to the wolf.*
accusative	lup	+	um	lupum	I love *the wolf.*
ablative	lup	+	ō	lupō	Run *from the wolf.*
vocative	lup	+	e	lupe	*Wolf,* come here!

In *Alice's Adventures in Wonderland,* Lewis Carroll has Alice give us a brief lesson in grammatical case. Alice has become very small and is swimming around in a pool of her own tears with a mouse whom she wishes to befriend:

> "Would it be of any use, now," thought Alice, "to speak to this mouse? Everything is so out-of-the-way down here, that I should think very likely it can talk: at any rate, there's no harm in trying." So she began: "O Mouse, do you know the way out of this pool? I am very tired of swimming about here, O Mouse!" (Alice thought this must be the right way of speaking to a mouse: she had never done such a thing before, but she remembered having seen in her brother's Latin Grammar, "A mouse—of a mouse—to a mouse—a mouse—O mouse!")

Alice gives an English "translation" of the nominative, genitive, dative, accusative, and vocative cases (she omits the ablative and locative).

Such an extensive case system (of which we have seen only part) was present in Latin, Ancient Greek, and Sanskrit. It was also present in Indo-European, the ancestor of all these languages. Modern languages such as Lithuanian and Russian retain much of the Indo-European case system, but these languages are in the minority. In most modern Indo-European languages, changes have all but obliterated the case system. English still retains the genitive case, calling it possessive (as in *a sheep in wolf's clothing*). Pronouns retain a few more traces: for example, *he/*

[2]E. Newman, *A Civil Tongue,* New York: Bobbs-Merrill, 1976.

she corresponds to the nominative, *him/her* to the accusative and dative, and *his/ hers* to the genitive case.

English has replaced its depleted case system with an equally expressive system of prepositions and with stricter constraints on word order (a "trade-off" between morphological and syntactic rules). For example, in Latin *lupus donum viro dat,* literally "the wolf a gift to the man gives," is only one of many possible word orders. In English this same meaning is normally conveyed in two ways: *The wolf gives a gift to the man,* in which the preposition *to* "marks" the dative case; or *The wolf gives the man a gift,* in which the word order determines the case structure, hence the meaning.

Old English also had a rich case ending system, as illustrated by the following noun forms:

Case	OE Singular		OE Plural	
nominative	stān	"stone"	stānas	"stones"
genitive	stānes	"stone's"	stāna	"stones'"
dative	stāne	"stone"	stānum	"stones"
accusative	stān	"stone"	stānas	"stones"

and pronoun forms:

Case	OE Singular		OE Dual		OE Plural	
nominative	ic	"I"	wit	"we two"	wē	"we"
genitive	min	"my-mine"	uncer	"our two"	ūre	"our-ours"
dative	mē	"me"	unc	"us two"	ūs	"us"
accusative	mec	"me"	uncit	"us two"	ūsic	"us"

In these examples, *stān* represents the principal "strong" masculine noun declension. There were "weak" declensions also. The plural of this strong declension in the nominative and accusative cases became generalized to all the English regular nouns in the following way.

In becoming Middle English, Old English underwent a change that lengthened the "stem" vowel and reduced the "suffix" vowel of certain word classes. Thus Old English *stānas,* /stɔnas/, "stones" became Middle English /stɔːnəs/. Another phonological rule change, mentioned earlier, resulted in the dropping out of certain short unstressed vowels, and this rule, together with the Great Vowel Shift, applied to the Middle English /stɔːnəs/ to give Modern English /stonz/ (with vowel length not indicated because it is not distinctive in Modern English). This change,

OE /stɔnas/ → ME/stɔːnəs/ → Mod. Eng. /stonz/

is representative of thousands of similar changes. When the "weak" syllables representing case endings in the forms of the singular, genitive plural, and dative plural were similarly dropped, only two distinct forms of the noun were left: *stone* and *stones.* English thus lost much of its case system; this morphological change resulted from changes that took place in the phonological rules of English.

Syntactic Change

The loss of case endings in English occurred together with changes in the rules of syntax, which constrained word order more than it had been. In Old English, word order was freer because the case endings alone disclosed the thematic or meaning relations in a sentence. Thus, the following sentences were all grammatical in Old English, and all meant "The man slew the king":

Se man sloh þone kyning.
þone kyning sloh se man.
Se man þone kyning sloh.
þone kyning se man sloh.
Sloh se man þone kyning.
Sloh þone kyning se man.

(*Se* was a definite article used only with the subject noun, and *þ*one was the definite article used only with the object noun.)

In Modern English only the first of the literal translations below means what the original meant, and four of the six are ungrammatical as sentences:

The man slew the king.
The king slew the man.
*The man the king slew.
*The king the man slew.
*Slew the man the king.
*Slew the king the man.

The syntactic rules of Modern English permit less variation in word order. Additionally, Modern English, as discussed in Chapter 3, is an SVO (Subject-Verb-Object) language. Old English was more of an SOV language;[3] thus the phrase structure rules that determine the word order of the basic sentences of the language changed in the history of English.

The syntactic rules relating to the English negative construction also underwent a number of changes from Old English to the present. In Modern English, negation is expressed by adding *not* or *do not.* We may also express negation by adding words like *never* or *no:*

I am going→I am not going
I went→I did not go
I go to school→I never go to school
I want food→I don't want any food; I want no food

---

[3]Old English had both SVO and SOV characteristics. Despite the freer word order, SVO and SOV were still the preferred word order of the basic sentences of the language.

In Old English the main negation element was *ne*. It usually occurred before the *auxiliary verb* or the verb, as illustrated by these examples from Old English manuscripts:[4]

þæt he *na*   siþþan geboren *ne* wurde
that he never after   born   not would-be
that he should never be born after that

ac hie *ne* dorston þær on cuman
but they not dared   there on come
but they dared not land there

In the first example the word order is different from that of Modern English, and there are two negatives: *na* (a contraction of *ne* + *a;* "not" + "ever" = "never") and *ne*. As shown, a "double negative" was grammatical in Old English, although double negatives are ungrammatical in Modern Standard American English.

In addition to the contraction of *ne* + *a* → *na*, other negative contractions occurred in Old English: *ne* could be attached to *habb-* "have," *wes-* "be," *wit-* "know," and *will-* "will" to form *nabb-, nes-, nyt-,* and *nyll-,* respectively.

Modern English has "contraction" rules that change *do* + *not* into *don't, will* + *not* into *won't,* and so on. In these contractions the phonetic form of the negation element always comes at the *end* of the word, because Modern English word order puts the *not* after the auxiliary. In Modern English, *not* must precede the main verb of the clause, and a *do* or *does* must be present if there is no auxiliary verb. In Old English, the negative element occurs at the beginning of the contraction, because it typically preceded the auxiliary in sentences. The rules determining the placement of the negative morpheme have changed. Such syntactic changes may take centuries to be fully completed, and there are often intermediate stages.

Another syntactic change in English affected the rules of "comparative" and "superlative" constructions. Today we form the comparative by adding *-er* to the adjective or by inserting *more* before it; the superlative is formed by adding *-est* or by inserting *most.* In Malory's *Tales of King Arthur,* written in 1470, double comparatives and double superlatives occur, which today are ungrammatical: *more gladder, more lower, moost royallest, moost shamefullest.*

When we study a language such as Elizabethan English (sixteenth century) solely from written records, we see only sentences that are grammatical, unless ungrammatical sentences are used deliberately. Without native speakers of Elizabethan English to query, we can only infer what was ungrammatical. Such inference leads us to believe that expressions like *the Queen of England's crown* were ungrammatical in former versions of English. The title *The Wife's Tale of Bath* (rather than *The Wife of Bath's Tale*) in *The Canterbury Tales* supports this inference. Modern English, on the other hand, allows some rather complex constructions that involve the possessive marker. An English speaker can use possessive constructions such as

---

[4]From E. C. Traugott, *The History of English Syntax,* New York: Holt, Rinehart and Winston, 1972. *Note:* þ, or "thorn," was pronounced [θ].

The girl whose sister I'm dating's roommate is pretty.
The man from Boston's hat fell off.

Older versions of English had to resort to an "*of* construction" to express the same thought (*The hat of the man from Boston fell off*). It is clear that a syntactic change took place that accounts for the extended use of the possessive morpheme *'s*.

Lexical Change

Curl'd minion, dancer, coiner of sweet words.
Matthew Arnold, *"Sohrab and Rustum"*

Changes in the lexicon also occur, including the addition of new words, changes in the meanings of words, and the loss of words.

New Words

Chapter 2 discussed ways in which new words can enter the language—for example, by *compounding,* the recombining of old words to form new ones with new meanings. Thousands of common English words have entered the language by this process, including *afternoon, bigmouth, chickenhearted, do in, egghead, force feed, g-string, icecap, jet set, longshoreman, moreover, nursemaid, offshore, pothole, railroad, sailboat, takeover, undergo, water cooler, x-ray,* and *zooecology.*

We also saw that new words may be formed by derivational processes, as in *uglification* or *finalize* (from which we get a "bonus," *finalization*). Other methods for enlarging the vocabulary that were discussed include word coinage, deriving words from names, blends, back-formations, acronyms, and abbreviations or clippings.

Borrowings

Another important source of new words is borrowing from other languages. Borrowing occurs when one language takes a word or morpheme from another language and adds it to its lexicon. Most languages are borrowers, so the lexicon can be divided into native and nonnative words (often called **loan words**). A *native word* is one whose history (or **etymology**) can be traced back to the earliest known stages of the language.

A language may borrow a word *directly* or *indirectly*. A *direct* borrowing means that the borrowed item is a native word in the language from which it is borrowed. *Feast* was borrowed directly from French and can be traced back to Latin *festum.* On the other hand, the word *algebra* was borrowed from Spanish, which in turn had borrowed it from Arabic. Thus *algebra* was indirectly borrowed from Arabic, with Spanish as an intermediary.

Some languages are heavy borrowers. Albanian has borrowed so heavily that few native words are retained. On the other hand, most Native American languages borrowed little from their neighbors.

English has borrowed extensively. Of the 20,000 or so words in common use, about three-fifths are borrowed. Of the 500 most frequently used words, however, only two-sevenths are borrowed, and because these "common" words are used over and over again in sentences, the actual frequency of appearance of native words is about 80 percent. Morphemes such as *and, be, have, it, of, the, to, will, you, on, that,* and *is* are all native to English.

The history of the English-speaking peoples can be followed by studying the kinds of loan words in the language and when they entered. Until the Norman Conquest in 1066, England was inhabited chiefly by the Angles, the Saxons, and the Jutes, peoples of Germanic origin who came to England in the fifth century C.E. and eventually became the English. (The word *England* is derived from *Anglaland*.) Originally, they spoke Germanic dialects, from which Old English developed directly. These dialects contained a number of Latin borrowings but were otherwise undiluted by foreign elements. These Germanic tribes had displaced the earlier Celtic inhabitants, whose influence on Old English was confined to a few Celtic place-names. (The modern languages Welsh, Irish, and Scots Gaelic are descended from the Celtic dialects.)

For three centuries after the Norman Conquest, French was the language used for all affairs of state and for most commercial, social, and cultural matters. The West Saxon literary language was abandoned, but regional varieties of English continued to be used in homes, in the churches, and in the marketplace. During these three centuries, vast numbers of French words entered English, of which the following are representative:

government	crown	prince	state	parliament
nation	jury	judge	crime	sue
attorney	property	miracle	charity	court
lechery	virgin	saint	pray	mercy
religion	value	royal	money	society

Until the Norman Conquest, when an Englishman slaughtered an ox for food, he ate *ox*. If it was a pig, he ate *pig*. If it was a sheep, he ate *sheep*. However, "ox" served at the Norman tables was *beef (boeuf)*, "pig" was *pork (porc)*, and "sheep" was *mutton (mouton)*. These words were borrowed from French into English, as were the food-preparing words *boil, fry, stew,* and *roast.*

English borrowed many "learned" words from foreign sources during the Renaissance. In 1476 the printing press was introduced in England by William Caxton, and by 1640, 55,000 books had been printed in English. The authors of these books used many Greek and Latin words, and as a result, many words of ancient Greek and Latin entered the language.

From Greek came *drama, comedy, tragedy, scene, botany, physics, zoology,* and *atomic.* Greek roots have also provided English with a means for coining new words. *Thermos* "hot" plus *metron* "measure" give us *thermometer.* From *akros* "topmost" and *phobia* "fear" we get *acrophobia* "dread of heights." An ingenious cartoonist, Robert Osborn, has "invented" some phobias, to each of which he gives an appropriate name:[5]

logizomechanophobia	"fear of reckoning machines" from Greek *logizomai* "to reckon or compute" + *mekhane* "device" + *phobia*
ellipsosyllabophobia	"fear of words with a missing syllable" from Greek *elleipsis* "a falling short" + *syllabē* "syllable" + *phobia*
pornophobia	"fear of prostitutes" from Greek *porne* "harlot" + *phobia*

Latin loan words in English are numerous. They include:

bonus	scientific	rape	exit
alumnus	quorum	orthography	describe

Latin, like Greek, has also provided prefixes and suffixes that are used productively with both native and nonnative roots. The prefix *ex-* comes from Latin:

ex-husband   ex-wife   ex–sister-in-law

The suffix *-able/-ible* is also Latin, borrowed via French, and can be attached to almost any English verb, as in:

writable   readable   answerable   movable

During the ninth and tenth centuries, the Scandinavians, who first raided and then settled in the British Isles, left their traces in the English language. The pronouns *they, their,* and *them* are loan words from the Scandinavian language Old Norse, from which modern Danish, Norwegian, and Swedish have descended. This period is the only time that English ever borrowed pronouns. Many English words beginning with [sk] are of Scandinavian origin: *scatter, scare, scrape, skirt, skin, sky.*

Bin, flannel, clan, slogan, and *whisky* are all words of Celtic origin, borrowed at various times from Welsh, Scots Gaelic, or Irish.

Dutch was a source of borrowed words, too, many of which are related to shipping: *buoy, freight, leak, pump, yacht.*

From German came *quartz, cobalt,* and—as we might guess—*sauerkraut* and *beer.*

From Italian, many musical terms, including words describing opera houses, have been borrowed: *opera, piano, virtuoso, balcony,* and *mezzanine.*

Words having to do with mathematics and chemistry were borrowed from Arabic, because early Arab scholarship in these fields was quite advanced. *Alcohol,*

[5]From *An Osborn Festival of Phobias.* Copyright © 1971 by Robert Osborn. Text copyright © 1971 by Eve Wengler. Reprinted by permission of Liveright Publishers, New York.

algebra, cipher, and *zero* are a representative sample. Arabic loan words have also entered English through Spanish, the original borrower.

Spanish has loaned us (directly) *barbecue, cockroach, guitar,* and *ranch,* as well as *California,* literally "hot furnace."

With the settlement of the "New World," the English-speaking colonists borrowed from Native American languages as well as from Spanish. Such languages provided us with *pony, hickory,* and *squash,* to mention only a few, and nearly half the state names of the United States are from Native American languages.

Hundreds of "place names" in the United States are of non-English origin. We certainly cannot call Native American names "foreign," except in the sense that they were foreign to English. Native American place names include:

Connecticut	Potomac	Ohio	Mississippi
Erie	Huron	Michigan	Allegheny
Appalachia	Ozark	Massachusetts	Kentucky
Wisconsin	Oregon	Texas	Chattanooga
Chicago	Milwaukee	Omaha	Passaic

Spanish place names include:

Rio Grande	Colorado	Sierra Nevada	Santa Fe
Los Angeles	San Francisco	Santa Barbara	San Jose

Dutch place names include:

Brooklyn	Harlem

The influence of Yiddish on English is interesting; Yiddish words are used by many non-Jews as well as by non-Yiddish-speaking Jews in the United States. There was even a bumper sticker proclaiming: "Marcel Proust is a yenta." *Yenta* is a Yiddish word meaning "gossipy woman" or "shrew." *Lox* "smoked salmon," *bagel* "a hard roll resembling a doughnut," and *matzo* "unleavened cracker" belong to American English, as well as Yiddish expressions like *chutzpah, schmaltz, schlemiel, schmuck, schmo,* and *kibitz.*

Other languages also borrow words, and many of them have borrowed from English. Twi speakers drank palm wine before Europeans arrived in Africa. Now they also drink [bia] "beer," [hwiski] "whisky," and [gɔrdɔn ǰin] "Gordon's gin."

Italian is filled with "strange" words like *snack* (pronounced "znak"), *poster,* and *puzzle* ("pootsle"), and Italian girls use *blushes* and are warned by their mothers against *petting.*

Young Russians have incorporated into their language words like *jazz, rock,* and the *twist,* which they dance in their *blue jeans* to *rock music.* When former President Nixon was considered for impeachment by the Congress, the official Communist party newspaper *Pravda* used the word *impeechmente* instead of the previously used Russian word *ustraneniye* "removal."

For thousands of years Japanese borrowed heavily from Chinese (to which it is unrelated). Because Japanese uses Chinese characters in its writing system, many native Japanese words coexist with a Chinese loan word. Japanese even has two ways of counting, one using native Japanese words and the other using Chinese loan words for the numbers.

In the past hundred years Japanese has borrowed heavily from European languages, especially American English. The Japanese have a special "syllabary" (similar to our alphabet, but see Chapter 9 on writing systems), which is used primarily to transcribe loan words. Japanese has many thousands of loan words from English, including technical vocabulary, sports terms, and the jargon used in advertising.

Loss of Words

Words also can be *lost* from a language, though an old word's departure is never as striking as a new word's arrival. When a new word comes into vogue, its unusual presence draws attention; but a word is lost through inattention—nobody thinks of it; nobody uses it; and it fades out of the language.

A reading of Shakespeare's work shows that English has lost many words, such as these taken from *Romeo and Juliet: beseem* "to be suitable," *mammet* "a doll or puppet," *wot* "to know," *gyve* "a fetter," *fain* "gladly," and *wherefore* "why."

Semantic Change

> His talk was like a stream which runs
> with rapid change from rocks to roses.
> It slipped from politics to puns;
> It passed from Mahomet to Moses.
>
> Winthrop Mackworth Praed, *"The Vicar"*

We have seen that a language may gain or lose lexical items. Additionally, the meaning or semantic representation of words may change, becoming broader, narrower, or shifted.

Broadening

When the meaning of a word becomes broader, that word means everything it used to mean, and then some. The Middle English word *dogge* meant a specific breed of dog, but it was eventually **broadened** to encompass all members of the species *Canis familiaris*. The word *holiday* originally meant "holy day," a day of religious significance. Today the word signifies any day on which we do not have to work. *Butcher* once meant "slaughterer of goats" (and earlier "of bucks"), but its modern usage is more general. Similarly, *picture* used to mean "painted representation," but today you can take a picture with a camera. A *companion* used to mean a person with whom you shared bread, but today it is a person who accompanies you. *Quarantine* once had the restricted meaning "forty days' isolation," and *bird* once meant "young bird." The invention of steam-powered boats gave the verb *sail* an opportunity to extend its dominion to boats without sails, just as the verb *drive* widened in meaning to encompass self-propelled vehicles.

Narrowing

In the King James Version of the Bible (1611), God says of the herbs and trees, "to you they shall be for meat" (Genesis 1:29). To a speaker of seventeenth-century English, *meat* meant "food," and *flesh* meant "meat." Since that time, semantic change has **narrowed** the meaning of meat to what it is in Modern English. The word *deer* once meant "beast" or "animal," as its German related word *Tier* still does. The meaning of *deer* has been narrowed to a particular kind of animal. Similarly, the word *hound* used to be the general term for "dog," like the German *Hund*. Today *hound* means a special kind of dog. The Old English word that occurs as modern *starve* once meant "to die." Its meaning has narrowed to become "to die of hunger," and in colloquial language "to be very hungry," as in "I'm starved." *Token* used to have the broad meaning "sign," but long ago was specialized to mean a physical object that is a sign, such as a *love token*. *Liquor* was once synonymous with *liquid, reek* used to mean "smoke," and *girl* once meant "young person of either sex."

Meaning Shifts

The third kind of semantic change that a lexical item may undergo is a shift in meaning. The word *bead* originally meant "prayer." During the Middle Ages the custom arose of repeating prayers (that is, *beads*) over and over and counting them by means of little wooden balls on a rosary. The meaning of *bead* shifted from "prayer" to the visible sign of a prayer. The word *knight* once meant "youth" but was elevated in meaning in time for the age of chivalry. *Lust* used to mean simply "pleasure," with no negative or sexual overtones. *Lewd* was merely "ignorant," and *immoral* meant "not customary." *Silly* used to mean "happy" in Old English. By the Middle English period it had come to mean "naive," and only in Modern English does it mean "foolish." The overworked Modern English word *nice* meant "ignorant" a thousand years ago. When Juliet tells Romeo, "I am too *fond*," she is not claiming she likes Romeo too much. She means "I am too *foolish*."

Reconstructing "Dead" Languages

The branch of linguistics that deals with how languages change, what kinds of changes occur, and why they occurred is called **historical and comparative linguistics.** It is *historical* because it deals with the history of particular languages; it is *comparative* because it deals with relations between languages.

The nineteenth-century historical and comparative linguists based their theories on the observations that there is a resemblance between certain languages, and that the *differences* among languages showing such resemblance are *systematic:* in particular, that there are regular sound correspondences. They also assumed that languages displaying systematic differences, no matter how slight in resemblance, had descended from a common source language—that is, were genetically related.

The chief goal of the nineteenth-century historical comparativists was to develop and elucidate the genetic relationships that exist among the world's languages. They aimed to establish the major language families of the world and to define principles for the classification of languages. Their work grew out of earlier research.

In 1786 Sir William Jones (a British scholar who found it best to reside in India because of his sympathy for the rebellious American colonists) delivered a paper in which he observed that Sanskrit bore to Greek and Latin "a stronger affinity . . . than could possibly have been produced by accident." Jones suggested that these three languages had "sprung from a common source" and that probably Germanic and Celtic had the same origin. The classical philologists of the time attempted to disprove the idea that there was any genetic relationship among Sanskrit, Latin, and Greek, because if such a relationship existed it would make their views on language and language development obsolete. A Scottish philosopher, Dugall Stewart, for example, put forth the hypothesis that Sanskrit and Sanskrit literature were inventions of Brahmans, who used Greek and Latin as models to deceive Europeans. He wrote on this question without knowing a single Sanskrit character, whereas Jones was an eminent Sanskritist.

About thirty years after Jones delivered his important paper, the German linguist Franz Bopp pointed out the relationships among Sanskrit, Latin, Greek, Persian, and Germanic. At the same time, a young Danish scholar named Rasmus Rask corroborated these results, and brought Lithuanian and Armenian into the relationship as well. Rask was the first scholar to describe formally the regularity of certain phonological differences between related languages.

Rask's investigation of these regularities was followed up by the German linguist Jakob Grimm (of fairy-tale fame), who published a four-volume treatise (1819–1822) that specified the regular sound correspondences among Sanskrit, Greek, Latin, and the Germanic languages. It was not only the similarities that intrigued Grimm and the other linguists, but the systematic nature of the differences. Where Latin has a [p], English often has an [f]; where Latin has a [t], English often has a [θ]; where Latin has a [k], English often has an [h].

Grimm pointed out that certain phonological changes that did not take place in Sanskrit, Greek, or Latin must have occurred early in the history of the Germanic languages. Because the changes were so strikingly regular, they became known as "Grimm's Law," which is illustrated in Figure 8–3.

Earlier stage:[6]	bh	dh	gh	b	d	g	p	t	k
	↓	↓	↓	↓	↓	↓	↓	↓	↓
Later stage:	b	d	g	p	t	k	f	θ	x (or h)

Figure 8–3
Grimm's Law (an early Germanic sound shift).

Grimm's Law can be expressed in terms of natural classes of speech sounds: voiced aspirates become deaspirated; voiced stops become voiceless; voiceless stops become fricatives.

By observing **cognates,** words in related languages that developed from the same word (and hence often, but not always, have the same meaning), we can observe sound correspondences and from them deduce sound changes. Thus, from the cognates of Sanskrit, Latin, and English (representing Germanic) shown in Figure 8–4, the regular correspondence *p–p–f* indicates that the languages are genetically related. Indo-European *p is posited as the origin of the *p–p–f* correspondence:[7]

Indo-European	Sanskrit	Latin	English
*p	p	p	f
	pitar-	pater	father
	pad-	pēs	foot
	No cognate	piscis	fish
	pasu	pecu	fee

Figure 8–4
Cognates of Indo-European *p.

A more complete chart of correspondences is given in Figure 8–5, where a single representative example of each regular correspondence is presented. In most cases *many cognate sets* exhibit the same correspondence, which leads to the reconstruction of the Indo-European sound shown in the first column.

---

[6]This "earlier stage" is the original parent of Sanskrit, Greek, the Romance and Germanic languages, and other languages—namely, Indo-European. The symbols *bh, dh,* and *gh* are "breathy voiced" stop phonemes, often called "voiced aspirate."
[7]The asterisk before a letter indicates a "reconstructed" sound. It does not mean an unacceptable form. This use of the asterisk occurs only in this chapter.

Indo-European	Sanskrit		Latin		English	
*p	p	pitar-	p	pater	f	father
*t	t	trayas	t	trēs	θ	three
*k	ś	śun[8]	k	canis	h	hound
*b	b	No cognate	b	labium	p	lip
*d	d	dva-	d	duo	t	two
*g	j	ajras	g	ager	k	acre
*bh	bh	bhrātar-	f	frāter	b	brother
*dh	dh	dhā	f	fē-ci	d	do
*gh	h	vah-	h	veh-ō	g	wagon

Figure 8–5
Some Indo-European sound correspondences.

Sanskrit underwent the fewest consonant changes, while Latin underwent somewhat more, and Germanic (under Grimm's Law) underwent almost a complete restructuring. Still, the fact that it was the phonemes and phonological rules that changed, and not individual words, has resulted in the remarkably regular correspondences that allow us to reconstruct much of the sound system of Indo-European.

Exceptions can be found to these regular correspondences, as Grimm was aware. He stated: "The sound shift is a general tendency; it is not followed in every case." Karl Verner in 1875 explained some of the exceptions to Grimm's Law. He formulated "Verner's Law" to show why Indo-European *p, t,* and *k* failed to correspond to *f,* θ, and *x* in certain cases:

> Verner's Law: *When the preceding vowel was unstressed,* **f,** θ, *and* **x** *underwent a further change to* **b, d,** *and* **g.**

A group of young linguists known as the **Neo-Grammarians** went beyond the idea that such sound shifts represented only a tendency, and claimed that sound laws have no exception. They viewed linguistics as a natural science, and therefore believed that laws of sound change were unexceptionable natural laws. The "laws" they put forth often had exceptions, however, which could not always be explained as dramatically as Verner's Law explained the exceptions to Grimm's Law. Still, the work of these linguists provided important data and insights into language change and why such changes occur.

The linguistic work of the early nineteenth century had some influence on Charles Darwin, and in turn, Darwin's Theory of Evolution had a profound influence on linguistics, and on all science. Some linguists thought that languages had a "life cycle" and developed according to evolutionary laws. In addition, it was believed that each language can be traced to a common ancestor. This theory of biological naturalism, called *Stammbaum* ("family tree") theory, has an element of

---

[8] ś is a sibilant different from *s*.

truth to it; but it is a vast oversimplification of the way languages change and evolve into other languages.

The Comparative Method

> . . . Philologists who chase
> A panting syllable through time and space
> Start it at home, and hunt it in the dark,
> To Gaul, to Greece, and into Noah's Ark.
>
> Cowper, *"Retirement"*

When the differences among two or more languages are systematic and regular, as exemplified by regular sound correspondences, the languages are likely to be related. Even if the "parent" language no longer exists, by comparing the "daughter" languages we may deduce many facts about the parent language. The method of **reconstruction** of a parent language from a comparison of its daughters is called the **comparative method.**

A brief example will illustrate how the comparative method works. Consider these words in four Romance languages.[9]

French	Italian	Spanish	Portuguese	
cher	caro	caro	caro	"dear"
champ	campo	campo	campo	"field"
chandelle	candela	candela	candeia	"candle"

In French [š] corresponds to [k] in the three other languages. This regular sound correspondence, [š]–[k]–[k]–[k], along with other facts, supports the view that French, Italian, Spanish, and Portuguese descended from a common language. The comparative method leads to the reconstruction of [k] in "dear," "field," and "candle" of the parent language, and shows that [k] underwent a change to [š] in French, but not in Italian, Spanish, or Portuguese, which retained the original [k] of the parent language, Latin.

To use the comparative method, analysts identify regular sound correspondences (not always easy to do) in what they take to be "daughter" languages; and for each correspondence, they reconstruct a sound of the parent language. In this way the entire sound system of the parent may be reconstructed. The various phonological changes that occurred in the development of each "daughter" language as it descended and changed from the parent are then identified. Sometimes the sound that analysts choose in their reconstruction of the parent language will be the sound that appears most frequently in the correspondence. This approach was illustrated above with the four Romance languages.

[9]Data from Winfred P. Lehmann, *Historical Linguistics,* 2nd ed. New York: Holt, Rinehart and Winston, 1973. (*Note:* ch = [š]; c = [k].)

Other considerations may outweigh the "majority rules" principle. The likelihood of certain phonological changes may persuade the analyst to reconstruct a "minority" sound, or even a sound that does not occur at all in the correspondence. For example, consider data in these four hypothetical languages:

Language A	**Language B**	**Language C**	**Language D**
hono	hono	fono	vono
hari	hari	fari	veli
rahima	rahima	rafima	levima
hor	hor	for	vol

Wherever Languages A and B have an *h,* Language C has an *f* and Language D has a *v.* Therefore we have the sound correspondence *h–h–f–v.* We might be tempted by the comparative method to reconstruct *h* in the parent language; but from other data on historical change, and from phonetic research, we know that *h* seldom becomes *f* or *v.* Generally the reverse is the case. Therefore linguists reconstruct an **f* in the parent, and posit the sound change "*f* becomes *h*" in Languages A and B, and "*f* becomes *v*" in Language D. The other correspondences are not problematic insofar as these data are concerned. They are:

$$o–o–o–o \quad n–n–n–n \quad a–a–a–e \quad r–r–r–l \quad m–m–m–m$$

They lead to the reconstructed forms **o, *n, *a, *r, *m* for the parent language, and the sound changes "*a* becomes *e*" and "*r* becomes *l*" in Language D. They are "natural" sound changes often found in the world's languages. Language D, in this example, is the most *innovative* of the three languages, as it has undergone three sound changes.

It is by means of the comparative method that nineteenth-century linguists, beginning with August Schleicher in 1861, were able to initiate the reconstruction of the long-lost parent language so aptly conceived by Jones, Bopp, Rask, and Grimm. This is the language, which we believe flourished about 6000 years ago, that we have been calling **Indo-European.**

Historical Evidence

You know my method. It is founded upon the observance of trifles.

Sir Arthur Conan Doyle, *"The Boscombe Valley Mystery," The Memoirs of Sherlock Holmes*

How do we discover phonological changes? How do we know how Shakespeare or Chaucer or the author of *Beowulf* pronounced their versions of English? We have no phonograph records or tape recordings that give us direct knowledge.

For many languages, historical records go back more than a thousand years. These records are studied to find out how languages were once pronounced. The spelling in early manuscripts tells us a great deal about the sound systems of older forms of modern languages. If certain words are always spelled one way, and other words another way, it is logical to conclude that the two groups of words were pronounced differently, even if the precise pronunciations are not known. For example, a linguist who did not know English but consistently found that the word that meant "deep hole" was written as *pit,* whereas the word for a domesticated animal was written as *pet,* would think it safe to assume that these two words were pronounced differently. Once a number of orthographic contrasts are identified, good guesses can be made as to actual pronunciation. These guesses are supplemented by common words that show up in all stages of the language, allowing their pronunciation to be traced from the present, step by step, into the past.

Another clue to earlier pronunciation is provided by non-English words used in the manuscripts of English. Suppose a French word that scholars know contains the vowel [o:] is borrowed into English. The way the borrowed word is spelled reveals a particular letter–sound correspondence.

Other documents can be examined for evidence. Private letters are an excellent source of data. Linguists prefer letters written by "naive" spellers, who will misspell words according to the way they pronounce them. For instance, at one point in English history all words spelled with *er* in their stems were pronounced as if they were spelled with *ar,* just as in modern British English *clerk* and *derby* are pronounced "clark" and "darby." Some poor speller kept writing *parfect* for *perfect,* which helped linguists to discover the older pronunciation.

Clues are also provided by the writings of the prescriptive grammarians of the period. Between 1550 and 1750 a group of prescriptivists in England known as **orthoepists** attempted to preserve the "purity" of English. In prescribing how people should speak, they told us how people actually spoke. An orthoepist alive in the United States today might write in a manual: "It is incorrect to pronounce *Cuba* with a final *r.*" Future scholars would know that there were speakers of English who pronounced it that way.

Some of the best clues to earlier pronunciation are provided by puns and rhymes in literature. Two words rhyme if the vowels and final consonants are the same. When a poet rhymes the verb *found* with the noun *wound,* it strongly suggests that the vowels of these two words were identical:

> BENVOLIO: . . . 'tis in vain to seek him here that means not to be found.
> ROMEO: He jests at scars that never felt a wound.

Shakespeare's rhymes are helpful in reconstructing the sound system of Elizabethan English. For example, the rhyming of *convert* with *depart* in Sonnet XI strengthens the conclusion that *er* was pronounced as *ar.*

Dialect differences may provide clues as to what earlier stages of a language were like. There are many dialects of English spoken around the world, including the United States. By comparing the pronunciation of various words in several dialects, we can "reconstruct" earlier forms and see what changes took place in the inventory of sounds and in the phonological rules. When we study different dialects it becomes apparent that all language change is not "hidden." We can actually observe some changes in progress.

For example, since some speakers of English pronounce *Mary, merry,* and *marry* with three different vowels (that is, [meri], [mɛri], and [mæri], respectively), we suspect that at one time all speakers of English did so. (The different spellings are also a clue.) For some dialects, however, only one of these sounds can occur before /r/, namely the sound [ɛ], so we can "see" a change taking place. This same change can also be seen in this "drinking song" of the University of California:

> *They had to carry Harry to the ferry*
> *And the ferry carried Harry to the shore*
> *And the reason that they had to carry Harry to the ferry*
> *Was that Harry couldn't carry any more.*

This song was written by someone who rhymed *Harry, carry,* and *ferry.* It does not sound quite as good to those who do not rhyme *Harry* and *ferry.*

The historical-comparativists working on Indo-European languages, and other languages with written records, had a difficult job, but not nearly as difficult as scholars who are attempting to discover genetic relationships among languages with no written history. Linguists have, however, been able to establish language families and reconstruct the histories of such individual languages. They first study the languages and dialects spoken today and compare the sound systems, the vocabularies, and the syntax, seeing what correspondences exist. By this method, Major John W. Powell, Franz Boas, Edward Sapir, Mary Haas, and others have worked out the complex relationships of Native American languages. Other linguists have worked with African languages and have established a number of major and minor language families in Africa, each containing many subgroups. They have established that over a thousand different languages are spoken in Africa.

The Genetic Classification of Languages

> The Sanskrit language, whatever be its antiquity, is of a wonderful structure, more perfect than the Greek, more copious than the Latin, and more exquisitely refined than either, yet bearing to both of them a stronger affinity, both in the roots of verbs and in the forms of grammar, than could possibly be produced by accident; so strong, indeed, that no philologer could examine all three, without believing that they have sprung from some common source, which, perhaps, no longer exists. . . .
>
> Sir William Jones (1786)

We have discussed how different languages descend from one language, and how historical and comparative linguists classify languages into families and reconstruct earlier forms of the ancestral language. When we examine the languages of the world, we perceive similarities and differences among them that provide further evidence for the "genetic" relatedness we know exists.

Counting to five in English, German, and Vietnamese shows similarities between English and German not shared by Vietnamese.

English	German	Vietnamese[10]
one	ein	mot
two	zwei	hai
three	drei	ba
four	vier	bon
five	funf	nam

This similarity between English and German is pervasive. Sometimes it is extremely obvious (*man/Mann*), at other times a little less obvious (*child/Kind*).

Because German and English are human languages, we expect to find certain similarities reflecting the Universal Grammar between them. English and German, however, are not related because they are highly similar. Rather, the particular kinds of similarities are the result of their being related. They are related because at one time in history they were the same language.

Fifth-century Germanic is the parent of Modern English and Modern German, which are its "daughters"; English and German are "sisters." Sisterhood is the fundamental genealogical relationship between languages. Similarly, the Romance languages of French, Spanish, Portuguese, Italian, and Romanian are daughters of Latin and sisters to one another.

Where there are mothers and sisters, there must be "cousins." At one time, well over 2000 years ago, an early form of Germanic and an early form of Latin were sisters. The respective offspring are cousins. The five Romance languages mentioned above are cousins to English and German. The numbers from one to three in English and two Romance languages, compared with the unrelated Japanese, reveal this relationship:

Spanish	French	English	Japanese
uno	un	one	ichi
dos	deux	two	ni
tres	trois	three	san

Norwegian, Yiddish, Danish, Icelandic, and Dutch are all close relatives of English. They, like English, are Germanic. Greek is a somewhat more distant cousin. The Celtic language gave birth to Irish, Scots Gaelic, Welsh, and Breton, all cousins of English. Breton is spoken by the people living in the northwest coastal regions of France, called Brittany. It was brought there by Celts fleeing from Britain in the seventh century and has been preserved as the language of some Celtic descendants in Brittany ever since. Russian is also a distant cousin, as are its sisters, Bulgarian, Serbo-Croatian, Polish, Czech, and Slovak. The Baltic language Lithuanian is related to English, as is its sister language, Latvian. A neighboring language, Estonian, however, is not a relative. Sanskrit, as pointed out by Sir William Jones, though far removed geographically, is nonetheless a relative. Its daughters, Hindi

---

[10]Tones are omitted for simplicity.

and Bengali, spoken primarily in India and Bangladesh, are distantly related to English. Even the Persian spoken in modern Iran is a distant cousin of English.

All the languages mentioned in the last paragraph, except for Estonian, are related, more or less distantly, because they descended from Indo-European.

Figure 8–6 is an abbreviated "family tree" of the Indo-European languages which gives a genealogical and historical classification of the languages shown. All the languages of the world may be similarly classified. This diagram is somewhat simplified. For one thing, the "dead ends"—languages that evolved and died, leaving no offspring—are not included.

A language dies when no children learn it. This situation may come about in two ways: either all the speakers of the language are annihilated by some cataclysm, or more commonly, the speakers of the language are absorbed by another culture that speaks a different language. The children, at first bilingual, grow up using the language of the dominant culture. Their children, or their children's children, fail to learn the old language, so it dies. This fate has befallen many Native American languages. Cornish, a Celtic language akin to Breton, met a similar fate in England in the seventeenth century. Today, however, there are "revival" movements among some peoples to resurrect their old languages. Hebrew is an example of a nearly extinct language that was brought back to life. For centuries it was used only in religious ceremonies, but today it is the national language of Israel and is spoken natively by a large number of people.

The family tree also fails to show a number of intermediate stages that must have existed in the evolution of modern languages. Languages do not evolve abruptly, which is why comparisons with the genealogical trees of biology have limited usefulness.

Finally, the diagram fails to show a number of Indo-European languages because of lack of space.

Obviously, most of the world's languages do not belong to the Indo-European family. Linguists have also attempted to classify the non–Indo-European languages according to their genetic relationships. The task is to identify the languages that constitute a family and the relationships that exist among them.

The results of this research are often surprising: faraway Punjabi is an Indo-European language, whereas Hungarian, surrounded on all sides by Indo-European languages, is not.

For linguists interested in the nature of human language, the number of languages in the many different language families provides necessary data. Although these languages are diverse in many ways, they are also remarkably similar in many ways. We find that the languages of the "wretched Greenlanders," the Maoris of New Zealand, the Zulus of Africa, and the native peoples of North and South America all have similar sounds, similar phonological and syntactic rules, and similar semantic systems. There is evidence, then, that we need a theory of language that aims at universality as well as specificity.

At the end of this chapter we offer Table 8.1, which includes a number of the world's languages, showing genetic relationships, the principal geographic areas

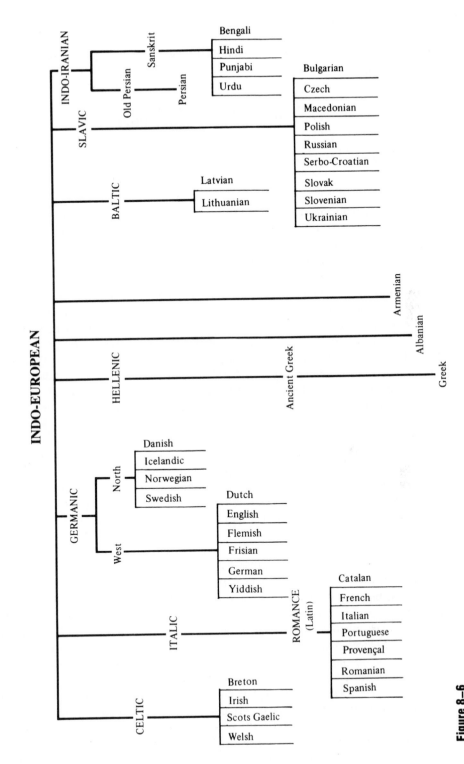

Figure 8-6

The Indo-European family of languages.

where the language is spoken, and the number of speakers (as nearly as that can be determined).

Why Do Languages Change?

Stability in language is synonymous with rigor mortis.

Ernest Weekley

No one knows exactly how or why languages change. As we have shown, linguistic changes do not happen suddenly. Speakers of English did not wake up one morning and decide to use the word *beef* for "ox meat"; nor do all the children of one particular generation grow up to adopt a new word. Changes are more gradual, particularly changes in the phonological and syntactic system.

Of course, certain changes may occur instantaneously for any one speaker. When a new word is acquired by a speaker, it is not "gradually" acquired, although full appreciation for all of its possible uses may come slowly. When a new rule is incorporated into a speaker's grammar, it is either in or not in the grammar. It may at first be an optional rule, so that sometimes it is used and sometimes it is not, possibly determined by social context or other external factors; but the rule is either there and available for use or not. What is gradual about language change is the spread of certain changes over an entire speech community.

A basic cause of change is the way children acquire the language. No one teaches a child the rules of the grammar; each child constructs a personal grammar alone, generalizing rules from the linguistic input received. As will be discussed in Chapter 10, the child's language develops in stages until it approximates the adult grammar. The child's grammar is never exactly like that of the adult community, because children receive diverse linguistic input. Certain rules may be simplified or overgeneralized, and vocabularies may show small differences that accumulate over several generations.

The older generation may be using certain rules optionally. For example, at certain times they may say "It's I" and at other times "It's me." The less formal style is usually used with children, who as the next generation may use only the "me" form of the pronoun in this construction. In such cases, the grammar will have changed.

The reasons for some changes are relatively easy to understand. Before television there was no such word as *television*. It soon became a common lexical item. Borrowed words, too, generally serve a useful purpose and their entry into the language is not mysterious. Other changes are more difficult to explain, such as the Great Vowel Shift in English.

We have some plausible explanations for some of the phonological changes in languages. Some of these changes are due to physiological mechanisms. Some sounds and combinations of sounds are "easier to pronounce" than others. One example is the simplification of geminate [f:] to single [f], which we noted earlier contributed to the phonemicization of [v] to /v/ in English.

Another example: Vowels are frequently nasalized before nasal consonants because it is difficult to time the lowering of the velum to produce nasality with the consonant articulation. As Chapter 6 explained, the effect of one sound on another is called **assimilation;** the vowel **assimilates** to the nasality of the nasal consonant. Once the vowel is nasalized, the contrast that the nasal consonant provided can be equally well provided by the nasalized vowel alone, and the redundant consonant may be deleted. The contrast between oral and nasal vowels that exists in many languages of the world today results from just such a historical sound change.

In French at one time, *bol* "basin," *botte* "high boot," *bog* "a card game," *bock* "Bock beer," and *bon* "good" were pronounced [bɔl], [bɔt], [bɔg], [bɔk], and [bɔn], respectively. Notice that in *bon* there was a final nasal consonant, which *conditioned* the nasalization of the preceding vowel. Due to a sound change that deleted nasal consonants in word-final position, *bon* is pronounced [bɔ̃] in modern French; the nasal vowel maintains the contrast with the other words.

Another example from English illustrates how such assimilative processes can change a language. In English *key,* the /k/ is articulated forward in the mouth in anticipation of the high front "palatal" vowel /i/. In *cot,* the /k/ is pronounced farther back in anticipation of the low back vowel /a/. The /k/ in *key* is slightly "palatalized." In Old English there were a number of words that began with a palatalized /k/, which is written as [kʲ]. When [kʲ] was followed by /i/, it became our modern palatal affricate /č/, as illustrated by the following words:

Old English (*c* = [kʲ])   **Modern English (*ch* = [č])**
ciese   cheese
cinn   chin
cild   child

The same process of palatalization that produced the /č/ in English from an older /k/ is also found in many other languages. In Twi, for example, the word meaning "to hate" was once pronounced [ki]. The [k] became first [kʲ] and then finally [č], so that today "to hate" is pronounced [či].

Such assimilative processes gave rise to a *"theory of least effort"* to explain linguistic change. According to this theory, sound changes are primarily due to an economy of effort. We tend to assimilate one sound to another, to drop out unstressed syllables, and so on.

Another kind of change that can be thought of as "economy of memory" results in a reduction of the number of exceptional or irregular morphemes. This kind of change has been called **internal borrowing**—that is, we "borrow" from one part of the grammar and apply the rule generally. It is also called **analogic change.** It may be by analogy to *foe/foes* and *dog/dogs* that speakers started saying *cows* as the plural of *cow* instead of the earlier plural *kine.* By analogy to *reap/reaped, seem/ seemed,* and *ignite/ignited,* children and adults are presently saying *I sweeped the floor* (instead of *swept*), *I dreamed last night* (instead of *dreamt*), and *She lighted the bonfire* (instead of *lit*).

The same kind of analogic change is exemplified by our "regularization" of exceptional plural forms, which is a kind of morphological change. We have borrowed words like *datum/data, agendum/agenda, curriculum/curricula, bandit/ banditi, memorandum/memoranda, medium/media, criterion/criteria,* and *virtuoso/virtuosi,* to name just a few. The irregular plurals of these nouns have been replaced by regular plurals among many speakers: *agendas, curriculums, memorandums, criterias, virtuosos.* In some cases the borrowed original plural forms were considered to be the singular (as in *agenda* and *criteria*) and the new plural is therefore a "plural-plural." Also, many speakers now regard *data* and *media* as nouns that do not have plural forms, like *information.* All these changes lessen the number of irregular forms that must be remen bered.

The "theory of least effort" does seem to account for some linguistic changes, but it cannot account for others. Simplification and regularization of grammars occur, but so does elaboration or complication. Old English rules of syntax became more complex, imposing a stricter word order on the language, at the same time that case endings were being simplified. A tendency toward simplification is counteracted by the need to limit potential ambiguity. Much of language change is a balance between the two.

Many factors contribute to linguistic change: simplification of grammars, elaboration to maintain intelligibility, borrowing, and lexical additions. Changes are realized by children learning the language, who incorporate them into their grammar. The exact reasons for linguistic change are still elusive, though it is clear that the "imperfect" learning of the adult dialects by children is a contributing factor. Perhaps language changes for the same reason all things change: that it is the nature of things to change. As Heraclitus pointed out thousands of years ago, "All is flux, nothing stays still. Nothing endures but change."

Languages of the World

> And the whole earth was of one language, and of one speech.
> Genesis 11:1

> Let us go down, and there confound their language, that they may not understand one another's speech.
> Genesis 11:7

How many people of the world can be brought together so that no one person understands the language spoken by any other person? Considering that there are over five billion inhabitants on the planet (the five-billionth was supposedly born on July 7, 1986), the number of mutually unintelligible languages is relatively small—somewhat over four thousand, according to most estimates. Table 8.1 lists some of these languages. Despite the seemingly large number of languages spoken in the world today, one-half of the world's total population speaks but eight languages. As the figures in the table show, if you speak Mandarin Chinese, English, Hindi, Spanish, and Russian, you can speak with over two billion people.

TABLE 8.1
Some Languages of the World[11]

Indo-European Family (see Figure 8–6)				
Subfamily	**Language**	**Principal Geographic Areas Where Spoken**	**Rank**	**Number of Speakers**
Germanic	Danish	Denmark		5,000,000
	Dutch	Netherlands, Indonesia		14,000,000
	English	North America, Great Britain, Australia, New Zealand	(2)	443,000,000
	Flemish	Belgium		6,000,000
	Frisian	Northern Holland		300,000
	German	Germany, Austria, Switzerland	(12)	118,000,000
	Icelandic	Iceland		251,000
	Norwegian	Norway		5,300,000
	Swedish	Sweden, Finland		9,000,000
	Yiddish	(diffuse)		4,000,000
Romance (Latin)	Catalan	Andorra, Spain, France		9,000,000
	French	France, Belgium, Switzerland, Canada	(10)	121,000,000
	Galician	NW Spain		3,000,000
	Italian	Italy, Switzerland	(17)	66,000,000
	Portuguese	Portugal, Brazil	(8)	173,000,000
	Provençal	Southern France		4,000,000
	Romanian	Rumania		25,000,000
	Spanish	Spain, Latin America	(4)	341,000,000
Celtic	Breton	Brittany (France)		900,000
	Irish	Ireland		500,000
	Scots Gaelic	Scotland		78,000
	Welsh	Wales		522,000
Hellenic	Greek	Greece, Cyprus		12,000,000
Baltic	Latvian	Latvia		2,000,000
	Lithuanian	Lithuania		3,000,000
Slavic	Bulgarian	Bulgaria		9,000,000
	Byelorussian	Belorus		10,000,000
	Croatian	Croatia		5,000,000

[11]These data are compiled from the 1992 *World Almanac* and Katzner (1986). Languages such as Dutch/Flemish (called collectively *Netherlandish*), which are close enough to be considered dialects, are nonetheless listed as separate languages out of political considerations. So are Norwegian/Danish, Hindi/Urdu, Malay/Indonesian, Thai/Lao, and Croatian/Serbian. Political changes in the former USSR and Yugoslavia may affect the names of some geographic areas.

TABLE 8.1
Some Languages of the World (continued)

Indo-European Family (see Figure 8–6)				
Family/ Subfamily	**Language**	**Principal Geographic Areas Where Spoken**	**Rank**	**Number of Speakers**
	Czech	Czechoslovakia		12,000,000
	Macedonian	Southern Yugoslavia		2,000,000
	Polish	Poland	(29)	43,000,000
	Russian	Russia, former USSR Republics	(5)	293,000,000
	Serbian	Yugoslavia		15,000,000
	Slovak	Czechoslovakia		5,000,000
	Slovene	Slovenia		2,000,000
	Ukrainian	Ukraine, Poland	(27)	4,000,000
Indo-Iranian	Bengali	Bangladesh, India	(7)	184,000,000
	Hindi	Northern India	(3)	352,000,000
	Marathi	Western India	(19)	64,000,000
	Persian	Iran, Afghanistan		32,000,000
	Punjabi	Northern India, Pakistan	(14)	84,000,000
	Urdu	Pakistan	(13)	92,000,000
Armenian	Armenian	Armenia, Azerbaijan		5,000,000
Albanian	Albanian	Albania, Yugoslavia		5,000,000
Amerindian Language Families and Subfamilies				
Algonquian	Arapaho	Wyoming		1,000
	Blackfoot	Montana		8,500
	Cheyenne	Montana		4,000
	Cree	Ontario (Canada)		89,000
	Ojibwa	Ontario		25,000
Athapaskan	Apache	Oklahoma		10,000
	Chipewyan	Alberta (Canada)		4,400
	Navajo	Arizona		125,000
Iroquoian	Cherokee	Oklahoma, North Carolina		27,000
	Mohawk	Northern New York		6,700
Mayan	Maya	Guatemala, Mexico		600,000
Quechumaran	Quechua (Incan)	Bolivia, Peru		7,000,000
Siouan	Sioux (Dakota)	South Dakota, North Dakota		15,000
	Crow	Montana		3,500
	Winnebago	Wisconsin, Nebraska		4,000

TABLE 8.1
Some Languages of the World *(continued)*

Family/Subfamily	Language	Principal Geographic Areas Where Spoken	Rank	Number of Speakers
Amerindian Language Families and Subfamilies				
Uto-Aztecan	Hopi	Northwest Arizona		7,900
	Nahuatl (Aztec)	Southern Mexico		1,200,000
	Pima-Papago	Southern Arizona		25,000
Other Language Families and Subfamilies				
Afro-Asiatic	Amharic	Ethiopia		17,000,000
(includes	Arabic	North Africa, Middle East	(6)	197,000,000
Semitic	Berber	Morocco		8,000,000
languages)	Oromo (Galla)	Somaliland, Ethiopia		10,000,000
	Hausa	Northern Nigeria		34,000,000
	Hebrew	Israel		4,000,000
	Somali	Somalia, Ethiopia, Kenya		7,000,000
Altaic	Japanese	Japan	(9)	125,000,000
	Korean	Korea	(15)	71,000,000
	Mongolian	Mongolia		5,000,000
	Tatar (Tartar)	Southwestern Russia		7,000,000
	Turkish	Turkey	(24)	55,000,000
	Uzbek	Uzbekistan		13,000,000
Austro-Asiatic	Khmer	Cambodia		7,000,000
	Vietnamese	Vietnam	(23)	57,000,000
Austronesian	Batak	Sumatra		2,000,000
	Chamorro	Mariana Islands (Guam)		63,000
	Fijian	Fiji Islands		270,000
	Hawaiian	Hawaii		15,000
	Indonesian	Indonesia	(11)	120,000,000
	Javanese	Java	(22)	58,000,000
	Malagasy	Madagascar		11,000,000
	Malay	Malaysia, Singapore		8,000,000
	Maori	New Zealand		100,000
	Samoan	Samoa		200,000
	Tagalog	Philippines		36,000,000
	Tahitian	Tahiti		66,000
Caucasian	Georgian	Georgia (of the former USSR)		4,000,000

TABLE 8.1
Some Languages of the World *(continued)*

		Other Language Families and Subfamilies		
Family/ Subfamily	**Language**	**Principal Geographic Areas Where Spoken**	**Rank**	**Number of Speakers**
Dravidian	Kannada	Southwest India	(30)	41,000,000
	Malayalam	Southwest India		34,000,000
	Tamil	Southeast India, Sri Lanka	(18)	65,000,000
	Telugu	Southeast India	(16)	68,000,000
Niger- Kordofanian*	Efik	Southeast Nigeria		6,000,000
	Ewe	Ghana		3,000,000
	Fulani (Fula)	Northeast Nigeria		13,000,000
	Ibo (Igbo)	Southeast Nigeria		16,000,000
	Luganda	Uganda		3,000,000
	Nupe	Nigeria		1,000,000
	Shona	Zimbabwe		7,000,000
	Swahili	East Africa	(28)	44,000,000
	Twi-Fante (Akan)	Ghana, Ivory Coast		7,000,000
	Yoruba	Nigeria		18,000,000
	Zulu	South Africa		7,000,000
Sino-Tibetan	Burmese	Burma		30,000,000
	Cantonese	South China	(20)	63,000,000
	Hakka	Southeast China		32,000,000
	Mandarin	North China	(1)	864,000,000
	Min	Eastern China, Taiwan	(25)	49,000,000
	Tibetan	Tibet		5,000,000
	Wu	East Central China	(21)	62,000,000
Tai	Lao	Laos		4,000,000
	Thai	Thailand	(26)	48,000,000
Uralic**	Estonian	Estonia		1,000,000
	Finnish	Finland		6,000,000
	Hungarian	Hungary		14,000,000
	Lapp	Northern parts of Norway, Finland, Sweden, Russia		35,000

*All languages given belong to the subfamily of Niger-Congo. Swahili, Luganda, Shona, and Zulu are Bantu languages.
**All languages given belong to the subfamily Finno-Ugric. The other Uralic subfamily is Samoyed.
Note: Obviously, we have omitted thousands of languages. These examples are only some of the languages in some of the language families and subfamilies.

Summary

All living languages change regularly through time. Evidence of linguistic change is found in the history of individual languages and in the **regular correspondences** that exist between different languages and dialects. **Genetically related** languages "descend" from a common "parent" language through linguistic change. An early stage in the history of related languages is that they are dialects of the same parent.

All parts of the grammar may change. That is, **phonological, morphological, syntactic, lexical,** and **semantic** changes occur. Words, morphemes, phonemes, and rules of all types may be added, lost, or altered. The meaning of words and morphemes may expand, narrow, or shift.

No one knows all the causes for linguistic change. Basically, change comes about through the restructuring of the grammar by children learning the language. Grammars are both simplified and elaborated; the elaborations may arise to counter the simplifications that could lead to unclarity and ambiguity.

Some sound changes result from physiological, **assimilative** processes. Others, like the Great Vowel Shift, are more difficult to explain. Grammatical changes may be explained, in part, as **analogic** changes, which are simplifications or generalizations. External borrowing from other languages also affects the grammar.

The study of linguistic change is called **historical and comparative linguistics.** By examining the internal structure of languages as well as comparing related languages, linguists are able to reconstruct earlier forms of particular language families. A particularly effective technique for reconstructing "dead" languages is the **comparative method.** By comparing the various "daughter" languages or dialects, the linguistic history of a language family may be partially reconstructed and represented in a "family tree" similar to Figure 8–6.

In spite of the differences between languages, there is a vast number of ways in which languages are alike. That is, there are language universals as well as differences.

References for Further Reading

Aitchison, Jean. 1985. *Language Change: Progress or Decay.* New York: Universe Books.

Anttila, Raimo. 1972. *An Introduction to Historical and Comparative Linguistics.* New York: Macmillan.

Baugh, A. C. 1978. *A History of the English Language,* 3rd ed. Englewood Cliffs, N.J.: Prentice-Hall.

Cassidy, Frederic G., ed. 1986. *Dictionary of American Regional English.* Cambridge, Massachusetts: The Belknap Press of Harvard University Press.

Comrie, Bernard, ed. 1990. *The World's Major Languages.* New York: Oxford University Press.

Hock, Hans Henrich. 1986. *Principles of Historical Linguistics.* New York: Mouton de Gruyter.

Hoenigswald, Henry M. 1960. *Language Change and Linguistic Reconstruction.* Chicago, Ill.: University of Chicago Press.

Jeffers, Robert J., and Ilse Lehiste. 1979. *Principles and Methods for Historical Linguistics.* Cambridge, Mass.: M.I.T. Press.

Katzner, Kenneth. 1986. *The Languages of the World.* London: Routledge and Kegan Paul.

Lehmann, W. P. 1973. *Historical Linguistics: An Introduction,* 2d ed. New York: Holt, Rinehart and Winston.

Pedersen, H. 1962. *The Discovery of Language.* Bloomington, Ind.: University of Indiana Press.

Pyles, Thomas. 1982. *The Origins and Development of the English Language,* 3rd ed. New York: Harcourt Brace Jovanovich.

Traugott, E. C. 1972. *A History of English Syntax.* New York: Holt, Rinehart and Winston.

Voegelin, Charles F., and Florence M. Voegelin. 1977. *Classification and Index of the World's Languages.* Amsterdam, Netherlands: Elsevier.

Exercises

1. Many changes in the phonological system have occurred in English since 449 C.E. Below are some Old English words (given in their spelling and phonetic forms), and the same words as we pronounce them today. They are typical of regular sound changes that took place in English. What sound changes have occurred in each case?

>   Example: OE hlud [xlu:d]→Mod. Eng. loud
>   Changes: (1) The [x] was lost.
>   (2) The long vowel [u:] became [aw].

>   OE   Mod E
>
>   a. crabbe [krabə]→crab
>   Changes:
>
>   b. fisc [fɪsk]→fish
>   Changes:
>
>   c. fūl [fu:l]→foul
>   Changes:
>
>   d. gāt [ga:t]→goat
>   Changes:
>
>   e. læfan [læ:van]→leave
>   Changes:
>
>   f. tēþ [te:θ]→teeth
>   Changes:

2. The Great Vowel Shift in English left its traces in Modern English in such meaning-related pairs as:

   a. serene/serenity [i]/[ε]
   b. divine/divinity [aj]/[ɪ]
   c. sane/sanity [e]/[æ]

   List five such meaning-related pairs that relate [i] and [ε] as in example *a*, [aj] and [ɪ] as in *b*, and [e] and [æ] as in *c*.

	[i]/[ε]	[aj]/[ɪ]	[e]/[æ]
i.			
ii.			
iii.			
iv.			
v.			

3. Below are given some sentences taken from Old English, Middle English, and early Modern English texts, illustrating some changes that have occurred in the syntactic rules of English grammar. (*Note:* In the sentences, the earlier spelling forms and words have been changed to conform to Modern English. That is, the OE sentence *His suna twegen mon brohte to þæm cynige* would be written as *His sons two one brought to that king,* which in Modern English would be *His two sons were brought to the king.*) Underline the parts of each sentence that differ from Modern English. Rewrite the sentence in Modern English. State, if you can, what changes must have occurred.

> Example: It *not* belongs to you. (Shakespeare, *Henry IV*)
> Mod. Eng.: *It does not belong to you.*
> Change: At one time, a negative sentence simply had a *not* before the verb. Today, the word *do,* in its proper morphological form, must appear before the *not.*

a. It nothing pleased his master.
   Mod. Eng.:
   Change:

b. He hath said that we would lift them whom that him please.
   Mod. Eng.:
   Change:

c. I have a brother is condemned to die.
   Mod. Eng.:
   Change:

d. I bade them take away you.
   Mod. Eng.:
   Change:

e. I wish you was still more a Tartar.
   Mod. Eng.:
   Change:

f. Christ slept and his apostles.
   Mod. Eng.:
   Change:

g. Me was told.
   Mod. Eng.:
   Change:

4. It is not unusual to find a yearbook or almanac publishing a "new word list." In the 1980s and 1990s several new words entered the English language, such as *teflon* and *liposuction.* From the computer field, we have new or incipient words such as *byte* and *biochip.* Other words have been expanded in meaning,

such as *memory* to refer to the storage part of a computer and *crack* meaning a form of cocaine.

a. Think of five other words or compound words that have entered the language in the last ten years. Describe briefly the source of the word.

   i.

   ii.

   iii.

   iv.

   v.

b. Think of three words that might be "on the way out." (*Hint:* Consider *flapper, groovy,* and *slay/slew.* Dictionary entries that say "archaic" are a good source.)

   i.

   ii.

   iii.

5. Here is a table showing, in phonemic form, the Latin ancestors of ten words in modern French:

Latin	French	
kor	kǿr	"heart"
kantāre	šãte	"to sing"
klārus	klɛr	"clear"
kervus	sɛrf	"hart" (deer)
karbō	šarbɔ̃	"coal"
kwandō	kã	"when"
kentum	sã	"hundred"
kawsa	šoz	"thing"
kinis	sãdrə	"ashes"
kawda ⎱ koda	kǿ	"tail"

Are the following statements true or false?

	True	False
a. The modern French word for "thing" shows that a [k], which occurred before the vowel [o] in Latin, became an [š] in French.	_____	_____
b. The French word for "tail" probably derived from the Latin word [koda] rather than from [kawda].	_____	_____

c. One historical change illustrated by these data is that [s] became an allophone of the phoneme /k/ in French. _____ _____

d. If there was a Latin word *kertus,* the modern French word would probably be *sert.* (Consider only the initial consonant.) _____ _____

6. Here is how to count to five in a dozen languages. Six of these languages are Indo-European and six are not. Circle the Indo-European ones.

	L1	L2	L3	L4	L5	L6
1	en	jedyn	i	eka	ichi	echad
2	twene	dwaj	liang	dvau	ni	shnayim
3	thria	tři	san	trayas	san	shlosha
4	fiuwar	štyri	ssu	catur	shi	arbaʔa
5	fif	pjeć	wu	pañca	go	chamishsha

	L7	L8	L9	L10	L11	L12
1	mot	ün	hana	yaw	uno	nigen
2	hai	duos	tul	daw	dos	khoyar
3	ba	trais	set	dree	tres	ghorban
4	bon	quatter	net	tsaloor	cuatro	durben
5	nam	tschinch	tasŏt	pindze	cinco	tabon

7. More than 4000 languages exist in the world today. State one reason why this number might grow larger and one reason why it might grow smaller. Do you think the number of languages will increase or decrease in the next hundred years? Justify your answer.

8. The vocabulary of English consists of "native" words as well as thousands of loan words. Look up the following words in a dictionary that provides the etymologies (histories) of words. Speculate how each word came to be borrowed from the particular language.

a. size
b. royal
c. aquatic
d. heavenly
e. skill
f. ranch
g. blouse

h. robot
i. check
j. banana
k. keel
l. fact
m. potato
n. muskrat

o. skunk
p. catfish
q. hoodlum
r. filibuster
s. astronaut
t. emerald
u. sugar

v. pagoda
w. khaki
x. shampoo
y. kangaroo
z. bulldoze

9. Consider the "Peanuts" cartoon below:

PEANUTS reprinted by permission of UFS, Inc.

a. Use a dictionary to find the source of this "phobia." (*Hint:* It has nothing to do with spiders.)

b. Using Latin or Greek loan words that you know or look up, make up three of your own phobias.

10. Analogic change and **internal borrowing** refer to a tendency to generalize the rules of language, a major cause of language change. We mentioned two instances, the generalization of the plural rule (*cow/kine* becoming *cow/cows*) and the generalization of the past tense formation rule (*light/lit* becoming *light/ lighted*). Think of at least three other instances of "nonstandard" usage that are analogic; they are indicators of possible future changes in the language. (*Hint:* Consider fairly general rules and see if you know of dialects or styles that overgeneralize them, for example, comparative formation by adding *-er*.).

11. Below is a passage from Shakespeare's *Hamlet,* Act IV, scene iii:

HAMLET: A man may fish with the worm that hath eat of a king, and eat of the fish that hath fed of that worm.

KING: What dost thou mean by this?

HAMLET: Nothing but to show you how a king may go a progress through the guts of a beggar.

KING: Where is Polonius?

HAMLET: In heaven. Send thither to see. If your messenger find him not there, seek him i' the other place yourself. But indeed, if you find him not within this month, you shall nose him as you go up the stairs into the lobby.

Study these lines and identify every difference in expression between Elizabethan and Modern English that is evident. (For example, in line 3, *thou* is now *you*.)

12. Consider these data from two American Indian languages:

Yerington Paviotso = YP	Northfolk Monachi = NM	Gloss
mupi	mupi	"nose"
tama	tawa	"tooth"
piwɨ	piwɨ	"heart"
sawaʔpono	sawaʔpono	"a feminine name"
nɨmɨ	nɨwɨ	"liver"
tamano	tawano	"springtime"
pahwa	pahwa	"aunt"
kuma	kuwa	"husband"
wowaʔa	wowaʔa	"Indians living to the west"
mɨhɨ	mɨhɨ	"porcupine"
noto	noto	"throat"
tapa	tape	"sun"
ʔatapɨ	ʔatapɨ	"jaw"
papiʔi	papiʔi	"older brother"
patɨ	petɨ	"daughter"
nana	nana	"man"
ʔatɨ	ʔetɨ	"bow," "gun"

A. Identify each sound correspondence. (*Hint:* There are ten different correspondences of consonants and six different correspondences of vowels: for example, *p–p, m–w, a–a,* and *a–e.*)

B. a. For each correspondence you identified in A not containing an *m* or *w,* reconstruct a proto-sound. (For example, for *h–h, *h; o–o, *o.*)

   b. If the proto-sound underwent a change, indicate what the change is and in which language it took place.

C. a. Whenever a *w* appears in YP, what appears in the corresponding position in NM?

   b. Whenever an *m* occurs in YP, what two sounds may correspond to it in NM?

   c. On the basis of the position of *m* in YP words, can you predict which sound it will correspond to in NM words? How?

D. a. For the three correspondences you discovered in A involving *m* and *w,* should you reconstruct two or three proto-sounds?

   b. If you chose three proto-sounds, what are they and what did they become in the two "daughter" languages, YP and NM?

   c. If you chose two proto-sounds, what are they and what did they become in the "daughter" languages? What further statement do you need to make about the sound changes? (*Hint:* One proto-sound will become two different pairs, depending on its phonetic environment. It is an example of a **conditioned** sound change.)

E. Based on the above, reconstruct all the words given in the common ancestor from which both YP and NM descended. (For example, "porcupine" is reconstructed as *mɨhɨ.)

CHAPTER 9
Writing: The ABCs of Language

The Moving Finger writes; and, having writ,
Moves on: nor all thy Piety nor Wit
   Shall lure it back to cancel half a Line,
Nor all thy Tears wash out a Word of it.

                Omar Khayyám, *Rubáiyát*

The palest ink is better than the sharpest memory.

                Chinese proverb

PEANUTS reprinted by permission of UFS, Inc.

In previous chapters, we emphasized the *spoken* form of language. The grammar, which represents one's linguistic knowledge, was viewed as the system for relating the sounds and meanings of one's language. The ability to acquire and use language represents a dramatic evolutionary development. No individual or people discovered or created language. As was discussed in Chapter 1 and will be discussed further in Chapters 10 and 11, the human language faculty appears to be biologically and genetically determined. This is not true of the written form of human languages.

Children speak without being taught and only later learn to write with instruction. Millions of people who have not been taught to write speak their native language fluently. A very large number of languages spoken today throughout the world lack a writing system. Among these people oral literature abounds, and crucial knowledge is memorized and passed between generations. However, human memory is short-lived, and the brain's storage capacity is limited. Writing overcame such problems and allowed communication across the miles and through the centuries. Writing permits a society to permanently record its literature, its history and science, and its technology. The creation and development of writing systems is therefore one of the greatest of human achievements.

By writing we mean any of the many visual (nongestural) systems for representing language, including handwriting, printing, and electronic displays of these written forms. It might be argued that today we have electronic means of recording sound and cameras to produce films and television, so writing is becoming obsolete. If writing became extinct, however, there would be no knowledge of electronics for TV technicians to study; there would be, in fact, little technology in years to come. There would be no film or TV scripts, no literature, no books, no mail, no newspapers. There would be some advantages—no bad novels, junk mail, poison-pen letters, or "fine print"; but the losses would far outweigh the gains.

The History of Writing

An Egyptian legend relates that when the god Thoth revealed his discovery of the art of writing to King Thamos, the good King denounced it as an enemy of civilization. "Children and young people," protested the monarch, "who had hitherto been forced to apply themselves diligently to learn and retain whatever was taught them, would cease to apply themselves, and would neglect to exercise their memories."

Will Durant, *The Story of Civilization 1*

There are many legends and stories about the invention of writing. Greek legend has it that Cadmus, Prince of Phoenicia and founder of the city of Thebes, invented the alphabet and brought it with him to Greece. (He later was banished to Illyria and changed into a snake.) In one Chinese fable, the four-eyed dragon-god Cang Jie invented writing, but in another, writing first appeared to humans in the form of markings on a turtle shell. In an Icelandic saga, Odin was the inventor of the runic script. In other myths, the Babylonian god Nebo and the Egyptian god Thoth gave humans writing as well as speech. The Talmudic scholar Rabbi Akiba believed that the alphabet existed before humans were created; and according to Islamic teaching, the alphabet was created by Allah himself, who presented it to humans but not to the angels.

Although these are delightful stories, it is evident that before a single word was written, uncountable billions were spoken; it is highly unlikely that a particularly gifted ancestor awoke one morning and decided, "Today I'll invent a writing system."

Pictograms and Ideograms

The seeds out of which writing developed were probably the early drawings made by ancient humans. Cave drawings such as those found in the Altamira cave in northern Spain, drawn by humans living over 20,000 years ago, can be "read" today. They are literal portrayals of aspects of life at that time. We have no way of knowing why they were produced; they may well be aesthetic expressions rather than pictorial communications. Later drawings, however, are clearly "picture

By permission of Johnny Hart and Creators Syndicate, Inc.

writings," or **pictograms.** Unlike modern writing systems, each picture or pictogram is a direct image of the object it represents. There is a **nonarbitrary** relationship between the form and meaning of the symbol. Comic strips minus captions are pictographic—literal representations of the ideas to be communicated. This early form of "writing" did not have any direct relation to the language spoken, because the pictures represented objects in the world, rather than the linguistic names given to these objects; they did not represent the sounds of spoken language.

Pictographic "writing" has been found among peoples throughout the world, ancient and modern: among African tribes, native Americans, Alaskan Eskimos, the Incas of Peru, the Yukagirians of Siberia, and the people of Oceania. Pictograms are used today in international road signs and in other places where the

Figure 9–1

Six of seventy-seven symbols developed by the National Park Service for use as signs indicating activities and facilities in parks and recreation areas. These symbols denote, from left to right: environmental study area; grocery store; men's restroom; women's restroom; fishing; amphitheater. Certain symbols are available with a *prohibiting slash*—a diagonal red bar across the symbol that means that the activity is forbidden. (National Park Service, U.S. Department of the Interior.)

native language of the region might not be adequate. The advantage of such symbols is that they can be understood by anyone, because they do not depend on the words of any language. To understand the signs used by the National Park Service, for example, a visitor does not need to know English (Figure 9–1).

Once a pictogram was accepted as the representation of an object, its meaning was extended to attributes of that object, or concepts associated with it. Thus, a picture of the sun could represent "warmth," "heat," "light," "daytime," and so on. Pictograms thus began to represent *ideas* rather than objects. Such pictograms are called **ideograms** ("idea pictures" or "idea writing").

Later pictograms and ideograms became stylized, possibly because of the ambiguities that could result from "poor artists" or creative "abstractionists" of the time. The simplifying conventions that developed so distorted the literal representations that it was no longer easy to interpret symbols without learning the system. The ideograms became *linguistic* symbols as they came to stand for the *sounds* that represented the ideas—that is, for the words of the language. This stage represented a revolutionary step in the development of writing systems.

Cuneiform Writing

> One picture is worth a thousand words.
>
> Chinese Proverb

Much of our information on the development of writing stems from the records left by the Sumerians, an ancient people of unknown origin who built a civilization in southern Mesopotamia over 5000 years ago. They left innumerable clay tablets containing business documents, epics, prayers, poems, proverbs, and so on. So copious are these written records that scholars studying the Sumerians are publishing a seventeen-volume dictionary of their written language. The first of these volumes appeared in 1984.

The writing system of the Sumerians is the oldest one known. They were a commercially oriented people, and as their business deals became increasingly complex, the need for permanent records arose. An elaborate pictography was developed along with a system of "tallies." Some examples are shown here:

star, sky, God	hand	corn	5 oxen[1]	13 fish

Over the centuries their pictography was simplified and conventionalized. The characters or symbols were produced by using a wedge-shaped stylus that was pressed into soft clay tablets, made from the clay found on the land between the Tigris and Euphrates rivers. This form of writing is called **cuneiform**—literally, "wedge-shaped" (from Latin *cuneus* "wedge"). Here is an illustration of how Sumerian pictograms evolved to cuneiform:

became became star

became hand

became fish

The cuneiform "words" do little to remind us of the meaning represented. As cuneiform evolved, its users began to think of the symbols more in terms of the *name* of the thing represented than of the actual thing itself. Ultimately cuneiform script came to represent words of the language, and hence became a **word-writing system.** In this kind of writing system the symbol stands for both the sounds used to pronounce the word and for the concept, which it may still resemble, however abstractly.

The cuneiform writing system was borrowed by the Assyrians (or Babylonians) when they conquered the Sumerians, and later by the Persians. In adopting cuneiform characters to their own languages, the borrowers used them to represent the *sounds* of the *syllables* in their words. In this way cuneiform evolved into a **syllabic writing system.**

In a syllabic writing system, each syllable in the language is represented by its own symbol, and words are written syllable by syllable. Cuneiform writing was never purely syllabic; there was always a large residue of symbols that stood for whole words. The Assyrians retained a large number of word symbols, even though every word in their language could be written out syllabically if it were desired. Thus they could write *mātu* "country" as:

---

[1]The pictograph for "ox" evolved, much later, into our letter A.

ma   +   a   +   tu

The Persians (ca. 600–400 B.C.E.) devised a greatly simplified syllabic alphabet for their language, which made little use of word symbols. By the reign of Darius I (522–468 B.C.E.) this writing system was in wide use. It is illustrated by the following characters:

da

di

fa

ma

tu

The Rebus Principle

B.C.   **BY JOHNNY HART**

By permission of Johnny Hart and Creators Syndicate, Inc.

When a graphic sign no longer has any visual relationship to the word it represents, it becomes a symbol for the sounds that represent the word. A single sign can then be used to represent all words with the same sounds—the homophones of the language. If, for example, the symbol ⊙ stood for *sun* in English, it could then be used in a sentence like *My ⊙ is a doctor*. This sentence is an example of **the rebus principle.**

A rebus is a representation of words or syllables by pictures of objects whose names *sound like* the intended syllables. Thus  might represent *eye* or the pronoun *I*. The sounds of the two monosyllabic words are identical, even though the meanings are not. In the same way, 🐝🍃 could represent *belief* (*be* + *lief* = *bee* + *leaf* = /bi/ + /lif/), and 🐝🍃🍃 could be the verb form, *believes*.

Similarly, 2 👄 —/tu/ + /lɪp/—could represent *tulip*. Proper names can also be "written" in such a way. If the symbol **/** is used to represent *rod* and the symbol ⚲ represents *man*, then **/** ⚲ could represent *Rodman,* although the name is unrelated to either rods or men, at least at this point in history. Such combinations often become stylized or shortened so as to be more easily written. *Rodman,* for example, might be "written" in such a system as **/**⚲ or even ⚡ .

This system is not an efficient one, because in many languages words do not lend themselves to subdivision into sequences of sounds that have meaning. It would be difficult, for example, to represent the word *English* (/ɪŋ/ + /glɪš/) in English according to the rebus principle. *Eng* by itself does not "mean" anything, nor does *glish*. In some languages, however, a rebus system of writing may lead to a syllabic writing system, which has many advantages over word writing; such a change occurred in the Semitic languages spoken many thousands of years ago in what is now the Middle East.

From Hieroglyphs to the Alphabet

At the time that Sumerian pictography was flourishing (around 4000 B.C.E.), a similar system was being used by the Egyptians, which the Greeks later called **hieroglyphics** (*hiero* "sacred" + *glyphikos* "carvings"). That the early "sacred carvings" were originally pictography is shown by the following hieroglyphics:

"eye"   "giraffe"   "to rule"[2]   "fresh" or "cool"[3]

Like the Sumerian pictograms, the hieroglyphs began to represent the sounds of the words they symbolized. This **phoneticization** of the pictography made hieroglyphics a word-writing system, paralleling the Sumerian cuneiform development. Possibly influenced by the Sumerians, the Egyptian system also became, in part, a syllabic writing system.

[2]The symbol portrays the Pharaoh's staff.
[3]Water trickling out of a vase.

In this advanced "syllabic" stage, hieroglyphics were borrowed by many people, including the Phoenicians, a Semitic people who lived on the eastern shores of the Mediterranean. By 1500 B.C.E. a system of twenty-two syllabic characters, the West Semitic Syllabary, was in use, in which a single symbol represented both a consonant and a following vowel (CV).

This syllabic system, first borrowed by the Greeks in the tenth century B.C.E., proved to be inefficient because Greek has a complex syllable structure. The simpler syllabic structure of Semitic languages, together with the fact that the vowel within a syllable is often grammatically predictable, made syllable writing more feasible for these languages than for others.

The ancient Greeks nevertheless borrowed the Phoenician writing system, using the symbols to represent the individual vowels and consonants of their language rather than syllables. The Phoenicians had taken the first step in this direction by using certain symbols to represent consonants alone. The language spoken by the Phoenicians, however, had more consonants than Greek, so when the Greeks borrowed the system they used the extra symbols to represent vowel sounds. The result was an **alphabetic writing system.** (The word *alphabet* is derived from *alpha* and *beta,* the first two letters of the Greek alphabet.)

Alphabetic systems are those in which each symbol typically represents one sound unit. Such systems are primarily *phonemic* rather than *phonetic,* as is illustrated by the fact that the *p* in both *pit* and *spit* in the English alphabet system is one rather than two "letters," even though the sounds are phonetically distinct.

There are arguments as to whether this event—the development of an alphabetic writing system—occurred more than once in history. Most scholars believe that all alphabetic systems in use today derive from the Greek system. This alphabet became known to the pre-Latin people of Italy, the Etruscans, who in turn passed it on to the Romans. The Roman Empire spread it throughout the world.

According to one view, the alphabet was not invented; it was *discovered.*[4] If language did not include discrete individual sounds, no one could have invented alphabetic letters to represent such sounds. When humans started to use one symbol for one phoneme, they had merely brought their intuitive knowledge of the language sound system to consciousness; they discovered what they already "knew." Furthermore, children (and adults) can learn an alphabetic system only if each separate sound has some psychological reality.

Modern Writing Systems

> . . . but their manner of writing is very peculiar, being neither from the left to the right, like the Europeans; nor from the right to the left, like the Arabians;

---

[4]Dr. Sven Ohman, Professor of Phonetics at the University of Uppsala, Sweden; paper presented at the International Speech Symposium, Kyoto, Japan, 1969.

nor from up to down, like the Chinese; nor from down to up, like the Cascagians,
but aslant from one corner of the paper to the other, like ladies in England.

Jonathan Swift, *Gulliver's Travels*

We have already mentioned the three types of writing systems used in the world:
word or *logographic writing, syllable writing,* and *alphabetic writing.* Of the world's
major languages, only Chinese and Japanese use as their primary writing system
non-alphabetic writing. Both languages, however, use alphabetic transcription systems for special purposes, which are sometimes learned in schools and which can
be used by foreigners.

There is some question as to whether the writing systems of Semitic languages
such as Hebrew or Arabic are truly alphabetic. These languages are written using
only consonants; vowels are often predictable from the context. For example, the
consonants *ktb* in Arabic form the "root" of words associated with "write." *katab*
means "to write," *aktib* means "I write"; *kitab* means "a book," and so on. Inflectional and derivational processes can be expressed by different vowels inserted into
the triconsonantal roots. Such writing systems are sometimes referred to as **consonantal,** and can be considered a fourth type of writing system.

Word Writing

PEANUTS reprinted by permission of UFS, Inc.

In a word-writing or logographic writing system the written character represents
both the meaning and pronunciation of a word or morpheme. The awkwardness of
such a system is obvious. For example, the editors of *Webster's Third New International Dictionary* claim more than 450,000 entries. All these words are written
using only twenty-six alphabetic symbols, a dot, a hyphen, an apostrophe, and a
space. It is understandable why, historically, word writing gave way to alphabetic
systems in most places in the world.

The major exceptions are the writing systems used in China and Japan. The Chinese system has an uninterrupted history that goes back more than 3500 years. For
the most part it is a word-writing system, each character representing an individual
word or morpheme. Longer words may be formed by combining two words or morphemes, as shown by the word meaning "business," *măimai,* which is formed by
combining the words meaning "buy" and "sell." This system, which could create
serious problems if used for English and other Indo-European languages, works for

Chinese because *spoken* Chinese has little affixation of bound morphemes (such as the *un-* in *unhappy* or the *-fy* in *beautify*).

Chinese writing utilizes a system of **characters,** each of which represents a morpheme or word. Chinese dictionaries and rhyme books contain tens of thousands of these characters, but a person "only" needs to know about 5000 to read a newspaper. In 1956 the Chinese government moved to simplify the characters. This process had started in 213 B.C.E., when Li Si published an official list of over 3000 characters, which eliminated the different characters representing the same words; but successive generations kept adding new characters and changing and complicating the characters. The character simplification efforts that have been under way in the last thirty years are therefore of major importance. An example of the simplifications is given below:[5]

Original	Simplified	Pronunciation	Meaning
餐	歺	cān	"meal"
酒	氿	jiǔ	"wine"
漆	沬	qī	"paint"
稻	秎	dào	"rice crops"
副	付	fù	"deputy"
賽	宓	sài	"to compete"

The Chinese government has adopted a spelling system using the Roman alphabet, called **Pinyin,** which is now used for certain purposes along with the regular system of characters. Many city street signs are printed in both systems, which is helpful to foreign tourists. It is not their intent, however, to replace the traditional writing, which is viewed as an integral part of Chinese culture. In addition, writing is an art—**calligraphy**—and thousands of years of poetry, literature, and history are preserved in the old system.

An additional reason for keeping the traditional system is that it permits all literate Chinese to communicate even though their spoken languages are mutually unintelligible. Thus writing has served as a unifying factor throughout Chinese history, in an area where hundreds of languages and different dialects of what we call "Chinese" exist. For example, in one county in the Fujian province, three major and over ten minor dialects are spoken. It is said that "people separated by a blade of grass cannot understand each other"; but all the dialects use the one writing system, and a common sight in a city like Hong Kong is for two people to be talking and at

---

[5]W.P. Lehmann (ed), *Language and Linguistics in the People's Republic of China,* Austin, Texas: University of Texas Press, 1975.

the same time drawing characters in the air with their forefingers to overcome their spoken linguistic differences.

This use of written Chinese characters is similar to the use of Arabic numerals, which mean the same in many different countries. The "character" 5, for example, stands for a different sequence of sounds in English, French, and Finnish. In English it is *five* /fajv/, in French it is *cinq* /sæŋk/ and in Finnish *viisi* /vi:si/, but in all these languages, and, in fact, in all the languages of the world, including Chinese, 5, whatever its phonological form means "five." Similarly, the spoken word for "rice" is different in the various Chinese languages, but the written character is the same. If the writing system in China were to become alphabetic, each language would be as different in writing as in speaking, and written communication would no longer be possible among the various language communities.

Syllabic Writing

Syllabic writing systems are more efficient than word-writing systems, and they are certainly less taxing on the memory. However, languages with a rich structure of syllables containing many consonant "clusters" (such as *tr* or *spl*) cannot be efficiently written with a **syllabary.** To see this difficulty, consider the syllable structures of English.

I	/ay/	V	*an*	/æn/	VC
key	/ki/	CV	*ant*	/ænt/	VCC
ski	/ski/	CCV	*ants*	/ænts/	VCCC
spree	/spri/	CCCV	*pant*	/pænt/	CVCC
seek	/sik/	CVC	*pants*	/pænts/	CVCCC
speak	/spik/	CCVC	*splints*	/splɪnts/	CCCVCCC
scram	/skræm/	CCCVC	*stamp*	/stæmp/	CCVCC
striped	/straypt/	CCCVCC			

With more than thirty consonants and over twelve vowels, the number of different possible syllables is immense, which is why English, and Indo-European languages in general, are unsuitable for syllabic writing systems.

The Japanese language, on the other hand, is more suited for syllabic writing, because all words in Japanese can be phonologically represented by about 100 syllables, mostly of the consonant-vowel (CV) type, and there are no consonant clusters. To write these syllables the Japanese have two syllabaries, each containing forty-six characters, called *kana.* The entire Japanese language can be written using kana. One syllabary, *katakana,* is used for loan words and for special effects similar to italics in European writing. The other syllabary, *hiragana,* is used for native words and may occur with Chinese characters, which the Japanese call *kanji.* Thus Japanese writing is part word writing, part syllable writing.

During the first millennium, the Japanese tried to use Chinese characters to write their language. However, the Japanese language is much different from Chinese, and a word-writing system alone was not suitable. Japanese is a highly inflected language; verbs may occur in thirty or more different forms. Using modified Chinese characters, the syllabaries were devised to represent the inflectional endings and other grammatical morphemes. Thus, in Japanese writing, Chinese characters will commonly be used for the verb roots, and hiragana symbols for the inflectional markings.

For example, 行 is the character meaning "go," pronounced [i]. The word for "went" in formal speech is *ikimashita,* written as 行きました, where the hiragana symbols きました represent the syllables *ki, ma, shi, ta.* Nouns, on the other hand, are not inflected in Japanese, and they can generally be written using Chinese characters alone.

In theory all of Japanese could be written in hiragana. There are many homophones in Japanese, however, and the use of word characters disambiguates a word that would be ambiguous if written syllabically. Also, like Chinese, Japanese kanji writing is an integral part of Japanese culture, and it is unlikely to be abandoned.

In 1821, Sequoyah, often called the "Cherokee Cadmus," invented a syllabic writing system for his native language Cherokee. Sequoyah's script, which survives today essentially unchanged, proved useful to the Cherokee people and is justifiably a point of great pride for them. The syllabary contains eighty-five symbols, many of them derived from Latin characters, which efficiently transcribe spoken Cherokee. A few symbols are shown here:

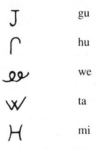

J	gu
∩	hu
ℓℓ	we
W	ta
H	mi

An alphabetic character can be used to represent a syllable in some languages. In words such as OK and bar-b-q, the single letters represent syllables (*b* for [bi] or [bə], *q* for [kju]).

Alphabetic Writing

Alphabetic writing systems are easy to learn, convenient to use, and maximally efficient for transcribing any human language.

The term **sound writing** is sometimes used in place of alphabetic writing, but it does not truly represent the principle involved in the use of alphabets. One-sound–one-letter is inefficient, because we do not need to represent the [pʰ] in *pit* and the [p] in *spit* by two different letters. It would also be confusing, because the non-phonemic differences between sounds are seldom perceptible to speakers. Except for the phonetic alphabets, whose function is to record the sounds of all languages for descriptive purposes, most, if not all, alphabets have been devised on the **phonemic principle.**

In the twelfth century, an Icelandic scholar developed an orthography derived from the Latin alphabet for the writing of the Icelandic language of his day. Other scholars in this period were also interested in orthographic reform, but the Icelander, who came to be known as "the First Grammarian" (because his anonymous paper was the first entry in a collection of grammatical essays), was the only one of the time who left a record of his principles. The orthography he developed was clearly based on the phonemic principle. He used minimal pairs to show the distinctive contrasts; he did not suggest different symbols for voiced and unvoiced [θ] and [ð], nor for [f] or [v], nor for velar [k] and palatal [č], because these pairs, according to him, represented allophones of the phonemes /θ/, /f/, and /k/, respectively. He did not use these modern technical terms, but the letters of this alphabet represent the distinctive phonemes of Icelandic of that century.

King Seijong of Korea (1417–1450) realized that the same principles held true for Korean when he designed a phonemic alphabet. The king was an avid reader, and he realized that the more than 30,000 Chinese characters that were being used to write the Korean language discouraged literacy among the people.

The alphabet was not reinvented by Seijong. Rather, the alphabetic principle was borrowed from the Hindu grammarians through Indian scholars who had visited Korea. Still, the Korean alphabet, called *hankul,* was conceived with remarkable insight. Originally hankul had eleven vowels and seventeen consonants (it is down to fourteen consonants and ten vowels at present). The characters representing consonants were drawn according to the place and manner of articulation. For example, ㅅ is meant to represent the teeth, and it is a part of each consonant character in which the tongue is placed behind the teeth (that is, alveolar or alveopalatal sounds). Thus ㅅ alone stands for /s/ (with allophones [s] and [š]). When crossed, ㅈ represents /ts/ (an alveolar affricate) with allophones [ts] and [tš] (= [č]). A bar above the character means aspiration, so ㅊ represents /tsʰ/. Hundreds of years later, the phonetician Henry Sweet (dramatized as Henry Higgins in *My Fair Lady*) used a similar principle to design a phonetic alphabet.

King Seijong constructed each of eleven vowel characters by using one or more of three "atomic" characters: ∘, ∣, and ▁; for example, ∣ is /i/, ▁ is /u/, and ∘ is /a/. The "strokes" used in drawing the vowels and consonants were also used in drawing the Chinese characters familiar to most Koreans.

Although Korean has the sounds [l] and [r], Seijong represented them by a single "letter" because they are allophonic variants of the same phoneme.[6] The same is true for the sounds [s] and [š], and [ts] and [tš]. Seijong knew that a narrow phonetic alphabet would be confusing to a Korean speaker.

Seijong's contribution to the Korean people has been recorded in a delightful legend. It is said that after he designed the alphabet he was afraid it would not be accepted, so he concocted a scheme to convince the people that it was a gift from

[6]See Exercise 1 of Chapter 6 (p. 265).

heaven. He wrote each one of the new letters in honey on individual leaves that had fallen from a tree in the palace garden. When the king walked with his soothsayer in the garden the next day, the insects had eaten the honey and the leaf fiber underneath, just as he had hoped, and the leaves were etched with the alphabetic letters. The soothsayer and the Korean people were convinced that these letters represented a message from the gods. It is essentially this alphabet that is used in Korea today.

In North Korea the alphabet is used exclusively. In South Korea it is mixed with Chinese characters. The alphabet is often used for inflectional affixes, whereas the Chinese characters represent the root. This mixture is similar to the way Japanese use kanji for roots and hiragana for affixing. In Korean the alphabetic characters are not always written linearly, but are grouped in squarish shapes according to the syllable structure. So Korean has a tinge of syllabic writing, and the unique style of Korean writing is unlike that of the Europeans, the Arabians, the Chinese, the Cascagians, or even "ladies in England."

Many languages have their own alphabet, and each has developed certain conventions for converting strings of alphabetic characters into sequences of sound (reading), and converting sequences of sounds into strings of alphabetic characters (writing). As we have illustrated with English, Icelandic, and Korean, the rules governing the sound system of the language play an important role in the relation between sound and character.

Most European alphabets make use of Latin (Roman) characters or letters, making minor adjustments to accommodate individual characteristics of a particular language. For instance, Spanish uses /ñ/ (an /n/ with a "tilde") to represent the palatalized nasal of *señor,* and German has added an "umlaut" for certain of its vowel sounds that did not exist in Latin (for example, in *über*). Such "extra" marks are called **diacritics.** The forty-six kana of the Japanese syllabaries are supplemented by diacritics in order to represent the one hundred plus syllables of the language. Diacritic marks are also used in writing systems of tone languages such as Thai to indicate the tone of a syllable.

Some languages use two letters together—called a **digraph**—to represent a single sound. English has many digraphs such as *sh* /š/ as in *she* /ši/, *ch* [č] as in *chop* /čap/, *ng* [ŋ] as in *sing* /siŋ/, *oa* [o] as in *loaf* /lof/, and so on.

Besides the European languages, languages such as Turkish, Indonesian, Swahili, and Vietnamese have adopted the Latin alphabet. Other languages that have more recently developed a writing system use some of the IPA phonetic symbols in their alphabet. Twi, for example, uses ɔ, ɛ, and ŋ.

The **Cyrillic** alphabet, named for St. Cyril, who brought Christianity to the Slavs, is used by many Slavic languages, including Russian. It is derived directly from the Greek alphabet without Latin mediation.

The contemporary Semitic alphabets, those used for Persian (Iranian), Urdu (spoken in Pakistan), and many languages of the Indian subcontinent including Hindi, are ultimately derived from the ancient Semitic syllabaries.

Figure 9–2 shows a greatly abbreviated "family tree" of alphabetic writing systems.

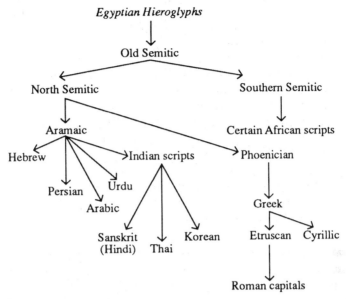

Figure 9–2
Family tree of alphabetic writing systems. (Adapted from Ernst Doblhofer, 1961. *Voices in Stone.* New York: Viking.)

Writing and Speech

> . . . Ther is so great diversite
> In English, and in wryting of oure tonge,
> So prey I god that non myswrite thee . . .
>
> Geoffrey Chaucer, *Troilus and Cressida*

The development of writing freed us from the limitations of time and geography, but spoken language still has primacy. Writing systems, however, are of interest for their own sake.

The written language reflects, to a certain extent, the elements and rules that together constitute the grammar of the language. The system of phonemes is represented by the letters of the alphabet, although not necessarily in a direct way. The independence of words is revealed by the spaces in the written string; but in languages where words are composed of more than one morpheme, the writing usually does not show the individual morphemes, even though speakers "know" what they are. In fact, many languages such as Japanese or Thai do not space between words, although speakers and writers are aware of the individual words. The sentences of some languages are indicated in the written form by capitals at the beginning and periods at the end. Other punctuation, such as question marks, italics, commas, and exclamation marks, is used to reveal syntactic structure, and to some extent intonation, stress, and contrast; but the written forms of many languages do not use such punctuation.

In Chapter 4, we discussed the difference in meaning between restricted and unrestricted relative clauses illustrated by the two sentences containing the relative clause *who were philosophers:*

(1) The Greeks, who were philosophers, loved to talk a lot.
(2) The Greeks who were philosophers loved to talk a lot.

Note that the unrestricted relative clause in (1) is set off by commas which "tells us" that the sentence means:

(1) The Greeks were philosophers, and they loved to talk a lot.

The meaning of the second sentence, without the commas, can be paraphrased as:

(2) Among the Greeks it was the philosophers who loved to talk a lot.

Similarly, by using an exclamation point or a question mark, the intention of the writer can be made clearer.

(3) The children are going to bed at eight o'clock. *(simple statement)*
(4) The children are going to bed at eight o'clock! *(an order)*
(5) The children are going to bed at eight o'clock? *(a question)*

These punctuation marks reflect the pauses and the intonations that would be used in the spoken language.

In sentence 6 *he* can refer to either John or someone else, but in sentence 7 the pronoun must refer to someone other than John:

(6) John said he's going.
(7) John said, "He's going."

The apostrophe used in contractions and possessives also provides syntactic information not always available in the spoken utterance.

(8) My cousin's friends *(one cousin)*
(9) My cousins' friends *(two or more cousins)*

Writing, then, somewhat reflects the spoken language, and punctuation may even distinguish between two meanings not revealed in the spoken forms, as shown in sentences 8 and 9.

In the normal written version of sentence 10,

(10) John whispered the message to Bill and then he whispered it to Mary.

he can refer to either John or Bill. In the spoken sentence, if *he* receives extra stress (called **contrastive stress**), it must refer to Bill; if *he* receives normal stress, it refers to John.

A speaker can usually emphasize any word in a sentence by using contrastive stress. Writers sometimes attempt to show emphasis by using all capital letters, italics, or underlining the emphasized word:

(11) *John* kissed Bill's wife. (Bill didn't)
(12) John *kissed* Bill's wife. (rather than hugging her)
(13) John kissed *Bill's* wife. (not Dick's or his own)
(14) John kissed Bill's *wife*. (not Bill's mother)

Although such "visual" devices can help in English, it is not clear that they can be used in a language such as Chinese. In Japanese, however, this kind of emphasis can be achieved by writing a word in katakana.

Written language is also more conservative than spoken language. When we write something—particularly in formal writing—we are more apt to obey the "prescriptive rules" taught in school, or to use a more formal style, than we are to use the rules of our "everyday" grammar. "Dangling participles" (for example, *While studying in the library, the fire alarm rang*) and "sentences ending with a preposition" (for example, *I know what to end a sentence with*) abound in spoken language, but may be "corrected" by copy editors, diligent English teachers, and careful writers. A linguist wishing to describe the language that people regularly use therefore cannot depend on written records alone.

Spelling

> "Do you spell it with a 'v' or a 'w'?" inquired the judge.
> "That depends upon the taste and fancy of the speller, my Lord," replied Sam.
>
> Charles Dickens, *The Pickwick Papers*

If writing represented the spoken language perfectly, spelling reformers would never have arisen. In Chapter 5 we discussed some of the problems in the English orthographic (spelling) system. These problems prompted George Bernard Shaw to write:

> . . . It was as a reading and writing animal that Man achieved his human eminence above those who are called beasts. Well, it is I and my like who have to do the writing. I have done it professionally for the last sixty years as well as it can be done with a hopelessly inadequate alphabet devised centuries before the English language existed to record another and very different language. Even

this alphabet is reduced to absurdity by a foolish orthography based on the notion that the business of spelling is to represent the origin and history of a word instead of its sound and meaning. Thus an intelligent child who is bidden to spell *debt,* and very properly spells it *d-e-t,* is caned for not spelling it with a *b* because Julius Caesar spelt the Latin word for it with a *b.*[7]

The irregularities between **graphemes** (letters) and phonemes have been cited as one reason "why Johnny can't read." The same spellings for different words pronounced differently, called **homographs,** such as *lead* /lid/ and *lead* /lɛd/, have fueled the flames of spelling reform movements. Different spellings for the same sound, "silent" letters, and "missing" letters also are cited as reasons why English needs a new orthographic system. The examples below (and those given in Chapter 5) illustrate the discrepancies between spelling and sounds in English:

Same Sound, Different Spelling	Different Sound, Same Spelling		Silent Letters	Missing Letters
/aj/	**th**ought	[θ]	**l**isten	use /yuz/
	though	[ð]	de**b**t	fuse /fyuz/
aye	**Th**omas	[t]	**g**nosis	
bu**y**			**k**now	
b**y**	**a**te	[e]	**p**sychology	
d**ie**	**a**t	[æ]	ri**gh**t	
h**i**	f**a**ther	[a]	**m**nemonic	
Th**ai**	m**a**ny	[ɛ]	arc**t**ic	
he**igh**t			ba**l**m	
g**ui**de			**h**onest	
			s**w**ord	
			bom**b**	
			cl**u**e	
			We**d**nesday	

Chapters 3 and 8 have discussed some of the reasons for the nonphonemic aspects of our spelling system. "Spelling is the written trace of a word. Pronunciation is its linguistic form."[8] The spelling of most of the words in English today is based on the Late Middle English pronunciation (that used by Chaucer) and on the early forms of Modern English (used by Shakespeare). The many changes that have occurred in the sound system of English, like the Great Vowel Shift, were not always reflected in changes in the spelling of the words that were affected.

When the printing press was introduced in the fifteenth century, not only were archaic pronunciations "frozen," but the spelling did not always represent even

[7]George Bernard Shaw, Preface to R. A. Wilson, *The Miraculous Birth of Language,* New York: Philosophical Library, 1948.
[8]D. Bolinger, *Aspects of Language,* New York: Harcourt Brace Jovanovich, 1968.

those pronunciations, because many of the early printers were Dutch and were unsure of English pronunciation.

During the Renaissance, in the fifteenth and sixteenth centuries, many scholars who revered Classical Greek and Latin became "spelling reformers." Unlike the later reformers who wished to change the spelling to conform to pronunciation, these scholars changed the spelling of English words to conform to their etymologies—the "original" Latin, or Greek, or French spellings. Where the Latin had a *b*, they added a *b* even if it was not pronounced; and where the original spelling had a *c* or *p* or *h*, these letters were added, as is shown by these few examples:

Middle English Spelling		**"Reformed" Spelling**
indite	→	indi**c**t
dette	→	de**b**t
receit	→	recei**p**t
oure	→	**h**our

Such spelling habits inspired Robert N. Feinstein to compose the following poem, entitled *Gnormal Pspelling:*[9]

Gnus and gnomes and gnats and such—
Gnouns with just one G too much.
Pseudonym and psychedelic—
P becomes a psurplus relic.
Knit and knack and knife and knocked—
Kneedless Ks are overstocked.
Rhubarb, rhetoric and rhyme
Should lose an H from thyme to time.

For these reasons, modern English orthography does not always represent what we know about the phonology of the language. The disadvantage is partially offset by the fact that the writing system allows us to read and understand what people wrote hundreds of years ago without the need for translations. If there were a one-to-one correspondence between our spelling and the sounds of our language, we would have difficulty reading the Constitution or the Declaration of Independence.

Today's language is no more static than was yesterday's; it would be impossible to maintain a perfect correspondence between pronunciation and spelling. We do not mean to say that certain reforms would not be helpful. Some "respelling" is already taking place; advertisers often spell *though* as *tho, through* as *thru,* and *night* as *nite*. For a period of time the Chicago *Tribune* used such spellings, but it gave up the practice in 1975. Spelling habits are hard to change.

In the case of homophones, it is helpful at times to have different spellings for the same sounds, as in the following pair:

[9]Reprinted with permission from *National Forum: The Phi Kappa Phi Journal,* Summer 1986.

The book was red.   The book was read.

Lewis Carroll once more makes the point with humor:

> "And how many hours a day did you do lessons?" said Alice.
> "Ten hours the first day," said the Mock Turtle, "nine the next, and so on."
> "What a curious plan!" exclaimed Alice.
> "That's the reason they're called *lessons,*" the Gryphon remarked, "because they *lessen* from day to day."

There are also reasons for using the same spelling for different pronunciations. In Chapter 4 it was shown that a morpheme may be pronounced differently when it occurs in different contexts, and that in most cases the pronunciation is "regular"; that is, it is determined by rules that apply throughout the language. The identical spelling reflects the fact that the different pronunciations represent the same morpheme.

Similarly, the phonetic realizations of the vowels in the following forms are "regular":

ay/ɪ	ɪ/ɛ	e/æ
divine/divinity	*serene/serenity*	*sane/sanity*
sublime/sublimate	*obscene/obscenity*	*profane/profanity*
sign/signature	*hyiene/hygienic*	*humane/humanity*

The spelling of such pairs thus reflects our knowledge of the sound pattern of the language and the semantic-morphological relations between the words.

Other examples provide further evidence. The *b* in "*debt*" may remind us of the related word *debit,* in which the *b* is pronounced. The same principle is true of pairs such as *sign/signal, knowledge/acknowledge, bomb/bombardier,* and *gnosis/prognosis/agnostic.*

It is doubtful that anyone would suggest that the plural morpheme should be spelled *s* in *cats* and *z* in *dogs.* The sound of the morpheme is determined by rules, in this case as in other cases.

There are also different spellings that represent the different pronunciations of a morpheme when confusion would arise from using the same spelling. For example, there is a rule in English phonology that changes a /t/ to an /s/ in certain cases: *democrat* → *democracy.* The different spellings are due in part to the fact that this rule does not apply to all morphemes, so that *art* + *y* is *arty,* not **arcy.* Regular phoneme-to-grapheme rules determine in many cases when a morpheme is to be spelled identically and when it is to be changed.

Other subregularities are apparent. A *c* always represents the /s/ sound when it is followed by a *y, i,* or *e,* as in *cynic, citizen,* and *censure.* Because it is always pronounced [k] when it is the final letter in a word or when it is followed by any other vowel (*coat, cat, cut,* and so on), no confusion results. The *th* spelling is usually pronounced voiced as [ð] between vowels (the result of an historical intervocalic voicing rule).

Such rules of orthography could be taught to children learning to read, which would lessen the difficulties they have with the spelling system. For example, by pointing out the alternate pronunciations of morphemes such as the [o] in *melodious* or the [g] in *signal,* teachers could make it easier for students to remember how to spell the related words *melody* or *sign*.

There is another important reason why spelling should not always be tied to the phonetic pronunciation of words. Different dialects of English have divergent pronunciations. Cockneys drop their "(h)aitches" and Bostonians and southerners drop their "*r*s"; *neither* is pronounced [niðər] and [niðə] by Americans, [nayðə] by the British, and [neðər] by the Irish; some Scots pronounce *night* as [nɪxt]; people say "Chicago" and "Chicawgo," "hog" and "hawg," "bird" and "boyd"; *four* is pronounced [fɔ:] by the British, [fɔr] in the Midwest, and [foə] in the South; *orange* is pronounced in at least two ways in the United States: [arənǰ] and [ɔrənǰ].

While dialectal pronunciations differ, the common spellings represent the fact that we understand each other. It is necessary for the written language to transcend local dialects. With a uniform spelling system, a native of Atlanta and a native of Glasgow can communicate through writing. If each dialect were spelled according to its own pronunciation, written communication among the English-speaking peoples of the world would suffer more than the spoken communication does today.

Spelling Pronunciations

> For pronunciation, the best general rule is to consider those as the most elegant speakers who deviate least from written words.
>
> Samuel Johnson (1755)

Despite the primacy of the spoken over the written language, the written word is often regarded with excessive reverence. The stability, permanency, and graphic nature of writing cause some people to favor it over ephemeral and elusive speech. Humpty Dumpty expressed a rather typical attitude: "I'd rather see that done on paper."

Writing has affected speech only marginally, however, most notably in the phenomenon of **spelling pronunciation.** Since the sixteenth century, we find that spelling has to some extent influenced standard pronunciation. The most important of such changes stem from the eighteenth century under the influence and "decrees" of the dictionary-makers and the schoolteachers. The struggle between those who demanded that words be pronounced according to the spelling and those who demanded that words be spelled according to their pronunciation generated great heat in that century. The "preferred" pronunciations were given in the many dictionaries printed in the eighteenth century, and the "supreme authority" of the dictionaries influenced pronunciation in this way.

Spelling also has influenced pronunciation in words that are infrequently used in normal daily speech. Many words that were spelled with an initial *h* were not pronounced with any /h/ sound as late as the eighteenth century. Thus, at that time no

/h/ was pronounced in *honest, hour, habit, heretic, hotel, hospital, herb.* Frequently used words like *honest* and *hour* continued to be pronounced without the /h/, despite the spelling; but all those other words were given a "spelling pronunciation." Because people did not hear them often, when they saw them written they concluded that they must begin with an /h/. *Herb* is currently undergoing this change; in Standard British English the *h* is pronounced, whereas in Standard American English it is not.

Similarly, many words now spelled with a *th* were once pronounced /t/ as in *Thomas;* later most of these words underwent a change in pronunciation from /t/ to /θ/, as in *anthem, author, theater.* "Nicknames" often reflect the earlier pronunciations: "Ka*te*" for "Ca*the*rine," "Be*tty*" for "Eliza*beth,*" "Ar*t*" for "Ar*th*ur." The words *often* and *soften,* which are usually pronounced without a /t/ sound, are pronounced with the /t/ by some people because of the spelling.

The clear influence of spelling on pronunciation is observable in the way place-names are pronounced. *Berkeley* is pronounced [bʌrkli] in California, although it stems from the British [baːkli]; *Worcester* [wʊstər] or [wʊstə] in Massachusetts is often pronounced [wʊrčɛstər] in other parts of the country; *Magdalen* is pronounced [mɔdlɪn] in England and [mægdələn] in the United States.

Although the written language has some influence on the spoken, it does not change the basic system—the grammar—of the language. The writing system, conversely, reflects, in a more or less direct way, the grammar that every speaker knows.

Summary

Writing is one of the basic tools of civilization. Without it, the world as we know it could not exist.

The first writing was "picture writing," which used **pictograms** to represent objects directly. Pictograms became stylized, and people came to associate them with the *sounds* that represented the object in their language. The Sumerians first developed a pictographic writing system to keep track of commercial transactions. It was later expanded for other uses and eventually evolved into the highly stylized (and stylus-ized) **cuneiform** writing. Cuneiform was borrowed by several nations and was adapted for use in syllabic writing systems by application of the **rebus principle,** which used the symbol of one word to represent any word or syllable with the same sounds.

The Egyptians also developed a pictographic system, which became known as **hieroglyphics.** This system was borrowed by many peoples, including the Phoenicians, who improved on it, using it as a **syllabary.** In a syllabic writing system, one symbol is used for each syllable. The Greeks borrowed the Phoenician system, and in adapting it to their own language they used the symbols to represent individual sound segments, thus inventing the first **alphabet.**

There are three types of writing systems still being used in the world: **word writing,** where every symbol or character represents a word or morpheme (as in

Chinese); **syllable writing,** where each symbol represents a syllable (as in Japanese); and **alphabetic writing,** where each symbol represents (for the most part) one phoneme (as in English). **Consonantal writing,** in which vowels are not explicitly represented, is considered by some scholars to be a fourth type of writing system.

Many of the world's languages do not have a written form, but this does not mean the languages are any less developed. We learn to speak before we learn to write, and historically tens of thousands of years went by during which language was spoken before there was any writing.

The writing system may have some small effect on the spoken language. Languages change in time, but writing systems tend to be more conservative. Thus spelling no longer accurately reflects pronunciation. Also, when the spoken and written forms of the language become divergent, some words may be pronounced as they are spelled, sometimes due to the efforts of "pronunciation reformers."

There are advantages to a conservative spelling system. A common spelling permits speakers whose dialects have diverged to communicate through writing, as is best exemplified in China, where the "dialects" are mutually unintelligible. We are also able to read and understand the language as it was written centuries ago. In addition, despite some gross lack of correspondences between sound and spelling, the spelling often reflects speakers' morphological and phonological knowledge.

References for Further Reading

Biber, Douglas. 1988. *Variation Across Speech and Writing.* Cambridge, England: Cambridge University Press.

DeFrancis, John. 1989. *Visible Speech: The diverse oneness of writing systems.* Honolulu, Hawaii: University of Hawaii Press.

Diringer, D. 1962. *Writing.* New York: Holt, Rinehart and Winston.

Doblhofer, E. 1961. *Voices in Stone: The Decipherment of Ancient Scripts and Writings.* New York: Viking Press.

Gaur, Albertine. 1984. *A History of Writing.* London, England: The British Library.

Gelb, I. J. 1952. *A Study of Writing.* Chicago, Ill.: University of Chicago Press.

Jensen, H. 1970. *Sign, Symbol and Script,* G. Unwin, trans. London, England: George Allen and Unwin.

Robertson, S., and F. G. Cassidy, 1954. *The Development of Modern English.* Englewood Cliffs, N.J.: Prentice-Hall, pp. 353–374 (on spelling and spelling reform).

Sampson, Geoffrey, 1985. *Writing Systems: A Linguistic Introduction.* Stanford, Calif.: Stanford University Press.

Wang, William S-Y. 1973. "The Chinese Language." *Scientific American* 228 (2): 50–63.

Wang, William S-Y. 1981. "Language Structure and Optimal Orthography." In *Perception of Print: Reading Research in Experimental Psychology,* O. J. L. Tzeng and H. Singer, eds. Hillsdale, N.J.: Erlbaum.

Exercises

1. A. "Write" the following words and phrases, using pictograms that you invent:

    a. eye
    b. a boy
    c. two boys
    d. library
    e. tree
    f. forest
    g. war
    h. honesty
    i. ugly
    j. run
    k. Scotch tape
    l. smoke

  B. Which words are most difficult to symbolize in this way? Why?

  C. How does the following sentence reveal the problems in pictographic writing? "A grammar represents the unconscious, internalized linguistic competence of a native speaker."

2. A *rebus* is a written representation of words or syllables using pictures of objects whose names resemble the sounds of the intended words or syllables. For example, might be the symbol for "eye" or "I" or the first syllable in "idea."

  A. Using the rebus principle, "write" the following words:

    a. tearing
    b. icicle
    c. bareback
    d. cookies

  B. Why would such a system be a difficult system in which to represent all words in English? Illustrate with an example.

3. A. Construct non-Roman alphabetic letters to replace the letters used to represent the following sounds in English:

    t r s k w č i æ f n

  B. Use these symbols plus the regular alphabet symbols for the other sounds to write the following words in your "new orthography."

a. character
b. guest
c. cough
d. photo
e. cheat
f. rang
g. psychotic
h. tree

4. Suppose the English writing system were a *syllabic* system instead of an *alphabetic* system. Use capital letters to symbolize the necessary syllabic units for the words below, and list your "syllabary." Example: Given the words *mate, inmate, intake,* and *elfin,* you might use: A = mate, B = in, C = take, and D = elf. In addition, write the words using your syllabary. Example: *inmate—* BA; *elfin—*DB; *intake—*BC; *mate—*A. (Do not use any more syllable symbols than you absolutely need.)

a. childishness
b. childlike
c. Jesuit
d. lifelessness
e. likely
f. zoo
g. witness
h. lethal
i. jealous
j. witless
k. lesson

5. In the following pairs of English words the boldfaced portions are pronounced the same but spelled differently. Can you think of any reason why the spelling should remain distinct? (Hint: *reel* and *real* are pronounced the same, but *reality* shows the presence of a phonemic /æ/ in *real.*)

A	B	Reason
a. I **am**	i**amb**	
b. goo**se**	produ**ce**	
c. fa**sh**ion	compli**c**ation	
d. New**ton**	or**gan**	
e. **n**o	**kn**ow	
f. hy**mn**	**h**im	

6. In the following pairs of words the bold-faced portions are spelled the same but pronounced differently. Try to state some reasons why the spelling of the words in column B should not be changed.

A	B	Reason
a. min**g**le	lon**g**	The **g** is pronounced in *longer.*
b. l**i**ne	ch**i**ldren	
c. **s**onar	re**s**ound	
d. **c**ent	mysti**c**	
e. crum**b**le	bom**b**	
f. cat**s**	dog**s**	
g. sta**gn**ant	desi**gn**	
h. se**re**ne	obs**ce**nity	

7. Each of the following sentences is ambiguous in the written form. How can these sentences be made unambiguous when they are spoken?

> Example: John hugged Bill and then he kissed him.

> For the meaning "John hugged and kissed Bill," use normal stress (*kissed* receives stress). For the meaning "Bill kissed John," contrastive stress is needed on both *he* and *him.*

a. What are we having for dinner, Mother?
b. She's a German language teacher.
c. They formed a student grievance committee.
d. Charles kissed his wife and George kissed his wife too.

8. In the written form, the following sentences are not ambiguous, but they would be if spoken. State the devices used in writing that make the meanings explicit.

a. They're my brothers' keepers.
b. He said, "He will take the garbage out."
c. The red book was read.
d. The flower was on the table.

9. Below are ten samples of writing from the ten languages listed. Match the writing to the language. There are enough "hints" in this chapter to get most of them. (The source of these examples, and many others, is *Languages of the World* by Kenneth Katzner. New York: Funk & Wagnalls. 1975.)

a. _____Cherokee

b. _____Chinese

c. _____German (Gothic style)

d. _____Greek

e. _____Hebrew

f. _____Icelandic

g. _____Japanese

h. _____Korean

i. _____Russian

j. _____Twi

1. 仮に勝手に変えるようなことをすれば.

2. Κι ὁ νοῦς του ἀγκάλιασε πονετικὰ τὴν Κρήτη.

3. «Что это? я падаю? у меня ноги подкашиваются»,

4. וְהָיָה ׀ בְּאַחֲרִית הַיָּמִים נָכוֹן יִהְיֶה הַר

5. Saá sàre yi bèŋ atɛkyé bí â mpɔ̀torɔ áhyɛ́

6. 既然必须和新的群众的时代相结合.

7. 𐒻𐒷𐓄 𐒹𐓓 𐒻𐓌𐒼𐓂 𐒿𐓍𐓊 𐒼𐒷𐒻𐓍.

8. Þótt þú langförull legðir sérhvert land undir fót,

9. Pharao's Anblick war wunderbar.

10. 스위스는 독특한 체제

10. The following appeared on the safety card of a Spanish airline. Identify each of the thirteen languages. (You will probably have to spend some time in the library and/or visit various departments of foreign languages.)

1. **Para su seguridad** _____

2. **For your safety** _____

3. **Pour votre sécurité** _____

4. **Für ihre Sicherheit** _____

5. **Per la Vostra sicurezza** _____

6. **Para sua segurança** _____

7. あなたの安全のために _____

8. **Для Вашей безопасности** _____

9. **Dla bezpieczeństwa pasażerów** _____

10. **Za vašu sigurnost** _____

11. **Γιά τήν ἀσφάλειά σας** _____

12. **Kendi emniyetiniz için** _____

13. من أجل سلامتك _____

PART 4
Biological Aspects of Language

The functional asymmetry of the human brain is unequivocal, and so is its anatomical asymmetry. The structural differences between the left and the right hemispheres are visible not only under the microscope but to the naked eye. The most striking asymmetries occur in language-related cortices. It is tempting to assume that such anatomical differences are an index of the neurobiological underpinnings of language.

Antonio and Hanna Damasio

[The brain is] the messenger of the understanding [and the organ whereby] in an especial manner we acquire wisdom and knowledge.

Hippocratic treatise "On the Sacred Disease," c. 377 B.C.E.

CHAPTER 10
Language Acquisition

The acquisition of language "is doubtless the greatest intellectual feat any one of us is ever required to perform."

Leonard Bloomfield, *Language* (1933)

"WHAT'S THE BIG SURPRISE? ALL THE LATEST THEORIES OF LINGUISTICS SAY WE'RE BORN WITH THE INNATE CAPACITY FOR GENERATING SENTENCES."

Every aspect of language is extremely complex; yet very young children—before the age of five—already know most of the intricate system we have been calling the grammar of a language. Before they can add 2 + 2, children are conjoining sentences, asking questions, selecting appropriate pronouns, negating sentences, forming relative clauses, and using the syntactic, phonological, morphological, and semantic rules of the grammar.

A normal human being can go through life without learning to read or write. Millions of people in the world today prove it. These same millions all speak and understand and can discuss complex and abstract ideas as well as literate speakers can. Therefore, learning a language and learning to read and write are somehow different. Similarly, millions of humans grow to maturity and never learn algebra or chemistry or how to use a typewriter. They must be taught these skills or systems, but they do not have to be taught to walk or to talk.

The study of the nature of human language itself has revealed a great deal about language acquisition, about what the child does and does not do when learning or acquiring a language.

1. Children do not learn a language by storing all the words and all the sentences in some giant mental dictionary. The list of words is finite, but no dictionary can hold all the sentences, which are infinite in number.
2. Children learn to construct sentences, most of which they have never produced before.
3. Children learn to understand sentences they have never heard before. They cannot do so by matching the "heard utterance" with some stored sentence.
4. Children must therefore construct the "rules" that permit them to use language creatively.
5. No one teaches them these rules. Their parents are no more aware of the phonological, syntactic, and semantic rules than are the children.

Even if you remember your early years, you will not remember anyone telling you to form a sentence by adding a verb phrase to a noun phrase, or to add [s] or [z] to form plurals. Children, then, seem to act like efficient linguists equipped with a perfect theory of language, who use this theory to construct the grammar of the language they hear.

In addition to acquiring the complex rules of the grammar (that is, linguistic competence), children must also learn the complex rules of the appropriate social use of language, what certain scholars have called communicative competence. These rules include, for example, the greetings that are to be used, the "taboo" words, the polite forms of address, the various styles that are appropriate to different situations, and so forth.

Stages in Language Acquisition

... for I was no longer a speechless infant; but a speaking boy. This I remember; and have since observed how I learned to speak. It was not that my elders taught me words . . . in any set method; but I . . . did myself . . . practice the sounds in my memory. . . . And thus by constantly hearing words, as they occurred in various sentences . . . I thereby gave utterance to my will.

St. Augustine (transl. F. J. Sheed, 1944), *Confessions* (circa 400 C.E.)

Children do not wake up one morning with a fully formed grammar in their heads or with all the "rules" of social and communicative intercourse. Linguistic knowledge develops by stages, and, it is suggested, each successive stage more closely approximates the grammar of the adult language. Observations of children in different language areas of the world reveal that the stages are similar, possibly universal. Some of the stages last for a short time; others remain longer. Some stages may overlap for a short period, though the transition between stages is often sudden.

Given the universal aspects of all human languages, signed and spoken, it is not surprising that deaf children of deaf signing parents parallel the stages of spoken language acquisition in their signing development.

The earliest studies of child language acquisition come from diaries kept by parents. More recent studies include the use of tape recordings, videotapes, and controlled experiments. Spontaneous utterances of children are recorded, and in addition various elicitation techniques have been developed so that the child's production and comprehension can be scientifically studied.

The First Sounds

An infant crying in the night:
An infant crying for the light:
And with no language but a cry.

Alfred Lord Tennyson, *"In Memoriam H.H.S."*

The stages of language acquisition can be divided into prelinguistic and linguistic stages. Most scholars agree that the earliest cries, whimpers, and cooing noises of the newborn, or neonate, cannot be considered early language. Such noises are completely stimulus controlled; they are the child's involuntary responses to hunger, discomfort, the desire to be cuddled, or the feeling of well-being. A major difference between human language and the communication systems of other species is that human language is creative, as discussed earlier, in the sense of being free from either external or internal stimuli. The child's first noises are, however, simply responses to stimuli.

During the earliest period, the noises produced by infants in all language communities sound the same.

The early view that the neonate is born with a mind that is like a blank slate is countered by the evidence showing that infants are highly sensitive to certain subtle distinctions in their environment and not to others. That is, the mind appears to be "prewired" to receive only certain kinds of information.

By using a specially designed nipple with a pressure-sensitive device that records sucking rate, it has been found that infants will increase their sucking rate when stimuli (visual or auditory) presented to them are varied, but will decrease the sucking rate when the same stimuli are presented over and over again. Experiments have shown that infants will respond to visual depth and distance distinctions, to differences between rigid versus flexible physical properties of objects, and to human faces rather than to other visual stimuli.

Similarly, newborn infants respond to phonetic contrasts found in some human languages even when these differences are not phonemic in the language spoken in the baby's home. A baby hearing a human voice over a loudspeaker saying [pa] [pa] [pa] will slowly decrease her rate of sucking; if the sound changes to [ba] or even [pʰa], the sucking rate increases dramatically. There will be no response to sound signals that are intermediate between, say, [pa] and [pʰa], differences that never signal phonemic contrasts in any human language. The infants could not have learned to make these phonetic distinctions; they seem to be born with the ability to perceive just those sounds that are phonemic in some language. Thus, children have the sensory and motor abilities to produce and comprehend speech, even in the period of life before language acquisition occurs.

Babbling

In the first few months, usually around the sixth month, the infant begins to **babble.** The sounds produced in this period (apart from the continuing stimulus-controlled cries and gurgles) seem to include a large variety of sounds, many of which do not occur in the language of the household.

One view suggests that it is during this period that children are learning to distinguish between the sounds of their language and the sounds which are not part of the language. During the babbling period children learn to maintain the "right" sounds and suppress the "wrong" ones. Babbling, however, does not seem to be a prerequisite for language acquisition. Infants who are unable to produce any sounds at this early stage due to physical motor problems begin to talk properly once the disability has been corrected.

It was once thought that deaf infants produced babbling sounds similar to those of normal children. This would suggest that the sounds produced do not depend on the presence of auditory input or that they are a first stage in language acquisition.

Recently, studies conducted by Laura Petitto and her colleagues of McGill University of vocal babbling of hearing children and manual babbling of deaf children suggest that babbling is a specifically linguistic ability related to the kind of language input the child receives. She reports that infants from four to seven months produce a restricted set of phonetic forms, vocally, if exposed to spoken languages, and manually if exposed to signed language, drawn from the set of possible sounds and possible gestures found in spoken and signed languages.

Babbling illustrates the sensitivity of the human mind to respond to linguistic cues from a very early stage. This is dramatically demonstrated in Petitto's comparative studies of hearing and deaf infants.[1] During the babbling stage of hearing

---

[1]Petitto, L. A. and P. F. Marantette. "Babbling in the manual mode: Evidence for the ontogeny of language." *Science* 251, pp. 1493–96. 22 March 1991.

infants, the pitch, or intonation contours produced by them begin to resemble the intonation contours of sentences spoken by adults. The semantically different intonation contours are among the first linguistic contrasts that children perceive and produce.

During this same period, the vocalizations produced by deaf babies are qualitatively different from those produced by hearing infants; they are unsystematic, nonrepetitive and random. In parallel, the manual gestures produced by hearing babies' language differ greatly from those produced by deaf infants exposed to sign language. The hearing babies move their fingers and clench their fists randomly with little or no repetition of the same gestures; the deaf infants, however, use more than a dozen different hand motions repetitively, all of which are elements of American Sign Language, or the other sign languages used by deaf communities in all countries.

Petitto's view is that humans are born with a predisposition to discover the units which serve to express linguistic meanings, and that at a genetically specified stage in neural development, the infant will begin to produce these units, sounds or gestures, depending on the language input the baby receives. Thus she suggests babbling is the earliest stage in language acquisition, in opposition to the earlier view that babbling was prelinguistic and simply neuromuscular in origin.

First Words

> From this golden egg a man, Prajapati, was born . . . A year having passed, he wanted to speak. He said bhur and the earth was created. He said bhuvar and the space of the air was created. He said suvar and the sky was created. That is why a child wants to speak after a year . . . When Prajapati spoke for the first time, he uttered one or two syllables. That is why a child utters one or two syllables when he speaks for the first time.
>
> Hindu myth

DOONESBURY copyright 1982 & 1984 G. B. Trudeau.

Sometime after one year (it varies from child to child and has nothing to do with how intelligent the child is), children begin to use the same string of sounds repeatedly to "mean" the same thing. They have learned that sounds are related to meanings, and they are producing their first "words." Most children seem to go through the "one word = one sentence" stage. These one-word "sentences" are called **holophrastic** sentences (from *holo* "complete" or "undivided" plus *phrase* "phrase" or "sentence").

One child, J.P., illustrates how much the young child has learned even before the age of two years. J.P.'s words of April 1977, at the age of sixteen months, were as follows:[2]

[ʔaw]	"not" "no" "don't"	[s:]	"aerosol spray"
[bʌʔ]/[mʌʔ]	"up"		
[da]	"dog"	[sʲu:]	"shoe"
[iʔo]/[siʔo]	"Cheerios"	[haj]	"hi"
[sa]	"sock"	[sr]	"shirt"
[aj]/[ʌj]	"light"		"sweater"
[ma]	"mommy"	[sæ:]/[əsæ:]	"what's that?"
[baw]/[daw]	"down"		"hey, look!"
[dæ]	"daddy"		

J.P.'s mother reports that before April he also had used the words [bʊ] for "book," [ki] for "kitty," and [tsi] for "tree" but seemed to have "lost" them.

What is more interesting than merely the list of J.P.'s vocabulary is the way he used these words. "Up" was originally restricted to mean "Get me up" when he was either on the floor or in his high chair, but later was used to mean "Get up!" to his mother as well. J.P. used his word for "sock" not only for socks but also for other undergarments that go over the feet, which illustrates how a child may extend the meaning of a word from a particular referent to encompass a larger class.

When J.P. first began to use these words, the stimulus had to be visible; but soon, it was no longer necessary. *Dog,* for example, was first only used when pointing to a real dog but later was used for pictures of dogs in various books. A new word that entered J.P.'s vocabulary at seventeen months was *uh-oh,* which he would say after he had an accident like spilling juice, or when he deliberately poured his yogurt over the side of his high chair. His use of this word shows his developing use of language for social purposes. At this time he also added two new words meaning "no," [do:] and [no]. He used these words frequently when anyone attempted to take something from him that he wanted or tried to make him do something he did not want to do. He used this negative either imperatively (for example, "Don't do that!") or assertively (for example, "I don't want to do that."). Even in his early

---

[2]We give special thanks to John Peregrine Munro for providing us with such rich data, and to Drs. Pamela and Allen Munro, J.P.'s parents, for their painstaking efforts in recording these data.

holophrastic stage, J.P. was using words to convey a variety of ideas, feelings, and social awareness.

According to some child-language researchers, the words in the holophrastic stage serve three major functions: they either are linked with a child's own action or desire for action (as when J.P. would say "up" to express his wish to be picked up), or are used to convey emotion (J.P.'s "no"), or serve a naming function (J.P.'s "Cheerios," "shoes," "dog," and so on).

At this stage the child uses only one word to express concepts or predications that will later be expressed by complex phrases and sentences.

Phonologically, J.P.'s first words, like the words of most children at this stage of learning English and other languages, were generally monosyllabic with a CV (consonant-vowel) form; the vowel part may be diphthongal, depending on the language being acquired. His phonemic or phonetic inventory (at this stage they are equivalent) is much smaller than is found in the adult language. It was suggested by the linguist Roman Jakobson[3] that children first will acquire the sounds found in all languages of the world, no matter what language they are exposed to, and in later stages will acquire the "more difficult" sounds. For example, most languages have the sounds [p] and [s], but [θ] is a rare sound. J.P. was no exception. His phonological inventory at an early stage included the consonants [b, m, d, k], which are frequently occurring sounds in the world's languages.

Many studies have shown that children in the holophrastic stage can perceive or comprehend many more phonological contrasts than they can produce themselves. Therefore, even at this stage, it is not possible to determine the extent of the grammar of the child simply by observing speech production.

The Two-Word Stage

Children begin to produce two-word utterances around the time of their second birthday. At first these utterances appear to be strings of two of the child's earlier holophrastic utterances, each word with its own single-pitch contour. Soon after this juxtaposition, children begin to form actual two-word sentences with clear syntactic and semantic relations. The intonation contour of the two words extends over the whole utterance rather than being separated by a pause between the two words. The following "sentences" illustrate the kinds of patterns that are found in children's utterances at this stage.[4]

---

[3]R. Jakobson, *Kindersprache, Aphasie, und Allgemeine,* Uppsala, Sweden: Almqvist and Wiksell, 1941. (English translation by A. Keiler. 1968. *Child Language, Aphasia, and Phonological Universals.* The Hague: Mouton.)

[4]All the examples given in this chapter are taken from utterances produced by children actually observed by the authors or reported in the literature. The various sources are listed in the reference section at the end of the chapter.

allgone sock	hi Mommy
byebye boat	allgone sticky
more wet	beepbeep bang
it ball	Katherine sock
dirty sock	here pretty

During the two-word utterance stage there are no syntactic or morphological markers—that is, no inflections for number, person, tense, and so on. Pronouns are rare, although many children use *me* to refer to themselves, and some children use other pronouns as well. Bloom has noted that in noun + noun sentences such as *Mommy sock,* the two words can express a number of different grammatical relations that will later be expressed by other syntactic devices.[5] Bloom's conclusions were reached by observing the situations in which the two-word sentence was uttered. Thus, for example, *Mommy sock* can be used to show a subject + object relation in the situation when the mother is putting the sock on the child, or a possessive relation when the child is pointing to Mommy's sock. Two nouns can also be used to show a subject–locative relation, as in *sweater chair* to mean "The sweater is on the chair," or to show conjunction, to mean "sweater and chair."

From Telegraph to Infinity

There does not seem to be any "three-word" sentence stage. When a child starts stringing more than two words together, the utterances may be two, three, four, or five words or longer. By studying the increasing lengths of the utterances that children use, however, a comparison across children as to stage of language acquisition can be made by the **mean length of utterances** (MLU) rather than by chronological age. That is, children producing utterances that average 2.3 to 3.5 morphemes in length seem to be at the same stage of grammar acquisition.

The first utterances of children longer than two words have a special characteristic. The small "function" words such as *to, the, can, is,* and so on, are missing; only the words that carry the main message—the "content" words—occur. Children often sound as if they are reading a Western Union message, which is why such utterances are sometimes called **telegraphic speech:**

Cat stand up table
What that?
He play little tune
Andrew want that
Cathy build house
No sit there

J.P.'s early sentences were similar:

[5]L. M. Bloom, *Language Development: Form and Function in Emerging Grammar,* Cambridge, Mass.: M.I.T. Press, 1972.

Age in Months

25 months	[dan ʔ i ʔ tˢɪʔ]	"don't eat (the) chip"
	[bʷaʔ tat]	"(the) block (is on) top"
26 months	[mamis tu hæs]	"Mommy's two hands"
	[mo bʌs go]	"where's another bus?"
	[dædi go]	"where's Daddy?"
27 months	[ʔaj gat tu dʲus]	"I got two (glasses of) juice"
	[do baj ʔ mi]	"don't bite (kiss) me"
	[kʌdər sʌni ber]	"Sonny color(ed a) bear"
28 months	[ʔaj gat pwe dɪs]	"I('m) play(ing with) this"
	[mamis tak mɛns]	"Mommy talk(ed to the) men"

Apart from lacking grammatical morphemes, these utterances appear to be "sentence-like"; they have hierarchical, constituent structures similar to the syntactic structures found in the sentences produced by the adult grammar.

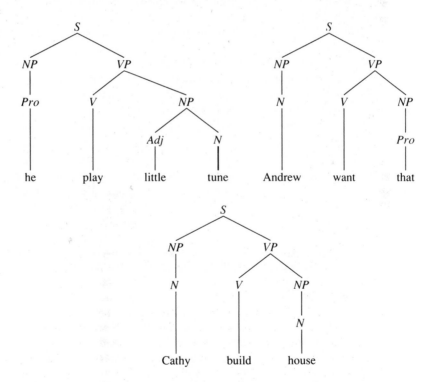

Children's utterances are not simply words that are randomly strung together, but from a very early stage reveal their grasp of the principles of sentence formation.

The examples cited above show that children's utterances adhere to the word order constraints of the language they are acquiring. The fact that children's sentences are structured is also revealed by the fact that children show subject-verb agreement in languages such as Italian, Polish, or Turkish, where this is required by the adult language. They would be unable to inflect the verb to agree with the subject Noun Phrase if they didn't know what a Noun or a Noun Phrase or a Verb was.

Though the utterances are described as "telegraphic," the child does not deliberately leave out the noncontent words as does an adult sending a telegram.

As children produce sentences that more and more closely approximate the adult grammar, they begin to use syntactic or grammatical function words and also to acquire the inflectional and derivational morphemes of the language. Brown and his associates at Harvard studied the spontaneous utterances of three children—Adam, Sarah, and Eve—over a long period of time, noting the appearance of grammatical morphemes, free and bound.[6] They found that the sentences of acquisition of the morphemes were the same for all three children, and this finding has been replicated by others. *-ing,* the ending that represents the present progressive form of the verb, as in *Me going,* was found to be among the earliest inflectional morphemes acquired. The prepositions *in* and *on* next entered the speech of the children studied, and then the regular plural ending, as in "two doggies" /tu dɔgiz/. It is interesting that the third person singular marker (as in *Johnny comes*) and the possessive morpheme (as in *Daddy's hat*), which have the same phonological shape as the plural /s/, entered the children's speech between six months and a year later, showing that acquisition of these morphemes is syntax-dependent.

Eventually all the other inflections were added, along with the syntactic rules, and finally the child's utterances sounded like those spoken by adults.

This feat is incredible, because the syntactic rules of all languages are complex; moreover, the child must "figure out" what these rules are from very "noisy" data. The child hears sentence fragments, false starts, speech errors, and interruptions; no one tells the child "this is a grammatical utterance and this is not." Somehow the adult grammar is acquired. A basic question is how the child accomplishes this task.

Theories of Child Language Acquisition

Do Children Learn by Imitation?

CHILD: *My teacher holded the baby rabbits and we patted them.*
ADULT: *Did you say your teacher held the baby rabbits?*
CHILD: *Yes.*
ADULT: *What did you say she did?*
CHILD: *She holded the baby rabbits and we patted them.*
ADULT: *Did you say she held them tightly?*
CHILD: *No, she holded them loosely.*

Courtney Cazden [7]

[6]R. O. Brown, *A First Language: The Early Stages,* Cambridge, Mass.: Harvard University Press, 1973.
[7]C. Cazden, *Child Language and Education,* New York: Holt, Rinehart and Winston, 1972, p. 92.

Various theories have been proposed to explain how children manage to acquire the adult language. There are those who think that children merely imitate what they hear. Imitation is involved to some extent, of course, but the sentences produced by children show that children are not imitating adult speech. From whom would children hear *Cat stand up table* or any of the utterances they produce?

> a my pencil
> two foot
> what the boy hit?
> other one pants
> Mommy get it my ladder
> cowboy did fighting me

Even when children are deliberately trying to imitate what they hear, they are unable to produce sentences that cannot be generated by their grammar.

ADULT: He's going out.	CHILD: He go out.
ADULT: That's an old-time train.	CHILD: Old-time train.
ADULT: Adam, say what I say: Where can I put them?	CHILD: Where I can put them?

Neither can the "imitation" theory account for another important phenomenon. There are children who are unable to speak for neurological or physiological reasons; yet these children learn the language spoken to them and understand what is said. When they overcome their speech impairment they immediately use the language for speaking.

Do Children Learn by Reinforcement?

> CHILD: Nobody don't like me.
> MOTHER: No, say "Nobody likes me."
> CHILD: Nobody don't like me.
>
> *(dialogue repeated eight times)*
>
> MOTHER: Now, listen carefully, say *"Nobody likes me."*
> CHILD: Oh, nobody don't likes me.

Another theory of language acquisition suggests that children learn to produce "correct" sentences because they are positively reinforced when they say something right and negatively reinforced when they say something wrong. This view assumes that children are being constantly corrected for using "bad grammar" and rewarded when they use "good grammar." Brown and his colleagues[8] report from their studies that reinforcement seldom occurs, and when it does, it is usually incorrect pronunciation or incorrect reporting of facts that is corrected. They report, for example, that the ungrammatical sentence *Her curl my hair* was not corrected because Eve's mother was in fact curling her hair. However, when the syntactically correct sentence *Walt Disney comes on on Tuesday* was produced, her mother corrected Eve because the program on television was shown on Wednesday. They conclude that it is "truth value rather than syntactic well-formedness that chiefly governs explicit verbal reinforcement by parents—which renders mildly paradoxical the fact that the usual product of such a training schedule is an adult whose speech is highly grammatical but not notably truthful" (p. 330).

Even if syntactic correction occurred more often, it would not explain how or what children learn from such adult responses or how children discover and construct the correct rules.

In fact, attempts to "correct" a child's language seem to be doomed to failure. Children do not know what they are doing wrong and are unable to make corrections even when they are pointed out, as shown by the example above and the following one:

CHILD: Want other one spoon, Daddy.
FATHER: You mean, you want *"the other spoon."*
CHILD: Yes, I want other one spoon, please, Daddy.
FATHER: Can you say "the other spoon"?
CHILD: Other . . . one . . . spoon.
FATHER: Say . . . "other."
CHILD: Other.
FATHER: Spoon.
CHILD: Spoon.
FATHER: Other . . . spoon.
CHILD: Other . . . spoon. Now give me other one spoon?

As already noted, such conversations between parents and children do not occur often. The above conversation was between a linguist studying child language and his child. Mothers and fathers are usually delighted that their young children are talking at all and consider every utterance to be a gem. The "mistakes" children make are "cute" and repeated endlessly to anyone who will listen.

Children Form Rules and Construct a Grammar

The "reinforcement" theory fails along with the "imitation" theory. Neither of these views accounts for the nonrandom mistakes children make, the speed with which the basic rules of grammar are acquired, the ability to learn language *without any formal instruction,* and the regularity of the acquisition process across diverse languages and environmental circumstances.

---

[8]Brown, *A First Language.*

Reprinted by permission of Newspaper Enterprise Association, Inc.

Between the ages of five and seven, children from diverse backgrounds reach the same stage of grammar acquisition irrespective of whether their parents talk to them constantly or whether they are brought up to be seen and not heard and are seldom spoken to.

The child appears to be equipped from birth with the neural prerequisites for the acquisition and use of human language just as birds are biologically "prewired" to learn the songs of their species. And just as birds of one species cannot learn the songs of other birds, so also children can only learn languages that conform to linguistic principles, like structural dependencies and universal syntactic categories, that pertain to all human languages and that determine the class of possible languages that can be acquired by children. Thus, children born of Zulu parents raised in an English-speaking environment will learn English, and vice versa, but no children will acquire a formal language (without specific instruction) which, for example, has a 'rule' to reverse the order of words in a sentence to form its negation. Such a rule is not in keeping with universal linguistic principles.

The different syntactic rules at any stage in acquisition govern the construction of the child's sentences at that period of development. Consider, for example, the increasing complexity of one child's negative sentences. At first the child simply added a *no* (or some negative morpheme) at the beginning or at the end of a sentence:

> no heavy
> no singing song
> no want stand head
> no Fraser drink all tea
> no the sun shining

Fraser did not hear such sentences. He used a simple way to form a negative, but it is not the way negative sentences are constructed in English. At some point he began to insert a *no* or *can't* or *don't* inside the sentence.

> He no bite you
> I no taste them
> That no fish school
> I can't catch you

The child progressed from simple rules to more complex rules, as is shown below:

Declarative:	I want some food.	
Negative 1:	No want some food.	(*no* added to beginning of sentence)
Negative 2:	I no/don't want some food.	(negative element inserted; no other change)
Negative 3:	I don't want no food.	(negative element inserted: negation "spread"—*some* becomes *no*)
Negative 4:	I don't want any food.	(negative element inserted correctly; *some* changed to *any*)

All children do not show exactly the same development as the child described above, but they all show similar regular changes. One child studied by Carol Lord first differentiated affirmative from negative sentences by pitch; her negative sentences were all produced with a much higher pitch. When she began to use a negative morpheme, the pitch remained high, but then the intonation became normal as the negative syntactic markers "took over."

Similar changes in the grammar are found in the acquisition of questions. One child first formed a question by using a "question intonation" (a rise of pitch at the end of the sentence):

> Fraser water?
> I ride train?
> Sit chair?

At the next stage the child merely "tacked on" a question word in front of the sentence; he did not change the word order or insert *do*.

> What he wants?
> What he can ride in?
> Where I should put it?
> Where Ann pencil?
> Why you smiling?

Such sentences are perfectly regular. They are not "mistakes" in the child's language; they reflect the grammar at a certain stage of development.

Errors or Rules?

> A final word about the theory of errors. Here it is that the causes are complex and multiple. . . .
>
> Henri Poincaré (1854–1912)

> Give me fruitful error any time, full of seeds, bursting with its own corrections.
>
> Vilfredo Pareto (1848–1923)

Children seem to form the simplest and most general rule they can from the language input they receive, and to be so "pleased" with their "theory" that they use the rule wherever they can.

Inflectional Errors

This "overgeneralization" of constructed rules is clearly revealed when children treat irregular verbs and nouns as if they were regular. We have probably all heard children say *bringed, goed, doed, singed,* or *foots, mouses, sheeps, childs.*

These mistakes tell us more about how children learn language than the "correct" forms they use. The child could not be imitating; children use such forms in families where the parents would never utter such "bad English." In fact, children may say *brought* or *broke* before they begin to use the incorrect forms. At the earlier stage they never use any regular past tense forms like *kissed, walked,* or *helped.* They probably do not know that *brought* is a "past" at all. When they begin to say *played* and *hugged* and *helped* as well as *play, hug,* and *help,* they have "figured out" how to form a past tense—they have constructed the rule. At that point they form all past tenses by this rule—they overgeneralize—and they no longer say *brought* but *bring* and *bringed.* The acquisition of the rule overrides previously learned words and is unaffected by "practice" reinforcement. At a later time, children will learn that there are "exceptions" to the rule, and only then will they once more say *brought.* Children look for general patterns, for systematic occurrences.

Phonological and Morphological Rule Acquisition

The child's ability to generalize patterns and construct rules is also shown in phonological development. In early language, children may not distinguish between voiced and voiceless consonants, for example. When they first begin to contrast one set—that is, when they learn that /p/ and /b/ are distinct phonemes—they also begin to distinguish between /t/ and /d/, /s/ and /z/, and so on. The generalizations refer, as we would expect, to natural classes of speech sounds.

The child's phonological and morphological rules emerge quite early. In 1958, Berko-Gleason[9] conducted a study that has now become a classic in our understanding of child language acquisition. She worked with preschool children and with children in the first, second, and third grades. She showed each child a drawing of a nonsense animal like the funny creature below and gave the "animal" a nonsense name. She would then say to the child, pointing to the picture, "This is a wug."

[9] J. Berko, "The Child's Learning of English Morphology," *Word* 14(1958):150–177.

Then she would show the child a picture of two of the animals and say, "Now here is another one. There are two of them. There are two _____ ?"

The child's "task" was to give the plural form, "wugs" [wʌgz]. Another little make-believe animal was called a "bik," and when the child was shown two biks, he or she again was to say the plural form [bɪks]. Berko-Gleason found that the children applied the regular plural-formation rule to words never heard before. Because the children had never seen a "wug" or a "bik" and had not heard these "words," their ability to add a [z] when the animal's name ended with a voiced sound and an [s] when there was a final voiceless consonant showed that the children were using rules based on an understanding of natural classes of phonological segments, and not simply imitating words they had previously heard.

PEANUTS reprinted by permission of UFS, Inc.

Such regular stages and patterns support the notion that language acquisition is grammar construction.

The investigation of the kinds of errors children make in forming their grammars shows that the mistakes are all in keeping with what we have called Universal Grammar, that is, the principles that constrain all grammars. Children do not construct "wild grammars"; their errors fall within the bounds of syntactic, phonological, and morphological natural linguistic processes. Such regular stages and patterns support the notion that language acquisition is grammar construction.

The Acquisition of Syntax

Children eventually acquire all the phonological, syntactic, and semantic rules of the grammar. This task is most difficult, and, in fact, seems to be an impossible one; yet not only is the child more successful than the most brilliant linguist, but the grammars of children, at each stage of their acquisition, are highly similar, and deviate from the adult grammar in highly specific constrained ways.

To account for the ability of children to construct the complex syntactic rules of their grammar, it has been suggested that the child's "grammar" is semantically based. This view holds that the child's early language does not make reference to syntactic categories and relations (Noun, Noun Phrase, Verb, Verb Phrase, subject, object, and so on) but rather solely to semantic roles (like agent or theme). Nina Hyams,[10] however, studying the language of Italian-speaking children of about two years old, shows clearly that their utterances can only be explained by reference to syntactic categories and relations.

This point is easier to see in Italian where there is subject–verb agreement than in English. The Italian verb is inflected for person and number to agree with the subject, as shown in the following utterances produced by an Italian child:

(1) Tu legg*i* il libro   "you read (2nd person singular) the book"
(2) Io vad*o* fuori   "I go (1st person singular) outside"
(3) Gir*a* il pallone   "Turns the balloon (3rd person singular)"
(4) Dorm*e* miao   "Sleeps (3rd person singular) the cat"

Subject–verb agreement cannot be semantically based, because the subject is an agent in utterances 1 and 2 but not in 3 and 4. Instead, agreement must be based on whatever noun phrase is the subject, a syntactic relationship.

Hyams upholds this position by reference to other kinds of agreement as well, such as the 'modifier–noun agreement' in the noun phrase as exemplified by 5, 6, and 7 where we see that the children have inflected the modifiers to agree with the gender and number of the noun they modify.

(5) E mi*a* gonna'   "(It) is my (feminine sg) skirt"
(6) Questo mi*o* bimbo   "This my (masculine sg) baby"
(7) Guarda quest*i* gialli   "Look at these (masculine plural) roosters"

As mentioned above, children learning other languages with similar agreement rules, such as Russian, Polish, or Turkish, show this same ability to "discover" the structures of their language. Their grammars from an early stage reveal their knowledge of the kinds of structure dependencies mentioned in Chapter 3.

Child language studies provide further support for the view that each stage of a child's early grammar is qualitatively similar to the adult grammar in that it includes both a syntactic and a semantic component.

Thus, just as human adult languages are governed by universal characteristics, the child's grammar while differing from the adult grammar in very specific ways,

---

[10]The data included in examples 1–7 were collected by M. Moneglia and E. Cresti and reported in Nina Hyams' *Language Acquisition and the theory of parameters,* Dordrecht, the Netherlands, Reidel Publishers, 1986.

also follows universal principles. This shows that language acquisition must be biologically based, which will be further discussed in the next section and also in Chapter 11.

Learning the Meaning of Words[11]

> Suddenly I felt a misty consciousness as of something forgotten—a thrill of returning thought; and somehow the mystery of language was revealed to me... Everything had a name, and each name gave birth to a new thought.[12]
>
> Helen Keller

Most people do not see the acquisition of the meaning of words as posing a great problem. The intuitive view is that children look at an object in their sight of vision, the mother says a word, and the child connects the sounds with the particular object being viewed. However, this is not as easy a task as one might think, as the following quote demonstrates.

> A child who observes a cat sitting on a mat also observes... a mat supporting a cat, a mat under a cat, a floor supporting a mat and a cat, and so on. If the adult now says "The cat is on the mat" even while pointing to the cat on the mat, how is the child to choose among these interpretations of the situation?[13]

Even if the mother simply says "cat", and the child by accident associates the word with the animal on the mat, the child may interpret "cat" as "Cat," the name of a particular animal or of an entire species, or with a particular part or attribute of the animal.

It is not surprising then that children often **undergeneralize** a word's meaning, as, for example, thinking that *dog* refers to the family pet only and not to the neighbor's dog and all dogs. They also **overgeneralize** the meaning of words. They may learn a word such as *papa* or *daddy* which they first use only for their own father and then extend its meaning to apply to all men. After the child has acquired her first seventy-five to one hundred words, the "overgeneralized" meanings become narrowed and the "undergeneralized meanings" extended until the meanings of these words are those of the other speakers of the language. How this occurs is also not easy to explain.

The mystery surrounding the acquisition of word meanings has intrigued philosophers and psychologists as well as linguists. It has been observed that children view the world in similar fashion. They first learn "basic level" terms like *cat* before learning the larger class word *animal*. Various studies have also shown that

---

[11]We wish to acknowledge the contribution to this section of Lila Gleitman and her chapter 'Language' in *Psychology*, 3rd Ed. H. Gleitman (ed.). New York: Norton, 1991.

[12]Helen Keller as quoted in Lash, J.P., *Helen and Teacher: The story of Helen Keller and Anne Sullivan Macy*, New York: Delacorte Press, 1980.

[13]Gleitman, Lila R., and Eric Wanner, *Language acquisition: The state of the state of the art*. Cambridge, England: Cambridge University Press, 1982, p. 10.

if an experimenter points to an object and uses a nonsense word to a child like *blick* saying *that's blick,* the child will interpret the word to refer to the whole object not one of its parts or attributes.

Furthermore, as a child is learning the meaning of words, she is also learning the syntax of the language and the syntactic categories. Psycholinguists like Gleitman suggest that the syntax helps the child acquire meaning, pointing out that a child will interpret a word like *blicking* to be a verb if the word is used while the investigator points to an action being performed, and will interpret the word *blick* to be a noun if used in the expression *a blick* or *the blick* while looking at the same picture. For example, suppose a child is shown a picture of some funny animal jumping up and down and hears either *See the blicking* or *See the blick;* later when asked to show "blicking" the child will jump up and down, but if asked to show a blick, will point to the funny animal. Gleitman calls this process "bootstrapping"; the child uses her knowledge of syntax to learn whether a word is a verb and thus has a meaning referring to an action, or whether the word is a noun and thus refers to an object of some kind.

The Biological Foundations of Language Acquisition

> Just as birds have wings, man has language.
> George Henry Lewes (1817–1878)

The ability of children to form complex rules and construct the grammars of the languages used around them in a relatively short time is indeed phenomenal. The similarity of the language acquisition stages across diverse peoples and languages supports the view that children seem to be equipped with special abilities to know what generalizations to look for and what to ignore, and how to discover the regularities of language. Children learn language the way they learn to walk. They are not taught to walk, but all normal children begin to do so at around the same age. "Learning to walk" or "learning language" is different than "learning to read" or "learning to ride a bicycle." Many people never learn to read because they are not taught to do so, and there are large groups of people in many parts of the world that do not have any written language. However, they all have language.

The "Innateness Hypothesis"

The child must be neurologically capable of utilizing the sounds (or sign language gestures) for language acquisition. Dogs and cats and other pets hear what we say. They are just unable to segment the sounds, attach meanings to them, and generalize from the regularities present in the signal to form the rules of grammar.

Chomsky explains the ability to acquire language in the following way:

> It seems plain that language acquisition is based on the child's discovery of what from a formal point of view is a deep and abstract theory—a generative

grammar of his language. . . . A consideration of the character of the grammar that is acquired, the degenerate quality and narrowly limited extent of the available data, the striking uniformity of the resulting grammars, and their independence of intelligence, motivation, and emotional state, over wide ranges of variation, leave little hope that much of the structure of the language can be learned by an organism initially uninformed as to its general character. . . . It may well be that the general features of language structure reflect, not so much the course of one's experience, but rather the general character of one's capacity to acquire knowledge.[14]

Copyright © 1983, 1984 by Chronicle Features.

It is this human capacity to acquire language that has led to "the innateness hypothesis" of child language acquisition, which posits that not only is the human species genetically "prewired" to acquire language, but that the kind of language is also determined. The principles that determine the class of human languages that can be acquired unconsciously, without instruction, in the early years of life has been referred to as Universal Grammar (or UG). This Universal Grammar underlies

[14]Noam Chomsky, *Aspects of the Theory of Syntax*, Cambridge, Mass.: M.I.T. Press, 1965.

the specific grammars of all languages. We are still far from understanding the nature of our genetic "prewiring," or the specific details of the language-learning device or Universal Grammar with which the human animal appears to be born; but there seems to be little doubt that the human brain is specially equipped for language acquisition. Chapter 11 will consider some aspects of the organization of the brain that appear to underlie our language abilities.

The "Critical Age Hypothesis"

It has been suggested that there is a "critical age" for language acquisition, or at least for language acquisition without special teaching and without the need for special learning. During this period, language learning proceeds easily, swiftly, and without external intervention. After this period, the acquisition of the grammar is difficult and, for some individuals, never fully achieved.

There have been a number of cases of children reared in environments of extreme social isolation who constitute "experiments in nature" for testing the critical age hypothesis. Such reported cases go back at least to the eighteenth century. In 1758, Carl Linnaeus first included *Homo ferus* (wild or feral man) as a subdivision of *Homo sapiens*. According to Linnaeus, a defining characteristic of *Homo ferus* was his lack of speech or observable language of any kind. All the cases in the literature support his view.

The most dramatic cases of children raised in isolation are those described as "wild" or "feral" children, who have reportedly been reared with wild animals or have lived alone in the wilderness. In 1920 two feral children, Amala and Kamala, were found in India, supposedly having been reared with wolves. A celebrated case, documented in Francois Truffaut's film *The Wild Child*, is that of Victor, "the wild boy of Aveyron," who was found in 1798. It was ascertained that he had been left in the woods when a very young child and had somehow survived.

There are other cases of children whose isolation resulted from deliberate efforts to keep them from normal social intercourse. As recently as 1970 a child, called Genie in the scientific reports,[15] was discovered; she had been confined to a small room under conditions of physical restraint, and had received only minimal human contact from the age of eighteen months until almost fourteen years. None of these children, regardless of the cause of isolation, was able to speak or knew any language at the time of reintroduction to society.

This linguistic inability could simply be because they received no linguistic input showing that the innate neurological ability of the human brain to acquire language must be 'triggered' by language. In the documented cases of Victor and Genie, however, it was found that they were unable to acquire language after exposure and even with deliberate and painstaking linguistic teaching.

Genie did begin to acquire some language, but while she was able to learn a large vocabulary, including colors, shapes, objects, natural categories, abstract as well as

---

[15]Curtiss, S., *Genie: A Linguistic Study of a Modern-Day "Wild Child,"* New York: Academic Press, 1977.

concrete terms, her syntax and morphology never fully developed. The UCLA linguist, Susan Curtiss, who worked with Genie for a number of years after she was found, reports that Genie's utterances were, for the most part, "the stringing together of content words, often with rich and clear meaning but with little grammatical structure." The case of Genie and other such isolated children supports the critical age hypothesis since they were exposed to language after the proposed critical age and were unable to acquire much of the syntactic component of the grammar.

The Acquisition of Bird Songs

The notion of a critical age for acquisition of cognitive knowledge pertains to other species as shown by studies of the development of bird songs and calls. Some bird species do not "learn" at all; the cuckoo will sing a fully developed song even if it never hears another cuckoo sing. These communicative messages are clearly innate. For other species, songs appear to be completely learned; the bullfinch, for example, will learn any song it is exposed to, even that of another species, however "unbullfinchlike" it may be. There do not appear to be any "bullfinch universals."

THE FAR SIDE copyright 1991, 1987, and 1986 Universal Press Syndicate. Reprinted with permission. All rights reserved.

The chaffinch represents a different acquisition pattern. Certain calls and songs of this species will vary depending on the geographical "dialect" area that the bird inhabits. The message is the same, but the "pronunciation" or form is different. Usually a young bird will exhibit a basic version of the song shortly after hatching, and then later on will undergo further learning in acquiring its final "dialect" version of the song. Since birds from the same brood will acquire different dialects depending on the area in which they finally settle, part of the song must be learned. Since a fledgling chaffinch will sing the song of its species in a simple, degraded form, even if it has never heard it sung, some aspect of "language" is biologically determined, that is, it is innate.

The chaffinch acquires its fully developed song in several stages, just as human children appear to acquire language in several stages. Furthermore, the chaffinch brain may also be lateralized for language, a subject which will be discussed in Chapter 11.

A critical age in the song learning of chaffinches, white-crowned sparrows, zebra finches, and other species has been observed. If these birds are not exposed to the songs of their species during certain fixed periods after their birth (the period differs from species to species) song acquisition does not occur. The chaffinch is unable to learn new song elements after ten months of age. If it is isolated from other birds before attaining the full "grammar" and is then reexposed after ten months, its song will not develop further. If white crowns lose their hearing during a critical period *after* they have learned to sing, they produce a song that differs from other white crowns; they need to hear themselves sing to produce particular whistles and other song features. If, however, the deafness occurs after the critical period, the songs are normal.

From the point of view of human language research, the relationship between the innate and learned aspects of bird songs is significant. Apparently the basic nature of the song of some species is biologically determined, but the details are learned, and can only be learned if exposure to the songs of their species occurs within a critical period. Similarly, it appears that the basic nature of human language is biologically determined, whereas the details of languages that make them different from each other are learned, and that the learning must occur within a critical period.

Sign Languages: Evidence for the Biology of Language

> It is not the want of organs that [prevents animals from making] . . . known their thoughts . . . for it is evident that magpies and parrots are able to utter words just like ourselves, and yet they cannot speak as we do, that is, so as to give evidence that they think of what they say. On the other hand, men who, being born deaf and mute . . . are destitute of the organs which serve the others for talking, are in the habit of themselves inventing certain signs by which they make themselves understood.
>
> **René Descartes,** *Discourse on Method*

Deaf children, who are unable to hear the sounds of spoken language, do not acquire spoken languages as hearing children do. However, deaf children of deaf parents who are exposed to sign language learn sign language in stages parallel to language acquisition by hearing children learning oral languages. These sign languages are human languages that do not utilize sounds to express meanings. Instead, hand and body gestures are the forms used to represent morphemes or words. Sign languages are fully developed languages, and those who know sign language are capable of creating and comprehending unlimited numbers of new sentences, just like speakers of spoken languages.

Current research on sign languages has been crucial in the attempt to understand the biological underpinnings of human language acquisition and use. Some discussion on sign languages is therefore essential.

About one in a thousand babies is born deaf, or with a severe hearing deficiency. One major effect is the difficulty the deaf have in learning a spoken language. It is nearly impossible for those unable to hear language to learn to speak naturally. Normal speech depends to a great extent on constant auditory feedback. Hence a deaf child will not learn to speak without extensive training in special schools or programs designed especially for the deaf.

Although deaf persons can be taught to speak a language intelligibly, they can never understand speech as well as a hearing person. Seventy-five percent of the words spoken cannot be read on the lips with any degree of accuracy. The ability of many deaf individuals to comprehend spoken language is therefore remarkable; they combine lip reading with knowledge of the structure of the language and the semantic redundancies.

If, however, human language is universal in the sense that all members of the human species have the ability to learn a language, it is not surprising that nonspoken languages have developed as a substitute for spoken languages among nonhearing individuals. The more we learn about the human linguistic ability, the more it is clear that language acquisition and use are not dependent on the ability to produce and hear sounds, but on a much more abstract cognitive ability, biologically determined, which therefore accounts for the similarities between spoken and sign languages.

American Sign Language (ASL)

The major language used by the deaf in the United States is American Sign Language (or AMESLAN or ASL). ASL is an independent, fully developed language that historically is an outgrowth of the sign language used in France and brought to the United States in 1817 by the great educator Thomas Hopkins Gallaudet. Gallaudet was hired to establish a school for the deaf, and after studying the language and methods used in the Paris school founded by the Abbé de l'Épée in 1775, he returned to the United States with Laurent Clerc, a young deaf instructor, establishing the basis for ASL. Like all living languages, ASL continues to change; only 60 percent of the present ASL vocabulary is of French origin. Not only have new signs entered the language, but the forms of the signs have changed, in ways similar to the historical changes in the phonological structure of words in spoken language. For example, many signs that were originally formed at waist or chest level are now produced at a higher level near the neck or upper chest.

ASL has its own morphological, syntactic, and semantic systems. Its formal units, corresponding to the phonological elements of spoken language, were originally called **cheremes**[16] (to correspond to the term phoneme) and are now more often referred to as **primes.** The signs of the language that correspond to morphemes or words of spoken language can be specified by primes of three different sets: hand configuration, the motion of the hand(s) toward or away from the body, and the place of articulation or the locus of the sign's movement.

Figure 10–1 illustrates the hand configuration primes.

There are minimal pairs in sign languages just as there are in spoken languages. Figure 10–2[17] shows minimal contrasts involving hand configuration, place of articulation, and movement.

The sign meaning "arm" can be described as a flat hand, moving to touch the upper arm. Thus it has three prime features: flat hand, motion toward, upper arm.

Just as spoken language has sequences of sounds that are not permitted in the language, so sign languages have forbidden combinations of features. They differ from one sign language to another, just as the constraints on sounds and sound sequences differ from one spoken language to another. A permissible sign in a Chinese sign language may not be a permissible sign in ASL, and vice versa. The linguistic study of ASL also reveals a complex system of morphological and syntactic rules that parallel those found in spoken languages.[18]

The other sign language used in the United States is called Signed English (or Siglish). Essentially, it consists in the replacement of each spoken English word (and morpheme) by a sign. The syntax and semantics of Signed English are thus approximately the same as those of ordinary English. It is thus a rather unnatural language similar to speaking French by translating every English word or morpheme into its French counterpart. Of course, there is not always a corresponding morpheme, and that would create problems just as it does in signed English.

If there is no sign in ASL, signers utilize another mechanism, the system of finger spelling. This method is also used to add new proper nouns or technical vocabulary. Sign interpreters of spoken English often finger spell such words. A manual

[16]W. C. Stokoe, Jr., D. Casterline, and C. Croneberg, *A Dictionary of American Sign Language on Linguistic Principles,* Washington, D.C.: Gallaudet College Press, 1965.

[17]Figures 10–1 and 10–2 are from E. S. Klima and U. Bellugi, *The Signs of Language,* Cambridge, Mass.: Harvard University Press, 1979, pp. 46 and 42.

[18]T. Supalla and E. Newport. "How Many Seats in a Chair? The Derivation of Nouns and Verbs in American Sign Language." In P. Siple, ed., *Understanding Language Through Sign Language Research.* New York: Academic Press, 1978, pp. 91–132.

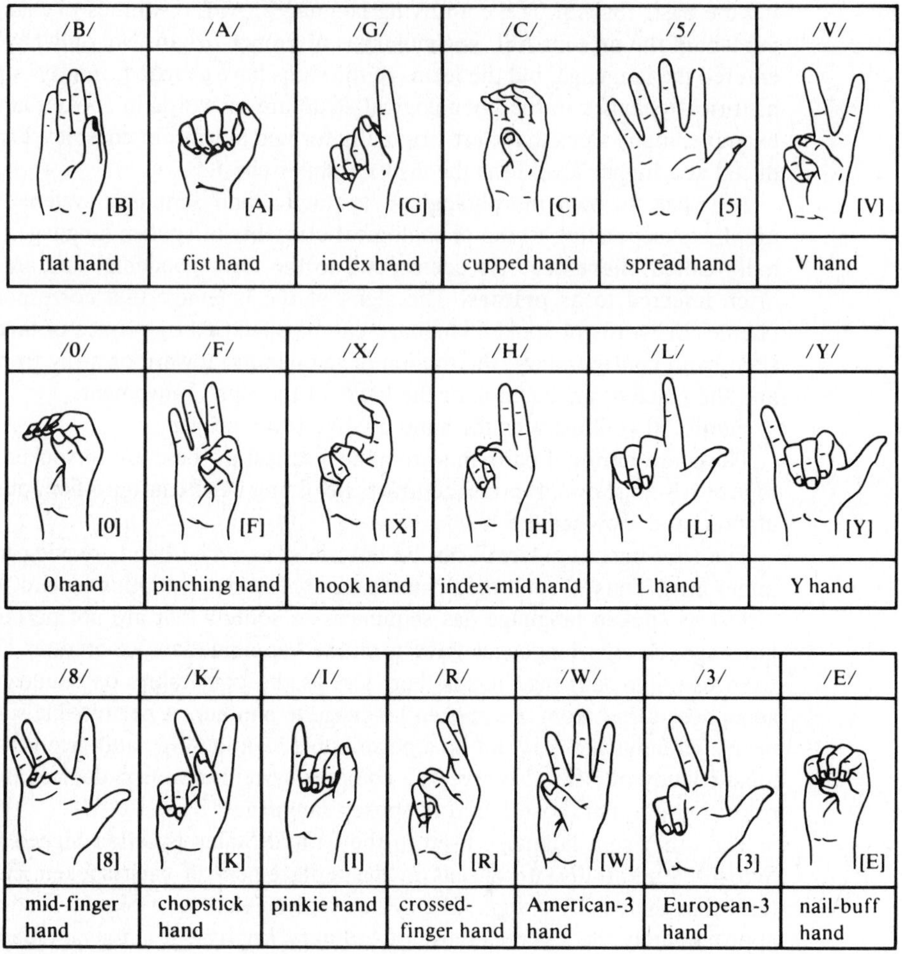

/B/	/A/	/G/	/C/	/5/	/V/
[B]	[A]	[G]	[C]	[5]	[V]
flat hand	fist hand	index hand	cupped hand	spread hand	V hand

/0/	/F/	/X/	/H/	/L/	/Y/
[0]	[F]	[X]	[H]	[L]	[Y]
0 hand	pinching hand	hook hand	index-mid hand	L hand	Y hand

/8/	/K/	/I/	/R/	/W/	/3/	/E/
[8]	[K]	[I]	[R]	[W]	[3]	[E]
mid-finger hand	chopstick hand	pinkie hand	crossed-finger hand	American-3 hand	European-3 hand	nail-buff hand

Figure 10–1

Hand configuration primes arranged in order of frequency (with descriptive phrases that are used to refer to them.)

alphabet consisting of various finger configurations, hand positions, and movements gives visible symbols for the alphabet and ampersand.

Signs, however, are produced differently than are finger-spelled words. "The sign DECIDE cannot be analyzed as a sequence of distinct, separable configurations of the hand. Like all other lexical signs in ASL, but unlike the individual finger-spelled letters in D-E-C-I-D-E taken separately, the ASL sign DECIDE does have

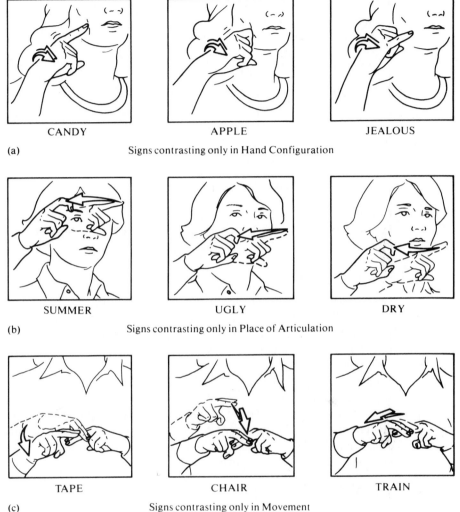

CANDY   APPLE   JEALOUS

(a)   Signs contrasting only in Hand Configuration

SUMMER   UGLY   DRY

(b)   Signs contrasting only in Place of Articulation

TAPE   CHAIR   TRAIN

(c)   Signs contrasting only in Movement

Figure 10–2
Minimal contrasts illustrating major formational parameters.

an essential movement but the handshape occurs simultaneously with the movement. In appearance, the sign is a continuous whole."[19] This sign is shown in Figure 10–3.

[19]Klima and Bellugi, *The Signs of Language*, pp. 38 and 62.

transition   sign   transition
a.   b.   c.

Figure 10–3

The ASL sign DECIDE. (a) and (c) show transitions from the sign; (b) illustrates the single downward movement of the sign.

An accomplished signer can "speak" at a normal rate, even when there is a lot of finger spelling. Television stations sometimes have programs that are interpreted in sign for the deaf in a corner of the TV screen. If you have ever seen such a program, you were probably amazed at how well the interpreter kept pace with the spoken sentences.

Language arts are not lost to the deaf. Poetry is composed in sign language, and stage plays such as Sheridan's *The Critic* have been translated into sign language and acted by the National Theatre of the Deaf (NTD). Sign language was so highly thought of by the anthropologist Margaret Mead that, in an article discussing the possibilities of a universal second language, she suggests using some of the basic ideas that sign languages incorporate.

The Acquisition of ASL

Given the universal aspects of sign and spoken languages, it is not surprising that deaf children of deaf signing parents parallel the stages of spoken language acquisition. They start with single signs similar to the single words in the holophrastic stage and then begin to combine signs. There is also a telegraphic stage in which the "grammatical" signs are omitted. Grammatical or function signs appear at around the same age for deaf children as function words in spoken languages.

Bellugi and Klima[20] point out that deaf children's acquisition of the negative morphemes in American Sign Language (ASL) shows much the same pattern as in spoken language. NO and NEG (a headshake) are frequently used signs in adult ASL,

[20]U. Bellugi and E. S. Klima, "The Roots of Language in the Sign Talk of the Deaf." *Psychology Today* 6 (1976): 60–64.

with different restrictions on their use. The children acquiring ASL use them interchangeably in initial position of a signed sentence, like hearing children starting negative sentences with *no* but unlike the ways in which negative signs are used in adult ASL. We see that the acquisition of ASL cannot be simple imitation any more than spoken language is acquired simply by imitation.

Hearing children of deaf parents acquire both sign language and spoken language when exposed to both, although studies have shown that the child's first signs emerge a few months before the first spoken words. It is interesting that deaf children appear to begin producing signs earlier than hearing children produce spoken words. It has been suggested that this timing may be because control of hand muscles develops earlier than the control of oral and laryngeal muscles.

Deaf children of hearing parents who are not exposed to manual sign language from birth suffer from a great handicap in acquiring language; yet language learning ability seems so strong in humans that even they begin to develop their own manual gestures to express their thoughts and desires. A study of six such children revealed that they not only developed individual signs but joined pairs and formed sentences (up to thirteen "words") with definite syntactic order and systematic constraints.

This fact, of course, should not be surprising; sign languages are as grammatical and systematic as are spoken languages. We saw in Chapter 1 that the signs are conventional or arbitrary and not imitative. Furthermore, because all languages change in time, just as there are many different spoken languages, there are many different sign languages, all of which (spoken and sign) reveal the same linguistic universals. Deaf children often sign themselves to sleep just as hearing children talk themselves to sleep; deaf children report that they dream in sign language as French-speaking children dream in French and Hopi children dream in Hopi. Deaf children sign to their dolls and stuffed animals; slips of the hand occur similar to slips of the tongue; finger fumblers amuse signers as tongue twisters amuse speakers. We see that sign languages resemble spoken languages in all major aspects, showing that there truly are universals of language despite differences in the modality in which the language is performed. This universality is predictable because it is language that is biologically based.

Learning a Second (or Third or . . .) Language

> He that understands grammar in one language, understands it in another as far as the essential properties of Grammar are concerned. The fact that he can't speak, nor comprehend, another language is due to the diversity of words and their various forms, but these are the accidental properties of grammar.
>
> Roger Bacon (1214–1294)

The Far Side. By Gary Larson. © 1983, 1984 Chronicle Features, San Francisco. Reprinted with permission. All rights reserved.

Anyone who has attempted to learn a second language in school or when visiting a foreign country knows that it is different from learning our first, native language. Even "talented language learners" require some instruction, or at least find a dictionary and "grammar" useful. Some of us are total failures at second language learning. We may be extremely fluent in our native language, we may get all As in composition and write beautiful poetry, but still find we are unable to learn another language.

The younger you are, the easier it seems to be to learn a language. Language is unique in that no other complex system of knowledge is more easily acquired at the age of two or three than at the age of thirteen or twenty.

Young children who are exposed to more than one language before the age of puberty seem to acquire all the languages equally well. Many bilingual and multilingual speakers acquired their languages early in life. Sometimes one language is the first learned, but if the child is exposed to additional languages at an early age they will also be learned.

The critical age hypothesis discussed above was first proposed to explain the dramatic differences between a child's ease in learning a first language and the difficulty in learning a second language (L2) after puberty. It was believed that these differences could not be fully accounted for by the psychological, physical, and sociological factors present in second language acquisition which could impede the learning process.

Many adults, for example, who are self-conscious about making mistakes, often find learning L2 very difficult. This is not a problem for children who are unaware that they are making mistakes. The situation in which second language learning takes place will also have an influence on one's success. Many individuals attempt to learn an L2 by taking a class in high school or college. The student is exposed to the language only in a formal situation and usually for no more than a few hours a week. Even in intensive courses, the learner does not receive constant input or feedback.

On the other hand, due to the universal characteristics of human language, adults who know one language, already "know" much about the underlying structure of every language. This is shown by the stages in second language acquisition, which are similar to those in first language acquisition. For example, Carol Chomsky[21] found that in the earliest years children learning English naively interpret sentences like *John is easy to see* as *It is easy for John to see*. French speakers learning English seem to go through a similar stage. Yet, this cannot be due to any "interference" from French grammar, because in this sense, French is similar to English. The acquisition of grammatical morphemes (both bound and free) in learning English as a second language proceeds in similar order as in children's acquisition no matter what the system is in the native language of the learner. However, interference from one's native phonology, morphology, and syntax can create difficulties which persist as a foreign "accent" in phonology and in the use of nonnative syntactic structures.

Theories of Second Language Acquisition

There are alternative theories regarding the acquisition of L2. Stephen Krashen has proposed a distinction between acquisition—the process by which children unconsciously acquire their native language—and learning, which he defines as "conscious knowledge of a second language, knowing the rules, being aware of them, and being able to talk about them."[22]

A similar view suggests that the principles of Universal Grammar hold only during the critical period mentioned above, after which general learning mechanisms, not specific to language acquisition, operate in learning L2.

A second theory proposes that L2 is acquired on the same universal innate principles that govern L1 acquisition, which is why one finds the same stages of

[21]Carol Chomsky. *The Acquisition of Syntax in Children from Five to Ten.* Cambridge, Mass.: M.I.T. Press, 1969.
[22]Stephen D. Krashen. *Principles and Practice in Second Language Acquisition.* Oxford, England: Pergamon Press, 1982.

"Gina is by lingal . . . that means she can say the same thing twice, but you can only understand it once."

DENNIS THE MENACE® used by permission of Hank Ketcham and © by North America Syndicate.

development even if the complete L2 grammar is not acquired due to nonlinguistic factors at work.

It is clear that children acquire their first language without explicit learning. A second language is usually learned but to some degree may also be acquired or "picked up" depending on the environmental setting and the input received by the second language learner.

More research and evidence is required before this interesting question can be resolved.

Can Chimps Learn Human Language?

> . . . It is a great baboon, but so much like man in most things . . . I do believe it already understands much English; and I am of the mind it might be taught to speak or make signs.
>
> Entry in Samual Pepys' Diary, August 1661

Reprinted courtesy Omni Magazine © 1987.

In this chapter, the discussion has centered on the biologically determined *human* language acquisition ability. Recently, much effort has been expended to determine whether nonhuman primates (chimpanzees, monkeys, gorillas, and so on) can learn human language. In their natural habitat, primates communicate with each other in systems that include visual, auditory, olfactory, and tactile signals. Many of these signals seem to have meaning associated with the animals' immediate environment or emotional state. They can signal "danger" and can communicate aggressiveness and subordination. Females of some species emit a specific call indicating that they are anestrous (sexually quiescent), which inhibits attempts by males to copulate. However, the natural sounds and gestures produced by all nonhuman primates show their signals to be highly stereotyped and limited in the type and number of messages they convey. Their basic "vocabularies" occur primarily as emotional responses to particular situations. They have no way of expressing the anger they felt yesterday or the anticipation of tomorrow.

Despite these characteristics of nonhuman primate *natural* systems of communication, there has been an interest in whether these animals may have a capacity for acquiring more complex linguistic systems that are similar to human language.

Gua

In the 1930s, Winthrop and Luella Kellogg raised their infant son with an infant chimpanzee named Gua to determine whether a chimpanzee raised in a human environment and given language instruction could learn a human language. Gua understood about one hundred words at sixteen months, more words than their son at that age; but she never went beyond that. Moreover, comprehension of language involves more than understanding the meanings of isolated words. When their son could understand the difference between *I say what I mean* and *I mean what I say,* Gua could not understand either sentence.

Viki

A chimpanzee named Viki was raised by Keith and Cathy Hayes, and she too learned a number of individual words, even learning to "articulate" with great difficulty the words *mama, papa, cup,* and *up.* That was the extent of her language production.

Washoe

Psychologists Allen and Beatrice Gardner recognized that one disadvantage suffered by the primates was their physical inability to pronounce many different sounds. Without a sufficient number of phonemic contrasts, spoken human language is impossible. Many species of primates are manually dextrous, and this fact inspired the Gardners to attempt to teach American Sign Language to a chimpanzee whom they named Washoe, after the Nevada county in which they lived. Washoe was brought up in much the same way as a human child in a deaf community, constantly in the presence of people who used ASL. She was deliberately taught to sign, whereas children raised by deaf signers acquire sign language without explicit teaching, as hearing children learn spoken language.

By the time Washoe was four years old (June 1969), she had acquired eighty-five signs with such meanings as "more," "eat," "listen," "gimme," "key," "dog," "you," "me," "Washoe," and "hurry." According to the Gardners, Washoe was also able to produce sign combinations such as "baby mine," "you drink," "hug hurry," "gimme flower," and "more fruit."

Sarah

At about the same time that Washoe was growing up, psychologist David Premack attempted to teach a chimpanzee named Sarah an artificial language designed to resemble human languages in some aspects. The "words" of Sarah's "language" were differently shaped and colored plastic chips that were metal-backed. Sarah and her trainers "talked" to each other by arranging these symbols on a magnetic board. Sarah was taught to associate particular symbols with particular meanings. The form–meaning relationship of these "morphemes" or "words" was arbitrary; a small red square meant "banana" and a small blue rectangle meant "apricot," while the color red was represented by a gray chip and the color yellow by a black chip. Sarah learned a number of "nouns," "adjectives," and "verbs," symbols for abstract concepts like "same as" and "different from," "negation," and "question."

There were drawbacks to the Sarah experiment. She was not allowed to "talk" spontaneously, but only in response to her trainers. There was the possibility that her trainers unwittingly provided cues, which Sarah responded to rather than the plastic chips.

Learning Yerkish

To avoid these and other problems, Duane and Sue Rumbaugh and their associates at the Yerkes Regional Primate Research Center began in 1973 to teach a different kind of artificial language, called Yerkish, to three chimpanzees, Lana, Sherman, and Austin. Instead of plastic chips, the words, called lexigrams, are geometric symbols displayed on a computer keyboard. The computer records every button pressed; certain fixed orders of these lexigrams constitute grammatical sentences in Yerkish. The researchers, however, are particularly interested in the ability of primates to communicate using functional symbols.

Koko

Another experiment aimed at teaching sign language to primates involved a gorilla named Koko, who was taught by her trainer, Francine "Penny" Patterson. Patterson claims that Koko has learned several hundred signs, is able to put signs together to make "sentences," and is capable of making linguistic jokes and puns, composing rhymes such as BEAR HAIR (which is a rhyme in spoken language but not ASL), and inventing metaphors such as FINGER BRACELET for ring.

Nim Chimpsky

In a project specifically designed to test the linguistic claims that emerged from these primate experiments, another chimpanzee, named Nim Chimpsky, who was taught ASL by an experienced teacher, was studied by the psychologist H. S. Terrace and his associates.[23] Under carefully controlled experimental conditions that

---

[23]Collaborating with Terrace were Laura Pettito, Richard Sanders, and Thomas Bever. The results of Project Nim are reported in H. S. Terrace, *Nim: A Chimpanzee Who Learned Sign Language*. New York: Knopf, 1979.

included thorough record keeping and many hours of videotaping, Nim's teachers hoped to show beyond a reasonable doubt that chimpanzees had a humanlike linguistic capacity, in contradiction to the view put forth by Noam Chomsky (after whom Nim was ironically named) that human language is species-specific. In the nearly four years of study, Nim learned about 125 signs, and during the last two years Nim's teachers recorded more than 20,000 "utterances" including two or more signs. Nim produced his first ASL sign (DRINK) after just four months, which greatly encouraged the research team at the start of the study. Their enthusiasm soon diminished when he never seemed to go much beyond the two-word stage. Terrace concluded that "his three-sign combinations do not . . . provide new information. . . . Nim's most frequent two- and three-sign combinations [were] PLAY ME and PLAY ME NIM. Adding NIM to PLAY ME is simply redundant," writes Terrace. This kind of redundancy is illustrated by a sixteen-sign utterance of Nim's: GIVE ORANGE ME GIVE EAT ORANGE ME EAT ORANGE GIVE ME EAT ORANGE GIVE ME YOU. This utterance does not sound much like the early sentences of children cited above.

Nim rarely signed spontaneously as do children when they begin to use language (spoken or sign). Only 12 percent of his utterances were spontaneous. Most of Nim's signing occurred only in response to prompting by his trainers and was related to eating, drinking, and playing; that is, it was "stimulus-controlled." As much as 40 percent of his output was simply repetitions of signs made by the trainer. Children initiate conversations more and more frequently as they grow older, and their utterances repeat less and less of the adult's prior utterance. Some children hardly ever imitate in conversation. Children become increasingly more *creative* in their language use, but Nim showed almost no tendency toward such creativity. Furthermore, children's utterances increase in length and complexity as time progresses, finally mirroring the adult grammar, whereas Nim's "language" did not.

The lack of spontaneity and the excessive "noncreative" imitative nature of Nim's signing led to the conclusion that Nim's acquisition and use of language is qualitatively different from a child's. After examining the films of Washoe, Koko, and others, Terrace drew similar conclusions regarding the signing of the other primates.

Signing chimpanzees are also unlike humans in that when several of them are together they do not sign to each other as freely as humans would under similar circumstances. There is also no evidence to date that a signing chimp (or one communicating with plastic chips or computer symbols) will teach another chimp language, or that its offspring will acquire language from the parent.

Clever Hans

Premack and the Rumbaughs, like Terrace, suggest that the sign language studies are too uncontrolled and that the reported results were thus too anecdotal to support the view that primates are capable of acquiring a human language. They also question whether each of the others' studies, and all those attempting to teach sign language to primates, suffer from what has come to be called the Clever Hans phenomenon.

Clever Hans, a horse owned by von Osten at the turn of the century, became famous because of his apparent ability to do arithmetic, read and spell, and even solve problems of musical harmony. He answered the questions posed by his interrogators by stamping out numbers with his hoof. It turned out, not surprisingly, that Hans did not know that $2 + 2 = 4$, but he was clever enough to pick up subtle cues conveyed unconsciously by his trainer as to when he should stop tapping his foot.

Sarah, like Clever Hans, took prompts from her trainers and her environment to produce the plastic chip sentences. In responding to the string of chips standing for

SARAH INSERT APPLE PAIL BANANA DISH

all Sarah had to figure out was to place certain fruits in certain containers, and she could decide which by merely seeing that the apple symbol was next to the pail symbol, and the banana symbol was next to the dish symbol. There is no conclusive evidence that Sarah actually grouped strings of words into constituents. There is also no indication that Sarah would understand a *new* compound sentence of this type; the creative ability so much a part of human language is not demonstrated by this act.

Problems also exist in Lana's "acquisition" of Yerkish. The Lana project was studied by Thompson and Church,[24] who were able to simulate Lana's behavior by a computer model. They concluded that the chimp's "linguistic" behavior can all be accounted for by her learning to associate or pair lexigrams with objects, persons, or events, and to produce one of several "stock sentences" depending on situational cues (like Clever Hans).

There is another difference between the way Sarah and Lana learned whatever they learned and the way children learn language. In the case of the chimpanzees, each new "rule" or sentence form was introduced in a deliberate, highly constrained way. As we noted earlier, when parents speak to children they do not confine themselves to a few words in a particular order for months, rewarding the child with a chocolate bar or a banana each time the child correctly responds to a command. Nor do they wait until the child has mastered one rule of grammar before going on to a different structure. Young children require no special training.

Kanzi

Research on the linguistic ability of nonhuman primates continues. Two investigators studied a male pygmy chimpanzee named Kanzi using the same plastic lexigrams and computer keyboard as used with Lana. They concluded that Kanzi "has not only learned, but also invented grammatical rules that may well be as complex as these used by human 2-year-old children."[25] The grammatical rule referred to was the combination of a lexigram (such as that meaning "dog") with a gesture

---

[24]Claudia R. Thompson and Russell M. Church, "An Explanation of the Language of a Chimpanzee," *Science* 208 (1980): 313–314.
[25]The study, conducted by UCLA psychologist Patricia Marks Greenfield and Georgia State University biologist E. Sue Savage-Rumbaugh, was reported in an article in *The Chronicle of Higher Education*, 26 September, 1990.

meaning "go". After combining these, Kanzi would then go to an area where dogs were located to play with them. Greenfield and Savage-Rumbaugh suggest that this "ordering" rule was not an imitation of his caretakers' utterances, who they suggest used an opposite ordering, in which "dogs" would follow "go" since it was Kanzi not the dogs going.

The investigators do report that Kanzi's acquisition of "grammatical skills" was much slower than that of human children, taking about three years (starting when he was five and a half years old when the study began).

Further grammatical progress has not been reported and certainly Kanzi does not reveal any of the kinds of linguistic knowledge (human or nonhuman) of a complexity equivalent to a three or four year old's knowledge of structure dependencies and hierarchical structure.

As often happens in science, the search for the answers to one kind of question leads to answers to other questions not originally asked. The linguistic experiments with primates have led to many advances in our understanding of primate cognitive ability. Premack has gone on to investigate other capacities of the chimp mind, such as causality; the Rumbaughs and Greenfield are continuing to study the ability of chimpanzees to use symbols. These studies also point out how remarkable it is that human children, by the age of three and four, without explicit teaching, and without overt reinforcement, create new and complex sentences never spoken and never heard before.

Summary

When children learn a language, they learn the grammar of that language—the phonological, morphological, syntactic, and semantic rules—as well as the words or vocabulary. No one teaches them these rules; children just "pick them up."

Before infants begin to produce "words," they produce sounds, some of which will remain if they occur in the language being acquired, and others that will disappear. Deaf children exposed at birth to sign languages also produce manual babbling, showing that **babbling** is universal in first language acquisition.

A child does not learn the language "all at once." The grammar is acquired by stages. Children's first utterances are one-word "sentences" (the **holophrastic** stage). After a few months, the two-word stage arises, in which the child puts two words together. These two-word sentences are not random combinations of words; the words have definite patterns and express both grammatical and semantic relationships. Later, but still in the very early years, in what has been called the **telegraphic stage,** longer sentences appear composed primarily of content words and lacking function of grammatical morphemes. The child's early grammar lacks many of the rules of the adult grammar, but is not qualitatively different from it, and eventually it mirrors the language used in the community.

A number of theories have been suggested to explain the acquisition process. Neither the imitation theory, which claims that children learn their language by imitating adult speech, nor the reinforcement theory, which hypothesizes that children are conditioned into speaking correctly by being negatively reinforced for "errors" and positively reinforced for "correct" usage, is supported by observational and experimental studies. Neither can explain how children form the rules that they then use to produce new sentences.

A **critical age hypothesis** has been proposed which suggests that there is a biological period during which a child may acquire its native language without overt teaching. Some song birds also appear to have a critical period for the acquisition of their calls and songs.

Deaf children exposed to **sign language** show the same stages of language acquisition as do hearing children exposed to spoken languages. Sign languages, including the major language of the deaf in America, called **American Sign Language (AMESLAN** or **ASL)**, are fully developed, complete languages with grammars comparable to those of spoken languages. The signs, representing the morphemes and words, are constructed from a finite set of primes—hand configurations, movement of the hands, places of articulation—that permit the generation of an infinite set of sentences. The grammars of sign languages include, in addition to their lexicons, rules of sign formation, morphology, semantics, and syntax.

The acquisition of a second or third language parallels the acquisition of one's first native language. If a second language is learned early in life, it is usually acquired with no difficulty. The difficulties encountered in attempting to learn languages after puberty may be due to the fact that they are learned after the critical age for language learning. One theory of second language acquisition suggests that the same principles operate that account for first language acquisition. A second view suggests that in acquiring a second language after the critical age, general learning mechanisms rather than principles specifically linguistic are used. There are a number of second language teaching methods that have been proposed, some of them reflecting different theories of the nature of language and language acquisition. These methods, however, do not explain the apparent differences between first and second language acquisition.

Questions as to whether language is unique to the human species have led researchers to attempt to teach nonhuman primates systems of communication that purportedly resemble human language. Chimpanzees like Sarah and Lana have been taught to manipulate symbols to gain rewards, and other chimpanzees, like Washoe and Nim Chimpsky have been taught a number of ASL signs. A careful examination of the "utterances" in ASL by these chimps show that unlike children, their language exhibits little spontaneity, is highly imitative (echoic), and reveals little syntactic structure. It has been suggested that the pygmy chimp Kanzi shows grammatical ability greater than the other chimps studied, but he still does not have the ability of even a three-year-old child.

The universality of the language acquisition process, of the stages of development, of the relatively short period in which the child constructs such a complex grammatical system without overt teaching, and the limited results of the chimpanzee experiments, suggest that the human species is "innately" endowed with special language acquisition abilities, that language is biologically and genetically part of the human neurological system.

All normal children everywhere learn language. This ability is not dependent on race, social class, geography, or even intelligence (within a normal range). This ability is uniquely human.

References for Further Reading

Bloom, L.M. 1972. *Language Development: Form and Function in Emerging Grammar.* Cambridge, Mass.: MIT Press.

Bowerman, M. 1973. *Early Syntactic Development.* Cambridge, Mass.: MIT Press.

Brown, R.O. 1973. *A First Language: The Early Stages.* Cambridge, Mass.: Harvard University Press.

Clark, H.H., and E.V. Clark. 1977. *Psychology and Language.* New York: Harcourt Brace Jovanovich.

de Villiers, Peter A., and Jill G. de Villiers. 1978. *Language Acquisition.* Cambridge, Mass.: Harvard University Press.

Ellis, R. 1985. *Understanding Second Language Acquisition.* Oxford, England: Oxford University Press.

Feldman, H., Goldin-Meadow, S., and L. Gleitman. 1978. "Beyond Herodotus: the Creation of Language by Linguistically Deprived Deaf Children." In A. Lock, ed., *Action, Symbol, and Gesture: The Emergence of Language.* New York: Academic Press, pp. 351–413.

Fischer, S.D., and P. Siple. 1990. *Theoretical Issues in Sign Language Research. Vol. 1. Linguistics.* Chicago, Ill.: University of Chicago Press.

Gleitman, H. 1991. *Psychology,* 3rd Ed. New York: W.W. Norton, chapter 10.

Hyams, Nina. 1986. *Language Acquisition and the Theory of Parameters.* Dordrecht, The Netherlands: Reidel Publishers.

Klima, E.S., and U. Bellugi. 1979. *The Signs of Language.* Cambridge, Mass.: Harvard University Press.

Krashen, Stephen D. 1982. *Principles and Practice in Second Language Acquisition.* Oxford, England: Pergamon Press.

Landau, Barbara, and Lila R. Gleitman. 1985. *Language and Experience: Evidence from the Blind Child.* Cambridge, Mass.: Harvard University Press.

Premack, Ann J., and D. Premack. 1972. "Teaching language to an ape." *Scientific American* (October): 92–99.

Rumbaugh, D.M. 1977. *Acquisition of Linguistic Skills by a Chimpanzee.* New York: Academic Press.

Sandler, Wendy. 1989. *Phonological Representation of the Sign: Linearity and Nonlinearity in American Sign Language.* Dordrecht, Holland: Foris Publications.

Sebeok, T.A., and Jean Umiker-Sebeok. 1980. *Speaking of Apes: A Critical Anthology of Two-Way Communication with Man.* New York: Plenum Press.

Sebeok, Thomas A., and Robert Rosenthal (eds.). 1981. *The Clever Hans Phenomenon: Communication with Horses, Whales, Apes, and People.* Annals of the New York Academy of Sciences, Vol. 364.

Terrace, Herbert S. 1979. *Nim: A Chimpanzee Who Learned Sign Language.* New York: Knopf.

Wanner, Eric and Lila Gleitman (eds.). 1982. *Language Acquisition: The State of the Art.* Cambridge, England: Cambridge University Press.

Exercises

1. "Baby talk" is a term used to label the word forms that many adults use when speaking to children. Examples in English are *choo-choo* for "train" and *bow-wow* for "dog." Baby talk seems to exist in every language and culture. At least two things seem to be universal about baby talk: the words that have baby talk forms fall into certain semantic categories (for example, food and animals) and the words are "phonetically simpler" than the adult forms (for example, *tummy* /tʌmi/ for "stomach" /stʌmək/). List all the baby talk words you can think of in your native language; then (1) separate them into semantic categories, and (2) try to state general rules for the kinds of phonological "reductions" or "simplifications" that occur.

2. In this chapter the way a child learns "negation" of sentences and "question formation" was discussed. Can they be considered examples of a process of over-generalization in syntax acquisition? If so, for each stage indicate *what* is being overgeneralized.

3. Find a child between two and four years old and play with the child for about thirty minutes. Keep a list of all words and/or "sentences" that are used inappropriately. Describe what the child's meanings for these words probably are. Describe the syntactic or morphological errors (including omissions). If the child is producing multi-word sentences, write a grammar that could account for the data you have collected.

4. Chomsky has been quoted as saying:

   It's about as likely that an ape will prove to have a language ability as that there is an island somewhere with a species of flightless birds waiting for human beings to teach them to fly.

   In the light of evidence presented in this chapter, comment on Chomsky's remark. Do you agree or disagree, or do you think the evidence is inconclusive?

5. Roger Brown and his coworkers at Harvard University (see *References,* above) studied the language development of three children, referred to in the literature as Adam, Eve, and Sarah. The following are samples of their utterances during the "two-word stage."

see boy	push it
see sock	move it
pretty boat	mommy sleep
pretty fan	bye-bye melon
more taxi	bye-bye hot
more melon	

A. Assume that the above utterances are "grammatical sentences" in the children's grammars.

(1) Write a mini-grammar which would account for these sentences.

Example: One rule might be: S→V N

(2) Draw phrase structure trees for each utterance.

Example:

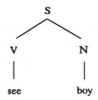

B. One observation made by Brown was that many of the sentences and phrases produced by the children were ungrammatical from the point of view of the adult grammar. The research group concluded, based on utterances such as those below, that a rule in the children's grammar for a Noun Phrase was:

NP→M N (where M = any modifier)

A coat	My stool	Poor man
A celery	That knee	Little top
A Becky	More coffee	Dirty knee
A hands	More nut	That Adam
My mummy	Two tinker-toy	Big boot

(3) Mark with an asterisk any of the above NPs which are ungrammatical in the adult grammar of English.

(4) State the 'violation' for each starred item.
For example, if one of the utterances were *Lotsa book* you might say: "The modifier *lotsa* must be followed by a plural noun."

6. In the holophrastic (one word) stage of child language acquisition, the child's phonological system differs in systematic ways from that in the adult grammar. The inventory of sounds and the phonemic contrasts are smaller, and there are greater constraints on phonotactics. (See Chapter 6 for discussion on these aspects of phonology.)

A. For each of the following words produced by a child, state what the substitution is.

Example: spook (adult) [spuk] (child) [pʰuk]
substitution: initial cluster [sp] reduced to single consonant; /p/ becomes aspirated, showing that child has acquired aspiration rule.

(1) dont   [dot]
(2) skip   [kʰɪp]
(3) shoe   [su]
(4) that   [dæt]
(5) play   [pʰe]
(6) thump   [dʌp]
(7) bath   [bæt]
(8) chop   [tʰap]
(9) kitty   [kɪdi]
(10) light   [wajt]
(11) dolly   [dawi]
(12) grow   [go]

B. Try to state some general rules that account for the children's pronunciation.

CHAPTER 11
Human Processing: Brain, Mind, and Language

The nervous systems of all animals have a number of basic functions in common, most notably the control of movement and the analysis of sensation. What distinguishes the human brain is the variety of more specialized activities it is capable of learning. The preeminent example is language.

Norman Geschwind (1979)

"Rabbit's clever," said Pooh thoughtfully.
"Yes," said Piglet, "Rabbit's clever."
"And he has Brain."
"Yes," said Piglet, "Rabbit has Brain."
There was a long silence.
"I suppose," said Pooh, "that that's why he never understands anything."

A.A. Milne, *The House at Pooh Corner*[1]

The attempts to understand the complexities of human cognitive abilities and especially the acquisition and use of language are as old and as continuous as history. The view that the brain is the source of human language and cognition goes back over 2000 years. Assyrian and Babylonian cuneiform tablets mention disorders of intelligence that may develop "when man's brain holds fire." Egyptian doctors in 1700 B.C.E. noted in their papyrus records that "the breath of an outside god" had entered their patients who became "silent in sadness." The philosophers of ancient Greece also speculated about the brain/mind relationship but neither Plato nor Aristotle recognized the brain's crucial function in cognition or language. Aristotle's wisdom failed him when he suggested that the brain is a cold sponge whose function is to cool the blood. But others writing in the same period showed greater insight. One of the Hippocratic treatises dealing with epilepsy referred to the brain as "the messenger to the understanding" and the organ by which "in an especial manner we acquire wisdom and knowledge."

A major approach in the study of the brain/mind relationship has been through an investigation of language. Research on the brain in humans and nonhuman primates, anatomically, psychologically, and behaviorally, is, for similar reasons, help-

[1]A.A. Milne, *House at Pooh Corner.* New York: E. P. Dutton, 1928.

ing to answer the questions concerning the neurological basis for language. The study concerned with the biological and neural foundations of language is called **neurolinguistics** and the study of the brain mechanisms underlying the use of language is called **psycholinguistics.** This chapter will discuss these two areas of linguistic research.

The Human Brain

The Two Sides of the Brain

It only takes one hemisphere to have a mind.

A.W. Wigan (1844)

"ROGER DOESN'T USE THE LEFT SIDE OF THE BRAIN OR THE RIGHT SIDE. HE JUST USES THE MIDDLE."

We have learned a great deal about the brain—the most complicated organ of the body—in the last two millenia. It lies under the skull and consists of approximately 10 billion nerve cells (**neurons**) and billions of fibers that interconnect them. The neurons or gray matter form the **cortex,** the surface of the brain, under which is the white matter, which consists primarily of connecting fibers. The cortex is the decision-making organ of the body. It receives messages from all the sensory organs, and it initiates all voluntary actions. It is "the seat of all which is exclusively human in the mind" and the storehouse of "memory." Somewhere in this gray matter the grammar that represents our knowledge of language resides.

The brain is divided into two parts (called **cerebral hemispheres**), one on the right and one on the left. These hemispheres are connected like Siamese twins right down the middle, as shown in Figure 11–1.

BACK

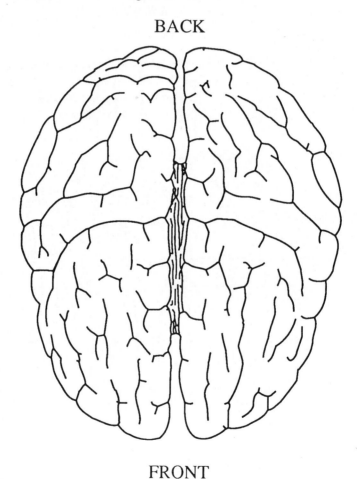

FRONT

Figure 11–1
The brain.

In general, the left hemisphere controls the movements of the right side of the body, and the right hemisphere the movements of the left side. If you point with your right hand, it is the left hemisphere which has "directed" your action.

Since the middle of the nineteenth century, there has been a basic assumption that it is possible to find a direct relation between language and the brain, and a continuous effort to discover direct centers where language capacities (competence and performance) may be localized.

In the early part of the nineteenth century Franz Joseph Gall put forth theories of **localization,** that is, that different human abilities and behaviors were traceable to specific parts of the brain. Gall's theory predates the findings of current research even though the bases for some of his views are amusing when looked at from our present state of knowledge. For example, he suggested that the frontal lobes of the brain were the locations of language because when he was young he had noticed that the most articulate and intelligent of his fellow students had protruding eyes, which he believed reflected overdeveloped brain material. This notion led Spruzheim, a follower of Gall, to establish the pseudo-science called "phrenology," the practice of determining personality traits, intellectual capacities and other matters by examination of the "bumps" on the skull. This led to elaborate maps and skull models such as the one shown in Figure 11–2, in which language is located directly under the eye.

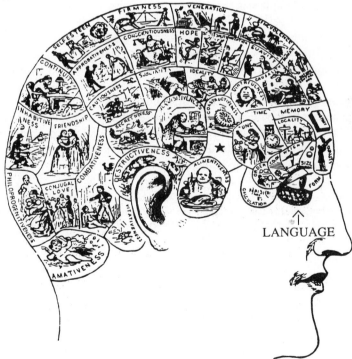

Figure 11–2
Phrenology skull model.

Although phrenology has long been discarded as a scientific theory—except for a few remaining adherents including a recent writer who refers to herself as "a practicing witch"—Gall's view that the brain is not a uniform mass and that some linguistic capacities are functions of localized brain areas has been upheld.

It was not until 1861 that language was specifically related to the left side of the brain. At a scientific meeting in Paris, Paul Broca stated that we speak with the left hemisphere on the basis of his finding that damage to the front part of the left hemisphere (now called **Broca's area**) resulted in loss of speech, whereas damage to the right side did not.[2] Language, then, is said to be **lateralized. Lateralization** is the term used to refer to any cognitive functions which are primarily localized to one side of the brain or the other.

Today, patients with such damage or lesions in Broca's area are said to have **Broca's aphasia. Aphasia** is the neurological term used to refer to language disorders that follow brain lesions caused by a stroke, a tumor, a gunshot wound, or an infection.

The speech output of Broca's aphasia patients is characterized by labored speech, word-finding pauses, loss of "function" words (grammatical morphemes), and quite often, disturbed word order. Auditory comprehension for colloquial conversation gives the impression of being generally good although controlled testing reveals considerable impairments when comprehension depends upon syntactic structure. Thus, Broca's aphasics show syntactic deficits.

In 1873, Carl Wernicke presented a paper that described another variety of aphasia shown by patients with lesions in the back portion of the left hemisphere. Unlike Broca's patients, Wernicke's spoke fluently with good intonation and pronunciation, but with numerous instances of lexical errors (word substitutions) and often with phonological errors. They also had difficulty in comprehending speech, revealing semantic and lexical difficulties.

The area of the brain that when damaged seems to lead to these symptoms is now, not surprisingly, known as **Wernicke's area,** and the patients are said to suffer from **Wernicke's aphasia.** Figure 11–3, drawn by the neurologist Hanna Damasio, shows these areas of the brain.

---

[2]Broca also held extremely racist and sexist views based on incorrect measurements of the brains of men and women and different races. His false view correlating brain size with intelligence is thoroughly demolished by Stephen Jay Gould in *The Mismeasure of Man*. New York: W.W. Norton, 1981.

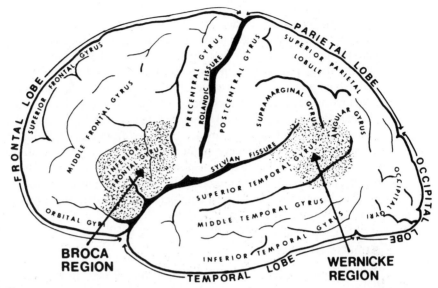

Figure 11–3

Lateral (external) view of the left hemisphere of the human brain. Note the position of Broca and Wernicke regions—two key areas of the cortex related to language processing.

There is now a consensus that the so called higher mental functions are greatly lateralized. Research, some of which will be discussed below, shows that though the nervous system is generally symmetrical—what exists on the left exists on the right and vice versa—the two sides of the brain form an exception.

Evidence for Brain Lateralization

PEANUTS reprinted by permission of UFS, Inc.

Although neurolinguistics is still in its infancy, our understanding has progressed a great deal since a day in September 1848, when a foreman of a road construction gang named Phineas Gage became a famous figure in medical history. He achieved his "immortality" when a four-foot-long iron rod was blown through his head. Despite the gaping tunnel in his brain, Gage maintained the ability to speak and understand and retained whatever intellectual abilities he had prior to the injury, although he suffered major changes in his personality (he became "cranky" and "inconsiderate"), in his sexual behavior, and in his ability to control his emotions or make plans. Both Gage and science benefited from this explosion. Phineas gained monetarily by becoming a one-man touring circus; he traveled all over the country charging money to those curious enough to see him and the iron rod. Nevertheless, he died penniless in an institution twelve years after the accident. Science benefited because brain researchers were stimulated to learn why his intelligence remained intact.

Aphasia Studies

The interest in aphasia goes back long before Broca. In the New Testament, St. Luke reports that Zacharias could not speak but could write. And in 30 A.D. the Roman writer Valerius Maximus describes an Athenian who was unable to remember his "letters" after being hit in the head with a stone. Pliny who lived from 23 to 79 C.E. also refers to this same Athenian noting that "with the stroke of a stone, he fell presently to forget his letters only, and could read no more; otherwise his memory served him well enough." The recognition of the loss of specific parts of language with the retention of other aspects of linguistic competence or performance and other cognitive abilities has important implications for our understanding of the neural basis for language and cognition and will be discussed further below.

It is primarily in the last fifty years that controlled scientific studies of aphasia have been conducted, providing unequivocal evidence that language is predominantly and most frequently a left-hemisphere function. In the great majority of cases, lesions to the left hemisphere result in aphasia but injuries to the right do not (although such lesions result in perceptual difficulties, defects in pattern recognition, and other cognitive deficits). If both hemispheres were equally involved with language this should not be the case.[3]

The language impairments suffered by aphasics are not due to any general cognitive or intellectual impairments. Nor are they due to loss of motor or sensory controls of the nerves and muscles of the speech organs or hearing apparatus. Aphasics can produce sounds and hear sounds. Whatever loss they suffer has to do only with the production or comprehension of language (or specific parts of the grammar).

---

[3]For some people—about a third of all left-handers—there is still lateralization, yet it is the right side that is specialized for language. In other words, the special functions are switched, but asymmetry still exists.

This fact is dramatically shown by the fact that deaf signers with damage to the left hemisphere show aphasia for sign language similar to the language breakdown in hearing aphasics. Bellugi and her colleagues at the Salk Institute have found that patients with lesions in Broca's area show language deficits similar to those found in hearing patients—severe dysfluent, agrammatic sign production.[4] While deaf aphasic patients show marked sign language deficits, they have no difficulty in processing nonlanguage visual spatial relationships, just as hearing aphasics have no problem with processing nonlinguistic auditory stimuli. Thus, the left hemisphere is not lateralized for hearing or speech, but for language.

As shown by the different symptoms of Broca's and Wernicke's aphasias, many aphasias do not show total language loss. Rather, different aspects of language are impaired. Broca's aphasics are often referred to as **agrammatic** because of their particular problems with syntax, as the following sample of the speech of an agrammatic patient with damage to Broca's area illustrates. The patient was asked what brought him back to the hospital and answered:

> Yes—ah—Monday ah—Dad—and Dad—ah—Hospital—and ah—Wednesday—Wednesday—nine o'clock and ah Thursday—ten o'clock ah doctors—two—two—ah doctors and—ah—teeth—yah. And a doctor—ah girl—and gums, and I.[5]

As this patient illustrates, agrammatic aphasics produce nongrammatical utterances, frequently omitting both free grammatical morphemes and bound inflectional affixes. They also have difficulty in interpreting sentences correctly when comprehension depends on syntactic structure. Thus, they have a problem with determining "who did what to whom" in passive sentences such as:

> (a) The girl was kicked by the boy.

where either the subject or the object of the sentence can be the sentence theme, since in real life girls and boys can kick each other. But they have less difficulty with

> (b) The ball was kicked by the boy.

where the meaning of the sentence agrees with their nonlinguistic knowledge. They know that balls do not under normal circumstances kick boys and so use that knowledge to interpret the sentence. Normal speakers will have no difficulty because they use the syntax for comprehension.

Wernicke's aphasics, on the other hand, produce fluent, but often unintelligible speech, have serious comprehension problems and difficulty in lexical selection. One patient replied to a question about his health with:

---

[4]Poizner, H., E. Kilma, and U. Bellugi, *What the Hands Reveal About the Brain,* Cambridge, Mass.: MIT Press, 1987.

[5]Harold Goodglass."Studies on the Grammar of Aphasics," in *Psycholinguistics and Aphasia.* Goodglass and S. Blumstein, eds. Baltimore, MD.: John Hopkins University Press, 1973.

> "I felt worse because I can no longer keep in mind from the mind of the minds to keep me from mind and up to the ear which can be to find among ourselves."

Some aphasics have difficulty in naming objects that are presented to them, which shows a lexical defect. Others produce semantically anomalous jargon such as the patient who described a fork as "a need for a schedule"; another, when asked about his poor vision said "My wires don't hire right." While some of these aphasics substitute words which bear no semantic relationship to the correct word, such as calling a chair an *engine,* others substitute words which, like normal speech errors, are related semantically, substituting for example, *table* for *chair* or *boy* for *girl.*

Another kind of aphasia called **jargon aphasia** results in the substitution of one phoneme for another. Thus *table* might be pronounced as *sable.* The substituted segments often share most of the distinctive features of the intended phonemes. An extreme variety of phonemic jargon results in the production of nonsense forms—nonoccurring but possible words. One patient, a physician prior to his aphasia, when asked if he was a doctor, replied:

> "Me? yes sir. I'm a male demaploze on my own. I still know my tubaboys what for I have that's gone hell and some of them go."

The kinds of language impairments found in aphasics provide information on the nature of the grammar. If we find that damage to different parts of the brain leads to impairment of different components of the grammar, this is good evidence to support the models proposed by linguistics.

Patients that produce long strings of "jargon," which sound like well-formed grammatical language but which are uninterpretable, show that the phonological and phonetic systems of language are separate components of language.

The substitution of semantically related words provides additional evidence to that of word substitution errors of non-aphasics in support of semantic features, as discussed in Chapter 4. Some of the most interesting examples of such substitutions are produced by aphasic patients who become dyslexic after brain damage. They are called **acquired dyslexics** because prior to the brain lesion they were normal readers (unlike developmental dyslexics who have difficulty learning to read). One group of these patients, when reading aloud words printed on cards, produced the kinds of substitutions shown in the following examples.[6]

Stimulus	Response 1	Response 2
act	*play*	*play*
applaud	*laugh*	*cheers*
example	*answer*	*sum*
heal	*pain*	*medicine*
south	*west*	*east*

[6]Patient G. R. as reported in F. Newcombe and J. Marshall, "Varieties of Acquired Dyslexia: A Linguistic Approach." *Seminars in Neurology* 4, no. 2. (1984): 181-195.

Note that these patients did not always substitute the same words in two different testing periods. In fact, at times they would read the correct word, showing that the problem was in performance (accessing the correct phonological form in the lexicon) not in competence, since they could sometimes get to the right word and produce it.

The substitution of phonologically similar words *pool* for *tool* or *crucial* for *crucible,* also provides information on the organization of the lexicon. Words in the lexicon seem to be connected to other words by phonology and semantics.

The difference between syntactic word classes is revealed in aphasia cases by the omission of grammatical morphemes in the speech of Broca's aphasics and in some cases of acquired dyslexia. Patient G.R., cited above, who produced semantically similar word substitutions was unable to read grammatical morphemes at all; when presented with words like *which* or *would,* he just says, "No" or "I hate those little words"; but he can read, though with many semantic mistakes, homophones of these words, as shown in the following reading errors.

Stimulus	Response	Stimulus	Response
witch	*witch*	which	*no!*
bean	*soup*	been	*no!*
hour	*time*	our	*no!*
eye	*eyes*	I	*no!*
hymn	*bible*	him	*no!*
wood	*wood*	would	*no!*

These errors suggest that the mental dictionary is divided into sublexicons, one consisting of major lexical content words and the other of grammatical morphemes.

Most of us have experienced word-finding difficulties in speaking if not in reading, as Alice did when she said:

> "And now, who am I? I will remember, if I can. I'm determined to do it!" But being determined didn't help her much, and all she could say, after a great deal of puzzling, was "L, I know it begins with L."

This "tip-of-the-tongue" (TOT as it is often referred to) phenomenon is not uncommon. But if you never can find the word you want, you can imagine how serious a problem aphasics have. Aphasics with such problems are said to suffer from **anomia.**

Split Brains

"It's finally happening, Helen. The hemispheres of my brain are drifting apart."
Drawing by Lee Lorenz: © 1980 The New Yorker Magazine, Inc.

Aphasia studies provide good evidence that language is primarily processed in the left hemisphere. Other evidence is provided by patients who have one of the hemispheres removed. If the right hemisphere is cut out, language remains intact, although other cognitive losses may result. Because language is such an important aspect of our daily life, surgical removal of the left hemisphere is only performed in dire cases of malignant brain tumor.

"Split-brain" patients provide important evidence for language lateralization and for understanding brain functions. In recent years it was found that persons suffering from serious epilepsy could be treated by cutting the corpus callosum. This "freeway" between the two brain halves consists of two million fibers connecting the cells of the left and right hemispheres. The corpus callosum is shown in Figure 11–4. When this pathway is split there is no "communication" between the "two brains."

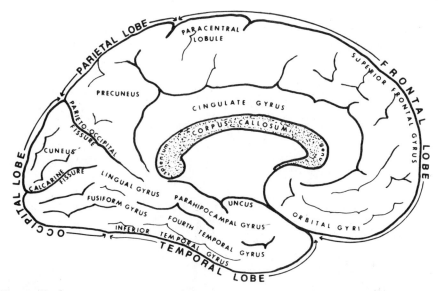

Figure 11–4

Internal view of the left hemisphere of the human brain. Note the position of the corpus callosum, which joins the structures of the left and right hemispheres across the midline.

The psychologist Michael Gazzaniga states:[7]

> With [the corpus callosum] intact, the two halves of the body have no secrets from one another. With it sectioned, the two halves become two different conscious mental spheres, each with its own experience base and control system for behavioral operations. . . . Unbelievable as this may seem, this is the flavor of a long series of experimental studies first carried out in the cat and monkey.

When the brain is split surgically, certain information from the left side of the body is received only by the right side of the brain and vice versa (because of the "crisscross" phenomenon discussed above). For example, suppose a monkey is trained to respond with its hands to a certain visual stimulus, such as a flashing light. If the brain is split after the training period, and the stimulus is shown only to the left visual field (the right brain), the monkey will perform only with the left hand, and vice versa. Many such experiments have been done on animals. They all show the independence of the two sides of the brain.

Persons with split brains have been tested by psychologists, showing that, like the monkey brain, the two human hemispheres are distinct. However, these tests showed that messages sent to the two sides of the brain result in different responses, depending on which hemisphere "receives" the message. If an apple is put in the left hand of a split-brain human whose vision is cut off, the person can use it appropriately but cannot name it. The right brain senses the apple and distinguishes it from

[7]Michael Gazzaniga, *The Bisected Brain*, New York: Appleton-Century-Crofts, 1970.

other objects, but the information cannot be relayed to the left brain for linguistic naming. By contrast, if a banana is placed in the right hand, the subject is immediately able to name it as well as describe it. (See Figure 11–5.)

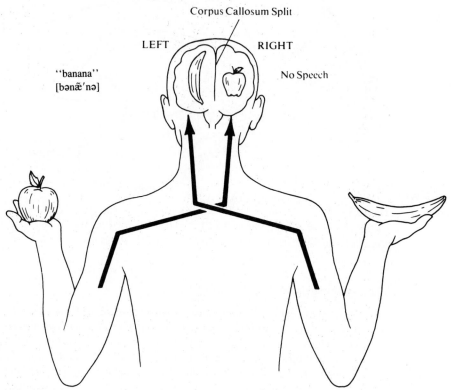

Figure 11–5
Sensory information is received in the *contralateral* (opposite) side of the brain from the side of the body from which it is sent. In a split-brain patient, the information in the right hemisphere cannot get across to the left hemisphere; for this reason, this patient cannot produce the word "apple."

Various experiments of this sort have been performed, all providing information on the different capabilities of the "two brains." The right brain does better than the left in pattern-matching tasks, in recognizing faces, and in spatial orientation. The left hemisphere is superior for language, for rhythmic perception, for temporal-order judgments, and for mathematical thinking. According to Gazzaniga, "the right hemisphere as well as the left hemisphere can emote and while the left can tell you why, the right cannot."

Studies of human split-brain patients have shown that when the interhemispheric visual connections are severed, visual information from the right and left visual fields becomes confined to the left and right hemispheres respectively. Because of the crucial endowment of the left hemisphere for language, written material delivered to the right hemisphere can not be read if the brain is split, because the information can not be transferred to the left hemisphere.

An image or picture that is flashed to the right visual field of a split-brain patient (and is therefore processed by the left hemisphere) can be named. However, when the picture is flashed in the left visual field and lands in the right hemisphere, it can not be named.

More Lateralization Evidence

Aphasia studies and split-brain research all involve "nonnormal" human subjects (in one way or another). Other experimental techniques that can be used with all human subjects have been developed to explore the specialized capabilities of the two hemispheres.

One such method, called **dichotic listening,** uses auditory signals. Subjects hear two different sound signals simultaneously through earphones. For example, a subject may hear "boy" in one ear and "girl" in the other, or "crocodile" in one ear and "alligator" in the other; or the subject may hear a horn tooting in one ear and rushing water in the other. When asked to state what they heard in each ear, subjects are more frequently correct in reporting linguistic stimuli (words, nonsense syllables, and so on) delivered directly to the right ear but are more frequently correct in reporting nonverbal stimuli (musical chords, environmental sounds, and so on) delivered to the left ear. That is, if subjects hear "boy" in the right ear and "girl" in the left ear, they are more likely to report the word heard in the right ear correctly. If they hear coughing in the right ear and laughing in the left, they are more apt to report the laughing stimulus correctly. The same acoustic signal may be processed in one hemisphere or the other depending on whether the subjects perceive it as part of their language system or not. Thai speakers show a right ear advantage (left hemisphere) in distinguishing between CV syllables that contrast in tone (pitch contours); English subjects do not show the right ear advantage when they hear the same stimuli, because English is not a tone language.

Both hemispheres receive signals from both ears, but the "crossed" contralateral stimuli (right to left and vice versa) compete successfully with the "same side" ipsilateral stimuli, either because they are received earlier, or because they are not weakened by having to cross the corpus callosum. The fact that the left hemisphere has an edge in linguistic processing and the right hemisphere is better at nonverbal material determines the accuracy with which subjects report on what they have heard.

These experiments are important in that they show that the left hemisphere is not superior for processing all sounds, but only for those that are linguistic in nature. That is, the left side of the brain is specialized for language, not sounds.

Other experimental techniques are also being used to map the brain and to investigate the independence of different aspects of language and the extent of the independence of language from other cognitive systems.

New technologies such as PET (an acronym for *P*ositron *E*mission *T*omography) and MRI (*M*agnetic *R*esonance *I*maging) now make it possible to detect changes in brain activities in extremely small areas of the brain and relate these changes to focal brain damage and cognitive tasks.

Even before these spectacular new technologies were introduced in the 1970s, researchers were taping electrodes to different areas of the skull and investigating the electrical activity of the brain, by comparing the signals emitted from these differently placed electrodes. In such experiments the electrical signals emitted from the brain in response to different kinds of stimuli (called evoked potentials or event-related potentials or erps) are measured. For example, electrical differences may result when the subject hears speech sounds and nonspeech sounds. These experiments show that neuronal activity in different locations varies with different stimuli and different tasks, and provide further support for the views on lateralization presented above.

The results of these studies, using different techniques and diverse subjects, both normal and brain damaged, are converging to provide the information we seek on the relationship between the brain and various language and nonlanguage cognitive systems.

The Evolution of Language

> As the voice was used more and more, the vocal organs would have been strengthened and perfected through the principle of the inherited effects of use; and this would have reacted on the power of speech. But the relation between the continued use of language and the development of the brain has no doubt been far more important. The mental powers in some early progenitor of man must have been more highly developed than in any existing ape, before even the most imperfect form of speech could have come into use.
>
> Charles Darwin, *The Descent of Man*

If the human brain is uniquely suited to the acquisition and use of language, how (and when) did this development occur? Two scholarly societies, the American Anthropological Association and the New York Academy of Sciences, held forums in 1974 and 1976 to review research on this question. It is not a new question, and seems to have arisen with the origin of the species as the discussion on the origin of language in Chapter 1 pointed out.

There is much interest today among biologists as well as linguists in the relationship between the development of language and the evolutionary development of the human species. There are those who view language ability as a difference in degree between humans and other primates, and those who see the onset of language ability as a qualitative leap. Many of those who support the "discontinuity" view believe that language is species-specific.

In trying to understand the development of language, scholars past and present have debated the role played by the vocal tract and the ear. For example, it has been suggested that speech could not have developed in nonhuman primates because their vocal tracts were anatomically incapable of producing a large enough inventory of speech sounds. According to this hypothesis, the development of language is linked to the evolutionary development of the speech production and perception apparatus. This, of course, would be accompanied by changes in the brain and the nervous system toward greater complexity. Such a view implies that the languages of our human ancestors of millions of years ago may have been syntactically and phonologically simpler than any language known to us today. The notion, "simpler," however, is left undefined. One suggestion is that this primeval language had a smaller phonetic inventory.

One evolutionary step must have resulted in the development of a vocal tract capable of producing the wide variety of sounds utilized by human language, as well as the mechanism for perceiving and distinguishing them. That this step is insufficient to explain the origin of language is evidenced by the existence of mynah birds and parrots, which have the ability to imitate human speech, but not the ability to acquire language.

More importantly, we know from the study of humans who are born deaf and learn sign languages that are used around them that the ability to hear speech sounds is not a necessary condition for the acquisition and use of language. In addition, the lateralization evidence from brain damaged deaf signers discussed above shows that the brain is neurologically equipped to learn language rather than speech.

The complexity of language argues against the notion that it could have been caused by a single event or one mutation in the evolution of the species. It is more likely that the language faculty originated from a convergence of a number of evolutionary developments.

The major step in the development of language most probably relates to evolutionary changes in the brain. It is not yet clear what role, if any, hemispheric lateralization played in its development. Lateralization certainly makes greater specialization possible. Research conducted with birds and monkeys, however, shows that lateralization is not unique to the human brain. Thus, while it may constitute a necessary step in the evolution of language, it is not a sufficient one.

The Autonomy of Language

In the last twenty years or so, a major issue being debated among linguists and other cognitive scientists concerns the question of whether the human mind and the brain which serves as its neural base is 'modular' in its anatomical structure and functional organization. That is, the question is being asked whether human language ability is an autonomous system, independent of other cognitive systems with which it interacts, or whether it is derivative of more general cognitive ability.

We have seen that after brain damage individuals will suffer different cognitive deficiencies, depending on the area of the brain that has been damaged. This would argue that at least in the mature brain, language can be impaired or preserved, independent of other cognitive systems or of general intellectual abilities. This does not tell us whether the language faculty from birth is domain specific.

The psychological literature documents numerous cases of intellectually handicapped individuals, traditionally known as "idiot savants" but more recently simply called "savants," who, despite their disabilities in certain spheres, show remarkable talents in others. The classic cases include individuals who are superb musicians, or artists, or draftsmen but lack the simple abilities required to take care of themselves. Some of the most famous savants are human calculators who can perform complex arithmetic processes at phenomenal speed or the calendrical calculators who can tell you almost instantaneously on which day of the week falls any date in the last or next century.

Until recently, most of the savants have been reported to be linguistically handicapped. They may be good mimics who can repeat speech like parrots but show meager creative language ability.

While such cases strongly argue for domain specific abilities and suggest that certain talents do not require general intelligence, they do not decisively respond to the suggestion that language is one ability that is derivative of general cognitive abilities.

The more recent literature is now reporting on cases of language savants who have acquired the highly complex grammar of their language (as well as other languages in some cases) without parallel non-linguistic abilities of equal complexity.

There are now a number of such studies of children who have few cognitive skills and virtually no ability to utilize language for meaningful communication and yet have extensive mastery of linguistic structure. Jeni Yamada[8] has studied one severely retarded young woman, named Laura, with a non-verbal IQ of 41–44, lacking almost all number concepts including basic counting principles, drawing at a preschool level, and processing an auditory memory span limited to three units, who when at the age of sixteen was asked to name some fruits, responded with "pears," "apples," and "pomegranates" and in this same period produced syntactically complex sentences like *He was saying that I lost my battery powered watch that I loved; I just loved that watch* or *Last year at school when I first went there, three tickets were gave out by a police last year.*

Laura cannot add 2 + 2. She is not sure of when "last year" is or whether it is before or after "last week" or "an hour ago," nor does she know how many tickets were "gave out" nor whether 3 is larger or smaller than 2. Although Laura produces sentences with multiple embeddings; can conjoin verb phrases, produce passives, inflect verbs for number and person to agree with the grammatical subject; and forms past tenses when the time adverbial structurally refers to a previous time, she can neither read nor write nor tell time. She does not know who the president of the United States is or what country she lives in and does not know her own age. Her drawings of humans resemble potatoes with stick arms and legs. Yet, in a sentence imitation task she both detected and corrected surface syntactic and morphological errors.

Laura is but one of many examples of children who display well developed phonological, morphological, and syntactic linguistic abilities; seemingly less de-

---

[8]Jeni E. Yamada, *Laura: A Case for the Modularity of Language,* Cambridge, Mass: Bradford Books, M.I.T. Press, 1990.

veloped lexical, semantic, or referential aspects of language; and severe deficits in non-linguistic cognitive development.

In addition, any notion that linguistic ability results simply from communicative abilities or develops to serve communication functions is also negated by studies of children with fully developed structural linguistic knowledge but with almost a total absence of pragmatic or communicative skills. The ability to communicate in a social setting seems to depend on different cognitive skills than the acquisition of language.

Another dramatic case of a twenty-nine-year-old "linguistic savant" named Christopher[9] has been reported. Christopher has a non-verbal IQ between 60 and 70 and is institutionalized because he is unable to take care of himself. Christopher finds the tasks of buttoning a shirt, cutting his fingernails, or vacuuming the carpet too difficult. Yet, when given written texts in some fifteen or sixteen languages, he translates them immediately into English. The languages include Germanic languages like Danish, Dutch, and German; Romance languages like French, Italian, Portuguese, and Spanish; as well as Polish, Finnish, Greek, Hindi, Turkish, and Welsh. He learned them either from speakers who used the languages in his presence or from grammar books. The investigators of this interesting man conclude that his linguistic ability is independent of his general conceptual or intellectual ability.

Such cases argue against the view that linguistic ability derives from more general cognitive "intelligence," since in these cases language develops against a background of deficits in general and non-linguistic intellectual abilities.

The Linguistic Mind at Work: Human Language Processing

> No doubt a reasonable model of language use will incorporate, as a basic component, the generative grammar that expresses the speaker-hearer's knowledge of the language; but this generative grammar does not, in itself, prescribe the character or functioning of a perceptual model or a model of speech production.
>
> **Noam Chomsky,** *Aspects of a Theory of Syntax*

Psycholinguistics is, as mentioned at the beginning of this chapter, the area of linguistics that is concerned with linguistic performance—how we use our linguistic competence, our knowledge of language in speech production and comprehension. The human brain is able not only to acquire and store the mental grammar, but to access that linguistic storehouse to speak and understand what is spoken.

How we process knowledge depends to a great extent on the **nature** of that knowledge. If, for example, language was not "open-ended," if language consisted of a finite store of fixed phrases and sentences, then speaking might simply consist of finding a sentence that expresses a thought we wish to convey with its phonological representation and producing it; comprehension could be the reverse—

---

[9]Neil Smith and Ianthi Tsimpli, *Linguistic Modularity: A Case-Study of a "Savant" Linguist.* Paper presented at meeting of Generative Linguistics of the Old World, Spain, 1991.

matching the sounds to a stored string which has been entered with its meaning. We know this is not possible because of the creativity of language. In Chapter 10, we saw that children do not learn language by imitating and storing sentences but by constructing a grammar. When we speak, we **access** our grammar to find the words, construct novel sentences, and produce the sounds that express the message we wish to convey. When we listen to someone speak and understand what is being said, we also access the grammar to process the utterances in order to assign a meaning to the sounds we hear.

The grammar contains the units and rules of the language which make speech production and comprehension possible. But the grammar does not describe the psychological processes which are used in producing and understanding utterances. A theory of linguistic performance describes the relationship between the mental grammar and the psychological mechanisms by means of which this grammar is accessed to permit speech and comprehension.

Comprehension

> "I quite agree with you," said the Duchess; "and the moral of that is—'Be what you would seem to be'—or, if you'd like it put more simply—'Never imagine yourself not to be otherwise than what it might appear to others that what you were or might have been was not otherwise than what you had been would have appeared to them to be otherwise.'"
>
> "I think I should understand that better," Alice said very politely, "if I had it written down: but I can't quite follow it as you say it."
>
> Lewis Carroll, *Alice's Adventures in Wonderland*

The difficulty Alice had in understanding this sentence is not surprising. What is surprising is that we usually do understand even long and complex sentences with multiply embedded relative clauses and many conjoined phrases and modifiers. Even young children can do this automatically and without conscious effort. Once in a while, of course, one stops and asks for clarification as Christopher Robin did in listening to a story about *Winnie-the-Pooh*.

> Once upon a time, a very long time ago now, about last Friday, Winnie-the-Pooh lived in a forest all by himself under the name of Sanders.
>
> (*"What does 'under the name' mean?" asked Christopher Robin.*
> *"It means he had the name over the door in gold letters, and lived under it."*) . . .[10]

If Christopher took the time to think about the meaning of the phrase "under the name of Sanders," he may have realized that it was an ambiguous sentence. In normal conversations, non-linguistic considerations like word frequency or what we expect to hear or what we are thinking can influence which meaning of an ambiguous sentence we come up with. One aim of psycholinguistic research is to clarify the processes by which speakers match one or more meanings to the strings of sounds they hear.

[10]A. A. Milne, *Winnie-the-Pooh*. New York: E.P. Dutton & Co., 1926.

We are not conscious of the complicated processes we use in order to understand speech. The comprehension of speech involves many psychological operations. Speech perception—analyzing the speech signal into strings of phonemes—is a necessary but not sufficient first step in comprehension. Some of the complexities of the speech perception process were discussed in Chapter 6 and will be further discussed in Chapter 12. To see how complex speech processing is, suppose you heard someone say:

>A sniggle blick is procking a slar.

and were able to perceive the sounds as

>/ə snɪgəl blɪk ɪz prakɪŋ ə slar/

You would still be unable to assign a meaning to the sounds, because the meaning of a sentence depends on the meanings of its words, and the only English lexical items in this string are the morphemes *a, is,* and *-ing.* The sentence lacks any English content words.

You can only know that the sentence has no meaning by attempting a **lexical lookup** of the phonological strings you construct; finding no entries for *sniggle, blick, prock* or *slar* in your mental dictionary tells you that the sentence is composed of nonsense strings.

If instead you heard someone say *The cat chased the rat,* through a lexical lookup process, you would conclude that an event concerning a cat, a rat, and the activity of chasing had occurred. You could only know this because you segmented the words in the continuous speech signal, analyzed them into their phonological word units, matched these units with similar strings stored in your lexicon, which also include the meanings attached to these phonological representations. This still would not enable you to tell who chased whom, since this is determined by syntactic processing. That is, processing speech to get at the meaning of what is said requires syntactic analysis as well as knowledge of lexical semantics.

Stress and intonation provide some cues to syntactic structure. We know, for example, from Chapter 6, that the different meanings of the sentences *He lives in the white house* and *He lives in the White House* can be signalled by differences in their stress patterns. Such prosodic aspects of speech also help to segment the speech signal into words and phrases; syllables at the end of a phrase are longer in duration than at the beginning. Intonation contours mark boundaries of clauses. Relative loudness, pitch, and duration of syllables thus provide information in the comprehension process.

Speech comprehension is very fast and automatic. We understand an utterance as we hear it or read it. We don't wait for a pause and then say, "Hold on. I have to analyze the speech sounds, look the words up in my dictionary, and **parse** (provide a syntactic analysis of) your utterance." But how do we understand a sentence?

Comprehension Models and Experimental Studies

>I have experimented and experimented until now I know that [water] never
>does run uphill, except in the dark. I know it does in the dark, because the pool
>never goes dry; which it would, of course, if the water didn't come back in the

night. It is best to prove things by experiment; then you know; whereas if you depend on guessing and supposing and conjecturing, you will never get educated.

Mark Twain, *Eve's Diary*

In this laboratory the only one who is always right is the cat.

Motto in laboratory of Arturo Rosenblueth

The psychological stages and processes that a listener goes through in comprehending the meaning of an utterance are very complex. Alternative models of speech processing have been proposed in the attempt to clarify the stages involved. Some psycholinguists suggest that speech perception and comprehension involve both **top-down** and **bottom-up** processing.

Top-down processes proceed from semantic and syntactic information to the sensory input. Using such 'higher level' information, it is suggested that we can predict what is to follow in the signal.

Bottom-up processes move step-by-step from the incoming acoustic signal to semantic interpretation, building each part of the structure on the basis of the sensory data alone.

Evidence for at least partial top-down processing is provided in a number of experiments. For example, subjects make fewer identification errors of words when the words occur in sentences than when they are presented in isolation. This suggests that subjects are using knowledge of syntactic structures in addition to the acoustic input signal. This is true even when the stimuli are presented in the presence of noise. Subjects also do better if the words occur in grammatically meaningful sentences as opposed to grammatically anomolous sentences; identification of words in ungrammatical sentences produced the most errors. This supports the idea that subjects are not responding simply to the input word by word. Top-down processing is also supported by the fact that when subjects hear recorded sentences in which some part of the signal is removed and a cough substituted, they "hear" the sentence without a missing phoneme, and, in fact, are unable to say which phonemic segment the cough replaced. Context plays a major role in determining what sounds the subjects replace. Thus, "[cough] eel" is heard as *wheel, heel, peel,* or *meal* depending on whether the sentence in which the distorted word occurs refers to an axle, shoe, orange, or food, respectively.

In a **shadowing** task, subjects are asked to repeat what they hear as rapidly as possible. A few exceptionally good shadowers can follow what is being said only about a syllable behind (300 milliseconds). Most of us, however, shadow with a delay of about a second (500 to 800 milliseconds). This is still quite fast. More interesting than the speed, shadowers often "correct" speech errors or mispronunciations unconsciously, and even add inflectional endings if they are absent. Even when they are told the speech they are to shadow includes errors and they should repeat the errors, they are unable to do so. Lexical corrections are more likely to occur when the target word is predictable from what has been said previously. These shadowing experiments show that speech perception involves more than simply processing the incoming signal.

One technique used in psycholinguistic experiments involves **response time** or **reaction time** measurements (often referred to as RTs). The assumption is that the longer the time it takes to respond to a particular task, the more processing is involved. Using such measurements, it has been found that ambiguous sentences take longer to process than nonambiguous sentences. It appears that even if subjects are not aware of the multi-meanings of an ambiguous sentence, both meanings are evoked and they interfere with each other.

Reaction time is also measured in experiments using a **priming** technique. It has been found, for example, that if subjects hear a word such as *nurse,* their response to *doctor* will be faster than to a semantically unrelated word such as *flower.* This may be due to the fact that semantically related words are located in the same part of the lexicon and once the "path" to that section has been taken it is easier to travel that way a second time. It may also be due to the fact that other words are triggered when we "look up" a semantically related word.

In priming experiments, the response required may be a **lexical decision.** That is, the subject is presented with a prime and then another stimulus, which may be a word or a nonsense string, and must respond by pressing a button if the second stimulus is an actual word.

An interesting finding in such experiments is that a lexically ambiguous word can be primed by a word referring to either meaning, even if the context of the ambiguous word disambiguates it. For example, either *harbor* or *wine* will prime the word *port* (result in faster response time) in the sentence

The ship is in port.

This suggests that, in listening to speech, all the meanings in our mental lexicons represented by a phonological form will be triggered. This however argues against top-down processing, since both words are accessed even when the preceding sentence disambiguates the ambiguous word. That is, if we use information other than what is contained in the incoming signal, the sentence that was heard earlier should influence which word is accessed.

Another experimental technique, called the naming task, asks the subject to read aloud a printed word. Subjects read real words faster than nonwords, and irregularly spelled words like *dough* and *enough* as fast as regularly spelled words like *doe* and *stuff,* and even faster than regularly spelled nonsense forms like *cluff.* This shows that the subjects first go to the lexicon to see if the word is there, access the phonological representation, and produce the word. They only use spelling-to-pronunciation rules if they canot find the string of letters listed.

The frequency of words—how often they are used in ordinary speech or writing—also affects response time, showing that comprehension performance involves both linguistic and nonlinguistic factors.

There has been more psycholinguistic research dealing with lexical access than with syntactic processing, possibly because the available experimental techniques can be more easily directed toward this question. In recent years, an increasing number of studies have concentrated on sentence processing.

One class of sentences that involves syntactic processing as distinguished from syntactic competence has been referred to as *garden path sentences,* illustrated by the following:

> *The horse raced past the barn fell.*

Many individuals, on hearing this sentence will judge it to be ungrammatical, yet will judge a sentence with the same syntactic structure as grammatical, such as:

> *The bus driven past the school stopped.*

Similarly, subjects will have no problem with:

> *The horse that was raced past the barn fell.*

The reason why the first sentence is called a "garden path" sentence is because, as the idiom implies, we are incorrectly led to interpret the word *raced* as the VP verb since it immediately follows the first Noun Phrase. To interpret the sentence correctly we have to retrace our processing when we come to the main sentence verb *fell* which becomes very confusing. Such retracking seems to put a burden on short-term memory and syntactic processors which creates comprehension errors. Such sentences highlight the distinction between syntactic competence and syntactic performance strategies.

The ability to understand and comprehend what is said to us is a complex psychological process involving the internal grammar, motivation, frequency factors, memory, and both linguistic and nonlinguistic context.

Speech Production

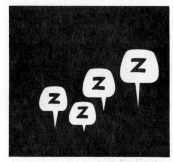

U.S. ACRES reprinted by permission of UFS, Inc.

> And has the reader never asked himself what kind of a mental fact is his intention of saying a thing before he has said it? . . . How much of it consists of definite sensorial images, either of words or of things? Hardly anything! Linger, and the words and things come to mind. . . . The intention welcomes them.
>
> William James (1890)

The speech chain starts with a speaker who, through some complicated set of neuromuscular processes, produces an acoustic signal that represents a thought, idea, or "message" to be conveyed to a listener, who must then **decode** the signal to arrive at a similar message. It is more difficult to devise experiments that provide information on how the speaker proceeds than to do so from the listener's side of the process. The best information has come from observing and analyzing spontaneous speech.

Planning Units

We might suppose that the thoughts of the speaker are simply "translated" into words one after the other through a semantic mapping process. Grammatical morphemes would be added as demanded by the syntactic rules of the language. The phonetic representation of each word in turn would then be mapped onto the neuromuscular commands to the articulators to produce the acoustic signal representing it.

We know, however, that this supposition is not a true picture of speech production. Although, when we speak, the sounds we produce and the words we use are linearly ordered, speech errors show that the prearticulation stages involve units larger than the single phonemic segment or even the word, as illustrated by the *U.S. Acres* cartoon. Phrases and even whole sentences are constructed prior to the production of a single sound. Errors show that features, segments, and words can be **anticipated,** that is, produced earlier than intended, or reversed (as in typical spoonerisms), so the later words or phrases in which they occur must already be conceptualized. This point is illustrated in the following examples (the intended utterance to the left of the arrow, the actual utterance, including the error, to the right of the arrow).

1. The *h*iring of minority *f*aculty. → The *f*iring of minority faculty.
   (The intended *h* is replaced by the *f* of *faculty,* which occurs later in the intended utterance.)
2. *a*d ho*c* → *o*dd ha*c*k
   (The vowels /æ/ of the first word and /a/ of the second are exchanged or reversed.)
3. *b*ig and *f*at → *p*ig and *v*at (The values of a single feature are switched:
   [+ voiced] becomes [− voiced] in *big* and [− voiced] becomes [+ voiced] in *fat.*)
4. There are many ministers in our church. → There are many churches in our minister.
   (The stem morphemes *minister* and *church* are exchanged; the grammatical plural morpheme remains in its intended place in the phrase structure.)
5. Seymour sliced the salami with a knife. → Seymour sliced a knife with the salami.
   (The entire noun phrases—article + noun—were exchanged.)

In these errors, the intonation contour (primary stressed syllables and variations in pitch) remained the same as in the intended utterances, even when the words were disordered. In the intended utterance of (5), the highest pitch would be on *knife*. In the disordered sentence the highest pitch occurred on the second syllable of *salami*. The pitch rise and increased loudness are thus determined by the syntactic structure of the sentence and are independent of the individual words. Thus syntactic structures also are units in linguistic performance.

Errors like those cited above are constrained in interesting ways. Phonological errors involving segments or features, as in (1), (2), and (3), primarily occur in content words, and not in grammatical morphemes, again showing the distinction between these lexical classes. In addition, while words and lexical morphemes may be reversed (exchanged), grammatical morphemes, bound inflectional affixes or free, are not exchanged. As example (4) illustrates, the inflectional endings are "stranded," left behind and subsequently attached, in their proper phonological form, to the moved lexical morpheme.

Such errors show that speech production involves different kinds of units—features, segments, morphemes, words, phrases, the very units that exist in the grammar. They also show that when we speak, words are structured into larger syntactic phrases that are stored in a kind of buffer memory before segments or features or words are disordered. This storage must occur prior to the articulatory stage. Thus, we do not select one word from our mental dictionary and say it, then select another word and say it. We organize an entire phrase and in many cases an entire sentence.

The constraints on which units can be exchanged or moved also suggest that grammatical morphemes are added at a stage after the lexical morphemes are selected. This provided one of the motivations for a two-lexicon grammatical model proposed by Chris Colston, one with lexical and derivational morphemes listed, and the other with inflectional and grammatical morphemes.[11]

Lexical Selection

> . . . Humpty Dumpty's theory, of two meanings packed into one word like a portmanteau, seems to me the right explanation for all. For instance, take the two words "fuming" and "furious." Make up your mind that you will say both words but leave it unsettled which you will say first. Now open your mouth and speak. If . . . you have that rarest of gifts, a perfectly balanced mind, you will say "frumious."
>
> Lewis Carroll, *Preface to The Hunting of the Snark*

In Chapter 4, word substitution errors were used to illustrate the semantic properties of words. Such substitutions are seldom random; they show that in speaking, in our attempt to express our thoughts through words in the lexicon, we may make an incorrect lexical selection based on partial similarity or relatedness of meanings.

Blends, in which we produce part of one word and part of another, further illustrate the lexical selection process in speech production; we may select two or more words to express our thoughts and instead of deciding between them, produce them

[11]Chris Golston, *Both Lexicons,* UCLA Ph.D. dissertation, 1991.

as "portmanteaus," as Humpty Dumpty calls them. Such blends are illustrated in the following errors:

1. splinters/blisters→ splisters
2. edited/annotated→ editated
3. a swinging/hip chick→ a swip chick
4. frown/scowl→ frowl

Application and Misapplication of Rules

> I thought . . . four rules would be enough, provided that I made a firm and constant resolution not to fail even once in the observance of them.
>
> René Descartes (1596–1650)

Spontaneous errors show that the rules of morphology and syntax, discussed in earlier chapters as part of competence, may also be applied (or misapplied) when we speak. It is hard to see this process in normal error-free speech, but when someone says *groupment* instead of *grouping, ambigual* instead of *ambiguous,* or *bloodent* instead of *bloody,* it shows that regular rules are applied to morphemes to form possible but nonexistent words.

Inflectional rules also surface. The UCLA professor who said *We swimmed in the pool* knows that the past tense of *swim* is *swam* but mistakenly applied the regular rule to an irregular form.

Morphophonemic rules also appear to be performance rules as well as rules of competence. Consider the *a/an* alternation rule in English. Errors such as *an istem* for the intended *a system* or *a burly bird* for the intended *an early bird* show that when segmental disordering changes a noun beginning with a consonant to a noun beginning with a vowel, or vice versa, the indefinite article is also changed so that it conforms to the grammatical rule.

Such utterances also reveal that in speech production, internal "editing" or monitoring attempts to prevent errors. When an error slips by the editor, such as the disordering of phonemes, the editor prevents a compounding of errors. Thus, when the /b/ of "bird" was anticipated and added to the beginning of "early" the result was not *an burly bird*. The editor applied (or reapplied) the *a/an* rule to produce *a burly bird*.

An examination of such data also tells us something about the stages in the production of an utterance. Disordering of phonemes must occur before the indefinite article is given its phonological form or the morphological rule must reapply after the initial error has occurred. An error such as *bin beg* for the intended *Big Ben* shows that phonemes are disordered before phonetic allophones are determined. That is, the intended *Big Ben* phonetically is [bɪg bɛ̃n] with an oral [ɪ] before the [g] and a nasal [ɛ̃] before the [n]. In the utterance that was produced, however, the [ɪ̃] is nasalized because it now occurs before the disordered [n], whereas the [ɛ] is oral before the disordered [g]. If the disordering occurred after the phonemes had been replaced by phonetic allophones, the result would have been the phonetic utterance [bɪn bɛ̃g].

Nonlinguistic Influences

The discussion on speech comprehension suggested that nonlinguistic factors are involved in and sometimes interfere with linguistic processing. They also affect speech production . The individual who said *He made hairlines* instead of *He made headlines* was referring to a barber. The fact that the two compound nouns both start with the same sound, are composed of two syllables, have the same stress pattern, and contain the identical second morphemes undoubtedly played a role in producing the error; but the relationship between hairlines and barbers may also have been a contributing factor.

Other errors show that thoughts unrelated structurally to the intended utterance may have an influence on what is said. One speaker said "I've never heard of classes *on April 9*" instead of the intended *on Good Friday*. Good Friday fell on April 9 that year. The two phrases are not similar phonologically or morphologically; yet the nonlinguistic association seems to have influenced what was said. This influence is a further example of the distinction between linguistic competence and performance.

The more we look at the brain/mind/language interface, the more we find that knowledge and processing of language are separate from the ability to acquire and process other kinds of knowledge. Furthermore, the asymmetry between general knowledge and linguistic knowledge supports the view that language is independent of general intellectual ability, and that language and other cognitive systems are distinct both anatomically and functionally.

Summary

The attempt to understand what makes human language acquisition and use possible has led to research on the brain-mind-language relationship. **Neurolinguistics** studies the brain mechanisms and anatomical structures underlying language representation and use. **Psycholinguistics** is concerned with the psychological processes involved in linguistic performance—speech comprehension and production.

The brain is the most complicated organ of the body, controlling motor and sensory activities and thought processes. Research conducted for over a century reveals that different parts of the brain control different body functions. The nerve cells that form the surface of the brain are called the **cortex,** which serves as the intellectual decision maker, receiving messages from the sensory organs and initiating all voluntary actions. The brain of all higher animals is divided into two parts called the **cerebral hemispheres,** which are connected by the **corpus callosum,** a pathway that permits the left and right hemispheres to communicate with each other.

Although each hemisphere appears to be a mirror image of the other, the left hemisphere controls the right hand, leg, visual field, and so on, and the right brain controls the left side of the body. Despite this seeming symmetry, there is much evidence that the left and right hemispheres are specialized for different functions. Evidence from **aphasia**—language disfunction as a result of brain injuries—and from surgical removal of parts of the brain, electrical stimulation studies, emission tomography results, dichotic listening, and experiments measuring brain electrical activity show a lack of symmetry of function of the two hemispheres. These results are further supported by studies of split-brain patients, who, for medical reasons, have had the corpus callosum severed.

For normal right-handers and many left-handers, the left side of the brain appears to be specialized for language. This **lateralization** of functions is genetically and neurologically conditioned.

Aphasia studies show impairment of different parts of the grammar. Patients with **Broca's aphasia** exhibit impaired syntax and speech problems, whereas **Wernicke's aphasia** patients are fluent speakers who produce semantically empty utterances and have difficulty in comprehension. **Anomia** is a form of aphasia in which the patient has word-finding difficulties. **Jargon aphasia** patients may substitute words unrelated semantically to their intended messages; others produce phonemic substitution errors, sometimes resulting in nonsense forms, making their utterances uninterpretable.

The evolution of the human brain is related to the development of language in the human species. Some scholars suggest that this occurred simultaneously, and that from the start the human animal was innately equipped to learn language. Studies of the evolutionary development of the brain provide some evidence for physiological, anatomic, and "mental" preconditions for language development.

Psycholinguistics is concerned with linguistic **performance** or **processing,** the use of linguistic knowledge (competence) in speech **production** and **comprehension.**

Comprehension, the process of understanding an utterance, requires the ability to access the mental lexicon to match the words in the utterance we are listening to with their meanings. In addition, to get the full meaning of an utterance we must **syntactically parse** the string into syntactic structures, since meaning depends on word order, constituent structure, and so on, in addition to the meaning of words. Some psycholinguists believe we utilize both **top-down** and **bottom-up** processes during comprehension. Top-down processing uses semantic and syntactic information in addition to the incoming acoustic signal; bottom-up processes utilize only information contained in the sensory input.

Psycholinguistic experimental studies are aimed at uncovering the stages and processes involved in linguistic performance. A number of experimental techniques have proved to be very helpful. In a **shadowing** task, subjects repeat what is being said to them as fast as possible; they often correct errors in the stimulus sentence suggesting that they use linguistic knowledge rather than simply echoing the sounds they hear. The measurement of **response times** in **priming, naming,** and **lexical decision** tasks show that it takes longer to comprehend ambiguous utterances, ungrammatical compared to grammatical sentences, nonsense forms as opposed to real words. We also appear to access all the meanings of a word despite the context of a previously heard sentence which should disambiguate the meanings. Other experiments reveal the processes involved in accessing the mental grammar and the influence of nonlinguistic factors in comprehension.

The units and stages in **speech production** have been studied by analyzing spontaneously produced speech errors. **Anticipation** errors in which a sound is produced earlier than in the intended utterance and **spoonerisms,** in which sounds or words are **exchanged** or reversed show that we do not produce one sound or one word or even one phrase at a time but construct and store larger units with their syntactic structures specified prior to mapping these linguistic structures on to neuromuscular commands to the articulators. In producing speech, we select words from the mental lexicon whose meanings partially express the thoughts we wish to convey. Word **substitutions** and **blends** may occur showing that words are connected to other words phonologically and semantically. The production of ungrammatical utterances also shows that morphological, inflectional, and syntactic rules may be wrongly applied or fail to apply when we speak, but at the same time show that such rules are actually involved in speech production.

References for Further Reading

Blumstein, S. 1973. *A Phonological Investigation of Aphasic Speech.* Janua Linguarum Series, 153. The Hague: Mouton.

Caplan, D. 1987. *Neurolinguistics and Linguistic Aphasiology.* Cambridge, England: Cambridge University Press.

Carroll, D.W. 1986. *Psychology of Language.* Monterey, Calif.: Brooks/Cole Publishing Co.

Coltheart, M., K. Patterson, and J.C. Marshall, (eds.). 1980. *Deep Dyslexia.* London, England: Routledge & Kegan Paul.

Fodor, J.A., M. Garrett, and T.G. Bever. 1986. *The Psychology of Language.* New York: McGraw-Hill.

Fromkin, V.A. (ed.). 1980. *Errors in Linguistic Performance.* New York: Academic Press.

Damasio, H. 1981. "Cerebral Localization of the Aphasias," in *Acquired Aphasia,* M. Taylor Sarno (ed.), New York: Academic Press, pp. 27–65.

Gardner, H. 1978. "What We Know (and Don't Know) About the Two Halves of the Brain." *Harvard Magazine* 80: 24–27.

Garnham, A. 1985. *Psycholinguistics: Central Topics.* London and New York: Methuen.

Garrett, M.F. 1988. "Processes in Sentence Production," in F. Newmeyer (ed.), *The Cambridge Linguistic Survey,* Vol 3, Cambridge, England: Cambridge University Press.

Gazzaniga, M.S. 1970. *The Bisected Brain.* New York: Appleton-Century-Crofts.

Geschwind, N. 1979. "Specializations of the Human Brain." *Scientific American,* September, 206: 180–199.

Grodzinsky, Y. (1990) *Theoretical Perspectives on Language Deficits.* Cambridge, Mass.: A Bradford Book. MIT Press.

Lieberman, P. 1975. *On the Origins of Language.* New York: Macmillan.

Lenneberg, Eric H. 1967. *Biological Foundations of Language.* New York: Wiley.

Lesser, R. 1978. *Linguistic Investigation of Aphasia.* New York: Elsevier.

Newcombe, F., and J.C. Marshall. 1972. "World Retrieval in Aphasia." *International Journal of Mental Health* 1:38–45.

Springer, S.P., and G. Deutsch. 1981. *Left Brain, Right Brain.* San Francisco, Calif.: W.H. Freeman.

Yamada, J. 1990. *Laura: A Case for the Modularity of Language.* Cambridge, Mass.: A Bradford Book. MIT Press.

Exercises

1. The Nobel Prize laureate Roger Sperry has argued that split brain patients have two minds:

> Everything we have seen so far indicates that the surgery has left these people with two separate minds, that is, two separate spheres of consciousness. What is experienced in the right hemisphere seems to lie entirely outside the realm of experience of the left hemisphere.

Another Nobel Prize winner in physiology, Sir John Eccles, disagrees. He does not think the right hemisphere can think; he distinguishes between "mere consciousness," which animals possess as well as humans, and language, thought, and other purely human cognitive abilities. In fact, according to him, the human aspect of human nature is all in the left hemisphere.

Write a short essay discussing these two opposing points of view, stating your own opinion on how to define "the mind."

2. A. Some aphasic patients, when asked to read a list of words, substitute other words for those printed. In many cases there are similarities between the printed words and the substituted words. The data given below are from actual aphasic patients. In each case state what the two words have in common and how they differ:

Printed Word	Word Spoken by Aphasic
a. liberty	freedom
canary	parrot
abroad	overseas
large	long
short	small
tall	long
b. decide	decision
conceal	concealment
portray	portrait
bathe	bath
speak	discussion
remember	memory

B. What do the words in groups a and b reveal about how words are likely to be stored in the brain?

3. The following are some sentences spoken by aphasic patients, collected and analyzed by Dr. Harry Whitaker of the University of Maryland. In each case state how the sentence deviates from normal nonaphasic language.

    a. There is under a horse a new sidesaddle.

    b. In girls we see many happy days.

    c. I'll challenge a new bike.

    d. I surprise no new glamor.

    e. Is there three chairs in this room?

    f. Mike and Peter is happy.

    g. Bill and John likes hot dogs.

    h. Proliferate is a complete time about a word that is correct.

    i. Went came in better than it did before.

4. A young patient at the Division of Neuropsychology of the Radcliffe Infirmary, Oxford, England, following a head injury, appears to have lost the spelling-to-pronunciation and phonetic-to-spelling rules that most of us can use to read and write new words or nonsense strings. He also is unable to get to the phonemic representation of words in his lexicon. Consider the following examples of his reading pronunciation and his writing from dictation.

Reading Pronunciation		Writing from Dictation
fame	/fæmi/	FAM
café	/sæfi/	KAFA
time	/tajmi/	TIM
note	/noti/ or /nɔti/	NOT
praise	/pra-aj-si/	PRAZ
treat	/tri - æt/	TRET
goes	/go-ɛs/	GOZ
float	/flɔ-æt/	FLOT

His reading and writing errors are not random, but rule governed. See if you can figure out the rules he uses to relate his (spelling) orthography to his pronunciation.

5. Speech errors, commonly referred to as "slips of the tongue" or "bloopers," illustrate a difference between linguistic competence and performance since our very recognition of them as errors shows that we have knowledge of well formed sentences. Furthermore, errors provide information about the grammar. The utterances listed below were actually produced deviations from the speakers' intended utterances. They are part of the UCLA corpus of over 15,000 speech errors, plus a few from Dr. Spooner.

    (a) For each speech error, state what kind of linguistic unit or rule is involved, that is, phonological, morphological, syntactic, lexical, or semantic.

    (b) State, to the best of your ability, the nature of the error, or the mechanisms which produced it.

(*Note:* the intended utterance is to the left of the arrow; the actual utterance to the right)

example: ad hoc→odd hack
          (a) phonological vowel segment   (b) reversal or exchange of
                                                      segments.

example: she gave it away→she gived it away
          (a) inflectional morphology   (b) incorrect application of
                                                        regular past tense rule to
                                                         exceptional verb

example: When will you leave?→When you will leave?
          (a) syntactic rule   (b) failure to "move the
                                                     auxiliary" to form a
                                                         question.

(1) brake fluid→blake fruid

(2) drink is the curse of the working classes→work is the curse of the drinking classes. (Spooner)

(3) we have many ministers in our church→ . . . many churches in our minister

(4) untactful→distactful

(5) an eating marathon→a meeting arathon

(6) executive committee→executor committee

(7) lady with the dachshund→lady with the Volkswagen

(8) stick in the mud→smuck in the tid

(9) he broke the crystal on my watch→he broke the whistle on my crotch

(10) a phonological rule→a phonological fool

(11) pitch and stress→piss and stretch

(12) big and fat→pig and vat

(13) speech production→preach seduction

(14) he's a New Yorker→he's a New Yorkan

(15) I'd forgotten about that→I'd forgot abouten that

PART 5
Language in the Computer Age

We should acknowledge that computers are not just another product of industrial society. They are not like automobiles, cameras, or telephones, which represent extensions of human physical or sensory capabilities. Computers are information processing systems. They manipulate symbols, and thus resemble us more closely in what we see as our essential being: a thinking person. In computers . . . we recognize . . . a new kind of intelligence different from ours, in some ways more powerful and in others much more limited. . . . We did not ask for this new world. But it is the opportunity of our generation to seize the computer revolution, make it ours, and bring it forth for the good of all humanity.

Heinz R. Pagels, "Introduction," *Annals of the New York Academy of Sciences,* Vol. 426, 1984.

Further information processing must be able to handle Japanese, English, and other natural languages. This is one of the core themes of artificial intelligence and at the same time, an area of linguistics: deep relations exist between theoretical linguistics and computers.

Kazuhiro Fuchi, "Fifth Generation Computers: Some Theoretical Issues,"
Annals of the New York Academy of Sciences, Vol. 426, 1984.

CHAPTER 12
Computer Processing of Human Language

BIZARRO by Dan Piraro. Copyright © 1991 by Chronicle Features. Reprinted by permission.

Throughout history only human beings have had the capability to process language. Today, it is common for computers to process language. **Computational Linguistics** is a subfield of linguistics and computer science that is concerned with computer processing of human language. It includes automatic machine translation of one language into another, the analysis of written texts and spoken discourse, the use of language for communication between people and computers, computer modeling of linguistic theories, and the role of human language in artificial intelligence.

Machine Translation

Egad, I think the interpreter is the hardest to be understood of the two!

R. B. Sheridan, *The Critic*

. . . There exist extremely simple sentences in English—and . . . for any other natural language—which would be uniquely . . . and unambiguously translated into any other language by anyone with a sufficient knowledge of the two languages involved, though I know of no program that would enable a machine to come up with this unique rendering. . . .

Yeshua Bar-Hillel

The first use of computers for natural language processing began in the 1940s with the attempt to develop **Automatic Machine Translation.** During World War II, United States scientists without the assistance of computers deciphered coded Japanese military communications and proved their skill in coping with difficult language problems. The idea of using deciphering techniques to translate from one language into another was expressed in a letter written to Norbert Wiener by Warren Weaver, a pioneer in the field of computational linguistics: "When I look at any article in Russian, I say: 'This is really written in English, but it has been coded in some strange symbols. I will now proceed to decode.' "[1]

The aim in automatic translation is to "feed" into the computer a written passage in the **source language** (the input) and to receive a grammatical passage of equivalent meaning in the **target language** (the output). In the early days of machine translation, it was believed that this task could be accomplished by entering into the memory of a computer a dictionary of a source language and a dictionary with the corresponding morphemes and words of a target language. The "translation" decoding program consisted of "matching" the morphemes of the input sentence with those of the target language. Unfortunately, what often happened was a process called by early machine translators "language in, garbage out."

Translation is more than word-for-word replacement. Often there is no equivalent word in the target language, and the order of words may differ, as in translating from a Subject-Verb-Object (SVO) language like English to a Subject-Object-Verb (SOV) language like Japanese. There is also difficulty in translating idioms, metaphors, jargon, and so on.

These problems are dealt with by human translators because they know the grammars of the two languages and draw on general knowledge of the subject matter and the world to arrive at the intended meaning. Machine translation is often impeded by lexical and syntactic ambiguities, structural disparities between the two languages, morphological complexities, and other cross-linguistic differences. It is

---

[1]W. N. Locke and A. D. Boothe (eds.), *Machine Translation of Languages,* New York: Wiley, 1955.

often difficult to get good translations even when humans do the translating, as is illustrated by some of the "garbage" printed on signs in non-English-speaking countries as "aids" to tourists:

> Utmost of chicken with smashed pot (restaurant in Greece)
> Nervous meatballs (restaurant in Bulgaria)
> The nuns harbor all diseases and have no respect for religion (Swiss nunnery hospital)
> All the water has been passed by the manager (German hotel)
> Certified midwife: entrance sideways (Jerusalem)

Such "translations" represent the difficulties of just finding the "equivalent" words; but word choice is a minor problem in automatic translation. The syntactic problems are more complex.

The greater recognition of the role of syntax and the application of linguistic principles over the past forty years have made it possible to use computers to translate "simple" texts grammatically and accurately between well-studied languages such as English and Russian. More complex texts require human intervention if the translation is to be grammatical and semantically faithful. The use of computers to aid the human translator can improve efficiency by a factor of ten or more, but the day when travelers can whip out a "pocket translator," hold it up to the mouth of a native speaker, and receive a translation in their own language is as yet beyond the horizon.

Text Processing

> [The professor had written] all the words of their language in their several moods, tenses and declensions [on tiny blocks of wood, and had] emptied the whole vocabulary into his frame, and made the strictest computation of the general proportion there is in books between the numbers of particles, nouns, and verbs, and other parts of speech.
>
> Jonathan Swift, *Gulliver's Travels*

Jonathan Swift prophesied one way computers would be put to work in linguistics—in the statistical analysis of language. Computers can be programmed to reveal such properties of language as the distribution of sounds, allowable word orders, permitted combinations of morphemes, relative frequencies of words and morphemes (that is, their "general proportion"), and so on.

Such analyses can be conducted on existing texts (such as the works of Shakespeare or the Bible) or on a collection of utterances gathered from spoken or written sources, called a **corpus.** One such corpus, compiled at Brown University, consists of over one million words from fifteen sources of written American English, including passages from daily newspapers, magazines, and literary material.[2] Because this corpus is available in computer-readable form, many scholars are able to use it in their research.

A corpus of *spoken* American English, similar in size to the Brown corpus, was also collected.[3] A computer analysis of this corpus was conducted and the result was compared with the Brown corpus, which provided a contrast between written and spoken American English. Not surprisingly, the pronoun *I* occurs ten times more frequently in the spoken corpus. Profane and taboo words are, as expected, more frequent in spoken language; *shit* occurs 128 times in the spoken corpus, but only four times in the written one. All of the prepositions except *to* occur more frequently in written than in spoken English, suggesting that different syntactic structures are used in written English than in spoken English.

A computer can also be used to produce a **concordance** of a literary text, which gives the frequency of every word in a text and the line and page number of each occurrence. Such analyses, once carried out painstakingly over many years, were only produced for the most eminent of texts (such as the Bible). Now a concordance can be accomplished in a short time on any text that has been entered into a computer. The use of concordances on *The Federalist Papers* helped ascribe the authorship of a disputed paper to James Madison rather than to Alexander Hamilton, by comparing the concordance of the paper in question with those of known works by the two writers.

A concordance of *sounds* by computer may reveal patterns in poetry that would be nearly impossible for a human to detect. Such an analysis on the *Iliad* showed that many of the lines with an unusual number of etas (/i/) related to youth and lovemaking; the line with the most alphas (/a/) was interpreted as being an imitation of stamping feet.

Poetic and prosaic features such as assonance, alliteration, meter, and rhythm have always been studied by literary scholars. Today, computers can do the tedious mechanical work of such analyses, leaving the human more time to contemplate new ideas.

Computers That Talk and Listen

The first generations of computers had received their inputs through glorified typewriter keyboards, and had replied through high-speed printers and visual displays. Hal could do this when necessary, but most of his communication with his shipmates was by means of the spoken words. Poole and Bowman could talk to Hal as if he were a human being, and he would reply in the perfect idiomatic English he had learned during the fleeting weeks of his electronic childhood.

Arthur C. Clarke, *2001, A Space Odyssey*

---

[2]H. Kučera and W. N. Francis, *Computational Analysis of Present-Day American English,* Providence, R.I.: Brown University Press, 1967.
[3]H. Dahl, *Word Frequencies of Spoken American English,* Essex, Ct.: Verbatim, 1979.

The ideal computer is multilingual; it should "speak" computer languages such as FORTRAN and human languages such as English. For many purposes it would be helpful if we could communicate with computers as we communicate with other humans, through our native language; but the computers portrayed in films and on television as capable of speaking and understanding human language do not yet exist.

Computers are at present severely limited in their ability to comprehend and produce spoken language, and programming them to do so is one of the most difficult and challenging goals of computational linguistics. Properly programmed, a computer can "understand" language fragments with vocabularies of 100 to 1000 words in an extremely narrow context (simple syntax and a limited semantic field). (The vocabulary can be larger for written language.) Computers can produce synthetic speech that imitates the human voice fairly well, but humans must program them to do it and tell them what to say.

Just as human speech production and comprehension differ in the psychological mechanisms involved (although they access the same mental grammar), comprehension and production of speech by computers require entirely different programs. In some cases the attempt is to model the human processor; in others, the goal is to get the computer to speak and understand, rather than to shed light on human performance.

Computer comprehension consists of **speech recognition,** the perception of sounds and words, and **speech understanding,** the interpretation of the words recognized. Some comprehension programs bypass speech recognition by processing written text. Visual scanners are able to "read" printed texts.

Speech production consists of **language generation**—deciding what to say— and **speech synthesis,** the actual creation of speech sounds. As in attempts at computer comprehension, different research groups concentrate on one aspect or another of speech production, and with different purposes.

The Speech Signal

> Be a craftsman in speech that you may be strong, for the strength of one is
> the tongue, and speech is mightier than all fighting.
>
> Ptahhotep, *Maxims* (c. 3400 B.C.E.)

Human beings generally have no difficulty producing and understanding the speech of any language they know. Computers have no innate capacity to acquire language as do humans; they must be carefully programmed for speech production or synthesis, and for speech perception or recognition. This task requires an understanding of the **speech signal,** an **acoustic signal** produced by speakers.

In Chapter 5 speech sounds were described according to the ways in which they are produced—the position of the tongue, the lips, and the velum, the state of the vocal cords, the airstream mechanisms, whether the articulators obstruct the free flow of air, and so on. All of these articulatory characteristics are reflected in the physical characteristics of the sounds produced.

Speech sounds can also be described in physical or **acoustic** terms. Physically, a sound is produced whenever there is a disturbance in the position of air molecules. The question asked by ancient philosophers as to whether a sound is produced if a tree falls in the middle of the forest with no one to "hear" it has been answered by the science of acoustics. Objectively, a sound is produced; subjectively, there is no sound. In fact, there are sounds we cannot hear because our ears are not sensitive to all changes in air pressure (which result from the movement of air molecules). Acoustic phonetics is concerned only with speech sounds, all of which can be heard by the normal human ear.

When we push air out of the lungs through the glottis, it causes the vocal cords to vibrate; this vibration in turn produces pulses of air, which escape through the mouth (and sometimes also the nose). These pulses are actually small variations in the air pressure, due to the wavelike motion of the air molecules.

The sounds we produce can be described in terms of how fast the variations of the air pressure occur, which determines the **fundamental frequency** of the sounds and is perceived by the hearer as **pitch.** We can also describe the magnitude or **intensity** of the variations, which determines the **loudness** of the sound. The **quality** of the sound is determined by the kind of vibrations, or **wave form,** which is determined by the shape of the vocal tract when the air is flowing through it.

An important tool in acoustic research is a machine called a **sound spectrograph.** When you speak into a microphone connected to this machine (or when a tape recording is plugged in), a "picture" is made of the speech signal. The patterns produced are called **spectrograms** or, more vividly, "visible speech." More recently these pictures have been referred to as **voiceprints.** A spectrogram of the words *heed, head, had,* and *who'd* is shown in Figure 12–1.

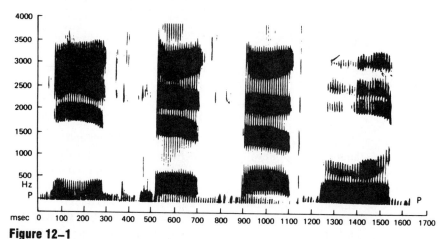

Figure 12–1

A spectrogram of the words *heed, head, had,* and *who'd,* as spoken with a British accent (Speaker: Peter Ladefoged, February 16, 1973).

Time in milliseconds moves horizontally from left to right; vertically, the "graph" represents pitch (or, more technically, frequency). Notice that for each vowel there are a number of dark bands that differ in their placement according to their pitch. They represent the **overtones** produced by the shape of the vocal tract and are called the **formants** of the vowels. Because the tongue is in a different position for each vowel, the formant frequencies, or overtone pitches, differ for each vowel. It is the different frequencies of these formants that account for the different vowel qualities you hear. The pitch of the entire utterance (intonation contour) is shown by the "voicing bar" marked *P* on the spectrogram. When the striations are far apart, the vocal cords are vibrating slowly and the pitch is low; when the striations are close together, the vocal cords are vibrating rapidly and the pitch is high.

By studying spectrograms of all speech sounds and many different utterances, acoustic phoneticians have learned a great deal about the basic acoustic components that reflect the articulatory features of speech sounds. For speech synthesis, then, a computer must simulate electronically the wave forms of the speech sounds it wishes to "utter."

Talking Machines (Speech Synthesis)

Machines which, with more or less success, imitate human speech, are the most difficult to construct, so many are the agencies engaged in uttering even a single word—so many are the inflections and variations of tone and articulation, that the mechanician finds his ingenuity taxed to the utmost to imitate them.

Scientific American, January 14, 1871

DOONESBURY copyright 1982 and 1984 G. B. Trudeau. Reprinted with permission of Universal Press Syndicate. All rights reserved.

Early efforts toward building "talking machines" were more concerned with machines that could produce sounds that imitated human speech than with machines that could figure out what to say. In 1779, Christian Gottlieb Kratzenstein won a prize for building such a machine ("an instrument constructed like the *vox humana* pipes of an organ which . . . accurately express the sounds of the vowels") and for answering a question posed by the Imperial Academy of St. Petersburg: "What is the nature and character of the sounds of the vowels *a, e, i, o, u* [which make them] different from one another?" Kratzenstein constructed a set of "acoustic resonators" similar to the shapes of the mouth when these vowels are articulated and set them resonating by a vibrating reed that produced pulses of air similar to those coming from the lungs through the vibrating vocal cords.

Twelve years later, Wolfgang von Kempelen of Vienna constructed a more elaborate machine with bellows to produce a stream of air such as is produced by the lungs, and with other mechanical devices to "simulate" the different parts of the vocal tract. Von Kempelen's machine so impressed the young Alexander Graham Bell, who saw a replica of the machine in Edinburgh in 1850, that he, together with his brother Melville, attempted to construct a "talking head," making a cast from a human skull. They used various materials to form the velum, palate, teeth, lips, tongue, cheeks, and so on, and installed a metal larynx with vocal cords made by stretching a slotted piece of rubber. They used a keyboard control system to manipulate all the parts with an intricate set of levers. This ingenious machine produced vowel sounds and some nasal sounds and even a few short combinations of sounds.

With the advances in the acoustic theory of speech production and the technological developments in electronics, machine production of speech sounds has made great progress. We no longer have to build actual physical models of the speech-producing mechanism; we can now imitate the process by producing the physical signals electronically.

Research on speech has shown that all speech sounds can be reduced to a small number of acoustic components. One way to produce artificial or **synthetic** speech is to mix these important parts together in the proper proportions, depending on the speech sounds to be imitated. It is rather like following a recipe for making soup, which might read: "Take two quarts of water, add one onion, three carrots, a potato, a teaspoon of salt, a pinch of pepper, and stir it all together."

This method of producing synthetic speech would include a "recipe" that might read:

1. Start with a tone at the same frequency as vibrating vocal cords (higher if a woman's or child's voice is being synthesized, lower for a man's).
2. Add overtones corresponding to the formants required for a particular vowel quality.
3. Add hissing or buzzing for fricatives.
4. Add nasal resonances for any nasal sounds.
5. Temporarily cut off sound to produce stops and affricates.
6. and so on. . . .

All these "ingredients" are blended together electronically, using computers to produce highly intelligible, more or less natural-sounding speech.

Most synthetic speech still has a machinelike quality or "accent," due to small inaccuracies in simulation and because suprasegmental factors such as changing intonation and stress patterns are not yet fully understood. Still, speech synthesizers today are no harder to understand than a person speaking with a slight "accent."

Of course, the machine used to produce synthetic speech does not "know" what it is saying. It may be reading a text, a useful function for persons unable to read for some reason, but this employs no linguistic knowledge of syntax or semantics. Speech synthesis in the future can be highly beneficial to mute patients with laryngectomies, advanced multiple sclerosis, or other medical conditions that prevent normal speech production.

When a computer produces synthetic speech it produces speech sounds corresponding to the input text it is "reading." It must be programmed with a complex set of text-to-speech rules that translate texts written in English orthography into a phonetic transcription from which speech sounds are synthesized and produced. Since, in its synthesis program, the computer uses no semantic or syntactic knowledge (even if such information has been put into its memory), it will read ungrammatical and nonsensical texts as easily (or as poorly) as grammatical ones.

Speech synthesis has important applications. It benefits blind persons in the form of "reading machines," now commercially available. Mute patients with laryngectomies or other medical conditions that prevent normal speech can use synthesizers to express themselves. For example, Eva K. Simmons at North Carolina State University developed a communication system for an individual with so severe a form of multiple sclerosis that he could utter no sound, and was totally paralyzed except for nodding his head. Using a head movement for "yes," and its absence as "no," this individual could select words displayed on a computer screen and assemble sentences expressing his thoughts, which were then "spoken" by a synthesizer.

Most of us these days hear synthesized speech when we call our bank and an "automatic bank clerk" tells us our bank balance, or when a telephone information "operator" gives us a requested phone number. You will have to decide for yourself if this is a benefit.

Knowing What To Say

> Speech was given to the ordinary sort of men whereby to communicate their mind; but to wise men, whereby to conceal it.
>
> Robert South, *Sermon* (1676)

PATIENT: Men are all alike.
  ELIZA: In what way?
PATIENT: They're always bugging me about something or other.
  ELIZA: Can you think of a specific example?
PATIENT: Well, my boyfriend made me come here.
  ELIZA: Your boyfriend made you come here?
PATIENT: He says I'm depressed much of the time.
  ELIZA: I am sorry to hear you are depressed.

Joseph Weizenbaum, *Eliza*

When a computer is "reading" a text it knows what to say, but in many applications the computer is called upon not only to speak, but to decide what to say, and to do so grammatically. This is the problem called **language generation.**

In the dialogue at the head of this section, ELIZA is a computer program designed to simulate a nondirective psychiatrist talking to a patient. ELIZA has a collection of "canned" phrases stored in memory such as "In what way?" or "Tell me more" that help keep the conversation going when it doesn't "understand" the patient. When ELIZA recognizes certain syntactic patterns, however, it turns them around to make a sensible response, as when it echoes "Your boyfriend made you come here?" ELIZA was programmed with a small bit of syntactic knowledge allowing it to make grammatical utterances based on the patient's statements, but no semantic knowledge at all. If a patient says "My sniggle is untherible" ELIZA would respond with "How long has your sniggle been untherible?"

In other applications the computer is given bits of knowledge in computer-digestible form (for example, the day's baseball scores), and then programmed to state that knowledge in fluent, grammatically and semantically correct language (for example, a report of the baseball scores on the news). This program requires adherence to the rules of syntax and semantics, as well as morphology and phonetics. In some sense the machine "knows" what it is saying, because if you changed the bits of knowledge fed to it, the statement of that knowledge would change too, providing it were correctly programmed. The most sophisticated language generation programs allow the computer to converse with a human. One such application is for repairing electronic circuits. The computer is programmed with knowledge of the circuit, and a method to enable it to understand and speak phrases and sentences within the context of the repair problem. The following dialogue was observed on one such system:[4]

> COMPUTER: This is the circuit fix-it shop. How may I help you?
> TECHNICIAN: I need to fix the RS111 circuit.
> COMPUTER: I am familiar with that circuit. The l.e.d. is supposed to be display-ing alternately blinking one and seven.
> TECHNICIAN: Where is the l.e.d.?
> COMPUTER: In the middle right of the blue region is the l.e.d.
> TECHNICIAN: No light.
> COMPUTER: What is the switch at when the l.e.d. is off?
> TECHNICIAN: The switch is down.
> COMPUTER: Put the switch up.

Once the computer has understood the technician's utterance, it uses rules of semantics and syntax, together with a lexicon of words and morphemes, to formulate a grammatical, sensible response, which its synthesizer program then speaks. The rules in many cases are similar to the phrase structure rules seen in Chapter 3, such as form a noun phrase from an article followed by a noun. It also has semantic rules that tells it to use *the* with the word *switch* since its "world knowledge" tells it that there is only one switch in that particular circuit.

---

[4]The system was developed at Duke University in collaboration with North Carolina State University.

Unlike a human, though, if the technician used unusual or complex syntax, the computer would be unable to answer because the grammar with which it is programmed is incomplete, as is any computer grammar. Similarly if the technician suddenly changed the subject and asked the computer "Who won the game last night?" or "How much is two plus two?" the computer would be stumped since both its world knowledge and linguistic knowledge are confined to the narrow realm of repairing circuits.

Machines for Understanding Speech

By permission of Johnny Hart and Creators Syndicate, Inc.

Understanding is a relative concept. We often complain that our parents or mates or children "don't understand" what we say, and we are probably at least partially right: one hundred percent understanding is an ideal goal toward which we strive in communication, including human-computer communication.

For a machine to understand speech, it must process the speech signal into sounds, morphemes, and words, which is *speech recognition,* and at the same time comprehend the meaning of the words as they occur in phrases and sentences, which is *speech understanding.* In many machine understanding systems these are separate stages with recognition preceding comprehension. In human language processing these two stages blend together smoothly as listeners recognize some words based on the speech signal alone, while other words have to be figured out from the meanings of words already understood.

Speech Recognition

B.C.   **BY JOHNNY HART**

By permission of Johnny Hart and Creators Syndicate, Inc.

Speech recognition is far more difficult than speech synthesis. It is comparable to trying to transcribe a spectrogram with only phonetic knowledge of the language spoken. As we have seen, the speech signal is not physically divided into discrete sounds. Human ability to "segment" the signal arises from knowledge of the grammar, which tells us how to pair certain sounds with certain meanings, what sounds or words may be "deleted" or "pushed together," and when two different speech signals are linguistically "the same" and when two similar signals are linguistically "different." The difficulty of programming a computer to have and use such linguistic knowledge in recognizing speech is enormous.

There are two kinds of speech recognizers. One recognizes speech at the word level, the other at the phoneme level. A word-level recognizer keeps the acoustic patterns of its vocabulary in its "memory." When it "hears" something, it matches the acoustic pattern of the input signal with all of its prestored acoustic patterns. The best match is chosen as the word or words recognized.

A phoneme-level recognizer operates in a similar manner, prestoring acoustic patterns of the sounds of the language and attempting to match them to incoming sound patterns. Phoneme-level recognition is more error-prone than word-level recognition because individual sounds are more confusable than individual words. That is, the machine is more likely to confuse the sound [b] with the sound [d] than it is to confuse the word *boy* with the word *dog;* words contain more redundant information than sounds, which helps to resolve confusions and ambiguities.

To ease the difficulties of recognition in some speech recognizer systems, the user must insert a short pause of about 1/3 second after each word spoken. (The pause between words must exceed the pause that occurs within words during stop and affricate articulation.) This pause shifts the burden of word boundary detection to the human speaker and makes the machine recognition process more accurate, but it is inconvenient to speak in this manner and reveals that the computer is not capable of "perceiving" in the way a human perceives.

Other speech recognizers accept continuously spoken speech, providing the speaker articulates carefully and clearly. In this case the speaker may not apply certain optional rules such as vowel reduction to schwa, vowel and/or consonant deletion, consonant assimilation at word boundaries, and so on; so *did you* is pronounced [dɪd ju], not [dɪǰə]. Natural, rapidly spoken continuous speech—the kind that humans usually use—is not yet machine recognizable with a useful degree of accuracy.

Speech Understanding

> A computer understands a subset of English if it accepts input sentences which are members of this subset, and answers questions based on information contained in the input.
>
> Daniel Bobrow

Computer comprehension of spoken language is so difficult that it is often divided into two stages: recognition and understanding. Even when recognition is successful, and a "written" transcription of the utterance is obtained, understanding is still an exacting task. Words may have several meanings, the syntactic structure of the utterance must be ascertained, and the meaning of the entire utterance must be built up using rules of syntax and the meanings of its parts. In cases of ambiguity, contextual knowledge may be needed to arrive at the intended meaning.

Understanding also is done in stages. One stage is **parsing,** which is discovering the syntactic structure, or structures, of the utterance. Another stage is semantic processing which combines the meanings of words, looked up in the computer's lexicon, into phrasal meanings, and so on until the entire utterance meaning is assembled. A third stage is applying contextual or world knowledge to disambiguate any utterances.

Parsing To understand a sentence you must know its syntactic structure. If you didn't know the structure of *dogs that chase cats chase birds,* you wouldn't know whether dogs or cats chase birds. Similarly, machines that understand language must also determine syntactic structure. A **parser** is a computer program that uses

Reprinted with special permission of North America Syndicate.

a grammar to assign a phrase structure to a string of words. Parsers may use a phrase structure grammar and lexicon similar to those discussed in Chapter 3.

For example, a parser may use a grammar containing the following rules: S → NP VP, NP → Art N, etc. Suppose the machine is asked to parse *The child found the kittens.* A **top-down** parser proceeds by first consulting the grammar rules and then examining the input string to see if the first word could begin an S. If the input string begins with an Art, as in the example, the search is successful, and the parser continues by looking for an N, and then a VP. If the input string happened to be *child found the kittens,* the parser would be unable to assign it a structure because it doesn't begin with an Art, which is required by this grammar to begin an S.

A **bottom-up** parser takes the opposite tack. It looks first at the input string and finds an Art (*the*) followed by an N (*child*). The rules tell it that this phrase is an NP. It would continue to process *found, the* and *kittens* to construct a VP, and would finally combine the NP and VP to make an S.

Occasionally a parser may have to **backtrack.** In a sentence like *The little orange rabbit hopped,* the parser might mistakenly assume *orange* is a noun. Later in the parse, when the error is apparent, the parser can return to *orange* and process it as an Adjective. To avoid backtracking, Mitch Marcus at M.I.T. invented the **look-ahead parser,** which is capable of scanning ahead. In the above example a look-ahead parser will find that the word following *orange* is not a verb, so that *orange* cannot be a noun and must be an adjective.

Even look-ahead parsers may have to backtrack when parsing "garden-path" sentences such as *The horse raced past the barn fell,* discussed in Chapter 11. The reason for this is that the amount of structure that must be scanned ahead is too great. Even if the parser is programmed to scan far enough ahead for some examples, cases will remain where it will fail, and have to backtrack. This is because the amount of structure that must be scanned ahead is, in principle, unbounded, as illustrated by *The horse with the long mane raced past the barn fell*.

In general, humans are far more capable of understanding sentences than computers. But there are some interesting cases where computers outperform humans. For example, try to figure out what the sentence, *Buffalo buffalo buffalo buffalo,* means. Most people have trouble determining its sentence structure, and are thus unable to understand it. A computer parser, with four simple rules and a lexicon in which *buffalo* has three entries as a noun, verb, and adjective, will easily parse this sentence as follows:

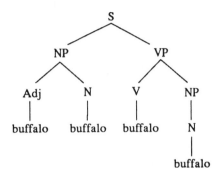

It means "Bison from the city of Buffalo deceive bison."

Regardless of details, every parser uses some kind of grammar to assign phrase structures to input strings. If a structure cannot be found, the input string is ungrammatical relative to that grammar.

A *morphological parser* uses rules of word formation, such as those studied in Chapters 2 and 6, to decompose words into their component morphemes. A morphological parser decomposes a word like *kittens* into *kitten* + *s*.

Morphological parsers also operate on morphologically complex words, such as *uncomfortably* to decompose them into the bound morphemes *un-, -able, -ly,* and the free morpheme *comfort,* all of which have regular meanings which may be looked up in the lexicon, and rules which determine the meanings of the combinations.

As suggested, just as humans store information about words and morphemes in their *mental* lexicon, a machine must also store such information in a lexicon in its "memory." Such information as syntactic category (parts-of-speech), pronunciation, spelling, subcategorization, plurality if irregular like *men,* tense if irregular like *found,* and elements of meaning are usually included in the computer's lexicon. Thus when a parser encounters *found,* it can use the spelling to look the word up in the lexicon, at which point the computer would "know" that it is a verb, that it is the past tense of *find* and that it is transitive, among other things.

A parser may use as its grammar **transition networks** which represent the grammar as a complex of **nodes** (circles) and **arcs** (arrows). A network that is the equivalent of the phrase structure rule S→NP VP may be illustrated as:

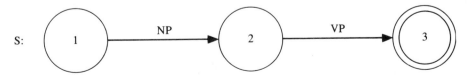

Transition Network for S → NP VP

The nodes are numbered to distinguish them; the double circle is the "final" node.

The parser would start at node 1, examine an input string of words, and if the string began with a Noun Phrase, "move" to node 2. (If it did not find a Noun Phrase, it would decide that the input string was not a sentence, unless there were other S networks in the grammar to try.) The parser would then look for a Verb Phrase, and if one were found the VP arc could be traversed to node 3. Because node 3 is a final node, the parser would indicate that the input string was a sentence consisting of a Noun Phrase and a Verb Phrase. The program would, of course, also have to specify what string of words constitutes an NP, VP, and so on.

Augmented Transition Networks (ATN) are transition networks in which each arrow not only indicates a syntactic category, but may carry other information essential to accurate parsing as well. For example, an ATN extension to the above example might carry a condition on the VP arc to ensure "agreement," as shown below:

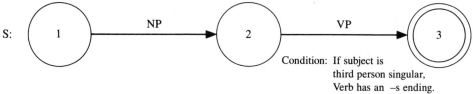

Augmented Transition Network for S →NP VP

Semantic Processing Once a sentence is parsed, the machine can try to find the meaning or semantic representation. This task requires a dictionary with the meaning of each word, and rules for combining meanings, as discussed in Chapter 4. The question of how to represent meaning is one that has been debated for thousands of years, and it continues to engender much research in linguistics, philosophy, psychology, and computer science.

One approach common to several semantic processing methods first locates the verb of the sentence—based on the sentence parse—and then identifies its thematic roles such as agent, theme, location, instrument, any complements, and so on.

Another approach is based on mathematical logic and represents the sentence *Zachary loves sushi* as

    LOVE (ZACHARY, SUSHI)

where LOVE is a "two-place predicate" with arguments *Zachary* and *Sushi*. A rule of semantic interpretation indicates that *Zachary* is the one loving, and *sushi* is the object loved.

Two well-known natural language processing systems from the 1970s used this logical approach of semantic representation. One, named SHRDLU by its developer Terry Winograd, demonstrated a number of abilities, such as being able to interpret questions, draw inferences, "learn" new words, and even explain its actions. It operated within the context of a "blocks world," consisting of a table, blocks of various shapes, sizes, and colors, and a robot arm for moving the blocks. Using simple sentences, one could ask questions about the blocks and give commands to have blocks moved from one location to another.

The second system is called LUNAR, developed by William Woods. The LUNAR program was capable of answering questions phrased in simple English about the lunar rock samples brought back from the moon by the astronauts. LUNAR translated English questions into a logical representation, which it then used to query a database of information about the lunar samples.

Semantic networks are also used to represent meaning. They are similar to ATNs in appearance, consisting of nodes and arcs, but they function differently. Here is how *Zachary loves sushi* might be represented, using semantic networks:

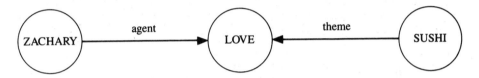

Semantic Network for *Zachary loves sushi*.

Semantic networks make thematic roles explicit, which is a crucial part of semantic interpretation.

Both logical expressions and semantic networks are convenient for *machine* representation of meaning because they are easily programmed and because the meanings thus represented can be used linguistically. For example, if the computer is asked "Who loves sushi?" it can search through its "knowledge base" for a node labeled *love*, look to see if an arc labeled "theme" is connected to *sushi*, and if so, find the answer by looking for an arc labeled "agent."

Pragmatics

GARFIELD reprinted by permission of UFS, Inc.

When a sentence is structurally ambiguous, such as *He sells synthetic buffalo hides,* the parser will compute each structure. Semantic processing may eliminate some of the structures if they are anomalous, but often some ambiguity remains. For example, the structurally ambiguous sentence *John found a book on the Oregon Trail* is semantically acceptable in both its meanings. To decide which meaning is intended, **pragmatic,** or contextual, or "real world" knowledge is needed. If John is in the library researching history, the "book *about* the Oregon Trail" meaning is most likely; if John is on a two-week hike to Oregon, the "book *upon* the Oregon Trail" meaning is more plausible.

Many language processing systems have a **knowledge base** containing contextual and world knowledge. The semantic processing routines can refer to the knowledge base in cases of ambiguity. For example the linguistic component of the electronic repair task system, referred to earlier, will have two meanings for *The l.e.d. is in the middle of the blue region at the top.* Its knowledge base, however, disambiguates because it "knows" that the l.e.d. is in the middle of the blue region, and the blue region is at the top of the work area, rather than the l.e.d. is in the middle, top of the blue region.

Computer Models of Grammars

I am never content until I have constructed a . . . model of the subject I am studying. If I succeed in making one, I understand; otherwise I do not.

William Thomson (Lord Kelvin), *Molecular Dynamics and the Wave Theory of Light*

A theory has only the alternative of being right or wrong. A model has a third possibility: it may be right, but irrelevant.

Manfred Eigen, *The Physicist's Conception of Nature*

The grammars used by computers for parsing are not the same as the grammars linguists construct for human languages, which are models of linguistic competence; nor are they similar, for the most part, to models of linguistic performance. Computers are different than people, and they achieve similar ends differently. Just as an efficient flying machine is not a replica of any bird, efficient grammars for computers do not resemble human language grammars in every detail.

Computers are often used to model physical or biological systems, which allows researchers to study those systems safely and sometimes even cheaply. For example, the performance of a new aircraft can be simulated and the test pilot informed as to safe limits in advance of actual flight.

Computers can also be programmed to model the grammar of a language. An accurate grammar—one that is a true model of a speaker's mental grammar—should be able to generate *all* and *only* the sentences of the language. Failure to generate a grammatical sentence means a "bug" in the grammar, because the human mental grammar has the capacity to generate all possible grammatical sentences—an infinite set. In addition, if the grammar produces a string that speakers consider to be ungrammatical, that too indicates a defect in the grammar; although in actual speech performance we often produce ungrammatical strings—sentence fragments, slips of the tongue, word substitutions and blends, and so on—we will judge them to be ill-formed if we notice them. Our grammars cannot generate these strings.

One computer model of a grammar was developed in the 1960s by the computer scientist Joyce Friedman to test a generative grammar of English written by syntacticians at U.C.L.A. More recently, computational linguists are developing computer programs to generate the sentences of a language and to simulate human parsing of these sentences using the rules included in various linguistic theories, such as Chomsky's government-binding theory. The computational models developed by Ed Stabler, Robert Berwick, Amy Weinberg, and Mark Johnson, among other computational linguists, show that it is possible, in principle, to use a transformational grammar, for example, in speech and comprehension, but it is still controversial whether human language processing works in this way. That is, even if we can get a computer program to produce sentences as output and to parse sentences fed into the machine as input, we still need psycholinguistic evidence that this is the way the human mind stores and processes language.

It is however because linguistic competence and performance are so complex that computers are being used as a tool in the attempt to understand human language and its use. We have emphasized some of the differences between the way humans process language and the way computers process language. For example, humans appear to do speech recognition, parsing, semantic interpretation, and contextual disambiguation more or less simultaneously and smoothly while comprehending speech. Computers, on the other hand, usually have different components, loosely connected, and perform these functions individually.

One reason for this is that typically, computers have only a single, powerful processor (or "brain"), capable of performing a single task at a time. Currently, computers are being designed with multiple processors, albeit less powerful ones, which are interconnected. The power of these computers lies both in the individual processors and in the connections. Such computers are capable of **parallel-processing,** or carrying out several tasks simultaneously.

With a parallel architecture, computational linguists may be better able to program machine understanding in ways that blend all the stages of processing together, from speech recognition through contextual interpretation, and hence approach more closely the way humans process language.

Language and Artificial Intelligence

Man is not a machine. . . . Although man most certainly processes information, he does not necessarily process it in the way computers do. Computers and men are not species of the same genus. . . . However much intelligence computers may attain, now or in the future, theirs must always be an intelligence alien to genuine human problems and concerns.

Joseph Weizenbaum

I propose to consider the question, "Can machines think?"

A. M. Turing, "The Imitation Game"

It is easier to fake intelligence than virginity.

Sir Alexander King

In answer to his question, Turing proposed that if a machine could impersonate a human being, apart from physical attributes, under any conceivable cross-examination, then the machine was thinking. The "Turing test" includes a command of human language such that a conversation between the machine and the human would be indistinguishable from a conversation between two humans.

Similarly, a computer may be said to have **artificial intelligence (AI)** when it exhibits intelligence ordinarily associated with human behavior—reasoning, learning, use of language, and so on. There are opposing philosophical viewpoints and research strategies in the field of AI as to whether computers should be programmed to imitate the way the human mind works, or whether computers should simply simulate human behavior in any way practical, whether or not that is the way people think. In linguistic terms the debate boils down to whether the grammars that machines use to communicate should be actual grammars of the language, or any kind of grammatical system that gives acceptable results.

All computer activity results from programs, usually written by humans, but sometimes written by the computer itself. A question of interest is how an AI program differs from a non-AI program. It is not always easy to distinguish between them, but computer scientists generally agree that an AI program is designed to process **knowledge** and that such processing includes **inferencing**—the ability to derive additional knowledge from the original knowledge base.

Most computer programs designed for natural language communication exploit AI techniques. In speech understanding, for example, knowledge may be stored in the form of acoustic patterns for recognizing sounds, grammatical rules for determining sentence structure, and semantic rules for determining meaning.

Inferencing capabilities are required, for example, to fulfill the task of determining phonemes from variable sounds or allophones. The phoneme underlying an alveolar stop whose voicing in the input signal is indeterminate—a /t/ or a /d/—can be inferred; if the sound occurs at the beginning of a word whose other segments are [ɪ] and [g], it must be a /d/ since *tig* is not a word but *dig* is. Similarly, an intelligent parser, faced with the sequence *the /si/ was* . . . would choose the noun *sea* rather than the verb *see,* because the presence of the article infers that a noun must follow.

Semantic inferencing has been widely researched since the 1960s. Suppose there is a knowledge base—information stored in the computer memory—that includes such facts as "Tweety is a canary," "a canary is a bird," "a bird is an animal," and "most birds can fly," which might be represented by the following semantic net:

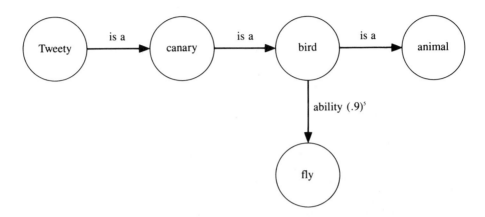

An intelligent computer program will use inferencing to deduce the further facts that Tweety is a bird, Tweety is an animal, and it is likely that Tweety can fly, none of which facts are directly represented in the original knowledge base.

If "intelligent computers" are ever developed, if artificial intelligence ever approaches human intelligence, it is clear that linguistics will play a major role in these developments, because human linguistic ability is the single most prolific manifestation of intelligence.

Summary

Computers can process language. They can be programmed to translate from a **source language** into a **target language,** and they can aid scholars analyzing a literary text or a **corpus** of linguistic data. They can also communicate with people via spoken human language.

The **speech signal** can be described in terms of the **fundamental frequency,** perceived as **pitch;** the **intensity,** perceived as **loudness,** and the **quality** perceived as differences in speech sounds, such as an [i] from an [a]. The speech wave can be displayed visually as a **spectrogram,** sometimes called a **voiceprint.** In a spectrogram, vowels exhibit dark bands where frequency intensity is greatest. These are called **formants** and result from **overtones** of the fundamental frequency, as determined by the shape of the vocal tract. Each vowel has a characteristic formant pattern different from that of other vowels. An understanding of the speech signal is necessary to program computers to speak and understand language.

Speech synthesis is accomplished by programming computers to imitate the human voice electronically. **Language generation** is the problem of determining

---

[5]The .9 on the "ability" arc shows the degree to which this ability occurs; it quantifies the concept "most" because not all birds fly.

what the computer should say. Sometimes **canned** or prepared speech is used. Other times the computer uses rules of grammar to assemble sentences from a lexicon of words and morphemes that express the intended meaning.

Speech understanding is a far more difficult task, because the physical speech signal alone is insufficient for understanding a spoken message; much linguistic knowledge is required. Machine comprehension of speech begins with **speech recognition,** which attempts to identify phonemes and words from the raw acoustic signal. To understand a string of recognized words, the machine must first **parse** the string to determine its syntactic structure. **Parsers** are computer programs that use a grammar to determine the structure of an input string. Parsers may operate **top–down** or **bottom–up. Look-ahead** parsers scan forward to avoid the need to **backtrack. Morphological parsers** decompose words into their component morphemes according to rules of word formation.

Once parsed, an utterance is analyzed semantically using **logical representations, semantic networks,** or other devices to represent meaning.

Computers may be programmed to model a grammar of a human language and thus rapidly and thoroughly test that grammar. Modern computer architectures include **parallel processing** machines that can be programmed to process language more as humans do in so far as carrying out many linguistic tasks simultaneously.

Artificial intelligence is the endowing of machines with humanlike intellectual capabilities. The use of language by machines to communicate with humans is one of the most important manifestations of artificial intelligence.

References for Further Reading

Allen, J. 1987. *Natural Language Understanding.* Menlo Park, Calif.: Benjamin/Cummings.

Barr, A., and E. A. Feigenbaum, (eds.). 1981. *The Handbook of Artificial Intelligence,* Los Altos, Calif.: I. William Kaufmann.

Berwick, R.C., and A.S. Weinberg. 1984. *The Grammatical Basis of Linguistic Performance: Language Use and Acquisition.* Cambridge, Mass.: MIT Press.

Gazdar, G., and C. Mellish. 1989. *Natural Language Processing in PROLOG: An Introduction to Computational Linguistics.* Reading, Mass.: Addison-Wesley.

Hockey, S. 1980. *A Guide to Computer Applications in the Humanities.* London, England: Duckworth.

Johnson, M. 1989. "Parsing as Deduction: The Use of Knowledge in Language." *Journal of Psycholinguistic Research* 18 (1): 105–128.

Ladefoged, P. 1981. *Elements of Acoustic Phonetics.* 2d ed. Chicago, Ill.: University of Chicago Press.

Lea, W. A. 1980. *Trends in Speech Recognition.* Englewood Cliffs, N.J.: Prentice-Hall.

Marcus, M.P. 1980. *A Theory of Syntactic Recognition for Natural Language.* Cambridge, Mass.: MIT Press.

Slocum, J. 1985. "A Survey of Machine Translation: Its History, Current Status, and Future Prospects." *Computational Linguistics* 11 (1).

Sowa, J. (ed.). 1991. *Principles of Semantic Networks.* San Mateo, Calif.: Morgan Kaufmann.

Stabler, E.P., Jr. 1992. *The Logical Approach to Syntax: Foundations, Specifications and Implementations of Theories of Government and Binding.* Cambridge, Mass.: MIT Press. Bradford Books.

Weizenbaum, J. 1976. *Computer Power and Human Reason.* San Francisco, Calif.: W. H. Freeman.

Winograd, T. 1983. *Language as a Cognitive Process.* Reading, Mass.: Addison-Wesley.

Winograd, T. 1972. *Understanding Natural Language.* New York: Academic Press.

Witten, I. H. 1986. *Making Computers Talk.* Englewood Cliffs, N.J.: Prentice-Hall.

Exercises

---

1. The use of spectrograms or "voiceprints" for speaker identification is based on the fact that no two speakers have exactly the same speech characteristics. List some of the differences you have noticed in the speech of several individuals. Can you think of any possible reasons why such differences exist?

2. Using a bilingual dictionary of some language you do not know, attempt to translate the following English sentences by looking up each word.

   The children will eat the fish.
   Send the professor a letter from your new school.
   The fish will be eaten by the children.
   Who is the person that is hugging that dog?
   The spirit is willing, but the flesh is weak.

   A. Using your own knowledge, or someone else's, give a *grammatically correct* translation of each sentence. What difficulties are brought to light by comparing the two translations? Briefly, mention five of them:

      a.
      b.
      c.
      d.
      e.

   B. Have a person who knows the "target" language translate the grammatical translation back into English. What problems do you observe? Are they related to any of the difficulties you mentioned in Part A?

3. Suppose you were given a manuscript of a play and were told that it is either by Christopher Marlowe or William Shakespeare (both born in 1564). Suppose further that this work, and all of the works of Marlowe and Shakespeare, were in a computer. Describe how you would use the computer to help determine the true authorship of the mysterious play.

4. Speech synthesis is useful because it allows computers to convey information without requiring the user to be sighted. Think of five other uses for speech synthesis in our society.

   a.

   b.

c.

d.

e.

5. Some advantages of speech recognition are similar to those of speech synthesis. A computer that understands speech does not require a person to use hands or eyes in order to convey information to the computer. Think of five other possible uses for speech recognition in our society.

a.

b.

c.

d.

e.

6. Consider the following ambiguous sentences. Explain the ambiguity, give the most likely interpretation, and state what a computer would have to "know" to achieve that interpretation.

Example: A cheesecake was on the table. It was delicious and was soon eaten.

Ambiguity: "It" can refer to the cheesecake or the table.
Likely: "It" refers to the cheesecake.
Knowledge: Tables aren't usually eaten.

a. John gave the boys five dollars. One of them was counterfeit.
Ambiguity:
Likely:
Knowledge:

b. The police were asked to stop drinking in public places.
Ambiguity:
Likely:
Knowledge:

c. John went to the bank to get some cash.
Ambiguity:
Likely:
Knowledge:

d. He saw the Grand Canyon flying to New York.
Ambiguity:
Likely:
Knowledge:

e. Do you know the time? (*Hint:* This is a pragmatic ambiguity.)
Ambiguity:
Likely:
Knowledge:

f. Concerned with spreading violence, the president called a press conference.
Ambiguity:
Likely:
Knowledge:

7. Here is a transition network similar to the one on page 485 for the Noun Phrase (NP) rule given in Chapter 3:

NP →Art (Adj)* N PP

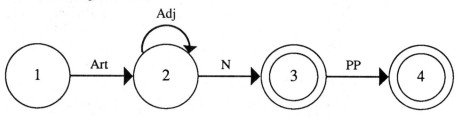

Using this as a model, draw a transition network for the Verb Phrase Rules:
VP→ V (NP) (PP)
(*Hint:* Recall from Chapter 3 that the above rule abbreviates four rules.)

8. Here are some sentences along with a possible representation in predicate logic notation.

i. Birds fly. FLY (BIRDS)
ii. The student understands the question. UNDERSTANDS (THE STUDENT, THE QUESTION)
iii. Penguins do not fly. NOT (FLY [PENGUINS])
iv. The wind is in the willows. IN (THE WIND, THE WILLOWS)
v. Kathy loves her cat. LOVES (KATHY, [POSS (KATHY, CAT)])

A. Based on the examples in the text, and those in part B of this exercise, give a possible semantic network representation for each of these examples.

i.
ii.
iii.
iv.
v.

B. Here are five more sentences and a possible semantic network representation for each. Give a representation of each of them using the predicate logic notation. (*Hint:* Review Chapter 4 for the meanings of *agent, theme, patient, goal,* and so on.)

    i. Seals swim swiftly.

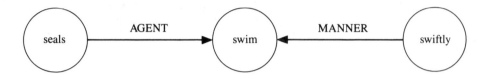

Logic:

    ii. The student doesn't understand the question.

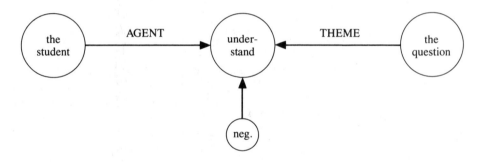

Logic:

    iii. The pen is on the table.

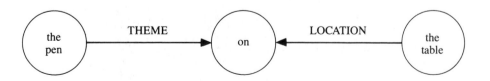

Logic:

iv. My dog eats bones.

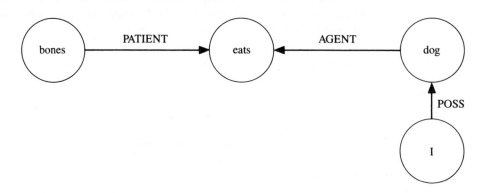

Logic:

v. Emily gives money to charity. (*Hint: Give* is a three-place predicate.)

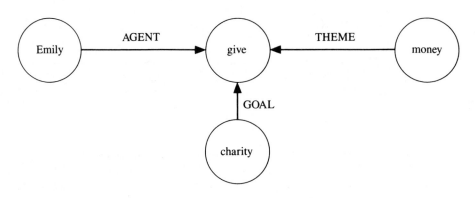

Logic:

Glossary

A

Abbreviation Shortened form of a word (e.g., *prof* from *professor*).

Accent (1) Prominence. Cf. **stressed syllable,** (2) the phonology or pronunciation of a specific regional dialect (e.g., southern accent), (3) the pronunciation of a language by a nonnative speaker (e.g., French accent).

Acoustic Pertaining to physical aspects of sound.

Acoustic phonetics The study of the physical properties of speech sounds.

Acoustic signal The sound waves produced by any sound source, including speech.

Acquired dyslexia Loss of ability to read correctly following brain damage by persons who were previously literate.

Acronym Word composed of the initials of several words (e.g., *PET scan* from *positron emission tomography scan*).

Active sentence A sentence in which the thematic role of the subject Noun Phrase is usually an agent; a sentence which is not passive (e.g., *George hugged Martha*). Cf. **Passive sentence.**

Adjective (Adj) The syntactic category of words that may precede nouns in Noun Phrases and have the semantic effect of modifying or qualifying the noun.

Affix Bound morpheme attached to a stem or root morpheme. Cf. **prefix, suffix, infix, circumfix.**

Affricate Sound produced by a stop closure followed immediately by a slow release, characteristic of a fricative; phonemically a sequence of stop + fricative.

Agent The thematic role of the Noun Phrase whose referent deliberately performs the action described by the verb (e.g., *George* in *George hugged Martha*).

Agrammatism Language disorder usually resulting from damage to Broca's region in which the patient has difficulty with syntax. Cf. **Broca's area.**

Agreement A relationship between words of a sentence in which the choice of one restricts the choice of the other (e.g., the choice of a pronoun is restricted by the person, number, and gender of its antecedent). See also **Subject Verb Agreement.**

Airstream mechanisms The ways in which air from the lungs or mouth is moved to produce speech sounds.

Allophones Predictable phonetic variants of phonemes (e.g., [p] and [pʰ] of the phoneme /p/ in English).

Alphabetic writing A writing system in which each symbol typically represents one sound segment.

Alveolars Sounds produced by raising the tongue to the alveolar ridge (the bony tooth ridge).

Ambiguous The term used to describe a word, phrase, or sentence with multiple meanings.

American Sign Language (ASL) The sign language used by the deaf community in the United States. Cf. **sign languages.**

Analogic change A language change in which a rule generalizes to forms hitherto unaffected (e.g., the plural of *cow* changed from the earlier *kine* to *cows* by the generalization of the plural formation rule). Also called **internal borrowing.**

Anaphor A pronominal expression such as a reflexive pronoun that always has an antecedent.

Anomalous Semantically ill-formed (e.g., *Colorless green ideas sleep furiously*).

Anomia A form of aphasia in which patients have word-finding difficulties.

Antecedent The Noun Phrase in a sentence or discourse with which a pronoun is coreferential (e.g., the antecedent of *he* in *John said he was tired* is *John*).

Antonyms Words that are opposite in meaning. Cf. **gradable pairs, complementary pairs, relational opposites.**

Aphasia Neurological term used to refer to language disorders following brain damage.

Arbitrary The term used to describe a property of language, including sign language, whereby there is no natural or intrinsic relationship between the way a word is pronounced (or signed), and its meaning (e.g., the sounds represented by *casa* in Spanish, *house* in English, *dom* in Russian, etc. have the same meaning).

Arc Part of the graphical depiction of a **transition network** represented as an arrow labeled with a syntactic category and connecting two nodes. Cf. **node.**

Argot The set of words used by a particular occupational group such as scientists, artists, musicians, bricklayers, etc. Also called **jargon.**

Article (Art) The syntactic category of words such as *the* and *a* which may combine with nouns to form Noun Phrases (e.g., *the boy* or *a pretty girl*).

Articulatory phonetics The study of how the vocal tract produces speech sounds.

Artificial intelligence (AI) Computer processing that purports to exhibit characteristics ordinarily attributed to human beings (e.g., the ability to play chess or understand spoken language).

Aspirated A term which refers to voiceless consonants in which the vocal cords remain open for a brief period after the release of the constriction resulting in a 'puff' of air (e.g., the [p] in *pit*). Cf. **unaspirated.**

Assimilation rules Phonological rules that change or spread feature values of segments to make them more similar.

Asterisk The symbol [*] used to indicate ungrammatical or anomalous examples (e.g., *cried the baby, *sincerity dances). Also used in historical and comparative linguistics to represent a reconstructed form.

Auditory phonetics The study of the perception of speech sounds.

Augmented transition network A transition network in which the arcs carry information necessary to parsing over and above their syntactic category label. Cf. **transition network, arc, node.**

Automatic machine translation The use of computers to translate from one language to another. Cf. **source language, target language.**

Autonomy of language The independence of language as a genetically conditioned cognitive system which is not derived from the general intellectual capacities of the human species.

Auxiliary verbs; Auxiliary (Aux) A closed category of words traditionally called "helping verbs" such as *will, can, would, could.* They are also called **modals.**

B

Babbling Sounds produced in the first few months after birth which include sounds that do and do not occur in the language of the household. Deaf children 'babble' with hand gestures similar to the vocal babbling of hearing children.

Back-formation A new word created by removing what is mistakenly considered to be an affix (e.g., *edit* from *editor*).

Backtrack The action in which a **parser** returns to a decision point where it went wrong and makes a different choice.

Back vowels Vowel sounds involving the back of the tongue.

Banned languages Languages or dialects which are by law not permitted in an attempt to maintain one official language.

Bilabials Sounds articulated by bringing both lips together.

Binary valued The two values of a distinctive feature (e.g., a segment is either nasal [+ nasal] or oral [− nasal]).

Black English (BE) A dialect of English used by some African Americans.

Blend Word composed of the parts of more than one word (e.g., *smog* from *smoke + fog*).

Borrowing The incorporation of a loan word from one language into another (e.g., English borrowed *buoy* from Dutch). Cf. **loan words.**

Bottom-up parser A parser which first examines the input sequence of words and then determines whether it conforms to the rules of grammar stored in the computer's memory. Cf. **parser, top-down parser.**

Bound Describes a pronoun which has an antecedent. Cf. **free, unbound.**

Bound morpheme Morphemes which can only occur in words attached to other morphemes; prefixes, suffixes, infixes, circumfixes. Cf. **free morphemes.**

Broadening A semantic change in which the meaning of a word becomes more extensive (e.g., *dog* once meant a particular breed of dog).

Broca, Paul A French neurologist who in 1861 suggested that the left side of the brain was the language hemisphere.

Broca's area or region A front part of the left hemisphere of the brain, damage to which causes telegraphic, agrammatic speech (Broca's aphasia).

C

Calligraphy Originally referred to the art of drawing Chinese characters; the profession or art of elegant writing.

Canned speech Speech recorded beforehand and stored digitally in a computer's memory for future use.

Case The morphological form of nouns and pronouns, and in some languages articles and adjectives as well, indicating the grammatical relationship to the verb (e.g., *I* is in the *nominative* case of the first person singular pronoun in English and functions as a subject; *me* is in the *accusative* case and can only function as an object).

Cerebral hemispheres The two parts of the brain, the left hemisphere controlling the movements of the right side of the body, the right hemisphere those of the left side.

Characters (Chinese) The units of Chinese writing, each of which represents a morpheme or word. Also called **ideographs,** or **ideograms.**

Chicano English (ChE) A dialect of English spoken by some bilingual Mexican Americans in the Southwest and California.

Circumfix Bound morpheme parts of which occur in a word both before and after the root.

Click A speech sound produced by a velaric airstream mechanism found in certain African languages. (One of the clicks is similar to the sound of disapproval made by speakers of non-click languages, often spelled *tsk, tsk.*)

Closed-class words Function words; a category of words which rarely if ever has new words added to it (e.g., prepositions, pronouns, conjunctions).

Cognates Words in related languages that developed from the same word (e.g., English *one,* Spanish *uno,* and French *une*).

Coinage The construction and addition of new words to the lexicon.

Communication A system for conveying information. Language is a linguistic system of communication; there are also nonlinguistic systems of human communication as well as systems used by other species.

Comparative linguistics The branch of linguistics that deals with language change by comparing related languages.

Comparative method The technique used by linguists to deduce forms in an earlier stage of a language by examining corresponding forms in several of its daughter languages.

Complementary distribution Phones which never occur in the same phonetic environment (e.g., [p] and [pʰ] in English). Cf. **allophones.**

Complementary pairs Two antonyms related in such a way that the negation of one is the meaning of the other (e.g., *alive* means not *dead*). Cf. **gradable pairs.**

Complementizer (Comp) A syntactic category of words that precede the S in an S-bar (e.g., *that* in *I know that you know*).

Compound A word composed of two words (e.g., *washcloth*).

Comprehension Understanding of sentences or utterances; providing a semantic interpretation to a sentence.

Computational linguistics A subfield of linguistics and computer science that is concerned with computer processing of human language.

Concordance An alphabetical index of all the words of a text which gives the frequency of every word and the location of each occurrence in the text.

Conditioned sound change A change in the phonological rules that depends on the phonetic environment (e.g., part of Verner's law states that /f/ changed to /b/ in words where the preceding vowel was unstressed, but not otherwise).

Consonant A speech sound produced with some constriction of the airstream.

Consonantal Phonetic feature distinguishing the class of obstruents, liquids, and nasals which are [+ consonantal], from other sounds which are [− consonantal].

Consonantal writing A writing system in which only symbols representing consonants are used; vowels are inferred from context (as in, e.g., Arabic).

Content words The nouns, verbs, adjectives, and adverbs constituting the major part of the vocabulary. Cf. **open class words.**

Continuants Sounds in which the airstream continues without complete interruption through the mouth.

Contour tones Tones in which the pitch glides from one level to another (e.g., from low to high—rising tone).

Contrastive stress Additional stress placed on a word to highlight it or to clarify the referent of a pronoun (e.g., in *Joe hired Bill and* he *hired Sam,* with contrastive stress on *he,* it is usually understood that Bill rather than Joe hired Sam).

Convention (conventional) The agreed on arbitrary relationship between the form and meaning of words.

Cooperative principle A maxim of conversation which states that a speaker's contribution to the discourse should be as informative as is required, neither more nor less.

Copula A verb, usually a form of *to be,* that equates the expressions on either side of it (e.g., *is* in *Bob is the professor*).

Coreference Two noun phrases with the same reference.

Coronals The class of sounds including labials, alveolars, and palatals.

Corpus A collection of utterances, gathered from spoken or written sources, used for linguistic research and analysis.

Corpus callosum The nerve fibers connecting the right and left cerebral hemispheres.

Cortex The approximately ten billion neurons forming the outside surface of the brain; also referred to as the *gray matter.*

Creative aspect of linguistic knowledge Speakers' ability to combine the linguistic units of their language to produce and understand an infinite range of novel sentences.

Creole A pidgin language adopted by a community as its native tongue and learned by children as their first language.

Critical Age The period between early childhood and puberty during which a child can acquire language without instruction.

Cuneiform The word-writing system of the Sumerians whose ideographs (words) were written using a wedge-shaped stylus.

Cyrillic alphabet The alphabet used by many Slavic languages, including Russian.

D

Daughter language A descendant of an earlier form of a language (e.g., French is a daughter language of Latin, which is the parent).

Definite A term referring to a unique object insofar as the speaker and listener are concerned.

Deictic, deixis Describes words or expressions whose reference relies entirely on context (e.g., *I, now, here*). Cf. **person deixis, time deixis, place deixis, demonstrative articles.**

Demonstrative articles Words such as *this, that* occurring in Noun Phrases and indicating that context is needed to determine the referent of the Noun Phrase (e.g., the referent of *this boy* can only be known in context).

Derivational morphemes Morphemes added to stem morphemes (lexical content morphemes) which may change the syntactic category or meaning of a word. For example, *ish* added to *boy* to form *boyish* changes the Noun to an Adjective.

Descriptive grammar A linguist's description or model of the mental grammar, the units, structures, and rules of speakers of a particular language. The attempt to state what speakers unconsciously know about their language.

Diacritics Symbols combined with segment symbols to specify various phonetic properties such as length, tone, stress, nasalization; extra marks added to a written character that change its usual value (e.g., the tilde [~] drawn over the letter *n* in Spanish represents a palatalized nasal rather than an alveolar nasal).

Dialect A language variety used by a particular group of speakers. Cf. **regional dialect, social dialect.**

Dialect atlas A book of maps showing the areas where specific dialectal characteristics occur in the speech of the region.

Dialect leveling Decreasing of dialect differences, thought by some to occur due to mass media use of one dialect.

Dialects The mutually intelligible forms of a language which differ in systematic ways from each other.

Dichotic listening Experimental method for testing brain lateralization in which subjects hear different auditory signals in the left and right ears.

Dictionary List of all morphemes and words; lexicon.

Digraph Two letters used to represent a single sound (e.g., *gh* represents [f] in *enough*).

Diphthong Vowel + glide.

Direct object The Noun Phrase immediately below the Verb Phrase immediately below the S in a phrase structure tree.

Discourse Linguistic units composed of several sentences.

Discourse analysis The study of discourse.

Dissimilation rules Phonological rules that change feature values of segments to make them less similar.

Distinctive features Phonetic properties of phonemes which account for the segmental contrasts (e.g., voicing, nasality, labiality).

Downdrift The lowering of pitch of a phrase or utterance.

E

Egressive airstream mechanism Method by which lung air is pushed out of the mouth.

Embedded sentence A sentence occurring within a sentence in a phrase structure tree (e.g., *You know that I know*).

Entailment The relationship between two sentences where the truth of one infers the truth of the other (e.g., *Corday assassinated Marat* entails *Marat is dead*). Also called **implication.**

Etymology The history of words; the study of the history of words.

Extension The **reference** of a Noun Phrase.

Euphemism A word or phrase that replaces a taboo word or is used to avoid reference to certain acts or subjects (e.g., *powder room* for *toilet*).

F

Finger spelling The use of hand gestures symbolizing the letters of the alphabet used when there is no sign in the sign language.

Flap See **tap.**

Folk etymology Nonscientific speculation about the origin of words.

Form, linguistic Phonological or gestural representation of a morpheme or word.

Formants The principal frequencies of a speech sound; the **overtones** of the speech signal. They are depicted by dark bands on **spectrograms.**

Free Describes a pronoun which refers to an object not explicitly mentioned in the sentence or discourse in which it occurs (e.g., *he* in the phrase *he is sick* if the person has not been specifically named, can only be interpreted by the nonlinguistic context). Also called **unbound.** Cf. **bound.**

Free morphemes Single morphemes which constitute words.

Free variation Alternative pronunciations of a word in which one sound is substituted for another without changing the word's meaning (e.g., pronunciation of *bottle* with a glottal stop as the medial consonant).

Frequency effect Influence on response time of how often words are used in speech and writing.

Fricatives Sounds produced in which the constriction in the mouth or at the lips is very narrow, creating a hiss or friction; sometimes called **spirants.**

Front vowels Vowel sounds involving front part of the tongue.

Function words Grammatical words including conjunctions, prepositions, articles, etc. Cf. **closed class words.**

Fundamental frequency In speech the rate at which the vocal cords vibrate, symbolized as F_0, called F-zero, perceived by the listener as **pitch.**

G

Gall, Franz Joseph A nineteenth century physiologist who proposed a theory of brain localization, i.e., that different parts of the brain were responsible for different abilities and actions.

Geminates A sequence of two identical sounds; an alternative way of representing long segments.

Generic terms The use of a word that ordinarily has the semantic feature [+ male] to refer to both sexes (e.g., *mankind* meaning "the human race"; the use of the [+ male] pronoun as the neutral form, as in *Everyone should do his duty*).

Genetically related Describes two or more languages which developed from a common, earlier language (e.g., French, Italian, Spanish, all developed from Latin).

Glides Sounds produced with little or no obstruction of the airstream which are always preceded or followed by a vowel (e.g., /w/ and /j/ in *we, you*).

Gloss A word in one language given to express the meaning of a word in another language (e.g., "house" is the gloss for the French word *maison*); a brief definition of difficult word or expression.

Glottalic airstream mechanism Method for production of implosive and ejective sounds.

Glottal stop The sound produced when the air is stopped completely at the glottis by tightly closed vocal cords.

Goal The thematic role of the Noun Phrase toward whose referent the action of the verb is directed (e.g., *the theater* in *The kids went to the theater*).

Gradable pairs Two antonyms related in such a way that more of one is less of the other (e.g., *warm* and *cool,* more warm is less cool and vice versa). Cf. **complementary pairs.**

Grammar Everything known about a language, including its phonology, morphology, syntax, semantics, and lexicon.

Grammatical A sequence of words conforming to the rules of syntax; **well formed** sequence.

Grammaticality The degree to which a string of words conforms to the syntactic rules for sentences.

Grammatical morpheme Free function word or bound morpheme required by the syntactic rules. Cf. **Inflectional morpheme.**

Graphemes The symbols of an alphabetic writing system; the letters of an alphabet.

Great Vowel Shift A sound change that took place in English sometime between 1400 and 1600 C.E. in which seven long vowel phonemes changed their quality.

H

Head The lexical category always present in the corresponding phrasal category (e.g., the noun of a Noun Phrase).

Hierarchical structure The subgroupings of words in a phrase or sentence.

Hieroglyphics A pictographic writing system used by the Egyptians around 4000 B.C.E.

Hispanic English A variety of English spoken by some native Spanish speakers or their descendants.

Historical linguistics The branch of linguistics that deals with how languages change, what kinds of changes occur, and why they occur.

Holophrastic Refers to the *one-word stage* in which children produce one-word sentences.

Homographs Different words spelled the same, which may or may not be pronounced the same (e.g., *lead* in "to lead a parade" or in "heavy as lead"; *bear* the animal or *bear* meaning "to carry").

Homonyms Different words pronounced, and possibly spelled, the same (e.g., *to, too, two,* or *bat* the animal, *bat* the stick, and *bat* as in *bat the eyelashes*).

I

Iconic relationship; iconicity A nonarbitrary relationship between form and meaning, such as the male and female symbols on toilet doors.

Ideogram, ideograph A character of a word-writing system, often highly stylized, which represents a concept, or the pronunciation of the word representing that concept.

Idiolect An individual's way of speaking, reflecting that person's grammar.

Idiom An expression whose meaning is not composed solely of the meaning of its parts (e.g., *to play possum* meaning "to feign death").

Ill-formed The term used to describe a sequence of words not conforming to the rules of syntax; **ungrammatical sequence** (e.g., *kiss boys girls to like*).

Illocutionary force The purpose of a speech act, such as a warning, a promise, a threat, a bet, etc. (e.g., the illocutionary force of *I resign!* is the act of resignation).

Implication Entailment.

Indo-European The descriptive name given to the ancestor language of many modern language families including Germanic, Slavic, Romance, etc.

Inference The derivation of additional knowledge from facts already known.

Infix A bound morpheme which is inserted in the middle of a word or stem.

Inflectional morpheme A bound grammatical morpheme.

Ingressive airstream mechanism A method of producing speech sounds in which air enters the vocal tract from outside.

Innateness hypothesis Scientific hypothesis which posits that the human species is genetically equipped to acquire universal grammar which is the basis for all human languages. Cf. **universal grammar (UG).**

Instrument The thematic role of the Noun Phrase whose referent is the entity used to carry out the action of the verb (e.g., *knife* in *Seymour cut the salami with the knife*).

Intension The **sense** of a Noun Phrase.

Intensity The magnitude of sound waves, perceived by the listener as **loudness.**

Interdentals Sounds produced by inserting the tip of the tongue between the upper and lower teeth.

Internal borrowing A language change in which the effect of a rule spreads to forms hitherto unaffected. Cf. **analogic change.**

Internal reconstruction The comparing of morphologically different forms of a word in a language to deduce facts about earlier stages of the language (e.g., pairs such as *please/pleasant* demonstrate a change involving front vowels in English).

International Phonetic Alphabet (IPA) The phonetic alphabet designed by the International Phonetic Association to be used to represent the sounds found in all human languages.

International Phonetic Association The organization founded in 1888 to further phonetic research and develop the IPA.

Intonation Pitch contour of phrase or sentence.

Intransitive A verb that must not be followed by a Noun Phrase direct object (e.g., *sleep*).

Inventory of sounds The phonetic segments of a language.

Isogloss The boundary separating one regional dialect or dialectal characteristic from another.

J

Jargon Special words peculiar to the members of a profession or group. Cf. **Argot.**

Jargon Aphasia Form of aphasia in which phonemes are substituted, often producing nonsense words.

K

Knowledge In **artificial intelligence** the term used to describe the storehouse of facts in the computer's memory; in linguistics, generally, refers to linguistic competence.

Knowledge base That part of a computer language-processing system containing contextual and world knowledge (e.g., in the expression *synthetic buffalo hides,* the meaning "hides of synthetic buffalo" is ruled out because there is no such animal as a synthetic buffalo in the knowledge base); in **artificial intelligence,** that part of the computer program housing the basic facts about the application and its context.

L

Labials Sounds articulated with the lips.

Labiodentals Sounds produced by touching the bottom lip to the upper teeth.

Language faculty That part of human biological and genetic makeup specifically designed for language acquisition and use.

Language generation A computer process in which grammatical sentences and discourses are constructed as part of a human-computer interaction.

Language purists Prescriptivists who attempt to establish a particular dialect or usage as the only correct one.

Lateralization Term used to refer to any cognitive functions localized to one or the other side of the brain.

Lax vowels Short vowels produced with very little tension in the vocal cords.

Length A prosodic feature referring to duration of segment. Two sounds may contrast in length (e.g., long vs. short).

Level tones Relatively stable (nongliding) pitch on syllables of tone languages. Also called **register** tones.

Lexical ambiguity Multiple meanings of words, or of sentences with ambiguous words.

Lexical category A syntactic category whose members are words (e.g., Noun, Verb, Article); those categories occurring only on the right side of phrase structure rules; those categories occurring just above the words in a phrase structure tree.

Lexical decision Task of subjects in psycholinguistic experiments who on presentation of a spoken or printed stimulus must decide whether it is a word or not.

Lexical gap Possible but nonoccurring words; forms obeying the phonological rules of a language for which there is no meaning (e.g., *blick* in English).

Lexical paraphrases Paraphrases based on synonyms (e.g., *She lost her purse* and *She lost her handbag*).

Lexicographer One who edits or works on a dictionary.

Lexicography The editing or making of a dictionary.

Lexicon The component of the grammar containing speakers' knowledge about morphemes and words; a speaker's mental dictionary.

Lingua franca The major language used in an area where speakers of more than one language live to permit communication and commerce among them.

Linguistic competence The knowledge of a language represented by the mental grammar which accounts for speakers' linguistic creativity. For the most part, linguistic competence is unconscious knowledge.

Linguistic performance The use of linguistic competence in the production and comprehension of language; behavior as distinguished from knowledge.

Linguistic theory The principles which characterize all human languages, the discovery of which is the goal of modern linguistics.

Liquids Sounds like /r/ and /l/ in which there is obstruction of the air but not sufficient to cause friction.

Loan words Words in one language whose origins are in another language (in Japanese *besiboru (baseball)* is a loan word from English). Cf. **borrowing.**

Location The thematic role of the Noun Phrase whose referent is the place where the action of the verb occurs (e.g., *her office* in *Vicki graded exams in her office*).

Logographic Word writing.

Logical representation Method of representing semantic information that utilizes notations from symbolic logic.

Lookahead parser A parser capable of scanning forward in a sequence of words to avoid mistaken assumptions.

Loudness The listener's perception of the magnitude of sound waves.

M

Main verb The verb immediately below the Verb Phrase immediately below the S in the phrase structure tree of a sentence.

Manners of articulation Phonetic features which reflect the way the air stream is obstructed as it travels through the vocal tract. Cf., e.g., **stop, fricative, continuant.**

Marked That member of a gradable pair of antonyms which is not used in questions of degree (e.g., *low* is the marked member of the pair *high/low* because we ask *How high is the mountain?* not **How low is the mountain?*). The polymorphemic form of a word that in male/female pairs usually refers to the female (e.g., *princess* vs. *prince*). Cf. **unmarked.**

Maxim of relevance A maxim of conversation which states "be relevant," that is, avoid abrupt changes in topic.

Maxims of conversation Conversational conventions such as the **cooperative principle.**

Meaning shift A semantic change in which the meaning of a word changes in time (e.g., *silly* once meant "happy").

Mean length of utterances (MLU) A measure used by child language researchers to refer to the number of words or morphemes in a child's utterance; a more accurate measure of the acquisition stage than chronological age of child.

Metaphor Nonliteral meaning (e.g., *The walls have ears,* meaning "you may be overheard").

Metathesis A phonological rule that reorders segments, often by transposing two sequential sounds.

Middle English The dialects of English spoken between 1100 and 1500 C.E.

Mimetic Similar to imitating, acting out, or miming.

Minimal pair (or set) A pair (or set) of words which are identical except for one phoneme, occurring in the same place in the string (e.g., *pain*/pen/, *bane*/ben/, *main*/men/).

Modal Verbs or Modals (M) Another term for Auxiliary Verbs.

Modern English The dialects of English spoken from 1500 C.E. to the present.

Monomorphemic Word consisting of one morpheme.

Monophthong Simple vowel. Cf. **diphthong.**

Morpheme Smallest unit of linguistic meaning.

Morphological parser A parser that uses rules of word formation to decompose words into their component morphemes.

Morphology The study of the structure of words; the component of the grammar which includes the rules of word formation.

Morphophonemic rules Rules which specify the pronunciation of morphemes; a morpheme may have more than one pronunciation determined by such rules (e.g., the plural morpheme in English is regularly pronounced /s/ /z/ or /əz/).

N

Narrowing A semantic change in which the meaning of a word changes in time to become less extensive (e.g., *deer* once meant "animal").

Nasal sounds Speech sounds produced with an open nasal passage permitting air to go through the nose as well as the mouth (e.g., /m, n, ŋ/). Cf. **oral sounds**.

Natural class A class of sounds characterized by a phonetic property or feature pertaining to all members of the set (e.g., class of stops).

Neo-Grammarians A group of nineteenth century linguists who claimed that sound shifts (i.e., changes in phonological systems) took place without any exceptions.

Neurolinguistics That branch of linguistics concerned with the brain mechanisms underlying the acquisition and use of human language.

Neuron Nerve cell.

Neutralization rules Phonological rules which obliterate the contrast between two phonemes in certain environments (e.g., in some dialects of English, /t/ and /d/ are both pronounced as voiced flaps intervocalically as in *writer, rider*).

Node A branch point in a **phrase structure tree**; part of the graphical depiction of a **transition network** represented as a circle, pairs of which are connected by **arcs**. Cf. **arc**.

Noun (N) The syntactic category of words that function as the **heads** of Noun Phrases, such as *book, Jean, sincerity*.

Noun Phrase (NP) The syntactic category of expressions containing some form of a noun; NP's function as the subject or object in a sentence (e.g., *a car, Sue, we*).

O

Obstruents The class of sounds consisting of nonnasal stops, fricatives, and affricates. Cf. *sonorants*.

Old English The dialects of English spoken between 449 and 1100 C.E.

Onomatopoeic, onomatopoetic Terms used to describe words whose pronunciations suggest their meaning (e.g., *meow, buzz*).

Open class words Lexical content words; a category of words which commonly adds new words (e.g., nouns, verbs).

Oral sounds Speech sounds produced by raising the tongue to the velum to close the nasal passage so that air can only escape through the mouth. Cf. **nasal sounds**.

Origin of language Throughout history there have been many attempts to explicate how human language arose including proposed 'theories' of divine origin, evolution, and human invention.

Orthoepists Prescriptivist grammarians in the sixteenth to eighteenth centuries who were concerned with the pronunciation of words and the spelling/pronunciation relationship.

Orthography The written form of a language; spelling.

Overgeneralization The process used by children to extend the meaning of a word (e.g., *papa* to refer to all men). Cf. **undergeneralization.**

Overtones The harmonics of an acoustic signal; the **formants** of a speech signal.

P

Palatals Sounds produced by raising the front part of the tongue to the palate.

Palate The section of the roof of the mouth behind the alveolar ridge.

Parallel processing The ability of a computer to carry out several tasks simultaneously due to the presence of multiple central processors.

Paraphrases Sentences with the same meaning, except possibly for minor differences in emphasis (e.g., *He ran up a big bill* and *He ran a big bill up*).

Parent language An earlier form of a language (e.g., Latin is the parent language of French, which is the daughter).

Parser A computer program which determines the grammaticality of sequences of words according to whatever rules of grammar are stored in the computer's memory, and assigns a linguistic structure to the grammatical ones.

Participle The form of a verb that occurs after the auxiliary verb *have* (e.g., *kissed* in *John has kissed many girls,* or *seen* in *I have seen trouble*).

Passive sentence A sentence in which the verbal complex contains a form of *to be* followed by a verb in its **participle** form (e.g., *The girl was kissed by the boy; The robbers must not have been seen*). Cf. **active sentence.**

Patient The thematic role of the Noun Phrase whose referent undergoes the action of the verb, usually called the **theme** (e.g., *Martha* in *George hugged Martha*).

Performative verb A verb, certain usages of which comprise a speech act (e.g., *resign* when the sentence *I resign!* is interpreted as an act of resignation).

Person deixis Noun Phrases with the semantic feature [+ human] such as *this boy,* in which context is needed to determine the referent. Cf. **deixis.**

Phone Phonetic segment.

Phonemes Sound segments that are distinctive, that contrast or distinguish words (e.g., /p/ as in *pit* and /b/ in *bit*).

Phonemic principle The principle underlying alphabetic writing systems in which one symbol typically represents one phoneme.

Phonemic representation The phonological representation of words and sentences prior to the application of phonological rules.

Phonetic alphabet Alphabetic symbols used to represent the phonetic segments of speech.

Phoneticization The process by which a pictographic writing system came to represent the sounds of the words it depicted.

Phonetic representation The pronunciation of words and sentences. Cf. **phonemic representation.**

Phonetics The study of linguistic sounds, how they are produced (articulatory phonetics), how they are perceived (auditory or perceptual phonetics), and the physical aspects of speech sounds (acoustic phonetics).

Phonological rules The statements in the phonological component of a grammar which account for the sound patterns and constraints in a language; rules which apply to phonemic representations to derive phonetic representations or pronunciation.

Phonology The sound system of a language; the component of a grammar which includes the inventory of sounds (phonetic and phonemic units) and rules for their combination and pronunciation; the study of the sound systems of all languages.

Phonotactics Sequential constraints; rules stating permissible strings of phonemes.

Phrasal categories Syntactic categories that are composed of other syntactic categories; those categories occurring on the left side of phrase structure rules.

Phrase structure rules Principles of grammar which specify the constituency of syntactic categories in the language (e.g., NP→ Art N).

Phrase structure tree A tree diagram with syntactic categories at each **node** that reveals both the linear and hierarchical structure of phrases and sentences.

Phrenology A pseudo-science developed by Spurzheim in the nineteenth century, the practice of determining personality traits and intellectual ability by examination of the bumps on the skull.

Pictograms A form of writing in which the symbols resemble the objects represented; a nonarbitrary form of writing.

Pidgins A simple but rule-governed language developed for communication among speakers of mutually unintelligible languages, often based on the language of one of the languages spoken.

Pinyin An alphabetic writing system for Chinese utilizing the characters of the Roman alphabet.

Pitch The fundamental frequency as perceived by the listener.

Place deixis Expressions like *here, there, that place* for which context is needed to determine the actual location being referred to. Cf. **deixis.**

Plosives Oral or nonnasal stop consonants, so called because the air that is stopped 'explodes' with the release of the closure.

Polymorphemic Word consisting of more than one morpheme.

Polysemous A single word with several closely related but slightly different meanings (e.g., *face,* as in the face of a person, a building, or a clock).

Pragmatics The study of how context influences the interpretation of meaning; considered by some to be a part of linguistic performance and by others to be a component of the grammar.

Predictable The descriptive term used of a phonetic feature that is nondistinctive, noncontrastive, or **redundant** (e.g., aspiration is a predictable feature of voiceless stops that occur initially in stressed syllables in English).

Prefix Bound morpheme which occurs before a root or stem of a word; affix which is attached to the beginning of a morpheme or word.

Preposition (P) The syntactic category of words that function as the **heads** of Prepositional Phrases, such as *to, at, with*.

Prepositional Phrase (PP) The syntactic category of expressions composed of a preposition and a Noun Phrase.

Prescriptive grammar Grammarians' attempt to legislate what speakers' grammatical rules should be, rather than what they are.

Presupposition Implicit assumptions about the world required to make an utterance meaningful or appropriate (e.g., *Take some more tea!* presupposes that you already had some tea).

Primes The basic formal units of sign languages corresponding to phonological elements of spoken language (originally called *cheremes*).

Priming The effect on response time of previously read or heard related word on the accessing of subsequent words.

Proper names Names of persons, places, and other entities with unique reference insofar as the speaker and listener are concerned. Usually capitalized in writing.

Prosodic feature Duration (length), pitch, or loudness of vowel sounds.

Psycholinguistics The branch of linguistics concerned with linguistic performance, language acquisition, and speech production and comprehension.

Pulmonic Referring to lungs; speech sounds produced by movement of lung air through the mouth, and sometimes the nose.

Q

Quality of sound The listener's perception of the **wave form** of speech, which differentiates the various speech sounds.

R

Rebus principle Using a pictogram for its phonetic value (e.g., using a picture of a bee to represent the verb *be,* or the sound [b]).

Reconstruction Using the comparative method to establish the forms of words in a parent language. Cf. **comparative method.**

Recursion The property of human language in which phrases of the same type occur within themselves, giving rise to the limitless and creative aspect of language.

Recursive Phrase structure rules in which the same syntactic category occurs on the left and right side (e.g., NP→Art N PP, PP→P NP), and which give rise to recursion.

Redundancy rules Principles in the lexicon stating generalizations between semantic features (e.g., a word that is [+human] is [+animate]).

Redundant The value (+ or −) of a phonetic feature is said to be redundant if it is predictable either from its context or other feature values of the segment (e.g., [+ voicing] is redundant for any nasal phoneme in English since all nasals are voiced).

Reference That part of the meaning of a Noun Phrase which is its referent. Also called **extension.**

Referent The entity designated by a Noun Phrase (e.g., the referent of *John* in *John knows Sue* is the actual person named John under discussion).

Reflexive pronoun A pronoun ending in *self* or *selves* (e.g., myself, yourselves).

Regional dialect The dialect spoken by people in a particular area of the language community.

Register tones Level tones; high, mid, or low tones.

Regular sound correspondence The occurrence of a phoneme in a word in one language or dialect with a corresponding phoneme in the same position of the word in another dialect or language with this parallel holding for a significant number of words in the two dialects or languages (e.g., /aj/ in nonsouthern American English corresponds to /a/ in southern American English). Also found between new and older forms of the same language.

Relational opposites Pairs of antonyms in which one describes a relationship between two objects and the other describes the same relationship when the two objects are mentioned in the opposite order (e.g., *parent* and *child*; *John is the parent of Susie* describes the same relationship between John and Susie as *Susie is the child of John*).

Response or reaction time (RT) The measurement of the time it takes subjects to respond in psycholinguistic experiments (e.g., in making lexical decisions, naming objects). RT is assumed to reflect processing time.

Retroflex Refers to sounds produced by curling the tip of the tongue back behind the alveolar ridge.

Roman alphabet The characters used in many of the alphabetic writing systems of the world (e.g., English, French, etc).

Rounded vowels Vowel sounds produced with rounding of lips (e.g., /o, u/).

Rules of syntax Principles of grammar which account for (1) the grammaticality of sentences; (2) word order; (3) structural ambiguity; (4) the meaning relations between words in a sentence; (5) structure-based paraphrases; (6) the creative ability; and more.

S

S bar (S′) A syntactic category composed of a **complementizer** and a sentence (e.g., . . .*that I know*).

Segment An individual sound that occurs in a language.

Semantic features A notational device for expressing the presence or absence of semantic properties by pluses and minuses (e.g., *baby* is [+ young], [− abstract]).

Semantic network A network of arcs and nodes used to represent semantic information about sentences.

Semantic properties The components of meaning of a word (e.g., "young" is a semantic property of *baby, colt, puppy*).

Semantics The study of the linguistic meaning of words and sentences; the component of the grammar which specifies these meanings.

Semantic Substitutions Common reading errors by one group of acquired dyslexic patients who produce semantically similar word substitutions (e.g., *hour* is read as *time*).

Sense That part of the meaning of a Noun Phrase which determines its referent. Cf. **reference.** Also called **intension** (e.g., knowing the sense or intension of *the president of the United States* allows one to determine that George Bush is the referent, as of this writing).

Sentence (S) A syntactic category of expressions usually composed of at least a Noun Phrase followed by a Verb Phrase.

Sibilants The class of sounds which includes alveolar and palatal fricatives, and affricates, characterized acoustically by a hissing sound.

Siglish The name used for Signed English, consisting of the replacement of each spoken English word (and morpheme) by a sign.

Sign Term used in traditional linguistics to refer to a form arbitrarily related to a meaning, that is, a word; a single gesture (possibly with complex meaning) in the sign languages used by the deaf equivalent to the term "word" in spoken languages.

Sign languages The languages used by the deaf in which hand and body gestures are the forms of morphemes and words.

Slang Words and phrases used in casual speech often invented and spread by close-knit social or age groups.

Slip of the tongue Speech error; involuntary deviation of intended utterance. Cf. **Spoonerism.**

Social dialect The variety of a language spoken by a class or group.

Sonorants The class of sounds which includes vowels, glides, liquids, and nasals; nonobstruents. Cf. **obstruents.**

Sound spectrogram Picture of a physical sound showing the harmonics (formants), amplitude (loudness), and fundamental frequency (pitch).

Sound spectrograph A device for depicting the wave forms of speech in the form of **spectrograms.**

Sound symbolism When sound and meaning are not arbitrarily related (e.g., **onomatopoeic** words, or semantically similar words that happen to begin with certain sound combinations such as *gl* in *gleam, glisten, glitter,* which all relate to sight).

Sound writing A term sometimes used to mean a writing system in which one sound is represented by one letter. Sound writing systems do not employ the **phonemic principle,** and are similar to phonetic transcriptions.

Source The thematic role of the Noun Phrase whose referent is where the action of the verb originated (e.g., *Paris* in *Franklin sent news from Paris*).

Source language In **automatic machine translation,** the language being translated. Cf. **target language.**

Spectrograms, speech spectrograms A graphical depiction of speech, plotting frequency (on the y-axis) as a function of time (on the x-axis). The intensity of the sound is represented by darker (more intensity) and lighter (less intensity) areas on the graph. Sometimes called "visible speech" or **voiceprints.**

Speech act The nonlinguistic accomplishments of an utterance, such as a warning or a promise, as determined in part by context (e.g., *There is a bear behind you* is a warning in certain contexts).

Speech processing Linguistic performance; speech production and speech perception or comprehension.

Speech recognition Computer processing for transcribing speech.

Speech signal The sound waves of speech.

Speech synthesis An electronic process in which speech is reproduced.

Speech understanding A computer process in which speech is interpreted semantically.

Spelling The alphabetic representation of words. Cf. **orthography.**

Spelling pronunciation Pronouncing a word as it is spelled, irrespective of its actual pronunciation by native speakers (e.g., pronouncing *Wednesday* as "wedness-day").

Spirant See **fricative.**

Split brain The result of an operation for epilepsy in which the corpus callosum is cut, thus separating the brain into its two halves; split brain patients are studied to determine the role of each hemisphere in cognitive and language processing.

Spoonerism Slip of the tongue in which phonemic segments are reversed or exchanged as in *tip of the slongue;* named for Reverend William Archibald Spooner, head of New College, Oxford, in nineteenth century, who was purported to have made many such errors.

Stages in language acquisition Periods from infancy to the age of five or six through which children learning all languages pass in acquiring their first language. Cf. **babbling, holophrastic, two-word stage, telegraphic speech.**

Standard The dialect (regional or social) considered to be the norm.

Standard American English (SAE) An idealized dialect of English which has never been objectively described or defined.

Stops Sounds in which the air flow is briefly but completely stopped in the oral cavity (e.g. /p, n, g/).

Stressed syllable, stress Syllable with relatively greater length, loudness, and/or higher pitch. Also called **accent.**

Structural ambiguity Multiple meanings based on structural differences (e.g., *He saw a boy with a telescope*).

Structure dependent Rules which apply to certain syntactic structural configurations irrespective of the words in the structure or their meaning (e.g., transformational rules are structure dependent).

Styles Situation dialects (e.g., formal speech, casual speech).

Subcategorization That part of the lexical entry of a verb specifying which syntactic categories can and cannot occur with it (e.g., specification that the verb *sleep* may not be followed by a Noun Phrase, but the verb *find* must be followed by a Noun Phrase).

Subject The Noun Phrase immediately below the S in the phrase structure tree of a sentence.

Subject-Verb Agreement The requirement in English that whenever the subject of a sentence is third person singular, the main verb have an "s" or "es" added to it (orthographically) (e.g., *The boys I know think* but *The boy I know thinks;* the addition of an inflectional morpheme to the main verb required by some property of the noun phrase subject such as number or gender.

Suffix Bound morpheme which occurs after the root or stem of a word; affix which is attached to the end of a morpheme or word.

Suprasegmentals Prosodic features (e.g. length, tone).

Syllabary The inventory of symbols used in a syllabic writing system.

Syllabic Sounds which may constitute the nucleus of syllables; all vowels are syllabic and liquids and nasals may be syllabic as in the words *towel, button, bottom.*

Syllabic writing A writing system in which each syllable in the language is represented by its own symbol.

Synonyms Different words with the same or nearly the same meaning (e.g., *purse* and *handbag*).

Syntactic categories Traditionally called *parts of speech;* expressions that can substitute for one another without loss of grammaticality (e.g., Noun Phrases).

Syntax The rules of sentence formation; the component of the mental grammar that represents speakers' knowledge of the structure of phrases and sentences.

Synthetic speech Speech produced electronically by simulating the acoustic components of actual speech.

T

Taboo A descriptive term used in reference to words (or acts) that are not to be used (or performed) in 'polite society.'

Tap Sound in which the tongue touches the alveolar ridge as in some British pronunciations of /r/. Also called **flap.**

Target language In **automatic machine translation,** the language into which the **source language** is translated.

Teaching grammars A set of language rules written to help speakers learn a foreign language or a different dialect of their language.

Telegraphic speech Utterances of children after the two-word stage when many grammatical morphemes are omitted. Cf. **mean length of utterances.**

Tense vowels Feature of vowels which are often slightly longer in duration and higher in tongue position and pitch than the corresponding lax vowels.

Thematic role The semantic relationship between the verb and the Noun Phrases of a sentence, such as **agent, theme, location, instrument, goal, source.**

Theme The thematic role of the Noun Phrase whose referent undergoes the action of the verb (e.g., *Martha* in *George hugged Martha*). Sometimes called **patient.**

Theta-criterion A proposed universal principle stating that a particular thematic role may only occur once in a sentence.

Time deixis Expressions like *now, then, last week* for which context is needed to determine the actual time being referred to. Cf. **deixis.**

Tone Contrastive pitch of syllables in languages where two words may be identical except for such differences in pitch. Cf. **register tones, contour tones.**

Top-down parser A parser which operates by first consulting the rules of grammar and then determining whether the input sequence of words conforms to those rules. Cf. **parser, bottom-up parser.**

Transformationally related Two sentences related to each other in a systematic way described formally by a **transformational rule** (e.g., *The boy is sleeping* and *Is the boy sleeping?*).

Transformation or **Transformational Rule** An operation relating two *classes* of sentences in a systematic way (e.g., declarative sentences of the form *The boy is sleeping* may be related to interrogative sentences of the form *Is the boy sleeping?* through the moving of the Auxiliary Verb to the front of the sentence).

Transition network A method for representing rules of grammar which can be graphically depicted by means of **nodes** connected by **arcs.**

Transitive A verb that must be followed by a Noun Phrase direct object (e.g., *find*).

Tree diagram A graphical representation of the hierarchical structure of a phrase or sentence.

Trill Sounds in which the tip of the tongue vibrates against the roof of the mouth.

Truth conditions The circumstances that must be known to determine whether a sentence is true, and therefore part of the meaning of declarative sentences.

Two-word stage Around the beginning of the second year, children produce sentences of two words with clear syntactic and semantic relations.

U

Unaspirated Voiceless sounds in which the vocal cords start vibrating immediately upon release of constriction (e.g., /p/ in *spit*). Cf. **aspirated.**

Unbound Describes a pronoun lacking an antecedent. Also called **free.** Cf. **free, bound.**

Undergeneralization Children's use of a general term such as *dog* to refer only to a single instance, e.g., the family pet.

Ungrammatical sequence Words not conforming to the rules of syntax; **ill-formed** sequence (e.g., **kiss boys girls to like*).

Uninterpretable A condition whereby a sentence cannot be interpreted because of nonsense words (e.g., *All mimsy were the borogoves*).

Universal grammar The principles or properties which pertain to the grammars of all human languages; the initial state of the language faculty. Cf. **language faculty.**

Unmarked The term used to describe that member of a gradable pair of antonyms used in questions of degree (e.g., *high* is the unmarked member of *high/low*). Cf. **marked.**

V

Velaric airstream mechanism Method by which clicks are produced in which there is a slight inflow of air into the mouth.

Velars Sounds produced by raising the back of the tongue to the soft palate or velum.

Velum The soft palate; the part of the roof of the mouth behind the hard palate.

Verb The syntactic category of words that function as the **heads** of Verb Phrases, such as *give, gives, gave.*

Verb Phrase (VP) A syntactic category of expressions containing a verb and, possibly, other elements such as a Noun Phrase (e.g., *fall, hit a ball, give a kid a dime*).

Voiced sounds Speech sounds produced with closed and vibrating vocal cords.

Voiceless sounds Speech sounds produced with open and nonvibrating vocal cords.

Voiceprints A popular term for **speech spectrograms.**

Vowel A sound produced without significant constriction of the air flowing through the mouth.

W

Wave form The variations in air pressure produced by sound. In speech, the wave form is determined by the shape of the vocal tract.

Well formed A term used to describe a sequence of words conforming to the rules of syntax; **grammatical** sequence.

Wernicke, Carl Neurologist who showed that damage to different parts of the left cerebral hemisphere cause differential language disorders.

Wernicke's area or region Back (posterior) part of the left brain which if damaged causes fluent but semantically empty speech production, i.e., *Wernicke's aphasia.*

Wh words Words in English typified by those beginning with *wh* that may function as question words (e.g., *who, what, when, which, where, whose*).

Word A free sound-meaning lexical unit, which may be simple (monomorphemic) or complex (polymorphemic) (e.g., *boy, boys*).

Word sets Words related by virtue of including the same root morpheme or stem, i.e., the same content morpheme (e.g., *phone, phonetic, phonetician, phonic, phoneme,* etc.).

Word writing A system of writing in which each character represents a word or morpheme of the language (e.g., Chinese). Sometimes called ideographic or logographic writing.

Wug An imaginary animal created by Jean Berko Gleason to test children's acquisition of morphological and phonological rules.

X

X bar theory A theory that emphasizes the head-centered characteristics of phrase structure rules, i.e., that X Phrases always contain a head of category X (e.g., Noun Phrases always contain a Noun).

Index